AMERICAN ECONOMIC HISTORY

SECOND EDITION

ROBERT C. PUTH
University of New Hampshire

THE DRYDEN PRESS

Chicago   New York   San Francisco
Philadelphia   Montreal   Toronto
London   Sydney   Tokyo

Acquisitions Editor: Elizabeth Widdicombe
Developmental Editor: Deborah Acker
Project Editor: Gale Miller
Design Supervisor: Jeanne Calabrese
Production Manager: Barb Bahnsen
Permissions Editor: Doris Milligan
Director of Editing, Design, and Production: Jane Perkins

Text and Cover Designer: Vargas/Williams Design
Copy Editor: JoAnn Learman
Indexer: Joyce Goldenstern
Compositor: Impressions, Inc.
Text Type: 10/12 Baskerville Roman

Library of Congress Cataloging-in-Publication Data

Puth, Robert Christian, 1936–
  American economic history.

  Bibliography: p.
  Includes index.
  1. United States—Economic conditions. I. Title.
HC103.P9   330.973   87-6782
ISBN 0-03-011892-1

Printed in the United States of America
789-090-987654321

Address orders:
111 Fifth Avenue
New York, NY 10003

Address editorial correspondence:
One Salt Creek Lane
Hinsdale, IL 60521

The Dryden Press
Holt, Rinehart and Winston
Saunders College Publishing

Cover: Sheeler, Charles. *American Landscape.* 1930. Oil on canvas, 24″ × 31″. Collection, The Museum of Modern Art, New York. Gift of Abby Aldrich Rockefeller. Photograph © 1987 The Museum of Modern Art, New York.

THE DRYDEN PRESS SERIES IN ECONOMICS

PREFACE

The recorded history of North America is now approximately four centuries old. The continent's economic development has been an extraordinarily rich process. The handful of starving colonists in the first European settlements were abjectly poor by any standard of comparison; but in little more than a century, Americans enjoyed one of the world's highest standards of living. Perhaps even more remarkably, their descendants have continued to do so to this day. If for no other reason than the dimensions of its success, the story of American economic development is well worth recounting. But the history of the nation's economic success involves far more than its quantitative dimensions, impressive though they have been.

No economic history that merely recounts what happened is complete. Modern scholarship requires that an adequate treatment also introduce the student to the causes and consequences of economic growth and their relative weights. Only in this way can we determine whether less fortunate nations can learn from the American example or why it may be unique.

The second edition of *American Economic History* presents an analysis of the growth of the American economy over time. As it makes clear, no single source of economic growth was dominant in all circumstances and at all times. Virtually every study of economic development has concluded that sustained growth in real output, particularly if it exceeds population growth, inevitably involves change not merely in the productive processes and the resources employed, but in the larger society. The U.S. economy and its colonial predecessors have undergone massive change in virtually all dimensions and characteristics. The country began as an agricultural and extractive economy, largely dependent on the soil, the forest, and the sea for its people's livelihood. In the nineteenth century the United States became the world's greatest industrial power. In the last four decades it has begun yet another transformation. It now appears that the generation and processing of information will become the major focus of U.S. economic activity.

The Theme of This Book

During all these changes, many factors contributed to the nation's growth. Natural resources shaped the nature of many early ventures. Americans forged the tools that extended their capabilities. Their labor has contributed more to economic growth than any other physical input. In all of these productive resources as well as their end uses, enormous change has occurred, and the pace has quickened. Today, few people can realistically expect to spend their working lives in the same occupation in which they began their careers.

To reiterate, U.S. economic growth has many sources, and no single one has consistently been dominant. Nevertheless, the theme of this book is that there was a special ingredient in this country's development. Total economic growth exceeded that produced by the increase in factors of production alone. America was able to produce so much more for so many of its people than other nations with many or more of the same initial advantages because of its superior use of human capabilities. From the time European settlement began, Americans developed attitudes and institutions more responsive to change and individual initiative than those of any other nation. Nor did the process begin and end there: America quickly began to devote more effort to further developing human productive capacity, both by providing a climate where such capabilities were recognized and rewarded and by creating institutions that encouraged their development and employment in both new and existing applications.

Even in the seventeenth and eighteenth centuries America made better use of its human talent than the most advanced and enlightened European economies. This is why the American economy was so uniquely capable of rapidly and extensively responding to new opportunities and, increasingly, to their production as well. The process has been cumulative, and it is one key to long-term economic growth. Moreover, it employs a resource capable of continuous enhancement—the human mind. Other factors have been influential, even dominant, in fostering economic development at various periods, but the rational use of human productive potential contributed to the process in America as it did nowhere else.

The Intended Audience

This book has been written for students rather than their instructors. Most of the factual contents, I am sure, are already familiar to persons sufficiently acquainted with American economic history to present the topic to others, even if the interpretation is new. My purpose is not to instruct my peers but to aid their efforts to enlighten others. Throughout, I have endeavored to explain events, their causes and nature, and their consequences for further development—which were not always positive. I have paid less attention to the research methods that led scholars to these conclusions (or controversies). Where I thought it useful, data on the quantitative dimensions of development have been incorporated.

New Economic Research

Economic history has made great strides in the past three decades. Through explicit models, new sources of data, and sophisticated methods of quantitative analysis, the discipline has been able to assess the relative importance of various influences on historical events and to determine the validity of established interpretations of history. In some cases, the new methods have produced coherent explanations of problems once thought to defy analysis or have made long-established views untenable. This book includes references to the studies that produced these results. My assessments of these scholarly efforts are also presented.

Organization of the Book

All aspects of any economic system are interrelated, whether directly or indirectly. In a world of scarcity, one use of resources precludes their employment elsewhere and affects future capabilities differently than alternative allocations. For this reason, the book is divided into five time periods usually bounded by major political events, such as wars. The intent is not to imply that these events denoted important economic transitions but rather to help keep developments in various sectors to manageable dimensions. It would not be easy, for example, to follow the entire course of U.S. agricultural history without some idea of events in the other parts of the economy that furnished agriculture with resources, markets, and a social context.

Unique and Notable Topic Coverage

The second edition retains the organization of the first edition. However, the entire text has been rewritten and the basic theme strengthened and more fully incorporated into the material. Much greater use has been made of public choice theory, particularly as presented by such authorities as Olson, North, Rosenberg and Birdzell, and Anderson and Hill. This should be especially evident in Chapters 9 and 16 and in all of Part V. The treatment of "Big Business" and of trends in competition between the Civil War and 1920 has been extensively revised. The final chapter (Chapter 22) has been completely revised to incorporate more modern analysis and a greater emphasis on the book's basic theme. Where new research has altered either quantitative or qualitative assessments of American economic history since the previous edition, new views have been noted and their significance assessed.

ACKNOWLEDGMENTS

One of the most pleasant duties of authorship is the recognition of one's debts to others. My thanks are extended to many individuals who over three decades gave me more than I can ever repay. While I was an undergraduate at Carleton College, Ada M. Harrison and Robert Will introduced me to the study of economics. Harold F. Williamson began my training in economic history at Northwestern University. My students have taught me as I taught them.

The first edition of this book benefited from the comments of Robert Gallman, University of North Carolina; Terry Anderson, Montana State University; Mary Yeager, UCLA; and Paul Koefod, University of Florida–Gainesville.

Professors Kenneth Ng, Fullerton State College; Thomas Ulem, University of Illinois; and William Hutchinson, Miami University of Ohio, gave me their insights on the complete manuscript of this edition. Louis Cain, Loyola University (Illinois); Tim Sullivan, Eastern Illinois University; Barry Eichengreen, Harvard; Pamela Nickless, University of North Carolina; Robert Higgs, Lafayette; Robert Kenney, Miami Dade Community College; and Donald R. Wells, Memphis State University, made other useful suggestions.

The services of Gavin Wright (formerly at the University of Michigan, currently at Stanford) extended beyond the call: he has read both editions in manuscript and final form. My colleagues at the University of New Hampshire—Allen Thompson, Dwayne Wrightsman, James Horrigan, Fred Kaen, Evangelos Simos, William Wetzel, and Kenneth Rothwell—provided insights and advice that made this a better book. The remaining imperfections reflect my inability to absorb all that these reviewers and consultants had to give me.

Other assistance took different but no less vital forms. My appreciation of the benefits of technological change has been strengthened far more by a Zenith word processor than by any study. The University of New Hampshire and Dean Dwight Ladd of the Whittemore School provided support in the form of a sabbatical leave and helped me acquire my computer. At the Dryden Press, Deborah Acker, Gale Miller, and Liz Widdicombe knew how to present deadlines in a manner that encouraged me to meet them. My wife and family gave me the support and forbearance that allowed me to master a new medium of authorship while expanding my vocabulary to include expressions hitherto unused since I left the Army. To all, my most profound gratitude.

Robert C. Puth
Dover, New Hampshire
December 1987

CONTENTS

POPULATION GROWTH MAPS

INTRODUCTION

THE AMERICAN SUCCESS STORY: ECONOMIC GROWTH AND ITS IMPORTANCE

Compared to other countries, the economic growth of the United States and its colonial antecedents is a success story. As Table I.1 reveals, per-capita incomes in the United States are very high. The current high standing of American income levels is generally recognized, but many U.S. citizens do not realize that their economy has been among the world's most successful for at least three centuries. Even less do they understand the sources of these high incomes or the reasons for their growth over time.

This book is an attempt to illustrate the economic growth of the United States and the colonies from which it sprang. Since the primary focus is on the sources and consequences of economic growth, more emphasis is placed on how and why such growth occurred than on chronologizing the achievement. To accomplish this, the book applies economic theory to historical events.

The Concept of Scarcity

The fundamental reason for the existence of economics as a discipline is scarcity. Scarcity does not necessarily refer to the quantities of a commodity available, but to their ability to satisfy human desires for that good. Mankind is engaged in a constant struggle between its productive capabilities and its desire for more and more varied goods. At any instant, productive capacity is limited by the amounts of natural resources, labor, and capital available and the technology for putting them to use. The amount of any single item that these resources may produce is further restricted because most resources may be employed in more than one use. The cost of producing most goods, then, is the alternatives foregone by making one item and not another. At the same time, the desire for more goods is restricted

1

**Table I.1   Per-Capita Income Levels and Recent
Growth Rates, Selected Countries***

Country	GNP/Capita, 1984	1960–1984 Average Annual Real Growth
United Arab Emirates	$21,920	—
Switzerland	16,330	1.4
United States	15,390	1.7
Norway	13,940	3.3
Canada	13,280	2.4
Sweden	11,860	1.8
Australia	11,740	1.7
Denmark	11,170	1.8
Germany (Fed. Rep.)	11,130	2.7
Japan	10,630	4.7
Saudi Arabia	10,530	5.9
France	9,760	3.0
Netherlands	9,520	2.1
United Kingdom	8,570	1.6
Libya	8,520	−1.1
Singapore	7,260	7.8
Italy	6,420	2.7
Hong Kong	6,330	6.2
Israel	5,060	2.7
Spain	4,440	2.7
Venezuela	3,410	0.9
Yugoslavia	2,120	4.3
South Africa	2,340	1.4
Argentina	2,230	0.3
Korea, Rep. of	2,110	6.6
Mexico	2,040	2.9
Brazil	1,720	4.6
Chile	1,700	−0.1
Turkey	1,160	2.9
Nigeria	730	2.8
Philippines	660	2.6
Indonesia	540	4.9
Pakistan	380	2.5
China	310	4.5
India	260	1.6
Uganda	230	2.9
Niger	190	−1.3
Mali	140	1.1
Bangladesh	130	.6
Ethiopia	110	0.4

*At market prices in 1984 U.S. dollars.
Source: World Bank, *World Development Report, 1986* (Washington, D.C., 1986), pp. 180–181.

only by the limits of human imagination. Consequently, aggregate desires consistently exceed the means available to satisfy them. Economic scarcity thus means that more of any good is obtainable only at a cost in alternatives foregone. Something—money, time, effort, or the opportunity to obtain something else from the same resources—must be sacrificed to obtain additional quantities of any scarce good.

Scarcity has been obvious throughout recorded history, and it shows no signs of abating. Although the stocks of productive resources have increased and the knowledge of how to employ them has risen spectacularly, human wants have increased at least as much—especially humanity's taste for variety—and the prices of goods remain positive. It seems clear that scarcity will always be the result of the race between productive capacity and imagination, and that scarcity is no less obvious today than at any other time.

Given scarcity, it follows that choices are necessary. We cannot have, in aggregate, all of everything that we want. Therefore, to maximize satisfaction, we must employ our scarce resources to produce those things we want most, and we must use them to obtain the largest possible output, since all we can produce is not going to fully satisfy our desires. Economics is thus the study of choices, of the application of scarce means toward satisfying as many of our most intense desires as possible. All economic decisions occur within this environment of scarcity and involve weighing costs against benefits. Economic history adds a time context; it surveys mankind's struggle against scarcity throughout history.

Economics is not a discipline that stands alone. It has links to other fields of study, in both its means and the ends toward which they are directed. To the economist, wants are given, meaning that it is accepted that the desire for commodities exists. But how these desires are generated and studied lies outside the purview of economics. In a wealthy economy like our own, the majority of our wants are determined

not by the need for physical survival, but by individuals' interactions in society. The desires for goods can be analyzed through sociology, anthropology, psychology, and the other social sciences, as well as biology. For example, why does eating lobster generally indicate a festive occasion in our society, while eating horse meat is a sign of deprivation? The causes are largely determined by our past and present interactions with other people.

The determinants of our ability to produce are likewise not a matter of primary concern to economists. For the answers to questions in this area, we must turn to the physical sciences and their applications in technology, and to the political and cultural rules we have developed to regulate the use of productive resources. These regulations can be very important; an economy's productive capacity depends not merely on physical resources and knowledge of how to use them, but also on the attitudes and laws that regulate their use. The ages at which people enter and leave the work force, the number of hours worked during any time period, attitudes toward safety, the preservation of environmental quality, future growth, and the trade-offs between cultural values and productive efficiency that the society accepts are all determined outside economics, but they influence what gets produced, how it is produced, and how it is distributed among the population. In short, they determine the limits within which economic activity can occur.

Theories of Economic Growth

If we are to attempt to explain the reasons behind America's economic success, we must make sense of the enormous array of facts revealed to us by history. We need some method of determining which facts are pertinent to our explanation and in what manner.

Theories are statements of cause and effect. The economic historian seeks to determine the factors that caused the growth of incomes in America, which were consequences of that growth, and which were not germane to the process. The formulation of an economic theory follows the methodology established in the physical sciences. Preliminary observations of some phenomenon are made and a hypothesis advanced about its causes or consequences. Then, to whatever extent possible, the explanation is compared to observed reality. Often this process involves the application of explicit statements of cause and effect (economic models) and employs statistical data and the conclusions drawn from their analysis. If the theory allows accurate predictions of subsequent events, or better explains the past than alternatives, the theory is accepted (not proved). If not, it is rejected. Two examples of the use of theory to explain American economic growth will illustrate the point. (The term "American" is used throughout the book to connote the United States of America and the colonies from which it was formed, not the entire Western Hemisphere.)

The Resource Endowment Theory

One widely discussed explanation for high American income levels holds that the large and varied natural resources possessed by this country are the chief source of its economic development. The United States is unusually well endowed with fertile soil, fuels, metals, and geographic features that either encourage their use or impose much lower barriers to use than elsewhere. For example, the United States has a much greater share of the earth's richest agricultural land than its portion of the earth's surface would indicate, and many other raw materials are also relatively abundant here. However, evidence both from America's and other nations' pasts casts grave doubt on the notion that abundant natural resources made American economic growth inevitable.

Table I.1 indicates that other countries, such as Canada and Australia, combine large natural resource endowments and high levels of per-capita incomes. But incomes are at least

as high in Denmark, the Netherlands, and Switzerland. The recent growth rates of the Japanese economy, if sustained, will produce the world's highest incomes. Nevertheless, all these countries are notoriously poor in natural resources. Nor does it appear that mere possession of natural bounty is any guarantee of economic success: Brazil and Indonesia both enjoy enormous and varied natural resources, plus head starts of 100 and 1,000 years, respectively, in civilization over the United States. Yet both are still poor. Brazil has commenced rapid economic growth only in the last few decades, and Indonesia remains one of the world's poor countries.

Even more damaging to this theory is the fact that America was a high-income economy long before its mineral wealth or even its most fertile soils had been discovered. Colonial Americans enjoyed some of the world's highest per-capita incomes when only the Eastern Seaboard's natural resources were available—and by no means were all of these known, far less exploited. It appears that natural resources or their absence can affect the nature of the initial development process, but economic success over time is much more heavily influenced by other factors that provide effective substitutes.

The Exploitation Theory

A second proposed explanation of American economic development sees the source of high incomes in U.S. ability to exploit other regions, reducing their welfare to raise that of America. As in the previous example, however, the sequence of observed events does not support this contention. In this discussion, we will employ Robert Zevin's definition of imperialism as "the formal or informal extension of sovereignty beyond the borders within which it was previously exercised."[1] For this explanation to hold, American power over foreigners must

[1] R. Zevin, "An Interpretation of American Imperialism," *Journal of Economic History* (March 1972).

have preceded income growth in this country. But America was a wealthy society, its citizens probably enjoying higher incomes than their British masters, while still a group of colonies. Further, incomes in the United States appear to have grown faster before our most blatantly imperialistic ventures—prior to 1898—than subsequently. Often too, the most explicitly imperialistic activity of the United States occurred in areas where markets, raw materials, or investment outlets paled in comparison to those at home. Before the United States possessed significant international political power, its principal foreign economic and political relations were with nations it could not hope to control. Even within North America, American territorial expansion did not typically involve the exploitation of the existing populations— although the efforts to destroy them cannot be approved by modern standards. Even after the United States became a world power, most overseas trade and investment has linked this country to nations well able to protect their own interests. American imperialism was real enough, but its motives were not economic, and its payoff was negative (See Chapter 14 for an elaboration on American imperialism.). In no way can the wealth of this country be explained as the proceeds of international exploitation: such activity was never large enough in aggregate nor crucial enough in detail to have a significant impact on the U.S. economy.[2]

The failure of these two theories to explain American economic growth brings out two important points. First, theories are linked to facts—they are not empty logical exercises. If a theory does not allow accurate predictions or if it cannot accommodate the observed reality it purports to explain, then the theory is wrong or misapplied. Things are *never* "all right in theory but not in fact." Second, we need theories to place facts in logical contexts and to draw conclusions from them.

As later chapters will show, there are many theories that purport to explain at least some elements of the economic growth of this country. Such theories must be evaluated in light of the factual evidence that adds to or detracts from their credibility. No single theory explains American economic growth over the past 375 years, at least in detail, better than all others. On the other hand, a theory need not be universally applicable to be useful.

The Value Of Growth

As a social science, economics deals with what has occurred or will occur and why: it cannot say what should have occurred or ought to occur. The ideal pace and pattern of economic growth must be drawn from value judgments, in which economists have no special expertise. However, it does appear that rising incomes— at least for individuals—raise the recipients' perceptions of their own happiness. Professor Richard Easterlin has found that most people become happier when their incomes rise in relation to those of others in their communities. However, no such increase in well-being occurs when all incomes rise at the same rate. These traits appeared to hold in a wide variety of circumstances: planned as well as market economies, societies with both high and low per-capita incomes, and those with both very rapid and very slow rates of growth.[3]

---

[2] Economic theory indicates that aggregate human welfare cannot be improved by armed conflict. Even if one party gains control of all the loser's goods, the winner can only acquire what his victim has lost. Since the conflict itself uses scarce resources, thus sacrificing alternative output, and often results in destruction of capital and labor, overall welfare is reduced, not increased. Particularly in the case of nineteenth- and twentieth-century imperialism, the areas over which conflict occurred were poorly endowed, and the efforts to acquire or control them often costly. It is difficult to perceive gains to the economies of any participants in such ventures.

[3] R. A. Easterlin, "Does Money Buy Happiness?" *The Public Interest,* Winter 1973.

In 1986, the average American enjoyed perhaps 12 times the real income of his or her eighteenth-century counterpart,[4] but was more satisfaction derived from this much higher income? We cannot measure the satisfaction derived by different generations from their lifestyles, but we can say with some assurance that late twentieth-century Americans would not be willing to exchange living standards with their ancestors in eighteenth-century Virginia. It also seems obvious that contemporary income levels cannot be significantly reduced except at the cost of emotional trauma. The amounts and variety of goods made possible by contemporary productive capabilities form our standards of comparison today, and, just as in the past, most people appear convinced that "more is better." In Easterlin's terms, individuals and societies are caught on a "hedonic treadmill."

Although more commodities cannot be proved to increase human welfare as time passes, reductions in current incomes will reduce well-being. Over time, if an unchanging income level could be achieved, it would probably decrease human happiness.

ECONOMIC COMPARISONS

The most commonly used comparison of individual well-being between nations is real per-capita income. Recent income trends, which may be good indicators of prospects for the immediate future, are also widely employed. It is generally agreed that the appropriate standard of comparison between countries is income per person rather than aggregate income. The total income of India, for example, is many times that of Sweden, but so many more Indians must share their economy's total output that output per person in Sweden is perhaps 50 times that of India.

[4] A. H. Jones, *Wealth of a Nation to Be* (New York: Columbia University Press, 1980), pp. 122–123, 303.

In concept, per-capita income calculation is simple: the money value of an economy's annual production of final goods and services (gross national product, or GNP) is divided by the population. But such figures should be viewed with caution. First, GNP is often compiled under rules that give more weight to convenience of data collection than to accuracy of measurement. Goods and services that are not sold are assigned arbitrary values, and their quantity is approximated. Second, figures for all countries must be quoted in some common unit to enable comparison. Normally the U.S. dollar is used. But the use of dollars to measure income changes in other countries means that fluctuations in exchange rates may affect income figures even when material output remains the same, or may mask greater real changes. The use of 1984 exchange rates in Table I.1, for example, has substantially improved the relative standing of the United States compared to that of a few years before. Also, the relative prices of goods that cannot be traded internationally (for example, housing and services) may be quite different in various countries. Finally, per-capita income figures are an arithmetic average of all incomes; they do not indicate the distribution of incomes within that average.

Despite these imperfections, large differences in per-capita incomes between nations are reasonably accurate reflections of the direction, if not the exact magnitude, of differences in real income per person. The huge gap between Indian and Swedish incomes indicates what we can readily observe—the average inhabitant of Stockholm has a far higher level of material well-being than his or her counterpart in Calcutta.

The Need for Economic Growth

Over time human wants increase rather than decrease, so economic growth appears necessary if economic well-being (the satisfaction gained from income rather than real income itself) is not to decline. The relevance of this point is especially clear if we observe the effects of very low incomes on human life-styles. Higher incomes allow people a wider range of choices, and very low incomes may impose extremely harsh constraints. In the recent past, the Eskimos practiced female infanticide and accepted the idea that in severe winters the elderly might have to die. Such attitudes reflected stark necessity, not cruelty or insensitivity. The Eskimo economy produced so little, at least in bad times, that the population had to be kept within the limits imposed by the available food supply, even if that meant reducing the current population. Lacking the ability to change their economic environment, the Eskimos had to adapt to its limits. If their society was to survive, the Eskimos could only support the unproductive from any surplus after the requirements of working adults were met. Until they gained knowledge of other societies' economic standards, their aspirations were limited by their own experience. In really poor economies, little effort can be devoted to providing anything other than physical necessities. The real difference between rich and poor societies, then, lies in the range of choices open to their citizens.

There can be little expression of artistic, social, or political values if all the resources of a society must be devoted to survival. Before people can begin those forms of activity that distinguish humanity from other life forms, some margin of output above subsistence is necessary. Throughout history, mankind's most noteworthy achievements—Egypt's pyramids and monuments, Indian philosophy, Chinese art and literature, Dutch painting, Elizabethan drama, and today's social and space programs—have come from societies that considered themselves rich. By expanding the range of attainable choices, economic development makes civilization possible. How the choices are used—with concern for others or in pursuit of the "good life" of private consumption, artistic expression, further growth, more leisure, or

war—is determined by the society's values and perhaps its experience during the development process. But enhanced capabilities are essential for choices to be available.

Costs of Growth

Like any other scarce good, economic growth is not free. Resources devoted to growth cannot simultaneously be used to enhance current consumption, nor can they be left in a natural state. Leisure, foregone consumption, and occasionally some deeply ingrained cultural values may be some of the costs of higher incomes. Moreover, economic growth produces new problems as well as new choices, and these may differ from any previously encountered as much as the new capabilities. Growth may produce income levels beyond the imaginations of previous generations, but it may also worsen the harried conditions of urban life and generate pollution and more threatening forms of warfare. The implications of these developments for human welfare, however, must be assessed in the context of the (usually greater) ability to meet them that is also generated. All of economics is a matter of weighing extra benefits against extra costs; only such cases involve meaningful choice.

The modern world suffers from pollution, epidemics, and crop failures, but these are hardly new problems. Formerly, their impact was much worse. City dwellers in the eighteenth and nineteenth centuries were also subjected to pollution, and their mortality rates indicate that the problem was much more serious then. Even if pollution has taken new forms, our abilities to reduce its threat have more than kept pace. Imagine, if possible, the terrifying impact of epidemic disease on societies that lacked all modern responses: medical knowledge to treat it, the biological, chemical, and engineering skills required to prevent it, and even an understanding of its causes in order to avoid it. Local crop failures still spell reduced incomes for the affected producers and consumers, but two or three centuries ago they meant famine. If we contrast the experiences of Germany and Japan in the Second World War and its aftermath with those of Central Asia in the wake of Genghis Khan or Germany after the Thirty Years' War, it is not even clear that modern war has (thus far) posed greater threats to civilization. In the past, recurrent energy crises, social upheavals, epidemics, and other phenomena appeared every bit as threatening to those experiencing them as contemporary problems do to us. With our capabilities, we might view the crises of the past as trivial, but those who faced them lacked our means.

SOURCES OF ECONOMIC GROWTH

If economic growth generally creates more benefits than problems, we must understand its sources, both in the United States and elsewhere, if we are to promote it. Is there any reason for the unique economic success of the United States? The theme of this book is that the American record owes a great deal to the superior short-run use of human potential and to institutions that in the long run both encouraged the development of that potential and allocated it and other inputs to their most productive uses. These have long been prominent characteristics of the American economy, and from the earliest days they yielded important economic gains. Other nations made less use of the productive potential of their people. They restricted geographic or occupational mobility or limited the number of people allowed to make their fullest contribution to a greater extent than in America.

American conditions and thinking from the earliest days of European settlement in the New World favored employment of available human talent in its most productive uses. For the entire formative period of the American economy, labor was too valuable to be wasted in uses that returned less than its maximum pos-

sible output. In addition, the prevailing economic circumstances fostered highly pragmatic assessments of change. From both inclination and necessity, Americans were more receptive to new tools, methods, and products and less tolerant of custom and tradition than were Old World societies. Not only were Americans inclined to select job candidates, tools, and methods on the basis of productivity, they pushed these concepts considerably further. Americans came to accept change as a continuous and largely beneficial element in their lives. Consequently, they developed institutions that accommodated and even encouraged it. Americans found it easier to change jobs, work methods, and locations than did people elsewhere. In this climate, innovations were not only rapidly adopted, but likely to produce a high proportion of their potential under American conditions. Americans prospered not merely because of superior opportunities in the New World, but because they made more of those opportunities.[5]

American superiority at recognizing and using human talent was (and to some extent remains) relative rather than absolute. By no means has every American always been free to make his or her maximum contribution or to develop the abilities to do so. Discrimination against women and blacks is only the most prominent example of the historical waste of talent that occurred in this country. Other nations, however, did much worse. There, the evaluation of human potential was more affected by considerations of race, sex, religion, social origin, or others of the thousand and one "reasons" people have developed to restrict or disregard the activities of others. In America, a job applicant's response to "What can you do, and how well?" carried more weight than that to "Who were your parents?"—if the latter

---

[5] D. North, *Structure and Change in Economic History* (New York: Norton, 1981) and M. Olson, *The Rise and Decline of Nations* (New Haven, Conn.: Yale University Press, 1982) are major contributions to the development of this theme.

were asked at all—than in even the most open European societies until the middle of the twentieth century. That degree of tolerance was unusual in Europe: many countries were far removed from the standards of Britain or the Netherlands.[6] European attitudes were often a major impetus to the migration of talented and ambitious individuals to this country.

The environment of seventeenth-century America provided harsh and conclusive evidence of job eligibility. Attitudes changed rapidly in the new surroundings. The very act of emigration guaranteed that America would obtain an unusually flexible subset of Europe's population, but New World circumstances forced even greater revisions in the first settlers' thinking. Initially, the only clear point about the optimum technology for American conditions was that traditional European methods were not the answer, and physical survival required rapid adaptation. Since most efforts were experimental, and initially no one had a monopoly on the right answers, Americans learned to judge actions by results rather than by their authors. In the process, they acquired a lasting appreciation of the potential benefits of change.

It is clear from both theoretical and empirical studies of economic development that change is an essential ingredient in the long-term growth recipe. Productive capabilities must be altered qualitatively if quantitative growth is to continue for very long. Any economy restricted to "more of the same" methods of raising output will soon discover that under such conditions output cannot rise much more than in proportion to the work force under the best of circumstances. Thus, there is a "lid" on per-capita incomes. Even these cannot be maintained indefinitely; growth within these restrictions can continue only as long as additional inputs of equal productivity remain available. With technology fixed, this could conceivably be the case for capital and labor, but natural resources cannot be expected to remain in perfectly elastic supply over large or long-term increases in production. The result is diminishing returns—additional increments of variable resources (capital and labor) produce smaller and smaller increases in output. Falling productivity, of course, implies rising costs; total output rises, but less than in proportion to inputs, and per-capita incomes fall. If substitutes for scarce resources can be developed or new, resource-saving methods introduced, diminishing returns need not impose a barrier to long-term growth. But such responses imply change.[7]

Attitudes toward Change

Economic change is usually a mixed blessing. New methods and products, however favorable their overall impacts, make life difficult for those with a stake in the old ways. Innovations can change the social status of individuals or produce competitive challenges to established views and products that are impossible to ignore.[8] Even if change is inevitable over time in any society, its pace and ultimate impact may be heavily influenced by prevailing attitudes and institutions. Is change viewed as a welcome vehicle for general improvement, as something to be tolerated in others but not encouraged, or as a destructive force to be grudgingly accommodated at minimum levels?

[6] E. H. Jones, *The European Miracle* (Cambridge, England: Cambridge University Press, 1981), Chaps. 8–10. See also J. R. Hughes, *Industrialization and Economic History: Theses and Conjectures* (New York: McGraw-Hill, 1970) and D. North and R. Thomas, *The Rise of the Western World* (Cambridge, England: Cambridge University Press, 1973).

[7] W. Parker, *Europe, America, and the Wider World: Essays in the Economic History of Western Capitalism* (Cambridge, England: Cambridge University Press, 1984), pp. 44–45.
[8] S. Kuznets, "Innovations and Adjustments in Economic Growth" in *Poverty, Ecology, and Technological Change* (Durham, N.H.: University of New Hampshire, 1973).

When social institutions and the popular opinions that underlie them allow a sizable portion of a society's work force to perform in occupations of each individual's choosing and to reap most of the positive or negative consequences, the economic environment encourages a continuous and widespread dispersion of new ideas throughout the system. Such circumstances reach their greatest development within a market economy. By making the authors of change responsible for the results of their innovations, the market system encourages changes that raise incomes and discourages those that reduce them, thus producing efficient responses to opportunity. Over time, the cumulative effects of such a climate are far-reaching indeed. The human mind appears capable of finding substitutes for any input or method, given sufficient time and incentives. This means that diminishing returns may be kept permanently at bay and that there are *no* ultimate restrictions on aggregate economic output. In encouraging these responses, the American economy gained an important advantage, and it did so earlier and more completely than any rival. The market system developed more by default than by any conscious choice as the basic framework for economic activity in America, but this was a most fortuitous accident.

All societies have to work out methods of developing, recognizing, and allocating human talent. Perhaps no other task has more profound long-run implications. How are important jobs assigned to people—on the basis of tradition, nepotism, political favoritism, bribery, social standing, inertia, or ability? No system has ever relied exclusively on a single criterion, but the weights assigned to choice factors have shown great variation. Several historical examples can illustrate this point.

In 1588, the king of Spain sought a commander for the armada. Military experience and ability were important considerations in his selection, but so was social standing. The Duke of Medina-Sidonia was chosen: he was an ex-perienced soldier, but also the scion of one of the oldest noble houses of Spain. Given Spanish values, neither the king's choice nor the duke's inability to refuse such a sign of high royal favor on grounds of ability (he had no naval experience whatsoever) were surprising. Elizabethan England, a more flexible society that was facing a life-or-death situation, used different weights in selecting leaders to oppose the armada. Perfunctory attention was given to social background, but Elizabeth's captains were seamen—or even ex-pirates—first, with other qualities a very distant second.

Over time, the allocation of human talent becomes even more important than in response to an immediate crisis. Toward what fields of endeavor does the society urge its "best and brightest?" By what standards are candidates appraised and trained, and what proportion of the population is considered? How are societal goals selected? The answers to these questions are critical to any society's long-term success.

Classical China, certain of the superiority of its traditional values, recruited its administrative class through a system of competitive examinations. Important jobs within the imperial government were filled on a merit basis, and most of the empire's male population was at least theoretically eligible to take the examinations. However, the subject matter of the tests and the tasks to which the successful candidates were assigned were the maintenance of China's ancient traditions and the exclusion of all things foreign. The system worked only too well. China became extremely resistant to change, particularly that originating outside its borders. The eventual Chinese response to pressures for which tradition allowed no effective answers was a traumatic restructuring that involved both enormous bloodshed and, at least temporarily, the almost total rejection of all aspects of traditional Chinese culture. Even in the United States, the stronghold of very different views, the change process has not always run smoothly—or peacefully.

In sum, then, if economic development is to be a major social goal, an economic system must alter both its productive capacities and the social institutions that govern their uses and determine their purposes. In the author's view no other system of economic organization aids this process as well as a price or market system. To a much greater degree than any other organization, markets not only foster the introduction of innovation, but provide accurate and automatic assessments of the costs and benefits involved. Since the eventual outcome of really significant departures from established norms can never be fully anticipated, this feedback process is vital for economic efficiency. No claim is made that mistakes are never made within a market system, but the pressures to undo them are generated more quickly and clearly than under any other form of economic organization. Markets also provide a near-ideal mechanism for diffusing new ideas throughout the economy, often producing a greater cumulative impact than the idea's initial introduction.

THE COURSE OF DEVELOPMENT

There is no single universally accepted theory of economic development. This book stresses one viewpoint—that much of America's success stems from its superior use of its human potential. But no claim is made that this was the sole source of American growth or the most important in all times and circumstances. Many theories stress other primary causes. Economic development has been claimed to stem from capital accumulation, entrepreneurs' efforts to introduce innovation, the success of an export sector, the sudden transformation of an economy's capabilities, and class strife and the exploitation of labor. This is only a sampling of some of the better-known theories. Various combinations of these and other theories have

also been proposed. The more prominent, together with the pertinent historical data, will be presented in later chapters.

The Importance of Continuity

If any single point emerges from studies of the development of modern economies, it is continuity. Much more than in political history, even the most significant events in economic history are best viewed as the consequences of prior events and as the basis for future changes. Even though dates may be assigned to important inventions based on patents or initial demonstrations, they seldom indicate the period in which the innovation had its greatest economic impact.[9] So too with the formation of institutions or laws: generally these are the culmination of previous activities. Once instituted, time is required before really different frameworks for economic activity have their full effects. Revolutions in economic capabilities do occur, based both on technology and the rules and attitudes governing the people who apply it. But the pressures that generate them and the culmination of their impacts may require years, decades, or even generations. The full impact of the Industrial Revolution, for example, is not yet apparent even in the countries where that epochal event first took place. Political manifestations of economic pressures are often as slow and incomplete as economic responses to change in the political environment.

Continuity is prominent in American economic history. The high incomes currently enjoyed by U.S. citizens result from a growth process at once more modest and longer-lived than that of most other countries. In addition, the incomes from which Americans began the process of continued growth were high by contemporary standards. Especially in relation to

[9] Ibid. See also N. Rosenberg, *Technology and American Economic Growth* (New York: Harper & Row, 1972).

the rates of economic growth achieved elsewhere since 1950, the American pace has not been outstandingly rapid. In the nineteenth and early twentieth centuries, the U.S. growth rate was among the world's fastest, but even then the pace did not match many of those in Table I.1. Since 1839, American per-capita incomes have risen at an average annual rate of about 1.6 percent. Before that time, the pace was apparently much slower and subject to considerable variation. It must be remembered, however, that this apparently insignificant rate of increase is compounded; one year's income gains become the base on which the next year's are based. Thus, a 1.6 percent compound growth rate doubles incomes every 45 years. Over the centuries, the cumulative effect can be enormous.

As the preceding pages have stressed, such growth could not have occurred without major alterations in the American economy. These have taken place; Americans now live and work in different manners and locations than their forebears. With economic development came specialization, which implies growing economic interdependence and exchange between an ever-widening variety of producers. Institutions and occupations that foster specialization—trade, transportation, communications, finance, marketing, education, and government—have enrolled a growing portion of the work force. The nature of production has also changed. Not only is the service component of the GNP accounting for a larger share than previously, but even within manufacturing and primary production the costs of capital and labor rather than raw materials increasingly determine prices. In some cases the change has been dramatic. Computer prices, for example, are far more heavily affected by the costs of labor and capital than by those of the copper and other raw materials that go into them.

The gains from American economic growth have been widespread as well as large. Income distribution has become more equal in the twentieth century than in other eras. Even change itself is now different. Increasingly it has become qualitative rather than quantitative, as reflected in the emphasis placed on research and education in the modern economy. Finally, as might be expected, not all the dimensions of economic change have been universally acclaimed.

We turn next to the background of economic growth in America.

SELECTED READINGS

Davis, L., et al. *American Economic Growth: An Economist's History of the United States*. New York: Harper & Row, 1972.

Hicks, J. *A Theory of Economic History*. New York: Oxford University Press, 1969.

Hughes, J. *Industrialization and Economic History: Theses and Conjectures*. New York: McGraw-Hill, 1970.

Kuznets, S. "Innovation and Adjustments in Economic Growth." In R. Puth, ed., *Poverty, Ecology, and Technological Change: World Problems of Development*. Whittemore School of Business. Durham, N.H.: University of New Hampshire, 1974.

———. "The Meaning and Measurement of Economic Growth." In *The Experience of Economic Growth*, edited by B. Supple. New York: Random House, 1963.

North, D. *Growth and Welfare in the American Past*. 2d ed. Englewood Cliffs, N.J.: Prentice-Hall, 1974.

———. *Structure and Change in Economic History*. New York: Norton, 1981.

Olson, M. *The Rise and Decline of Nations*. New Haven, Conn.: Yale University Press, 1982.

Parker, W. *Europe, America, and the Wider World: Essays on the Economic History of Western Capitalism*. Cambridge, England: Cambridge University Press, 1984.

Rosenberg, N., and L. Birdzell. *How the West Grew Rich*. New York: Basic Books, 1986.

Temin, P., ed. *New Economic History*. Baltimore, Md.: Penguin, 1973.

World Bank. *World Development Report, 1984*. Washington, D.C.: Government Printing Office, 1984.

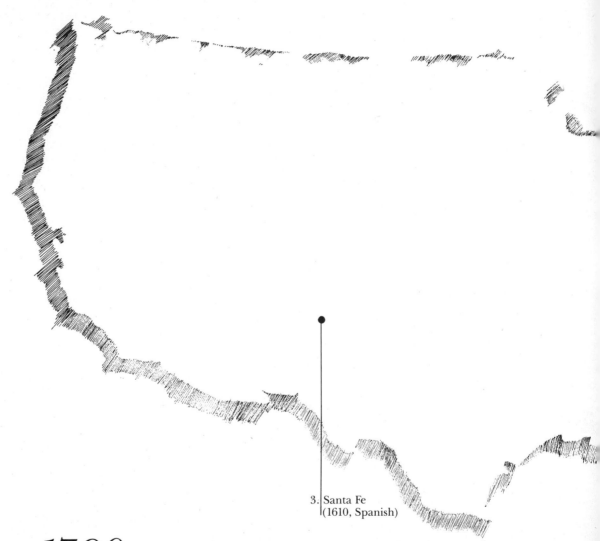

3. Santa Fe
(1610, Spanish)

1790 Dates for all the above taken from: *Timetables of American History.* Laurence
Urdang, edition introduction by H.S. Commanger. Simon & Schuster, Inc., 1981.

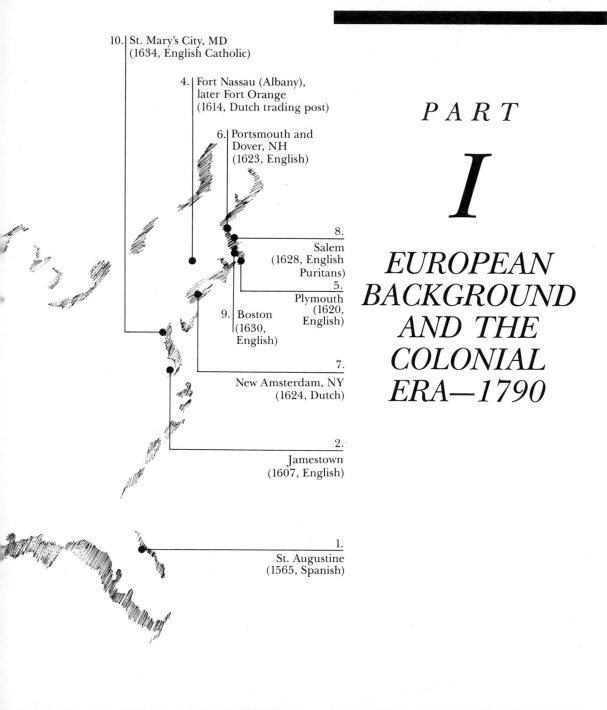

10. St. Mary's City, MD
(1634, English Catholic)

4. Fort Nassau (Albany),
later Fort Orange
(1614, Dutch trading post)

6. Portsmouth and
Dover, NH
(1623, English)

8.
Salem
(1628, English
Puritans)

5.
Plymouth
(1620,
English)

9. Boston
(1630,
English)

7.
New Amsterdam, NY
(1624, Dutch)

2.
Jamestown
(1607, English)

1.
St. Augustine
(1565, Spanish)

PART

I

*EUROPEAN
BACKGROUND
AND THE
COLONIAL
ERA—1790*

CHAPTER

1

INITIAL SETTLEMENTS AND THE EUROPEAN BACKGROUND

THE NORSE

The first European attempt to settle in North America ended in utter failure. Not only were the settlements abandoned, but even the memory of the discovery was almost totally forgotten. Nevertheless, for approximately the first two decades of the eleventh century, the Norse made a series of efforts to establish colonies in what is now Newfoundland. These rugged seafarers had already colonized Iceland, where they displaced the original Irish settlers. Shortly before A.D. 1000, the Icelandic colonists in turn established two settlements in Greenland. In the course of voyages to these colonies, northeastern North America was discovered. The Norse achievements were recounted in sagas, a type of epic poetry, but for a long time the sagas were regarded as mere legends. Only in the twentieth century was it realized that the sagas were also sailing directions, and that their references to attempts to settle land to the west recounted facts. By following the sagas' instructions, modern researchers have discovered the remains of a Norse village at the northern tip of Newfoundland.[1]

The physical evidence discovered in Newfoundland strongly supports the sagas. The Norse not only reached North America—at least some of them came to stay. The Newfoundland site's ruins are those of permanent buildings. The group that lived there included women, and at least one saga mentions that the settlers brought cattle to the new land. Yet in only a few years the settlements were abandoned, and the Norse retreated to Greenland.

[1] H. Ingstad, *Land Under the Pole Star* (New York: St. Martin, 1966) and *Westward to Vinland* (New York: St. Martin, 1969).

The Norse Settlements' Failure

Why did the Norse settlements nearly half a millenium before Columbus fail? The immediate cause appears to have been conflict with the indigenous population, either Indian or Eskimo. Their encounters with non-Europeans appear to have shocked the Norse, who at that time had met no other humans in Greenland.[2] The Irish, whom they had driven from Iceland, were familiar; indeed, they appear to have been seeking refuge there from Norse attacks on Ireland itself.

The Norse settlements in Newfoundland were very small and peopled by farmers and fishermen. Outnumbered and surprised by the natives, the Norse felt threatened. Yet these settlers were at most a generation or two removed from the Vikings who had raided and conquered along the coasts and rivers of Europe, from Russia and the Black Sea in the East to the British Isles, Normandy, and Sicily in the West. The Norse had met and overcome larger, better equipped, and better organized forces than any they would meet in the New World, and many of the Icelanders and Greenlanders had been exiled from Scandinavia for excessive violence. Further, by the standards of Greenland and Iceland, the new lands were rich. Newfoundland had a milder climate and more varied and plentiful resources—timber, game, arable land, and fisheries—than did either Iceland or Greenland. The Norse were able to maintain their Greenland colony for at least four centuries and the Iceland settlement was permanent. Why did the attempt in a more promising area fail?

In the long run the most likely reason for the Norse failure in America was economic, as it was for the demise of the Greenland settlements in the fourteenth or fifteenth century. At the time, the cost of establishing and maintaining a North American colony exceeded the returns. The costs could only have been borne by Europe. Iceland and Greenland were closer to the new area, but they were poor and Greenland in particular had only a tiny population of probably less than a thousand people. Output per person in both areas was low: what little production margin existed above direct subsistence had to support essential imports from Europe, such as grain and metal. Thus the established colonies could not spare the goods, ships, or people for a settlement effort large enough to promise success, particularly in the face of native opposition.

The Importance of European Support

European support was essential for any colony. Goods and tools that the colonists could not hope to make for themselves were required both to establish a colony and to maintain its living standards at European levels. Over time, these requirements could be obtained only if there were a payoff to the European suppliers. Reports from the initial contacts indicated the new area had few potential exports with good European markets. Furs, fish, and timber were readily available in Scandinavia itself at low cost. North America appeared to offer no gold, its native population allowed only slight opportunities for trade or plunder, and further exploration would involve high costs with no certainty of better returns. As the long-suffering inhabitants of coastal Europe could testify, the Norse were only too willing to undertake hazardous voyages—but there had to be some prospect of gain to tempt them into sustained efforts. In comparison to North America, eleventh-century Europe appeared to offer opportunities both more lucrative and more certain. In A.D. 1000, the Norse homeland was too poor, thinly populated, and disorganized to generate

[2] S. Morison, *The European Discovery of America: The Northern Voyages* (New York: Oxford University Press, 1971), pp. 55–57.

resources for ventures no more promising than the North American discoveries.

THE EUROPEAN SETTING AND ITS DEVELOPMENT

The Europe from which Columbus—very much by accident—rediscovered America had undergone profound changes since the Norse discoveries. Its capabilities were much greater; not only were there far more resources—people, ships, and other goods—but technological change had enhanced their performance. Attitudes and institutions had changed in manners that further supported economic activity, particularly long-distance trade. Nation-states were able to draw on resources from large areas and to marshal them toward a given end much more effectively than Medieval Europe could. For our purposes, the important results of these new capabilities were the great voyages of discovery and the establishment of colonies and trading posts in areas previously unknown to Europeans. Once begun, these efforts became more systematic than any that had occurred previously.

Some of the European changes were obvious. By the end of the fifteenth century, Europe possessed many more ships than it had 500 years previously. The ships were larger and more seaworthy, and navigation had improved; mariners could now cross the sea with some idea of the relative position of origin and destination. They could now determine their approximate location on the earth's surface, at least in terms of latitude, even on the open sea. The exchange of information between sources and the accuracy with which it was transmitted were facilitated by increasingly sophisticated maps and rutters (books of sailing directions), which allowed better comparisons of information from different sources. More widespread literacy aided information transfer as well, particularly when the original discoverer could not be consulted directly.

The Importance of Nation-States

The nation-states that had appeared by Columbus's time had both the capability and the motive to direct resources toward voyages of discovery. Information has many public good characteristics; its production requires scarce resources, yet the returns may accrue to the wider community, not the explorer. There was also a growing realization that political power had an economic base, so the development of new trade routes and products merited investment by the state.

The availability of gunpowder and improved naval tactics were less important than the advances in navigation, the ability to support exploration, and the determination to do so. But the combination of more maneuverable ships, cannon, and tactics that made the most of these advantages no doubt gave Europe's mariners more confidence in contemplating voyages into the unknown. In this era, all strangers were assumed hostile until proven otherwise, and at least at sea European technology could offset superior numbers. On land, Europeans had no overwhelming military superiority in either the Far East or the New World.

European Attitudes

The change in attitudes was at least as important as the change in physical capacity for overseas ventures. Medieval Europeans had viewed both human existence and the physical world in essentially static terms. Life was thought to be a preparation for the hereafter. The emphasis was much less on changing people's earthly circumstances, which were to be accepted, than on preparing for an afterlife. The philosophy of the Middle Ages did not view the world as subject to physical laws, the mastery of which might allow human betterment. There was great emphasis on the views of Aristotle or Ptolemy as the final answers in natural science or geography, often with little consideration of how well the ancients' ideas accorded with observed reality. The social, economic, and political institutions of most medieval European nations were largely based on tradition, and change was viewed as something to be avoided or minimized wherever possible. But very gradually the idea that improvements in the conditions of material life were both desirable and possible began to replace the older views. In pursuit of the new goals, people developed more rational and systematic methods of thought based more on observation and less on tradition.

THE STRUCTURE OF THE MEDIEVAL ECONOMY

There were reasons why economic change took so long to accelerate during the Middle Ages. The single dominating reality of the medieval economy was that output per person was very low, especially in agriculture. Since each farm family produced only a small surplus of food over its own needs, only a minority of the population could engage in nonagricultural pursuits. Further, a lack of production by any member of the agricultural community imposed severe burdens on the available surplus. Medieval cities were small, and trade was limited. Since the really significant changes most people could imagine were generally for the worse—war, famine, epidemics, or other disasters—the pervasive existence of institutions that made change difficult is not surprising. Nearly all persons were born into the jobs, locations, and social status they would retain for

their entire lives. Only a handful of people ever got the opportunity to qualify for a task on the basis of ability alone. Group activity in agriculture was the rule; fields were shared among families, and planting and harvesting were done as common exercises. Each village was responsible for the welfare of all its residents. Adherence to established methods was very strong; the consent of the entire community was necessary before new methods could be adopted. As a consequence, productivity improvements in agriculture were inhibited. There were some productivity-raising changes in medieval agriculture, but the pace was glacial.

Feudalism

Medieval economic and social systems were both land-based. Theoretically, in a feudal system all land belonged to the king. In return for military service and a variety of other payments, the king allowed nobles to control the administration of various regions within his realm. In turn, the nobles (often in several hierarchical levels) provided military services and administered justice for the peasants. In an era of constant armed strife, protection for the people who actually farmed the land was essential. The peasants supported the nobility with labor services on land under their lord's direct control, part of their own output, and various fees. The size of the peasants' contribution was determined by agricultural productivity, the peasants' mobility (if there were other nobles close by who desired additional workers, the lord's ability to exact more labor or higher fees was restricted), and compulsion. Tradition played a major role in the determination of each party's rights and obligations. Peasants also supported the church, which functioned as a secular as well as a religious institution; the local lord might be a bishop.

Given the state of military technology and the incredibly difficult transportation problems of the Middle Ages, the local nobility had a great deal of autonomy. Most of the king's political power was derived from the resources under his direct control: strong kings were usually great landlords in their own names. It was difficult for the king to obtain resources from the nobles for purposes that they opposed.

The End of the Medieval Economy

The economic system outlined here was largely static. Total output could be increased, but only by "more of the same" methods, at least in agriculture. Workers, tools, and land had to be increased in roughly the same proportions, because farming methods were essentially fixed. This also implied that the urban population was limited by the size of the agricultural surplus. With its fixed or very slowly changing technology, the Medieval European economy was very vulnerable to diminishing returns. If unused land of equal quality to that already utilized was not available as population increased, increases in agricultural production could only be obtained at increasing costs—and costs were already very high. The price of sizable increases might be insuperable. Population increases were therefore restricted by the supply of natural resources, in particular, unused agricultural land. This description of the medieval economy and the following discussion are based on the work of Professors North and Thomas.[3]

North and Thomas hypothesize that from the tenth through the thirteenth centuries, Europe's economic output rose as a growing population was employed on previously unused arable land. Increases in agricultural ouput allowed growth in the number and size of cities, which in turn facilitated regional specialization and trade. Since the technology of the urban economies was not fixed, productivity growth

in the cities initially permitted some growth in per-capita incomes. By 1300, however, diminishing returns in European agriculture were increasingly obvious. Little unused high-quality land remained to be brought into use; as the population grew, each additional laborer added less and less to the food supply. Not only were there more workers per unit of land, but the remaining additions to Europe's arable land were of lower fertility than those previously farmed.

Landlords' bargaining power rose as that of the peasants declined. The supply of labor was rising relative to that of land. In addition, real food prices rose. Landlords responded by increasing rents and labor services required of their tenants in an attempt to capture a larger share of agricultural output. Not coincidentally, Europe began to experience growing social unrest. In the early fourteenth century, the European economy collapsed in a catastrophic series of plagues (the bubonic plague—"Black Death"—outbreak of 1348–1351 may have killed a third of Europe's population), famines, and wars that left no area untouched. In some regions, population fell by as much as one-half over the next century. The sources of decline were viciously reinforcing. Malnutrition made the people more susceptible to epidemics, and epidemics in turn disrupted agriculture. Wars not only had a direct impact, but armies spread disease and disrupted or destroyed normal economic activities.

The Development of New Economic and Social Systems

During the long, painful recovery from these disasters, some areas of Europe developed new economic and social systems. The decrease in population reduced the pressures of diminishing returns. Now the scarce factor of production was labor rather than land, which improved the peasants' bargaining position with the land-

[3] D. North and R. Thomas, *The Rise of the Western World* (New York: Cambridge University Press, 1973).

lords. More significant for the long run were the changes in agricultural patterns and techniques that resulted from the change in factor proportions. These changes were more conducive to increases in agricultural productivity, which in turn allowed a rise in the nonagricultural portion of the population and further productivity gains. In Western Europe, North and Thomas claim, one crucial change was the development of private property rights to land. The old joint cultivation and common effort system was replaced by one in which individuals owned or rented land and were free to determine their own production methods. In Eastern Europe, the landlords' response to the population decline was an increase in physical coercion, which permanently bound the peasants to the soil as serfs. In Western Europe, however, the old constraints on agricultural change were reduced. Individuals could now try new methods without first gaining the consent of the entire community. Land was increasingly oriented toward production for the market instead of local subsistence needs, the preservation of the status quo, and risk minimization. The results were a reduction in the incidence of famine, rising urban populations, enhanced markets for all types of goods, and better use of human talent.

In a few countries where the new agricultural methods could be combined with low-cost water transportation, the food supply rose at a long-term pace first equaling and then exceeding that of population. Technological progress also occurred in mining, metallurgy, textiles, printing, and shipbuilding. These developments were most significant in Britain and the Netherlands after 1450. The innovations were less significant in France and still less so in Spain. Italy and Germany, formerly the centers of medieval technology, urbanization, and trade, were least affected, losing ground to the rest of the region, particularly after 1600. By that time, nation-states were combining the city-states' use of human resources with superior military and political power. The result was a further erosion of the old immobilities, but the process had no more than begun when the voyages of discovery commenced.

Changes in Political Structure

Changes in productive capacity were linked to changes in political power. Central governments gained at the expense of the traditional landowning nobility. In the struggle between the old and new power centers, the kings found allies in the towns and the merchants, who found the legal institutions of fragmented agricultural societies unsuited to their needs and slow to change. Economies of scale in the use of force increased: mercenary armies employing new weapons and tactics proved superior to the feudal levies of the nobility. Kings now had a source of political power independent of the nobles and greater than that which could be supported from their own lands—if it could be financed. The new armies were expensive and could not be funded from the traditional revenue sources. In exchange for new laws better suited to trade, finance, and manufacturing, the towns' taxes financed the central governments. Urban success in gaining a quid pro quo for taxes was an important influence on further development. In the Netherlands and England, the consent of parliaments was required before taxes could be levied, and this consent was generally forthcoming only as the property rights of individuals were further secured.[4] Gradually, too, it became clear that it was easier to obtain additional taxes if the economy that generated the revenues was growing. The new central governments did not eliminate war between nations, but they greatly reduced the local conflicts between nobles that had plagued the Middle Ages. Nation-states allowed traders to operate in larger areas under uniform laws and with greater security, and the volume of trade and specialization increased.

---

[4] Ibid., Chaps. 8–10.

Trade

The medieval view of trade was that economic activity, particularly that involving exchanges, was a zero-sum game in which one party's gain was another's loss. Once it became accepted that both parties to a transaction might gain, attitudes became more secular and rational. Interest in economic matters, especially trade, increased. Exchanges with distant regions whose customs, standards, and often religions were different posed the necessity of responding to customers' wishes. Tradition could not be invoked among peoples whose cultures differed from those of their would-be trading partners, and trade thus became profoundly subversive of rules based on long-established custom. Cities, whose very existence presupposed some trade, had always shown greater response to new ideas than the countryside. This was especially so where cities controlled their own governments. In Italian and German city-states, innovation flourished and opportunities existed for individuals to rise on the basis of talent even during the Middle Ages. The expansion of trade and urban populations in the fifteenth and sixteenth centuries spread these conditions to wider areas of Europe.

The Advent of Empirical Thought

The relaxation of tradition encouraged a view of the natural world as potentially understandable. Moreover, better knowledge might be usable in improving human welfare. Complete and consistent explanations of observed phenomena were now sought, and answers relying on appeals to faith or references to classical authorities no longer found ready acceptance.[5] Means of accurately transmitting the new knowledge improved. Printing reduced the cost of books, literacy became more widespread, and education began to be oriented toward prac-

tical subjects. Although these changes did not result in the complete triumph of attitudes comparable to modern scientific thought, it was obvious that horizons had broadened and that inquiry was becoming more efficient.

The new attitudes fostered different means of allocating human resources. Slowly the idea that people should be allowed to do those jobs that they performed most efficiently gained at the expense of the old rules assigning work on the basis of parents' occupations or social group. For the new jobs produced by innovation, this view developed by default; there were no traditional groups whose members had always done such work. Selection on the basis of ability had obvious advantages, both for talented individuals and for society. The new methods gained favor, particularly in Britain and the Netherlands. In these countries, institutions such as guilds, which had formalized the old methods of allocation, began to lose ground. These trends were strongest in Dutch and British export industries, where sellers had little choice about matching competitors' efficiency. Elsewhere in Europe, however, guild control over manufacturing probably increased.

Changes in Religious Thought

The profound religious changes of this period also influenced the economic transformation. It is inappropriate to regard the medieval Catholic Church as fundamentally opposed to economic activity or the development of rational thought. Even though the Church is linked with the doctrines of just price, prohibition of interest, and asceticism, these views were seldom enforced by 1400. Northern Italy, where the Church's religious control was never in doubt, was the cradle of both the Renaissance and the basic institutions of capitalism. Nor, despite the views of their later disciples, were John Calvin and Martin Luther particularly pro-business. Yet it is true that many of the new ideas were developed further or applied more generally either within Protestant countries or by ad-

---

[5] D. Landes, *The Unbound Prometheus: Technological Change and Industrial Development in Western Europe from 1750 to the Present* (Cambridge, England: Cambridge University Press, 1969), Chap. 1.

herents of minority religions within Catholic nations. The Reformation probably contributed to the separation of religious and secular thought, but no religion of this era advocated freedom of thought, and all were prone to violent repression of free expression and accepted employment discrimination as an expression of moral policy.

THE EXPANSION OF EUROPEAN VISION

These changes made the Europe of Christopher Columbus more motivated to mount overseas ventures than it had been in Leif Ericson's time. It was also far more capable of supporting them. Europeans were interested in the wider world for the sake of knowledge, but now it was also realized that foreign lands might produce material gains. If more and better goods were desired than those locally available, trade appeared to be the most efficient vehicle by which they could be obtained. It was not easy to learn foreigners' techniques, and the limited technology then available could not offset disadvantages in climate, raw materials, or skills. Thus, really different foreign products were hard to duplicate.

Some trade had always existed both within Europe and between that continent and Africa and Asia. Europe had maintained some cities since the Roman era, and cities cannot exist without trade. Regional specialization and the exchanges it made possible had increased through the twelfth century and again after 1400. The growth of nation-states reduced the risks of trade and sometimes improved transportation. European regions especially suited to the production of wine, wool, salt, timber, fish, grain, and cloth began to exchange these items for those that they could not make as well or as cheaply. The specialization process favored urban growth. Cities were collection

and distribution centers. They also provided the services, such as finance, primitive forms of insurance, and transportation, which supported trade. Eventually some towns became manufacturing sites as well.

Southern Europeans had exchanged their salt, wine, fruit, and manufactures for the fish, timber, metals, and wool of the North in the Middle Ages. The volume of this trade increased, and great market centers developed. Initially these were in Northern Italy and Southern Germany. Later, as seaborne commerce replaced overland trade, the Low Countries (modern Belgium and the Netherlands) supplanted Southern Germany. By the fifteenth century, the focus of intra-European trade had begun to shift from the Mediterranean to the North and Baltic Seas, and to the commodities of the North. Concentration on these bulky, high-volume goods had important repercussions on ship design and navigational techniques.

The Low Countries

The Low Countries were a centrally located exchange point, dominated politically as well as economically by cities devoted to trade and the processing of imported materials. As a result, the area developed market institutions earlier and more fully than other parts of Europe. Since many of their customers had access to other sellers, Low Country producers quickly learned competitive responses. In order to reduce costs and maintain markets, efficiency had to be continually improved. The Low Countries' resources were engaged in a wider variety of occupations than were those of nations still bound by tradition. This fostered comparisons of relative productivity in domestic as well as foreign trade.

Consequently, production methods in the Low Countries emphasized both current productivity and the rapid innovation of new technology. In addition to manufacturing innovations, cities in the region developed institutions to support their merchants' trade, such as banking, financial services, and practices that provided accurate information on current markets and prices. Antwerp and then Amsterdam became known as cities in which trade was easier, cheaper, and less risky than anywhere else in Europe. Capital was available there at low interest rates, and both buyers and sellers enjoyed a wide range of choices. Both parties to transactions made in these markets could be confident that contracts would be enforced and that materials and payments would meet the specified terms.

The Gains from Trade

If exchange is informed and voluntary, both parties gain. The gains from trade are greatest, however, when the capabilities and values of the trading parties differ widely. Thus, the profits from trade between Europe and distant areas could be very large. Europeans could not produce the fine fabrics, spices, rugs, jewels, and luxury manufactures of the Orient for themselves. Consequently, they were willing to pay high prices to those bringing such items to European markets. But obtaining Oriental goods was a slow, difficult, and often dangerous process, especially when overland transport was necessary. A round trip even to the Eastern Mediterranean required months, and one to China years—with a good chance the merchant might never return. Such trade also required that merchants obtain knowledge of the markets and customs of different regions, which generally could be gained only through personal experience. Chinese and Indian goods were expensive to transport, often passing through the hands of several sets of middlemen who took advantage of their monopoly positions. Moslems controlled the trade centers of the Levant, and religious as well as political conflicts raised the risks and costs of trade. The merchants of various Italian cities, especially

Venice and Genoa, were the first to overcome these obstacles and develop trade with the Orient. Their access to goods that Europe could obtain nowhere else made the Italian trading cities wealthy, and gains also accrued to regional distributors within Europe.

The Italian cities' trade-generated wealth was obvious to other Europeans. So too, if not as great, was that of the towns of the Hanseatic League, which controlled the trade in northern goods from the Baltic. As usual, the evidence of such gains provoked attempts to emulate the traders' success. Cities and states that did not share in these trade monopolies began to search for alternative products, markets, and routes. Since maritime transportation was much cheaper than overland, it seemed obvious that an all-water route to the Orient would provide its discoverer with a major advantage, especially after the Turks gained control of the Moslem world and imposed new restrictions on trade through the eastern Mediterranean. New goods' potential for gain was equally apparent.

These incentives encouraged British, French, and Portuguese fishermen to search for new fishing grounds to supplement those of the North Sea and the Baltic. Their intent was to break into markets currently controlled by the Hanseatic League and the Dutch. There was a steady demand in Southern Europe for dried, salted, or pickled fish, chiefly herring. The northern fishermen used the proceeds to finance imports from the Mediterranean and the Orient. As they developed their maritime skills, the Atlantic nations of Europe probed farther afield. All nations sent ships north and west into the great ocean, and the Portuguese sent expeditions south along the African coast. Most of these efforts were financed by individuals or groups of merchants, but Portuguese exploration was increasingly systematic. That nation established a school of navigation in the fifteenth century that both compiled much useful information and developed navigational aids and methods to make further use of it, particularly maps on which Portuguese discoveries were accurately portrayed.[6] During these early voyages, some encouraging discoveries were made.

Mercantilism

The increasing European emphasis on secular values was not confined to private citizens. Rulers began to see that a strong economy was an important base for aspirations to political power. Initially, monarchs had developed policies favoring the interests of merchants and towns as the price for tax revenues to support the struggle against the nobility. But soon it appeared that the costs of military power rose at even faster rates than rulers' ambitions, especially when the opposition was another nation-state. It was easier and safer to obtain revenues from a larger tax base than it was to simply raise rates. In pursuit of the goal of political power, efforts were made to expand and enrich the economy through a series of measures called *mercantilism*. To mercantilists, strong economies were a base for political power. The primary mercantilist policies were:

1. *Economic self-sufficiency*. Ideally, all domestically consumed goods were to be produced within the country. If some necessary item or input could not be made at home, it was to be obtained without granting any gains to the nation's rivals—that is, from distant producers or from the mercantilistic nation's colonies. All imports were to be in raw-material form and imported via domestic shipping to obtain the income generated by transporting and processing. To further these aims, nations were to develop import substitutes and obtain colonies where raw materials could be produced.

2. *An export surplus*. Mercantilism discouraged imports, especially of manufactured goods. Simultaneously, it encouraged exports, especially of highly processed items and luxuries. Foreigners were to pay the difference between their purchases and their sales to the mercantilistic nation in gold and silver, which could readily be used to obtain the services of mercenary armies at the time. A brimming treasury could easily be converted to military power.

3. *Widespread government direction and control of the economy in pursuit of these goals*. Massive state intervention was to be employed both to mobilize the nation's productive resources and to use them for mercantilist purposes. Labor effort was required from all, and coercion might be employed to discourage "idling" or divert labor from "unproductive" activities that neither increased exports nor substituted for imports. Luxury consumption was discouraged at home while it was promoted abroad. To increase exports, the state was to regulate their quality. Imports were fended off by tariffs, subsidies to domestic producers, and efforts to steal rivals' trade secrets while safeguarding any the mercantilist nation might have. Preferential treatment was given to products from colonial possessions.

4. *Strong military and naval forces*. As both a means and an end of mercantilist policy, military might and arms production had a high priority.

Obviously, every nation cannot sell more to foreigners than it buys from them. Perhaps only a little less clearly, mercantilistic policies were intended to injure rivals—one nation's gains were necessarily another's losses. No nation interested in mercantilism followed all its prescriptions. But even partial adherence to mercantilist policies could and did produce conflict. From the fifteenth through the seventeenth centuries, Europe was already well

---

[6] G. Walton and J. Shepherd, *The Economic Rise of Early America* (New York: Cambridge University Press, 1969), Chap. 1.

supplied with motives for war, and mercantilism added to the list. There were direct economic incentives for conflicts at sea. Most long-distance trade was waterborne, and goods' origins and owners might be difficult to establish. There were plenty of buyers willing to take advantage of bargains and nations that regarded anyone damaging rival trade as a public benefactor. Piracy flourished in such an atmosphere.

The Increase in Trade

Despite the interferences with trade that mercantilism fostered, Europe's internal and external trade increased after 1450. Transportation costs fell as shipping improved, markets grew larger, and information became more accurate. Even the armed forces developed under mercantilism played a positive role. The navies were used in peacetime to suppress piracy on some of the most heavily traveled routes, particularly in the North and Baltic Seas. After 1550 this allowed ships to carry more cargo, smaller crews, and lighter armament. Ships designed as specialized cargo carriers rather than quasi warships were more efficient transport vehicles. Since they did not carry cannon, they could be built more lightly, without the heavy timbers necessary to withstand the guns' weight and recoil. Their crews were only large enough to sail the vessels, rather than to deter attack. In an era when transport costs were a large portion (often 20 percent to 50 percent) of the price of foreign goods, these changes yielded important savings.[7]

Ironically, the very expansion of trade sought by mercantilism undermined its values. Many countries found it expedient to trade with their neighbors even if they were political rivals, to export precious metals, and to tolerate higher levels of domestic consumption, which produced more effective incentives to increase output than mercantilist compulsion. Expanded foreign trade produced a fundamental lesson: it was easier to sell foreigners what they wanted to buy than to persuade them to take what mercantilism said the nation ought to export. To sell in markets where buyers had alternative sources of supply, exporting nations were forced to substitute economic rationality for mercantilist doctrine.

The Oriental Trade.

One primary difficulty arose in trade with the East. A ready market existed throughout Europe for Oriental goods; any surplus over the importer's domestic needs could easily be reexported. But the Orient was not willing to accept European goods, especially the manufactures European mercantilists wanted to export, on terms favorable to Europe. Woolens were almost the only finished good in which Europe had a comparative advantage, and the market for them in the East was limited. The one commodity always acceptable in exchange for Oriental goods was precious metals. But aside from the opposition of mercantilist doctrine, Europe produced barely enough gold and silver for its own monetary needs and internal trade. Consequently, searches for both new sources of precious metal and other goods suitable for Oriental markets were intensified as Europeans sought new trade routes to the East.

Portugal

This tiny country on the Atlantic made the first effective responses to these difficulties, finding both trade routes and the commodities—or rather services—to supply them. Long before Columbus sailed, Portuguese efforts to improve navigation had been producing useful methods and information. In 1492 Portugal had not yet reached India by sea, but the southern tip of Africa had been rounded in 1488, indicating that the voyage could be made. In 1498, the first ship returned to Portugal from India with an enormously valuable cargo of spices. Spices were used both to preserve foods, particularly meat, and to disguise the taste of

[7] C. Cipolla, *Before the Industrial Revolution: European Society and Economy, 1000–1700* (New York: Norton, 1976), pp. 254–255. See also Morison, *The European Discovery.*

those stored too long. Portugal's efforts to develop an all-water route to the Orient had generated some direct benefits as well as geographic information. A trade in gold, ivory, low-grade pepper, and slaves had been developed along the west coast of Africa. Islands in the Atlantic had been discovered—Madeira (1333), the Canaries (1341), and the Azores (1431). These, Europe's first non-Mediterranean colonies in several centuries, proved to be valuable producers of wine and sugar. In the North Atlantic the rich fisheries that eventually made codfish a staple of European diets—perhaps even those of the Grand Banks—were being discovered.

These discoveries, rich as they may have seemed, paled in comparison with those of the next 50 years. In that short space of time, Europeans not only reached areas they had never known existed, but they also established trade relations and even political authority in vast regions.

THE NEW EMPIRES

The characteristics of the populations and products of the newly contacted—if not always newly discovered—regions determined the nature of the economic and political relationships that Europeans developed with them. In India, Europeans found themselves dealing with an ancient, highly developed civilization, skilled in the production of the goods so desired in Europe and well able to maintain its political independence. The tiny crews of the first ships to reach India quickly realized that their only option was trade: they could not hope to control the powerful Indian states. Worse, they had little that India would accept in trade.

The Portuguese Conquest

Notwithstanding these handicaps, the Portuguese quickly became a major factor in India's trade with Europe. It was obvious that the key to this trade lay in control of the Indian Ocean. If they could deny their trading rivals access to the sea routes from India to the Middle East and Egypt, the Portuguese could supplant Venice and Genoa by cutting off the supplies of the Arab middlemen from whom the Italians obtained their Oriental goods.

In a breathtakingly audacious move, the Portuguese gained naval dominance of the Indian Ocean. There, thousands of miles from home, the Portuguese navy destroyed the Moslem fleet (some of which, they found, had Venetian gunners aboard) in the Battle of Diu (1509). Once victorious, the Portuguese consolidated their position, using sea power to blockade the outlets to the Red Sea and the Persian Gulf. These measures greatly restricted (but did not eliminate) Arab traders' access to the Indian Ocean and cheap sources of Indian goods. After this, the Portuguese had no need to control India itself, since they controlled its best trade routes to the West. Trade along the traditional routes through the Mediterranean did not disappear, but henceforth the growth in trade would be on the new all-water routes around Africa.[8] Attempts to control the production of Oriental goods would have been futile. Europeans had no expertise in these areas, and they lacked the means to achieve the political control on land provided by their ships and cannon at sea.

Although the Portuguese gained control of trade in an area stretching from the east coast of Africa to Japan, their hold was precarious. The Portuguese "empire" was a string of small forts and trading posts, all dependent on the support of naval forces never more than barely adequate to meet local challenges. It could not withstand a challenge from any nation possessing modern sea power.

Portuguese domination of Oriental trade lasted less than a century. The population of Portugal was too small to supply the manpower needed to fully exploit her gains. The labor

[8] Walton and Shepherd, *The Economic Rise*, pp. 15–16.

shortage in Portugal was so severe that it was the only country in Europe to use African slaves domestically as well as in its overseas colonies. Other problems were even more serious. Portugal did not market the proceeds of its Oriental trade within Europe; they were distributed by the Italians and the Dutch after arrival in Lisbon. The country did not develop industries to produce trade goods for the East or for Africa. Portuguese social institutions were not flexible enough to make maximum use of the available human skills; royal control over trade became ever more extensive and rigid. Portugal itself was annexed by Spain in 1580, and its Eastern empire proved unable to withstand pressure from the Netherlands, which by 1600 had become one of Europe's most formidable sea powers.

The Netherlands

The Dutch role in Oriental trade was more enduring than the Portuguese. Although a small country with a limited population and even more limited natural resources than Portugal, the Netherlands was far more successful in offsetting its deficiencies. Until the latter half of the sixteenth century, the Netherlands was ruled by Spain. The Spanish seemed to view the Netherlands largely as a source of tax revenues to be devoted to causes that were anathema to the Dutch. From this unpromising base, the Netherlands became the wealthiest country in the world and maintained that position for several centuries. The Dutch made the most of what they had—a favorable location for trade and the talents of their people. Dutch institutions used the country's human resources, allowing more scope for competition and innovation than elsewhere; consequently the Netherlands was able to counter rivals' quantitative superiority with efficiency and a shrewd grasp of opportunities.

The Low Countries had shaken free of rigid medieval institutions as early as any other area in Europe. Dutch markets were highly developed and open to merchants of all nations. The Netherlands became Europe's market center and the Dutch its delivery service. The Dutch economy produced little from the nation's own resources except fish; manufacturing in the Netherlands involved the processing of imported raw materials. As middlemen, the Dutch enjoyed no markets in which their position could not be challenged; they had no choice but to compete, and they were formidable competitors indeed. Their situation forced a pervasive economic rationality on the entire economy. Access to jobs was decided far more on the basis of ability than elsewhere in continental Europe. The Dutch learned to tolerate religious diversity while other Europeans were still at each others' throats over this issue. The country welcomed refugees possessing useful talents; both French Protestants and English Pilgrims found refuge in the Netherlands. The Dutch nation was not completely free of the grasp of tradition, nor was it a democracy by modern standards, but the Netherlands had come far closer to both than any other country in Europe, with the possible exception of England.

The Dutch achieved a great deal more than high incomes. Theirs was the first economy to achieve sustained growth in per-capita incomes, but it also supported accomplishments in other fields. The Netherlands produced Rembrandt, Erasmus, and many other great names in art and science, reflecting the high levels of individual freedom that made inquiry possible. Although they preferred to trade, the Dutch were a formidable military power as well, especially on the sea. They used military force to prevent the recovery of Antwerp as a rival to Amsterdam and to replace the Portuguese in the Far East.

In the long run, however, the Dutch were vulnerable. As middlemen, they had no markets secure from foreign competition. As a trading nation, the Netherlands was injured by other countries' mercantilist policies. They had no secrets that others could not learn, and they failed to develop manufacturing to the extent the English did. Although their decline was relative, not absolute, the Dutch lost ground to the English and the French in the eighteenth century. Like the Portuguese, their trading empire in the Far East was based on the control of seaborne trade, not commodity production. As a result, there were no extensive Dutch settlements, and their position was weakened as other naval powers expanded into Oriental seas.

SPAIN IN THE NEW WORLD

Spain was the first European country to establish colonies in America, and the Spanish colonies differed from European ventures in the Far East almost as much as Spain herself differed from the Netherlands. There could be no greater difference than that between the attitudes of Spain and the Netherlands. The Dutch were pragmatic, flexible traders; Spain was a nation consumed by ideology. Spanish values ranked religion, tradition, and military prowess far above material success, and these goals were pursued both internally and in foreign policy. In foreign endeavors, the Spanish sought "God and gold"—not necessarily in that order. The Dutch welcomed religious refugees; Spain created them. A crusade might sound ludicrous to the Dutch, but no term better describes the zeal with which Spain tried to push back the Moslems, reestablish Catholicism in Protestant Europe, and further Spain's great-power aspirations. All these efforts were marked by the utter disregard of costs and economic reality that has always characterized fanaticism.

The Spanish Government

Spain's government was controlled by the king and the Church. The merchant community had a much smaller voice than in most other European countries. Spain's military adventures were both far-reaching and never-ending, and internal policy was largely oriented toward the immediate generation of tax revenues. Consequently, established revenue sources were favored over new industries, especially if the formation of new activity might involve a short-term loss of taxes. Even worse, property was not secure in Spain, particularly in the newer forms possessed by merchants and manufacturers. Even older forms were subject to arbitrary taxation or confiscation; there was no effective popular control over the king's claims on his subjects' wealth. Spanish commercial agriculture was retarded in favor of the *Mesta*, the wool producers' association that furnished most of the country's internal revenues. This policy kept Spanish agriculture unproductive and subjected the nation to recurrent famines. Spain had achieved a precarious sort of political unity only a few years before Columbus's voyage—but through the marriage of King Ferdinand of Aragon to Isabella, Queen of Castile, and the new sovereigns' conquest of Granada in 1491, rather than through the development of new institutions. The nation had been willing to pay a high price for a government that could maintain internal order, but some Spanish subjects considered it excessive. The Netherlands, a far greater source of tax revenues than Spain's New World empire, eventually revolted because of the exactions of the Spanish Crown. In the long run, these policies made change very difficult in Spain. The country did have active merchant communities, particularly in Barcelona and Seville, but merchants and their views were scorned by the soldiers and churchmen who constituted Spain's administrative force.[9]

Columbus and Spain

Given these rigidities, it may seem strange that Columbus sailed from Spain rather than from some country where trade was better regarded.

---

[9] North and Thomas, *The Rise of the Western World,* pp. 127–131.

In this case, the centralization of authority in the Spanish Crown proved helpful in assembling the resources for the voyage. Although the Crown did not finance Columbus, it did use political pressure to obtain funds, ships, and men from the cities.

Within Spain, the initial exhilaration over Columbus's discoveries quickly became disappointment when it was realized that the West Indies were not the gateway to the Orient, but the outliers to a great barrier to that goal. Nor did the islands offer quick payoffs in themselves. There were some opportunities for ranching and mining on Cuba, Jamaica, and Hispaniola, but the Spanish conquest, mistreatment of the natives, and European diseases soon all but eliminated the native Indians. Few Spaniards were willing to go to the New World to work for others, and interest in the New World waned.

The Conquest of the Spanish Main

The conquest of the great Aztec (1519–1521) and Incan (1534–1536) empires of the mainland (financed from existing settlements in the islands)[10] sparked another abrupt change in Spanish regard for the potential of the New World. Not only was there enormous loot in precious metals (chiefly silver), but the structure of the Indian societies facilitated the Spanish conquest at ridiculously low cost (Pizarro began the attack on Peru with 134 men) and aided the formation of colonial societies highly congenial to Spanish values.

The Spanish could overcome large, highly developed, and warlike Indian empires in the first half of the sixteenth century because both the Aztecs and the Incas had formed strongly centralized, hierarchical societies. Spanish military superiority was at best marginal. In both conquests, the Spanish gained access to the rul-

ers and killed them or forced them to cooperate, leaving the opposition leaderless. In addition, there were plenty of Indians willing to ally themselves with the Spaniards to settle old scores with the Aztecs and Incas. Once the Indian leadership was eliminated, the Spaniards replaced it with their own, leaving many of the society's basic institutions intact. They were thus directing nations with large agricultural labor forces accustomed to devoting much of their output to the needs of the state.

The values of the Spanish conquistadores were feudal, and they found the new circumstances much to their liking. Even better, the payoff to Spain grew: European mining methods made the mines of Mexico and Peru far more productive than under the Indians. Since labor appeared abundant and its products were valuable, the Spanish used Indian workers harshly. Labor in the mines killed many Indians, and diseases to which they had no resistance proved even more lethal.[11] Under Spanish rule, the economy of the mainland became one of great landed estates, owned by the conquistadores or their descendants, which provided agricultural products to support the labor forces of the mines and ports. Spain's primary interest in the colonies was in maintaining the flow of treasure to the royal coffers.

In the long run, the New World produced items far more valuable than precious metals. Food crops developed by the American Indians—maize (corn), white and sweet potatoes, and manioc—are now staples of the human diet in many parts of the world. Some of these crops have enormously enhanced the productivity of agriculture, particularly in tropical areas. Peanuts, beans, squashes, peppers, tomatoes, and cocoa have also contributed to the quality and variety of human diets. Tobacco has had a less benign influence. Several of these crops, particularly maize, spread rapidly through the Old

---

[10] Walton and Shepherd, *The Economic Rise,* p. 20.

[11] A. Crosby, Jr., *The Columbian Exchange: Biological and Cultural Consequences of 1492* (Westport, Conn.: Greenwood Press, 1972), Chap. 2.

World after importation from South America.[12]

The Results of Spain's Imperial Rule

The new empire, which at first appeared to be a mercantilist dream come true, in the long run did very little to further Spain's economic development. In the colonies, the feudal attitudes that so impeded change in Spain herself were strongly reinforced. There was no mass migration from Spain to America. New Spain's overlords did not encourage the formation of new attitudes and institutions, and the Spanish Colonial Office was even more rigid. The Spanish ruling class was in a position to extract huge incomes for itself with little regard for the effects on the colonies' economy.

Starvation, disease, overwork, and violence decimated the Indian population of Spanish America. In the century after the conquest, the native population of Peru fell by more than one-half; that of Mexico, by as much as 90 percent.[13] Nor did Spanish rule even produce order. Their new status did not incline the conquistadores to humility. The conquest of the Inca Empire required only two years; suppressing rebellions among the Spaniards who accomplished that feat required 34 more.

Economic activity in Spanish America was largely confined to mining, ranching, and agriculture. European domestic stock thrived on the rich pastures of the New World. But aside from new landownership patterns and the introduction of cattle, sheep, horses, and pigs, there were few innovations. Markets were small; the Spanish rulers were few and the Indians both poor and discouraged from acquiring European goods. In particular, there were few innovations in urban life.

Spain had no interest in changing the colonies' economies as long as they continued to produce revenues; if anything, stability made administration easier. Ironically, the flow of New World treasure probably postponed within Spain the adaptive responses to changing conditions that were transforming the Dutch and English economies. Spain used the New World treasure to finance a long and ultimately disastrous series of European wars rather than to stimulate its own internal development. The colonies were kept under tight mercantilist control, their trade regulated by monopolies whose main purpose was to generate more taxes. Spain produced few of the goods shipped to the colonies; American silver was used to buy supplies for the empire and for Spain itself elsewhere in Europe.

The beneficial results of increased demand and a larger money supply were technological change and increases in production, but these occurred in England, France, and the Netherlands, not Spain. It seems clear that the sixteenth and seventeeth centuries were a period of substantial technological progress, especially in industry. Manufactured goods' real prices fell, even though rising population generated substantial increases in food prices, indicating much smaller productivity gains in agriculture.[14]

So great were Spain's ideological aspirations that treasure flowed out of the country even faster than it could be acquired. Efforts to increase the Crown's share of New World treasure and ever-increasing domestic taxation were preferred to changes that might have allowed the economy to produce more. Much the same policy was followed in the other parts of the Spanish empire. Indeed, it was increasing tax burdens as much as religion that drove the Netherlands to fight for and win independence.

To better control her colonial trade, Spain restricted all trade to one or two great fleets each year. The flotillas brought European goods

[12] Ibid., Chap. 5.
[13] Walton and Shepherd, *The Economic Rise*, pp. 31–33.
[14] Ibid., pp. 21–28.

to the colonies and returned with treasure. To ensure the collection of taxes, all goods—regardless of their ultimate destination within the colonies—had to be shipped via the Caribbean, a clumsy, slow, and expensive system. Both Spanish colonists and the Europeans who were their source of goods found that direct exchanges were more lucrative. Spain made little effort to adjust its regulations to New World conditions and granted local authorities little autonomy. Their requests for change might not be answered for two years—and often the Colonial Office's response would be a request for more information. Even officials selected for their loyalty to the Crown made adjustments contrary to their instructions from Spain. Spanish colonists began to trade directly—and illegally—with other Europeans, an exchange from which both parties received larger benefits than from legal trade.

Other European nations were anxious to obtain some of the treasure produced on the "Spanish Main" (the South and Central American portions of the continent). English, French, and Dutch ships combined trade and piracy as advantage dictated. Spain was frequently at war in Europe, and at times military strategy was turned to economic advantage. In 1628 the Dutch navy captured every ship in the annual treasure flotilla, the most successful of many such efforts. Piracy was endemic in the unsettled political climate of the Caribbean, the more so as privateering (legalized piracy) was widely employed in wartime. At times the pirate forces grew strong enough to attack not only shipping, but even some of the major ports, such as Panama (1662) and Porto Bello (1668), through which treasure was shipped to Spain.

The Slave Trade

The decline of the Indian population of Spanish America encouraged a new trade in the Caribbean, that in African slaves. The virtual disappearance of the natives created a demand for labor from Spanish planters, ranchers, and miners. Early in the sixteenth century, Europeans found that they could earn high profits by buying slaves on the West African coast and selling them in the New World from Brazil to Mexico. Later, North America furnished an additional market. So lucrative was this business that Europeans fought wars over the control of the slave trade.

Other European Settlements in the Caribbean

Traders, pirates, and navies all required bases. After 1600, non-Spanish Europeans began to acquire islands that the Spanish had not settled, and shortly after, to attempt the conquest of some of Spain's more weakly defended possessions, such as Jamaica (1664). Even earlier, pirates and traders had established less formal settlements. Occupation led to the production of a variety of goods on the islands: fine woods, a few spices, tobacco, and preserved beef for ships' stores (*boucan,* meaning "smoked beef," is the origin of the word *buccaneer*—a reflection of the pirates' alternative occupation).

The islands' real value became apparent to Europeans only after sugar cultivation was introduced, chiefly in the seventeenth and eighteenth centuries. Sugar was an ideal mercantilist good; it was in high demand throughout Europe, yet could not be produced there, save on a few Mediterranean islands. Better still, Caribbean production replaced imports from the Spanish empire and Brazil, and any surplus beyond domestic needs could readily be sold to other European nations. Large plantations worked by slave labor had lower production costs than other forms of organization. Many Caribbean islands became highly specialized sugar producers, performing few of the other activities necessary to sustain their populations. Instead, they used their exports of sugar to finance imports of much of their food and nearly all their manufactured goods, and to pay for the services of foreign shippers.[15] Sugar production resulted in another large market for slaves, and not merely because the demand for the product expanded; with slaves readily available at low prices, it was cheaper for planters to work them to death and rely on continuous imports of fresh slaves rather than natural reproduction to maintain a labor supply. Tropical diseases also reduced slaves' longevity. So valuable were the Sugar Islands to Europe that in 1763 England seriously debated which of its conquests from France to retain after the Seven Years' War—all of Canada or Guadeloupe and a few other tiny islands.

As succeeding pages will make clear, understanding the economic history of Latin America and especially the Caribbean is essential to comprehension of the economic development of the North American colonies. All European colonies in the Americas were parts of an integrated economic system, and in some cases their relations with each other were fully as important as those with Europe.

NORTH AMERICAN SETTLEMENTS

Europeans colonized the Caribbean and the mainland from Mexico south to Argentina earlier, and initially in larger numbers, than they

did North America. Even after the first settlements on that continent were established in the sixteenth and seventeenth centuries, their growth was very slow and punctuated with disasters. In 1565, the Spanish established St. Augustine in what is now Florida to protect the route of their treasure flotillas. But the town and its hinterland produced nothing that could not be obtained elsewhere, and St. Augustine remained little more than a garrison post.

Farther north, prospects were no better. There were no obvious rewards of the type that beckoned from the Caribbean or the Spanish Main. The Indians had little of immediate value to Europeans except furs, the populations were too small to furnish a labor force if subdued, and conquest of the less developed tribes in both North and South America often proved much more difficult than had that of the great Indian civilizations. Tribes lacking cities to attack, agriculture to tie them to a given area, or rigid leadership patterns proved able to resist European domination for long periods, sometimes centuries.

Early Exploration and Settlements

Shortly after the resumption of European contact with North America, it became clear that if Europeans were to obtain anything from the area, they would have to do so themselves. Rumors of gold, highly developed cities, and easy trade routes to China all proved disappointing. (Hope died hard: in 1634 a French explorer landed in what is now Little Suamico, Wisconsin, in full regalia for the Chinese court; several expeditions from seventeenth-century Virginia hoped to find the Pacific Ocean just beyond the Blue Ridge.) Even though the first voyages to North America followed closely in Columbus's wake (Cabot in 1497), serious attempts at settlement did not occur for half a century, and none succeeded until Jamestown (1607) and Quebec (1608), whose success was any-

---

[15] Several economists, notably Harold Innis and Douglass North, have propounded growth theories in which the development of an economy is based upon the growth of its export commodity, or "staple." They contend that the overall pattern of development depends upon the nature of the export industry and the effects of its expansion upon other sectors, as well as the disposition of the income which it generates. If the staple's production expands rapidly and has substantial linkages with the rest of the economy, as a source of markets or supplier of goods and services that aid the development of other sectors—or if a substantial part of the income generated by the staple is plowed back into the economy—the staple's growth will generate overall economic development. See H. Innis, *The Fur Trade in Canada* (Toronto, University of Toronto Press, 1970), and D. North, *The Economic Growth of the United States, 1790–1860* (Englewood Cliffs, NJ: Prentice-Hall, 1961).

■ Sir Richard Grenville led the expedition to settle Roanoke Island as a base for raiding Spanish shipping.
Source: De Bry, *America*, Part I. 1590.

thing but clear for years more. Permanent settlements with a high degree of self-sufficiency would be required before the full potential of North America could be assessed. The Caribbean, South America, the Orient, and Europe itself seemed to offer better prospects than did North America.

Early attempts at settlement did nothing to change this opinion. There were at least two Spanish, four French, and several English efforts north of Florida in the sixteenth century. All failed, and several colonies vanished without a single survivor. Europeans held wildly unrealistic ideas of New World conditions that all but guaranteed disaster. The English, for example, believed that latitude determined climate. To play it safe, they established a colony well south of England—at the latitude of the Riviera. The survivors of a winter at the mouth of Maine's Kennebec River claimed that the theory needed major modification. The French tried to establish a colony on Sable Island, a windswept sandbar in the midst of the North Atlantic's worst weather, from 1598 to 1603. They rescued 11 insane and probably cannibalistic survivors.[16]

[16] Morison, *The European Discovery: Northern Voyages*, pp. 480–481.

Explorers and settlers alike never seemed to realize that the feasts with which the local Indians greeted them indicated hospitality rather than an unlimited food supply. Attempts to obtain food from the Indians were a frequent source of trouble in the early days of several settlements and may have caused at least one colony's disappearance. Even after Europeans became more realistic about American conditions, other mistakes continued. Many colonies were badly located in terms of harbors, potential food and water sources, defense, and disease. Survivors of these early efforts had grim tales of hunger, deadly new diseases, Indian raids, and extremes of climate. For Europeans, hot American summers were almost as great a surprise as the cold and snow of the new land's winters. If only the most fortunate of the earliest settlers survived to return to Europe, and none improved his welfare, there is little wonder that Europe concentrated its efforts elsewhere. Until early in the seventeenth century, St. Augustine and a few fishermen sun drying their catches on northeastern shores made up the entire colonial effort in eastern North America.

FRENCH AND DUTCH COLONIES

In view of North American conditions and the region's apparent potential, the fur trade appeared to offer the best chance to get quick returns from small investments overseas. Since the French and Dutch intended to trade with the Indians for furs rather than do their own trapping, only a few people would be needed, and returns would not be long delayed. Little long-term investment was necessary to establish trading posts. Both nations had gained some experience in fur trading as a sideline to their fishing ventures in the North Atlantic.

The Dutch in America

Given their objectives, the Dutch picked a good location. In 1614, they established a post at Fort Orange (Albany) that gave the easiest access to the interior on the Atlantic coast south of Canada. New Amsterdam, on the present site of New York City, was settled later. Fort Orange possessed the essential element for success in the fur trade—access to a vast hinterland by low-cost water transportation.

Rather surprisingly, in light of their policies at home, the Dutch did not establish colonial institutions particularly conducive to individual effort and initiative. No real effort was made to encourage settlement in New Netherlands, perhaps because the limited Dutch population already had so many other alternatives, both in their homeland with its growing incomes and in other trade locations. Indeed, some policies discouraged mass settlement. It was not easy for the average Dutch citizen to obtain clear title to usable land in the colony. For farm land to have any real value, it had to have access to water transportation so produce could be brought to market. But much of the land along the Hudson River was granted in great estates to landowners called *patroons*, who were more willing to rent land than to sell it. The patroons' rental terms were more favorable to tenants than were those in Europe, but few people were willing to risk the Atlantic voyage and settlement in a new land without the prospect of landownership. Patroons had near-feudal political and social control over their estates, and since their boundaries were ill-defined, title to land outside their immediate claims was uncertain.[17] Land along the coast was somewhat easier to obtain, but Dutch expansion to the north was soon restricted by Yankees moving down from New England. Movement to the south was contested by Swedes

[17] S. Kim, *Landlord and Tenant in Colonial New York, Memorial Society, 1664–1775* (Chapel Hill, NC: University of North Carolina Press, 1978).

and other English settlers. Although New Netherlands did grow and even managed to annex the Swedish settlements in the Delaware Valley and New Jersey, ambitious Dutch settlers apparently saw better opportunities elsewhere.

Much of the population of New Netherlands was not Dutch; one governor claimed to rule people speaking 23 different languages. The fur trade never had the profit potential of Dutch ventures in other parts of the world, and the colony was always more or less neglected. When the English assaulted it in 1664 (and offered the inhabitants liberal terms of government), neither the Dutch nor the colony's inhabitants offered resistance. But the English did recognize the patroons' land claims, and the colony grew slowly for a long time.

French North America

It might be argued that even with correct policies, the Dutch simply lacked sufficient resources to establish a successful North American colony. But France was different. In the early seventeenth century, France had the largest population in Western Europe and a government both able and willing to marshall the resources for a colony. But although the French endured for over a century and a half and left an indelible cultural imprint, New France too was eventually taken over by the English.

The Fur Trade

Once again, the root of New France's long-term problem appears to lie in the colony's orientation toward the fur trade. French decisions, given that choice, were excellent, but in the long run the selection of the colony's basic industry was a fatal handicap. The location of their initial settlement in the St. Lawrence River valley gave the French the best route to the interior of North America on the entire East Coast, and they later gained control

of the Ohio and Mississippi River valleys as well. But the fur trade had implications for the settlement and conduct of the colony that hindered expansion and eventually made its survival impossible. The pursuit of furs encouraged the French to explore the interior and establish territorial claims, but it also reduced their ability to hold territory devoted to that purpose.

Too great a production of furs from any area wiped out the animal populations on which the trade was based, so the fur trade's volume could be expanded only by increasing the territory in which it was conducted. Territorial expansion was costly: transportation expenses were high, and there was the ever more complicated problem of maintaining good relations with mutually antagonistic tribes. Samuel de Champlain's early intervention in one tribal war (1616) was a serious mistake; it earned the French the lasting enmity of the Iroquois Federation. This powerful group of tribes menaced New France's communications with the interior and, for many years, the very existence of the colony itself. Most of all, the fur trade depended on the continued existence of the wilderness and of good relations with the Indians, who actually collected the furs. The French were traders, not trappers.

The fur trade's primacy sharply restricted the type and extent of other economic activity within New France. Above all, European-style agriculture and the population densities it allowed were utterly incompatible with the fur trade.[18] Since New France had to produce its own food, this precluded a large population. Given the difficulties of trans-Atlantic communication, the fact that the St. Lawrence was icebound for at least four months each year, and the memory of New France's forced surrender in 1632 when the English captured that year's supply ships, dependence on outside food

---

[18] For an excellent discussion of the land needs of Indians versus those of agricultural peoples, see S. Lebergott, *The Americans: An Economic Record* (New York: Norton, 1984), Chap. 2.

supplies was unacceptable. A small population allowed little specialization and thus lower productivity gains and increases in incomes. Limited specialization increased the colony's dependence on France. The French government's attitude toward migration to the colony was consistent with its choice of New France's primary activity. Little was done to encourage French citizens to settle in the New World, except for some efforts to provide New France with a continuous reservoir of military manpower. Some Frenchmen who might have made unusually productive colonists were forbidden to emigrate. Unlike the English, who allowed or even encouraged troublesome religious minorities to form colonies within the empire, the French either exiled their Protestants or allowed them to settle in private colonies outside the governmental protection of France. The Huguenots made two such efforts; one colony was abandoned, and the second was wiped out by Spain. When they left France for Britain, the Netherlands, or the British colonies, the Huguenots compiled an unusual record of economic achievement. France forced them to make their contributions to other nations' economies, very much to her own loss.

The Attraction of Landownership

If there was one lure that proved irresistible in attracting seventeenth-century Europeans to North America, it was the prospect of acquiring land. Landownership meant more than mere income to Europeans; it was the major determinant of social status. The ownership of land—especially a lot of land—conveyed a standing unmatched by any other form of wealth. But immigrants to New France could not normally obtain clear title to land; they found that much of the colony's desirable acreage was in the hands of landlords who imposed conditions of tenancy not much more favorable than those of France itself. New France was also a closely controlled, stratified society. Even within the limits imposed by the

small population, there was not much scope for individual initiative in the settled areas.

Despite these limitations, the French had remarkable success. They were proficient traders. Even though their trade goods were higher priced and qualitatively inferior to those of the English, they compensated through lower transportation costs and better relations with the Indians. Until the Hudson's Bay Company was established in 1670, the French alone had access to the area that produced the highest quality furs. Since they regarded the fur trade as a long-term proposition, the French got along better with the Indians than did the British, for whom the fur trade was generally a prelude to settlement and the Indians a potential nuisance. In the context of the era, French efforts to Christianize the Indians implied an obligation to treat them more nearly as equals. The English policy of mass settlement and agricultural development made the coexistence of English and Indian cultures impossible. The French needed the Indians both as trade partners and as military allies: the English did not.

French Limitations

In the long run, however, concentration on the fur trade made New France unable to resist English and colonial pressure. Not only did it result in a population too small to hold New France, but the income it produced was never enough to give France a real incentive to protect its colony. The French were willing to cede all of New France to Britain in order to retain a few Caribbean sugar islands at the close of the Seven Years' (French and Indian) War in 1763. When French authority in North America finally ended, there were about 60,000 persons of French descent in all of New France. Pitted against them were over two million people in British North America.

New France was vast, but the physical presence of French settlers was restricted to a narrow strip of settlement in the St. Lawrence valley, a few locations in the Maritimes, and, in the eighteenth century, New Orleans and its environs. Elsewhere, there were only isolated forts, trading posts, and a few tiny villages. Only geography and British military ineptitude enabled the French to retain control as long as they did.

ENGLISH COLONIES

In terms of wealth, indigenous population, and the generation of institutions suited to the new conditions, the English colonies developed far beyond those of any other nation. Thus, it might be assumed that the English avoided the mistakes made in the early years of other nations' colonies. Such is not the case: the British made as many or more errors than the French, Dutch, or Spanish. But the English did learn from their mistakes and adapted better to New World conditions than did their rivals.

The first successful colony was established at Jamestown in Virginia (which then connoted the entire Middle Atlantic coast) in 1607. Yet for some years after the initial landings, the colony's survival was in doubt. Many lessons had to be learned by trial and error in circumstances where the stakes often were survival. European experience was often a hindrance rather than a help. Ironically, even those nations that had gone farthest in developing flexible institutions seemed determined to reestablish in their colonies the very systems they had discarded at home. It seems particularly ironic that such efforts were made in Virginia by the English; the initial ownership of the colony was vested in a private, profit-seeking corporation. Nor did it appear that subsequent colonies took the hard-won experience of their predecessors to heart; the same recipes for disaster were repeated, and the same lessons learned through suffering and death.

England in the Seventeenth Century

No country except the Netherlands had produced institutions so favorable to economic development as had seventeenth-century England. The country had settled its form of government early and had been wise enough to exploit its island position in trade, limiting its participation in continental wars. England had an able merchant community that was, as new participants in markets generally are, both responsive to new opportunities and engaged in a search for new trade routes and markets. Like the Netherlands, England had to compete its way into established markets.[19] In the process, she had gone as far as any European nation in freeing her economy from medieval regulations intended to preserve the status quo. As befits interlopers, the English were opposed to monopolies—at least to those that restricted English opportunities.

Royal grants of monopoly at home encountered increasing opposition on both economic and political grounds (they were sold by the sovereign, giving the Crown a revenue source outside the control of Parliament). The English foreign trade in both woollen textiles and fish had been developed in the face of foreign monopolies. English labor was as free and mobile between occupations as Dutch, and a wide spectrum of the population, from nobles to common laborers, took advantage of economic opportunity with less restraint from established custom than elsewhere. Like the Dutch, the English developed markets and the institutions that improved their performance. English law was highly favorable to property rights in ideas as well as physical possessions. Coupled with a receptive attitude toward new technology (England sought new methods, wel-

---

[19] W. Parker, *Europe, America, and the Wider World* (New York: Cambridge University Press, 1984), pp. 36, 44–45.

comed foreigners possessing them, and rewarded its own inventors), this produced a climate in which new ideas were generated and rapidly adopted.[20] Because they were forced to compete their way into established markets, the English had developed an appreciation of competitive efficiency and the institutions that promoted it.

Other English institutions reflected this attitude. Education, at least outside the ancient universities, was increasingly practical and vocational, which aided the transmission of new information. New types of business organizations had been developed to pool the savings of large numbers of people and reduce individual investors' risks—the joint stock companies. By 1600, England was technically proficient, possessed great maritime capabilities, and had an ambitious merchant class eager to employ these advantages along the lines of economic rationality. Although the influence of tradition, nepotism, and other productivity-inhibiting influences on the use of human talent was still strong, the assessment of human talent was growing more pragmatic. Since the most promising avenue for success open to young men with more ambition than inherited status was "adventures" (which meant anything from piracy or mercenary soldiering to trade and exploration), there was no lack of talent for the merchants' aspirations.

Early English Ventures in the New World

English merchants—particularly those of the West Country, who had not yet found secure markets and trade routes—were active in backing exploration, trade, and colonies in the New World. The early ventures were disappointing.

Cabot's first voyage (1497) discovered nothing but fish, and he never returned from the second. Several efforts to establish settlements failed. Martin Frobisher's voyages to Baffin Island (1576–1578) generated an initial burst of euphoria when it appeared he had discovered not only gold but the Northwest Passage, but both failed to materialize. Exploration was costly, and there was no guarantee that the information it generated could be retained by those who had financed the voyages. The English government was interested in discoveries but unwilling to finance them. Colonies might be more lucrative than exploration, but founding them required even larger sums. In North America, any returns from colonies would probably be long delayed. Even worse, these returns were more likely to accrue to the colonists themselves than to their financial backers in England. The Caribbean and the Orient appeared to offer better prospects, and action followed impression. In 1640, Barbados had a larger British population than the Virginia and Massachusetts Bay colonies combined.[21]

Virginia

One of the new joint-stock companies, the London Company, financed the 1607 investment at Jamestown. In terms of return on investment, the financiers' experience was even more disastrous than the settlers'. A very few of the first arrivals in America survived, but the investors lost every penny. A second colony was attempted in Maine at the same time, and its few survivors returned to England the next spring.

The Initial Struggle

Although the first batch of colonists had strong economic motivation—they had come to America to get rich—they had no idea of the con-

---

[20] J. Hughes, *Industrialization and Economic History: Theses and Conjectures* (New York: McGraw-Hill, 1970), Chaps. 3 and 4; D. Landes, *The Unbound Prometheus,* Chap. 2; North and Thomas, *The Rise of the Western World,* Chap. 12.

[21] V. Parry, *The Age of Reconnaissance* (New York: World Publishing, 1963), p. 276.

■ Comparison with modern maps quickly reveals the inadequacy of these seventeenth-century maps of America.
Source: Courtesy of Elizabeth Widdicombe.

ditions that awaited them. The goals assigned them by the London Company reflected complete innocence of the conditions under which the colonists would live, work, and die. The colonists were instructed to produce items that England currently had to import—wine, silk, and tropical crops. They were to search for precious metals and copper and find a new trade route to the Orient. At least in England, it was expected that all these goals could be met quickly and easily. Certainly the initial group of settlers was prepared only for easy achievements; very few were accustomed to sustained hard work, and fewer still possessed skills useful in the new surroundings. Jamestown had plenty of soldiers, ex-servants, and "gentlemen," but few carpenters or farmers. The plans for the colony's operation made the worst of these disadvantages. Jamestown was to be operated along military lines; the men marched to work in the fields to the beat of a drum. Whatever was produced was to be shared equally among all the colonists. There were no women in the first group—a strong indication that few if any of the settlers intended to stay in Virginia.

It quickly became apparent that the colony would have to produce its own food. Prior events should have indicated that: Sir Walter Raleigh's Roanoke colony had depended on English supplies, and the relief expedition bringing them arrived three years behind schedule, in 1590. It found no trace of the colony. Transportation costs were too high to depend on imported provisions, even had communications with England not been slow and uncertain. Jamestown had another reason to

produce its own food: for the first few years the colony produced nothing for its English backers but requests for more supplies and people, and even the most optimistic investors were beginning to seek ways of cutting costs. Achieving self-sufficiency in food was not easy. The colony's labor force was unaccustomed to farm work of any sort, and conditions in Virginia were particularly difficult. There were no draft animals, the tools were not suited to American conditions, and clearing virgin forests was brutally hard work under the best conditions. Given the character of the settlers, the conditions under which they labored, the bitter disappointment that grew as hopes for quick fortunes evaporated, and the manner in which output was distributed, the work effort was far below the colony's meager potential. A system better designed to discourage maximum effort

■ This view of Jamestown in 1607 is reconstructed from available evidence.
Source: The Bettman Archive, Inc.

from each individual could hardly be imagined. The communal agricultural system not only produced far less food than possible, but it made change and adaptation to Virginia conditions more difficult. Starvation added to the toll already imposed by malaria, Indian raids, and work in a climate much harsher than England's. Over half the original 120 settlers died within the first two years. For the first decade, additional immigrants fared even worse.[22]

The Necessity for Change

In such conditions the colony could not survive unless changes were made. Work rules were altered to force a contribution from every individual ("He that doth not work, neither shall he eat"). Later a transition was made to greater individual responsibility. The first step was to allow each person a small plot of his own to farm as he wished, with all produce the property of the owner. After 1623, the communal effort was abandoned; each settler was assigned his own land and was expected to support himself from the results. Not every colonist proved up to the harsh new system, but it was a decided improvement over its predecessor. Where adaptation to new conditions was so important, it encouraged a variety of methods and rapid innovation of those that appeared successful. Jamestown's margin above starvation was so tiny that anything less than the maximum effort from all concerned or anything that reduced the incentives of the capable was intolerable. Had the colony's founders possessed knowledge of effective methods when settlement occurred, a cooperative effort might have been more successful, but the death rate was grim evidence that such information was lacking. To be successful, planning requires realistic goals, accurate information, and a knowledge of the available resources and techniques. The London Company's directors lacked all three.

Incentives were further strengthened by the arrival of women. This encouraged effort likely to pay off only over time, because now settlers might regard their migration as permanent and attempt to build up estates for their families. Even so, the colony barely survived the first years. On one occasion a relief expedition from England arrived to find the colonists already abandoning Jamestown.

Solving Jamestown's food problems did not ensure the survival of the colony. The chief remaining problem was that the colony produced almost nothing with which to finance imports from England. Without English tools and manufactured goods, the colonists could not hope to live much better than the Indians. But with no return on previous investment, the London Company could not be expected to provide for them indefinitely. The company was reorganized to provide additional capital. Nevertheless, it failed in 1623, and the colony's charter reverted to the Crown.

Tobacco

The colony desperately needed a larger population, but potential settlers were reluctant to brave its appalling death rates without the prospect of higher incomes. Even the chance to acquire land meant little if the land could not produce something salable. Tobacco changed this situation. In 1612 the colony began to produce tobacco, and Virginia found its export staple. The Virginia Company (the reorganized, renamed London Company) and even King James abandoned their objections to the "stinking weed" when it appeared that tobacco was an ideal mercantilist commodity. Virginia tobacco not only replaced imports from the Spanish colonies but could be reexported to Europe in huge quantities. Production required unskilled labor, for the most part, and tobacco was easy to ship. Although it could be grown on farms of any size, there were economies of scale in curing operations and in the maintenance of soil fertility that favored large-scale producers. The prospect of cheap land in

---

[22] Walton and Shepherd, *The Economic Rise*, pp. 37–38.

Virginia became more alluring with the advent of a profitable cash crop, and migration to the colony was stimulated.

Solving the Labor Problem

The demand for labor in Virginia rose sharply, and the colonists began to offer inducements, chiefly in the form of grants of land, both to emigrants and to those who arranged their passage. The voyage to Virginia cost about as much as the average Englishman earned in a year, so few new arrivals had been able to pay their own way. Typically, the emigrant's passage fees were paid by a ship captain or Virginia planter, who in turn received the rights to three to seven years' labor from the new arrival. This contract could be transferred to other employers, so for its duration, the emigrant was an assured labor source for its owner. In return for labor, the indentured servant received food, clothing, and other maintenance, but no wages. Training was also given—a valuable commodity in the very different environment. When the indenture expired, the now-free individual was entitled to "dues" intended to make him or her self-supporting (and to increase the incentives to fulfill the indenture contract): a plot of land, tools, and sometimes a small cash payment. The risks of such a program were high. The trans-Atlantic passage alone killed an estimated one-fifth of those attempting it, and the emigrant was exposed to new diseases and hard labor. Such circumstances, when they became known in England, were no spur to recruitment, but as time passed the survival rate in Virginia improved and most indentures were voluntary. Demand for labor in Virginia continued, and awards of land were made to new settlers, their families, and those arranging the migration of others.[23]

Some indentured servants had little choice but to emigrate. They were prisoners from various sources: common criminals, victims of the civil and political turmoil that beset Britain (especially Ireland and Scotland) in the seventeenth and eighteenth centuries, or victims of kidnappers.[24] Recent research has indicated that only a minority of indentured servants fit this category, but there is evidence that servants furnished a less than ideal work force. Planters not only had to buy the servants' contracts, maintain and train them, and furnish freedom dues on the contracts' expiration, they had to accept the risk that servants might die or run away before the contracts matured. As the colony's population and knowledge of survival skills grew, it became easier for servants to escape. There were no means of identification such as fingerprints or Social Security numbers, and few persons were well known more than a few miles from home. In Virginia it was not wise to inquire too closely into the backgrounds of "strangers," given the pasts of even some now-respectable settlers. As mortality rates declined, a greater proportion of servants survived their indentures, and freedom dues imposed higher costs on planters. Political problems within the colony also increased with the growing numbers of landless workers and small farmers. (Bacon's Rebellion in 1676 pitted frontiersmen and the landless against the established planters and the governor.)

Since European labor was expensive and risky, the colonists tried to find other workers. The local Indians were impossible to retain on the plantations, and efforts to force them into such labor led, understandably, to violent conflict. Europeans had long employed Africans as slave labor in the Caribbean, the Atlantic islands, and South America, and as the seventeenth century wore on, indentured Europeans were increasingly supplemented by blacks. These involuntary immigrants were sold by governments concerned only with the price obtained for them, rather than their long-term

---

[23] E. Perkins, *The Economy of Colonial America* (New York: Columbia University Press, 1980), pp. 69–70.

[24] A. Smith, *Colonists in Bondage* (Chapel Hill, N.C.: University of North Carolina Press, 1947), p. 3.

■ The tobacco plantation was a primary source of income for farmers in Virginia and Maryland.

prospects in America. Before long they were regarded as "servants for life," and in 1664 slavery was declared to be hereditary.

The initial price of a slave was higher than that of an indentured European (an indication of the treatment both races received on the Atlantic passage), but the slave's services were obtained for life, and if slaves had children, a permanent source of labor was obtained. Once both types of labor began to survive beyond the usual indenture period, slaves became cheaper labor than indentured servants. In addition, it was much more difficult for blacks to escape successfully. Still, as late as 1700 only

11 percent of the colonial population was black, although by then the slave population was growing faster than the colonial aggregate.

Plymouth and Massachusetts

The Pilgrims and Plymouth

Settlement in New England began shortly after that in Virginia. Plymouth was founded in 1620, New Hampshire in 1623, and Massachusetts Bay in 1629. The Pilgrims repeated most of Jamestown's errors and added a few of their own. They paid in starvation, disease, and death before learning the lessons of survival in the New World. The colony's primary motives were noneconomic. The Pilgrims were apparently as concerned with getting away from Europe for religious reasons as they were with the conditions they would encounter in their new home. The unsurprising result was that the history of Plymouth's early years reads like a list of the things to avoid when founding a colony.

Unlike Jamestown's settlers, the Pilgrims were closely knit by religion and possessed a sense of group unity. At the same time, they may have had even less material and intellectual equipment to face the rigors of settlement. They were largely townspeople, lacking the skills required in the new environment. They seem to have chosen additional people over tools or other equipment. The Pilgrims were not eager to include outsiders who might have skills they lacked. They expected to settle in a mild climate just north of Virginia, but delays, supply shortages, and navigational errors forced them to come ashore nearly 500 miles north of their intended landfall. They arrived in November, with no time to search for a good site. The group was already weakened by sickness when the Plymouth site was chosen.

Plymouth's chief attraction was cleared fields, formerly cultivated by an Indian tribe which had been wiped out by disease a few years previously. (To the Pilgrims, the Indians' demise was clear proof of God's blessing.) The

■ The Mayflower Compact was written in 1620.
Source: Culver Pictures.

Pilgrims by that time did not have the manpower to clear enough land for European-style agriculture.[25] That winter, food supplies were very limited and disease was especially deadly among the cold, half-starved little group. By spring only 39 survivors from the original group of 106 remained. As if the difficulties imposed upon them were not affliction enough, the Pilgrims tried the same form of communal agriculture that had failed in Jamestown. When it was finally abandoned for a system of family-owned and cultivated plots, the work effort

[25] J. Furnas, *The Americans: A Social History of the United States* (New York: Putnam, 1969), pp. 34, 55.

greatly increased. Women and children who had not worked in the fields when all crops were shared began to do so when each family became responsible for its own welfare.[26]

In such circumstances, the courage and perseverance that sustained Plymouth were dubious assets. Even after survival was assured, the colony's growth was very slow. The harbor was not well suited to shipping, and the soil was far less fertile than Virginia's. More important was the lack of exports; in addition to their ongoing requirements of tools and manufactured goods, the Pilgrims had borrowed part of the funds to establish their colony. Shipments of what was available—furs and timber— were made, but even though Plymouth established trading posts along the coast and in the interior, only small amounts of furs could be obtained. Timber was simply too difficult to ship. The company that had financed the Pilgrims soon gave up and allowed them to buy the colony's charter at a fraction of the original sum. The small population did not permit any great degree of specialization, so incomes rose slowly.

The Puritans and the Massachusetts Bay Colony

Later colonies took some of the experience of Jamestown and Plymouth to heart; a few even made efforts to prepare for American conditions. Nine years after the founding of Plymouth, the Puritans established the Massachusetts Bay Colony. They sought information about their destination, sending an advance party to chose a site for the settlement. The result was an excellent harbor at the site of Boston—and more than 80 deaths in a group of 180 before the main group of settlers arrived. The Puritans made other preparations; they sought advice from Captain John Smith, of Virginia fame, and others. Despite their strong religious feelings, the Puritans admitted, even recruited,

"strangers" who possessed skills not found within their ranks. In a world where most religions extended tolerance chiefly to those too strong to be exterminated for any deviation in faith, this was a significant concession. There would be no interference from English financiers: the colony was controlled by its members and brought its charter to Massachusetts. Finally, the Puritans came in large numbers, nearly 20,000 in the first decade. A population of this size allowed a good deal of specialization, which resulted in more and better products at lower cost. Within the first two decades, Massachusetts had established two colonies of its own, Rhode Island and Connecticut, both in part because of religious differences. It had also set up trading posts inland and on the Maine coast.

Early New England Agriculture

New England agriculture never produced much more than enough to feed its own population, and by 1700 not even that. Yankees quickly realized that their fields would not produce the exports they needed, so they turned to the sea and the forest and sent New England products to areas specializing in other goods. As early as 1635, Massachusetts had begun to "look to the West Indies for a trade," sending fish, leather and wood products, and livestock to the Sugar Islands, and providing shipping services as well. In return, New England received sugar, rum, molasses, and gold, which could be exchanged for European products. Few New England farmers depended on crops alone for income. Some turned out preserved meat and dairy products; others spent the long winters producing tools, shoes, harness, and other leather goods, barrel staves, and virtually anything else that could be made from wood. Many farmers were fishermen between spring planting and fall harvests and either lumbermen or traders during the winter.

Because of the multitude of small-scale producers, each also a consumer, concentration points for exports were necessary. Towns

[26] J. Hughes, *Industrialization*, p. 112.

were important in New England from the beginning of settlement. Urban concentrations were also encouraged by activities such as shipbuilding, which required large labor forces. To New Englanders, shipbuilding furnished a means of transporting their own exports, a device for earning transport charges from other areas, and an export good—ships were one of New England's few exports that could be sold in Britain. For the first century of settlement, most New England farmers lived in villages rather than amidst their own fields.

Maryland

It was possible to learn from others' experience in the tobacco colonies also. Founded in 1634, Maryland benefited from the examples of previous settlements. The colony was intended to serve two purposes: to be a refuge for English Catholics and to generate income from a large land grant that the Calvert family had received from the king. To meet the latter goal, it was necessary to admit members of other faiths. It was soon obvious that the colony's owners were more tolerant than its settlers; it proved difficult to combine settlers of different faiths, particularly those who provoked animosities among English Protestants. Nevertheless, the colony prospered. Its soil and climate were so similar to Virginia's that there was no groping for an export good. It soon became apparent to the proprietors of the colony that they could obtain income from their land only by attracting settlers to it. This they did by making land available on easy terms, with only nominal quitrents (annual payments to the proprietor) and without the regulations imposed by European landlords. Although they had the legal right to do so, the proprietors of Maryland did not establish a hereditary nobility or impose restrictions on the sale or use of land. The combination of easy access to land and ready markets for its products attracted settlers, and Maryland was

the most successful of the early British colonies in North America.

THE FIRST COLONIES

By 1650, Europeans were firmly established on the Atlantic coast of North America. There were perhaps 50,000 Europeans (most of them English) and 1,000 to 2,000 blacks scattered from Canada to Florida. Long stretches of coastline without any European settlements still remained; even within the colonies, most land was still forested. Nevertheless, further growth now appeared probable. Survival was no longer an issue within most colonies, and positive adjustments to American conditions had been made. Some valuable lessons had been learned.

First, the New World environment required new goals and methods unimaginable from a European point of view. Spectacular wealth might be gained in a short time in other parts of the world—generally at others' expense—but there were no such opportunities in North America. Increases in income and wealth were possible, but only as the result of sustained hard work. Permanent settlement in large numbers was required if Europeans were to take advantage of North America's potential. This point had profound implications; one had to become an American to profit from this land.

Second, each colony needed an agricultural base; food had to be produced locally, and under very different conditions from those in Europe. There were few guides to optimum measures other than trial and error. Indian crops and farming methods may have saved some colonies from starvation in their formative periods, but Indian agriculture was not intended to support dense populations. In all of North America beyond Mexico, there were no more than two million Indians at the time of European settlement; clearly, limited food supplies controlled their numbers. A combination of Indian and European crops and techniques was evolving and being adapted to the new conditions. Corn (maize) could be grown on land that was not fully cleared; wheat was much more difficult to raise under such circumstances. Factor proportions were very different in America: labor was much scarcer than in Europe, and land more abundant. Thus the cost of bringing wilderness land up to the standards of European farmland was very high and that of maintaining soil fertility even greater. New methods of determining the potential fertility of raw land and the proper crops to grow on it had to be developed. Allowing each production unit to make its own adjustment to new conditions generated a wide range of useful information quickly. Necessity and the settlers' intense economic motivations helped to ensure rational evaluation of alternatives and rapid adoption of those that worked. They also taught that there were benefits from abandoning less effective methods. Those who refused to learn from others might not last very long in America.

Third, unless the colonists were willing to live solely on what they could produce for themselves, they had to make something that could be exchanged for European goods. This was more than a matter of tastes: tools were needed for the new style of agriculture even more than they were under English conditions, because labor was so scarce. Lacking both capital and skilled labor, the colonists could not hope to produce manufactured goods at costs or qualities comparable to those of Europe. It was far cheaper to make tools indirectly, by trading American products for them.

Finally, population in general and labor in particular were in short supply in all colonies, and efforts to increase both paid rich dividends. Large populations were not only more secure from attack and able to generate larger aggregate surpluses, but they had important advantages in land clearing, building, and shipbuilding. The larger the colonial population, the wider the range of specialized occupations it could support and the higher the quality of their goods. Specialization increased the incomes of the community as well as of the specialists themselves.

Even at this early date, colonial responses were apparent. The response to the labor shortage was a high birthrate and a continuing welcome to immigrants. The colonists recognized that even indentured servants required incentives, so they offered what they had—prospects of cheap land and, increasingly, of high standards of material welfare. With slaves, coercion would suffice, but even slaves were expensive labor; it paid owners to use methods that produced maximum output per worker and maintained slaves over long working lives.

The colonists had also learned, often through bitter experience, what not to do. Those settlers most firmly committed to religious or political ideology at the expense of economic rationality often paid a high price. Such thinking might be a barrier to survival, to say nothing of prosperity. The settlers recognized how greatly their initial ideas had needed to change. Even more, experience in the New World convinced the colonists that no ideas would be imposed on them by people utterly unfamiliar with colonial circumstances.

If America taught the colonists anything, it was the value of pragmatism. They learned to respect and adopt whatever produced results, be it a method, a tool, or a person. In the next century, the application of this lesson was to garner a rich reward.

SELECTED READINGS

Cederberg, H. *An Economic Analysis of English Settlement in North America, 1583–1635.* New York: Arno Press, 1977.

Cipolla, C. *Before the Industrial Revolution: European Society and Economy, 1000–1700.* New York: Norton, 1976.

Clough, S., and R. Rapp. *European Economic History: The Economic Development of Western Civilization.* 3d ed. New York: McGraw-Hill, 1975.

Crosby, A., Jr. *The Columbian Exchange: Biological and Cultural Consequences of 1492.* Westport, Conn.: Greenwood Press, 1972.

Davis, R. *The Rise of the Atlantic Economies.* Ithaca, N.Y.: Cornell University Press, 1973.

Furnas, J. *The Americans: A Social History of the United States.* New York: Putnam, 1969

Hechser, E. *Mercantilism.* 2 vols. London: Allen & Unwin, 1935.

Hughes, J. *Industrialization and Economic History: Theses and Conjectures.* New York: McGraw-Hill, 1970.

Morison, S. *The European Discovery of America: The Northern Voyages.* New York: Oxford University Press, 1971.

———. *The Southern Voyages.* New York: Oxford University Press, 1974.

North, D., and R. Thomas. *The Rise of the Western World: A New Economic History.* New York: Cambridge University Press, 1973.

Parker, W. *Europe, America, and the Wider World. Vol. I: Europe and the World Economy.* New York: Cambridge University Press, 1984.

Parry, V. *The Age of Reconnaissance.* New York: World Publishing, 1963.

Tawney, R. *Religion and the Rise of Capitalism.* New York: Peter Smith, 1952.

Walton, G., and J. Shepherd. *The Economic Rise of Early America.* New York: Cambridge University Press, 1979.

CHAPTER

2

THE COLONIAL ECONOMY

*B*y 1750, the colonies that would one day comprise the United States had substantially increased their shares of the population and income of the British Empire and the North Atlantic economy. There were now nearly 1,200,000 colonists, as opposed to 50,000 in 1650, and in another 20 years there would be over 2,000,000. The details of colonial population growth are outlined in Table 2.1.

Population had increased at an annual average rate of 3.4 percent during the colonial era.[1] This rate would be considered high by modern standards; in the eighteenth century it was unprecedented. Surprisingly, the major source of the high population growth rate was natural increase rather than immigration. As early as 1650, a majority of the colonists were born in America, and the proportion grew with time.

The pace of internal population growth is determined by the difference between birth and death rates. American birthrates were somewhat higher than European, and death rates were considerably lower.

Children are an economic asset in any unmechanized agricultural society. This was particularly so under colonial conditions. Not only was there a chronic labor shortage, there was also plenty of cheap, unused land to which a growing population could spread. Parents could have large families and gain the labor services of their children without fear that the family farm might have to be divided into uneconomically small holdings, or that satisfactory jobs might not be available for the children who left

[1] U.S. Department of Commerce, Bureau of the Census, *Historical Statistics of the United States: Colonial Times to 1970,* 2 vols. (Washington, D.C., 1975), p. 1168. See also J. Potter, "The Colonial Period," in *Readings in United States Economic and Business History,* eds. R. Robertson and J. Pate (Boston: Houghton Mifflin, 1966).

Table 2.1 Estimated Colonial Population (Thousands)

Colony	1650	1680	1710	1750	1770
New Hampshire	1.3	2.0	5.7	27.5	62.4
Massachusetts*	16.6	46.2	62.4	188.0	266.3
Rhode Island	.8	3.0	7.6	33.2	58.2
Connecticut	4.1	17.2	39.4	111.3	183.9
New York	4.1	9.8	21.6	76.7	162.9
New Jersey	—	3.4	19.9	71.4	117.4
Pennsylvania	—	.7	24.5	119.7	240.1
Delaware	.2	1.0	3.6	28.7	35.5
Maryland	4.5	17.9	42.7	141.1	202.6
Virginia	18.7	43.6	78.3	231.0	447.0
North Carolina	—	5.4	15.1	73.0	197.2
South Carolina	—	1.2	10.9	64.0	124.2
Georgia	—	—	—	5.2	23.4
Kentucky	—	—	—	—	2.5
Tennessee	—	—	—	—	.2
Total**	50.4	151.5	331.7	1,170.8	2,148.1

*Massachusetts figures include Maine and Plymouth.
**Figures may not add to totals because of rounding.
Source: U.S. Bureau of the Census, *Historical Statistics of the United States: Colonial Times to 1970*, vol. 2, 1975, p. 1168.

home. High birthrates were a logical response to colonial circumstances. Hired labor was scarce, expensive, and unreliable; slaves or indentured servants required large cash outlays; and children were the best alternative source of labor. From a very early age, children were expected to "earn their keep" by doing chores and gradually gaining the experience needed to manage their own farms later. The average age at first marriage was lower in the colonies than in Europe, and families tended to be larger.

The colonies' lower death rates appear to have been the result of a more abundant and regular food supply, smaller urban populations, and lower incidences of epidemic disease than in Europe. These factors were interrelated. Throughout the colonial era most colonists lived close to the sea. Consequently, it was easier to transport food to offset local crop failures than it was in the interior of Europe, where frequent local famines indicated the very high costs of overland transport of provisions. In aggregate, the colonies produced a consistent food surplus and certain regions, such as the Sugar Islands and New England, were able to depend on food imports from the Middle Atlantic and Southern colonies. Diets were hearty, although inadequate by modern nutritional standards. Still, colonial diets were more varied than those of most Europeans, and apparently they furnished greater resistance to epidemic disease. Only in America were substantial amounts of grain used for animal feed rather than direct consumption, indicating both high levels of food production and more protein consumption than in other countries.

Urban Demography

Today we tend to think of cities as places where better medical care more than offsets a less healthy environment. But until well into the nineteenth century, European cities had death rates far above their birthrates, so that even maintenance of urban populations required a continual influx from rural areas. Eighteenth-century London was by no means the worst of these cities, yet an estimated 50 percent of all children born in London died before reaching the age of five.[2]

At this time, there were virtually no public health measures to counteract the effects of large populations crowded into small areas. Since there was no mass transport, the poor had to live within walking distance of their jobs. Tall buildings were impractical given the prevailing construction methods, so crowding was the only way to accommodate urban populations. The means by which diseases spread were unknown. Without metal pipes and modern pumps, water supplies were frequently contaminated. Only primitive methods of food preservation were available, so urban populations ate a poorer and less varied diet than country people.

In sum, the cities of this period were death-traps. They were at least as polluted as modern cities, probably more crime-ridden, and subject to recurrent fires. American cities offered no real improvements over their European counterparts except that they were generally smaller—although Philadelphia's 38,000 people constituted the second largest urban population in the British Empire on the eve of the Revolution. Still, about 95 percent of all Americans lived in the countryside. Americans appear to have been less subject to catastrophic events such as war and epidemic disease than were Europeans.

Despite favorable comparisons to contemporary Europe, the colonies were no paradise. Life expectancy was short by modern standards—about 40 years—largely due to high infant and maternal mortality. The homes of all but the wealthy were dark, poorly heated, and frequently vermin-infested. Diseases that we now know largely from history, such as malaria and typhus, were deadly menaces to people who understood neither their causes nor their treatment.

Further Immigration

Immigration continued throughout the colonial era, but in later years the pattern differed from that of the initial settlement period. A smaller number of the later arrivals were English. There were more Scots, Irish, and Scotch-Irish (Protestants from what is now Northern Ireland), and, especially in the Middle Colonies, southern Germans. These "Pennsylvania Dutch" joined smaller numbers of Huguenots, Swiss, Dutch, and Swedes. A high proportion of the total immigration, perhaps more than half, was indentured. Over time, however, indenture became less prevalent, and it was never common in New England. Some indentured servants were fleeing oppression in their native lands—both the Irish and the Scotch-Irish were victims of a repressive British policy toward Ireland, and Highland Scots of that toward Scotland. To the "Pennsylvania Dutch," government in their native lands had meant taxes, tyranny, and military conscription from which young men often did not return. Other immigrants may have found migration the best way out of personal difficulties.

Despite the considerable "push" element, the "pull" of attractive conditions in America was at least as large a motive for immigration. It now appears clear that the new arrivals not only had surprisingly accurate information about New World conditions, but they also had a good deal of bargaining power over the terms of their indentures. By no means were all who offered their services in return for passage across the Atlantic victims of economic desperation or refugees. Records from the Philadelphia market where many indenture contracts were sold indicate that the servants possessed above-average literacy and a wide va-

---

[2] P. Deane, *The First Industrial Revolution*, 2d ed. (Cambridge, England: Cambridge University Press, 1979), p. 261.

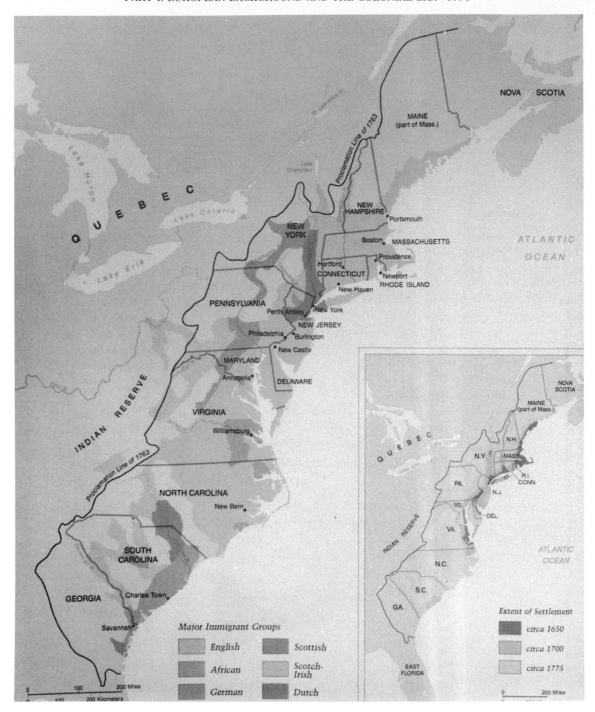

■ The 13 colonies exhibited definite patterns of settlement according to immigrant nationalities.

Source: From *America Past & Present*, Volume I, by Robert A. Devine and T. H. Breen, front page. Copyright © 1984 by Scott, Foresman and Company. Reprinted by permission.

riety of job skills. Moreover, indenture contracts' terms (determined in Europe before the servant took passage) reflected the individual's learning capacity, health, and skills, often obligated the employer to provide training in some occupation, and invariably specified the length of service required and the "freedom dues" to be paid at the end of the indenture period.[3]

The servants' settlement patterns strongly reinforce this evidence. They tended to choose colonies where land access was easy, the family farm was the standard production unit, and they could obtain what they had lacked in Europe. New England, with its tightly knit communities, block settlement of new land, limited supply of good, arable soil, and grudging tolerance of strangers, attracted relatively few. Over time, the numbers of servants choosing the plantation colonies also declined. The Middle Colonies, especially Pennsylvania, were more appealing to immigrants. There, once indentures were over, cheap, fertile land was available from a government that granted secure titles and welcomed all Christians.

Even in Pennsylvania, however, immigrants sometimes encountered less than even-handed treatment. The Germans settling just west of the original Quaker colony had little enough involvement in governmental affairs, but the Scotch-Irish, who located farther west, fared even worse. The colony regarded them as a buffer against French and Indian raids (which they sometimes provoked) and provided them so little support that on one occasion they marched on Philadelphia. New arrivals and frontier dwellers were underrepresented in most colonial legislatures. They often claimed to pay more than their share of colonial taxes, although the major seaports considered themselves the primary victims of tax discrimina-

tion.[4] Still, immigrants' letters to the "old country" leave no doubt that most of them considered the colonies in general and Pennsylvania in particular "the best poor man's country" in the world.[5]

Slavery

For another large group of immigrants, both the reasons for coming to America and the long-term prospects were less benign. In the eighteenth century, the proportion of blacks in the colonial population nearly doubled, to about 20 percent in 1770. Although most blacks were slaves employed in southern agriculture, there were free blacks as well as slaves in all colonies. By no means were all unskilled farm laborers; colonial blacks had noteworthy achievements in craft skills, science, and literature.

Slaves were a labor alternative to indentured servants, whose prices rose in the late seventeenth and eighteenth centuries. Economic conditions in Europe improved, and the life expectancy of indentured servants rose. This meant that not only would colonial employers have to grant more favorable terms of indenture (shorter indentures, implying higher long-term training costs), but they would also have higher and more certain obligations for freedom dues. At the same time, the costs of bringing slaves to America had fallen and slaves' increased life expectancy had raised their value to North American purchasers—both because of the longer stream of services obtained from each slave and because of improved prospects for a continuous labor supply through slave reproduction. While this explains the greater influx of slaves after 1700, it does not explain their concentration in plantation agriculture.

The most likely cause of the observed geographic distribution of slaves in North America

[3] D. Galenson, "Immigration and the Colonial Labor System: An Analysis of the Length of Indenture," in *Explorations in Economic History* 14 (1977) and R. Heavner, "Indentured Servitude: The Philadelphia Market," *Journal of Economic History* (September 1978).

[4] E. Perkins, *The Economy of Colonial America* (New York: Columbia University Press, 1980), p. 127.
[5] J. Lemon, *The Best Poor Man's Country: A Geographical Study of Early Southeastern Pennsylvania* (Baltimore: Johns Hopkins University Press, 1972).

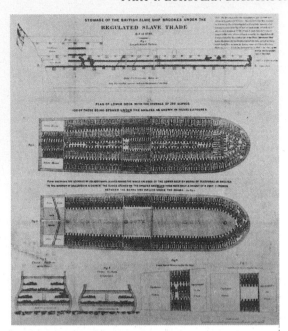

■ In the eighteenth century, the British were forced to make regulations for stowing human cargo to prevent overcrowding aboard slave ships.
Source: Library of Congress.

is twofold. The crops of the plantation colonies required nearly year-round attention. Those of the North, especially wheat, had very high labor requirements at sowing and reaping, but required little labor in between. Such labor requirements greatly influenced the prevalence of slavery, which is best suited to tasks requiring more or less constant effort. Significantly, even slave-worked plantations needed to supplement their slave-based work forces, and hired free labor for the wheat harvest when it could be obtained.[6] The second point concerns the high cost of slaves. Slave prices in North American markets were determined by conditions in the Caribbean slave markets. Slaves were employed in high-productivity uses there (sugar was an extremely valuable crop that generated huge profits), and the cost of transporting them to North America was added to their prices here (which implied higher prices in New England and the Middle Colonies than the South). Therefore, they could be profitably employed only where supervisory costs per slave were low and the value of their output high. These conditions were satisfied largely in plantation agriculture.[7]

American slaves apparently received much better physical treatment than did those in the Caribbean, especially those on the sugar plantations. One authority claims that colonial slaves' "incomes" of food, shelter, and clothing compare quite favorably with those of most inhabitants of contemporary continental Europe.[8] Better treatment probably owed much less to the colonists' humanitarian principles than to economics. In North America, slave prices were high and the costs of adequate maintenance low. Under such circumstances, it was in their masters' best interests to preserve slaves' health. Economics also helped to shape the demographic parameters of the colonies' slave population. Women were unsuited to the grueling work of sugar production, so female slaves were relatively cheaper on the continent. It paid to allow the slaves to form families and have children, since there was a greater possibility here than in the Caribbean that these children would eventually add to their owner's work force. Aside from the possibility of better treatment (which was under owners' control), slaves in North America were much less subject to epidemic diseases than were those working in tropical climes. The Caribbean slave population could only be maintained by continuous imports, but North American slaves had a rate of natural increase about equal to that of the aggregate population. The more rapid overall

---

[6] E. Perkins, *The Economy of Colonial America*, p. 77.

[7] G. Wright, *The Political Economy of the Cotton South* (New York: Norton, 1978), pp. 11–12.
[8] Perkins, *The Economy of Colonial America*, Chap. 8.

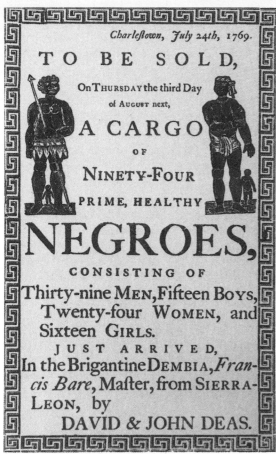

Charleſtown, July 24th, 1769.

TO BE SOLD,

On THURSDAY the third Day
of AUGUST next,

A CARGO

OF

NINETY-FOUR

PRIME, HEALTHY

NEGROES,

CONSISTING OF
Thirty-nine MEN, Fifteen BOYS,
Twenty-four WOMEN, and
Sixteen GIRLS.

JUST ARRIVED,
In the Brigantine DEMBIA, *Francis Bare*, Maſter, from SIERRA-
LEON, by

DAVID & JOHN DEAS.

■ This advertisement for slaves posted in Pennsylvania in the 1760s notes that the slaves speak English and have already had smallpox.

rate of increase among blacks was due to proportionally higher "immigration." Although only 6 percent of the Africans carried across the Atlantic from 1500 to 1870 (the vast majority had arrived by 1800) were sent to North America, that region had 25 percent of the New World's black population by 1825.[9] Even

for slaves, then, American conditions encouraged rational use of human talent. Survival, of course, is hardly the only measure of the fate of slaves in various regions, but it cannot be denied that it is an important one.

At its origins in Africa, the slave trade was just that—a trade. European (and a few American) slave traders purchased slaves from other Africans who had captured them in tribal wars or specialized slave-raiding expeditions. By no means was this a matter of militarily dominant whites forcibly kidnapping previously free blacks. The slave-trading tribes were quite capable of defending themselves against Europeans. Since the gathering of slaves unquestionably increased because of American demand for them, whites were hardly free of complicity in this inhuman traffic. But they originated neither African slavery nor the methods by which slaves were obtained.[10] Horrifying as the tales of filth, brutality, disease, and death aboard the slave ships during the "Middle Passage" may be, the voyage to America killed fewer Africans than the raids and tribal wars in which the victims were obtained.

GEOGRAPHIC EXPANSION

The colonial population did more than just grow—it expanded into new areas. By 1750, the frontier had been pushed well inland for most of the expanse from Maine to Georgia. Settlements were now established in the valleys of the Appalachians, and by the 1770s, the first tentative efforts at colonization beyond the mountains had begun in Kentucky and Tennessee. New England's expansion to the west and north was still hampered by the French in

[9] R. Fogel and S. Engerman, *Time on the Cross: the Economics*

of American Negro Slavery, 2 vols. (Boston: Little, Brown & Co., 1974), pp. 13–20.
[10] R. Thomas and R. Bean, "The Fishers of Men," *Journal of Economic History* (December 1974).

1750, but elsewhere existing colonies had begun to push into regions far from salt water.

North Carolina was settled by people moving overland from Virginia rather than from the coast. For a long time the colony's lack of access to the sea (and thus a low-cost outlet for its cash crops) was a serious handicap to the growth of incomes, if not population. It influenced the nature of North Carolina agriculture, which had fewer plantations and more family farm, subsistence-oriented agriculture than other southern colonies.

By 1700, South Carolina was established as a highly successful plantation colony specializing initially in tobacco, then in rice. Just before 1750 rice cultivation was supplemented by that of indigo, a blue vegetable dye. All these crops were best suited to production on large-scale plantations, and South Carolina's specialization in that mode was revealed by its population patterns. Blacks constituted a majority of South Carolina's population, as they did in no other mainland colony. As such, its demographic patterns were similar to those of the Sugar Islands.[11] Charleston, with its excellent harbor, was the only colonial city south of Norfolk.

Georgia was the last colony to be established, in 1733. Once more, altruistic principles clashed with economic reality in the founding of a colony. Georgia had been established by English philanthropists to give people imprisoned for debt a second chance. The colony's charter established rules that proved to be obstacles to settlement. Initially, the size of landholdings was restricted and slavery prohibited. These rules meant that Georgia would have higher tobacco production costs than other colonies, and rice production was all but out of the question. Without the attraction of a competitive cash crop, Georgia grew very slowly. In the late 1740s the colony's laws were revised,

but Georgia was barely past its formative stage by the Revolution. In 1750, its population was only 5,000, by far the smallest of any seaboard colony.

COLONIAL AGRICULTURE

Although the majority of every colony's population was engaged in agriculture, often in combination with other extractive industries such as fishing, whaling, or lumbering, distinct regional patterns had emerged by 1750. Agricultural products furnished the bulk of colonial exports and enabled the colonists to trade for manufactured goods that could not have been produced as easily, if at all, from domestic resources. Low agricultural productivity also forced the concentration on agriculture. Each colonial farm produced only a small surplus, limiting the proportion of the population that could follow nonagricultural pursuits.

Another feature common to all colonies' agriculture was a great contrast in factor proportions relative to those of Europe. Since colonial populations were small and land relatively abundant, each unit of labor was combined with a great deal more land than normal European practice dictated.

It is important to realize that colonial land was never free. Even if it could be obtained without a cash payment, rendering it suitable for use involved sizable costs. Nevertheless, land costs were far lower than they had been in Europe, and social considerations reinforced the strong economic incentives for landownership. Hired labor was scarce and expensive throughout the colonial period. The colonists' response to their factor cost situation was rational; they used land far more lavishly than did European farmers. It was cheaper for colonists to clear new land when fields lost their fertility than to expend the extra labor required to maintain soil quality. This practice made good sense as long as a supply of additional land remained

[11] G. Walton and J. Shepherd, *The Economic Rise of Early America* (New York: Cambridge University Press, 1972), pp. 56–57.

available, but it confused European observers, whose values were based on abundant labor and a nearly fixed endowment of arable land. European agriculture maximized output per unit of land, while colonial practice was to seek maximum production per unit of labor. Although European observers accused Americans of "mining" their land, there is little evidence of declining yields per acre over the colonial period.[12]

Land Speculation

Low land prices and the practice of keeping a reserve of untilled land encouraged land speculation in colonial America. Farmers typically held far more land than they cultivated, both as a defense against reduced yields from their current arable land and as a potential source of income from sale. As populations increased and settlements became more dense, land prices tended to rise. Raw land was initially available at very low prices; under the headright system, payment to those assuming the transportation expenses of indentured servants was often in land. Many colonial governments gave transferable land warrants to military veterans. Politically influential persons, especially plantation owners, might obtain title to land far beyond the current limits of settlement. Land could be held at little or no expense, given colonial tax rates. Since colonial population growth was so rapid, the risks of investment in land were low; it was all but certain to appreciate in value after its carrying costs were met.

Nonagricultural Activity

Many farming households engaged in nonagricultural activity as well. They produced furniture, buildings, tools, and land improvements for their own use. Many produced distilled beverages and beer, using almost anything that could be induced to ferment as raw material, including pumpkins. Especially during the first

years on a new farm, the output of field crops would be low and expenses heavy, so there was a great incentive to produce commodities that could be sold or bartered for goods the household could not make for itself, or even for additional food. Before adequate cropland had been cleared to allow specialization in cash crops, lumber, furs, potash, pearlash, maple sugar, or honey might be exchanged for salt, metal goods, ammunition, grindstones, and the services of such specialists as blacksmiths, lawyers, and ministers.

Most roads were suitable only for pack animals, and transportation by this method was expensive. Wherever possible, colonial farmers sought access to water transportation, and so bad were the alternatives that their assessments of stream navigability appear almost suicidally optimistic today. In addition, crops were processed into less bulky or more easily transported forms. Grain was sent to market as flour, whiskey, or fattened livestock, all of which represented higher value in smaller bulk.

Clearing land was extremely slow and difficult work. Trees were huge, and often the settler had only an axe and a few other hand tools with which to attack the forest. There were also many other demands on his time in the first few years. Buildings had to be constructed, some type of crop raised and harvested, firewood cut, and many other tasks performed. In addition, unless the family had accumulated a reserve before it made the settlement, something had to be produced to exchange for goods the family could not make for itself. Twenty years might pass before a farm family had cleared as much land as its members could cultivate, and another score might pass before it had erected a full complement of permanent buildings and fences. The timetable depended on the nature of the land, luck, weather, and the number of able-bodied workers available. In a world in which draft animals were not always available or suited to the necessary tasks, more hands meant that basic demands could be met in less time. The response could be di-

---

[12] Perkins, *The Economy of Colonial America*, p. 45.

rect: one colonial family achieved prosperity because it contained "26 strong, healthy sons."[13] Consumption on colonial farms, particularly in the early years, might be modest, but this gave a misleading impression of income. Clearing ground, constructing buildings, building up livestock herds, and other such activities were in fact investments that would add to the family's ability to consume or produce still more in the future.

New England

By the mid-eighteenth century, it was apparent that New England had no comparative advantage in agriculture versus the Middle Colonies or the South. Not only did those regions have more and better soil per capita as well as longer growing seasons, but their climates allowed the production of crops for export. In contrast, after 1700 New England was a net importer of food. This fact may reveal as much about the growing efficiency of ocean shipping as about differences in agricultural capabilities. New England's response in part took the form of an exodus of young men seeking better farming opportunities. In most of New England, landholdings tended to be small and not very productive even by colonial standards, and their average size declined over the eighteenth century.

Especially in its early years, New England's agricultural patterns reflected social and religious influences as well as economic responses to a harsh environment. In most cases, the initial agricultural settlements were made by the members of a church congregation moving into a new area en masse. The congregation would build a village in the midst of the fields cultivated by its members. Each family would have a small garden or orchard plot close to its house,

plus a number of strips of land in the town's fields and the right to graze livestock on the common pasture. The fields were cooperatively farmed; joint action was needed for planting and harvesting.

This type of settlement had some advantages. In New England, it allowed for better defense against the French and their Indian allies. It provided a larger pool of labor for construction and other activities best accomplished through joint effort and allowed members access to the group's reserves in emergencies. Above all, however, such a settlement pattern kept every individual under the watchful eye of the minister and other church officials, ensuring the enforcement of community standards of conduct. Members of the congregation had a voice in community affairs, but the voice of the church spoke very loudly indeed, particularly by modern standards.

As populations grew and the threat of attack receded, this system increasingly clashed with more secular values. Making everyone live in town certainly promoted church attendance, but as the town's cleared land and population increased, it also increased commuting time to fields distant from the village. Inheriting land rights also became more complicated; either heirs had to receive shrinking allocations within each of a larger number of common fields, or some mechanism for determining the relative worth of land parcels in different fields had to be devised. Gradually private ownership of individual parcels of land developed, and families began to live in farmhouses surrounded by their own acres rather than in villages. By 1750 land in New England was largely in the hands of individual owners, as in other regions.

But the rise of a private market in land failed to offset New England's other agricultural shortcomings. After a promising start, cultivation of wheat had been halted by plant diseases. The staple crop of New England became corn, which was suited to the region's small fields and short growing season. Other crops often raised in the cornfields were beans,

---

[13] J. Furnas, *The Americans: A Social History of the United States* (New York: Putnam, 1969), Chapter 3.

pumpkins, squash, and peas. Fruit, particularly apples, was grown and used in many ways: fresh, dried, and in cider and applejack. Livestock was also produced; some areas, such as Rhode Island, exported horses. But most New England farmers had to supplement their incomes from crops and husbandry by lumbering, fishing, whaling, trading, or producing shoes, harness, wooden items, and other handicrafts.

The nature of New England agriculture, with its many small-scale producers, and the region's other activities encouraged the formation of towns as export and import distribution centers. The towns also furnished a growing market for farm produce.

The Middle Atlantic Colonies

The region from New York south to Maryland (and, in later years, even parts of Virginia) developed a more productive agriculture than New England. Fertile soils and the development of social institutions that attracted some of the most skillful farmers in America made Pennsylvania a colonial success story. In this region, wheat and meat were produced in large quantities as cash crops. Both were exported, and the requirements of the export trade gave rise to industries such as milling, which transformed wheat into flour, raising its unit value and decreasing its bulk, and bakeries, which converted flour into still more portable ships' biscuits or hardtack. The region also produced much corn, a portion of which was fed to the hogs and cattle eventually exported as pickled or salted meat.

The Middle Atlantic colonies were a stronghold of the family farm—larger units had no economic advantages in the production of the region's principal exports. As in New England, the presence of many commercially oriented farms encouraged the growth of towns. Philadelphia was a seaport, a market center, and the seat of government. Businesses in the town milled flour, packed meat, and made the

barrels and ships in which the products of Pennsylvania, Delaware, and southern New Jersey farms were sent to other colonies, the West Indies, and Southern Europe.

New York City performed similar services for its hinterland, the farming areas of Long Island, northern New Jersey, and the Hudson Valley. Later the produce of the Mohawk Valley added to New York's exports. Like Philadelphia, New York transformed its hinterland's output into more portable forms: the city was a shipbuilding center and baked biscuit and hardtack. In these rapidly growing towns the colonists made some of their first efforts at insurance, finance, and small-scale manufacturing.

The Pennsylvania Dutch were unique among colonial American farmers. Rather than girdling trees and farming among the dead trunks until they could be destroyed by decay or fire, the tireless Dutch cleared the land of roots and stumps in the first year of cultivation. Their methods allowed the use of animal-drawn plows, which most American farmers did not use. Having made the move to America, the Pennsylvania Dutch were not eager to move again. They maintained the fertility of their land and modified their methods, achieving increased yields per acre over time. They originated many of the innovations that later generations of American farmers found so useful during the western movement: the barn with hayloft and inclined ramp above and animal stalls below, plow and wagon designs, and the "Kentucky" rifle. Pennsylvania, where advanced agricultural techniques were by no means universal, and South Carolina present the only clear evidence of increases in agricultural productivity over the colonial era.[14]

Pennsylvania's combination of religious and ethnic tolerance, low-cost land with secure ti-

[14] G. Walton and D. Ball, "Agricultural Productivity Change in 18th Century Pennsylvania" *Journal of Economic History* (March 1976). See also the comments of R. Menard in this article.

tles, and a light governmental hand owed much to William Penn. Combined with the colony's natural advantages, these institutions produced rapid growth and a prosperous, diversified economy. Pennsylvania was virtually unsettled in 1680, but by 1770 the colony's population was 240,000. Penn's was one of only two proprietary colonies that may have returned a profit to its owners. Maryland, which followed similar policies, was the other.

The Southern Colonies

Although both regions furnished markets for English exports, neither New England nor the Middle Atlantic colonies could be termed ideal possessions from a mercantilist standpoint. Neither produced much of use to England, although New England's mast trees had strategic importance. Many New England exports actually competed with those of the mother country. The Middle Colonies' exports in large part were sent to other colonies or outside the British Empire. The southern colonies, however, closely approached the mercantilist ideal. They were large-scale exporters of tobacco, rice, and indigo, all useful within Britain and as reexports. Their sizable populations, particularly in Virginia and Maryland, furnished good markets for English exports. And the region produced little that competed with British overseas trade.

Although the plantation dominated the region's agriculture, by no means were all the southern colonies' farms plantations. Parts of the region had been settled too recently for such development, and even in the more established areas most farms were worked by the owner, his family, and perhaps one or two servants or slaves. Nor were tobacco, rice, and indigo the only cash crops. Particularly toward the end of the colonial period, the South exported sizable amounts of corn and other foodstuffs, and it always provided for its own consumption. Nevertheless, the influence of the plantation was pervasive.

Plantations were large-scale production units. A plantation's output would typically be a sizable portion of a merchant ship's capacity. Plantations tended to trade directly with England, loading their products from their own docks onto the ships that had brought imported goods. The plantation was also a large-scale import purchaser. Some planters used their purchasing advantages to operate stores from which they sold imported goods to neighboring farmers, thus taking the place of the merchants in other colonies. One result was that towns were less necessary than in other regions.

Most plantations were located on tidal rivers with direct water transportation links to Europe. Since plantations tended to keep sizable land reserves, using only the most fertile acreage available, plantation-colony populations tended to be scattered rather than concentrated. Many areas without convenient access to navigable water long remained lightly populated. The initial land grants in many southern colonies lacked well-defined boundaries, which also discouraged close settlement. As a result, there were few large-scale markets in the southern colonies accessible from a single point.

Plantations often maintained their own blacksmiths, carpenters, coopers, and other skilled workers. What the plantation could not produce from its own resources was purchased from England. Trans-Atlantic shipping costs for English goods tended to be lower than those for colonial exports. Southern exports tended to be bulky; they required more space than the manufactured goods for which they were exchanged. Thus ships coming to the colonies were often less fully loaded than those coming from the colonies and were willing to accept any cargo (including people) that paid more than its handling costs. The result was another major discouragement to manufacturing in the southern colonies. For a long time, Williamsburg was the only real town in Virginia, and it was a government and social center, active only while the legislature was in session. Charleston, with its secure harbor on a dangerous coast, was the regional metropolis of the Carolinas as well as a government center, but the South remained even more rural than the rest of the colonies.

Tobacco

Tobacco had been responsible for the growth of the plantation colonies. Initially, planters in the Tidewater regions sent their crops to English merchants, who sold the tobacco for them on commission. The merchants then used the proceeds to pay for the planters' orders of British goods. Since many planters in several colonies had no cooperative policies, there was no way to control the supply of tobacco, which increased very rapidly in the seventeenth century. Prices fluctuated considerably, but the long-run trend was down until about 1720. After that, low but stable prices prevailed.[15]

Some planters borrowed from English merchants in years of low prices or pressing need for imports, pledging the next year's crop as security. The Tidewater planters were difficult customers. There was no standard grading system initially, and the planters sold each barrel of tobacco individually. They demanded explanations if prices did not vary in accordance with their estimates of quality.[16]

Late in the seventeenth century, tobacco markets began to change. A shift in Europe's preferences from chewing to smoking tobacco increased the demand for Virginia tobacco and reduced that for Brazilian, which was better suited for chewing. When coupled with the declining price of Chesapeake tobacco, this meant that larger quantities could now be sold, particularly in continental Europe. England began to export large amounts of American tobacco. This trend accelerated when the French government tobacco monopoly began to buy its supplies in England.

The old consignment system of marketing was not suited to large-scale sales, and a few great merchants in Glasgow, London, and Whitehaven controlled the French business. Since these merchants had an assured market for a large portion of the total crop, they were in a better position to extend credit to American producers. Also, they were interested in large amounts of uniform-quality tobacco. The merchants began to open stores in the tobacco colonies. These establishments purchased tobacco, sold English goods, and extended credit to farmers.

At the same time, it became obvious to the colonies that the new markets required a different response, and that the key to profits lay in lower production costs, not in haggling over prices. Consequently, the Chesapeake colonies developed uniform grading systems and improved packing methods so that larger quantities of tobacco could be shipped in the same amount of space. One result of these changes was that tobacco production began to shift from the large-scale planters to smaller production units, and from its old stronghold in the Tidewater region to the Piedmont. The new producers were less sensitive to price variations, since tobacco sales were a smaller portion of their total incomes.[17] Many Tidewater planters began to produce wheat, corn, and meat as cash crops, spurring the rise of Baltimore and Norfolk as export centers for these crops. Throughout the colonial period, however, tobacco was the most important export of the North American colonies, accounting for nearly half of the total export values.[18]

---

[15] J. Price, "The Economic Growth of the Chesapeake and the European Market, 1697–1775," *Journal of Economic History* (December 1963).
[16] Ibid.

[17] Perkins, *The Economy of Colonial America*, p. 54.
[18] Price, "Economic Growth."

Rice, Indigo, and Naval Stores

Another change in export crops occurred in the Carolinas. Originally both colonies had produced tobacco as their major cash crop. In the period of falling tobacco prices after 1650, rice cultivation was begun along the coast, chiefly in South Carolina. After it was discovered that the crop could be irrigated via a system of dikes and the natural pressure of the tides, which forced fresh water back up the coastal rivers, rice production boomed. Suitable land was limited, however, and the required investment in dikes, sluices, and milling machinery quickly made rice cultivation a rich man's business. But there were growing markets for rice in Southern Europe as well as in England, and exports rose from 10,407 pounds in 1698 to an average of 78,485,000 pounds in the 1770–1774 period.[19]

An additional source of income for rice planters appeared when the British government began offering bounties (subsidies) for indigo, a blue vegetable dye used on textiles. Eliza Lucas, one of America's first female entrepreneurs, showed planters how the crop was grown and processed for export, and by 1750 Carolina indigo had replaced Britain's previous supply from the French West Indies. Indigo ideally complemented rice cultivation. The crop grew on land unsuitable for rice, and its chief labor requirements occurred while there was little to do in the rice fields. But the British bounty was necessary to make indigo production worthwhile.

Another English bounty went to Carolina's producers of "naval stores"—the pitch, turpentine, and tar so vital for the preservation of wooden ships. Together with masts and spar timbers, naval stores were crucial to the maintenance of Britain's naval supremacy. The Royal Navy's alternate sources were in the Baltic, which might be inaccessible in wartime, and Britain's own inadequate production.

COLONIAL MANUFACTURING

In general the colonies were severely handicapped as producers of manufactured goods. Their products had to compete with those from England, even in colonial markets, so colonial producers had to meet English quality and prices. This was possible with few items. England had more and cheaper capital and English labor costs were considerably lower; the typical English worker produced more output for lower wages than his colonial counterpart. Because emigration to the colonies was concentrated among people who hoped to better their situations, the colonies attracted few skilled workmen or others who were already receiving above-average incomes in Europe. In addition, English manufacturers had better access to new technology, and since their markets were larger, they were better situated to take advantage of any economies of scale. Finally, British manufacturers enjoyed equal access to markets in all colonies as well as in Britain itself and the areas outside the empire. Under these circumstances, even the costs of trans-Atlantic shipping (which might raise delivered prices by 20 percent or more over those in England) were not enough to increase British goods' prices above colonial production costs.

These economic considerations, rather than the regulations of British mercantilism, were the chief barriers to colonial manufacturing. The colonists' resources could produce higher incomes if employed in trade and agriculture rather than industry. In most types of manufacturing, the colonists could not hope to compete with England until the advantages of the mother country diminished.

[19] U.S. Department of Commerce, *Historical Statistics,* vol. 2, pp. 1192–1193.

English mercantilists were not very receptive to the idea of colonial manufacturing. Even so, legal restraints on colonial industry were often ineffective. In 1750, Parliament forbade the production of nails in the colonies. Three colonial legislatures subsequently passed laws offering bounties to anyone producing nails within their borders, in open defiance of British law. In most cases, the British government was not totally unresponsive to colonial needs, and laws were sometimes changed or repealed if the products or activities involved were important to the colonists.

Britain's manufacturing advantages, although great, did not hold equally for all products. For some goods, particularly those where shipping costs were a high proportion of final price, the colonies were able to compete. Accordingly, the colonies made most of their own beer, furniture, bricks, and similar items.

Iron Production

Colonial manufacturing of two items was considerable despite the fact that both required skilled labor and large amounts of capital. In each case the reason for colonial success lay in the product's raw materials requirements. England in the seventeenth and eighteenth centuries experienced a growing shortage of wood. The problem was more acute in timber than in fuel, because the charcoal used to smelt iron could be made from small trees or brush. Even so, all types of wood were far more expensive in England than in America. Iron making required huge amounts of fuel: a typical iron furnace in the eighteenth century required no less than 10,000 acres of woodland to fuel continuous production. Charcoal could not be transported any great distance without deterioration, and far more fuel than iron ore was required to make a ton of iron, so smelting furnaces had to be located at the fuel source rather than at markets or at the source of the ore. This meant that iron smelting was a rural industry.

Iron was smelted in all the colonies, using local ore deposits, but by 1750 the industry had become concentrated in the Middle Colonies. It has been estimated that by that date the American colonies were producing about one-seventh of the world's iron. Most colonial iron was shipped to Britain for fabrication into finished products. Skilled ironmasters were recruited in England and Europe and brought to America to apply their craft to the abundant resources of the New World.

Shipbuilding

The other manufacturing sector in which it proved efficient to send skilled labor and capital to raw materials was shipbuilding. Timber was cheap in the colonies, and there was plenty of high-quality oak for ship frames and planking and white pine for masts, spars, and decks. England had increasing shortages of oak, but the really critical problem for British shipbuilders was material for masts and spars. Britain had few suitable trees, and there were no satisfactory substitutes. But colonial white pine—tall, straight, and strong—had no equal anywhere in the world. England's sources of ship timber were her own dwindling domestic reserves plus imports from the Baltic and Scandinavia, which produced the only satisfactory mast timber. The imports were uncertain in wartime, just when assured supplies were crucial, and even in peace could be obtained only for gold. Colonial shipbuilding thus satisfied mercantilist ideas better than did most other American industry.

From their founding, most colonies had produced small ships for local use, and the industry quickly expanded to produce a wide variety of vessels. England waived mercantilist regulations restricting the emigration of shipwrights, and between the development of colonial skills and the infusion of new talent, shipbuilding became one of the few areas in which colonial skills matched British. The colonies produced many high-quality, inexpensive ships for both their own use and for sale to the British merchant marine, and even some warships for the Royal Navy. Perhaps one-third of all the empire's merchant ships were colonial-built just before the Revolution.

Other Manufacturing

Some colonial manufacturing was necessary to support other activities. Barrels, for example, filled the roles of today's oil drums, plastic bags, tin cans, and cardboard boxes, so there was a continuous demand for the coopers' output. Goods especially adapted to colonial needs, such as axes and rifles, were also made. Although population growth relaxed some of the restrictions imposed by small markets in the later eighteenth century, for many items the size of markets still restricted specialization. Paul Revere lived in Boston, one of the largest and weal-

thiest colonial cities, but he was not able to restrict his manufacturing to silversmithing. He produced clock faces, branding irons, false teeth, and surgical instruments and also performed copperplate engraving. After the Revolution, he made an even wider variety of manufactured goods. Like other craftsmen, he was versatile in order to be fully employed. In small towns, the blacksmith-wheelwright-dentist and tanner-harnessmaker-cobbler were typical.

By the close of the colonial period, a few signs of more complete specialization were apparent. In some of the larger cities, specialized producers and stores existed. In the Middle Colonies, capital-intensive mills produced flour and gunpowder with the most modern techniques in the world, employing waterpower and sophisticated machinery. These culminated in Oliver Evans' flour mill, one of the world's first

■ Although whale oil was a major Yankee export to England, it still did not prevent New England's trade deficit.
Source: The Bettmann Archive.

examples of automation. Evans' mill unloaded, weighed, ground, bolted, and barrelled as many as three bushels of grain per hour. It used hand labor largely to close flour barrels. The mill did not commence operations until 1785, however, and the techniques it pioneered did not spread beyond milling. Elsewhere in the colonies, factories—in the sense of labor forces working as coordinated teams, using powered machinery, and performing specialized, interdependent operations on a common product—were almost unknown even at the end of the eighteenth century.

COLONIAL TRADE

Given their disadvantages in manufacturing, the colonies had little choice but to engage in trade. The tools and luxury goods obtained through trade enabled them to maintain and improve their standards of living.

The Colonial Trade Network

Colonial trade was much more than a simple exchange of the colonies' raw materials for British manufactures. The colonists participated in a network of exchanges involving the entire North Atlantic rather than merely the British possessions. The Americans realized that they could not finance the volume of British goods they desired through direct trade with the mother country. By the end of the colonial period, they were buying from one and one-half to three times as much from England as the value of their direct sales to her.

Over time, any country can import more than it exports in trade with any other single nation through three devices. It can borrow to finance its trade deficit, it can provide services ("invisible exports"); or it can pay the difference in cash. In the eighteenth century, cash meant specie—gold or silver. The colonists were willing enough to borrow, but the British were reluctant to lend to them. Aside from limited amounts of short-term credit, this means of import financing was not available. At this time, Eastern North America did not produce precious metals. The colonists did sell services (and ships) to the English, and British government spending in the colonies provided another source of funds. Still, a sizable gap remained between the income produced by these efforts and the colonies' purchases from England. It was filled largely through selling more goods and services to other areas than the value of colonial purchases there. The dimensions of the colonies' trade with England just before the Revolution are given in Table 2.2.

The colonies sold more goods to Southern Europe and Africa (a quantitatively insignificant trading partner) than they purchased from them. In addition, they sold far more shipping services to those areas and the Caribbean than they bought. The total volume of this trade was less than that with England, but it was nevertheless crucial to maintaining colonial trade with England. It provided a means of financing most of the trade imbalance that the colonies incurred in their direct trade with Britain. Thus, the extent to which the colonies could fulfill one mercantilistic rule—to furnish markets for home-country exports—depended on their violation of another—to have no trade with rival nations or their colonies.

French sugar-producing islands provided especially tempting business opportunities for colonial traders. Their sugar was cheaper and at least equal in quality to British sugar. Moreover, the French merchant marine was inferior to colonial shipping, so large profits could be made in both direct trade and shipping earnings.

Such trade was often illegal and always in violation of mercantilistic ideals. However, economic theory predicts that given great opportunities for gain in some activity, laws prohibiting it will be violated unless a high probability of detection, conviction, and severe

Table 2.2 Balance of Payments for the 13 Colonies, Yearly Averages, 1768–1772 (In Thousands of 1774 Pounds)

	Debit	Credit
Commodities		
Exports		2,800
Imports	3,920	
Balance of trade	1,120	
Ship sales		140
Invisible earnings		
Shipping earnings		600
Merchant commissions, risk, and insurance		220
Balance of current account from trade	160	
Payments for human beings		
Indentured servants	80	
Slaves	200	
British collections and expenditures in colonies		
Taxes and duties	40	
Salaries of British civil servants		40
Military expenditures		230
Naval expenditures		170
Capital and monetary flows		
Specie and indebtedness		40

Source: G. Walton and J. Shepherd, *The Economic Rise of Early America* (Cambridge, England: Cambridge University Press, 1979), p. 101.

punishment exists. The British made only sporadic efforts to enforce their trade regulations until the latter half of the eighteenth century. Most of those attempts were made through colonial courts, whose juries tended to regard smugglers as public benefactors. Under such circumstances, practice followed theory. The colonists were quite willing to trade with the French—and the Spanish, Dutch, Portuguese, and on occasion, pirates. Until the end of the French and Indian War in 1763, British trade regulations could be violated with almost complete impunity. If goods could not be smuggled, corrupt customs officials could be bribed and conscientious ones intimidated. In the unlikely event of prosecution, colonial courts held few terrors for colonists accused of trade violations.

The three colonial regions developed differing trade patterns, based on their varying commodity production and maritime capabilities.

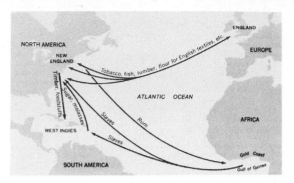

■ The West Indies were an integral part of American trade routes in 1770.
Source: From *The American Pageant*, eighth edition by Thomas A. Bailey and David M. Kennedy. Copyright © 1987 by D. C. Heath and Company. Reprinted by permission of the publisher.

The South

This region sent its tobacco, indigo, and naval stores, plus much of its rice, directly to Britain. Most of this trade was carried in English ships. We now know, however, that the South also sent substantial amounts of food to the West Indies and Southern Europe. Southern colonies' direct exports to England made up as much as 80 percent of the colonial total. For most of the colonial period, exports from the South more than equalled the value of imports from England, and much of the balance was used to finance imports of slaves. After 1750 the plantation colonies began running trade deficits with Africa and the West Indies, largely because of slave imports.

The Middle Colonies

The Middle Colonies ran a consistent trade deficit with Britain, buying from two and one-half to seven times the value of their direct exports. The difference was made up by sales of grain, flour, bread, and meat to Southern Europe, the West Indies, and other American colonies. In addition, the Middle Colonies' merchants were more successful in obtaining British trade credit than were those of other regions, and they also sold ships and shipping and financial services to the British.

New England

From its earliest days, New England ran a large trade deficit with Britain. The major Yankee exports—fish, livestock, whale oil, and shipping services—either competed with English domestic exports or had few markets in Britain. There was a market for lumber in England, but transport costs were very high. Yankees found it more profitable to export wooden products than the wood itself. New England also bought more goods in the West Indies than it sold there, but ran a large surplus on shipping services in that region. Combined with merchandise and service surpluses in Yankee dealings with Southern Europe and Africa, this financed the New England trade deficit with Britain. The carrying trade to Southern Europe, in which New England transported both its own fish and the Middle Colonies' meat and breadstuffs, was especially important. Voyages to this area produced wine, salt, fruit, and some manufactured goods, as well as hard money to apply against the trade deficit with England. Ship sales were another source of British funds for New England.[20]

British Government Spending

The final source of colonial income that could be used to finance overseas trade was British government spending in the colonies. In the latter part of the eighteenth century, Britain spent about 400,000 pounds sterling annually to fulfill its military and governmental obligations in the colonies. Since the colonists paid virtually no direct taxes to the mother country, almost this entire amount could be credited against the trade deficit. A conservative assessment of the colonies' balance of payments over the 1768–1772 period by Professors Walton and Shepherd concluded that no more than 40,000 pounds remained to be paid to England

[20] Walton and Shepherd, *The Economic Rise*, pp. 96–101.

each year by the colonies. Most of this was settled by British extension of trade credit. The total volume of trade at the time was over 4,000,000 pounds annually.[21]

Although the inflow of gold and silver from the West Indies and Southern Europe was important to the colonies, the proportion of this specie used to finance imports from Britain was no less important to the mother country. Specie was a necessary export component of two vital elements of Britain's foreign trade. It financed imports of timber, iron, naval stores, and hemp from the Baltic, all necessary for the maintenance of Britain's merchant shipping and navy. In addition, that region furnished grain when Britain's own harvest fell short of its needs—a frequent event after 1750. The second trade requiring specie exports was that with the Orient, where precious metals could be exchanged for tea, spices, artwork, and rare fabrics unobtainable elsewhere. Such goods were the basis of a lucrative reexport trade for Britain. Thus, Britain had vital political and economic interests in maintaining the flow of specie from the colonies.

Trade Patterns

Historians once believed that colonial overseas trade typically consisted of voyages to a succession of foreign ports. These ventures generally involved a variety of export goods and exchanges of cargoes at each port. An example might be the carriage of a cargo of rum from Newport to West Africa, where it would be exchanged for slaves and perhaps a little gold. The slaves would be carried to the West Indies and exchanged there for sugar, molasses, and hard money, which would be brought back to New England. There the sugar would be distilled into more rum, and the voyage repeated. This trade route has been called the Triangular Trade. New England shippers were thought to be especially partial to such ventures, whose patterns might be triangular, quadrangular, or even more complicated. In each port visited, the ship would sell as much of its cargo as possible, or even the ship itself, reload with whatever item could be obtained on the most favorable terms, and sail off to take advantage of the best opportunities offered by the new cargo.

Recent research has found that although such voyages did occur, they were uncommon. In particular, less than 3 percent of all New England voyages were to Africa, and not all of these involved slaving. Colonial shippers preferred direct voyages and returns wherever possible, and they liked to restrict the variety of commodities in which they dealt.

The reason behind these preferences was obvious. To be profitable, multileg voyages depended on either luck or superior access to information (in relation to trade rivals). In the eighteenth century, information about markets in distant ports was generally at least a month out of date when received. Even if it indicated a chance for high profits, an immediate response was seldom possible: assembling the appropriate cargo and sailing without delay required unusually fortuitous circumstances. Even then, risks were high: prices in most ports could be drastically changed by the sale or purchase of a single ship's cargo. The chances of adverse price movements probably increased at least in proportion to the number of legs in the voyage. Colonial merchants could not avoid risk, but they certainly did not seek it either: wherever possible, they preferred trade ventures involving only one commodity and voyages as short and direct as they could make them. To obtain current information, many merchants tried to have correspondents in each port where they did business. The correspondents' duties were to send market information and their assessments of any developments that might change it as often as possible.

---

[21] Ibid., pp. 102–103.

New Englanders were willing enough to engage in the slave trade, but they suffered competitive disadvantages in relation to the English. The African slave sellers demanded manufactured goods as well as rum, and English traders could obtain these more cheaply. Colonial ships were smaller and more lightly crewed than English, increasing both carrying costs per slave and the risks of a slave mutiny. In addition, English slave traders had better business connections with the slave "factories" where human cargoes were assembled for shipment. The great majority of slaves imported into North America did not arrive in American ships.

THE IMPORTANCE OF TRADE

Trade was important to the colonies in several senses. It was one of two methods by which a colonist of ordinary income could hope to become rich. (The other was plantation agriculture.) Even from a beginning as a common seaman, it was possible for an ambitious young man to progress to ship's officer, and then to ship's captain, while still in his twenties. In addition to their pay, seamen had a minor opportunity to trade on their own account. Officers were entitled to a certain portion of the ship's cargo space for their own use. The proceeds from wise or lucky use of this opportunity could far exceed even the captain's pay for the voyage. Such gains could finance the purchase of shares in later ventures and a possible rise to shipowner and merchant. This was by no means a certain or an easy road to wealth—war, pirates, shipwreck, and other catastrophes were common, and business risks were high. A dead-end job as a common sailor was another possible outcome. However, since a New England farm offered no hope at all for a high income, there was no lack of seaman

recruits throughout the colonial period. Such circumstances forced the development of business skills and responses to opportunity to very high levels.

Rising Trade Productivity

Incomes generated by trade increased over the history of the colonies because the volume of trade increased, shipping became more efficient, and the very existence of trade allowed a greater degree of specialization within the colonial economy, raising the output given levels of resources could generate. Through the century ending in 1775, the productivity of ocean shipping approximately doubled: by 1775, a unit of goods could be shipped the same distance at half the 1675 cost.[22]

This gain resulted from two developments, one ashore and the other at sea. As populations grew, the time required to assemble or dispose of a cargo declined. Packaging of exports, especially tobacco, became more efficient. Consequently, a ship could make more voyages and carry a greater value of cargo in each during a given time period. Port facilities such as docks, cranes, and warehouses also improved, further reducing turnaround time. Minor improvements in ship design and rigging, and possibly in navigation methods as well, increased efficiency, although ship speeds did not rise.

The major factor in the increase in shipping efficiency was the reduction in piracy. When the risks of attack by pirates were high, even merchant ships had to carry large crews and plenty of cannon for defense. Ship designs had to emphasize naval attributes at the expense of mercantile; cannon and the structural strength to accommodate their recoil cut down on cargo capacity. Some prospective voyages were curtailed because of the risks of pirate activity. But after 1675, the Royal Navy protected merchant shipping in American waters, and the danger from pirates fell. Consequently,

[22] Ibid., pp. 117–130.

not only could merchant ships carry a much higher proportion of "payload," but they could be redesigned to be more specialized and efficient cargo carriers rather than quasi warships. Ships plying waters where naval protection was not available or carrying particularly valuable cargoes still retained their defensive capabilities. Those designed for the East Indian trade, for example, could readily be converted to military purposes, as was John Paul Jones's *Bonhomme Richard.*

In addition to the colonies' overseas trade, there was an extensive coastal commerce in various North American products. The New England colonies imported foodstuffs, tobacco, and naval stores from the other colonies, in addition to dried fish (for reexport) from the Canadian Maritimes. The Middle Colonies imported fish, flax, candles, cheese, and the results of New England's overseas trade—rum and molasses. They also distributed the proceeds of their Southern European trade—wine, salt, and some dried and citrus fruit.[23] The South sent corn, wheat, hemp, tobacco, and naval stores to other areas of North America. Some trade in American manufactured goods such as soap, beer, furniture, and shoes also occurred.

Not only did external trade account for a considerably higher proportion of the total economic activity of the colonies than it does for the United States today (about 15 percent of total output compared to 10 or 12 percent), but to a much greater extent than today, it produced otherwise unobtainable goods. In this era, technology could not offset differences in climate or natural resource distribution. Even foreign production techniques often proved difficult to transport.

[23] J. Shepherd and S. Williamson, "The Coastal Trade of the British North American Colonies," *Journal of Economic History* (December 1972). See also G. Walton and J. Shepherd, *Shipping, Maritime Trade, and the Economic Development of Colonial North America* (New York: Cambridge University Press, 1972).

Specialization

It is no accident that productivity gains in foreign trade and related activities were much greater than the average recorded by the colonial economy. Trade promoted specialization. Specialization increased productivity both directly and through "learning by doing," the gains that come from greater experience with any economic activity. Most of the colonies' trading was carried out in a highly competitive atmosphere. Most colonial exports had to compete their way onto world markets in the face of existing substitutes. Moreover, these products were typically produced by large numbers of small-scale makers operating under the separate political jurisdictions of from two to six colonies. Such conditions further encouraged pragmatic evaluation of methods and efficient allocation of labor. They also increased the incomes of the entire North Atlantic economic community. Specialization and exchange increased colonial welfare and produced conditions leading to further gains, and this was well understood at all levels, from the great colonial merchants to the frontier farmer seeking to improve the forest trail that linked him to markets.

THE MONEY SUPPLY

Money is a good traded in all markets, a commodity whose most important economic quality is ready convertibility into anything else. Thus, money increases the efficiency of markets; it fosters trade between two individuals when one commodity (other than money) is desired by the other. Use of money fosters specialization, both directly and by making exchanges easier, and specialization increases productivity. By reducing the time lost in barter transactions and encouraging specialization, the use of money allows the same real resources to produce more output.

But if a little money is good, more is not necessarily better. Money's value depends on its scarcity; this is true for any commodity used as money, even gold and silver. If over any considerable period of time the supply of money increases faster than the supply of goods and services, the purchasing power of a unit of money will decline (in other words, inflation occurs). When American gold and silver flowed into Spain in the sixteenth century, the real output of the Spanish economy did not rise in proportion, and prices expressed in money rose even though in every sense of the term "money was as good as gold."

There were no gold or silver mines in British North America, so specie had to be obtained from other areas by trade or some substitutes for "hard money" developed. Substitutes—Indian wampum, furs, tobacco and warehouse receipts for it, musket balls, and many other items—were used extensively in all colonies. All had disadvantages as money. Their alternative uses affected their supply and hence their value as money. Some commodities' supply could not be controlled at all, and units of others were not of uniform quality. Some were not readily transportable or storable or came in units of inconvenient size or value for most transactions, and many were not accepted outside the colony that had designated them as money. Nonacceptance as payment for imports was a serious drawback. Consequently, the colonists had to either exchange exports of equivalent value for whatever they imported in each transaction (barter), or obtain some form of money acceptable to trading partners. The first method was highly inconvenient, so the second was used. By selling more to certain areas than they bought there, the colonists generated a trade balance in their favor that was paid in coins or bullion. The chief sources of this specie inflow were the Caribbean, Latin America, and Southern Europe.

Coins at this time were valued by all nations in proportion to their gold or silver content. If a Spanish silver dollar contained 4.5 times as much pure silver as an English shilling, it would exchange for 4.5 shillings. Coins of any nation could thus be used in trade in most markets. The colonies' trade produced a supply of bullion and foreign coins, chiefly Spanish silver dollars (which were sometimes cut into as many as eight "bits," or pieces, to make change). But in trade with England, a steady outflow of specie covered the excess of imports over colonial exports to Britain.

The colonies' trade balance with Britain grew increasingly adverse during the eighteenth century, but British manufactured goods were better and cheaper than any other nation's, and the colonists were not willing to reduce their imports to retain specie. The colonists' complaints about the specie drain to England appear exaggerated: while no doubt there was a net specie flow from the colonies to England, colonial prices expressed in specie rose during the eighteenth century, indicating that "hard money" was becoming more rather than less plentiful in the colonies.[24] Nevertheless, it was true that the cost of maintaining a large colonial supply of coin and bullion was a reduction in British imports.

Paper Money

As a substitute for money, paper currency had some obvious advantages. The low production costs of paper money meant a smaller sacrifice of alternative products of the real resources employed to make it. But the same low costs also tempted suppliers to produce too much and cause inflation. The supply of metallic money was limited by the amount of specie in the world and, for the colonies, by the size of their trade surplus. The surplus in turn depended on the colonists' ability to produce exports and to limit nonmoney imports. Thus limits on the supply of specie did not hold for

[24] Perkins, *The Economy of Colonial America*, pp. 101–102.

paper money. If paper currency was to retain its value, its supply had to be controlled, either by requiring the issuing authorities to maintain some fixed value between paper currency and other forms of money or by simply limiting the amount issued.

Today, commercial banks furnish the bulk of our money supply. But in the colonial era, no commercial banks in the modern sense existed. There were land banks, institutions that issued notes secured by land or mortgages thereon. These notes circulated and were used as money until the issuing institutions redeemed them or failed. Land banks were forbidden by the English Parliament in 1741. In the colonial period, governments were the primary source of paper money. Nevertheless, in terms of purchasing power rather than nominal value, specie was always the largest component of colonial money supplies.[25] Frequently, colonial governments' paper money issues were interest-bearing notes.

Most colonial governments that issued paper money (and all had by 1755) did so with caution. In such cases, paper money's exchange ratio with specie and English money remained fairly constant. Notes issued by Virginia, Maryland, New York, and Pennsylvania depreciated less than 1 percent annually during the eighteenth century. But in Massachusetts, Rhode Island, and the Carolinas, paper money was issued in large amounts and prices expressed in this medium rose. Such currency depreciated relative to specie or more stable forms of paper money.

Legislatures were generally willing to issue paper money to finance military expenditures. Thus, colonial money supplies rose in wartime while real output declined owing to the diversion of resources to wartime uses. Increased demands for goods by the colonial and British military interacted with this reduced supply to produce rapid price increases—a pattern repeated in later periods. After peace returned, the first paper money issues were retired; currency was accepted in payment of taxes, and by limiting government expenditures to less than tax revenues, it could be removed from circulation. But if a surplus was generated too quickly, it might reduce the amount of real output as well as the price level. In any case, taxes have always been less popular than government spending; it was much more politically popular to place money in circulation than to take it out. Over time, this meant that colonial paper money remained in circulation for longer periods, and new issues were made for a growing variety of reasons in addition to the needs of war.

Real output in the colonies was growing at more than 3 percent annually: this meant that the money supply could grow at the same rate without inducing inflation. In the colonial context, the money supply could rise a little faster since, as the volume of economic activity employing money rather than barter increased, more currency would be required. Increasingly, colonists favored issues of paper money as an aid to economic growth. So did most colonial governors, at least after they had gained some experience with the results of a well-managed currency and colonial reluctance to finance governmental activity through taxes.

Problems with Paper Money

The British view of colonial paper money was less favorable. Information about the purchasing power of colonial currency grew more out of date the farther from its point of issue. People who knew that Rhode Island currency circulated at much less than its nominal value might take advantage of those lacking this information. British merchants feared that they would receive colonial money that had depreciated at greater than average rates, and that they would have great difficulty forcing colonial debtors to pay the full value of their obligations. Even so, there is little evidence that British merchants suffered serious losses.

[25] Perkins, *The Economy of Colonial America,* p. 105.

Still, English merchants were represented in Parliament and the colonists were not, and they were increasingly successful in restricting colonial paper money issues. As usual, politics and economics made uneasy partners. Although the chief concern of the merchants was to avoid losses caused by inflation, the one situation in which colonial currency issues were sure to be permitted was for wartime military expenditures, when they were certain to be inflationary. Moreover, Parliament's initial restrictions generally applied to all colonial uses of paper money, not just those involving Britons. The restrictions were very unpopular in the colonies, even among conservatives. After all, most currency issues had not produced the effects that the British feared, and the alternatives to paper money were costly.

In the Currency Act of 1764, Parliament forbade the colonies to authorize private note-issuing banks. In 1751, an act restricting New England currency issues and forbidding them legal tender status even within the issuing colonies had been passed, following the restrictions placed on South Carolina, another chronic offender, in 1731. These laws were enacted with no regard for the state of economic activity within the colonies, and the 1764 legislation worsened a serious business slump. The laws affecting colonial currencies' legal tender status were repealed in 1773, with the proviso that they were not legal tender for private debts, thereby protecting British merchants. Further accommodations to colonial needs were made, often after strong colonial protests, but little doubt existed that Parliament was far more responsive to noncolonial interests and its consideration of its actions' effects on the colonies was minimal.[26]

Monetary Flexibility

Another colonial effort to increase domestic money supplies involved the minting and circulation of coins that were overvalued in terms

of their silver content. Colonial legislatures sometimes did the same thing with the Spanish silver dollar, quoting a high legal-tender value. Although these measures attracted specie (sometimes from pirates seeking favorable exchange rates for their booty), prices eventually would rise, and coins would flow out to purchase imports at prices determined by their silver content, not the official valuation.

The development of monetary substitutes and means of "stretching" existing money supplies reveals the ingenuity and flexibility that permeated colonial economic activity. The colonists made extensive use of credit, borrowing wherever and whenever they could. Merchants demanded credit from British exporters, often on the grounds that they were obliged to extend it to their own customers. A wide variety of payments in kind and collateral were employed, and funds were pooled for large endeavors by temporary partnerships, loans from friends or relatives, and even marriages. The corporate form of business, however, was rarely employed and never used in normal production or exchange at this time.

Whatever their failings, and despite the complaints they generated, colonial monetary and financial institutions were successful. Investment was high by contemporary standards, although most of it was financed quite differently than it might be today. Above all, the source of most colonial capital was internal. The farmer's cleared land, buildings, and livestock increase; the merchant's ships, wharves, and inventories; the increases in plantation labor forces; and increases in individual skills at every level resulted from devoting a portion of current output to expanding future productive capabilities rather than current consumption. No doubt a highly developed capital market would have encouraged more efficient applications of savings to the investment projects with the highest rates of return and wasted less effort in a search for funds, but there is little evidence that promising investment projects were not undertaken because of a lack of funds.

[26] Perkins, *The Economy of Colonial America*, pp. 114–115.

TRENDS IN
COLONIAL INCOMES

To compare the incomes generated by the colonial economy with those we enjoy today, we must combine a strong dose of impressions with any quantitative data. Many economists are dissatisfied with modern statistics as indicators of real income. For the entire colonial period, we still have no data of comparable accuracy or scope. Most conclusions on colonial incomes, trends, and distribution are based on probate records, which indicate the wealth bequeathed at death, on food and fuel consumption (and their relation to total income), and on imports per capita. Such data allow inferences—and even some strong conclusions—about income trends, but these depend upon our views of how such data are related to income and how representative the surviving samples are of the entire record. Evidence from productivity trends and supplies of factors per capita are also useful.[27] We must also remember that comparisons between colonial and modern income levels cannot really be made in money figures alone. The colonists lived—and aspired to live— very differently from modern Americans.

Per-capita income figures for even the close of the colonial period vary by as much as 50 percent. Estimates for earlier periods show still greater variation. Estimates of rates of income growth also vary widely in both amount and trends over time. Nevertheless, the limits of the debate are narrower today than previously, and some broad agreements have emerged.

First, aggregate income for the colonies (the total received by all colonists combined) grew at an annual average of something over 3.4 percent. It is known that the colonial population grew at that rate, and the bulk of the evidence suggests that there was at least some increase in per-capita income. The least optimistic view is that incomes per colonist were static for long periods, but that some growth did occur, particularly in the first few decades of each colony's history. Since colonial population growth was very rapid by eighteenth-century standards, and only a few other economies could have been experiencing per-capita income growth at that time, the colonial economy was the world's fastest-growing.

Second, especially in view of the dismal economic conditions during the formative days of so many colonies, the pace of income growth was probably quite rapid for the first two or three decades of most colonies settled before 1700. From starvation levels or worse, colonists progressed to income levels affording a growing margin above mere subsistence. Evidence of the accumulation of productive assets (wealth) strongly reinforces this conclusion; assets bequeathed per person grow more numerous and varied over the colonial period, indicating more comfortable standards of living.

Third, it is probable that per-capita income growth after the initial adjustment spurt was quite modest, and its pace may well have slowed. Throughout the colonial period, the vast majority of the population was engaged in agriculture, where technology and productivity changed very little after the first few decades. Thus, at least 80 percent of the population was employed in a sector where output per worker rose very slowly, if at all. Also, as the colonial era progressed, the proportion of the population in new colonies or on the frontier, where increases in agricultural productivity were most likely, diminished. A few modest gains in farm-

[27] The primary reference is Alice H. Jones, *Wealth of a Nation to Be* (New York: Columbia University Press, 1980). Other useful works are T. L. Anderson, "Wealth Estimates for the New England Colonies, 1650–1709," *Explorations in Economic History* (April 1975); M. Egnal, "The Economic Development of the Thirteen Continental Colonies, 1720–1775," *William and Mary Quarterly* (April 1975); A. H. Jones, "Wealth Estimates of the New England Colonies About 1770," *Journal of Economic History* (March 1972); and R. Gallman, "The Pace and Pattern of American Economic Growth," in Davis et al., *American Economic Growth: An Economist's History of the United States* (New York: Harper and Row, 1972).

ing efficiency, such as those achieved by the Pennsylvania Dutch and some rice and indigo planters, affected only a small portion of the agricultural population.[28]

Fourth, some sectors of the colonial economy, such as shipping, achieved gains in productivity. Growth in the size of markets allowed for increased specialization, perhaps lower inventory costs, and gains from better and more current information. In a few cases, notably tobacco planting, new institutions increased the efficiency of operations. At the close of the colonial era, manufacturing productivity rose to some extent; there was greater use of waterpower and more capital per worker. It must be stressed, however, that these gains were achieved by small minorities within the work force.

Finally, colonial imports, for which the data are fairly reliable, increased faster than the population from 1700 to 1770. Since imports were largely tools and luxury goods, this trend indicates that both the standard of living and the ability to produce were increasing. The proportion of slaves to the total colonial population rose over this era, so rising imports per free colonist almost certainly indicate rising incomes.

Growth in Incomes

In the eighteenth century, per-capita incomes probably rose by less than 1 percent annually (some estimates are a little higher)—not a rate that made year-to-year gains obvious to the people generating them. Nor is this a high pace by modern standards (see Table I.1). A pace of only .5 percent annually, however, would imply that per-capita incomes doubled over the colonial period. The typical colonist could expect to live considerably better than his or her

grandparents had at the same age, and later generations could expect further gains. Elsewhere in the world, continuous growth in incomes was very much the exception.

Not only were colonial incomes growing, but they were also very high by world standards. In the eighteenth century, only England and the Netherlands could have had higher levels of income, and at best the difference in money income levels could only have been slight. It is at least equally probable that American incomes exceeded those of Europe's wealthiest nations. Moreover, an equivalent money income provided a higher "quality of life" in America than in Europe. It must also be remembered that incomes above subsistence in America went disproportionately to the free population. Britain and the Netherlands contained few slaves, so it is probable that the free population of the colonies enjoyed the highest real incomes in the world in 1750. In 1980 dollars, colonial incomes have been estimated at from $420 to $1,000 per person in 1750—well above those of much of the present-day world.[29] It should also be noted that the colonists paid much lower taxes than their British or Dutch counterparts while still receiving many services from the British government. At the same time, they were able to evade most governmental activity that reduced incomes.

Income Disparities

Arithmetic averages can be deceiving as indicators of the situation of the majority of the population: the distribution of income is also significant. Again, although the data are not sufficient to establish exact quantitative positions, they appear strong enough to support

---

[28] Walton and Shepherd, *The Economic Rise*, pp. 130–133. See also A.H. Jones, *Wealth of a Nation to Be*, pp. 304–305.

[29] Figures are from Walton and Shepherd, *The Economic Rise*, pp. 140, 207–208n. Perkins, *The Economy of Colonial America*, p. 145, gives an estimate of $845, somewhat above that of England. A.H. Jones concluded that colonial incomes were slightly less than English. Since her figures are pre-tax, they support the conclusion that American real income levels exceeded the English (*Wealth of a Nation to Be*).

comparisons with other countries. It is obvious that colonial incomes were not evenly distributed, either over the population or geographically. Some colonists, especially the great merchants and plantation owners, received incomes well above the colonial average. The colonial homes that have been preserved mainly belonged to these groups, so it is easy to gain an exaggerated idea of real income levels from "museum evidence." Incomes and wealth were higher in the South than in the Middle Colonies, and higher still relative to New England, even after deducting slave maintenance from incomes and slave values from wealth. Slaves and indentured servants obviously had below-average nonmonetary incomes—from slightly more than half to about 70 percent of the colonial average, respectively.[30] Details of the geographic distribution of colonial incomes in 1774 are given in Table 2.3. The cities had their poor as well, and the lot of a farmer's or fisherman's widow was not pleasant. Farmers with small or infertile holdings or physical disabilities did not share in the general prosperity.

Several studies have concluded that colonial income disparities increased over time, with the merchants and planters—especially in South Carolina—gaining a larger share of both income and wealth. Since both groups were experiencing productivity gains (and planters were able to obtain a large share of the income produced by their growing labor forces), this is to be expected. One study of colonial Boston indicated a sharp increase in the share of total wealth held by the wealthy few, but more recent work indicates stability or modest increases in inequality.[31] Boston's circumstances were atypical of the colonies; slowly growing cities would be expected to generate increased income inequalities. Nevertheless, even in the countryside, income distribution was probably becoming less equal, although the disparities were less than in the cities.

Even so, it is virtually certain that income distribution was considerably more equal in the colonies than in Europe. Despite approximate equality in average incomes between the colonies and Britain, the richest Americans had far less income and wealth than their counterparts in England, and even slaves received a substantial portion of the income received by the average free colonist. And abundant evidence suggests that much of the inequality in colonial incomes was based on economic performance rather than inherited status. The proportion of individuals who could reasonably expect their incomes to rise above the average (for example, young adults and indentured servants) was much higher in the colonies than in Europe. This aspect of colonial demography reinforces the conclusion that income distribution was more nearly equal than Europe's despite age distribution and social features that should have produced less equality. Because the aged have had more time to accumulate productive assets than the young, they generally hold disproportionate shares of total wealth.

In these relatively open colonial societies, with their acceptance of change, competitive structure, and range of opportunity, individuals had substantially greater opportunities to raise their relative income levels—or to lose standing by poor performance—than in Europe. This is the essence of income mobility: not that the poorest individuals be able to rise to the highest incomes of the community, or the reverse, but that people can reasonably hope to change their incomes relative to the average. The colonial economy was closer to this ideal than elsewhere. Although by 1750 there were instances of substantial inherited wealth, the colonies were an economic meritocracy by European standards.

[30] Perkins, *The Economy of Colonial America*, pp. 75, 151.
[31] J. Henretta, "The Economic and Social Structure of Colonial Boston," *William and Mary Quarterly* (January 1965). See also G. Warden, *Boston 1689–1776* (Boston: Little, Brown, 1970).

Table 2.3 Regional Distribution of Income, 1774
(In Pounds Sterling*)

	Population	Per-Capita Income (mean)	Aggregate Income	Percentage
Southern Colonies				
Free persons	652,585	£26.5	£17,293,000	49.3
Slaves	433,106	7.0	3,032,000	8.6
Indentured	19,786	9.0	178,000	.5
Subtotal	1,105,477		20,503,000	58.4
Middle Colonies				
Free persons	585,149	13.1	7,665,000	21.8
Slaves	34,172	7.0	239,000	.7
Indentured	21,374	9.0	192,000	.5
Subtotal	640,695		8,096,000	23.0
New England				
Free persons	582,285	10.8	6,289,000	17.9
Slaves	13,654	7.0	96,000	.3
Indentured	11,856	9.0	107,000	.3
Subtotal	607,795		6,492,000	18.5
Total	2,353,967		£35,091,000	

*£1 is equal to $65 in 1980 dollars.
Source: E. Perkins, *The Economy of Colonial America* (New York: Columbia University Press, 1980), p. 154. Data originally from A. Jones, *The Wealth of a Nation to Be: The American Colonies on the Eve of the Revolution* (New York: Columbia University Press, 1980).

COLONIAL GOVERNMENTS

If the initial colonists' material equipment was often insufficient, their intellectual baggage was almost equally excessive. During the seventeenth century, all aspects of human conduct—social, religious, and political as well as economic—were subject to intensive public regulation. While the colonists might dispute the type of restraints imposed—or, more often, who was to wield such power—they accepted the idea that most activity was properly the concern of the community and not merely a matter for individual choice. All colonies made attempts to restrict economic and other activities to acceptable community standards. But New World conditions forced changes in laws and attitudes just as they had in the tools and production methods brought from Europe.

The colonists had no intellectual commitment to free markets, or for that matter to free choice in most areas, particularly for "outsiders." Colonial governments were assigned a variety of tasks, and their performance varied widely. But the actual impact of government on the colonists was considerably less than initially had been intended. Over the colonial era, the influence of governments declined. Some governmental goals were found to be unobtainable or in conflict with other objectives. Over time, governmental activity based on religious or group attitudes of the early colonists waned. In addition, the colonists were not eager to fund law enforcement.

Colonial governments successfully defined the terms by which individuals could obtain land. Early in the colonial era, it became apparent that any governmental system that precluded individual ownership of land that could be sold, assigned, or inherited without restraint or subject only to minimal obligations such as tax payments was a severe barrier to the immigration all colonies desired. Europeans simply would not voluntarily migrate to colonies that offered no prospect for at least eventual ownership of land.

Defense, too, was largely provided through government (although the burden was shifted from colonial to British government in the eighteenth century). Efforts were made to prevent and punish crimes. Courts were provided to enforce contracts and settle disputes. The degree to which other public facilities were provided varied. New England strongly supported education; the goal was to enable the entire population to read Scripture. To ensure the maintenance of an educated clergy with the proper ideas, colleges were established soon after the founding of some colonies (Harvard in 1636).

Particularly in the seventeenth century, there was a great deal of interaction between religion and secular government; in many colonies, the established Church received tax support. Most colonies also made some effort to provide roads through taxes paid in labor, goods, or money. The destitute were grudgingly supported. Legal-tender laws were established; colonial success in establishing and controlling monetary systems has already been discussed. The enforcement of slavery and indenture contracts also appears to have been accomplished. In the eighteenth century, the tobacco colonies set up grading and warehousing systems for their primary export.

Other governmental efforts were obvious failures. As with all but the most authoritarian governments since, efforts to control speech, sexual activity, the use of alcohol, and appearance offensive to the established order were unsuccessful. This was not for lack of effort: there were numerous laws against blasphemy, fornication, drunkenness, and inappropriate dress. Efforts to formally stratify society, as in Maryland and South Carolina, were quickly abandoned.

Government and the Economy

Many early attempts to extend governmental authority over economic matters were unsuccessful. Massachusetts attempted to fix wages at English levels in an economy where both factor proportions and prices were very different from the mother country's. Virginia attempted to reduce the supply of tobacco to raise its price without making an agreement with the other tobacco colonies. Both attempts to defy economic reality were short-lived.

Attempts to control the quality and location of work, to limit access to certain jobs, and to set standards in general probably had some of the intended effects, but it is difficult to measure their impact on the colonial economy. It is possible to make a few conjectures, however. Regulatory laws were frequently changed, indicating that their effects were not all that had been intended. Compulsory militia training and work on the roads, especially, were often mere drunken frolics. Further, the very low levels of government spending in most colonies indicate limited enforcement of most laws.

In effect if not intent, government was a far less pervasive influence on the colonial economy than it was in Britain at that time or in the United States today. It performed fewer functions to a lesser extent than we are accustomed to today. It did affect noneconomic life to a degree many modern Americans would find offensive. Ideologically, the colonists seldom opposed the use of government's coercive powers to achieve its goals. But over time there was a tacit recognition that some early objectives of governmental action either could not be achieved or were not worth their costs; the assessment of government's role became increasingly pragmatic, especially in the case of regulations imposed by distant governments.

There was always concern over tax levels, access to land, and disputes with other colonies. Political ties between most colonies were through their relations with England: outside New England, few formal provisions for direct relations between colonies existed. Most colonists considered themselves citizens first of their colony, then of the British Empire, and lastly of America. Their major political interests were in the actions of colonial governments, not the British Parliament. Particularly in the eighteenth century, as migration between colonies became easier, the ability of any single colonial government to impose restrictions not found in other colonies diminished. This plurality of governmental authorities has consistently encouraged innovation and diversity, from the Greek city-states to the modern world.

The British Influence

In general the colonies' legal systems and traditions were based on those of England. Although the ultimate political authority remained the British Parliament, the colonies' internal legal powers were broad. In general, they could pass any law not contrary to those of England. By 1700, most colonies were royal colonies, with governors appointed by and directly responsible to the king. Only Maryland and Pennsylvania, which were proprietary colonies, and Connecticut and Rhode Island, which owned their own charters, remained exceptions.

All colonies had legislatures with at least one elected house. Most placed various restrictions on the franchise that today would be thought highly discriminatory. Only New En-gland had universal manhood suffrage. Tradition strongly dictated that "the people" be consulted before the enactment of major political changes in all colonies. The king appointed all high court judges, but most judges and all juries were colonists. Legislatures frequently had the right to deny governors the funds needed to carry out their policies and were not reluctant to exercise it. Unpopular governors might find their salaries unpaid for years. While taxes were a source of political controversy, they were very light by the standards of the day: perhaps 1.5 percent of income.[32] Moreover, taxes were devoted entirely to the purposes of colonial rather than British government.

Another recurring political issue was the conflicting claims of many colonies to territory in the West. Since such land could be acquired cheaply and held for speculative purposes, the validity of individual titles to land was a major concern. The status of individual claims was of course determined by those of the colony in which they were made. In addition, land sales were a major revenue source for some colonies, and restricted access to western land might mean higher taxes.

Governmental activity always increases in wartime, but the colonists became increasingly successful in shifting their defense burdens to the British army and navy after 1700. In successive wars the colonies' military effort probably declined relative to their population and wealth, perhaps because the bulk of the colonial population was now beyond the effective reach of the French and Indians. Often the British reimbursed them for wartime expenditures. In addition, the colonists gouged the British forces to whom they sold supplies and services—and were not averse to providing the same goods to the French if the prices were right.

---

[32] Perkins, *The Economy of Colonial America*, p. 125.

THE COLONIAL PEOPLE

By 1750, the colonists' response to the opportunities offered by the New World was obviously successful. They had achieved economic growth beyond that of any other nation, and in doing so had developed some distinctive characteristics. No one would have confused the colonists with their European forebears by this time. Those who had emigrated had not been typical of the European populations from which they came: over 99 percent of all Europeans had stayed at home. Courage and a much greater than normal willingness to face new and different situations were requisites for the trans-Atlantic passage. It must be remembered that theirs was a world in which "strange" meant "dangerous," and minor differences in religion, speech, or customs could provoke hostility even among Europeans. If crossing the Atlantic involved indenture, as it did for so many, there was no return. Even for most others, the costs of a return voyage were beyond reach. Given the risks of the voyage itself, few could have taken emigration lightly. Those undertaking the journey must have been extremely motivated. There were a variety of reasons to come to the New World—religion, politics, and in a few cases, an aversion to being hanged—but the primary motive of most emigrants was economic. The desire to obtain more than their lot in the Old World appears to have been all but universal. The people who would dare such enormous risks were not only more flexible than most of their contemporaries, they were also better informed and educated. Most had at least some idea of what would be required of them in America.

Change and Adaptation

Nevertheless, American conditions furthered the emigrants' educations and placed more stress on their ability to adjust than they had anticipated, as the initial death rates grimly testify. Many traditional European methods were unsuited to New World conditions—some disastrously so. Many that did not have to be abandoned completely required extensive adaptation. The colonists initially tried to build the same type of houses they had known in Europe. But in a world where labor and tools to shape timbers were far scarcer, more immediate shelter from harsh weather was needed, and there was no need to economize on wood, log cabins were a more effective response. The colonists still preferred the European-style house and built modified versions of it after they achieved secure food supplies and met other pressing needs. But they recognized that this was not the thing to do in new settlements. By 1750, the cumulative results of many such adaptations had fulfilled many dreams of a better life beyond the sea.

The adjustment process created an appreciation of the benefits of change. New circumstances placed a premium on rational evaluation of people and opportunities as well as methods, and the competitive structure of colonial economies ensured that this lesson would be stressed long after basic survival needs were met. In the process, ancient prejudices weakened, although they did not disappear. Nevertheless, under American conditions vital contributions to survival and improvement could and did originate in human sources that Europe would have disregarded had it allowed them to speak at all. Professional soldiers, women, slaves, Indians—even people who were in America "to make Europe better"—all added to the new nation's economic knowledge and received recognition for their efforts. Often too, those who had been leaders when settlements were founded proved least able to adapt, prosper, or even survive. The lessons of adjustment were both positive and negative. The basic structure of American institutions owes more to those first desperate years in new colonies than is commonly realized. The lessons were not forgotten, and they served America well.

SELECTED REFERENCES

Bridenbaugh, C. *Cities in the Wilderness: The First Century of Urban Life in America, 1625–1742.* New York: Oxford University Press, 1955.

Bruchey, S., ed. *The Colonial Merchant: Sources and Readings.* New York: Harcourt, Brace, and World, 1966.

Davis, L., et al. *American Economic Growth: An Economist's History of the United States.* New York: Harper and Row, 1972.

Furnas, J. *The Americans: A Social History of the United States.* New York: Putnam, 1969.

Hughes, J. *Social Control in the Colonial Economy.* Charlottesville, Va.: University Press of Virginia, 1976.

Jones, A. *The Wealth of a Nation to Be: The American Colonies on the Eve of the Revolution.* New York: Columbia University Press, 1980.

Nettles, C. *The Roots of American Civilization: A History of American Colonial Life.* New York: Irvington, 1938.

North, D., et al. *Growth and Welfare in the American Past.* 3d ed. Englewood Cliffs, N.J.: Prentice-Hall, 1983.

Perkins, E. *The Economy of Colonial America.* New York: Columbia University Press, 1980.

Smith, A. *Colonists in Bondage: White Servitude and Convict Labor in America, 1607–1776.* Chapel Hill, N.C.: University of North Carolina Press, 1947.

U.S. Department of Commerce, Bureau of the Census. *Historical Statistics of the United States: Colonial Times to 1970.* 2 vols. Washington, D.C., 1975.

Walton, G., and J. Shepherd. *The Economic Rise of Early America.* New York: Cambridge University Press, 1979.

———. *Shipping, Maritime Trade, and the Economic Development of Colonial North America.* New York: Cambridge University Press, 1972.

CHAPTER

3

CAUSES AND CONSEQUENCES OF INDEPENDENCE

*U*p to 1750, British rule imposed no appreciable hardships on the colonial economy. Indeed, it appeared preferable to any realistic alternative. As long as the French and Spanish remained politically powerful in North America, the colonies could not hope to retain political independence if it were achieved. They had small populations and limited military capabilities, and were anything but united. Further, they were rich enough to tempt aggressors. This combination made colonial independence from all European powers most unlikely in the political climate of the eighteenth century. Under these circumstances, British colonial status appeared preferable to French or Spanish rule because it allowed the colonists far more control over their own affairs.

Mercantilism was never carried as far in Britain as in continental Europe, and for most of the colonial era Britain made little sustained effort to enforce regulations that the colonists found irksome. For all practical purposes, the colonists made their own laws and obeyed only those British rules that appeared likely to increase colonial incomes. Colonial economies had developed almost entirely along the lines dictated by comparative advantage—resources were devoted to whatever uses produced the greatest income, with no regard for the mercantilistic ideals of the mother country. Parliament made few laws affecting colonial economic affairs and was not insensitive to colonial views on trade regulations and other matters, although it did tend to respond to colonial protests rather than incorporate American views in original legislation. Several laws that the colonists disliked had been modified or rescinded, and the colonies were allowed broad discretion in their application of British law. They made full use of it, both in their courts and in their choice of measures to enforce and ignore. In general, Britain followed a policy of benign neglect: it paid little attention to colonial affairs.

By the mid-eighteenth century, then, few colonists had much reason to question the overall benefits of British rule. Colonial incomes were high by world (and British) standards, and rising. The explicit cost of British control was very low. The colonists paid no taxes directly to Britain, and as Chapter 2 indicated, few of any kind. Nevertheless, they were beneficiaries of the most efficient services provided by the British government. Military protection was essential to colonial economic welfare, on both land and sea, and Britain had proved herself the most effective military power of the era. At the same time, the colonists were spared the most negative aspects of British government—the direct mercantilistic interventions in economic activity denounced so eloquently by the economist Adam Smith. These rules undoubtedly reduced the overall level of incomes within Britain by more than they raised the incomes of their beneficiaries.

The American colonists enjoyed free access to the British market, by that time the largest single aggregation of purchasing power in Europe. They could obtain English manufactured goods and trade credit on terms that allowed maximum benefits from British efficiency in these important activities. In dealing with other nations, the colonists could call on the British diplomatic service for support. For all these benefits the colonists paid very little explicitly and even less when all costs and benefits were considered.

Colonial taxes were very low and devoted entirely to the support of colonial rather than British governmental activity. In the early 1770s, the British were spending 400,000 pounds sterling annually on governmental services for the American colonies, chiefly for military and naval protection. This sum represented perhaps 1 percent of colonial gross product; it was far more significant for the colonial trade balance than its aggregate dimensions indicate.[1] There is no doubt that the colonists found British military protection valuable; after achieving independence, they taxed themselves to provide similar services. From the British viewpoint, the colonists were "free riders," consumers of services for which they did not pay.

■ Colonial tax protests vividly demonstrated the colonists' attitude.
Source: Library of Congress.

THE BACKGROUND TO REVOLUTION

The British colonial policy of benign neglect began to change after 1750. Previously, Britain had paid little attention to the colonies because their economic importance had been slight; the colonies accounted for only a minor (though growing) portion of the empire's overseas trade. But as incomes and populations increased, so did the economic importance of British North America. By 1773, the colonies had become the

[1] G. Walton and J. Shepherd, *The Economic Rise of Early America* (New York: Cambridge University Press, 1979), pp. 102–103.

largest single market for British exports and accounted for growing portions of British imports and reexports as well.[2] Moreover, as previously noted, some aspects of colonial trade were more important to Britain both economically and politically than their quantitative dimensions might indicate.

As the size and growth of colonial trade spurred British interest, it became clear that the colonies—or some of them—were the only regions within the empire that did not fit comfortably into the mercantilist mold. Not only did these colonies trade outside the empire, but they also competed with British producers and traders within it. Although these activities made the colonies better markets for English goods, that was an indirect result of an obvious violation of mercantilist doctrine. And the injured parties had better access to Parliament than did the colonists.

The colonies' political situation also changed in a manner that had deep significance for both them and Britain. The conclusion of the Seven Years' War (known to Americans as the French and Indian War) ended the French and Spanish presence in eastern North America. England acquired both Canada and Florida, and with them all territorial claims made by France and Spain. The only remaining threat to the security of the colonies was the Indians, who by this time posed little or no danger to the bulk of the colonial population.

These developments made political independence a realistic possibility for the colonies. There were significant consequences for Britain as well. The war had been enormously expensive. Large-scale military and naval operations had occurred in Europe and the Orient as well as in the Americas. Although the British government had levied heavy wartime taxes on its citizens, these had not sufficed to finance the entire cost of the conflict. Heavy

borrowing had been necessary, and the British national debt had grown alarmingly. Repayment of this debt implied continued high taxes within Britain unless some other source of revenue could be found. Britain had borne most of the war's costs even within the colonies; British troops had done most of the fighting, especially in the final conquest of Canada. Much of the military spending undertaken by colonial governments had been subsidized either then or later by Britain. The colonists had often used these revenues to reduce their own tax levels.[3] They had done little to endear themselves to British forces during the war and had often benefited at the empire's expense.

Colonists who sold supplies to British forces had charged what appeared to be high prices. Worse, their sales to the French delayed or, in the case of Haiti, even prevented eventual British victory.[4] Returning Englishmen carried bitter memories of the colonists' role in what the British viewed as a war fought for their benefit. They also brought better information about the actual levels of colonial wealth and income. Previously, British lack of interest in the colonies had allowed the impression that the colonists were poor to govern attitudes toward them. It was assumed that the colonial tax base was small. But now it became known that the colonists were anything but poor. Understandably, Britain began to consider taxing them to relieve British taxpayers and reduce the national debt. When it became clear that defense of the colonies against the Indians would continue to generate heavy British expenditures, the case became even more compelling, at least in British eyes. The colonists appeared both well able to pay and legally obligated, as citizens of the empire, to do so. But at the same time, the results of the war gave the colonists a new alternative to British rule. The clash between

[2] P. Deane and W. Cole, *British Economic Growth, 1688–1959: Trends and Structure,* 2d ed. (Cambridge, England: Cambridge University Press, 1969), p. 87.

[3] E. Perkins, *The Economy of Colonial America* (New York: Columbia University Press, 1980), pp. 130–131.
[4] Walton and Shepherd, *The Economic Rise,* p. 162.

these changed impressions on both sides eventually produced the American Revolution.

THE ECONOMIC BASIS OF REVOLUTION

Most American students have been taught to view the Revolutionary War as a protest against actual or proposed taxation by the British. These taxes supposedly threatened colonial well-being. But this no longer appears to be the case. If British rule did reduce the colonists' welfare, it was through other measures, particularly the laws imposed on the colonies' overseas trade.

Trade Regulations

The Navigation Acts were a series of laws enacted by Parliament from 1651 onward. Their purpose was to extend and increase the maritime strength of the British Empire. Later the acts were extended to achieve a wider range of mercantilistic objectives. All trade between Britain and her colonies was reserved to ships built and owned within the empire, and crews had to be at least three-quarters British. Foreigners could ship their domestic products only to British, not colonial, ports. They could carry British exports only directly to their own countries. Trade with countries unable to furnish their own shipping was reserved to British vessels. Colonial vessels, crews, and owners were regarded as British under the provisions of the Navigation Acts.

The purpose of the acts was to take as much of the international carrying trade from the Dutch as possible and to make Britain the trade center of Europe. The American colonists benefited from these laws, particularly before 1750. Since the Dutch were now less able to compete for the empire's extensive carrying trade, the demand for colonial ships and shipping services rose. Colonial efficiency in these areas—always high—continued to improve at the expense of both the British and the Dutch, apparently more than offsetting any resultant increase in the cost of imported goods. Thus, this part of the Navigation Acts stimulated colonial economic activity in an area to which colonial resource patterns were already well suited.

Other aspects of the Navigation Acts had less favorable impacts on the colonial economy. The acts required that certain colonial products, called "enumerated goods," be shipped through British ports regardless of their ultimate destinations. For goods ultimately consumed outside Britain, this law imposed the expenses of longer voyages, port fees, and transshipping and sometimes warehousing goods in Britain. It affected American imports from non-British sources, too. The resultant burdens were shared by buyers and sellers. Since the extra costs raised prices to final purchasers, the quantity sold and the price received by the original producers decreased. The difference between the prices paid by consumers and those received by producers accrued to British middlemen. But the services of British middlemen were necessary only because of the law requiring goods to pass through England. The enumeration laws reduced both the volume of colonial exports and the prices received by colonial producers, and consequently their incomes. Regulations on non-British imports raised their prices for colonial consumers and improved the competitive position of British substitutes.

At first, enumeration affected only a few items, but by 1770 the list of enumerated colonial goods exempted only fish, rice, and breadstuffs among major colonial exports. Even in those cases, free export was allowed only to European points south of Cape Finisterre, a point in northwest Spain. For all practical purposes, direct trade between the colonies and industrial areas of continental Europe was illegal. Moreover, as time passed the laws were more strictly enforced. Since a high proportion of enumerated exports originated in the plantation colonies (especially tobacco, indigo, and some rice), the burden of these laws was especially great there.[5]

Enumeration benefited British shippers and distributors at the expense of the colonists and other Europeans, but the British recognized that these gains could be had only while trade continued; it would not pay to raise costs so high that trade fell sharply or ceased altogether. Some laws that made it difficult for colonial exports to compete in world markets were relaxed or eliminated. In addition, domestic production of tobacco was forbidden in Britain, and rebates were granted on duties paid for colonial products later reexported from Britain. The colonists reduced the burden of enumeration by smuggling and a variety of other illegal actions. They were at least equally ingenious in obtaining European goods outside the law.

The impact of these laws was uneven. Trade regulation burdens rested disproportionately on high-income groups in the colonies—planters and merchants—and on the towns, which benefited from the largest possible volume of shipping activity.[6]

Additional Regulations

Parliament also attempted to regulate or restrict other colonial economic activity. The regulations placed on banking were described in Chapter 2. As of 1775, there was no evidence that these laws had any severe adverse impact (the colonial economy continued to thrive), and the most restrictive had already been repealed,

but their long-term consequences could not be favorable. Further, as with many other laws affecting the colonies, they were applied to all colonies without considering whether each had contributed to the problem or not.

Parliament also passed laws restricting colonial manufacturing or export of manufactured goods, but these had little real effect. First, colonial manufacturing was such a small portion of the economy that even prohibitions would have had only a minute impact on aggregate colonial incomes. Second, nearly all of the manufactured goods the colonies did produce were for their own use, not for export. The fact that potential incomes were much greater in agriculture and maritime activity than in manufacturing was a much greater barrier to the growth of industry than was British trade policy. Nor did Parliament forbid manufacturing in general; its restrictions applied only to a few specific items, such as hats. And the laws were widely evaded, ignored, or defied by the colonists, as were most other regulations they found inconvenient. Historical evidence strongly supports the conclusion that British regulation did not greatly influence American industrialization. Even after independence, industrialization did not really get under way in the United States for 30 or 40 years, in spite of a legal climate which now aided rather than opposed it.

The Impact of British Taxes

British taxes also had minimal real impact on the colonies. The tax laws that generated such vehement protests were in fact almost never put into effect. Most of the revenue measures enacted by Parliament after 1763 were rescinded after a few years and yielded little or no revenue while in force. Those on specific items (with the exception of tea and sugar) were met with colonial boycotts, particularly in the Middle Colonies, effective enough to cause British merchants to petition Parliament for

[5] Perkins, *The Economy of Colonial America,* p. 30.
[6] Ibid., pp. 35–36. See also M. Egnal and J. Ernst, "An Economic Interpretation of the American Revolution," *William and Mary Quarterly* (January 1972), for a somewhat different view.

their revocation. Britain spent an estimated 5 pounds on tax collection in the colonies for every pound of revenue actually collected before 1768. After that date, the new laws and revised rates of some longstanding duties on sugar and molasses raised approximately 17,000 pounds yearly. This was a minor burden, representing a maximum of 5¢ per colonist when yearly incomes were at least $100.[7] By the time of the Revolution, the colonists appear to have resolved the question of British taxation in their own favor. No new British taxes had been proposed since 1770, and the burden of those actually imposed was infinitesimal. Table 3.1 indicates that the colonists could hardly be termed overtaxed relative to the British and Irish. It also helps to explain British interest in raising revenues from the colonies.

Table 3.1 Index of Per-Capita Tax Burdens in 1765

	Relative Tax Burdens, 1765
Great Britain	100
Ireland	26
Massachusetts	4
Connecticut	2
New York	3
Pennsylvania	4
Maryland	4
Virginia	2

Source: Derived from estimates by G. Palmer as given in G. Gunderson, *A New Economic History of America* (New York: McGraw-Hill, 1976), p. 89. Quoted in G. Walton and J. Shepherd, *The Economic Rise of Early America* (New York: Cambridge University Press, 1979), p. 163.

BENEFITS OF BRITISH RULE

Although British trade regulations imposed costs on the colonists, benefits from British rule went far to offset them. If we minimize the value of British naval, military, and diplomatic services by assuming that it was no greater than U.S. spending for the same purposes after 1789, we find that they were worth between $1 million and $3 million annually.[8] Since the American forces provided by these expenditures were far smaller and at least initially less respected abroad than their British counterparts, we may be quite confident that these figures understate the value of the British contribution. In addition, Britain paid subsidies to colonial producers of indigo, timber, and naval stores, increasing their incomes. Colonial incomes from shipping services performed outside the empire were reduced by the Navigation Acts, but one scholar has concluded that, within the area of British rule, they increased by about as much.[9]

Attempts have been made to quantify the net impact (benefits and costs) of British imperial policy upon the colonial economy. Although the necessary data for an exact determination do not exist, a number of careful studies conclude that the net burden per colonist could not have exceeded $1 per year, and there is some possibility that British rule *raised* colonists' incomes rather than reduced them. Since colonial per-capita incomes were about $100 per year in 1770 dollars, the conclusion that Britain imposed intolerably high

[7] J. Hughes, *Social Control in the Colonial Economy* (Charlottesville, Va.: University Press of Virginia, 1976), p. 158. See also Perkins, *The Economy*, pp. 137–138.
[8] U.S. Department of Commerce, Bureau of the Census Historical Statistics of the United States, *Colonial Times to 1970*, 2 vols. (Washington, D.C.: Government Printing Office, 1975), vol. 1, p. 1115.

[9] R. Thomas, "A Quantitative Approach to the Study of British Imperial Policy Upon Colonial Welfare: Some Preliminary Findings," *Journal of Economic History* (December 1964).

costs on the colonists appears unjustified.[10] It is not even clear that the burden was increasing in the years immediately preceding the Revolution.

WHY A REVOLUTION?

Since the Revolution *did* occur, but the case for economic causation is shaky, what was its cause? Remember that there was no guarantee that the Revolution would succeed. Even after the war began, its outcome was uncertain for years. The colonists could have held few illusions about the risks involved: many Highland Scots and Irish in America could furnish grim firsthand accounts of British treatment of unsuccessful rebels. If potential risks were so great, the prospective gains so small, and colonial incomes both comfortably high and rising, why would the colonists rebel?

If the Revolution is viewed as an economic proposition, the colonists, or some of them, viewed the costs and benefits differently than presented here, or the benefits and burdens were unequally shared (or recognized), or our analysis has omitted something of importance to the colonists. Otherwise, the American Revolution cannot be viewed as having a largely economic cause. There is some support for all of these points.

Economic Factors

The costs of trade regulation were only too obvious to colonial planters and merchants. The Navigation Acts required that about three-quarters of all colonial exports be shipped through British ports. About 85 percent of these goods were later reexported. Thus, about two-thirds of all colonial exports were subject to laws that reduced both the volume and prices of exports. Approximately one-fifth of all colonial imports originated in continental Europe and cost the colonists more than was economically necessary because of the rerouting imposed by the Navigation Acts.[11] These are maximum estimates, since some of this export and import trade would be (and after independence was) shipped through Britain without legal compulsion. Britain was, after all, the greatest trade center in Europe. Large-scale traders were most heavily affected by the Navigation Acts. But planters were shipping a declining portion of colonial tobacco exports after 1740, and the portion of smaller farmers' income derived from tobacco was much smaller than that of the great planters.[12]

Still, the great planters and the merchants of the colonial cities were the colonies' political as well as economic leaders; developments that affected them had a disproportionate impact on British-colonial relations. Some analysts believe the changes in British regulations threatened both the monopoly power of the colonial elite (as distributors of imports and credit) and the political power on which it was based. These elite groups supported the nonimportation agreements of 1766 and 1768–1769 both to regain control over import markets from British firms' auction sales and tobacco factors and to dispose of excessive inventories of imported goods.[13]

The artisans and workers of the ports were also adversely affected by measures that reduced the volume of trade. Supposedly, they also saw increased colonial autonomy as a source of more jobs through increased manufacturing activity, the lifting of debt obligations to British exporters, and a greater voice

---

[10] Ibid. See also G. Walton, "The New Economic History and the Burdens of the Navigation Acts," *Economic History Review* (November 1971), and Perkins, *The Economy*, pp. 138–141.

[11] Thomas, "A Quantitative Approach."
[12] Perkins, *The Economy of Colonial America*, pp. 52–55.
[13] Egnal and Ernst, "An Economic Interpretation."

in the domestic affairs of the colonies.[14] The latter point, however, does not appear well supported as an important cause of the Revolution. The "lower orders'" influence was small because they were such a tiny portion of the population, and it is difficult to understand how they felt injured by British policies that reduced the prices of both imported goods and credit. In addition, in the years immediately preceding the Revolution, trade volume was clearly influenced more by colonial actions (boycotts) than by British policy.

The chief benefits from British rule were easy for the aggrieved colonists to overlook. When the Royal Navy was most effective in protecting colonial shipping, merchants and sea captains seldom saw the frigates that drove pirates from the sea lanes. When the navy was visible, it often appeared to be doing little but interfering with the pursuit of peaceful trade. The drastic fall in maritime insurance rates produced by the navy's efforts in the eighteenth century was also easily taken for granted or attributed to other causes.[15]

Most colonists had a low opinion of the British army's Indian-fighting ability, perhaps justly so. But their own record was also poor. The colonists may have suffered from 30 to 50 casualties for every one they inflicted on the Indians.[16] The Indians were generally able to control the time and place of battle, which was a major handicap to frontiersmen and militia with other claims on their time. After the British army was withdrawn, Americans found it necessary to replace it with their own and support it with taxes. The United States Army also had to learn Indian fighting the hard way.

The costs and benefits of British military protection were apportioned very unevenly over the colonial population. A frontier settlement with limited access to outside trade might gain

as much in expanded sales to a nearby garrison as in improved security; its overall benefits would be great. Merchants in New York or Philadelphia might well take a different view. To them the taxes that Britain was attempting to collect might appear a greater threat than the Indians. More rigorous enforcement of trade regulations by customs officials able to call on the protection of a sympathetic British military might cost the towns more than they could earn by selling provisions and services to the army or navy. The Quartering Act of 1765, which obliged colonial towns to house British troops in civilian dwellings if the towns would not provide barracks, was probably the most unpopular single measure proposed in this era so rich in British "provocations."

THE PATH TO REVOLUTION

Perhaps the most alarming development from the colonial viewpoint was Britain's growing determination after 1763 that its regulations should be obeyed. In pursuit of this goal, the British developed increasingly sophisticated measures more difficult for the colonists to evade. After 1763, the trade laws were no longer to be enforced by the colonists themselves in their own courts or by officials dependent on the colonists for salaries or security. Customs officials were ordered to their posts in the colonies (the necessity of such an order is eloquent testimony to previous efforts at law enforcement) and informed that they would be paid from the revenues they collected. Colonial governors were given larger staffs and granted more freedom from the colonists' legislative and judicial control. Revisions were made in the tax laws that made evasion far more difficult. Taxes on tea and sugar were reduced, which made legal imports cheaper. At the same time, the more active customs efforts raised the

---

[14] Ibid.
[15] Walton and Shepherd, *The Economic Rise,* pp. 120–121.
[16] J. Furnas, *The Americans: A Social History of the United States* (New York: Putnam, 1969), p. 38.

cost of goods smuggled in from French or Dutch sources, sometimes above those of legal goods.

Political Considerations

In their attempts to influence the laws, the colonists had severe political handicaps. They were, of course, not represented in Parliament. Even had they been represented in proportion to their numbers, the colonial delegation would have been a minority voice, unable to defend colonial interests in any straightforward clash of regional interests. In 1770, Britain's population was more than four times that of the colonies. Worse, although the colonists were not directly represented in Parliament, several groups strongly opposed to them were. British landlords who paid most of the property taxes that furnished much of the government revenue comprised the largest single group in Parliament. Merchants, whose interests wavered between expanding their American markets and minimizing the risks of existing trade, also formed a sizable portion of Parliament's members. Indirectly, even the British West Indies had a strong legislative voice.

Unlike the North American immigrants who remained for the rest of their lives, many British planters returned to England after making their fortunes in the Caribbean. In eighteenth-century England, politics was a socially acceptable hobby for a retired man of wealth, and many seats in Parliament were more or less sold to the highest bidder. The sugar interests were strongly opposed to competition from the French sugar-producing islands that colonial traders had found to be such lucrative sources of income.

Englishmen paid taxes and to a limited extent voted in parliamentary elections. The colonists did neither. They admitted that Parliament was the ultimate political authority within the empire but disputed its right to pass laws with which they disagreed. Even Englishmen favorably disposed toward the colonists found it impossible to defend so self-serving a position.

British Land Policies

A final major source of friction between Britain and her colonies was land policy. Various colonial charters had either left the region's western boundary undefined or extended it to the Mississippi River or even the Pacific. Sales of western land had allowed colonial governments to raise revenue without taxation, which was understandably popular among Americans. The value of western land appreciated as colonial populations grew and settlement expanded. Also, it was thought—apparently without much factual evidence—that soil fertility near the seaboard had declined or might decline. Most colonists were land speculators. Early settlers or those with political influence could often obtain and hold land for virtually nothing, so the potential gains from its appreciation appeared limited only by the landholder's optimism.

After the French surrender in 1763, the British faced a difficult decision. If peace could not be maintained between the colonists and the Indians, they would be faced with the expenses of yet another war, this time almost entirely for the colonists' benefit. The Indians were uneasy because their French allies were gone. But precisely because the French no longer supported Indian opposition to new settlements, the colonists were eager to extend the frontier westward. Faced with a choice between paying for further wars or incurring continuous expenses for keeping the antagonists apart, and under heavy domestic pressure to reduce taxes, the British decided to govern the lands west of the Appalachians along the lines pioneered by the French. Settlement west of the Atlantic watershed was prohibited, and colonial, though not British, land speculators' claims west of this "Proclamation Line" were denied.

To the British, this decision seemed better than any alternative. There had already been one serious Indian war (Pontiac's Rebellion) in 1763, which had been very costly in both money and the lives of British troops. If the colonists would not pay their own defense costs, they had to be kept away from the Indians, even if land claims had to be disallowed.

Colonial pressure induced Parliament to shift the Proclamation Line slightly farther west in 1768, but in 1774 the Quebec Act was passed. This legislation transferred ownership of all western lands north of the Ohio River to Canada, reserved large tracts south and east of that region for the Indians, and raised the price of land in the areas remaining open to settlement. As if to add insult to injury, French Canadians were granted liberal terms of government that upheld many of their political and religious institutions. The colonists were outraged. Not only did most of them dislike Catholics and nearly all harbor an intense hatred of Indians, but many dreams of prosperity financed by land sales were abruptly replaced by the nightmare of higher taxes. The Quebec Act had a direct impact on far more colonists than did trade regulations. Even though a great deal of uncultivated land remained within most colonies, it was clear that rapid population growth and static agricultural technology made access to additional land necessary for the long-term growth of the colonial economy. Since the colonists had no intention of paying taxes to Britain, the fact that the Quebec Act would reduce the empire's defense costs had little if any offsetting weight.

poor Irish paid more.[17] Most of the laws that the colonists were now to obey had long been on the statute books. This consideration appeared very different to the colonists, who had ignored them. One thing that Parliament could not accept was open defiance, especially of laws intended to benefit both the colonists and the mother country. The English were not trying to raise taxes for their own sake; their program was to keep overall taxes as low as possible by combining tax policy with laws reducing the need for expenditures.

Efforts to separate the colonists and the Indians would, if successful, reduce military expenses and the taxes required to support them. The colonists had provided little aid to the British war effort; they could do so now. Parliament was willing to compromise on details. Taxes were changed and in some cases abolished in the face of colonial protests—possibly a serious error. What Parliament saw as flexibility, the colonists may have viewed as the ability to reverse any law they disliked. Moreover, the means employed by the colonists were extralegal—boycotts, protests, and sometimes mob violence. Parliament had taken several stands on principal and had backed down in the face of colonial opposition each time; the Stamp Act and the Townshend Acts had been repealed. It may have been difficult for the colonists to realize that they could push too far.[18] Ominously, even in revoking some measures the colonists opposed, Parliament had restated its ultimate authority over the colonies.

The British View

The British saw the situation differently. To them, the new regulations and attempts to raise tax revenues seemed not only legal but eminently reasonable. The colonists were British subjects and therefore obligated to support the government. They were being asked to pay only about one-fourth the tax burden already imposed on Englishmen; even the desperately

Colonial Defiance

Initially, however, the colonists won the clash of wills. In 1765 Parliament passed the Stamp Act. This law required that revenue stamps sold

[17] G. Gunderson, *A New Economic History of America* (New York: McGraw-Hill, 1976), pp. 88–89. See also Perkins, *The Economy*, pp. 163–164.

[18] L. Harper, "Mercantilism and the American Revolution," *Canadian Historical Review* (March 1942).

■ Special seals to validate legal documents were required by the Stamp Act.
Source: Prints Division, New York Public Library, Astor, Lenox and Tilden Foundations and The Colonial Williamsburg Foundation.

by the British government be attached to all documents—even newspapers and playing cards—to give them legal standing. The burden of the act fell on merchants, lawyers, planters, and newspaper publishers; in short, on all the politically active and articulate groups in the colonies. It provoked massive colonial opposition, including an effective boycott of British goods in most colonies, and was repealed the next year. No revenue was collected while it was in force. In colonial cities, mobs often including merchants, lawyers, legislators, and other members of the colonial "establishment" intimidated the men appointed to administer the Stamp Act.[19] Two years later, boycotts in protest of the Townshend duties on a variety of colonial imports proved so effective that British merchants petitioned Parliament to repeal the taxes.

Mutual Provocations

Other developments, minor in themselves, added to the colonists' list of grievances or to British conclusions that the colonists refused

[19] J. Hughes, *Industrialization and Economic History: Theses and Conjectures* (New York: McGraw-Hill, 1970), pp. 106–110.

any of the responsibilities of citizenship while claiming all its privileges. The Royal Navy was often less than polite in its searches for contraband and in its insistence that colonial ships perform elaborate salutes to the flag. Some crews of British customs cutters, already unpopular for their very presence, helped themselves to colonial livestock, firewood, and other property. British troops in colonial garrisons were continually harassed, in one instance (1770) provoking the Boston Massacre. The British needed tall, straight white pines for warship masts and spars. Timber cruisers were sent through New England forests to locate suitable trees and mark them with the broad arrow that designated them as government property. But often when navy crews arrived to cut the tree, only a stump remained, and no one in the neighborhood had noticed that the tree had been cut. Since felling and moving such a tree required a large work force and from 50 to 80 yoke of oxen—the entire draft animal force for miles—the British found colonial protestations of ignorance hard to accept.

The inevitable challenge came in 1773. The East India Company, a British trading company with a monopoly on oriental trade, was in financial trouble. To increase its revenues, Parliament allowed it to ship tea directly from India to the colonies and reduced the tax on tea. These measures reduced the price of legal tea in the colonies to less than that of smuggled tea from Dutch suppliers. Colonial consumers benefited, but merchants and smugglers did not. In colonial ports, the tea ships met a hostile reception, and many sailed to England without even attempting to land their cargoes.

In Boston, a mob boarded the tea ship *Beaver* and threw its cargo into the harbor—the famous Boston Tea Party. This affront exhausted parliamentary patience. The response was a series of laws making it clear that Parliament was finally determined to show that it was the ultimate authority within the empire and would brook no further colonial opposition (the Port of Boston Act). Boston was

■ The Boston Tea Party, 1773, revealed the colonists' resistance to taxed tea arriving in Boston.
Source: Culver Pictures.

closed to all shipping until the East India Company received restitution for its tea, British officials charged with crimes committed in the enforcement of trade regulations were to be tried outside the colonies, the hand of the royal governor was strengthened, and more troops (whose expenses were to be paid by Boston) were sent to enforce the laws. There could be no mistaking Parliament's intentions. To Bostonians, these laws were the "Intolerable Acts."

It now appeared that England was not merely trying to force the colonists to buy British goods, but restricting their ability to pay for them. Boston could not exist without trade; the city depended on imported food. Once again, Parliament refused to notice variations in colonial behavior: Annapolis had burned its tea, ship and all, and only the discretion of tea-ship

captains had prevented similar incidents in other colonial ports. There seemed no way for the colonists to evade these penalties now, as they had in the past.

Other changes in trade regulations after 1765 outraged the colonists. Smuggling cases were now tried in admiralty courts. Since these courts were staffed by Royal Navy officers who received a share of any confiscated cargo, their decisions were not characterized by excess leniency. Colonial merchants now lost cases with the same regularity with which colonial courts had once acquitted them.

The Revolution's Base of Support

Even at this time, few Americans advocated more than the redress of what they regarded as legitimate grievances. Although American activists concluded over a year after armed conflict began that no solution could be found short of independence, they failed to convince a majority of the colonial population. The American Revolution was not a mass movement. Only about a third of the colonists supported it to varying degrees. A slightly smaller group, the Tories, was equally active in opposing the Revolution. The rest of the population tried to remain neutral. Although support for the Revolution was strong in the urban centers, with less than 5 percent of the population the towns could not have achieved independence without rural support.

Trade regulations may have been important issues to colonial townspeople, but the overwhelming majority of colonists were small-scale farmers. Their attitudes were determined largely on political, not economic, grounds. To them, the issue was that they had always made their own political decisions, and now the British were challenging those rights. Another group of colonists had little choice about supporting the revolt. The frontier had normally felt more oppressed by colonial governments than by the British. But changes in land acquisition policy began to alter this view. Also, after hostilities began, the British recruited Indians to fight for them. The Indians attacked those colonists who posed the greatest threat to their interests: the frontier settlements. The frontier found itself supporting the Revolution as a matter of survival.

Not all the planters and merchants supported the Revolution. If they bore the greater burdens of British rule, they remained wealthy after such costs were met. Nor was their position determined on economic grounds alone; some had strong loyalty to the king. Even on purely economic grounds, the Revolution's appeal to the wealthy must have been limited. When established authority is overthrown, the rich have much to lose. It could not have been clear that high-income groups would prosper from the Revolution.[20]

---

[20] Egnal and Ernst ("An Economic Interpretation") view

THE ECONOMICS OF THE REVOLUTION

The military situation favored Britain. She had an experienced professional army, plus command of the sea that allowed easy concentration of forces. The British military could draw on vastly greater resources than could the Continental Army. In contrast to the colonists' situation, the authority of the British government was unchallenged in its homeland. Britain had other assets: a much greater population, more manufacturing resources, and greater wealth. Even within the colonies, it was not likely that the Americans would be able to assemble superior forces. Total population was slightly over two million people, but only a small portion would be available to the Continental Army or the state militias. Half the population was female, one-fifth were slaves, and of the remainder, two-thirds did not support the Revolution. Even if over half the remaining manpower pool were capable of military duty, this was perhaps 150,000 men. But only a fraction of this number could serve as soldiers. Because output per person was low, most had to continue their civilian occupations. Any large-scale diversion of manpower to the army would have resulted in a disastrous drop in the production of food and other goods.

The Patriots also had difficulty concentrating large numbers of troops at any given point. Transportation and supply were especially difficult. The Royal Navy was strong enough to make any large-scale movement of American troops by sea too risky, and there was no way to transport large numbers of men overland. Political difficulties added to the Americans' problems. Complete unity of purpose was an ideal the 13 colonies never attained. There was no political authority that

---

this as a point increasing the pressures on the colonial elite to regain political domination—as they did.

could compel individual colonies to send troops or even supplies outside their own borders. Even should their governments be willing, individual soldiers were often reluctant to serve far from home or for long periods. Consequently, Washington never commanded more than about 20,000 troops and usually led about a third of that number.

Every new military location caused a qualitative decline in the Continental Army until men from the new area could be recruited, trained, and disciplined. America had to find its military leaders by trial and error. Many of the officers initially appointed owed their positions to political influence rather than military skill—and proved it in battle. The colonists also depended on access to foreign supplies of arms and munitions; control of some major seaports was essential. Fortunately, British forces were never sufficient to occupy all the major ports simultaneously.

The Sources of Victory

Despite all these handicaps, the Revolution succeeded. The Americans won because the British, for a variety of reasons, failed to make full use of their military superiority. Since the British were fighting in many parts of the world as well as in America, they were never able to commit sufficient troops to overwhelm the Continental Army. Nor did British generals make particularly good use of available resources. For the most part, the English sent second-rate generals to America. Some failed to live up to their reputations.

The Americans learned from a variety of mistakes, aided by British failure to follow up on advantages. They did not give up under difficult circumstances, and they received efficient foreign help. Saratoga (1777) and Yorktown (1781) were the two decisive battles of the war. Saratoga was won by the colonists with French arms and supplies. At Yorktown, a naval victory by the French was crucial; it trapped a British army, enabling a combined American and French force to beseige and defeat it.

The entry of France into the war in 1778 resulted in combat in Europe, the Caribbean, and even the Orient, spreading British forces very thin. At sea, a rejuvenated French fleet required almost the full attention of the Royal Navy. Few ships were available to blockade the American coast, and the Patriots could obtain supplies from Europe.

In addition, swarms of American privateers attacked British merchant shipping. Over 1,600 letters of marque ("privateering licenses") were issued to Massachusetts ships alone.[21] Though they never threatened Britain's control of the sea, the privateers greatly increased the costs of Britain's overseas trade—even in European waters—and forced the Royal Navy to use warships for convoy duty. Cargoes captured by privateers helped offset the reduction in American trade with Britain. Many Americans found privateering a means of combining patriotism and profit. Successful privateering ventures paid much better than service in the army.

In the end, the British found the cost of suppressing the Revolution too high. Given the costs also incurred by the colonists, perhaps the British were more realistic. Britain's gains from political control of the colonies, if any, could not have been great, and it was obvious that enforcing exploitation would henceforth be much costlier.

FINANCING THE WAR

The Revolutionary War lasted from 1775 to 1783, and there was considerable fighting in all but the last two years. Wars are always expensive, but the Patriots faced several unique problems. First, support for the war was not

---

[21] S. Morison, *The Maritime History of Massachusetts: 1783–1860* (Boston: Northeastern University Press, 1961 and 1979), p. 29.

universal among the colonial population. The Tories not only refused their help, but actively aided the British. Colonists living in areas under British control were in no position to offer aid, regardless of their sympathies. It was risky to press the neutral third of the people very hard. Even among the Patriots, a revolution against British taxation was hardly the ideal basis for raising revenues. The taxes that were levied were imposed by state governments, not the Continental Congress, which had to depend on whatever funds the individual states were willing to allocate.

Military demands diverted resources from other uses and thus reduced total output and incomes. War damage further reduced the tax base. Borrowing was a time-honored method of financing wars, but for the Patriots it also was difficult. Even fewer Americans were willing to buy war bonds than to pay taxes. The value of such bonds obviously depended on the buyer's assessment of the war's progress. A British victory made bond sales more difficult just when funds to replace lost equipment, train new troops, and above all pay and supply those already enlisted were most needed. Foreigners might be persuaded to lend to America, but again, their views of the military situation influenced their lending. In addition, the British would interpret such a loan as an act of war. Borrowing from neutral countries was not easy, and only France was openly allied with the Patriots before 1779. In total, domestic and foreign borrowing raised only about $14 million.

Paper Money Problems

Faced with soaring military expenses, the Patriots used one of the few sources of finance remaining: they printed money. The states issued $209 million in paper currency from 1775 to 1779, and the Continental Congress issued another $241 million. This amount equalled nearly two years' income for every resident of the colonies at prewar levels; it was an enormous increase in the money supply. Its infla-

tionary potential was increased still further because not everyone would accept such currency, and the supply of goods and services available for purchase had been reduced by the diversion of resources to war.

At the same time, the Continental Army's purchasing agents had to compete with those of the British and French, who paid in gold, not paper. The huge increase in the money supply resulted in runaway inflation. Paper currency rapidly lost value both in purchasing power and in relation to metallic money. By 1781, prices peaked at 135 times their prewar levels. Efforts at price controls during this period had little effect because the real source of inflation was the increased supply of paper money relative to goods—higher prices were merely the result.[22] After 1781, prices fell rap-

■ Inflation consumed the value of Continental currency, bringing about the saying "not worth a Continental."
Source: National Numismatic Collections, National Museum of American History, Smithsonian Institution—Photographer: Charles E. Rand.

[22] A. Bezanson, "Inflation and Controls: Pennsylvania 1774–1779," *Journal of Economic History* Supplement (1948): pp. 1–20.

idly as state money issues were repudiated and governments refused to accept them in payment of taxes. As a result, the state money became unacceptable and ceased to circulate.

The Burdens of War

Who paid for the Revolutionary War? Little of the financial cost was paid by taxpayers per se: only a small part of the total cost of the war was tax-financed. Those who bought bonds then found that Congress was unable to pay even the interest on its obligations, let alone redeem them on the specified terms, obviously paid more than they had expected. When the bonds eventually were redeemed some years later, current bondholders gained at the expense of those who paid the taxes that financed the redemption. But by 1792, the composition of both bondholding and taxpaying groups was very different from when the bonds were issued. Some of the bondholders had acquired bonds at a fraction—sometimes one-eighth—of their original value. Those who accepted paper currency and underestimated the rate at which it would lose purchasing power also paid for their errors. Taxation in the usual sense had been replaced by "taxation" through inflation, currency repudiation, and the imposition of less favorable terms of debt repayment than originally offered. Most veterans also paid by being the victims of promised rewards that were either undelivered or long overdue. Obviously, some people paid in physical terms—they were killed, wounded, or imprisoned during the war, or they lost property. This group included Tories as well as Patriots and those who suffered confiscation of property or were coerced into accepting paper money in payment on terms that they would not have freely accepted. To the extent that the war reduced the economic activity, the entire population incurred reductions in income.

THE WAR'S IMPACT

The war caused distortions within the colonial economy, but overseas trade expanded after 1777. There was now no reason to obey the Navigation Acts, and the Royal Navy had few ships to spare for customs patrols. Even trade with Britain did not cease entirely. A small volume of trade from areas under British control continued, and the Patriots were able to obtain some British goods by smuggling and trading in neutral ports, such as St. Eustatius in the West Indies. Privateering and raids supplemented the goods received through voluntary exchange. Trade with continental Europe expanded.

There was a considerable expansion of colonial manufacturing of both military goods and substitutes for imported goods that were now more expensive and erratic in supply. As is generally the case during periods of rapid inflation, economic activity was high, although efforts to offset the effects of higher prices meant that not all of it was productive. Nearly all of the new manufacturing depended upon the continuation of the war, which raised the prices of imported industrial products far above peacetime levels, allowing high-cost American producers to compete.

Little permanent damage to productive resources occurred. Human casualties were low in relation to the population and in comparison to later wars, although they were about one-eighth of military personnel—high compared to subsequent military ventures.[23] The Loyalists who felt compelled to leave the country after the war represented a loss of capabilities much greater than their numbers would suggest; they were disproportionately members of highly productive groups. Since the war had been

[23] S. Lebergott, *The Americans: An Economic Record* (New York: Norton Press, 1984), p. 41.

fought chiefly in the countryside, aggregate property destruction was not great. It was difficult to do lasting damage to agricultural areas with eighteenth-century weapons.

The war's impact on geographic regions varied. New England was virtually untouched after 1775, with a few exceptions in coastal areas. The South was the scene of much of the later combat and the only area where the British employed economic warfare. Some 50,000 slaves were carried off by the British, and deliberate destruction of buildings, crops, and livestock in the Plantation Colonies was considerable. Markets for grain expanded, but those for rice and tobacco shrank sharply, and indigo production dwindled without the British subsidy, which now went to West Indian producers.

Before 1781, overseas trade expanded and a new maritime activity (privateering) appeared, but the war also hurt some maritime activities. American fishing and particularly whaling fleets proved as vulnerable to British privateers as the empire's trade vessels were to American letter-of-marque ships. Britain had been the colonies' principal market for whale oil, and this was now lost. However, the Middle Colonies benefited from increased demand for their food exports.

The impact of the war was equally varied for individuals. Importers, those who supplied the French and British armies, debtors, and successful privateers all gained. Tories, those suffering physical damage, many shippers, creditors, and those few persons living on fixed incomes endured reduced standards of living.

THE POSTWAR SITUATION

Once the war ended, the citizens of what was now the United States of America quickly found that the absence of British rule did not solve all the country's problems. Indeed, some were worse. The Navigation Acts no longer restricted trade outside the British Empire, but they could be applied against Americans who wished to trade within it. Other European nations had mercantilistic regulations of their own, and these were often more stringent and more capriciously applied than the British laws had been. Shortly after the war's end British manufactured goods reappeared in American markets. Without the protection of wartime trade disruptions, the war-baby American industries found it impossible to match British efficiency. The specie balances that had accumulated in the last years of the war flowed out as payment for imports, and domestic prices fell.

Nor did the absence of British rule produce an alternative form of government. The colonists had not decided what form of government to adopt. Under the Articles of Confederation, adopted in 1777, there was little central authority. Congress was unable to effectively control the economic activity of the individual states in their relations with foreign countries or each other. Congress had no authority to levy or enforce a uniform tariff on imports, and the states could not agree among themselves. A low-tariff state would gain a high proportion of foreign trade, which would more than compensate for any loss in manufacturing income and employment.

Restoring International Commerce

Maritime activity was slow to recover from the war. Despite ample shipbuilding capacity, wartime losses in the fishing and whaling fleets were not replaced for the first decade after the war, indicating a lack of demand for the end products of these industries. In countries now open to American trade, it took time to develop contacts, adjust to different regulations, and obtain new sources of finance because Americans could draw on little prewar experience. Since few countries extended full recognition to the United States, and only minimal American diplomatic services had yet been established, great uncertainty about the rules of American overseas trade prevailed.

Debt Burdens

Prices fell to prewar levels by 1785. A declining price level seldom encourages business, and deflation was particularly hard on debtor groups. In the United States, many small farmers, particularly on the frontier, were debtors. States' policies for repaying their war debts varied. Some states levied taxes to pay off the debts they had incurred during the Revolution; others did not.

In one instance, a state's effort to discharge its bonded debt led to serious trouble. Massachusetts imposed taxes to redeem the bonds it had issued during the Revolution. The taxes were levied on real estate and thus bore most heavily on the agricultural regions of the state, but most bondholders were seaboard merchants. Deflation worsened the farmers' lot: a given amount of farm products now produced less money income, but the debt retirement required fixed sums. Thus, it took more farm produce to finance a given amount of bond principal and interest, and tax burdens rose. If farmers' welfare was reduced by these changes, bondholders benefited; they received money with increased purchasing power. Some farmers in western Massachusetts refused to pay their taxes. In 1786 this group seized an armory and convinced Daniel Shays, a former Continental Army captain, to lead them. The state militia, aided by Harvard students, suppressed the revolt, but Shays' Rebellion frightened many people. Had the state forces not been sufficient, there was no prospect of aid from the central government. Southern states feared slave rebellions for the same reason. Deflation created increasing political pressure on state governments for debt moratoria and paper money issues—neither of which would further economic stability.

A Weak Central Government

The central government faced no more urgent problem than its financial difficulties. Congress lacked the power to levy taxes and could only ask the states for funds to carry out its duties. In one postwar year, its receipts from the states paid only one-third of the interest due on the national debt, with nothing whatever left over for other expenses of government. The United States' failure to pay even the interest on its foreign debt hardly encouraged international respect for the new country. Even if treaties could be negotiated with foreign powers, Congress could not require the states to comply with their terms. Britain and Spain continued to occupy territory that the Treaty of Paris had granted to the United States. The nation was no better equipped to secure respect abroad than to enforce the central government's authority at home. There was no navy, and the 718-man army's pay was so long overdue that it was considering mutiny.

Pirates took full advantage of the fact that U.S. shipping was no longer protected either by a navy, or, in North African waters, by British bribes to the rulers of Algiers, Tunis, and Tripoli. Resolving other problems, such as relations with the Indians and the disposal of western lands, also required an effective central government. Even so, matters could have been worse. Despite the shortcomings of the Articles of Confederation, for the most part states did act responsibly in economic matters, particularly in regard to monetary policy. But little assured the continuation of this trend, and fears persisted that at best the states might prove unable to enforce their laws or to relate them coherently to those of other states. It still appeared possible that the states might enact measures imperiling economic stability and the long-term investment projects it encouraged.

Postwar Progress

Even so, the United States under the Articles of Confederation was not entirely hostile to economic development. There were some achievements in both the private and public sectors from 1783 to 1789. States provided minor improvements in access to land and flexibility in its use by breaking up some of the large estates previously owned by Tories (most, however, passed intact into the hands of wealthy Patriots) and by restricting entail (which allowed heirs the use of but not the right to sell estates) and primogeniture. Quitrent payments to colonial proprietors were abolished. However, these actions affected only a small portion of the land; changes on the western frontier had greater significance.

The frontier population was expanding rapidly in this period, especially in Kentucky, Tennessee, upstate New York, and northern New England. The Northwest Ordinances of 1784 and 1785 provided a highly favorable climate for the westward movement. Land in regions covered by these ordinances was to be sold only after accurate surveys established a township system and ensured secure land titles. This aided dense settlement, promoted social stability by providing for the basic functions of local government such as education, and increased the value of land by making it easy to sell. The states ceded their claims to western land to the central government. New states were to be admitted to the Union on an equal political footing with the original 13. One potential source of conflict had been avoided: the United States would have no colonies, at least not within its contiguous area.

Trade Recovery

American merchants began actively searching for new trade commodities and routes that took their ships to the Baltic, the eastern Mediterranean, the East Indies, and even China and Arabia. The new markets represented only a minor fraction of overseas trade in this period, but some had potential for considerable expansion. The terms of trade immediately after the war moved in favor of the United States; a unit of exports would now finance more imports than in the prewar period. This advantage did not last, however. By 1790 the terms of trade were at prewar levels.[24] Institutions that aided both internal and external trade, such as banks and insurance companies, now appeared. Population growth was rapid, and given America's chronic labor shortage, a larger work force enhanced the economy's potential. In international affairs, Dutch bankers were somehow persuaded to lend the U.S. government money to pay the interest on its foreign debts.

In assessing America's economic development in this era, we are forced to rely on indirect evidence; data on incomes are incomplete. Contemporary observers' conclusions about U.S. economic circumstances in the 1780s range from guarded optimism to the deepest pessimism, and in the absence of accurate statistics on per-capita incomes, cannot be validated. Figures on the volume of international trade indicate that prewar trade volumes had been regained in physical terms by 1788; in monetary terms, the recovery was somewhat quicker. The prices of tobacco, wheat, and rice, the principal U.S. exports, all rose in relation to import prices. But trade recovery was uneven. Most of New England had regained prewar levels of per-capita exports and shipping earnings by the early 1790s, but New Hampshire failed to share in this recovery. Rising exports of breadstuffs and meat benefited most of the Middle Atlantic states; wheat and its products replaced tobacco as the most valuable U.S. export at this time. Nevertheless, Pennsylvania experienced a serious economic slump. In the South, particularly the Carolinas and Georgia, conditions were less favorable. Increased prices for tobacco and rice did not

---

[24] Walton and Shepherd, *The Economic Rise,* p. 185.

generate rising output, and indigo production declined but by no means disappeared.[25]

Trade volume itself is only one indication of economic welfare. Even though the United States had regained prewar volumes of trade and probably of shipping earnings by 1790, the country's population had nearly doubled since 1770. On a per-capita basis, then, foreign trade was still considerably below prewar levels, and since the structure of the economy had not changed significantly, it held the same importance as an indicator of individual welfare and income as in colonial times. Most of the "growth" of the 1780s was thus merely a recovery of lost ground. The long-term outlook did not appear promising. Markets for the traditional plantation staples were not expanding, and incomes in the South were heavily dependent on exports. Slow urban growth produced scant prospects for internal markets for agricultural products. Some scholars have suggested that the economic prospects were even worse than suggested here.[26] Independence had proved no economic panacea for most Americans by 1790, and adequate responses to both internal and external barriers to growth had yet to be developed.

THE ECONOMICS OF THE CONSTITUTION

The internal problems related to government were addressed in 1789. With the Constitution, the United States provided an effective institutional framework for economic activity. Most of the previous failings of the central government were resolved by strengthening its powers relative to those of the states. Above all, the new federal government was granted the right to levy its own taxes; it would no longer be dependent on the states' largesse—or crippled by their niggardliness. Treaties negotiated with foreign countries by the federal government superseded state laws, and the states were forbidden to interfere with interstate commerce. The federal government was also given control over monetary matters: the Constitution prohibited issues of money by the states. Thus, in the areas where the states' economic performance had been poor or a source of potential difficulties, economic control was shifted to the federal government.

One immediate result of this transfer of powers was the formation of a "common market" consisting of the entire United States. Buyers or sellers in any part of the country were free to participate in the markets of all states without any government-imposed barriers to the movement of goods and services. This encouraged maximum utilization of the available opportunities for specialization and economies of scale. Federal control of interstate commerce might not have had substantial effects in 1789. However, as transportation costs fell and production technology changed, it would generate important economic gains for the United States by increasing competition and thus encouraging greater productive efficiency. The Constitution strongly supported property rights, including, at least implicitly, property rights in slaves.

The enforcement of contracts was upheld, and government was not allowed to change the provisions of agreements already made. A system of federal courts was established, with the power to hear appeals from state court decisions. Since the Constitution gave the federal government its own powers of taxation, the implicit control of the central government by the states was now ended: they could not "veto" central government measures by refusing to fund them. The federal government could now support an effective standing army and established a navy. The federal structure of government also potentially aided new economic

---

[25] Ibid., pp. 182–189.
[26] G. Bjork, "The Weaning of the American Economy: Independence, Market Changes, and Economic Development," *Journal of Economic History* (December 1964).

activity by reducing the possibility that established producers could forestall innovation and new competition.[27]

The Economic Orientation of the Constitution

The Constitution has been described as a class-oriented document, more protective of property rights than human rights, and especially tender toward the interests of delegates to the Constitutional Convention. This charge at least implies that such a slant came at the expense of other groups within America. Many of the convention delegates were wealthy, but the evidence indicates that the document they produced found broad acceptance among the general population. The Constitution apparently was an effective response to what most Americans saw as the major governmental problems of the day. By no means were all convention delegates doctrinaire conservatives; many had voted for paper money issues and debt-relief measures as state legislators. Nor do their voting patterns indicate that they were motivated largely by possible gains from redemption of the outstanding debts of preceding governments. The concern with property rights in the body of the Constitution may be explained by two factors. First, the vast majority of all American voters were property owners; the United States at this time was a nation of owner-occupied farms. Land values clearly depended on the security of property rights. Second, the Constitution was a response to failures of the previous system rather than

an attempt to build on its successes. Human rights were better protected under the Articles of Confederation than were property rights.

In any case, the Constitution was ratified by large majorities in both agricultural states and those where commercial interests were strong. Although no women, very few blacks, and in some cases only those white males who met property qualifications were eligible to vote, this was still a wider franchise than in any other country in 1789. There is no evidence that those excluded from the polls were largely opposed to the Constitution. A statement of human rights (the Bill of Rights, 1791) was added to the Constitution via a set of ten amendments to the main body of the document.

The Application of New Economic Powers

In economic matters, the Constitution is largely a permissive document. It defines what various levels of government *can* do but not what they *must* do or *how* they are to do it. Decisions were still necessary within the constitutional framework on how the federal government would use its new powers over money, taxes, and international trade, and toward what ends. Would the United States seek economic self-sufficiency or a continuation of the international specialization and exchange of the previous era? What would be done about the outstanding debts of all levels of government, state as well as central? This point was complicated. Not only did the amounts of state indebtedness vary widely, but some states had already repaid at least part of their indebtedness, while others had made no such effort. Further, the original purchasers of some government bonds, despairing of ever receiving payment, had sold their bonds for far less than their face value to speculators. If the bonds were redeemed at par, some bondholders would receive large windfall profits. The same considerations applied to some of the benefits promised to veterans. What type of taxes would be levied by the federal government? What type of money would the new country use? The federal government had

---

[27] Diversity among political jurisdictions has received increasing attention as a source of long-term economic growth. See J. Hicks, *A Theory of Economic History* (New York: Oxford University Press, 1969); M. Olson, *The Rise and Decline of Nations* (New Haven, Conn.: Yale University Press, 1982); N. Rosenberg and L. Birdzell, *How the West Grew Rich* (New York: Basic Books, 1986); and E. Jones, *The European Miracle* (Cambridge, England: Cambridge University Press, 1981).

■ On September 17, 1787, 39 of the 55 delegates of the Constitutional
Convention in Philadelphia signed the Constitution.
Source: The Bettmann Archive.

inherited title to vast expanses of western land.
How would it use this resource?

Decisive Actions

The answers to many of these questions were
interrelated. The policies established by the
Northwest Ordinances were continued; the
public domain would be sold by the government to private individuals. Revenues for the
federal government would come from land
sales, excise taxes on a few domestically produced goods, and modest tariffs on imported
goods. Several of these decisions had wider implications. The excise tax on whiskey provoked
defiance by some producers—the "Whiskey Re-

bellion"—which the federal government suppressed with its new powers, backed by the
army. One primary objective of the Constitutional Convention had been achieved: an effective central government could now enforce
its control against illegal opposition. The decision to use the tariff to produce revenue
rather than to protect domestic producers indicated another policy. A tariff can protect domestic producers by raising the prices of foreign
goods so high that few imported items are sold,
or it can yield revenue because goods on which
the tax is levied continue to enter the country,
but it cannot do both efficiently under normal
circumstances. The decision to use the tariff

for revenue meant that the United States would continue to employ its productive resources along the lines of comparative advantage.

Solutions to the Debt Problem

In another momentous decision, the federal government assumed responsibility not only for the outstanding debts of central government, but for those of the states as well. These would be paid off at their face value rather than the much lower current prices reflecting financial markets' skepticism that they would ever be redeemed. In the long run, this decision proved very beneficial to the United States. Europeans reasoned that if Americans would pay taxes to allow their government to repay its debts, surely the citizens would also repay their private obligations. America and its people were now regarded as good credit risks, which enabled them to borrow in Europe's financial markets.

Since capital was particularly scarce under U.S. economic conditions, access to European money markets was a valuable asset. Most capital employed in the American economy was generated by citizens, who restricted their consumption and used the balance of their incomes to raise future output. But the use of European savings allowed Americans to make fewer short-run sacrifices than if only domestically generated funds had been available.

The Monetary Standard

The monetary unit of the United States was defined as the dollar. The Spanish milled silver dollar had been the most common coin in circulation in the colonies, and the new monetary unit contained the same amount of silver. Unfortunately, the U.S. dollar was defined in terms of both gold and silver, resulting in difficulty when their relative values as metal changed. If silver became more abundant, for example, its market value in relation to gold would fall. But since the U.S. mint offered to buy and sell both metals at fixed prices in dollars, silver could be exchanged for dollars at the price fixed by the mint. The dollars could be taken to the mint,

exchanged for gold, and the gold used to buy a larger amount of silver in the metal markets than did dollars at the official exchange rate. These transactions could be repeated until the government ran out of gold or fixed a new rate of exchange between gold and silver.

By defining the dollar in terms of a fixed amount of precious metal, its value in relation to the currencies of other countries following similar policies was determined. For example, a British pound could be exchanged for 4.56 times as much gold as an American dollar, and thus the pound exchanged for $4.56. As long as American internal prices were free to rise and fall, Americans could readily compute the prices of foreign goods, as could foreign customers of American producers. Consequently, international trade and specialization were encouraged.

JEFFERSON VERSUS HAMILTON

The resolution of the questions just discussed provided a largely favorable climate for economic activity in the United States. Secure property rights, easy access to markets, and a defined currency all encouraged Americans to produce and to make long-term economic commitments. But the direction of economic development had not been determined. Two very different visions of America's economic future were proposed by Thomas Jefferson and Alexander Hamilton.

The Jeffersonian Ideal

Jefferson's ideal was a nation of owner-occupied farms, with each farm and the nation as a whole providing a high proportion of its own consumption needs. He wanted little if any urbanization and manufacturing and thought that foreign trade should only provide necessities that could not be produced domestically. Jefferson advocated minimal government intervention in the economy and opposed concentrations of power in any form. The Jeffersonian goal was a nation of informed, independent yeoman farmers who placed a major emphasis on individual freedom. Jefferson had been profoundly and unfavorably impressed by the conditions of life in European cities, which were horrible by modern standards or even relative to his own experience in contemporary rural America. Wage labor may also have implied a loss of personal independence to Jefferson.

Hamilton's Vision

Hamilton's views were more closely allied with those of European mercantilists. He wanted rapid American industrialization and proposed that the government serve as a development agency. Tariffs and subsidies were appropriate mechanisms to encourage manufacturing and would, he thought, eventually produce an economically self-sufficient United States. To Hamilton, industrialization was the most efficient route to national power, and the sooner the United States chose it, the better. Hamilton's view emphasized the interests of the state rather than the individual.

Conflict between Flawed Models

Both visions were highly idealistic and contained a large element of political ideology. Like most other ideological proposals, they ignored some inconvenient realities. Jefferson's program glossed over the actual conditions of small-farm life in eighteenth-century America. Farmers had to work long hours with few mechanical aids to substitute for their own muscles. More-

over, their lives were insecure. Farmers were vulnerable to weather, illness, injury, and adverse market conditions (even Jefferson realized that some goods would have to be obtained from nonfarm producers). The living conditions imposed by farm life left little time for the individual expression so valued by Jefferson, and small farmers' incomes restricted their ability to change their circumstances. One wonders whether even informed and educated yeomen would have much interest in discussing the great issues of the day after a 14- to 16-hour workday at harvest time. It must be remembered that Jefferson's own agricultural experience was hardly that of a small farmer totally dependent on his own labor.

Had Jefferson cared to look, he might have found considerable evidence that many American farmers wanted something other than the self-sufficient life he advocated. Improved transportation—especially if it gave better access to markets—labor-saving devices, and a wide range of creature comforts were all sought by the agricultural population. Their enthusiasm for change and material betterment was seldom tempered by thoughts that they increased farmers' interdependence with the rest of the economy. To most economists, the Jeffersonian program would lead to long-run stagnation, with incomes and opportunities never changing. The typical American viewed increased income as highly desirable and welcomed change if it furthered progress toward that goal. A crucial long-run deficiency was that the agrarian ideal had no effective answer to the rapid growth of the American population.

Even though in 1790 North America was still an underpopulated continent, the Jeffersonian scheme could only accommodate population growth by using more land in the same way since it envisioned no change in technology or occupational patterns. Thirteen years later, when Jefferson signed the Louisiana Purchase, he thought he had provided land for a thousand years' growth. But U.S. territory as of 1803 plus more than a million square miles of additional land were occupied in less than a century, largely by people born in America.

Hamilton's proposals involved the risk of major mistakes in direction as well as certain high short-run costs. In 1790 the productive resources of the United States were not well suited to manufacturing. In particular, the human skills and large amounts of capital required for industrialization simply did not exist. Consequently, American manufactured goods cost far more than those from Europe. These costs reflected alternatives foregone; Americans could earn high incomes producing agricultural and primary products and providing shipping services and had to be compensated accordingly to work in manufacturing instead. Furthermore, the incomes already enjoyed by Americans were if anything higher than those of "more developed" economies. Hamilton's ideas implied shifting American resources from high- to low-productivity uses. The result would have been reduced total output from the same resources: a fall in income. This was the short-run cost of Hamilton's proposals. The adverse effects might have been even greater than those directly induced by resource misallocation. Diverting resources from export-producing occupations to production of import substitutes would reduce the incomes foreigners could earn from trade with the United States. Thus, their demand for the remaining American exports would fall. American consumers would find both the total volume of goods available to them and their real incomes reduced.

If subsidies to American producers were employed instead of tariff protection, taxpayers would have to pay for them. Manufacturing might have developed faster under the Hamiltonian scheme than it actually did, through "learning by doing" and higher rates of industrial investment, which would reduce America's shortages of industrial resources. But the program's short-run costs appear inescapable. Furthermore, the extent to which American manufacturing became efficient relative to foreign producers depended on the government's ability to direct its support only to industries whose efficiency would eventually equal that of overseas competitors. The government could not hope to support all industries simultaneously; it lacked the resources. But such a strategy involved many risks. Some of the industries selected might never meet foreign competition without aid, and their American products would always cost more than imports. Even in sectors where American producers became competitive with foreigners, Hamilton's proposals could not be deemed economically successful unless the aid or protection was then terminated. The history of government assistance programs offers little hope that such "infant industries" would ever willingly give up aid. If government-assisted industries never relinquished aid even after achieving full maturity, they might benefit, but consumers and taxpayers would not. Finally, Hamilton's proposals assumed a degree of foresight and restraint that government has yet to exhibit in providing industrial aid.

THE NEW ECONOMIC ENVIRONMENT

Ultimately, the United States did little to foster either Hamilton's or Jefferson's ideas. As mentioned, the tariff was low and furnished only minimal protection to American producers. The fishing and shipbuilding industries received modest subsidies, and the market for coastal shipping was reserved to U.S. vessels. Only in arms manufacture did the government actually establish its own factories. These armories were a fertile source of new tools and techniques that proved to have important applications in other industries. But these limited efforts represented total government aid to industrialization. Although the government continued to sell land to individuals, and American support for education was strong by international standards, little else was done to further the Jeffersonian goals.

Instead, the United States presented its citizens with a highly permissive climate for all types of economic activity. People were largely free to produce whatever and however they pleased and to sell the results for whatever prices they could obtain. Their security in the proceeds of these market activities was guaranteed by the Constitution and a series of laws and court decisions. American markets allowed wide freedom of entry; the legal climate opposed monopoly.

Property rights to existing goods were secured by the Constitution, and patent and copyright laws gave similar rights to the producers of new ideas. Such laws are a major incentive to inventive activity. If an inventor bore the full costs and risks of developing a new product or method, only to discover that others were free to use the fruits of his work at no cost to themselves, the search for new goods and activities would be discouraged. Most inventive activity is undertaken in the hopes of a reward for success, not merely to benefit society. Moreover, new ideas and their practical applications are necessary both to ward off diminishing returns and to avoid economic stagnation. This point is central to the recent work of several students of the development process.[28] Other governmental measures that encouraged economic growth were the establishment of a postal system and the adoption of uniform weights and measures.

---

[28] D. North et al., *Growth and Welfare in the American Past: A New Economic History*, 3d ed. (Englewood Cliffs, N.J.: Prentice-Hall, 1983), Chap. 2. See also D. North, *Structure and Change in Economic History* (New York: Norton, 1981); D. North and L. Davis, *Institutional Change and American Economic Growth* (New York: Cambridge University Press, 1971); and M. Olson, *The Rise and Decline of Nations: Economic Growth, Stagflation, and Social Rigidities* (New Haven, Conn.: Yale University Press, 1982).

Promotion of Trade and Exploration

The new government sought information about the economic potential of distant areas and made it available to the public. The diplomatic service furnished reports on economic conditions in the countries where embassies and consulates were located. Within the United States, the government sent out expeditions such as those of Lewis and Clark (1804–1806) and Pike (1805–1807), and published their reports. These efforts supplemented information from American merchants and the mountain men. The army began (with varying success) to protect the frontier and the navy to protect American merchant shipping in the Caribbean and Mediterranean.

Efficiency versus Politics

Relations between government and the economy were not entirely along the lines dictated by economic efficiency, however. Sometimes goals conflicted: the desire to transfer western land into private hands and to foster western settlement was tempered by the U.S. Treasury's need for revenue from land sales. Sometimes decisions were made on purely political grounds. Contracts to build the new navy were allocated to as many shipyards as possible instead of restricted to those yards capable of building the types of warships actually required. The initial result was a number of small gunboats, all of limited military value and many not even oceanworthy. But the real product sought was votes from shipbuilders, not the most efficient naval protection for the United States.[29]

---

[29] A. Mahan, *Sea Power in Its Relations to the War of 1812*, 2 vols. (New York: Greenwood Press, 1969), vol. 1, p. 187; vol. 2, pp. 154–161.

In general, the role of government in the American economy was determined by pragmatic rather than ideological considerations. There was little advocacy of laissez-faire for its own sake. Americans were quite prepared to pursue economic goals through government action where it promised better results than the available private alternatives. If most economic activity was left to private markets, subject only to a framework of rules intended to improve their efficiency, it was because this was deemed likely to result in the greatest total well-being. Political values occasionally ruled: the eventual technological efficiency of the armories that produced government weapons was not the primary reason for their existence. The political costs of depending on Europe for arms appeared too great, whatever the economic considerations. The Constitution's provisions indicate that Americans believed that government had a definite role to play in economic activity. The U.S. Treasury, under Alexander Hamilton, played a leading role in most of the activities of the federal government in the 1790s, helping to determine the form and extent of tax and tariff programs, the distribution of revenues, land disposal, banking, overseas commerce, and foreign relations.[30]

INDEPENDENCE

It has been claimed that the United States and its colonial predecessors were in fact independent long before the Treaty of Paris (1783) that ended the Revolutionary War. Alternatively, it has been argued that not for many years after 1783—perhaps not until after the American Civil War—did the United States achieve true independence from Europe. It appears that the

proponents of these positions use different criteria to reach their conclusions.

For most of their history, the American colonies determined their own laws, subject to only the loosest British controls. When the British finally made a serious effort to impose their wishes against colonial opposition, they failed—the Revolution succeeded. In this largely political sense, independence was achieved long before 1776. But it is equally true that Americans maintained important economic ties with Europe and other parts of the world long after the ratification of political independence. To the extent that American needs for European manufactured goods, credit, and markets made it necessary to respond to a customer's preferences, independence was never fully attained. But Americans preferred meeting customers' requests rather than bear the costs of self-sufficiency. In this sense, the rest of the world was not fully independent of the United States. After 1792, events in Europe would greatly influence the American economy, both economically and politically.

SELECTED REFERENCES

Beard, C. *An Economic Interpretation of the Constitution of the United States.* New York: Free Press, 1913.

Bjork, G. *Private Enterprise and Public Interest: The Development of American Capitalism.* Englewood Cliffs, N.J.: Prentice-Hall, 1969.

Hughes, J. *The Governmental Habit: Economic Controls from Colonial Times to the Present.* Charlottesville, Va.: University Press of Virginia, 1977.

———. *Social Control in the Colonial Economy.* Charlottesville, Va.: University Press of Virginia, 1976.

Main, J. *The Social Structure of Revolutionary America.* Princeton, N.J.: Princeton University Press, 1965.

McDonald, F. *We the People.* Chicago: University of Chicago Press, 1958.

Nettles, C. *The Emergence of a National Economy, 1775–1815.* New York: M.E. Sharpe, 1961.

North, D. *Structure and Change in Economic History.* New York: Norton, 1981.

---

[30] L. Hacker, "Secretary of the Treasury," in *Alexander Hamilton in the American Tradition* (New York: McGraw-Hill, 1957), pp. 127–146.

North, D., and L. Davis. *Institutional Change and American Economic Growth.* New York: Cambridge University Press, 1971.

North, D., et al. *Growth and Welfare in the American Past: A New Economic History.* 3d ed. Englewood Cliffs, N.J.: Prentice-Hill, 1983.

Olson, M. *The Rise and Decline of Nations: Economic Growth, Staflation, and Social Rigidities.* New Haven, Conn.: Yale University Press, 1982.

Perkins, E. *The Economy of Colonial America.* New York: Columbia University Press, 1980.

Walton, G., and J. Shepherd. *The Economic Rise of Early America.* New York: Cambridge University Press, 1979.

1790-1865 Census figures refer to year 1790.

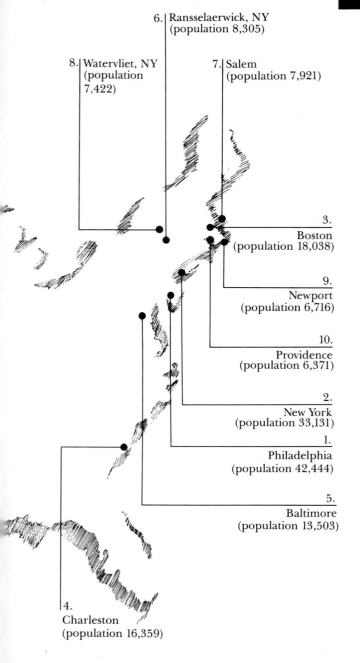

6. Ransselaerwick, NY
(population 8,305)

8. Watervliet, NY
(population 7,422)

7. Salem
(population 7,921)

3.
Boston
(population 18,038)

9.
Newport
(population 6,716)

10.
Providence
(population 6,371)

2.
New York
(population 33,131)

1.
Philadelphia
(population 42,444)

5.
Baltimore
(population 13,503)

4.
Charleston
(population 16,359)

PART

II

*The Emergence of
an American
Economy,
1790–1865*

*L*ittle change occurred between the economy of colonial America and that of the United States before 1815. Political independence had been achieved and some steam engines were in use—developments that would have appeared unprecedented in colonial eyes. Other changes were new to this country if not to the world: cotton cultivation in the South, a few factories in the North, and new financial institutions (banks and insurance companies). The economy had expanded. Population had risen to over seven million by 1815, and the area of settlement had grown. Still, the basic elements of economic life in America were similar to those prevailing in 1700. The economy was overwhelmingly agricultural and rural, and most manufactured goods were obtained through trade with Europe. Tools and methods were basically the same as in colonial days, and in most occupations output per worker was only slightly greater.

Dimensions of Economic Growth

By 1860, however, great changes occurred. First, the economy had expanded in all physical dimensions. Settlements now extended to the Pacific, and about one-fifth of the 32 million Americans were now urban dwellers. But the most significant differences were increases in per-capita incomes and their rate of growth. Real domestic output per person is thought to have risen 60 percent from 1800 to 1840, and the pace was quickening. According to one study, annual per-capita income growth rose from a range of 1.0 percent to 1.5 percent in the early decades of the nineteenth century to slightly over 1.5 percent in the 1840–1860 era. The increase was not continuous; incomes may have fallen from 1807 to 1820 and again in the early 1840s.[1] By 1860, U.S. per-capita incomes were higher than those of at least half the world's population today.

Increases in per-capita income of this magnitude imply qualitative changes within the economy; they indicate how production methods and the ends toward which they were directed had changed. Between 1815 and 1860 there were three major sources of such growth. Labor shifted into higher-productivity jobs, a larger proportion of the population was in the labor force, and productivity rose within existing sectors of the economy. Although these productivity gains were greater than those achieved in the colonial

[1] P. David, "The Growth of Real Product in the United States Before 1840: New Evidence, Controlled Conjectures," *Journal of Economic History* (June 1967). See also R. Gallman, "The Pace and Pattern of American Economic Growth," in L. Davis *et al.*, *American Economic Growth: An Economist's History of the United States* (New York: Harper & Row, 1972) pp. 15–60.

period, the pace was not high by modern standards; most of the growth in aggregate economic output in this period resulted from simple increases in the amount of productive factors available—"more of the same"—just as previously. As population, usable natural resources (chiefly land), and capital increased, they generated more income. Increases in the output generated by each unit of productive factors accounted for only a minor portion of aggregate growth, but the fraction was greater than in the earlier period, and it was growing.

Sources of Growth

The rate and time pattern of per-capita income growth have been controversial matters. At one time it was thought that American incomes stagnated or even declined from 1810 to as late as 1830. Maritime activity was a shrinking portion of the economy, and other high-income activities were thought to have grown too slowly to take up the slack before 1830 or even 1840. Some economists thought that agricultural productivity might have declined in this era, as the movement to western lands might have failed to offset declining soil fertility in the East. Since no comprehensive figures on income in this period have been developed, the question must be answered by theoretical inference from what data is available.

Shifts in the allocation of labor and growth in labor force participation rates unquestionably increased per-capita income. Both raised output per person, one through the transfer from low- to high-productivity jobs, and the second by increasing the ratio of workers (and consequently aggregate output) to the total population. However, if agricultural productivity declined, the dominance of the agricultural sector in the American economy could swamp more favorable developments elsewhere. Recent inquiries, however, conclude that the evidence points to an increase in agricultural productivity rather than a decrease. Moreover, the increase in farm efficiency was significant, perhaps as much as 30 percent over 1800–1840. When these gains are combined with those achieved in manufacturing, the result is an increase in per-capita incomes of between 55 percent and 62 percent for the period. Growth was particularly rapid from 1800 to 1807, from 1820 to 1835, and again in the late 1840s. Rates of growth approached the modern pace as early as 1820.[2]

[2] David, "The Growth of Real Product."

The Rise of Manufacturing

By 1860 the United States ranked no worse than fourth and probably second only to Britain among the world's manufacturing nations. However, America's was still primarily an agricultural economy. Manufacturing employed nearly one-fifth of the U.S. work force in 1860; it accounted for about 30 percent of the value of aggregate output. The proportions are significant, because the above-average incomes generated in the manufacturing sector imply that it would continue to grow faster than the overall economy and draw resources away from less productive applications. Manufacturing was concentrated in the cities and helped to account for their relatively rapid growth in this era. American manufacturers turned out a growing variety of products by 1860 and had begun adjusting methods and products to the unique characteristics of American markets and resources, just as agriculture had two centuries earlier. Some of their products and techniques were considered the best in the world.

Improvements in Transportation

During this period, the cities of America were linked to each other and to their hinterlands by a network of canals, river transport, and railroads that made inland transportation of bulky goods practical for the first time. The new transport network also encouraged the development of commercial agriculture by reducing the cost of moving produce to market. By 1860 agricultural activity was oriented toward markets rather than consumption by the farm family. Reapers, steel plows, and many other implements unknown in colonial times were in widespread use. If it had ever been a reality, the Jeffersonian ideal of the independent farmer was fading rapidly as agriculture became tied to other sectors both for inputs and markets. In the South, the production of plantation staples, particularly cotton, was expanding in a highly commercialized farming sector.

The Role of Attitudes

These changes and many more were fostered by the attitudes of the American people as both producers and consumers. Not only were they as willing as in colonial times to develop and adapt production methods and to relocate to more promising locations or occupations, but they were also highly receptive to the new products that resulted. The increasing variety of products raised the standard of living; the increasing variety of jobs created better opportunities for efficient use of the varied talents of the work force and furthered their development. Since the range of occupations and the ease of movement, between both jobs and regions, was much greater than in previous periods, so was the potential for efficient allocation of the labor force. Human mobility was a prominent feature of the American economy, and it had important implications for economic growth. The distinctive—and often highly productive—features of American economic activity made better use of resources than simple imitation of other nations' achievements could have done.

Models of Economic Growth

Rostow's "Stages of Growth" Model

Two well-known models of economic growth attempt to explain the growth of the American economy in this period. The first is the "Stages of Growth" model of W.W. Rostow.[3] In this model, all economies pass through a series of distinct periods in the course of economic development. The critical stage is the "takeoff," which marks the transition to sustained economic growth from earlier periods when economic stagnation or only episodic growth were the norm.

In Rostow's view, the takeoff period for the American economy as a whole was from 1843 to 1860, and railroads were the "leading sector" whose growth caused the rest of the economy to develop. Critics have noted, however, that the U.S. economy had begun to generate sustained growth in per-capita income (supposedly the distinctive feature of the takeoff) well before 1843—certainly by the 1820s and in all probability much earlier.

Although both incomes and the proportion of income devoted to capital formation increased in the nineteenth century, the time pattern is not consistent with Rostow's theory, which views the takeoff as an abrupt departure from previous conditions—an economic revolution. Instead, the empirical evidence now points to a gradual increase in the pace of growth extending over most of the century. Moreover, the railroads, which Rostow claimed were the leading sector, appeared well after growth was under way and even then had only modest effects on the rest of the economy. Railroad construction and operations could not have influenced development which preceded them. Thus, there is little evidence that the U.S. economy (or any other) ever experienced anything resembling a Rostovian takeoff.[4]

[3] W. Rostow, *The Stages of Economic Growth* (Cambridge, Mass.: Cambridge University Press, 1960).
[4] H. Rosovsky, "The Takeoff into Sustained Controversy," *Journal of Economic History* (June 1965).

The pattern of American economic growth was a gradual acceleration, based on simultaneous development in many sectors, rather than an abrupt transition narrowly based in one or a few sectors of the economy. Still, it is true that the American economy changed greatly over this period, and its capabilities for growth increased. The process was less dramatic than posited by Rostow, but the consequences were no less significant.

North's Staple Model

The second model developed to explain the economic growth of the United States in the pre-Civil War era is that of Douglass North. This model views the international cotton trade and its repercussions on the United States as the primary sources of development.[5]

Cotton made up more than half the value of all America's exports from 1815 to 1860, and it reached a peak of 63 percent in the 1830s. In North's view, American cotton production would increase rapidly in response to rising British demand for raw materials for the textile industry. Planters could shift land from other crops and bring previously unused acreage into production in no more than two years. But once almost all suitable land was employed in cotton production, further increases in British demand for cotton would increase its price rather than the quantity produced. Since this phenomenon did not raise planters' costs of production, their profits would increase sharply. Higher profits increased the incentives to expand cotton production, resulting in land booms as planters bought more acreage and pushed settlement farther west. Once the new lands' output came onto the market, however, the abrupt increase in supply would generate a sharp decline in cotton prices, lowering profits and altering planters' expectations. In the less euphoric circumstances, some growers would switch to other crops and to growing more of their own food. Efforts to cultivate new land would be inhibited until British demand rose enough to catch up with actual and potential cotton-growing capacity in America, after which the cycle would be repeated.

In this view, the cotton cycle influenced the rest of the American economy. When cotton prices were high the South specialized heavily in its production, buying its food and draft animals from the Ohio Valley. Increased southern demand for western food in turn produced higher incomes in the West, generating another land boom much the same as those caused by the demand for cotton. Increased incomes in southern and western agriculture

[5] D. North, *The Economic Growth of the United States, 1790–1860* (Englewood Cliffs, N.J.: Prentice-Hall, 1961).

meant higher demand for the manufactured goods of the North and for its shipping and financial services. Prosperity also encouraged foreign investment in the United States, which increased the money supply and consequently economic activity. The three regions of the United States are interdependent in North's model, but the South's cotton exports were the ultimate source of growth for all areas. Even though the influence of cotton was waning in the 1850s, North considered it the most important source of economic growth.

Critics of the North model charge that its view of the interdependence of the three areas of the United States—particularly of the South on western food and northern manufactured goods—is overstated. In fact, the South produced nearly all its own food even in boom times. Most of what food the southern planters did purchase was grown either on smaller farms within the South or in the border states, which were southern in everything but their ability to grow cotton. Although shipments of western food down the Mississippi River were substantial, most were for export or for eastern cities.[6] For its shipping and financial services and manufactured goods, the South had an alternative supplier in Britain.

The linkages between the North and the West, however, were strong and growing—particularly after 1845, when both western development and the completion of efficient rail and water transportation links encouraged interregional trade. Others have concluded that the price of cotton was influenced more by demand changes than by the "surges" and short-term restrictions in supply so prominent in North's model.[7]

Broad-Based Growth

American economic growth now appears to have been broadly based; no one industry, with the possible exception of transportation, appears critically important. Some development continued even when the cotton trade was depressed. Thus, although cotton was a major industry and had linkages to

[6] A. Fishlow, "Antebellum Interregional Trade Reconsidered," in *New Views on American Economic Development,* ed. R. Andreano (Cambridge, Mass.: Schenkman Books, 1965), pp. 187–200. See also Fishlow's "Postscript," pp. 209–212. A more sympathetic treatment of the North model's views on interregional trade, at least for the period before 1840 (when its volume was not large) is L. Mercer, "The Antebellum Interregional Trade Hypotheses: A Reexamination of Theory and Evidence," in R. Ransom et al., *Explorations in the New Economic History: Essays in Honor of Douglass C. North* (New York: Academic Press, 1982).

[7] P. Temin, *The Jacksonian Economy* (New York: Norton, 1969), pp. 91–112; and G. Wright, *The Political Economy of the Cotton South* (New York: Norton, 1978), p. 93.

others, it cannot be presented as the mainspring of American economic growth prior to 1860.

Even though neither of the models developed specifically to explain the economic growth of this period appears to offer a complete explanation, there is something to be explained. In terms of aggregate growth, the development of new sectors, and the changes within sectors, the pace and pattern of American economic development from 1815 to 1860 was quite different from anything preceding it. Not only had the scope of American economic capabilities broadened, but domestic events influenced activity much more heavily than in the colonial era. The population's response to the opportunities generated by technological change and the western movement was more swift and widespread than in any other nation. With the Constitution and early legal interpretations of its clauses by the courts, the United States had developed an institutional setting that provided maximum incentives for individual economic effort. Its people's attitudes ensured an enthusiastic response to these opportunities in many different regions and industries.

Selected References

Andreano, R. *New Views on American Economic Development*. Cambridge, Mass.: Schenkman Books, 1965.

Davis, L., et al. *American Economic Growth: An Economist's History of the United States*. New York: Harper & Row, 1972.

Lee, S., and P. Passell. *A New Economic View of American History*. New York: Norton, 1979.

North, D. *The Economic Growth of the United States, 1790–1860*. New York: Norton, 1966.

———. *Structure and Change in Economic History*. New York: Norton, 1981.

Ransom, R., et al. *Explorations in the New Economic History: Essays in Honor of Douglass C. North*. New York: Academic Press, 1982.

Rostow, W. *The Stages of Economic Growth: A Non-Communist Manifesto*. Cambridge, Mass.: Cambridge University Press, 1960.

Temin, P. *The Jacksonian Economy*. New York: Norton, 1969.

CHAPTER

4

MARITIME PROSPERITY AND "SECOND BEST" MANUFACTURING

In 1790, prospects for the U.S. economy were not particularly bright. The nation still had roughly the same economic capabilities it had possessed before the Revolution. The economy was not well equipped to undertake new types of economic activity. It lacked the capital, labor, and concentrated internal markets required for industrialization. Agricultural productivity was rising imperceptibly, if at all. There were a few bright spots: a growing population, territorial expansion, and the improved institutions either provided by the Constitution or legislated after its ratification.

Trade Problems

Some of the most serious problems centered on the country's foreign trade. As noted in Chapter 3, by 1790 trade had regained or slightly surpassed its pre-Revolutionary War volume but had not reached the old levels in per-capita terms. It appeared unlikely to soon do so.

Even though independence had freed U.S. overseas trade from the British controls imposed during the colonial era, Americans still had to contend with the mercantilistic restrictions imposed by other nations. In addition, British diplomatic assistance and low-cost trade credit were no longer available on favorable terms. Instead, the ex-colonists were now treated as foreign rivals by the British. Even with other nations, access did not necessarily guarantee trade. American traders had to gain familiarity with foreigners' product preferences, financial institutions, and legal climates—a costly process, particularly in the

123

political turmoil sweeping much of Europe after 1700.

Britain sharply limited U.S. trade with her West Indian possessions to boost Canada as a supplier of the fish, timber, food, and shipping services the islands had formerly obtained from America. American indigo producers had lost their British markets as well as the subsidy. Forbidden to compete with the British Caribbean for England's markets, they found it difficult to develop new ones. Although the United States was treated relatively favorably in direct trade with Britain compared to other nations, its ability to export to the leading trade center of the world was reduced. Britain would no longer buy American-built ships, and no markets were found elsewhere to replace this loss. Although U.S. trade with other nations' American colonies increased, it encountered tariffs, prohibitions, and frequent legal changes.[1] The Navigation Acts of other nations restricted American access to the carrying trade.

Foreign trade was hardly near collapse. But European markets for traditional American exports did not appear to be growing. Selling directly to the nations that consumed American rice, tobacco, wood products, grain, and fish allowed U.S. producers a higher portion of the final price than previously, but these gains had obvious long-term limits. The United States had not increased its exports in proportion to its own population growth. Thus, even though Americans might want more European goods, their ability to pay for them was not expanding. From 1790 to 1792 no significant increase in U.S. exports occurred. Only a slight increase in the proportion of trade carried by American ships brightened the gloomy prospects.[2] Since trade was still a major source of high and growing incomes relative to most domestic alternatives, this lull had serious implications.

THE WARTIME BOOM

In 1793, American trade prospects improved dramatically because of political developments in Europe. The Napoleonic Wars began, eventually involving nearly the entire continent. The hostilities continued with only brief pauses until 1815. The English and their allies, as well as the French, sought to destroy their enemies' overseas trade. While the United States was able to maintain its position as the only major neutral maritime nation, it reaped great gains. In terms of the familiar production-possibility frontier concept, the range of opportunities open to the American economy, particularly its foreign trade sector, had increased; the curve had shifted outward. U.S. shipping services could now be exchanged for far larger quantities of European goods than before the war.

The war created a huge increase in Europe's demand for American shipping services and exports and an entirely new market for reexports. The Royal Navy and British privateers were able to drive French, Dutch, and Spanish merchant shipping from the seas. The demands of a major war and French attacks on shipping left the British merchant marine unable to meet Britain's domestic needs. The war restricted or cut off British access to the grain, lumber, and other items traditionally imported from the Continent, just as continental Europe lost direct access to the products of its American colonies. It also reduced Europe's overall production and disrupted traditional patterns of trade. For both combatants, the choice was now between American goods and services or doing without or with much less from traditional sources. Almost overnight, the war increased demand for U.S. exports and, even more, for American shipping.

[1] C. Nettels, *The Emergence of a National Economy, 1775–1815* (New York: M.E. Sharpe, 1962), Chap. 3.
[2] G. Walton and J. Shepherd, *The Economic Rise of Early America* (New York: Cambridge University Press, 1979), pp. 197–198.

Maritime Prosperity

Both Britain and France found it expedient to change their regulations to allow American ships to carry their overseas trade—particularly that of their colonies, which they had previously tried to reserve for their own ships. Not only did the belligerents suspend their Navigation Laws to permit American carriage of their own goods, they also grudgingly allowed U.S. merchant shipping to carry goods between their European enemies and those nations' overseas colonies. A legal subterfuge was required under existing laws, but it greatly increased the profits of American shippers.

The trade was made indirect. For example, an American ship might load a cargo of sugar in the French West Indies for ultimate delivery to France. If carried directly to France, the sugar was considered an export of a French possession and subject to seizure by the British. To avoid this, the sugar would first be sent to a U.S. port where American duty was paid on it, then reexported to France. (A large portion of the U.S. duties were refunded to the shipper.) On passage from the United States to France, the sugar would now be regarded as a U.S. export, protected by American neutrality from British interference. Trade between Britain and her colonies gained similar protection from French attacks through routing via American ports: a sort of mirror image of the situation under the Navigation Acts.

The demand for American shipping greatly increased not merely because it substituted for European vessels, but also because voyages were now longer. American shippers, ports, and tax coffers gained at Europe's expense. Moreover, the terms of trade became more favorable—a unit of American exports now purchased more European goods. Neither the British nor the French had any illusions about the reexport trade, but both found it too useful to stop American trade with their adver-saries and risk a cutoff of their own trade in retaliation. The temptation to strike at the enemy's supply lines grew stronger, however—especially after 1805, when the war appeared to reach a stalemate. The French were supreme on land, Britain controlled the seas, but neither nation was able to inflict crippling blows on its adversary.

The Export Boom

While the opportunity for gains from such commerce existed, the United States took full advantage of it. Exports of domestically produced goods more than doubled from 1790 to 1807, the peak year of "maritime prosperity." Reexports grew from negligible amounts—about 5 percent of domestic exports in 1790—to equal or exceed the volume of exports originating in the United States, despite the export boom. The aggregate value of American exports (including reexports) more than quintupled from 1790 to 1807.[3] Not surprisingly, the earnings of American shipping also rose. Shipping prices increased and more cargo was carried in American vessels, producing a sevenfold increase in income from the carrying trade. The increase in gross income did not produce a rise in shipping costs per unit; on the contrary, they fell. Ships spent more time at sea and less in port waiting for cargoes, and they tended to carry full loads more often than in normal times. (See Table 4.1.)

Other Economic Activity

Foreign trade may have generated as much as 25 percent of U.S. gross national product in the peak years of 1805–1807. The major ports (Boston, New York, Philadelphia, and Balti-

---

[3] U.S. Bureau of the Census, *Historical Statistics of the United States: Colonial Times to 1970* (Washington, D.C.: Government Printing Office, 1975), vol. 2, p. 886.

Table 4.1 Trade Statistics, 1790–1816
(In Thousands of Dollars)

Date	Total Exports*	Reexports	Total Imports**	Net Income from Carrying Trade
1790	$ 20,205	$ 300	$ 23,800	$ 5,900
1791	19,012	500	30,500	6,200
1792	20,753	1,000	32,500	7,400
1793	26,110	1,750	32,550	11,900
1794	33,044	6,500	36,000	15,550
1795	47,989	8,300	71,300	19,000
1796	67,064	26,300	82,936	21,600
1797	56,850	27,000	77,379	17,100
1798	61,527	33,000	70,551	16,600
1799	78,666	45,523	81,069	24,200
1800	70,972	49,131	93,254	26,200
1801	94,116	46,643	113,364	31,000
1802	72,483	35,775	78,333	18,200
1803	55,800	13,594	65,667	23,700
1804	77,699	36,232	87,000	26,900
1805	99,566	53,179	125,525	29,700
1806	101,537	60,283	136,562	34,600
1807	108,343	59,644	144,740	42,100
1808	22,431	12,997	58,101	23,000
1809	52,203	20,798	61,029	26,200
1810	66,758	24,391	89,366	39,500
1811	61,317	16,023	57,888	40,800
1812	38,527	8,495	78,789	29,000
1813	27,856	2,848	22,178	10,200
1814	6,927	145	12,968	2,000
1815	52,558	6,583	85,357	20,600
1816	81,920	***	151,367	16,900

*Includes reexports
**Includes goods intended for reexport
***Not available
Source: D. North, *The Economic Growth of the United States, 1790–1860* (New York: Norton, 1961), appendices I, II.

more) benefited disproportionately from this commerce, apparently in large part because of the economies of scale inherent in some of the services that supported overseas trade, particularly finance. The costs of insurance, banking, and information services do not increase in proportion to the number of customers. The larger ports also offered more competition, wider markets for imports, and shorter turn-around times.[4] The populations of the major ports rose nearly half again as rapidly as that of the entire country. By 1810, about 1 American in 14 lived in a "city" of 2,500 or more people.

[4] G. Taylor, "American Urban Growth Preceding the Railway Age," *Journal of Economic History* (September 1967).

Since imports also rose during the trade boom, distributional activities benefited, too. Specialized occupations requiring a large market to fully occupy their practitioners became more common. Shipbuilders, warehousers, and chandlers flourished when the shippers to whom they sold goods or services prospered. The growth of the big ports was obvious to contemporary observers, who remarked on new buildings, luxury consumption, and other signs of growing affluence. Baltimore, with its services as a major port for the export of breadstuffs combined with flour milling and shipbuilding, grew especially fast.[5] Financial services that had expanded largely to serve maritime activities also spurred the growth of the domestic economy. In 1790 only three commercial banks existed in the entire United States; by 1800 there were 29, and by 1811, 89.[6]

Banks can improve the allocation of investment funds because they are a knowledgeable link between savers and investors and can allocate savings to their most productive uses. By reducing savers' risks, they may raise the proportion of income available for capital formation as well as increase its productivity. In addition, commercial banks can increase the money supply by extending their debt in the form of checking accounts or, especially in this era, currency to borrowers. Insurance activity in America antedated the Revolution, but it greatly expanded from 1792 to 1807. Insurance companies do more than reduce risks for those insured; they also are links between savers and investors, using their premium income to buy securities of various types. The maritime boom was concentrated in a few towns and on a small proportion of the population, so it increased their incomes spectacularly. But the rest of the economy was not stagnant.

---

[5] The picture of this era as one of unprecedented prosperity has been questioned. See D. Adams, Jr., "American Prosperity and Neutrality, 1793–1804: A Reconsideration," *Journal of Economic History* (December 1980).
[6] Nettels, *Emergence*, p. 296.

THE RISE OF KING COTTON

A new export—cotton–began to gain a prominent position in American foreign trade. The new crop was the result of an invention that shattered a technological bottleneck. Eli Whitney's cotton gin was unquestionably the most significant agricultural invention of the early nineteenth century. The cotton gin had an enormous economic impact because it allowed rapid and extensive responses in both supply and demand. Prior to the cotton gin, cotton was a profitable American crop only along a narrow strip of coast in the Carolinas and Georgia. Nowhere else could sea island cotton be grown. This variety of cotton produces long, soft fibers still valued for fine fabrics today. In the eighteenth century, however, the value of sea island cotton lay in the fact that the raw cotton could easily be separated from its seeds, allowing the fibers to be spun into thread. Other varieties of cotton grew well in the southern interior but were unprofitable because their seeds were so difficult to remove from the fiber. It was a full day's work to clean a single pound of upland cotton; under American conditions, even slave labor was too expensive for this task.

Whitney's cotton gin (1792) smashed this bottleneck. The machine was a simple arrangement of screens and roller brushes. It was cheap and easy to construct and simple to operate. And it worked: it may have increased productivity as much as fiftyfold. Like many other innovations, Whitney's machine was not a completely new idea, but it was the first really successful response to the cotton-cleaning problem. Although Whitney patented his invention, the machine was so easy to build and profits from its use so high that he was unable to enforce his patent monopoly. Use of the gin spread like wildfire and it was improved in the process, making cotton production still more profitable.

■ Eli Whitney's 1793 invention of the cotton gin increased the market for American cotton by mechanically removing the seeds. Afterwards, cotton became the most significant crop in much of the South.
Source: The Bettmann Archive.

The Southern Cotton Boom

The cotton gin's reception in the South was linked to both supply and demand factors. It represented a cheap and simple way to increase the income that other factors of production—land and labor—could produce. The soil and climate of the American South were ideally suited to cotton cultivation. At this time, the South's agricultural capacity was underutilized. In particular, the slave population had grown faster than the markets for traditional plantation crops. Not only did natural increase among the slaves equal that of the free population, but slave imports in the previous decade had been large. A provision in the Constitution prohibited the international slave trade after 1807, and many planters had fled the slave revolts in Haiti, bringing their bondsmen with them to the United States.

Cotton was well suited to plantation labor conditions, since it required nearly year-round work, but it could also be produced on smaller farms.[7] Cotton gave the South a new cash crop and a new export.[8] Production expanded rapidly. By 1807 the United States was Britain's most important source of cotton, and by 1810 cotton was the country's most valuable single export.

Cotton fiber was made into cloth in Britain. Cotton textile factories employed machinery and experienced rapid productivity increases in a highly competitive industry. Consequently, producers were forced to pass their lower costs on to consumers through lower textile prices, which fell until cotton became the first really cheap cloth the world had ever known. Demand for cotton cloth proved to be highly price elastic: a price decrease spurred a more than proportionate increase in the quantity sold. So productive were the new spinning and weaving methods (and so large were England's supplies of female and child labor) that by the early nineteenth century Britain was able to sell cotton cloth even in India. There textiles from British factories replaced the traditional hand-made fabrics with cheaper and better substitutes.

The demand for raw cotton from the United States grew as textile sales increased, and cotton prices remained at levels highly profitable to American planters. Throughout the nineteenth century, economic activity in the American South centered on cotton. At least one economic historian has claimed that the growth of the entire American economy before 1860 was shaped by the requirements of cotton agriculture and foreign demand for cotton.[9]

Transportation Gains

The transmontane West, which previously had sent only a trickle of high-value, low-bulk goods back over the mountains, now began to ship

[7] G. Wright, *Old South, New South: Revolutions in the Southern Economy Since the Civil War* (New York: Basic Books, 1986), pp. 107–110. See also G. Wright, *The Political Economy of the Cotton South* (New York: Norton, 1978).
[8] Wright, *The Political Economy*, pp. 18, 28.
[9] D, North, *The Economic Growth of the United States, 1790–1860* (Englewood Cliffs, N.J.: Prentice-Hall, 1961).

■ The cotton buyer was the intermediary between the cotton farmer and the manufacturer of cotton cloth.
Source: The Bettmann Archive.

■ By 1860, the American economy had achieved growth well beyond the initial boundaries of settlement.
Source: The Bettmann Archive.

bulky exports through New Orleans. There was great agitation for improvements in internal transportation to aid this trade. The result was an improved road network and a completely new travel mechanism—steamboats. These will be discussed in Chapter 5.

Gains in Manufacturing and Agriculture

Because of high potential profits, trade generally attracted more investors than did manufacturing. Industry did, however, expand somewhat. Some items essential to the merchant marine, such as sails, rope, cable, and anchors, were made in the United States. Textile mills appeared in New England and some of the larger cities, using copies of British machines. A rising portion of American wheat exports was processed into flour before leaving the country. These developments and the increase in both domestic and foreign demand for farm products caused widespread gains in income. Although few people in these sectors obtained the spectacular gains achieved in maritime activities, the aggregate increase in in-

comes from manufacturing and agriculture has been claimed to be greater than that generated by foreign trade.[10]

The Costs of Neutrality

Whatever the impact of the various sources, it appears that American incomes rose substantially from 1790 to 1807. But the path to riches was neither smooth nor steady. In particular, changes in European political conditions could end America's favorable trade position as quickly as they had generated it. Trade fell off sharply in 1802–1803, when Britain and France temporarily ceased hostilities (see Table 4.1). And as the two great antagonists sought to ruin each other's economies and cut their enemies off from foreign trade, American cargoes bound to enemy ports were increasingly regarded as

[10] C. Goldin and F. Lewis in "The Role of Exports in American Economic Growth during the Napoleonic Wars, 1793 to 1807," *Explorations in Economic History,* (January, 1980), find that foreign trade may have furnished as little as one-quarter of the total increase in incomes.

war contraband subject to seizure. Often the ship was confiscated together with its cargo. In all, some 2,000 U.S. merchant vessels were taken by the French and British between 1790 and 1812.[11]

Maritime prosperity was not without its costs. The British, desperately in need of seamen, often forced ("impressed") crewmen captured from American ships into the Royal Navy, sometimes despite evidence that the sailors were U.S. citizens rather than British deserters (the legal pretext for impressment from foreign ships). The United States fought an undeclared naval war with France between 1796 and 1800. The pirates of the Barbary Coast had been preying on American shipping ever since the Revolution stripped away the shield of British naval protection and bribes. In 1805 the new United States Navy forced an end to these raids. No doubt some American seamen paid a high physical price and some shippers suffered severe financial losses. U.S. protests of what were regarded as violations of neutral rights were common. But on the whole, American gains outweighed losses, and trade continued.

The Louisiana Purchase

Another development arising from political events in Europe was to have momentous consequences for the United States. Under the terms of the Treaty of Paris, which had concluded the Revolution in 1783, the southwestern boundary of the United States did not extend to the mouth of the Mississippi River or include the port of New Orleans. Spain controlled both and in the 1790s restricted American use of both river and port. Since the Mississippi was the only low-cost outlet for products from the rapidly growing agricultural areas of Tennessee and the Ohio Valley, restricted use of the river—even if only poten-

[11] Nettels, *Emergence*, pp. 324–325.

tial—impeded western settlement. Land had little value without a means of sending its products to market. After Spain ceded New Orleans to France in a secret treaty (1803), the United States offered to buy the city. The American diplomats presenting the offer were astounded when Napoleon's response was a proposal to sell the entire Louisiana Territory, a tract of 827,000 square miles. Acquisition of this region would nearly double the land area of the United States.

President Thomas Jefferson and Secretary of the Treasury Albert Gallatin overcame their distaste for deficit financing in the face of such a bargain (the French asked for $15 million). The government borrowed the funds before Napoleon could change his mind (or lose the territory to the British), making use of its newly developed creditworthiness. The Louisiana Purchase must be considered one of the most productive triumphs of pragmatism over ideology in American history. Once concluded, Jefferson sent expeditions led by Lewis and Clark and Zebulon Pike into the new territory to determine its economic potential.

The purchase gave the United States another new plantation crop. In 1795, French planters fleeing slave revolts in Haiti succeeded in growing sugar cane in the Mississippi Delta below New Orleans. Like rice, sugar was a capital-intensive crop restricted to a small area by natural conditions (in this case climate), but it was very profitable.

EMBARGO AND WAR

Foreign trade's contribution to American prosperity came to an end in 1807. The war between Britain and France had resumed in 1803, and by this time was a desperate struggle of opponents attempting to destroy each other by any means possible. Increasingly they began to strike at their rivals' foreign trade. The British proclaimed a blockade of all French-controlled ports in Europe, denying even neutral ships the right to trade there. Only if neutral shipping received British permission and paid duties in England was trade with the Continent allowed. The French forbade all trade with Britain. Napoleon's Milan Decree (1806) proclaimed that any neutral ship that entered a British port or even submitted to British search was subject to French seizure.

The dilemma of the United States was obvious. The price of continued trade with either country was the forfeiture of all trade with the other. Still worse, war with the nation to which America denied its trade was likely. To accede to the demands of either side would imply not only a surrender of U.S. sovereignty over its foreign commerce, but at least implicit support of the war against the other belligerent. The United States Navy was far too weak to protect American commerce against either party, especially in European waters. Under these circumstances, President Jefferson requested the authority to restrict American commerce with the warring nations. In December 1807 Congress passed the Embargo Act, which forbade practically all trade with foreign nations and placed strict limits even on American coastal trade.

The Impact of the Embargo

The reasoning behind the Embargo Act appeared to be that since both Britain and France would lose more through the absence of American exports, shipping services, and markets than they could gain in damage to each other, they would have to ease their restrictions on American commerce. The alternative to such a U.S. response appeared to be a war for which the nation was not prepared, on behalf of one of the states that had already inflicted damage on American trade. But the emotions generated by all-out war are no aid to rational consideration, and both Britain and France were more concerned with damaging each other than

with the costs their actions imposed on their own economies.

The effect of the abrupt halt of trade on the maritime sector of the economy was disastrous. Exports of both American and foreign origins plummeted, as did shipping earnings. Unemployment was concentrated in the ports, where there was plenty of evidence of economic distress: idle ships and seamen, bankrupt merchants, and jails bursting with imprisoned debtors. The rest of the economy did not escape. The prices of many exports fell, reducing the incomes of middlemen and producers alike. Smuggling and loopholes in the act mitigated its effects somewhat, but the economy was severely and adversely affected. There had been no time to prepare for the embargo's impact; all adjustments had to be made after it was imposed.

Trade with nations other than France and Britain resumed in 1809, and the Macon Bill (1810) reopened trade with them as well, but briefly: trade with Britain was suspended again in 1811.[12] Still, as Table 4.1 indicates, trade volume never regained pre-embargo levels. With the onset of the War of 1812, American overseas trade all but collapsed. After the Battle of Trafalgar (1805), there was no French fleet to occupy the Royal Navy, and the blockade of American ports proclaimed by Britain became increasingly effective. By 1814, it was almost impossible for American vessels to leave or enter U.S. ports.

ALTERNATIVES TO TRADE

Even before the political interference with American overseas commerce culminating in the War of 1812 became significant, some resources had been diverted into domestic economic activity. Some seaboard merchants had

---

[12] Nettels, *Emergence*, pp. 329–330.

become rich, and in the face of increasing risks in trade, they sought new areas of investment. Some began to consider producing substitutes for imported manufactured goods, using new technology and labor with limited employment possibilities under existing conditions.

The Textile Industry

The largest single category of imported manufactures had long been textiles.[13] In the absence of imports, factories were set up to produce woolen and especially cotton cloth in America. They were concentrated in New England and the port cities, where capital, cotton, and many underemployed or unemployed women and children were available (New England agriculture was highly seasonal, and the ports had few jobs for such workers). New England had abundant waterpower sites close to the coast to power the new machinery. After the embargo, labor of all types became abundant. British machines and techniques were copied, often by persuading trained workers who had memorized machinery designs to leave British factories. Mercantilistic regulations forbade both the export of machines and the emigration of skilled labor, but a number of such workers evaded the law and brought their knowledge to the United States. Americans also undertook some industrial espionage to obtain British technology. Among the workers who emigrated was Samuel Slater. He came to Rhode Island in 1790 at the invitation of a local merchant, whose capital combined with Slater's knowledge established one of the first cotton textile factories in America. The first mechanized cotton textile mill in the United States, however, was built in South Carolina, just before Slater's venture. The Carolina mill was unsuccessful.[14]

Only after the embargo and war restricted textile imports did U.S. cloth producers make

■ At the time of the Industrial Revolution, New England became the center of the textile industry.
Source: Yale University Art Gallery, Mabel Brady Garvan Collection.

real progress. Despite efforts to copy British techniques, they were unable to compete. Even after paying trans-Atlantic passage and tariffs, which domestic producers did not face, British textiles sold for less than American goods. Once the trade interferences significantly handicapped imports, however, the American industry grew rapidly. By 1815 there were over 200 factories making cotton textiles: there had been less than 20 in 1800.[15] Production of woolen cloth also increased, but to a lesser extent, because woolens were less suited to machine production. Substantial amounts of woolen cloth were produced by home manufacture in most regions of the United States—indicating that even the British had not yet fully mastered factory production of that commodity.

The First Factories

The new textile establishments were noteworthy because they were true factories, employing powered machinery (driven by water) and the

[13] Walton and Shepherd, *The Economic Rise*, p. 85.
[14] Wright, *Old South, New South*, p. 126.

[15] Ibid., p 275.

coordinated efforts of workers. They were not mere assemblages of labor using traditional methods to duplicate the techniques of the one-man shop, or cottage production on a larger scale.[16] Since they were so different from the previous production methods in America, it is not surprising that they required time to become efficient.

Other Manufacturing

Other types of manufacturing appeared in addition to textiles. Some developed from colonial beginnings, such as flour milling and iron and lead smelting. But progress also occurred in paper, glass, leather, and gunpowder output, in printing, and in a variety of other processing and finished goods industries. Rising population and income, as well as improved transportation, increased the markets for these goods and for traditional handicrafts. Lists of specialized occupations, particularly in the larger ports, grew longer. In many cases factory production did not represent a net increase in commodity output, it often replaced goods that people had made for themselves in their homes. The increasing range of production using new methods (at least by American standards) generated useful experience. In a few cases, the lessons learned allowed American producers to survive the return of British competition after 1815.

Arms

Another industry heavily affected by political considerations (in this case antedating the embargo) was the manufacture of arms. American armories developed a number of ingenious wood- and metalworking tools, such as lathes, milling machines, and jigs, taps, and gauges. These plants developed and applied the idea of interchangeable parts, although they did not originate the basic concept.

Transportation

War and the British blockade encouraged development of internal transportation. With coastal shipping now threatened by British frigates, New England built and used more roads, finding them a thoroughly inferior and vastly more expensive means of moving goods. The West, with its greater distances, bulky agricultural products, and extensive river systems, developed a wide variety of water craft—from simple rafts and flatboats to schooners and steamboats. Sometimes it was possible to export both cargo and container; the Ohio Valley built some oceangoing sailing ships and sent them downriver with loads of farm produce. In such cases both ship and cargo were exports, since sailing ships could not return against the current. Steamboats solved the problem of two-way travel on rivers. They were employed on the Ohio and Mississippi within a few years of Robert Fulton's voyage on the Hudson. The first steamboat reached Louisville from New Orleans in 1815.

Although most early manufacturing efforts were premature, they illustrate once again the flexibility and rapid adjustment to new circumstances that characterized the American economy. Resources were switched to new and very different uses in just a few short years. Moreover, the same willingness to learn from "strangers" that had served the country so well in colonial days was still evident. It cannot have been easy for Americans used to very different work styles to accept the direction of foreigners in factories, or to entrust hard-earned fortunes to them. But they did, and apparently with much less friction than when the same technology was transferred to continental Europe a few years later.[17] We must remember that most people

---

[16] Ibid., p. 269.

[17] D. Landes, *The Unbound Prometheus* (Cambridge, England: Cambridge University Press, 1969), Chap. 4.

who adapted so readily had never encountered power sources other than muscle, wind, and water. They certainly were not accustomed to factory work conditions, where machines or the overall establishment controlled the pace, rather than the individual worker, as was true in agriculture.

The War of 1812

The usual cause cited for the outbreak of America's second war with England is British interference with American shipping, especially the impressment of American seamen. The British had impressed about 4,000 American seamen, but the French were hardly innocent of the same offenses. Some Americans, particularly the "war hawks" of the western states, saw a chance to seize territory from Canada and Florida, then under British and Spanish control. American frontiersmen regarded both as havens for fugitive slaves and arsenals for hostile Indians, as well as rich potential conquests. New England did not share the enthusiasm for war, and when the British blockade became an even more effective restriction on trade than all those suffered in the preceding years, some exasperated Yankees considered seceding from the Union (the Hartford Convention, 1814) to regain the shipping incomes they had lost.

American war objectives were not achieved. At the war's end, the United States was on the defensive almost everywhere. Most of the victories gained by American armies were repulses of attempted British invasions. At sea, American privateers took over 2,000 British prizes during the war. The American navy gained some stunning (particularly in British eyes) victories in single-ship actions. But by the end of the war, the weight of British seapower prevailed; few American ships remained at sea. Perhaps the results are best summarized by noting that Americans entered the war with the slogan "On to Canada!" and ended it on a rather different note, "Not One Inch of Territory Lost or Ceded."

The Consequences of War

The War of 1812 generated the usual inflation. Real output fell as efficient uses of American resources gave way to military demands and even to civilian occupations that generated lower incomes than peacetime alternatives. The government borrowed heavily to finance its military efforts. Borrowing from the banks increased the supply of paper money, while hard currency supplies did not rise. Banks outside New England "suspended payment"—they refused to redeem the paper currency they had issued for its face value in coin. Nevertheless, the banks continued to operate and their notes to circulate as money. Such currency's specie value depended on public opinion of the probability and imminence of its eventual redemption in coin.

One potentially useful result of the demands of war finance was the formation of the Second Bank of the United States. The First Bank of the United States had been chartered by the federal government in 1791. With its federal charter, the bank could and did operate throughout the country rather than in a single state, but its charter had been allowed to lapse in 1811. Although neither the First nor the Second Bank of the United States was a central bank in the modern sense, their many branches and their position as government depositories afforded some monetary control. The Second Bank of the United States failed to achieve one objective that had figured heavily in its establishment. Bank stock could be purchased with government bonds. The intent was to make it easier to sell these securities to finance the war. But the Second Bank did not receive its charter until 1816.

Political events had produced industrialization in the United States when peacetime conditions would not. But the return to normal conditions revealed that economic realities had changed far less than the political situation between 1807 and 1815. When the war ended and British goods once again became available to American customers, all but a handful of the war baby domestic firms were unable to survive the competition. At the same time, however, traditional American economic activity flourished after a brief period of adjustment to peacetime conditions. Both exports of American goods and carrying trade earnings were far above 1790 levels in 1815 and 1816. Thus the wartime diversion of American resources into manufacturing was a "second best" use of their productive capacity that could endure only as long as political conditions prohibited their employment where productivity was greatest. A few American firms did survive the onslaught of British competition. Apparently at least some Americans began to search for effective responses to foreign producers. It would not be long before they met increasing success.

SELECTED REFERENCES

Davis, L., et al. *American Economic Growth: An Economist's History of the United States.* New York: Harper and Row, 1972.

Nettels, C. *The Emergence of a National Economy, 1775–1815.* New York: M.E. Sharpe, 1962.

North, D. *The Economic Growth of the United States, 1790–1860.* Englewood Cliffs, N.J.: Prentice-Hall, 1961.

North, D., et al. *Growth and Welfare in the American Past: A New Economic History.* 3d ed. Englewood Cliffs, N.J.: Prentice-Hall, 1983.

Temin, P. *The Jacksonian Economy.* New York: Norton, 1969.

U.S. Bureau of the Census. *Historical Statistics of the United States: Colonial Times to 1970.* 2 vols. Washington, D.C.: Government Printing Office, 1975.

CHAPTER

5

TRANSPORTATION FOR A GROWING ECONOMY

*I*n 1808, Secretary of the Treasury Albert Gallatin proposed a series of transportation improvements to Congress. In Gallatin's plan, the federal government was to finance the construction of a major highway along the East Coast and four canals through the major peninsulas, which would allow sheltered-water navigation from Cape Cod to the Carolinas. To aid east-west transportation, Gallatin proposed four improved river and road links between the Atlantic Coast and the Mississippi Valley, plus a canal connecting the Mohawk River with Lake Ontario. Within regions, canals would be built to circumvent major obstacles to river travel, such as Niagara Falls and the Falls of the Ohio at Louisville, and improved roads would be constructed in the West. Finally, in a gesture that modern politicians would appreciate, Gallatin proposed that $3,400,000 be spent for internal improvements in areas not directly benefited by the other routes.[1]

Such "sweeteners" proved to be essential ingredients in large-scale governmental transport improvement schemes throughout the early nineteenth century. They may have persuaded taxpayers in regions far from efficient transport routes to support construction, but they often greatly increased the costs of government aid to transport projects.[2] The Gallatin proposals were never carried out: the tariff revenues he thought would finance them were sharply reduced by the Embargo Act.

TRANSPORTATION NEEDS

Gallatin's proposal was a response to a very real need. The difficulty of overland transportation in the United States during the early nine-

[1] C. Goodrich, "National Planning of Internal Improvements," *Political Science Quarterly* (March 1948).
[2] S. Lebergott, *The Americans: An Economic Record* (New York: Norton, 1984), Chap. 10.

teenth century probably ranks as the foremost obstacle to economic development. It is hard to appreciate the incredible obstacles to moving people, goods, or even information that confronted Americans at this time. For example, letters sent from Philadelphia to Boston required five days to reach their destination. But this was along the best-developed routes; elsewhere, conditions were worse. Mail carried by express rider took two to three weeks to pass from Philadelphia to Nashville. Communications could, of course, move no faster than the people conveying the information.

Overland travel was slow, expensive, and not infrequently dangerous. Thomas Jefferson had to swim his horse across five of the eight rivers between Washington and Monticello; there were neither ferries nor bridges. The travel conditions encountered by the President of the United States in Virginia, one of the longest-settled and most populous of all the states, were by no means unusually bad. Although the United States had about 20,000 miles of roads in 1800, they were neither surfaced nor drained. Many roads had been "constructed" with axes, not picks and shovels. Several regions had laws specifying that no stumps over 18 inches high were to be left in the right of way. In dry weather roads were dusty; in wet weather they became quagmires. Many such roads did not permit the passage of wheeled vehicles, and even where wagon travel was possible, loads were severely limited. Only on the very best roads could stagecoaches achieve speeds of six miles an hour, and then at the cost of great discomfort. Stagecoaches had only the most primitive springs to soften road shocks, and most wagons had none at all. In addition to frequent breakdowns and accidents, travelers might encounter bandits or hostile Indians.

Travel Costs

Travel was costly as well. One passenger reported spending $21 on 36 hours of continuous travel from Philadelphia to New York

Table 5.1 Passenger Speed, 1840

Transport Mode	Miles per Hour
Sailing vesels	2.5
Canal boats	3.9
Stages and sleighs	4.9
Railroads, horse-drawn	6.0
Steamboats, river	9.0
Steamboats, lake	10.0
Railroads, steam	15.0

Source: *The American Almanac, 1841,* p. 87. Quoted in Lebergott, *The Americans: An Economic Record* (New York: Norton, 1984), p. 113. Based on a report by a "foreign gentleman" who traveled 10,330 miles throughout the United States.

City.[3] Stagecoach lines typically charged about 6¢ per mile, and consequently they were restricted to the wealthy. Food and lodging brought the total monetary costs of travel close to 10¢ per mile. The real costs were much higher, however. Not only were nineteenth-century prices far lower—perhaps only one-eighth their 1986 levels—but real incomes were lower still. Nor is this a full measure of the costs: time consumed in travel could not be devoted to other purposes, creating an additional expense. Table 5.1 gives some idea of travel speeds, but it should be remembered that by 1840 substantial improvement over conditions a few decades earlier had occurred. Nineteenth-century travel costs were high even compared to the less efficient modern forms, such as one person driving a large car. The expense of transporting goods was even greater. Frequently, the charges for moving goods a hundred miles or less exceeded their sales price. Under such circumstances, most regions were forced to produce a high proportion of all that they consumed, even though other areas might make some of these items at much lower cost.

[3] Professor Robert Gallman has suggested that this was an unusually expensive trip, at least in money costs.

Small wonder that Americans preferred travel by water. Along the coast, almost all freight went by sea. Inland, shippers used virtually any stream capable of floating even a canoe in approximately the right direction. Rapids, low water, ice, indirect routes, and the occasional attentions of river pirates notwithstanding, bulky goods could be moved cheaper by water than by any other means available. If goods were large or heavy, often it was physically impossible to transport them any other way.[4]

Transportation Difficulties

West of the Appalachians, transportation was even more difficult. Only a few high-value, low-bulk items such as ginseng, furs, and whiskey could be shipped over the mountains profitably. Cattle and hogs could be driven to markets in the East, but en route they lost a good deal of weight, not a few of their numbers, and any vestige of tenderness their meat might ever have possessed. Most western produce was sent down the Ohio and Mississippi rivers to New Orleans, where ocean-going ships could carry it to the Eastern Seaboard. The frontiersman who sold a boatload of whiskey, flour, or preserved meat in New Orleans (and then the boat, to be broken up for lumber or firewood) faced the problem of getting home with the proceeds. Neither a keelboat voyage up the Mississippi nor an overland journey along the Natchez Trace offered much certainty of a safe return. Ironically, the money obtained in New Orleans would in large part go to pay the costs of transporting goods purchased there over the same mountains that barred direct access to eastern markets. Shipping goods by wagon was often unprofitable; even a 40-mile journey might cost more than the load of grain or other crops would bring.

[4] G. Taylor, *The Transportation Revolution, 1815–1860* (New York: M.E. Sharpe, 1962), Chapter 7.

Distances in America, even east of the Mississippi, were longer than those in Western Europe. The land mass of the United States was far greater than that of any developed country in Europe.

Nor did Britain, the Netherlands, and Northern France contain any geographic barriers comparable to the Appalachian Mountains.

Financial and Political Obstacles to Better Transportation

Although Americans recognized the need for improved transportation, providing it was difficult. The first problem was financial: the sums required to build roads, canals, and railroads were far beyond the resources of any single individual. Institutions would have to be developed to pool the funds of many savers. Once this became apparent, Americans turned to the only institution with such capabilities already in existence: government was used to finance many early transportation improvements. Its taxing power and superior access to credit allowed government to raise the large sums required.

Another obstacle to private financing was the difficulty of collecting the full value of transport improvements from the people who used them. The benefits of improved transportation are often far greater than the reduced charges for freight or passenger movement. Consumers pay lower prices for goods, and producers receive a higher portion of the final price. The value of productive assets rises because their products can reach wider markets. In addition, long-term benefits may occur if improved access to markets leads to improved production methods. Economies of scale may now be worth utilizing, and costs may fall because of greater experience with the production process. But the users of transportation improvements and their customers tended to receive more of these benefits than the owners, which made the incentives to construct roads or canals lower than their aggregate economic contribution.

ROADS

Even road construction strained the early nineteenth-century American capacity for capital generation. Partnerships were not well suited to road finance. Roads often required large sums, which in turn meant either an unworkable number of partners or high risks for the individual members of such an agreement. Returns would be gained only over a long period, which also made partnerships difficult. To acquire the necessary capital, the corporate form was used. Groups of investors petitioned state legislatures for corporate charters giving them the rights to build roads and charge traffic for their use. By 1830, 22,000 miles of turnpikes had been constructed, mainly in New England and the Middle Atlantic states. But few of these proved profitable for their owners. In some cases, the volume of traffic was too small to pay for maintaining the road, much less amortizing the initial investment or providing a return to the turnpike owners.[5]

One problem was technological: even good roads allowed draft animals to pull only a fraction of the loads they could move over rails or along canals. Furthermore, roads were expensive to build and maintain, so at the charges of 12¢ to 17¢ per ton-mile needed to cover costs of construction and maintenance, only small volumes of high-value goods traveled by roads of any type. Those few roads built to serve large existing volumes of traffic, such as the routes between Lancaster and Philadelphia and some New England turnpikes, showed good financial performance, but they were exceptional. Even where traffic was heavy, tolls were not easy to collect. Travelers could often detour around the tollgate where a "pike" was lowered across the road to make them stop and pay tolls. At best, roads could not provide a national transportation network. Most were short, and there was no incentive to link them.

Government's Role in Road Construction

Government played a limited role in turnpike construction and operation. Such roads were usually private ventures, although the governments of Ohio, Virginia, and especially Pennsylvania did help fund construction costs. The federal government built the National Pike,[6] which reached a western terminus in Vandalia, Illinois, in 1852, but this was the only federal road project. Even though the federal government could provide the large initial investment required to construct a first-class road through its tax powers and better access to credit than private investors, its role was restricted. Sec-

■ In 1811, the Cumberland Road was built to aid travel and commerce between western Maryland and Illinois.
Source: From *The American Pageant*, eighth edition by Thomas A. Bailey and David M. Kennedy. Copyright © 1987 by D. C. Heath and Company. Reprinted by permission of the publisher.

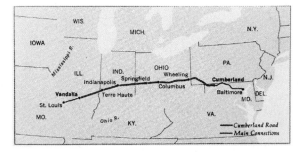

---

[5] Davis et al., *American Economic Growth: An Economist's History of the United States* (New York: Harper and Row, 1972).

[6] Ibid., p. 475

tional rivalries—particularly objections from areas that had already built their own roads and did not want to be taxed for the benefit of other regions—were common. If these were resolved by providing government projects in return for votes, they resulted in increased costs. Some people had doubts about the constitutionality of federal road building. The role of the federal government was largely restricted to providing surveys and training engineers at West Point. It was more active in improving water transportation; rivers and harbors bills became a favored means of obtaining federal funds for local projects very early in the history of Congress.

The limited role of government in road building may not have been a disadvantage for the economy. As noted, most roads generated financial losses for their investors. The evidence that they generated compensating increases in income for the rest of the economy is slight. The location of economic activity does not appear to have been affected by turnpikes, nor did property values along such roads increase above the average. As long as the traffic using roads was limited to animal power, roads were not the answer to America's transportation problems.

STEAMBOATS

Most turnpike builders failed to recover their investments,[7] but steamboat owners enjoyed modest financial success in the antebellum era. Steamboats could be constructed by individuals or small partnerships, but more importantly, they used existing waterways and had no problems collecting fees. At least in upstream travel, steamboats faced effective competition only from their own kind for several decades. Before the advent of steamboats, American rivers had been extensively used for transport, but except for those few streams broad enough to allow the use of sails or slow enough to make rowing possible, river travel was largely with the current.

On the Ohio and Mississippi rivers, a wide variety of craft, ranging from simple rafts to some ocean-going sailing ships, could be sent downstream. But upstream passage was extremely difficult. Keelboats made the journey upriver from New Orleans to Louisville in from three to four months, with the crew rowing, poling, or towing the boat from shore. (As a young man, Abraham Lincoln made the journey to New Orleans several times, traveling downstream via raft or flatboat and taking keelboat passage or walking back to Illinois.) But the only way to generate adequate muscle power for this feat was to employ a crew so large that there was little space left over for cargo or passengers. Losses from accidents were high, and the brawny, brawling rivermen were not famed for honesty.

Under such circumstances, there was great interest in alternative means of upstream transport, and steamboats appeared on western waters soon after Fulton's successful voyage on the Hudson River in 1807. The first steamboat from Pittsburgh reached New Orleans in 1811. A few problems remained to be solved; the first boats lacked the engine power to return against the current, but by 1815 two-way traffic had begun.

Steamboat charges for upstream travel soon fell to less than 10 percent of keelboat rates.[8] The journey from New Orleans to Louisville took the first steamboats slightly more than a month, but this fell to less than a week by the 1850s. Steamboats provide a classic example of the benefits of competition. Profits earned by the first boats were very high, but entry barriers in steamboating were low; when others realized

---

[7] Ibid.

[8] E. Haites et al., *Western River Transportation: The Era of Early Internal Development, 1810–1860* (New York: Kenikat, 1975), p. 637.

■ Although one of the first steamboats was called "Fulton's Folly," Robert Fulton's Clermont (1807) and its successors reduced the cost of river transportation.
Source: I. N. Phelps Stokes Collection
Miriam and Ira D. Wallach Division of Art, Prints, Photographs
The New York Public Library
Astor, Lenox and Tilden Foundations.

that some of the early boats repaid their investment in just a few years, the number of boats increased rapidly. Freight charges were forced down to little more than costs. Furthermore, costs continued to fall. One study found that steamboat productivity rose at an annual rate of 4 percent to 6 percent up to 1860.[9] Improvements in productivity in an open industry employing new technology might be expected: over time, boat operators could increase profits only by reducing costs faster than their rivals. The chief beneficiaries of this improved efficiency were the customers.

Especially on western waters, steamboats were modified to increase speed and carrying capacity and to reduce draft, which enhanced their ability to operate in times of low water. By 1850, some steamboats on the larger rivers could achieve speeds of 15 miles per hour. Steamboats were practical on American rivers,

where wood was available at every landing so their high fuel consumption made little difference. On the ocean, both fuel and payload for practical journeys entirely under power could not be carried. Most freight continued to cross the sea in sailing vessels until well after the Civil War, although passenger travel, at least in the coastal trade, shifted to steamers.

Steamboats' Limitations

Even though they were a marked improvement over previous modes of river travel, steamboats had their disadvantages. Like other river craft, they could be used only on natural bodies of water. Rarely did a direct water route connect two cities, and no route whatever existed between the Eastern Seaboard and the Ohio Valley. Steamboats could not be used on canals because their wakes eroded the banks. River travel had its hazards: ice, drought, snags, sandbars, and floating debris. The operating methods of many early steamboat captains created

[9] J. Mak and G. Walton, "Steamboats and the Great Productivity Surge in River Transportation," *Journal of Economic History* (September 1972).

other problems. The quest for speed often caused overloaded boilers, and uncertain metallurgy and unreliable pressure gauges gave only the most drastic evidence of the limits of machinery. Boiler explosions, collisions, and fires—often during races—ended the careers of many riverboats. The average life of a steamboat on western waters was only about five years.

In the 1850s, steamboats began to suffer from railroads' competition. Although the absolute amount of tonnage carried by steamboats continued to rise, railroads were taking an increasing proportion of total freight and a disproportionate percentage of the more valuable cargoes. On the larger rivers, steamboats could still compete by 1860 (as could sailing ships on the Great Lakes), but on smaller streams they had lost the battle.

CANALS

Americans tried another approach to the high cost of overland transportation: they created man-made waterways. The canals built in three "booms" between 1815 and 1860 added significantly to U.S. economic development. Some were profitable to their owners as well. The most successful of these ventures was the Erie Canal.

The Erie Canal

In 1817, the state of New York began constructing a canal from Albany, at the junction of the Mohawk and Hudson Rivers, to Lake Erie. This project had been proposed several times before, and work had actually commenced at least once. This time, however, the project was not only completed but so successful that it touched off a canal boom that spread to regions of the United States who considered their natural waterways inadequate av-

enues for commerce. The Erie Canal was an immediate financial success. Revenues from the first sections completed financed construction of the final portions linking the Eastern Seaboard to the Great Lakes. When the canal was finished in 1825, New York City became the only Eastern seaport with an all-water link to the interior. No project of comparable size had ever been undertaken in the United States. The canal's construction symbolized the optimism, vision, and determination of early nineteenth-century Americans. It also illustrated the country's ability to allocate the right people to perform important tasks.

The canal's construction was supervised by two lawyers. In this era, legal work was heavily concerned with land titles, so properly trained lawyers were also surveyors. Few engineers with formal training were available; only West Point gave such academic instruction. The canal became a massive on-the-job training project for its builders. The only tools available were black powder and horse-drawn scrapers; most of the work was done by men with shovels. After construction was under way, the builders discovered that some sections of the canal would not hold water. The invention of waterproof cement solved this problem, and others were overcome by persistence, effort, and good fortune. The canal's route covered a distance of 364 miles and a vertical rise of 655 feet. Its locks were paired to allow continuous two-way traffic.

A Profitable Undertaking

The Erie Canal returned at least 8 percent on the capital invested in it by the state. The reasons for its profitability were obvious. It connected a major seaport with a rich and well-populated hinterland, initially in upstate New York and later in the entire Great Lakes Basin, and, with the help of additional canals, the Ohio Valley as well. Since the terrain crossed by the Erie was relatively level, traffic on the canal was unusually quick and convenient. From the first, the Erie Canal was heavily used. In the 1820s and 1830s, most of the traffic in both directions originated within New York State, but after 1846 a majority of the eastbound shipments had been generated farther west. The canal was an important factor in New York City's rise to preeminence among eastern seaports. It also contributed greatly to the growth of Buffalo at its western terminus, where cargo was transferred from lake vessels to canal barges.

Other Canals

The Erie Canal generated extensive benefits for the state: population and industry grew rapidly in the regions that it served.[10] It spurred nationwide interest in canals. Once the Erie was built, other seaports had to find some way to match New York City's connections with the interior or forfeit both existing trade and a large share of future trade as western settlement increased. New York State was already expanding its canal system (much less profitably) to Lakes Champlain and Ontario and the region south of the Erie Canal.

■ Canals extended the American transportation system.
Source: Courtesy of the New York Historical Society, New York City.

But nature had been less kind to Philadelphia and Baltimore than to New York City. Boston's geographic position was even worse: it could not hope to do more than eventually tap into New York's system, and it could not even do that until railroads became practical. Baltimore attempted to build a canal linking the Potomac and Ohio rivers, but the Baltimore and Ohio Canal was never extended past Cumberland, Maryland, which it reached in 1850—too late and far short of its goal.

Philadelphia also attempted to build a route to the Ohio. The route was far more difficult than that traversed by the Erie Canal—the vertical rise in the Alleghenies was over 2,000 feet. The technical capabilities of the time made construction of an all-water route over such terrain impossible. Construction on the Pennsylvania Main Line Canal began in 1826 and took eight years to complete. The engineer chosen to supervise the project initially recommended a railroad, but canal construction promised more jobs, and with an election in the offing, he was persuaded to change his plan.[11] When completed, the Main Line was a canal, a horse-drawn railroad, and a series of inclined planes up which canal boats were pulled by stationary steam engines. It had no less than 174 locks. The frequent transitions between modes of transport slowed traffic, and the heavy construction expenses made the Main Line's tolls high. Although it did tap the Ohio River Valley, which was densely settled before the Great Lakes region, the Main Line never fulfilled its builders' expectations. Construction of a series of branches to other regions of the state added more expenses than revenues.

Ohio built two canals that linked the Ohio River with Lake Erie, one at each end of the state. Indiana constructed another, and Illinois connected Lake Michigan with the Illinois River and, through it, the Mississippi. The Ohio canals, particularly the Ohio and Erie, may have

[10] Davis et al., *American Economic Growth*, pp. 477–485.

[11] Lebergott, *The Americans*, p. 107.

been financial successes. Most canals, especially those in the western states, were not. Canals in that region tended to be long and required much time and expense to complete. Many were built to promote settlement in sparsely populated regions rather than to link existing markets. Projects begun in the later 1830s and the 1840s soon encountered competition from the railroads. Many western canals failed to earn back their construction costs and few, if any, generated returns equal to alternative uses of capital.

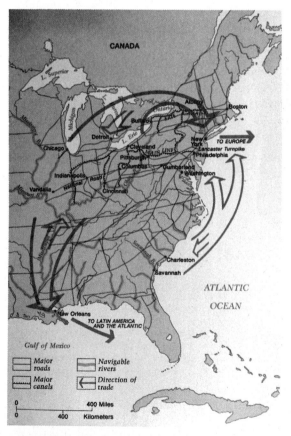

■ Commerce and transportation depended on rivers, roads, and canals to move goods and people both east-west and north-south.
Source: From *America Past & Present, Volume I,* by Robert A. Devine and T. H. Breen, p. 251. Copyright © 1984 by Scott, Foresman and Company. Reprinted by permission.

The Canal Boom

There were three cycles of canal building. During the first, between 1815 and 1834, 2,188 miles of canals were built. In the second, from 1834 to 1844, another 1,172 miles were added. The third era extended from 1844 to 1860, when 894 miles of new canals were added, but by the 1850s existing canals may have been abandoned as rapidly as new ones were built. In all, some 4,200 miles of canals were built in the antebellum era, at a total cost of $188 million.[12]

With the exception of the Erie Canal and a few others, canals proved poor investments for their owners. In some cases, tolls did not even cover operating expenses. But canals' impact on the economy was more positive than the private returns (or their absence) suggest. Ton-mile shipping charges on the canals were a tenth or less of those charged for wagon transportation, and canals shipped some goods that wagons simply could not handle. Population density increased sharply and economic activity became more diversified in regions served by canals, compared to similar regions that lacked them. Regional specialization increased and local monopolies declined as the canal network expanded, suggesting that canal tolls did not represent the full value of the services rendered by these waterways. Part of the rise in incomes produced by canals accrued to canal users, not owners. Any calculation of the precise external benefits depends heavily on the analyst's assumptions about what would have occurred in the absence of canals. Little consensus exists, especially for individual canals. But canals' impact on the aggregate economy was almost certainly positive.[13]

[12] C. Goodrich, ed., *Canals and American Economic Development* (New York: Columbia University Press, 1961), pp. 172–173.
[13] R. Ransom, "Canals and Development: A Discussion of the Issues," *American Economic Review* (May 1964): pp. 365–376. H. Segal, "Canals and Economic Development," in *Canals,* ed. Goodrich; and Davis et al., *American Economic Growth,* pp. 474–485.

Keys to Canal Success

Canals built between two areas that had already undergone some economic development—particularly if they specialized in different products—proved to have better economic records than those constructed as incentives for settlement. Easy construction usually was a good indicator of economic success: low construction costs resulted in modest tolls, greater speed, and higher traffic volume. Difficult, costly construction generally indicated that the canal would be inconvenient and expensive to use. The first canals (which were built where the advantages were obvious) had longer operating periods before railroad competition appeared.

Some special-purpose canals also generated good financial records. Those linking eastern Pennsylvania coal mines with Philadelphia are examples. They were short and answered an existing demand, and because the demand for fuel tended to be price-elastic, the reduced price of coal caused by lower transport costs resulted in large increases in traffic volume. Bulky, low-value items like coal were especially well-suited to water transportation.

Canal Benefits

The canals' contribution should not be underestimated. Without railroads' competition, their financial record might have been better. But it was the canals, not the railroads, that produced most of the fall in freight rates before the Civil War. The lower transportation costs allowed regional specialization and the use of comparative advantage. In a nation with such varied resource patterns, this yielded important income gains because the same resources could produce more output. Competition from more producers meant that consumers paid lower prices; over time, it also pressured producers to reduce their costs by improving the efficiency of their plants. Resources' value increased when their products could be sold in larger markets. Even though canals could not be extended to all regions of the country, they furnished the first low-cost transport links between the East and the West, encouraging the development of both regions.

Canal Limitations

Canals had their limits as well. Canal transportation might involve low money tolls, but the time costs were still high since canal travel was very slow. Basically, the speed limit on canals was the walking pace that draft animals could sustain—two to four miles per hour—and even this pace was reduced by traffic congestion or many locks. Locks, low water, floods, and incompatibility between parts of the canal system also slowed traffic. Canals' widths, depths, and lock dimensions varied, which often forced shippers to transfer their cargoes between boats. Weather imposed another time delay. Most of the canal network was closed by winter several months every year. Delays caused higher inventory costs, losses in shipment, and higher risks for those dependent on the canals than with more rapid transportation. Finally, canals could not be developed into a true national transportation system because terrain and water supply constraints restricted the construction of east-west canals.

Government's Role in Canal Financing

Investment in canals usually required the commitment of a large sum, perhaps millions of dollars, and the certainty of a long wait before any returns. Thus, canals were difficult for private investors to finance. The high proportion of income gains captured by customers rather than owners was another problem for investors. In the early years of canal construction, few institutions designed to raise large sums from private sources had been developed. As a consequence, state governments played a prominent role in canal financing. The states issued bonds to be redeemed by canal tolls and projected increases in tax revenues stemming from the economic development promoted by canals. Although the federal government made several grants to the Baltimore and Ohio Canal, in general it played only a minor role in canal financing.

Canal bonds were sold to investors in both the United States and Europe. Perhaps one-third of all canal construction funds were raised in Europe.[14] In the 1830s, the credit rating of the federal government was very high in Europe, and many investors there either did not understand the difference between federal and state governments or thought that the central government was responsible for the debts of the states as well as its own. It had, after all, assumed state debts at the time the Constitution was adopted. But when a number of states defaulted on their bonds in the early 1840s, these investors learned a painful lesson. European investors shied away from American securities for years after these defaults or demanded high risk premiums. There was an internal reaction as well: many western states that had borrowed heavily to finance development programs now demonstrated a strong aversion to further government-financed projects and borrowing. Bonds had been very easy to sell in the euphoric atmosphere of the mid-1830s, and some canal projects were apparently launched for little more reason than the ready availability of funds.

RAILROADS

By 1860, railroads had become the dominant and fastest growing form of transportation in the United States. Nevertheless, antebellum railroads had surprisingly small effects, through either forward or backward linkages, on the rest of the economy.[15] They clearly did not cause American industrialization, since it was well under way when the first railroads appeared. Railroads consumed relatively small proportions of the economy's output of machinery, engineering services, and (until the 1850s) even iron. As we have seen, the railroads were not responsible for the large drop in transportation costs in the antebellum era—canals and steamboats generated much greater reductions in shipping costs.

Nevertheless, railroads were an advance over earlier forms of transportation. The fact that they were able to divert business away from other transport modes is proof enough. Railroads influenced more than just shipping costs and passenger charges. Competition, the structure of business firms, the location of industry, financial institutions, and relations between government and the economy were all changed by the appearance of the railroads. But the U.S. economy was neither static nor technologically incapable of responses to transportation problems before the railroad era, as the growth in per-capita incomes and diversity of activities that it produced indicate. In sum, railroads in the antebellum era aided economic growth, but they did not make it possible.

The First Railroads

Before the invention of the steam locomotive, it had already been discovered that horses could pull far greater loads over iron rails than on even the best roads. England built the first steam railroad, the Stockton and Darlington, in 1825. Americans were quick to try out the new idea; in 1829, an English steam engine was imported and tested, though not very successfully. Still,

[14] H. Segal, "Cycles of Canal Construction," in *Canals,* ed. Goodrich, pp. 188–192.

[15] R. Fogel, "Railroads in American Economic Growth," *Journal of Economic History* (June 1962). A. Fishlow, *American Railroads and the Transformation of the Antebellum Economy* (Cambridge, Mass.: Harvard University Press, 1965) assigns greater impact to the railroads than does Fogel.

the new mechanism showed promise, and America had an obvious need for improved transportation.

Once again, an idea from overseas required considerable modification to achieve its potential under American conditions. The railroad had been invented in England, a country of short distances, relatively abundant labor and capital, and efficient water transportation. No point in Britain is more than 70 miles from the sea, and few real mountains or other obstructions exist. In addition, the English already had a system of canals and improved rivers. As a result, British railroads were built slowly and designed for a long life. English construction methods reflected resource patterns. Tunnels, bridges, and grades were all designed to minimize operating costs and to reflect the available alternatives. In Britain, really heavy or bulky goods would continue to move by water.

American Adaptations

These concepts did not suit American circumstances. Distances were greater in this country and water transportation less available. Natural obstacles were more challenging, and labor and capital were scarcer, while fuel was much cheaper than in Europe. By the 1840s, American railroads exhibited some distinct responses to the conditions under which they operated. Speedy construction and operation were emphasized. Wood was used more extensively than on English railways. Not only were American wood supplies large but wood required far less skilled labor than did other materials, such as the stone the British employed in ties as well as bridges. In America, sometimes even rails were made of wood topped with a strip of iron. Grades and curves were sharper than on British railroads.

Experience yielded the appropriate methods, but only after much trial and error. Many errors occurred; few Americans (or any other nineteenth-century humans) had the formal engineering skills to accurately predict the strength of bridges, the tolerable radius of curves in the track, or the slope of grades. Nobody at all had practical experience in operating machinery of such mass and speed—or the brakes required to stop it. Before the invention of the telegraph in 1844, the human eye was the primary instrument of traffic control and speeds sometimes exceeded stopping ability within line of sight. Wood-and-iron rails produced "snakeheads"; the iron would separate from the wood and curl up as trains passed over, often penetrating the floors of cars. Boilers were no safer than in steamboats, although at least the passengers were farther away. But as with any other widely used new technology, productivity gains were rapid; output per unit of input doubled in the railway industry between 1839 and 1859.[16] After prolonged experimentation, the "T" rail of solid iron replaced earlier varieties. Swivel trucks, improved brakes and signals, and more experience increased output and safety. Trains grew heavier, faster, and more powerful.

New Organizational Forms. As railways grew longer, new forms of organization were necessary for efficient operation. Lines of authority had to be worked out, because local agents often had to decide loads, adjust schedules, and keep track of rolling stock while fitting local operations into an integrated whole. In addition, the requirements of railroad finance, in which large amounts of capital had to be obtained for long periods, strengthened the corporate form.[17]

Man-Made Barriers. There was no lack of opposition to the railways. Canal boatmen, wagoners, and the innkeepers and stable operators who supported them saw the threat to their

[16] Davis et al., *American Economic Growth*, p. 484.
[17] See A. Chandler, *The Railroads: The Nation's First Big Business* (New York: Harcourt, Brace, and World, 1965) and *The Visible Hand: The Managerial Revolution in American Business* (Cambridge, Mass.: Harvard University Press, 1977), Chap. 3.

jobs and reacted accordingly. Also, the railroads were obviously new and "unnatural" in an age where such phenomena were far less commonplace than in our own. Debates raged over the effects of prolonged speeds of 20 miles per hour or even more on the human body, or whether speed attained by such means violated divine law. Since railroads required government help in acquiring corporate charters, obtaining rights of way in settled areas, and often financing, social opposition could not be disregarded.

Railroad Advantages

But it was soon clear that the railroads had advantages possessed by no other form of transportation. They could traverse land with too many hills or too little water for canals, and they carried far more than wagons. Railroads were easier and cheaper to build than canals. Once railroad operators realized that the efficient way to operate a railroad was to run their own trains rather than rent tracks to others using their own rolling stock, fare collection posed no problems. Above all else, however, the railroads were faster than other forms of transportation. Speeds over the ground were greater than those of canal boats or most steamboats, but in addition routes were more direct. And the railroads ran all year.

Since railroads' charges per ton-mile were two or three times those of canals,[18] the shippers who chose them over water transport obviously placed a high value on time. Initially, most railroad business was passenger traffic, but as technology improved, freight accounted for a growing portion of revenues. By 1850 freight constituted the majority of the railroads' business. Inventory costs fell as additional goods could be obtained with much less delay. Railroads could be much more flexible in response to shippers' needs than canals; in many cases, a spur could be constructed to the factory door. Speed gave railroads particularly great advantages in shipping perishable cargoes, but canal barges continued to carry a large share of coal, grain, and other raw materials. As Table 5.2 indicates, the U.S. rail network expanded rapidly after 1845.

Expansion of the Rail Network

By 1840 there were almost 3,000 miles of railroad track in the United States, and all Eastern Seaboard cities were linked. A decade later, 9,000 miles of railroads extended into all regions of the country, and by 1860, the United States could be said to possess a railway system. As Table 5.2 reveals, there were then 30,000 miles of railroad, and it was possible to travel by rail between nearly all the country's large cities, although not always directly. In the 1850s extensive construction occurred in the West and South. Raw statistics give a somewhat misleading picture, however. Since neither standard track gauges nor central (union) terminals existed, both passengers and freight often had to transfer from one railroad to another, many times by wagon. But by 1860 it was possible to

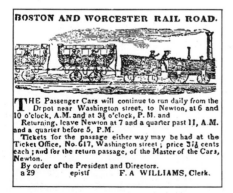

■ Above is an advertisement for Massachusetts' first passenger train in May of 1834.
Source: History of the American Nation by Andrew C. McLaughlin (New York: D. Appleton, 1901) p. 316.

[18] Davis et al., *American Economic Growth,* p. 484.

Table 5.2   Railroad Mileage and Construction, 1830–1860

Date	Total Mileage Operated	Construction (Each Year, in Miles)
1830	23	40
1835	1,098	133
1840	2,818	491
1845	4,633	277
1850	9,021	1,261
1855	18,374	2,453
1860	30,625	1,500

Source: U.S. Department of Commerce, Bureau of the Census, *Historical Statistics of the United States: Colonial Times to 1970* (Washington, D.C.: Government Printing Office, 1975), vol. 2, pp. 733–734.

travel from any of the great East Coast ports to Chicago or St. Louis and thence to New Orleans at speeds inconceivable only 30 years earlier.

State and Local Government's Role

The federal government was not active in financing the railways until it began to make land grants to them in the 1850s. State governments played a major role only in the South, where they provided about half the funds required. Local governments contributed to railroads' construction expenses in various ways: through land donations, favorable tax treatment, or guarantees of interest payments on railroad bonds. Cities and towns were quick to recognize that they could gain if a railroad served them—or lose population, industry, and jobs to rivals if they were bypassed. The railroads recognized this as well, and were not bashful about requesting aid. Nevertheless, private funds furnished the bulk of the capital for antebellum railroad construction in America.

The Role of Private Investors

Financing railroads posed the same types of problems as financing canals. A large sum had to be raised, far beyond the means of even the wealthiest individual investors, and no returns could be expected for a long period. Since the primary source of funds was private savers, railroads were organized as corporations.

The corporate form has many advantages as a device to pool the savings of many individuals in a common enterprise. Shares of corporate stock are transferable; they can be bought and sold, although securities markets were limited at this time. In a partnership, the entire agreement must be renegotiated each time a partner is added or deleted. Further, corporate shares carry limited liability. Shareholders cannot lose more than the purchase price of their stock or its face value, whichever is greater, no matter what happens to the corporation. Members of a partnership, on the other hand, are liable for its debts to the full extent of their personal wealth, regardless of the size of their investment or their participation in its management. Thus, corporations were better instruments for raising capital for new ventures such as railways. The lower risks involved made it easier to raise the large sums needed. Corporate charters had to be granted by state legislatures, initially on a case-by-case basis with strict limits on the type of activity permitted. Over time, however, states became

■ In the decade before the Civil War, the railroad network grew unevenly in the North and South.
Source: The Bettmann Archive.

more willing to grant wider powers to the holders of corporate charters.[19]

The European Connection. Especially after 1850, when memories of earlier American investments had begun to fade, Europeans bought large amounts of American railroad securities. The bulk of the investment remained American, but funds from Europe provided some advantages. The cost of raising a given sum was often lower in Europe, where wealth was more concentrated and financial markets better organized than in the United States. Western railroads, which had to build over long distances in regions where few investors had sizable amounts to invest, found access to European capital especially advantageous. Investors along the Eastern Seaboard had plenty of other promising alternatives and often were not as willing to hazard their funds in the West as were Europeans. As the interest in railroad securities increased, institutions to market them and aid in the transfer of existing issues were developed. By 1860, most large cities had "stock exchanges," dealing largely in government and railroad bonds rather than stocks.

There were other means to minimize the initial investment required. The attempts to obtain government aid have already been noted. Most railroads, particularly those built in the 1830s and 1840s, were short. They served local markets, connecting complementary economic activities. At least in this period, railroads were not built ahead of existing settlement, and most were profitable shortly after they began operations.[20] This record made it easier to raise funds for later projects.

Federal Assistance

An indication of the future participation of the federal government in railroad finance occurred in 1850. The Illinois Central Railroad was given several million acres of federally owned land in that year. The idea was that the railroad would sell most of the land (it had been granted far more than was needed for a right of way) to settlers, using the funds it obtained for construction. Since the land would eventually be close to a railroad, it could be sold at premium prices compared to similar land lacking transportation services. This procedure would achieve several governmental objectives. Western settlement would be increased and the railroad constructed (it appeared that sufficient funds could not be obtained from conventional sources of finance). At the same time, sales of the remaining government-owned land in the

---

[19] Chandler, *The Visible Hand*, pp. 89–94.

[20] Fishlow, *American Railroads*, Chaps. 4 and 5.

region would be easier. The cost to the Treasury was essentially zero, since the government then held more land than it could sell, in many cases because the land's produce could not be marketed. As with the corporate form, this procedure would be greatly expanded in later years.

CONSEQUENCES OF THE TRANSPORTATION SYSTEM BY 1860

The East

On the eve of the Civil War, little of the American transportation system had been operating for more than a few decades, but it had already begun to influence regional specialization and interdependence. The Middle Atlantic and New England regions now devoted fewer resources to agriculture and more to manufacturing, commerce, and finance. A growing share of the food consumed in these regions came from the Midwest via the Erie Canal, the railroads, and coastal shipping. The remaining eastern farmers had been forced to react to the competition from more fertile western soils by switching from grain production to wool production, dairying, and truck farming. Other eastern farmers had abandoned agriculture there and moved either to midwestern farms or to the cities.

The Midwest

In the Midwest, aggregate population rose sharply. Potential agricultural incomes in the region were now higher because food could be shipped cheaply to eastern markets. Not everyone found the changes desirable. Prior to the advent of efficient transportation, considerable small-scale, locally oriented manufacturing had developed in the Midwest. When transportation costs declined, many of these firms were unable to meet competition from larger, more specialized producers.[21] Yankee farmers regarded the invasion of their markets by midwestern produce with no more enthusiasm. The result, however, was that American resources produced more output because they were better allocated toward their most efficient uses. As Table 5.3 indicates, transportation costs were now as little as one-tenth their 1816 levels.

Returns to Transportation

Not only were regions now able to specialize in producing those items best suited to their resources, but lower transport costs forced them to pass on the gains in efficiency to their customers. Before 1860 most firms were tiny compared to their modern counterparts in absolute size, but not in terms of their markets. Though small, they often had monopoly power both as sellers of products and as purchasers of inputs. Their workers often had little bargaining power because only one or two potential employers were within walking distance of their homes. The firms' customers had few more alternatives.

Lower transportation costs now increased the range of choices in many markets and reduced (but hardly eliminated) the power of many local monopolies. By increasing the number and incomes of potential customers for any single producer, they encouraged the use of techniques that increased the volume of output and often reduced its unit costs as well. Tranportation improvements did much to produce the mass market that was one of the distinctive features of the American economy and a major source of its further growth.

[21] D. North, *The Economic Growth of the United States, 1790–1860* (New York: Norton, 1966), pp. 157 and 163.

Table 5.3 **Average Freight Rates per Ton-Mile**
(Cents per Ton-Mile)

Mode	1816	1853	1860
Turnpikes	30.00	15.00	15.00
Mississippi-Ohio downstream	1.30		.37
Mississippi-Ohio upstream	5.80		.37
Erie Canal		1.10	
Ohio canals		1.00	
Pennsylvania Main Line Canal		2.40	
New York Central Railroad		3.40	2.40
Erie Railroad		2.40	1.84
Western railroads (Buffalo-Chicago)		2.50	
Pennsylvania Railroad		3.50	1.96

Source: Adapted from G. Taylor, *The Transportation Revolution* (Armonk, N.Y.: M.E. Sharpe, 1977), p. 442.

As previously noted, the contribution of transport improvements is hard to quantify, but one study found that the railroads had produced a social saving of 5 percent of gross national product by 1860; that is, aggregate U.S. income was 5 percent higher because of the railroads than it would have been been without them.[22] Since the railroads' contribution built on the achievements of the canals and steamboats, it seems clear that the developments in antebellum transportation made very substantial differences in the economic alternatives available to Americans.

SELECTED REFERENCES

Chandler, A. *The Railroads: The Nation's First Big Business*. New York: Harcourt, Brace, and World, 1965.
————. *The Visible Hand: The Managerial Revolution in American Business*. Cambridge, Mass.: Harvard University Press, 1977.

[22] Fishlow, *American Railroads.*

Davis, L., et al. *American Economic Growth: An Economist's History of the United States*. New York: Harper and Row, 1972.
Fishlow, A. *American Railroads and the Transformation of the Antebellum Economy*. Cambridge, Mass.: Harvard University Press, 1965.
Goodrich, C., ed. *Canals and American Economic Development*. New York: Kenikat, 1975.
Haites, E., et al. *Western River Transportation: The Era of Early Internal Development, 1810–1860*. New York: Kenikat, 1965.
Kirkland, E., *Men, Cities, and Transportation*. 2 vols. New York: Russell and Russell, 1968.
Klingamen, D., and R. Vedder, eds. *Essays in Early 19th Century Economic History: The Old Northwest*. Athens, Ohio: Ohio University Press, 1975.
North, D. *The Economic Growth of the United States, 1790–1860*. New York: Norton, 1966.
North, D., et al. *Growth and Welfare in the American Past: A New Economic History*. 3d ed. Englewood Cliffs, N.J.: Prentice-Hall, 1983.
Scheiber, H., *The Ohio Canal Era*. Athens, Ohio: Ohio University Press, 1969.
Taylor, G. *The Transportation Revolution, 1815–1860*. New York: M.E. Sharpe, 1962.
U.S. Department of Commerce, Bureau of the Census. *Historical Statistics of the United States: Colonial Times to 1970*. 2 vols. Washington, D. C.: Government Printing Office, 1975.

CHAPTER

6

AGRICULTURAL EXPANSION AND CHANGE

More people earned their livings in agriculture than in any other occupation from 1815 to 1860. Thus, developments in agriculture directly affected most Americans. Even so, agriculture's importance to the economy declined; in 1860, it employed 53 percent of the work force as against 79 percent four decades earlier.[1] Farming's share of the value of total output declined from 60 percent to less than 40 percent over the same period. The numbers indicate that the relative decline of agriculture within the U.S. economy was not over in 1860; resources were more productive (and earned larger incomes) in other sectors. Incomes had grown more quickly elsewhere in the economy, and would continue to do so.

AGRICULTURAL CHANGES

But agriculture was neither declining nor even static in absolute terms. From 1815 to 1860, both agricultural exports and the proportion of the U.S. population living in cities increased, indicating that output per farmer had risen. This was indeed the case. In 1860, each farmer supplied the food and fiber needs of a larger number of people than in 1815. Total agricultural production had increased sharply, but output rose faster elsewhere in the economy.

Two major trends characterized American agriculture from 1815 to 1860. First, huge aggregate increases occurred in virtually all its dimensions: work force, total product, cultivated area, and amount of land available. Second, a variety of developments increased individual farmers' productive capacities. Pro-

[1] L. Davis et al., *American Economic Growth: An Economist's History of the United States* (New York: Harper and Row, 1972), p. 187.

155

ductivity rose far more than it had in the colonial era.

In the first half of the nineteenth century, the United States increased its land area to 3.4 times that of 1789. A combination of purchase, coercion, and annexation added the Louisiana Purchase, East and West Florida, Texas, Oregon, and the vast territory taken from Mexico. Together with its initial area, the acquisitions gave the United States large areas of some of the richest agricultural land on earth, plus a vast endowment of timber and mineral wealth. In 1860, most of the new areas had not been settled and were still raw frontier. Yet settlement extended far beyond previous boundaries. These new lands often required adjustments from their owners. Soil, climate, and productive capabilities differed from those along the Atlantic Coast. By 1860, settlers had started to determine the potential of western lands and forge the tools to reach it. But much still remained to be learned, and still more to be applied.

As Table 6.1 indicates, substantial numbers of people had moved to the new areas. Both the Midwest and the "New South"—the area west of Georgia, particularly the lower Mississippi Valley—had populations rivaling those of any of the older settled areas on the eve of the Civil War.

LAND POLICY AND THE PUBLIC DOMAIN

This vast area initially was the property of the federal government. Most of it was sold to private citizens on increasingly lenient terms, as Table 6.2 reveals. Widespread defaults forced the government to discontinue sales on credit after 1820, but by that time more than enough land for a family farm could be obtained for $100. The land was sold at auction, and the prices listed in the table were the minimum bids required. So much land was available that prices seldom rose above the minimum. Land purchased at government auctions had been surveyed and bore secure titles. It could be

Table 6.1   U.S. Population by Region

Region	1820		1860	
	Number	Percentage of Total	Number	Percentage of Total
New England	1,660,071	17.2%	3,135,283	10.0%
Mid-Atlantic	2,699,845	28.0	7,458,985	23.7
East North Central	792,719	8.2	6,926,884	22.0
West North Central	66,586	.7	2,169,832	6.9
South Atlantic	3,061,063	31.8	5,634,703	17.1
East South Central	1,190,489	12.4	4,020,991	12.8
West South Central	167,680	1.7	1,747,667	5.6
Mountain	—	—	174,923	.5
Pacific	—	—	440,053	1.4
Total	9,638,453	100.0	31,442,321	100.0

Source: U.S. Department of Commerce, Bureau of the Census, *Historical Statistics of the United States: Colonial Times to 1970* (Washington, D.C.: Government Printing Office, 1975), vol. I, pp. 22, 23.

Table 6.2 Land Sale Provisions and Prices, 1785–1854

Date	Minimum Purchase Allowed (Acres)	Minimum Bid (Price per Acre)	Sale Terms
1785	640	$1.00	Cash
1796	640	2.00	½ cash; rest in one year
1800	320	2.00	¼ cash; rest over four years
1804	160	2.00	¼ cash; rest over four years
1820	80	1.25	Cash
1832	40	1.25	Cash
1841	*	1.25	Cash
1854	40	**	Cash

*The Preemption Act of 1841 allowed squatters who had settled on surveyed land without legal title to buy up to 160 acres at the $1.25 per acre minimum price.

**The Graduation Act reduced prices on land that remained unsold after ten years. The minimum price was 12½¢ per acre for land unsold for 30 years.

Source: E. Kirkland, *A History of American Economic Life,* 4th ed. (New York: Appleton Century Crofts, 1969), pp. 86, 87.

transferred readily, and land speculation was at least as widespread as in the colonial era.

Public Land Sale Policy

In 1841 and 1854, the Preemption Act and Graduation Act eased land acquisition still further. The first enabled squatters who had settled on surveyed land without purchase to buy up to 160 acres of the land they occupied at the $1.25 per acre minimum price. It more or less recognized reality; squatters were prone to discourage those who sought to gain their land through legal means by threats or outright force, and Congress had legitimized their acquisitions several times previously. The second law provided that land unsold at $1.25/acre for more than ten years would be sold on a sliding scale, reaching 12½¢ per acre for land that had not been sold after 30 years. In itself, the Graduation Act indicated that there was no shortage of first-quality land at existing prices. Land could also be obtained from state and local governments, and military veterans were rewarded with land warrants. These were transferable, often at per-acre prices below those charged for direct purchase from the government.

Although some people believed that the government should have given the land away to encourage the growth of family farms, the speed of settlement indicates that land costs could hardly have been a major barrier to settlement. Had the land been given away, the government would have had to develop an alternative source of revenue. What's more, by 1860 the cost of land was only a small portion of the total cost of developing a commercially viable farm. The amounts required for livestock, tools, building materials, land clearance, travel, and first-year maintenance of the settler and his family might total ten times the land's purchase price. Another question that the free land proposal did not resolve was the criteria by which land was to be distributed—who would receive how much? Obviously, each potential recipient had an incentive to overstate the amount needed if the land's marginal costs were zero.

The Impact of Speculation

Land was not kept from small farmers by large-scale land speculators. It is quite true that many persons, including most small farmers, bought land—often in large amounts—in hopes of re-selling it at higher prices. But the market for land was highly competitive: buyers had their choice of many parcels from a variety of sellers. As noted, the stable prices of government land indicate that it was not growing scarcer. Also, the more speculators, the lower their ability to drive up prices.[2] Since more land was settled in this 45-year period than in the previous two centuries, the overwhelming bulk of it by small farmers, it is difficult to make a convincing case for speculation's inhibiting effects on settlement. Tracts with special properties—cleared fields, a desirable location, or special appeal to the buyer—might bring high prices, but in general it was a buyer's market for ordinary land.[3]

The Safety Valve Theory

The availability of western land was once thought to improve the bargaining power of eastern workers versus their employers'. According to this "safety valve" theory, if wages fell workers could always leave their jobs, buy land, and become farmers. This idea is almost certainly invalid for individual workers, and probably for the economy as a whole, at least over most periods. Wages in manufacturing, on the average, exceeded farmers' incomes, and thus a move from industrial work to agriculture would be a switch from an above-average to a below-average income. Nor would entry into farming be easy for most urban workers by 1860. Years of saving would be required for the investment needed to buy a fully equipped farm—difficult indeed if the worker thought his wages too low. Credit was hard for the average individual to obtain at this time, particularly on the frontier. And by 1860 farming had become a specialized occupation requiring skills few urban workers or recent immigrants possessed.

Patterns of migration during this period tend not to support the safety valve theory. Few if any city workers switched to agriculture, but some farmers—or their children—moved to the cities. The urban population of the United States rose from 7.2 percent to 19.7 percent of the total during this period (1800–1860).[4] Movement to the West was most pronounced during good times, not in periods of unemployment and falling wages. In short, population movements indicate that the western movement was a response to opportunity, not a flight from adversity.

Today it may be possible to romanticize life on a nineteenth-century farm, but the reality was less appealing. Work on farms in a time when power was supplied almost exclusively by human or animal muscles was brutally hard. Hours at planting or harvest time were limited only by available daylight. Even contemporary factory jobs might look easy in comparison. Frontier farmers generally had fewer tools and some even more demanding tasks, such as land clearing and construction, making their lives

---

[2] See A. Bogue and M. Bogue, "Profits and the Frontier Speculator," *Journal of Economic History* (March 1957); and R. Swierenga, *Pioneers and Profits: Land Speculation on the Iowa Frontier* (Ames, Iowa: Iowa State University Press, 1968).

[3] The results of speculation are often confused with the intentions of speculators, which are not at all the same thing. Speculators certainly hope to resell the commodities they have purchased at higher prices than they paid. But when such activity has a significant effect upon markets, it tends to be self-defeating. By adding to current demand, speculators raise prices at the time they make their purchases. When they resell, they add to the (then) current supply, pushing prices down. Speculation might not influence prices at all if on a small scale, but it cannot fulfill speculators' hopes if there are enough of them to influence prices. Speculation reduces the margin between current and future prices rather than increasing it. This analysis appears especially pertinent to the highly competitive land markets of the nineteenth century.

[4] U.S. Department of Commerce, Bureau of the Census, *Historical Statistics of the United States: Colonial Times to 1970* (Washington, D.C.: Government Printing Office, 1975), vol. I, p. 12.

harder than those of their counterparts in long-settled regions.

It has also been argued that the American frontier served as a safety valve for social non-conformists. Empirical evidence provides little support for this view. As the Mormons discovered at great cost, the frontier was not particularly tolerant of those with different social or religious views. Cities have always been more receptive to a variety of opinions and life-styles than has the countryside.

Despite this, it would be a serious error to conclude that the West had no impact on the economic life of the East. By furnishing a growing market for eastern goods, western economic growth increased the demand for industrial workers and hence raised their wages. Parts of the West were developing their own cities, and the demand for labor there was greater than in older areas. Cheaper food from the West also raised eastern workers' real incomes. For farm laborers in the East, the safety valve theory may well be valid: the West offered higher wages and better access to land.

PRODUCTIVITY GROWTH IN AGRICULTURE

Although yields per acre changed very slowly, output per farmer rose, indicating that the average size of farms was increasing. Corn, wheat, and cotton output doubled from 1839 to 1859, a period in which the agricultural work force increased by about 65 percent.[5] Man-hours required to produce given amounts of all three major crops had begun to fall even earlier, in the 1800–1840 period.[6] Gains of this magnitude indicate that production methods had changed.

[5] Ibid., pp. 512, 518.
[6] Ibid., p. 500.

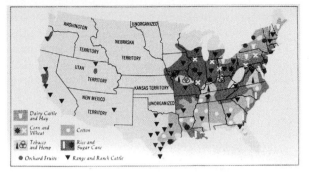

■ This map indicates the distribution of American agricultural production in 1860.
Source: From *The American Pageant,* seventh edition by Thomas A. Bailey and David M. Kennedy. Copyright © 1987 by D. C. Heath and Company. Reprinted by permission of the publisher.

Technological Change

The sources of these productivity gains are varied. Western land was more fertile than much of the East, but movement to more fertile land accounted for only minor gains. Improved knowledge also made only a limited contribution. Farmers were now able to cultivate larger acreage, and the major factor in this development was the appearance of new machinery. Some improvement and innovation in agricultural tools had been apparent since 1800, but in the 1840s and 1850s new mechanical devices came into widespread use, giving farmers greater capabilities than ever before.[7]

The changing conditions of American agriculture had by 1860 provoked a series of highly successful responses. Increased output could now be sold in larger markets to which farmers had better access, increasing the incentives for commercial rather than subsistence farming. The chief barrier to increased

[7] W. Parker and J. Klein, "Productivity Growth in Grain Production in the United States, 1840–1860 and 1900–1910," in National Bureau of Economic Research, *Output, Employment, and Productivity in the United States after 1800,* Studies in Income and Wealth (Princeton, N.J.: Princeton University Press, 1966), vol. 30.

production in American agriculture had always been the shortage of labor. Since land if anything became less scarce, the emphasis of productivity-raising innovation was on devices that allowed individual workers to farm more land: on labor-saving equipment. Since land was cheap and labor scarce, it paid to combine the limited amounts of labor available with additional land as long as output rose. The new machinery allowed a given number of man-hours to cultivate far more land than previously.

The Search for New Techniques

There was scope for productivity gains in the introduction of scientific, or at least systematic, techniques in animal husbandry and other areas of agriculture, but efforts in these areas were as yet less productive than the introduction of mechanical implements. Without an understanding of the basic scientific principles of heredity and soil chemistry, progress in selecting new breeds of stock, strains of seed, and fertilizers had to be achieved by trial and error. Some new breeds of sheep and cattle were introduced. In plant cultivation, attempts to develop strains resistant to disease and insect attack occurred.[8] These points were particularly obvious in cotton cultivation, perhaps because the large production units were able to maintain records of innovative efforts and use control groups that increased confidence in the results.[9] Despite the appearance of agricultural journals, fairs, and other devices for conveying information, innovations were likely to spread mainly after direct demonstration. If the innovation did not produce the same results for new users that it had for its inventor, there was no way of determining why it had failed.

The Introduction of Machinery

Mechanical aids, on the other hand, could be devised on a small scale by observation and experiment and used familiar concepts. They did not require the application of formal scientific principles. Particularly in wheat and hay cultivation, the results of mechanical innovations were easy to assess and attribute to the proper sources, so both invention and innovation were rapid.[10]

Since farm production was limited largely by the amount of labor available, especially for the harvest, efforts concentrated on increasing output per labor-hour and on harvesting rather than planting. Scythes replaced sickles early in the nineteenth century, and the cradle further increased productivity in grain harvesting. Plows were also improved. Early plows were wooden, difficult for a team to pull, susceptible to damage, and incapable of deep plowing. Iron was gradually added to plows to reduce friction and increase resistance to wear. Improved designs allowed farmers to make straighter, deeper furrows with less effort.

In 1819 the first cast iron plows appeared, and by the 1850s John Deere's steel plow, better suited to western soils, was in widespread use. Seed drills, reapers, and threshers became common in the same decade. Reapers and threshers had been invented several decades before, but considerable improvement was needed before they became economically useful. Since labor was not usually available to harvest the crop if the reaper broke down, the machines had to be made reliable and easy to repair. In addition, producers had to build up organizations to market, finance, and service these expensive and complicated devices at the local level.

But the real impetus to mechanical reaping was the movement of wheat production to the larger, more level fields of the Midwest. The

---

[8] I am indebted to Professor Robert Gallman on this point.
[9] S. Lebergott, *The Americans: An Economic Record* (New York: Norton, 1984), pp. 164–167.

[10] N. Rosenberg, *Technology and American Economic Growth* (New York: M.E. Sharpe, 1972), pp. 25–26.

machines performed better in this environment, and their high initial cost could be spread over a greater volume of output, reducing capital costs per bushel of wheat harvested.[11] The relocation and mechanization of production were linked to the development of a transportation network capable of carrying the larger volumes of grain to market. Horse-drawn rakes and cultivators reduced the labor needed to harvest hay and increased corn yields. Corn harvesting and shelling, however, remained a labor-intensive bottleneck throughout this era.

EASTERN AGRICULTURE

Prior to the improvement of transportation, eastern farmers had the markets of the seaboard cities to themselves. However, as western produce became more available at competitive prices, farmers in this region were forced to readjust. The West's great tracts of fertile land were better suited to labor-saving machinery than the smaller, less level farmlands of the East. In grain production, the West's comparative advantage was so large that eastern farmers had to find new products.

Eastern cities offered increasing markets for "truck" fruits and vegetables, hay, high-quality meat, dairy products, and, as the textile industry expanded, wool. The demand for dairy products in the cities exceeded the amounts that rural areas could deliver in this age of primitive cooling and preservation techniques. Improvements in distribution systems and in refrigeration were prerequisites to reallocating productive capacity to dairy products. Consequently, dairy herds were maintained within the cities.

Farmers in the East also attempted to compete with the West by improving the quality of both their output and their resources. They tried to improve the quality of eastern farmland through experiments with fertilizers and crop rotation. Merino sheep, whose wool production far exceeded that of domestic breeds, were imported from Spain. Crossbreeding American and European cattle raised the productivity of beef and dairy strains, and horses and hogs were also improved. Animal weights rose substantially. Given the need for improved techniques, there was widespread interest in innovation. Devices to disseminate new ideas, such as agricultural magazines and county fairs (which were devoted largely to business rather than social purposes), appeared.

In some cases, the response to western competition took a different form. Some farms, especially those on marginal soils, unsuited to the new methods, or badly located, were simply abandoned. This process was more widespread in New England than in the Middle Atlantic states. Despite the population movements of the 1970s, some rural areas in New England have yet to regain the population peaks recorded over a century ago.

THE OLD NORTHWEST

The valleys of the Ohio and the upper Mississippi contain some of the richest agricultural land on earth. Fertile, well-watered, and level, this area is immensely productive. Settlement of the region began in Kentucky and the southern Ohio Valley, with the first immigrants arriving from Virginia and the Carolinas in the 1770s. Abraham Lincoln was born in Kentucky, spent his boyhood in Indiana, and began his adult career in Illinois, a typical migration

[11] P. David, "The Mechanization of Reaping in the Antebellum Midwest," in *Technical Choice, Innovation, and Economic Growth*, P. David, ed. (Oxford, England: Oxford University Press, 1975). David's conclusions have been the subject of some controversy. See L. Jones, "The Mechanization of Reaping and Mowing in American Agriculture: A Comment," *Journal of Economic History* (June 1977); and A. Olmstead, "The Mechanization of Reaping and Mowing in American Agriculture, 1833–1870," *Journal of Economic History* (June 1975).

pattern for an ambitious young man of the region.

After 1800, another stream of migration began. Originating in New England and upstate New York and later strongly supplemented with immigrants, this group settled the northern halves of Ohio, Indiana, and Illinois, as well as southern Michigan and Wisconsin. When settlement reached the prairies, it faltered briefly: farmers had traditionally assessed the soil quality of new land by the types of trees growing on it. But they soon realized that the prairies were not inferior soil, but in fact so rich that the grass smothered tree seedlings (or promoted prairie fires which killed them) and in addition were far easier to bring into cultivation than forest land. After that, grain and livestock production expanded rapidly.

Much of the actual pioneering effort was concentrated in a small group of frontiersmen, typified by Daniel Boone and John Sevier. After making the initial settlements, these specialists would sell their landholdings to those with more settled inclinations and move west again to repeat the process. While the frontiersmen practiced subsistence agriculture, lumbering, trapping, and trading, their chief source of income was land speculation.

Mixed Farming

The chief agricultural products of the Old Northwest were corn, wheat, pork, and to a lesser extent, beef. The characteristics of these goods and the nature of their production processes shaped the region's economic development. Cattle could be driven east on the hoof, if distances were not too great, but mobility and food quality were not easily combined in hogs. Pork was generally exported in preserved forms—smoked into hams or bacon, salted, or pickled. Grain crops, especially corn, also required processing to improve their portability. Given the available agricultural technology, corn, wheat, beef, and pork were all well suited

to production on farms worked by the owner and his family; there were no economies of scale open to larger units.

The region grew spectacularly. In 1800, the leading wheat- and corn-producing states were all on the Atlantic Seaboard. By 1840 Kentucky, Ohio, and Tennessee were challenging the leaders, and by 1860 more than half of all the wheat grown in the United States originated in Illinois, Missouri, Indiana, Ohio, Michigan, and Wisconsin. The Midwest was a large-scale corn producer as well, but corn was grown almost everywhere that Americans farmed. It was widely used as food for both man and beast but not easily transported before a practical method of getting the kernels off the cob had been developed. Kentucky, Tennessee, and Missouri also produced tobacco, hemp, and mules.

Agriculture's Links to Urban Growth

The Midwest's chief crops could all be exported more easily if they were processed. Most corn left the Ohio Valley as fattened pork or whiskey. Before the railroads appeared, live hogs were more difficult to transport than preserved pork. Wheat was more expensive to ship than flour. There were economies of scale in the processing of all these items; unit costs fell when much larger amounts than the average farm turned out were milled, distilled, or slaughtered and packed by specialist firms rather than the farmers themselves. Once large-scale processing appeared, it paid to utilize such by-products as hides, tallow, mash, and bran. Plants making shoes, harness, soap, candles, lard, and feed complemented the mills, distilleries, and packing plants or combined with them. The large amounts of regional exports required containers—barrels at this time—and boats, especially since much of the region's output was sent to New Orleans on one-way flatboats or rafts. All these activities required sizable work forces and so contributed to urban growth. Urbanization increased the markets for foodstuffs and wood. The towns also served as distribution centers for manufactured goods from the East and Europe.

The Ohio Valley became thickly settled, with a substantial urban population, as a result of this concentration on commercial agriculture. The Old Northwest depended on eastern markets for its exports and on eastern factories for its industrial goods. Thus, there was great interest in developing efficient transportation links. Initially, goods were sent down tributary streams to the Ohio and Mississippi rivers and then to New Orleans for export or shipment to the East. Later, canals and railroads gave more direct access to seaboard markets. The many small-scale producers of basic export commodities required concentration points for exports and both local and regional distribution centers for the goods those exports purchased.

The Stronghold of the Small Town

Few midwestern farmers were more than a day's wagon ride away from a town where they could exchange agricultural products for other goods and services. Typically, the small town had its general store, which did duty as a tavern and social club. There farm products could be sold or bartered for tools, cloth, salt, whiskey, and many other items. The town would also offer the specialist services of a blacksmith and a saw-mill, gristmill, and perhaps others, to process goods. There might be a distillery and some small-scale manufacturing, along with banks, churches, and lawyers (specializing in land sales). Some local government functions would also be available: at least the circuit judge on occasion, and more if the town were a county seat.

The town would also have a school, and others would probably be scattered through the countryside. Education was valued in the Midwest. It enabled the new generation to read

Scripture, but it also equipped them for economic activity. Each midwestern farm was a small business, where information had to be assimilated and evaluated and decisions made about the type of crops produced and the techniques used under intensely competitive conditions. Farmers found the ability to read, write, and "cipher" useful. Land speculation required a knowledge of the law and surveying. Schools thus provided useful services to the population and were established and supported by government. Before the financial debacles of the early 1840s, public support through state government was likely to be available for transportation improvements, and sometimes for banks as well. After that time, the basis of support shifted from state to local government and to private enterprise.

Regional Centers

The Old Northwest was not merely an agricultural region. The very nature of the area's agriculture and products necessitated considerable urban development. Cities such as Cincinnati, Pittsburgh, Louisville, Cleveland, St. Louis, and Chicago began as lake or river ports and centers for processing and distribution, but they quickly developed further. Transportation and the processing industries, as noted, encouraged a variety of related activities. Overall population and income growth fueled an ever-expanding range of other economic activities.

Since agricultural implements were bulky and difficult to ship, manufacturers decided early to locate their production facilities near their midwestern markets, rather than in the more industrialized East. Chicago, using its position as a lake port for prairie exports as well as a regional distribution center, became the largest lumber market in the world. Here the forest products of the upper Midwest could be distributed to prairie dwellers who lacked local timber or exported to the East. Other industry began to exploit the coal, copper, lead, and iron ore of the region. By 1860, Cincinnati was still a meat-packing center, but it was also making locomotives, an outgrowth of its early steamboat industry. Chicago was spewing out the network of railroads that would make it the regional metropolis. Major industrialization of the Midwest would occur after the Civil War, but the region's diversification from agriculture was under way.

The Innovative Environment

Grain and meat production from a host of small family-operated farms provided a receptive atmosphere for innovation. Each farm's income was limited by the amount of labor available; the more each produced, the higher its income. Since there were thousands of such farms, no one unit's production could influence the price of the region's agricultural staples. Changes that increased productive capacity were therefore welcome. Innovation was also a defensive procedure. Even though no single farmer's increased output could reduce prices, a simultaneous rise in production by many farms might increase supply faster than demand, driving prices down. Under such circumstances, the individual farmer's only hope of maintaining or increasing income lay in reducing costs of production faster than prices fell. Thus there was keen interest in any innovation that promised to increase the output of each unit of labor. Labor supplies themselves were difficult to increase: hired help was scarce and undependable, and even children would eventually grow up and leave home.

If natural conservatism was a barrier to innovation, it was overcome by the highly competitive nature of midwestern agriculture and the demonstrated effectiveness of the new methods. It should not be forgotten that many of the new machines saved long hours of grueling labor in addition to raising incomes; some might have been adopted even if they had no effect on money incomes. The nature of the land and the variety of commodities that it could produce also favored innovation. Large, level fields were especially suited to machinery. The shortage of wood on the prairies forced new solutions to building, fencing, and heating. Farther west, the lack of surface water would encourage another search for new methods. The midwestern farm was thus a training school for rational decision making.[12]

SOUTHERN AGRICULTURE

The antebellum South was vastly different from other regions of the United States. In its major exports, the nature of much of its agriculture, its relative lack of urbanization, and—above all—the existence of slavery, the agricultural economy of the South was unique.

The Cotton Kingdom

The southern frontier moved westward nearly as rapidly as the northern (see Table 6.1). Because cities were almost totally absent in the South, population density was less than in the North Central region. Both areas thus had many frontier characteristics in common, but they also differed significantly. Midwestern farmers produced a variety of cash crops and livestock products, but in the South, agricultural expansion centered overwhelmingly on cotton. After the cotton gin made upland cotton a profitable crop, its cultivation spread rapidly. Cotton could be grown on a wide variety of soils, but just as in the Old Northwest, yields rose as cultivation moved west. Upland Georgia was more productive than South Carolina, and Mississippi and Alabama soils were better still. The deep alluvial soil of the lower Mississippi valley in Arkansas, Louisiana, and East Texas proved best of all.

[12] Davis et al., *American Economic Growth*, p. 396.

Cotton could be grown on farms of almost any size.[13] In most years from 1815 to 1860, prices made its cultivation highly profitable. Britain's appetite for raw cotton appeared insatiable, and the growing textile industries of the northeastern United States and continental Europe added to the demand. As a supplier, the American South had no peer: Egypt and India could not match its productivity. Through this entire period, it was the largest single producer in the world. Cotton's importance among American exports has already been discussed.[14]

The South's concentration on its principal cash crop shaped the entire region's economic development. While the South also produced and exported tobacco, rice, sugar, and hemp, and some areas produced surpluses of food and livestock, the combined value of all other antebellum southern exports was never more than a fraction of that of cotton. Even so, it is indicative of the productivity of nineteenth-century agriculture that corn cultivation required more land than any other southern crop.[15]

Settlement Patterns in the South

Unlike the Midwest's agricultural exports, cotton required little processing to make it portable. The South possessed an extensive network of navigable rivers that allowed easy shipment to coastal ports for export. These characteristics did not encourage the growth of cities and towns. In the entire "New South," only New Orleans and Mobile were among the 25 largest cities in America, and Mobile was 25th. Even New Orleans owed its development more to its status as the port of the Midwest than to regional activity. Most cotton was produced by plantations rather than family-operated farms, further reducing the need for local concentra-

tion and distribution centers. Among all southern states, only Louisiana did not rank at the bottom of an index of urbanization, and Louisiana owed its rank almost entirely to New Orleans.[16]

Industry

Since there were few cities and towns, the range of other economic activities was more restricted in the South than in either the Midwest or the East. There was much less manufacturing than in the East, although it has been claimed that southern industry compared quite favorably with that of the Midwest—particularly in cotton textiles[17]—and fewer and less varied service activities than in the other regions. The South might produce cotton, but its major crop was financed, insured, transported, and processed into cloth by Britain and the American North. Southern manufacturing also was handicapped by the region's concentration on cotton exports. This nullified any protection from competition that distance from foreign industrial centers might otherwise have provided. Cotton was very bulky in relation to manufactured goods. Consequently ships traveled to southern ports only partly full, and might even make the trip in ballast, because they could be certain of obtaining a cargo there. Shippers would be willing to carry any freight that paid more than its cost of loading and unloading and would charge very low rates for shipments to southern ports. The region's concentration on agriculture and the existence of slavery also reduced the potential industrial work force; the South had nothing comparable to the "mill girls" who staffed New England's cotton mills.[18]

[13] G. Wright, *The Political Economy of the Cotton South* (New York: Norton, 1978), pp. 18, 28.
[14] D. North, *The Economic Growth of the United States, 1790–1860* (Englewood Cliffs, N.J.: Prentice-Hall, 1961), table A–VIII, p. 233. See also the introduction to this section and Chapter 4.
[15] Wright, *The Political Economy*, p. 18.

[16] North, *The Economic Growth*, p. 130. See also A. Niemi, *U.S. Economic History: A Survey of the Major Issues* (Chicago: Rand McNally, 1975), pp. 143–145.
[17] F. Bateman and T. Weiss, "Comparative Regional Development in Antebellum Manufacturing," *Journal of Economic History* (March 1975).
[18] G. Wright, "Cheap Labor and Southern Textiles before 1880," *Journal of Economic History* (September 1979).

Education

Education was also less developed in the South than elsewhere in the United States. Because of slavery, a smaller portion of the population was legally eligible for schooling in any case, and the area's lack of urbanization increased costs per student. Planters, who dominated the South's political as well as economic life, appeared unwilling to support schooling that did little to benefit them—especially since they as owners of most of the taxable property would have to finance it.[19] Planters' children were taught by tutors or attended private schools. The point should not be overstressed: literacy rates were lower among free southerners than in the North, but the difference was on the order of 85 percent versus 95 percent.[20] Further, the immediate impact of lower levels of education is open to question; it may have hindered adjustment to changed conditions after the Civil War, but literacy was not needed for most nineteenth-century industrial jobs.

The Myth of Southern Underdevelopment

Much of the contemporary view of the antebellum South is inaccurate. The lack of cities, limited manufacturing, and the existence of staple-crop agriculture, plantations, and slavery have perpetuated ideas that are not valid. First, most planters in the "New South" were not the heirs of ancient wealth. Apart from older areas along the Mississippi and the colonial settlements in Virginia and the Carolinas, most of the South, like the Midwest, was in 1860 only a generation or so removed from

primitive wilderness. The great plantation houses in the interior evidenced very recent ascents to wealth, often by the current inhabitants. Many who lived in the "big house" had settled the region when it was still raw frontier, and not a few had worked alongside their slaves clearing the land and planting the first crops. Income status in the South was not fixed. With luck and favorable cotton prices, it was possible to expand a family farm into a plantation, although this became more difficult after 1850. It is true, however, that many plantations were offshoots of those on the seaboard, the direct result of migration by all or part of the work force of some Tidewater planter—perhaps under the direction of a younger son—to new and more fertile soil.

The South's income distribution was not particularly unequal by contemporary standards. The picture of the free southern population as a small class of planters and a much larger group of subsistence farmers who had little or no connection to the market economy is false. Most farms in the South (52 percent) were operated by owners and their families, with no slaves and little hired labor, a pattern quite similar to that in the North. Many planters, particularly in the sugar region, would be millionaires in today's terms, but income distribution in the South was more even than it was in northern cities and differed little from that of the agricultural Midwest.[21] Plantations did not concentrate exclusively on cotton production; most produced enough food for their

[19] D. North, *Growth and Welfare in the American Past*, 2d ed. (Englewood Cliffs, N.J.: Prentice-Hall, 1974), pp. 89—91. This point is not repeated in the latest edition.

[20] In 1860, literacy rates for free adult southerners ranged from 77 percent to 90 percent; the average for the United States was 91.7 percent. A. Niemi, Jr., *United States Economic History*, 2d ed. (Chicago: Rand McNally, 1980), pp. 172–173.

[21] R. Fogel and S. Engerman, *Time on the Cross: The Economics of American Negro Slavery*, 2 vols. (Boston: Little, Brown, and Co., 1974), vol. I, p. 254. As in many other areas, Fogel and Engerman's views have been contested. It appears that wealth distribution in the rural South was far less equal than in the North, due largely to slaveholding, but income distribution among nonslaveholding rural southerners may have been quite similar to that of the rural North. See D. Yang, "U.S. Rural Wealth Distribution in 1860," *Explorations in Economic History* (January 1984); and M. Schmitz and D. Schaefer, "The Parker-Gallman Sample and Wealth Distributions for the Antebellum South: Reply," both in *Explorations in Economic History* (April 1985).

own labor forces, and some sold surpluses. Whatever additional food was needed was purchased locally from smaller farms or from areas too far north for cotton cultivation, but still within the South.

The southern economy was rural and heavily concentrated on agriculture, but it was not static. Settlement and population were expanding, and even more significantly, cotton production per slave rose from 119 pounds in 1808–1810 to 759 in 1859–1860. Comparable gains occurred in other crops as well. The figures overstate actual productivity gains, considering the increasing concentration on cash crops during the period and unusually favorable climatic and market conditions in 1859 and 1860.[22] But they do indicate that the South's economic efficiency was increasing, at least within its chief occupation.

The South was also able to reallocate its resources in response to market stimuli—again, within the agricultural context. Cotton production moved toward more fertile land, paralleling a similar movement in the Midwest. But when necessary, the South could marshal resources for nonagricultural purposes. The region's extensive railroad construction after 1850 received more support from the planter-dominated state legislatures than did similar ventures elsewhere.[23] By the least favorable method of comparison, southern per-capita incomes at least equalled those of the Midwest (an area often viewed as "dynamic") and rose more rapidly. In sum, the antebellum South was neither poor nor incapable of change.

The Economics of Slavery

Especially when inflicted by one race upon another, slavery is not an easy topic to analyze dispassionately. In the following discussion,

Cotton Production 1800–1860

= 200,000 bales of cotton

Slave Population 1800–1860

= 200,000 slaves

■ From 1800 to 1860, both the production of cotton and the number of slaves grew.
Source: *Rise of the American Nation*, Volume I, Liberty Edition, by Lewis Paul Todd and Merle Curti. (New York: Harcourt Brace Jovanovich, Inc., 1982) p. 298. Used with permission.

[22] A. Conrad and J. Meyer, "The Economics of Slavery in the Antebellum South," *Journal of Political Economy* (April 1958). On the influence of the 1859 and 1860 crop years, see D. Schaefer, "The Effect of the 1859 Crop Year Upon Relative Productivity in the Antebellum South," *Journal of Economic History* (December 1983).
[23] G. Taylor, *The Transportation Revolution, 1815–1860* (New York: M.E. Sharpe, 1962), p. 92.

words such as *efficient*, *profitable*, and *viable* do not have any connotation of good or bad, either in themselves or when used in conclusions about the economics of slavery. The involuntary servitude of black Americans was a monstrous injustice, but its economic and historical analysis requires more than moral judgments. This holds for any phenomenon that inspires strong emotions.

Profitability

After prolonged debate, some consensus has been reached on the economics of slavery in the antebellum South. First, it was profitable, both to those who sold slaves and to those who employed them. Detailed studies have confirmed slavery's profitability for cotton, sugar, rice, and mixed-crop farming under a variety of conditions. The same results emerge from different methods of analysis.

At one time it was argued that observed trends in slave prices (which rose) and cotton prices (which fell) demonstrated that slave agriculture was unprofitable, or at least becoming so. Slavery served, it was thought, as a device for social control or as a manifestation of conspicuous consumption on the part of impractical planters.[24] But if slaves are regarded as a capital good, a human "machine" that could be used to produce income, the data indicate that under most circumstances slaveholders received income from the sale of slave-produced crops about equal to that obtainable from contemporary industrial securities of comparable risk. If the cost of food, clothing, shelter, medical care, taxes, tools, and other items required to maintain a male slave's production (these expenditures may be viewed as the slave's income) are deducted from the value of the slave's output, there will still be a surplus in most years of the slave's adult life. If this surplus is discounted over the slave's entire life, an estimate

of the value of the slave to his owner may be obtained. Quantitative studies indicate that this value was usually greater than the price of purchase. Alternatively, the returns on investments in slaves exceeded the rates charged to those borrowing to make such investments. Rental rates for slaves (whose short-term services could be purchased from their owners) indicate that slaveholders could obtain incomes from hiring out their chattels approximately equal to those received by owners of other forms of capital of equal value.[25]

The calculation is more complicated for female slaves because they produced children as well as field crops. Slave children began work at six years of age and produced more than the cost of their upkeep at twelve. The value of these children, who could be sold or added to the work force, offset the lower field productivity of female slaves. The evidence on this point is quite conclusive: hiring rates (rentals) were lower for female slaves than for males, but sale prices, which entitled the new owner to offspring, were about equal.

Returns to slave agriculture varied with soil fertility, the prices obtained for slaves' output, and slaves' mortality and birth rates; but in general, slave owners would be hard-pressed to find alternative investments yielding significantly higher returns. In areas where agriculture itself did not produce high incomes, slaveholders could sell their surplus slaves for additional income.

That slavery in the antebellum South was profitable should be no great surprise. An institution so widespread must have generated returns equal to alternatives, unless noneconomic reasons fostered its continuation. But the noneconomic motives do not appear strong. If slaves were investment that could be acquired by large numbers of owners, reasonably efficient markets would ensure that the return on

---

[24] Whether this view was ever really held by historians is in dispute. See G. Wright, "New and Old Views on the Economics of Slavery," *Journal of Economic History* (June 1973).

[25] Lebergott, *The Americans*, pp. 213–217. See also J. Reid, Jr., "Antebellum Southern Rental Contracts," *Explorations in Economic History* (January 1976).

an investment in slaves would approximately equal that obtainable on other assets, holding risks of ownership constant.

Viability

Moreover, slavery was viable: the costs (including interest) of rearing slaves were less than the prices at which they could be sold, and the differential widened between 1815 and 1860.[26] There is no reason to doubt that slavery was primarily an economic institution. Slave prices rose and fell in accordance with those of major crops and individual slaves' productive capabilities and skills. Since slave prices were at an all-time high in 1860 (both in absolute terms and in relation to their rental prices), slaveholders apparently expected the profitability of the institution to continue or improve; one does not pay more for a capital asset if its prospective return is becoming smaller or less certain.

The Prevalence of Slavery

Slaveholding was not universal among southern whites, and not all slaveholders were plantation operators. About half of all southern white families owned one or more slaves. But most slaves were held by only 12 percent of all slave owners, and approximately half held no more than four slaves each.[27] The proportion of all slaves held by large-scale owners was rising by 1860; the proportion of slave owners within the white population was declining.

Slave Prices

Slaves were expensive: the price of a prime field hand rose from $700 in 1810 to $1,800 in 1860. The profitability of slaveholding and slaves' high prices greatly influenced the treatment accorded slaves. Owners of such expensive and

[26] Y. Yasuba, "The Profitability and Viability of Plantation Slavery in the United States," *Economic Studies Quarterly* (September 1961).
[27] A. Niemi, *U.S. Economic History,* pp. 149, 161.

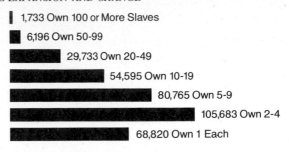

1,733 Own 100 or More Slaves

6,196 Own 50-99

29,733 Own 20-49

54,595 Own 10-19

80,765 Own 5-9

105,683 Own 2-4

68,820 Own 1 Each

■ The number of slave-owning families in 1850 is shown in this graph.
Source: The American Pageant, A History of the Republic, 7th ed., by Thomas A. Bailey and David M. Kennedy. (Lexington, MA: D. C. Heath and Co., 1983) p. 333. Used with permission.

profitable assets might be expected to try to keep them productive. This would mean giving slaves adequate food, housing, and other maintenance. It would also mean encouraging increases in slave numbers.

Trends in the Slave Population

The broad data are consistent with what we might deduce from economic theory. The slave population of the United States rose from 894,000 in 1800 to 3,954,000 in 1860. This was a rate of increase roughly comparable to the domestic growth of the white population. Immigration further increased whites' numbers but did little to raise slave numbers. After 1808, U.S. imports of slaves were forbidden through a provision of the Constitution. Although some slaves were smuggled in after that date, the largest estimate for the 1808–1860 period is 250,000, and most are much smaller. Since slave productivity also increased at least as much as that of the general population, it follows that the treatment of slaves, at least in physical terms, was adequate to produce both population growth and productivity increases similar to those achieved by free Americans.

Most slaves were employed in agriculture, but some worked in mining, lumbering, manufacturing, and domestic service. Since there were fewer substitutes for slaves in plantation agriculture than in urban occupations, where slaves were alternatives to free labor, urban slave populations fluctuated more than did those of rural slaves. Nor should we assume that all slaves were unskilled, either in agriculture or other occupations.

Slavery's Future in 1860: The Economic Indicators

Slavery on the eve of the Civil War was not threatened by economic factors. Not only was the institution profitable and viable at current costs and prices, but the South had plenty of unused land suitable for plantation agriculture, and cotton prices remained high at least through 1890. So profitable was it to rear slaves that their prices could have fallen by one-half before the profitability of slaveholding was endangered. There is also considerable evidence that slaves could be profitably employed in nonagricultural occupations.

Evidence for slavery's profitability and viability, of course, is not an endorsement of the institution. But it does indicate that the major threats to slavery in 1860 were political, ethical, social, and those personified in John Brown and his supporters, rather than economic. From the viewpoint of an 1860 slaveholder, the economic results generated by slavery were strong arguments for its continuation. And economic considerations, while not the only influence on slave owners, explain a great deal of their conduct. Planters responded to changes in cotton prices, slave productivity, and other income opportunities like rational, well-informed, and economically motivated businessmen, rather than impractical romantics or "cavaliers." Few slaveholders could have doubted slavery's benefits to them.

For small farmers, the most obvious route to wealth was to acquire a slave work force—a method they had seen enrich so many others. Planters with large work forces were wealthy men; 50 slaves in 1860 were worth at least $350,000 in 1985 dollars and would generate an income many times that of the average citizen. And yet 50 slaves was not a large work force. The owners of such valuable assets would no more abuse their slaves than their counterparts today would neglect the maintenance of expensive machinery.

New Slants on Established Views

About a decade ago, a book appeared that claimed that economic rationality drove planters well beyond providing adequate treatment to maintain or increase slave numbers and productivity. It claimed that slave owners offered a variety of positive incentives for improved performance to their work forces.[28] Even more than this, the authors claimed that the slaves responded to these incentives, in a sense cooperating with their masters. Fogel and Engerman do not deny that coercion was used— indeed, it is the very nature of slavery—but they claim that positive incentives were at least as commonly used to elicit greater effort as were whippings and loss of privileges. Bonuses, gifts, grants of leisure time, rights to garden plots, and the encouragement of a competitive spirit among the slaves were, they found, both used and effective. Perhaps the strongest incentive was one not normally associated with slavery: the chance to rise in status as the driver of a work gang, a skilled worker, or even a plantation overseer. The authors concluded that much of all work supervision on plantations was done by the slaves themselves, with virtually all work gang leaders and perhaps 75 percent of all overseers (the top nonownership management) being bondsmen.[29] In responding to positive incentives, and even more in directing the labor of others, slaves accepted their condition. Fogel and Engerman do not claim that slaves welcomed their servitude, merely that

---

[28] Fogel and Engerman, *Time on the Cross.*
[29] Ibid., p. 212.

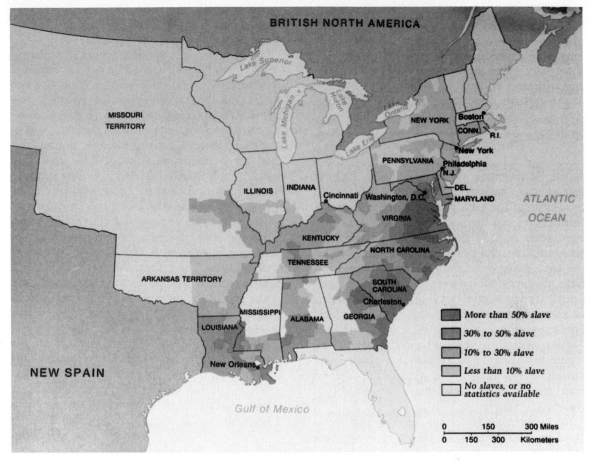

■ This map illustrates the concentration of slaves in 1820.
Source: From *America Past & Present, Volume I,* by Robert A. Devine and T. H. Breen, p. 330.
Copyright © 1984 by Scott, Foresman and Company. Reprinted by permission.

they took advantage of what limited opportunities their condition afforded.

The living conditions of American slaves described in *Time on the Cross* compare quite well with those of contemporary urban industrial workers. Diets, while monotonous and far short of modern nutritional standards, were hearty. Slaves could supplement their rations; most families had garden plots to grow food for themselves or even for sale and a chance to raise livestock as well. Some could use their leisure time for hunting or fishing. Housing,

according to this view, was comparable to that of northern workers, although standards varied widely between plantations. Clothing and medical care were adequate by contemporary standards. The treatment of slaves was surprisingly mild: the typical slave was whipped perhaps once a year, and care was taken to avoid serious injury. While this is not "mild" treatment by modern standards, whipping and beating were by no means unknown punishments for free Americans in the nineteenth century. Hours of labor were if anything fewer than those of free

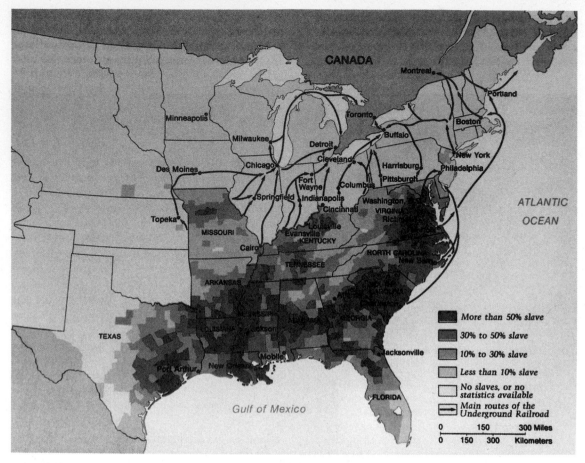

■ By 1860, slaves were more widely distributed than they had been in 1820.
Source: From *America Past & Present, Volume I,* by Robert A. Devine and T. H. Breen, p. 331.
Copyright © 1984 by Scott, Foresman and Company. Reprinted by permission.

agricultural labor, although slave work was more intense.

Fogel and Engerman also found that economic rationality governed slave owners' attitudes toward slaves' family lives. They claim that the nuclear family was strongly supported by slaveholders. Although slave marriages had no legal standing, planters encouraged them because they made for a more tranquil and productive work force and a higher birthrate. To further these goals, it was claimed, slave marriages were seldom broken up by the sale of one partner. Most slaves sold were single young adults, and sales of young children were uncommon, perhaps no more than the incidence of orphans. Promiscuity, forced marriages, and interracial sexual relations were strongly opposed by most slaveholders not only because they were immoral, but even more because they reduced productivity. Slaves were exploited in that they received less than the value of what they produced (if not, there was no economic basis for slavery), but the extent of exploitation was surprisingly small if all costs of slave maintenance were considered. Slaves were also exploited, however, by working conditions that free laborers, white or black, would not accept—the gang system and the requirement that slave women perform field labor.

The Economic Efficiency of Slavery

The authors of *Time on the Cross* concluded that such treatment of slaves paid off. Slaves can be considered an intermediate good in the production process. In this analysis, slave maintenance costs ("income") are subtracted from free southerners' incomes and slaves are deducted from the total southern population. This process considers slaves to be a productive asset, but not the consumers toward whose wishes economic activity is directed. With this approach, southern incomes compare favorably with those in other regions of the United States, both in amount and rate of growth (see Table 6.3).

If slave incomes and population are incorporated in the totals, southern per-capita incomes for 1860 were exceeded only by Australia, Britain, and the northern United States. Even if, as has been claimed, Fogel and Engerman understated slave maintenance costs by 60 percent, these conclusions would not substantially change. By contemporary world standards, the South was wealthy, and by some criteria, it generated incomes equal or superior to those of any other area.

Southern Agricultural Productivity

Since these southern incomes originated in a largely agricultural economy, and manufacturing incomes were much higher than agricultural for the country as a whole, they imply that southern agriculture was considerably more efficient than other regions'. In Fogel and Engerman's view, southern agriculture was in aggregate 35 percent more productive than northern (the South produced 35 percent more output per unit of input). Slave-using farms in general were 40 percent more efficient, and large plantations in the "New South," which combined efficiently organized slave work forces, economies of scale, and especially fertile soil, were a startling 53 percent more productive. Even southern farms employing only free labor were 9 percent more efficient than their northern counterparts.[30]

The portrait of the antebellum South and slavery that emerges from *Time on the Cross* departs considerably from the conventional picture. In the Fogel and Engerman study, slavery did not retard southern economic development; instead, it contributed greatly to the achievements of a wealthy and dynamic regional economy. The slaves themselves had a share in the incomes and opportunities produced (albeit a limited one with many jobs beyond the aspirations of even the most talented slave and incomes, at least in the short run, gained at the sufferance of the master and their form determined by him). Slaves responded positively to incentives. The South was agricultural and rural, but this structure was merely a logical response to its region's comparative advantages and conveyed economic gains rather than imposed income penalties.

The Fogel and Engerman study is controversial, but it must be evaluated on the grounds staked out by its authors, not the distorted views attributed to it by others. In no way did Fogel and Engerman conclude that slavery was "good" or "justified" or that the slaves liked it. Nor do they imply that slaves received "fair" or "just" shares of the income resulting from their work.

[30] Ibid., pp. 192–196.

**Table 6.3 Per-Capita Income and Rates
of Increase by Region, 1840–1860**

Region	Per-Capita Income with Slaves Considered as Consumers		Growth in Per-Capita Income over Period (Total Population)
	1840	1860	
North	$109*	$147	29%
Northeast	129	181	40
North Central	65	89	37
South	74	103	39
South Atlantic	66	84	27
East South Central	69	89	29
West South Central	151	184	22
United States	96	128	33

Region	Per-Capita Income with Slaves as Intermediate Goods		Growth in Per-Capita Income over Period (Free Population)
	1840	1860	
North	$110	$142	29%
Northeast	130	183	41
North Central	66	90	36
South	105	150	43
South Atlantic	96	124	39
East South Central	92	124	35
West South Central	238	274	15
United States	109	144	32

*All dollar values in 1860 dollars. In 1860, the purchasing power of the dollar was approximately eight times that of 1985.
Source: Adapted from S. Engerman, "The Effects of Slavery upon the Southern Economy," *Explorations in Economic History* (Winter 1967).

The Conditions of Life under Slavery

Slavery reduced human beings to the status of intelligent work animals and was brutal by its very nature. Slaves were forced to work under conditions such as the gang system (in which tasks were assigned to a work group supervised by a "driver"), which free labor would not accept at any wage payable by the proceeds of such toil. In addition, slaves had only minimal control over their own fate. They could be sold, and they had no defense against a sadistic or lecherous overseer in the short run, or against a similarly inclined master in the long run. Fogel and Engerman conclude that slaves simply made the best life possible given the restricted opportunities open to them. If they could not change their circumstances, responding to positive incentives at least made their lives a bit more comfortable. It might even be said that the Fogel and Engerman view is less patronizing than those stressing blacks' "difficulties" adjusting to freedom after 1865.

Achieving freedom by flight or revolt was not a very realistic possibility for slaves. Whether from fear of the unknown (often a powerful influence on the uneducated) or from a realistic assessment of the opportunities available to free blacks outside the South, incentives to escape were not strong. The famous "Underground Railway" apparently freed only some 25,000 slaves in the entire antebellum period. Plantations operated for half a century along the Ohio River, where a slave had only to find a boat or even a log to cross to free territory on a summer night. Although the prospects of slave revolts were widely discussed, less than a half dozen organized rebellions by slaves occurred in the entire history of the institution in North America. Nor does the conduct of plantation owners indicate that they felt any serious threat. On the typical plantation, slave owners were heavily outnumbered and had no means of summoning help rapidly. Yet they slept in wooden houses among their slaves and felt no compunctions about close contact with work forces using potentially lethal tools. Most adult white males had little hesitation over leaving their farms to fight in the Civil War.

It must be remembered that the conclusions in *Time on the Cross* are based on aggregate data. The authors do not argue that there were no exceptions, for better or worse, to the averages they compiled—only that those averages give a more typical picture than do individual cases out of context.

Opposing Views: The Critique of Time on the Cross

The work of Fogel and Engerman may be more valuable for the discussion and study that it provoked on the issue of slaves' treatment and response than for any claims initially made. Subsequent work has both supported and criticized their study.[31]

[31] For an extensive summary of the debate, see P. Passell

Diets and Medical Care

Some points are now fairly clear. The conclusion that the slaves received adequate diets for the work they performed is supported by both demographic data and analyses of the diet itself. Slave death rates were about the same as those of free southerners, and their population and output increased in a similar manner. It has, however, been claimed that the diets of slave children below working ages were seriously deficient, even though those of their parents were adequate.[32] Some of the alternative diets that Fogel and Engerman's critics proposed combined poorer nutritional value with higher money costs to slave owners; others imply that slaveholders would knowingly risk $1,500 slaves for savings of $3 per year.[33] Similar criteria apply to medical care; nineteenth-century doctors might not be very effective, but what slave owner able to calculate the changes in slave values caused by a quarter-cent variation in cotton prices would begrudge fifty cents for a doctor's visit?

Housing and Work Incentives

Fogel and Engerman's favorable comparisons of slave housing and apparel to those of northern workers appear overstated. They apparently matched slaves against the poorest northern slum dwellers, thus seriously understating the living standards of most urban laborers: the typical worker did not live in what then was considered a slum, but *Time on the Cross* compares northern slums to slave quarters. Likewise, that work is probably too optimistic on the subject of slave treatment and incentives. The available data are insufficient for firm conclusions on the incidence of phys-

and S. Lee, *A New Economic View of American History* (New York: Norton, 1978), Chaps. 8 and 9. Lebergott, *The Americans,* Chaps. 18 and 19, contributes a well-reasoned presentation of the quantitative data.

[32] R. Steckel, "A Peculiar Population: The Nutrition, Health, and Mortality of American Slaves from Childhood to Maturity," *Journal of Economic History* (September 1986).
[33] Lebergott, *The Americans,* Chap. 18, Appendix A.

ical punishment and slaves' reactions to it. Both sides appear to miss the real point regarding slaves' access to supervisory or overseer jobs. It is not so much the portion actually held by slaves that is germane, but whether enough openings were available to furnish incentives for greater effort on their part.

Family Stability

Data on family stability and the degree to which slave owners encouraged or discouraged it are insufficient to support a firm conclusion. Both sides' arguments about the effect of sales on family stability appear suspect. Fogel and Engerman concluded that the majority of slaves entering the "New South" from the older plantation states came through the migration of entire labor forces with their owners. Their critics emphasize a much greater role for the sale of individual slaves, but their arguments rely heavily on data from Maryland, the one major slaveholding state whose slave population was falling in the mid-nineteenth century—an indication that slave sales or migration were much more common there than throughout the South. No firm conclusion has been reached on the question of slave family stability, but the aggregate data appear to support Fogel and Engerman more than their critics.[34] Still, whatever the statistical probabilities, slaves could not control this source of family disruption and it may have generated a great deal of fear.

Exploitation

The discussion on the amount of exploitation of slaves has reached little common ground, aside from a consensus that it existed. Fogel and Engerman view the question as an investment, as the slave owner might. In this case, the costs of slave ownership include not only the current maintenance of adult slaves, but also rearing costs (including expenditures on slaves who died before reaching maturity) and costs for the nonworking elderly, plus interest on such expenses. Others have approached the problem from the viewpoint of the adult slave and treated the entire difference between current maintenance costs and the value of the slave's production as the burden of exploitation."[35]

This approach yields a much greater burden than does the Fogel and Engerman method. The largest beneficiaries of this exploitation were not the slave owners, but the consumers of cotton cloth, whose aggregate gains were far greater. Cotton planting was a highly competitive industry, and prices were continually pushed down toward production costs. Cheap cotton cloth was in part a consequence of the exploitation of American slaves, and this fabric was used throughout the nineteenth-century world.

The Economics of Southern Agriculture

The efficiency of southern agriculture is another area of controversy. It is difficult to determine whether the South's undeniable poverty after 1865 was a new development unless we know the region's antebellum income levels. It has been pointed out that much of what Fogel and Engerman regarded as "greater southern efficiency in agriculture" might instead be credited to a variety of factors: the South's ability to produce semitropical crops to which the North was unsuited, the effects of two extraordinarily favorable crop years (1859–1860), and the different working conditions of slave and

---

[34] R. Sutch, "The Breeding of Slaves," in S. Engerman and E. Genovese, *Race and Slavery in the Western Hemisphere: Quantitative Studies* (Princeton, N.J.: Princeton University Press, 1978), and H. Gutman, *The Black Family in Slavery and Freedom* (New York: Pantheon Books, 1976).

[35] See Fogel and Engerman, *Time on the Cross*, pp. 244–246; and R. Ransom and R. Sutch, *One Kind of Freedom: The Economic Consequences of Emancipation* (Cambridge, England: Cambridge University Press, 1977), pp. 3–4.

free labor.[36] The economies of scale of large plantations have also been downplayed, since the large plantation could concentrate on cash crops more fully than could the small owner-operated farm.

Efficiency and Farm Size

Planters could grow mainly cash crops and buy any food they were unable to produce. If crops failed or prices dropped, they had access to credit, slaves for collateral, and possibly cash reserves to tide the plantation over to the next crop. The small farmer could only borrow against the farm itself and risked losing his land if things turned out badly. In addition, the small farm maximized welfare while the plantation chiefly maximized money income. Leisure for his family had a very different value to the small farmer than did leisure for the slaves to the planter. Risk considerations and the limits imposed on total crop size by labor constraints also reduced cotton's returns to small farmers.[37] Such arguments appear to have a good deal of merit, but they do not alter the fact that the South's agricultural system was able to generate incomes that were high by contemporary standards—and rising. At least in comparison to other farming areas, it is difficult to describe the South as inefficient.

Regional Incomes and Trends

A final point involves the comparative growth rates of northern and southern incomes. If the arguments for excluding slaves from income figures for the South are accepted, income growth for the South as a whole was much higher than for any subregion within it (see Table 6.3). This resulted from the relocation of resources from regions where incomes were low to those where they were high: from the Old to the New South. Gains from this source could not continue indefinitely. Was this evi-

dence of real growth in incomes? Was the southern economy capable only of reallocating resources between regions, but not between occupations? (Income growth in other regions of the United States also was increased by this factor, albeit not to the same extent.)

Income gains within subregions of the South, while lower than the U.S. average, were still respectable. Thus, the charge that the South could not raise its per-capita income cannot be fully accepted; continued growth in southern productivity was possible. Whether such gains could have kept pace with the North is problematical. Some analysts have concluded that the South, burdened with slavery and its alleged inflexibilities plus a lack of educated, adaptable free labor, would have found the transition to industry difficult if not impossible. Others have pointed out that the South did not industrialize at this time because it had little economic incentive to do so; its comparative advantage in agriculture generated incomes and growth comparable to those of the manufacturing regions. The antebellum South *did* not change, but can it be concluded that it *could* not change? To free southerners in 1860, the need to industrialize cannot have appeared very pressing. Specialization along traditional lines did not appear to have handicapped the South at that time. Slavery would have to be abolished for noneconomic reasons—as it was.

GROWTH AND DIVERSITY IN AGRICULTURE

Agriculture remained the principle occupation in America in 1860, as it had been in 1815. But the pace of change was increasing rapidly for American farmers. Competition from distant producers now affected their markets, and they sold more of their output than they had in the colonial era. Far more choices now had to be made as to location, types of crops, access

[36] See Schaefer, "The Effect of the 1859 Crop Year."
[37] G. Wright, *The Political Economy*, p. 3.

to markets, methods, and particularly the use of available machinery. The growth of other sectors of the economy allowed farmers to consider movement to new jobs as well. Wider alternatives offered greater scope for efficient reallocation of people; rising incomes indicated that even within agriculture, people were taking advantage of the new opportunities.

SELECTED REFERENCES

Bogue, A., and M. Bogue "Profits and the Frontier Land Speculator." *Journal of Economic History* (March 1957).

Conrad, A., et al. "Slavery as an Obstacle to Economic Growth in the United States." *Journal of Economic History* (December 1967).

Conrad, A., and J. Meyer "The Economics of Slavery in the Antebellum South." *Journal of Political Economy* (April 1958).

David, P., et al. *Reckoning with Slavery*. Oxford, England: Oxford University Press, 1976.

David, P., and P. Temin. "Slavery: The Progressive Institution?" *Journal of Economic History* (September 1974).

Fogel, R., and S. Engerman. *Time on the Cross: The Economics of American Negro Slavery*, 2 vols., Boston: Little, Brown & Co., 1974.

Genovese, E. *The Political Economy of Slavery*. New York: Random House, 1967.

———. *Roll, Jordan, Roll: The World the Slaveowners Made*. New York: Random House, 1976.

Genovese, E. and S. Engerman. *Race and Slavery in the Western Hemisphere: Quantitative Studies*. Princeton, N.J.: Princeton University Press, 1978.

Goldin, C. *Urban Slavery in the American South*. Chicago: University of Chicago Press, 1976.

Gray, L. *History of Agriculture in the Southern United States to 1860*. Washington, D.C.: Kelley, 1933.

North, D. *The Economic Growth of the United States, 1790–1860*. Englewood Cliffs, N.J.: Prentice-Hall, 1961.

North, D., et al. *Growth and Welfare in the American Past: A New Economic History*. 3d ed. Englewood Cliffs, N. J.: Prentice-Hall, 1983.

Parker, W., ed. *The Structure of the Cotton Economy of the Antebellum South*. Washington, D.C.: Agricultural History Society, 1970.

Ransom, R. and R. Sutch. *One Kind of Freedom: The Economic Consequences of Emancipation*. Cambridge, England: Cambridge University Press, 1977.

Rosenberg, N. *Technology and American Economic Growth*. New York: Harper & Row, 1972.

Stampp, K. *The Peculiar Institution*. New York: Knopf, 1956.

U.S. Department of Commerce, Bureau of the Census. *Historical Statistics of the United States: Colonial Times to 1970*. Washington, D.C.: Government Printing Office, 1975.

Wright, G. *The Political Economy of the Cotton South*. New York: Norton, 1978.

Yasuba, Y. "The Profitability and Viability of Plantation Slavery in the United States." *Economic Studies Quarterly* (September 1961).

CHAPTER

7

THE ORIGINS
OF INDUSTRY

*I*n 1860, the U.S. economy was still basically agricultural. Almost 53 percent of the work force earned its living from the land, and the total value of agricultural products exceeded that of any other sector of the economy.[1] But the economy had made noteworthy strides in manufacturing, and agriculture's preeminence was fading. One worker in seven was employed in industry, and almost as many others worked at distributing, financing, or transporting manufactured goods or in construction. About one-third of the total value of U.S. output originated in manufacturing.[2]

This disparity betwwen the shares of employment and production in industry is significant: it indicates that productivity and incomes in that sector were about double the national average. The figures do not necessarily mean that the average manufacturing worker's wages were twice the average American's income, but they do indicate that resources employed in the industrial sector produced higher incomes for their owners than did most alternatives. Consequently, manufacturing was likely to continue to grow faster than the rest of the economy, as owners reallocated their capital, labor, and raw materials to uses that produced higher incomes. This is a typical pattern for new sectors of the economy: high resource productivity generates high rates of growth.

EARLY NINETEENTH-CENTURY MANUFACTURING

Accurate estimates of the value of aggregate output in the early nineteenth century are dif-

[1] U.S. Department of Commerce, Bureau of the Census, *Historical Statistics of the United States: Colonial Times to 1970,* 2 vols. (Washington, D.C.: Government Printing Office, 1975), 1:139, 239.
[2] Ibid., p. 239.

ficult to make. Most American families were far more self-sufficient than they are today, making many of their capital goods as well as most of what they consumed. For example, land clearance was a major investment for farmers on new land and a major component of the country's total investment, but its value is difficult to calculate.[3]

In this period, Americans, particularly farmers, made most of the clothing, tools, and other items used in their households. Sometimes they did everything from gathering raw materials to finishing the product; often they combined purchased components with home finishing. Yarn or cloth might be purchased and made into clothing, or the metal parts of tools from factories or the local blacksmith might be fitted with handles in the home. Food was virtually always processed into the form in which it reached the table by housewives. Specialists might be employed to process or finish homemade materials: masons might build a chimney or traveling cobblers make shoes or harness from leather the family had cured. But even in the absence of detailed data, it is clear that manufacturing grew. Some of its products replaced items previously made in the home and others were substituted for imports. From 1815 to 1860, industry and its products grew faster than the aggregate economy. After 1820, the importance of home manufactures declined, and the variety and state of finish of purchased goods increased.

Some American manufacturing for market existed even in colonial days. Ships, tar, iron, and salt were produced by specialized units that often employed considerable work forces. By the Revolution, flour milling and shoe production were developing along those lines as well. Especially in the North, farms often had a surplus of home manufactures for sale or barter. By 1860, however, manufacturing was the province of specialized producers for a

much greater range of items than just a few decades earlier. Some of industry's products had not existed in 1800. Only where transportation costs made factory-produced goods extremely expensive, as on the frontier, were home handicrafts still able to compete by 1860.

Sources of Economic Growth

Even though manufacturing grew faster than the aggregate economy and thus "pulled" it forward, industrialization was not the only source of American economic growth. As Chapter 6 indicated, agriculture was growing, although not at the same rate. Finance, banking, trade, construction, and transportation also grew, sometimes at rates as high as industry's. In 1860, even after very considerable growth, the manufacturing sector simply was not a large enough part of the overall economy to account for all of the increase in economic activity over the previous decade. Total U.S. output was increasing at about 5 percent annually in the 1850s, and about a third of total value added was in manufacturing. Had industry been the source of all growth, it would have had to grow at three times the rate of the entire economy, or about 15 percent per year. This is a most unlikely rate of growth for any broadly defined sector to sustain over a decade or more, especially considering that industry was well established several decades earlier. The growth of manufacturing undoubtedly increased the aggregate growth rate of the economy, but it was hardly the source of all economic development.

EARLY INDUSTRIALIZATION PATTERNS

The upswing in manufacturing apparently began quite early in the 1815–1860 period, probably in the 1820s. The cotton textile industry

[3] M. Primack, "Land Clearing under Nineteenth-Century Techniques: Some Preliminary Calculations," *Journal of Economic History* (December 1962).

was expanding rapidly then, and the production of woolen goods, carpets, paper, lead, refined sugar, salt, glass, steam engines, and preserved meat appears to have risen faster than population in this decade. This list includes only those items for which reasonably conclusive data are available; there may have been others as well.

Industrial growth continued over the next 30 years, although certainly not at a steady pace. Initially, especially for truly new products, demand may grow rapidly as consumers buy an item for the first time or substitute it for other goods. But once these needs are met, the rate of growth declines, and sales rise only at the pace of population and income growth, or even less. After a new industry's initial growth spurt begins to wane, the economy's growth leaders are other industries whose products are still being purchased for the first time by consumers and industrial users. Thus, new industries are a vital element in long-run economic growth. It should be noted that manufacturing activity in America not only began early in the country's history, but from the start involved a wide variety of items.

In 1860, the United States might still have been primarily an agricultural economy, but so were nearly all other nations. Industrialization here compared quite favorably with that in the rest of the world. By most estimates, the total value of manufactured goods produced in the United States was second only to that of Britain, at that time the acknowledged "workshop of the world." Even the least optimistic view ranked the United States no lower than fourth among the world's industrial powers.[4] Evidence that this country possessed a sizable, varied, and rapidly growing industrial sector from the 1820s on casts considerable doubt on the "takeoff" into sustained growth that Professor Rostow dates from the last two decades of the antebellum period. It also invalidates the idea that the American Civil War caused industrialization.

Adjustments after 1815

Manufacturing, especially as it had developed by 1860, was a new type of activity for most of the Americans it employed. The adjustments required for the transition were much greater than we might imagine today. As they had in agriculture, Americans began with European techniques and modified them to suit New World conditions. American factor proportions and markets differed from those of Britain; it soon became obvious that, in their original forms, British tools and methods were not ideal for American conditions. Factory production required adjustments from managers, workers, and consumers alike. Considerable foresight was required to see the potential in some innovations. Most Americans' incomes allowed little margin over basic needs in 1815, making completely new products very risky. Many of the first factories therefore concentrated on substitutes for imported goods, because markets for such items already existed.[5]

Moving from farm labor with hand tools to industrial work with powered machinery required difficult adjustments for many individuals. Working under somebody else's direction was hard enough for people accustomed to the individualism of farming, but now the pace of work was set by other people or, worse, machines. Nor did early machines always perform sufficiently better than older methods to "buy" immediate acceptance. Most new machines required a considerable period of testing and operation before they operated as expected, and even then might be only slightly better than the technology they replaced.

The reception innovations received could be crucial to their eventual success or failure.

---

[4] D. North, *The Economic Growth of the United States, 1790–1860* (Englewood Cliffs, N.J.: Prentice-Hall, 1961), p. v.

[5] Lebergott, *The Americans, An Economic Record* (New York: Norton, 1984), p. 130.

It makes a great deal of difference whether new machines are regarded as basically good ideas with "bugs" that need to be worked out, or as something new, different, and either inherently unworkable or threatening to established jobs. Workers had to adjust to life outside the factory as well; most industry was located in cities, and the contrast between rural and urban life was as great then as it has ever been. The American response appears to have been more favorable than that of other nations, including Britain.[6] New methods and products were welcomed, if not always universally, and attitudes and social institutions modified to accommodate them, rather than vice versa.

The Putting-Out System

In part because of these difficulties adjusting to new methods and new surroundings, some industries developed an intermediate step between domestic production and the factory. Called the putting-out system, it was especially prevalent with goods whose production required a great deal of hand labor. The putting-out system attempted to use resources that had few or low-productivity alternative uses, because they might be obtained at low cost.

Many farms, particularly in the North, had seasons when agricultural tasks did not fully occupy the available work force. The putting-out system used this labor force without requiring it to relocate to towns. Further, the workers supplied their own tools. Manufacturers or their agents brought raw materials to the farms, left instructions for completing the work, and returned later to pick up the finished goods and pay the workers. Labor remained largely independent under this system; the pace of work and to some extent its timing were determined by the individual. At a time when both social attitudes and transportation difficulties made it hard for women to work outside their homes, the putting-out system allowed them to earn a cash income. To the manufacturers, the putting-out system was a response to the chronic American shortages of capital and labor: not only might wages be lower than full-time workers would demand, but the investment in capital was far lower.

Drawbacks to the Putting-Out System

The putting-out system had disadvantages as well. It could be used mainly to produce items made by traditional hand methods, such as shoes, textiles, and clothing. It was difficult, if not impossible, to introduce new methods, because output came from numerous, scattered workers who owned their tools. The system did not allow any great degree of specialization, and in most cases did not provide full-time work. Workers and employers squabbled continuously over the amounts of raw materials furnished and the quantity and quality of goods made from them. Selling these products could be a nightmare: quality control and dependable delivery dates were all but impossible to achieve. In some seasons, the system competed with agriculture's demand for labor. For a few goods whose production could not be mechanized and required large amounts of unskilled labor working to its own schedules, the system persisted for a long time. "Panama" hats, for example, were produced in this manner. But for goods suited to factory production, the putting-out system was an inferior technique.[7]

---

[6] Landes, *The Unbound Prometheus: Technological Change and Industrial Development in Western Europe from 1750 to the Present* (Cambridge, England: Cambridge University Press, 1969), Chaps. 2, 3.

[7] For a theoretical discussion of the economics of centralized and decentralized control of production, see A. Alchian and H. Demsetz, "Production, Information Costs, and Economic Organization," *American Economic Review* (December 1972). A more historical treatment is A. Chandler, Jr., *The Visible Hand: The Managerial Revolution in American Business* (Cambridge, Mass.: Harvard University Press, 1977), Chaps. 1–4.

Table 7.1 Regional Manufacturing Comparisons, 1860

Region	Number of Establishments	Capital ($000,000)	Employees (000)	Total Output ($000,000)	Capital per Establishment (4)
New England	20,671	257	392	469	12,456
Middle states	53,287	435	546	802	8,164
Western states	33,350	174	189	347	5,216
Southern states	24,081	116	132	193	4,827
Pacific states	8,777	23	50	71	2,664

Region	Employment per Establishment	Output per Establishment ($)	Out per Employee ($)	Value Added per Employee ($)	Output per Capita ($)
New England	19	22,669	1,196	569	149
Middle states	10	15,057	1,168	656	96
Western states	6	10,395	1,838	769	38
Southern states	6	8,034	1,466	641	19
Pacific states	6	8,115	1,419	851	165

Source: Adapted from F. Bateman and T. Weiss, "Comparative Regional Development in Antebellum Manufacturing," *Journal of Economic History* (March 1975).

Regional Manufacturing Patterns

Manufacturing was not evenly distributed through the United States. It centered in the Middle Atlantic states and New England in this period. There was less activity in the Midwest, although indications of future growth appeared early. The South was not devoid of manufacturing activity,[8] but the high returns available in plantation agriculture deterred industrial investment. Nevertheless, as Table 7.1 reveals, southern manufacturing compared well with nearly every region of the United States except New England, the nation's industrial heartland. The very low output per capita figure for the South, however, reveals that only a small portion of that region's population was engaged in manufacturing.

In the Northeast, population densities were high by contemporary standards: there was a substantial rural population as well as more urbanization than elsewhere. New England farms appeared to produce people at least as easily as they did crops. Although the South had a substantial population, it had few urban concentrations, a lower overall density than New England, and greater opportunities in agriculture. In addition, slave labor's prices in industry were conditioned by national rather than local conditions, because slave labor was far more mobile than single females (an important source of labor, although not the most important).[9]

[8] F. Bateman and R. Weiss, "Manufacturing in the Antebellum South," *Research in Economic History* (Greenwich, Conn.: JAI Press, 1976), vol. I.

[9] G. Wright, "Cheap Labor and Southern Textiles before 1880," *Journal of Economic History* (September 1979).

■ The Assabet Manufacturing Company in Maynard, Massachusetts, is a prime example of Massachusetts' role in the American Industrial Revolution.
Source: The Bettmann Archive.

Large cities such as Philadelphia and New York combined access to labor, capital, and markets with the services of specialists in finance, construction, engineering, and distribution required to build factories and distribute their output. As seaports, they also had good access to transportation. With the exception of power sources and fuel for the iron industry, access to natural resources does not appear to have been a major constraint on the location of most industrial ventures in the antebellum period. Many of the early factories either used locally available materials or took advantage of water transportation.

The Cotton Textile Industry

From eighteenth-century England to contemporary Korea and Singapore, the manufacture of cotton textiles has been one of the first industries to appear in the process of economic development. The capital requirements are modest and technologically simple. The labor skills necessary for textile workers are readily learned by women and children, who are often less than fully employed in agricultural societies.

Textile production held other attractions: the demand for cotton cloth was expanding rapidly and was, at least prior to 1833, highly price elastic. Cotton cloth was more easily cleaned than wool and could be dyed in bright colors or even printed much like paper. Compared to linen, the only other lightweight fabric then available, it was much cheaper. The appearance of the first really inexpensive cloth allowed ordinary people some variety in their clothing. Prior to this time, cloth was so expensive that persons making wills carefully listed every article of clothing they possessed and assigned it to an heir. Now other innovations such as underwear, bed sheets, curtains, and a variety of other ornamental and useful items were within the reach of most of the population.

In Britain, where the new production methods were first developed, they reduced unit costs, especially at large volumes of output. The expanded production was easy to sell. Cotton cloth was initially a substitute for other materials, but as its price fell it became practical for a growing variety of uses as well as within the means of more and more customers.

Machine-Made Cotton Textiles

Efforts to produce cotton textiles with machinery in the United States date back to the 1790s. Copies of English machines were employed in these early efforts, with mixed results. The British had made breakthrough discoveries in the mechanization of textile production. In the latter half of the eighteenth century, they developed a series of machines, such as the spinning jenny, water frame, and mule, that produced unprecedented quantities of yarn and were soon adapted to water or steam power. Later, after prolonged development, power-operated looms came into use.

Machine production increased both the quantity and quality of cotton cloth, transforming it from a luxury fabric to an everyday material used by all economic classes. The new textile machines were simple to build and operate, and the cost of a fully equipped factory was low enough to allow even men of moderate means, singly or in partnership, to enter the industry. Consequently, cotton textile production expanded very rapidly. Highly competitive conditions (not only was entry easy, but few firms had a significant market share) forced producers to pass on the results of rapid technological progress to consumers. By 1820, Britain was selling its textiles all over the world.

The American Response. The English-style factories set up in the United States were not a great success at first. The machines so carefully copied from British originals were designed for an economy where capital and labor were more plentiful than in America. Given their higher costs for the required mix of inputs, American producers had great difficulty competing with imports from Britain. After 1808, embargo and then war furnished protection from overseas production, and the industry expanded rapidly, only to suffer a near-total collapse when British goods once again became available in 1815. By 1820, a few American producers were able to meet British competition within the American market—aided by transport costs and the U.S. tariff. In doing so, they learned some valuable lessons.

American producers modified British machines to obtain higher operating speeds and developed new types of power-driven looms. Because American capital costs were higher, it made sense to maximize output per machine-hour, particularly since scarce American labor as well as technological limits made multiple labor shifts impossible. Apparently, the experience gained in early operations was an important source of further productivity increases through "learning by doing."[10] The real price of cotton cloth fell steadily before 1860, a reflection of both productivity gains and a highly competitive industry.

The New Factory Work Force. Innovations were necessary in other areas as well. Prior to this time, America had only a tiny industrial work force, and almost no means of housing large numbers of workers in a limited area existed. Nor was it clear who should be recruited to work in the early factories. Two systems were developed. Factories from Rhode Island south along the Atlantic Seaboard hired entire families: husband, wife, and children all worked in the mills. From Massachusetts north, the bulk of the cotton mills' labor force was single young

[10] P. David, "Learning by Doing and Tariff Protection: A Reconsideration of the Case of the Antebellum United States Cotton Textile Industry," *Journal of Economic History* (September 1970).

women from rural areas. Few of these "factory girls" expected to spend more than three or four years in their jobs. To attract the women (or rather, to persuade their parents to allow them to take the new jobs), dormitories had to be built near the factories, and a full range of services—churches, stores, social facilities, and especially supervision—provided. Recruiting a labor force in northern New England was made easier by the scarcity of alternative jobs for respectable young women who wished to leave home before marriage.

A Formula for Success. The Boston Manufacturing Company discovered the formula that enabled American firms at last to meet the British challenge with some chance of success. Industrial espionage in Britain, improved looms at home, a plant integrating spinning and weaving, and a work force of young women were the main ingredients. Production was concentrated on a type of plain white cloth—a decision that maximized the protection afforded by shipping costs and tariffs. In addition, the firm was much larger and better capitalized than most American companies. It was founded in 1813, when the War of 1812 precluded effective competition during the critical shakedown

■ "Mill girls" were plentiful in Lowell, Massachusetts, during the 1830s. These young farm girls worked long hours in the textile mills because other opportunities were limited.
Source: Courtesy Massachusetts Historical Society.

period, another aid to survival. The Boston Company was one of just a handful of American textile firms to survive the British onslaught in 1815.

Initially, many American mills did not produce cloth. Instead, they made yarn, which was sold for home weaving. By 1824, however, the mills wove all the yarn they produced into cloth within their own walls.[11]

The Importance of Waterpower

The new spinning and weaving machinery required power, and in this New England was well favored. The region had plenty of well-situated waterpower. Especially north of Boston, the fall line (the point at which stream gradients increase) is often directly on the coast, allowing the textile mills to combine cheap water transportation for raw materials and finished goods with a source of power for their machinery. Initially, small- and medium-sized streams were used, since available engineering techniques could neither effectively dam large rivers nor harness the power they produced. By 1850, however, these problems had been overcome, and mills were built on the Merrimack and Connecticut rivers (where the dams exterminated the Atlantic salmon). By 1840, another source of power was available: steam power was becoming competitive with water even in New England.[12]

Waterwheels were improved over time, and by the 1850s the water turbine further increased the efficiency of waterpower. So important was waterpower to the budding textile industry that whole new towns—not merely the mills themselves—were built at favorable sites, such as Lowell, Lawrence, and Fall River in Massachusetts and Manchester in New Hamp-

---

[11] R. Zevin, "The Growth of Cotton Textile Production after 1815," in *The Reinterpretation of American Economic History*, eds. R. Fogel and S. Engerman (New York: Harper & Row, 1971), pp. 122–147.
[12] P. Temin, "Steam and Waterpower in the Early 19th Century," *Journal of Economic History* (June 1966).

shire. Up to 1860, waterpower appeared adequate for New England's needs, although nearly every possible dam site within 50 miles of the coast was in use. New England had no coal, and transporting it from producing areas was expensive. Firewood was barely adequate for residential needs in an era when wood was the only heating and cooking fuel and stoves were far less efficient than today. Perhaps the worst problem, however, was the difficulty of transporting wood.

Setting Up Shop

Would-be textile producers had to start by building their own machinery. England was more successful in prohibiting the export of machinery than in restricting the emigration of people who knew how to construct and operate it. British workers learned that Americans would pay well for technological expertise, and Samuel Slater was by no means the only English millwright to respond to Yankee dollars.

Machinery Production. Once machinery was constructed and operating, firms discovered that fewer skilled workers were required to keep it going than to set it up. Textile producers found new uses for their millwrights' skills: they began to produce textile machinery, as well as cloth, for sale. Initially just a sideline to textile production, machinery construction paid off in two ways. First, experience in machine construction yielded rapid technological progress as the basic designs became more productive. But the expertise gained had other applications. A growing range of other tools—even locomotives—was produced by the machine shops. Improved machinery was instrumental in reducing cotton textile prices to one-quarter their 1815 levels by 1860.[13]

Originally, machines were produced by large integrated mills such as the Boston Associates' Waltham plant or the Amoskeag Mills

in New Hampshire. By 1860, however, the numbers of textile producers had increased sufficiently to allow specialized machinery producers to appear. Increasingly, the textile factories "spun off" those functions for which they could not achieve full economies of scale and concentrated on those where they were most efficient. To produce textile machinery, the shops developed tools that proved to have widespread applications beyond their initial uses, in addition to a growing range of finished products.

Meeting British Competition

American producers initially could compete with the British only in coarse fabrics, where their deficiencies in labor skills were least important and their lower costs for raw materials significant. Here too, shipping costs and the tariff, which was levied on a per-unit basis, were larger portions of British firms' costs. By 1860 American mills had learned how to produce a variety of fabrics, including some of high quality. Even more significantly, they were now exporting some textiles to markets also open to British producers, so in these cases American textiles could survive in "fair" competition. Although the proportion of American textiles exported was not large, and many grades of American cloth could not compete in overseas markets, great progress had been made. In 1815, American textiles could not even hold their domestic markets.

Population growth as well as changes in supply increased the production of cotton textiles. Incomes were rising and transportation costs falling, which also tended to increase demand. The real price of textiles fell until 1860, indicating that supply was increasing faster than demand, particularly after 1833.[14] As in many other circumstances, American manufacturers responded to the growth of the market with

---

[13] Zevin, "The Growth of Cotton," pp. 141–143.

[14] Ibid.

innovations designed to increase production and reduce unit costs.

Other Textiles

Cotton was more easily adapted to machine spinning and weaving than was wool, because cotton fibers were more easily straightened and twisted into yarn. Nor did the woolen industry fully solve the problems of using power-driven looms until 1840. Both coarse cloth from home industry and fine imported fabrics competed effectively with the products of American factories throughout this period. Even though American efficiency in woolen textiles apparently had not improved in proportion to that in cotton, the production of woolen cloth rose sufficiently to keep that industry among the ten largest in the United States in 1860 (see Table 7.2). American woolen manufacturers developed several machines for carding (straightening) fibers and removing burrs during the antebellum period.

Production of other fibers and some non-cloth items made from them also increased. Carpets, hemp bagging, rope, and twine were produced in large quantities. Linen was the only other fabric produced in the United States to any extent. Its manufacture was not mechanized until just before the Civil War. Linen suffered heavily in competition with cotton.

Cotton Spurs a Fabric Revolution

Momentous changes resulted from the availability of new, cheaper fabrics. Competition from cotton forced a response from producers of the more traditional textiles, whose prices fell even as their quality improved. Cottons, which took dye more easily and could be printed in many patterns, must have been a welcome change from the often dull colors of traditional fabrics. Cotton could also be washed without shrinkage, making higher standards of cleanliness possible.

Cloth produced by hand was not only more expensive to make but tended to be more uneven in quality than the machine-made article. The specialization in clothing production en-

Table 7.2 United States Manufacturing Industries, 1860

Item	Number of Employees	Value of Product	Value Added by Manufacture*	Rank
Cotton goods	114,955	$107,337,783	$54,671,082	1
Lumber	75,595	104,928,342	53,569,942	2
Boots and shoes	123,026	91,899,298	49,161,124	3
Flour and meal	27,682	248,580,365	40,083,056	4
Men's clothing	114,800	80,830,555	36,680,803	5
Iron (cast, rolled, forged, and wrought)	48,975	73,175,332	35,685,275	6
Machinery	41,223	52,010,376	32,565,843	7
Woolen goods	40,597	60,685,190	25,002,489	8
Carriages, wagons, and carts	37,102	35,552,842	23,654,560	9
Leather	22,697	67,306,542	22,785,715	10

*Value added is calculated by deducting the value of raw materials from that of an industry's finished product. It thus measures the contribution of the manufacturing process.

Source: *Eighth Census of the United States: Manufactures.* Reprinted in R. Robertson, *History of the American Economy,* 3d ed. (New York: Harcourt Brace Jovanovich, 1973), p. 220.

abled by increased textile output raised the quality of clothing rather than lowered it, as is often assumed. With the advent of the sewing machine, another barrier to inexpensive clothing for the average citizen was reduced. More people could now afford a change of clothing, something many had previously not enjoyed.

Iron

In 1815 cheap metal was no more common than cheap cloth. Wood was used instead of iron in an amazing range of applications in antebellum America—even in the frames of steam engines and other machinery. Often all but the cutting or bearing edges of tools were made of wood. The reason was simple: in the early nineteenth century, iron and all other metals were very expensive. Iron was so scarce that many families burned their old homes when they moved to recover the nails. An adequate supply of metal was essential for successful industrialization. Despite American ingenuity in woodworking, wood simply could not withstand the stresses produced by high-speed machinery.

In colonial times, America had been one of the world's leading producers of iron. Although American iron production increased faster than population from 1815 to 1860, particularly after 1840, domestic supply failed to keep up with increased demand. The balance of the country's needs was made up by imports from Britain, especially of large items such as railway rails. Only in the late 1850s did domestically produced rails begin to replace imports.

Limitations of Early Iron Technology

Antebellum iron production is a study in the limits of early nineteenth-century technology. Smelting iron ore requires a great deal of fuel. Because wood fires were not hot enough, mankind had traditionally employed charcoal. Although charcoal's basic raw material is wood, which America had in abundance, charcoal manufacture is a highly labor-intensive process. Further, charcoal deteriorates badly if transported far in large quantities. Thus, furnaces had to be located near their fuel sources.

Coke Smelting. Britain had the labor and skills necessary for iron production, but her supplies of wood were becoming increasingly scarce in the eighteenth century. After prolonged trial and error, the British learned to use coke, a coal product, for smelting. Although British coal supplies were ample, problems still remained.

Iron smelted with coke did not produce wrought iron (the soft, tough, nearly pure iron still used for ornamental railings) of equal quality to the charcoal-smelted variety. Cast iron, which contains impurities, could be made just as well with coke as with charcoal. Cast iron is hard and brittle and cannot be worked once cast. It could be used for kettles, stove pans, and other uses where rigidity was important, but much of the demand was for wrought iron. The reason for coke's partial failure as a smelting fuel was that its impurities passed into the molten metal when fuel came in contact with it during the smelting process. Still, the price of British iron fell sharply, at first because the cheaper fuel could be used to make at least one type of iron and was better suited to the larger, more efficient blast furnaces that employed steam engines to increase the draft. Later, the price fell because refining methods which avoided contact between the fuel and metal were developed. Puddling and rolling, as the new methods were called, greatly increased the economies of scale in iron production.

Luck and Chemistry. Unlike their counterparts in the textile industry, American ironmasters were slow to follow the British lead in smelting techniques, although they did adopt puddling and rolling. The reason was not conservatism, but the sulfur content of American coal. The only American coal available for blast-furnace fuel contained sulfur that combined with the iron to make metal that was all but useless. British coal contained no sulfur, and thus made satisfactory iron.[15] In addition, most of the bituminous (soft) coal yet discovered in America lay west of the Appalachians, while the major markets for iron were in the East.

American ironmasters did not know the chemical reason for the failure, but they quickly learned that British methods did not work west of the Atlantic. Consequently, they continued to use charcoal, and this limited the size of furnaces and restricted their location. Iron production could only be expanded by "more of the same" methods, and so the price of domestic charcoal-smelted iron did not fall.

"Hot Blast" Furnaces. American producers did adopt another British innovation—preheating the air blown through blast furnaces to increase combustion—within six years of its discovery. These "hot blast" furnaces allowed another innovation: they burned with suffcient heat to allow the use of anthracite (hard coal). Anthracite had been impossible to burn in earlier furnaces, but there was plenty of it in eastern Pennsylvania, and it contained no sulfur. The new method spread rapidly, and by 1856 half of all the iron produced in America was smelted with anthracite.[16]

By 1860, the iron industry was concentrated around its fuel sources in Pennsylvania. The combination of hot blast and anthracite fuel allowed the use of larger, more efficient furnaces, and iron prices began to fall. Faced with this threat, the owners of older charcoal furnaces worked hard to improve their efficiency, with considerable success. This response is common when new technology threatens the very existence of older methods. Just before the Civil War, sulfur-free soft coal was discovered near Connellsville, Pennsylvania, allowing the use of British methods.

[15] N. Rosenberg, *Technology and American Economic Growth* (New York: Harper & Row, 1972), pp. 78–80.
[16] Ibid., pp. 79–81.

The Influence of Demand on Technology

The persistence of old-fashioned production methods may have owed a good deal to the nature of American demand for iron. Much of the charcoal-smelted iron in which American producers specialized was used for tools, nails, and other highly fabricated items where performance was nearly as important as price. Once demand for large items such as beams and rails became a larger portion of the total, cost considerations weighed more heavily, and lower-quality British metal and American anthracite-smelted iron had the advantage. Tariffs on imported iron had to be reduced when American producers could not supply the needs of the railroads. New methods' effects on the supply and price of cast iron (and rising prices for wood) allowed the production of cast-iron stoves to expand rapidly in the 1850s.

Iron firms, particularly after the introduction of the new methods, were sizable concerns, perhaps larger on average any other private organizations except railroads. They profited from developments in other sectors, such as easier incorporation, wider financial markets, and better transportation (see Chapter 8). The development of steam power had both forward and backward linkages to the iron industry. Steam engines and railroads consumed growing portions of the industry's production and also aided the operation of large furnaces and rolling mills.

Steel

Through the antebellum period, the industry concentrated its productive efforts on iron, not steel. Steel is iron containing small amounts of carbon; it combines the most useful characteristics of cast iron and wrought iron. Cast iron contains more carbon that does steel; wrought iron contains none. Steel had been produced in very small quantities for at least a thousand years. It was so expensive that it could only be used where performance was paramount, such as in springs, instruments, and weapons.

Steelmaking was still an art, rather than an applied science, in 1860. It required vast experience and judgement—the only available substitutes for scientific knowledge. Like the process followed by a first-rate cook, the product might be high-quality but the process difficult to duplicate with any degree of accuracy. Even when a process for large-scale steelmaking was simultaneously invented by William Kelly in America and England's Henry Bessemer, it was not widely used for another decade. When others attempted to replicate the inventors' work, the results were imperfect for unknown causes. Progress in industrial chemistry was necessary before steelmaking became systematic and predictable.

THE APPEARANCE OF THE FACTORY

Everyone knows what a factory is. Unfortunately, as in many other instances of "common knowledge," individual definitions' only common quality is diversity. If we define a factory as an aggregation of capital and labor performing interdependent tasks, using powered machinery to produce large amounts of some good, we capture the essential features of the institution. In factory production, labor and capital must be integrated; each worker and machine are parts of a unified production process, not used alone to make finished items from raw material. In factories each unit of capital or labor performs only a part of the production process. This need not imply an assembly line, but that is perhaps the ultimate illustration of such integration. In relation to alternative production systems, factories are large-scale production units. The use of large amounts of capital is profitable only if the result is large total revenues ("sales"); hence factories are practical only for large volumes of output.

Factories and Product Quality

Factories and some factory equipment allowed people to accomplish previously impossible tasks. This was especially true in cases involving a great weight of material or sustained high-speed operations. In addition, powered machinery made an important contribution to the increase in aggregate production. Human physical effort greatly decreased, but even so, steam and water power had by no means completely supplanted muscles. In 1850, just over 70 percent of the total horsepower generated by nonhuman effort in the United States was just that—it was furnished by work animals.[17] Still, the demands on human muscles were now lower in proportion to output than ever before.

Adjustment Problems

Factories allowed more output per worker with less physical effort, but they also had their drawbacks. Control of work pace was no longer in the hands of the individual laborer, nor were hours of work in any integrated production process where each step had to be performed in a fixed order. Factories imposed a new and unwelcome discipline on people accustomed to work on family farms, and their owners attempted to enforce it with penalties for absence and tardiness. But this point should not be overstressed. Farmers, particularly those with livestock, have only limited control over their workdays (and no days free from all work). The

---

[17] U.S. Department of Commerce, Bureau of the Census, *Bicentennial Statistics* (Washington, D.C.: Government Printing Office, 1976) p. 401.

seasons impose harsh penalties on those who fail to plant or harvest at the proper times. Factory organization allowed higher wages than agriculture: in 1849, industrial wages averaged more than twice those in agriculture.[18] Despite high turnover, this appeared to be adequate compensation to maintain a factory labor force.

Waterpower versus Steam Power

Power for the new machines initally was furnished largely by falling water, especially in New England. In regions with fewer waterpower sites or in industries where location could not be dictated by power availability, steam power offered an increasingly effective alternative. Waterpower required a large initial investment; dams, particularly on large streams, were expensive. Once installed, however, waterpower's operating and maintenance costs were very low. Yet despite considerable progress in capturing and applying stream flows, only a fraction of the power potential could be harnessed. Nor could waterpower be made very flexible. Poor engineering and the inevitable losses to friction in power transmission further reduced actual yields. At this time there was no method of obtaining strength in shafts and gears other than to make them large and heavy, so much of the power generated by steam or water went to overcoming their inertia. Waterpower was vulnerable to disruption by flood, drought, and ice, but its greatest disadvantage was its location. Machines had to be brought to the dam or falls, and this might be far from markets, inputs, or both.

Steam power was far more mobile. It could be used anywhere that fuel and a little water were available; thus, many of the factories built in existing cities used steam power. Although the initial investment required for steam power was likely less than for waterpower, operating costs were higher, particularly in regions where fuel was expensive. Nor were steam engines fully reliable until the 1850s.

For most of the antebellum period, the overall advantage appeared to lie with waterpower. In 1860, over half of all power generated for manufacturing came from water. Steam power was often used in the Midwest, a region whose rivers were far better suited to transporting the area's cheap coal than to driving waterwheels. This preference was undoubtedly reinforced by the region's high capital costs. But in 1860, the Midwest was far from the center of American manufacturing it later became.[19]

Steam Power and U.S. Adaptations

American steam engine design reflected the country's resource endowments as well as the uses to which it put steam power. Britain favored low-pressure steam engines, expensive to build but relatively fuel-efficient and long-lasting. The United States preferred high-pressure engines, fuel-hungry and less durable but cheaper to construct and better suited to transportation needs. In Britain, capital was relatively cheap, fuel costs high, and most steam engines in stationary installations. In the United States, the pattern of costs was reversed. So were the uses: in 1838, over 60 percent of American steam engines were installed in steamboats.[20]

An Overview of Antebellum American Industry

As Table 7.2 reveals, the major industries of antebellum America fall into two groups: those that processed raw materials (lumber, grain

---

[18] J. James and J. Skinner, "The Resolution of the Labor-Scarcity Paradox," *Journal of Economic History* (September 1985).

[19] Temin, "Steam and Waterpower."
[20] Ibid. See also Rosenberg, *Technology*, pp. 65, 71.

milling, iron, and leather) and those whose capital requirements were modest (textiles, boots and shoes, clothing). The distribution reflects American resouce endowments. Capital was scarce relative to Europe and Americans used it rationally, where it would produce a great deal of product per unit of capital.

The machinery and transportation equipment industries may be less of an exception than they appear. These products, like iron smelting, required large "lumps" of capital and could be purchased from foreign producers with lower capital and labor costs. But both were so expensive to transport that their delivered prices in America were higher than those of domestic producers. Nor were European machinery and transport equipment always well suited to American conditions.

Another point illustrated by the data is that value added per employee was low in textiles, clothing, and footwear, indicating the rather small amounts of simple machinery at each employee's disposal in those labor-intensive industries. Value added per employee in milling, where small work forces labored in highly mechanized mills, reflected very different conditions. Finally, by no means was all U.S. industry concentrated on light manufacturing. Nor had Americans been unable to generate capital. By 1860, the aggregate investment in U.S. industry totaled over $1 billion.

NEW TECHNOLOGY

Although American industrial technology had its roots in European methods, the United States developed distinctive patterns of production for many goods, as well as distinctive features in the goods themselves. The difference was one of degree rather than kind, but it was quite obvious to contemporary observers. Europeans observed and commented on American industrial methods, and even copied a few of them. The "American system of man-

ufacturing," as the British called it, featured a series of machines developed in response to the technical problems Americans found especially pressing.[21]

The reasons behind the development of these machines are unclear. American producers, operating in an economy where labor was scarce, generally have been thought to have substituted capital for high-priced labor. This raised production per worker and produced further increases in wages. There is no doubt that productivity increases allowed higher wages, but capital was also more expensive in America than in Europe, giving Americans an incentive to develop capital-saving methods as well. In any case, the source of any cost reduction is less important than its amount. Businessmen strive to reduce costs in general, rather than those of one particular input.[22]

Incentives for Productivity Growth

Since both capital and labor costs were higher in the United States than in Europe, it would seem that economic pressures would have encouraged increases in the productivity of both. But was captial substituted for labor in the United States to a greater extent than elsewhere? Output per worker would rise if hand tools were replaced by powered machinery, and output per machine would increase if a second labor shift were added. The aggregate capital stock per worker was lower in the United States than it was in Britain before 1860, so it is difficult to maintain that, in general, capital was substituted for labor in America.[23] The only

[21] Rosenberg, *Technology*, pp. 87–90.
[22] L. Davis et al., *American Economic Growth: An Economist's History of the Unites States* (New York: Harper & Row, 1972), p. 251.
[23] A. Field, "Land Abundance, Interest/Profit Rates, and Nineteenth-Century American and British Technology," *Journal of Economic History* (June 1983).

available change in factor proportions that would increase the profits of American manufacturers was a rise in the proportion of raw materials relative to capital and labor.

Natural Resources in U.S. Manufacturing

Natural resources, particularly wood, were cheap in America and were used lavishly and for purposes unheard of in Europe. Wherever possible, natural resources were substituted for both capital and labor. Log-burning fireplaces economized on labor for woodchopping and required less capital than stoves. Once firewood prices began to rise—particularly in urban areas—and iron became more plentiful, the fuel-saving but capital-using properties of stoves were more widely used.[24] American woodworking equipment operated rapidly and required little maintenance, but it reduced (in European eyes) an appalling portion of the log to sawdust. European observers were impressed, but they did not adopt American woodworking techniques. Log cabins and balloon-frame houses are other examples of attempts to cope with scant labor supplies. Log cabins economized on unskilled labor; balloon-frame construction saved on the highly skilled labor needed to construct a post-and-beam building.[25]

In some cases, the choice of factor proportions went beyond what might be indicated by current prices of inputs. For most of the nineteenth century, American wage rates were rising and both capital and raw material prices were falling. Manufacturers' decisions in many cases indicate that they expected these trends to continue, because the methods they chose tended to be even more capital- and materials-intensive and labor-saving than existing prices would dictate. In addition, a bias toward raw materials also tends to produce a more capital-intensive technology.[26] A recent study concluded that there was no single "American system"; industries employing skilled workers tended to be more and those employing unskilled labor less capital-intensive in America than in Britain.[27] Whether American industry was capital- or labor-intensive is still under discussion, and it appears that there may not be a single answer.

Another output-increasing option was to change the inputs themselves: use not more machines, but better machines, or more skilled workers. Also, efforts could be made to use existing equipment and workers more efficiently. Both patterns were followed, with considerable interaction between them.

Innovation as a Source of Lower Capital Costs

High capital costs in antebellum America have been thought to favor technological change. American machinery tended to be lightly built and operated at high speeds—features which increased output per investment dollar. One consequence was that such machinery had to be replaced more frequently than European machinery built and run with an eye to long life. It was thus easier to incorporate innovations as they appeared in America, and fewer held the fallacious but widespread view that any capital good had to be operated "until it repaid its cost." In any case, few American manufacturers hesitated to replace machinery of any age with capital that promised superior performance. The high and rising rate of aggregate investment in the United States helped to ensure that at any time a large portion of the nation's capital equipment was relatively new.

---

[24] Rosenberg, *Technology*, p. 29. It should also be noted that during winter in rural areas, the opportunity costs of woodchopping might be very low—a point reinforced by faster adoption of stoves in cities.

[25] Ibid., pp. 27–29.

[26] L. Cain and D. Paterson, "Factor Biases and Technical Change in Manufacturing: The American System, 1850–1919," *Journal of Economic History* (June 1981).

[27] James and Skinner, "The Resolution of the Labor-Scarcity Paradox."

SOURCES OF INVENTION

Throughout the antebellum era, the United States borrowed European ideas and adapted them to American conditions. The original American inventions from this period, with the important exceptions of the telegraph and vulcanized rubber, are applications of mechanics involving rather straightforward principles of cause and effect. None are based on really sophisticated science, and most owe more to dogged trial and error than to mastery of basic principles.

In the area of basic science, and even in its formal applications in technology, the United States lagged far behind Europe in 1860. Until the middle 1850s, only the United States Military Academy at West Point offered formal training in engineering, and only one scientific journal was published in the entire country. Nevertheless, the country had an ambitious, well-informed, and imaginative population, which went far to compensate for other deficiencies. Workmen tended to be literate and well versed in basic mechanical relationships. Further, they were eager to use new equipment, quick to learn how to repair and maintain it, and often able to make improvements or apply its basic principles in new ways. With its labor shortages, America welcomed both new ideas and new people and tried to develop their potential.

Interchangeable Parts

The development of interchangeable parts typifies the American response to new methods. The basic idea of making many identical parts, each easily fitting into a complex mechanism in lieu of any other, originated in Europe. Its first really successful application, however, was in American arms manufacture. Although Eli Whitney's role in introducing this technique has been widely publicized, the real credit should probably go to Simeon North.[28]

Production of military weapons was a logical field for the first application of this principle. Until interchangeable parts were developed, each gun was literally custom made. All but a few minor parts were handmade and, more importantly, hand fitted into the complete mechanism. The process was slow and required highly skilled hand labor: it took years of experience to learn to make and fit together a complicated mechanism such as a gunlock using only hand tools and the crudest measuring devices. Even though defense needs might require large numbers of guns, it was impossible to expand production quickly while skilled labor remained such a bottleneck. This was hardly less true of wooden components than of metal. Irregular shapes such as gunstocks required much hand labor, and the result had to be painstakingly fitted to the metal parts. Repairing guns made by such procedures was equally time consuming.

Two things were necessary to make interchangeable parts practical: machines capable of producing large quantities of components to a standardized design, and measuring devices and controls to ensure that each conformed to standard dimensions. To meet the first need, a series of machines—lathes, milling machines, and grinders—was developed by 1845. Accuracy was achieved with the introduction of calipers, jigs, taps, and gauges. By 1860, irregular wooden and metal shapes were being turned out in quantity by power-driven machines. The principle could be applied to many different products. The new technique did not merely increase the supply or reduce the price of manufactured goods. It made all

[28] R. Woodbury, "Eli Whitney and the Legend of Interchangeable Parts," *Technology and Cultural Change* 2, no. 1 (1960). Whitney apparently regarded the contract he had been awarded to produce muskets with interchangeable parts as a source of funds for lawsuits over infringements of his cotton gin patents, more than as a business venture in itself.

■ Many nineteenth-century factories relied on belts and shafts for power.
Source: *Scribner's Popular History of the United States*, Vol. 4 by William Cullen Bryant, Sidney Howard Gay, and Noah Brooks. (New York: Charles Scribner's Sons, 1896) p. 292.

but the most basic items of industry available to the average citizen for the first time.

Substituting machine-produced uniformity for expensive hand fitting greatly increased productivity and reduced costs. After watching a workman at the Springfield Arsenal assemble ten muskets, using only a screwdriver to fit together parts taken from guns made in ten different years, a British investigating committee paid the "American system" the most sincere compliment possible. It bought a complete duplicate plant and shipped it to England. The American workman had assembled one musket every three and a half minutes. Using traditional methods, a skilled workman could not make two such guns in an entire day.[29]

[29] Rosenberg, *Technology*, pp. 90–91.

Linkages to Other Industries

Interchangeable parts could be readily adapted to the production of almost any complex mechanism, such as watches, clocks, furniture, agricultural machinery, and sewing machines. Entrepreneurs quickly realized that interchangeable parts meant more than just low initial cost. If an item with interchangeable parts broke down, its owners could simply put a new part in place themselves. Previously, only a skilled workman—sometimes only the original producer—could make and hand fit a new component. The risks of employing machinery in place of labor fell because ease of repair meant decreased downtime if breakdowns occurred. The cost of items made with such machines also fell.

Many of the new developments interacted. Sewing machines and cheaper cloth made more and better clothes possible for the average person, and allowed some attention to fashion. In turn, sewing machines benefited from interchangeable parts—no seamstress would buy such an expensive machine without assurance that it could be easily and cheaply repaired. Meat packing produced large numbers of hides, which could be combined with improved sewing machines in boot and shoe factories. Ready-made clothing still was handicapped by inadequate statistical knowledge: there was no accurate information about the proportion of people of different dimensions and sizes. The railroads benefited from the telegraph, an obvious aid to both traffic control and the problems of obtaining current information from distant station managers. Producers of all types of machines found cheap iron useful for rigid equipment that had to withstand heavy stress.

Regularly, machines developed in response to one industry's needs proved to have even more significant applications in another. Moreover, some machines were equally effective in producing more machines. The United States began producing machine tools. These tools are the very core of industry: they determine the technical limits within which users can operate.[30] At first machine tools had to be built by each firm to meet its own needs, but when specialized machine-tool builders appeared, the new ideas embodied in such devices could be spread throughout industry much faster.

Better Goods or Cheaper Goods?

The resulting products should not be regarded as a flood of cheaply made goods that displaced the high-quality products of craftsmen. This may have been the case in a few instances, but goods made by the old methods generally remained available to those willing to pay for them. Far more often the new manufactured goods, especially mechanical items, now made available to ordinary people what before only the rich had been able to obtain. Before the machine age, low-priced goods could be produced only by skimping on materials or labor. The poor thus made do with inferior goods, attempted to make their own, waited for the castoffs of the rich, or, most commonly, did without. Nor did quality necessarily decline. Machine-made items might be well designed; if a good was to be produced by the thousands, it might well pay to spend more care on its design than on one that was to be unique.

American conditions spurred innovative responses. Given the vast distances of the interior, the list of significant American contributions to transportation and communications improvements should not be surprising. Inventors generally direct their efforts to areas of perceived need.

The Role of the Frontier

Frontier conditions also spurred innovation. Commanche warriors could keep a stream of six or more unpleasantly well-aimed arrows in

the air from the back (or far side) of a horse at full gallop. Few riflemen could reload their weapons without stopping. The survivors of encounters with such formidable combat technology were highly receptive to the new technology of Samuel Colt's six-shooters—although few were in any hurry for a return engagement.

In some cases a new machinery spurred further innovation as experience was gained in its use. Increased train weights and operating speeds stimulated the search for effective brakes and traffic control mechanisms.

The Influence of American Markets

The characteristics of the market for the new goods were important influences on both manufactured items and manufacturing technology. American population and per-capita incomes were both rising, and improving transportation further expanded the markets open to most producers. In 1860, most Americans were still living in widely dispersed rural populations with income distributions considerably more equal than those of Europe. Such consumers wanted goods that performed effectively; they were not willing to pay for features that only enhanced appearance or the producer's sense of technical perfection. The fact that an item was already in widespread use did not inhibit American consumers, as it might European—European consumers preferred one-of-a-kind manufactured goods, while American consumers accepted mass-produced items, even if the family next door owned the same item. This attitude was enhanced by the high proportion of tools among the new products. Americans were buying items they would use to make a living, not for prestige displays.

The Importance of Price

Under such circumstances, price was a major consideration in most American markets. In most cases, several sellers competed for buyers' favor, so at least some competition was present. Consumers' interest in low prices resulted in ready acceptance of design changes that made

[30] Ibid., pp. 96–100.

items easier to manufacture. The European consumer with his preference for distinctive features might be willing to buy fewer, hand-made goods at higher prices if these could not be incorporated in machine-made items. His American counterpart felt differently. If changes that made products easier to manu-facture reduced price, Americans were willing to adapt their tastes to what machines could produce.[31] American manufactured goods were seldom highly finished, and their designs were often no more than adequate, but they could be made by machines in large quantities and sold at low prices. Many of these simple, straightforward designs proved to be highly functional as well. American agricultural ma-chinery, locks, clocks, and small arms per-formed better than European products, and proved it in international competitions.

Other Innovations

Where the product or the nature of inputs de-fied mechanization, innovations in organiza-tion were developed. Meat-packing plants could not use machines for butchering, because an-imals are not uniform in size or proportion. However, where a large number of animals was to be processed, specialization and high pro-ductivity were achieved through the introduc-tion of a "disassembly line," a conveyor on which carcasses moved past workmen who each performed one specific task. This system was well established before the Civil War.

Despite the advances detailed in this chap-ter, American manufacturing in 1860 was not a sector of giant firms using highly mechanized production techniques (see Table 7.1). On the eve of the Civil War, the typical manufacturing firm was an individual proprietorship or part-nership, not a corporation. It employed fewer than ten workers, still relied heavily on human

[31] Ibid., pp. 44–51.

muscle, and served a local or at most a regional market. In only a few industries were there ex-ceptions.

NEW OPPORTUNITIES AND NEW RESPONSES

Periods of rapid economic growth tend to be periods of substantial technical change, and the antebellum U.S. economy typifies this theory—particularly in industry, which for all practical purposes was a brand new sector. The range of alternatives open to Americans expanded greatly in this era. There is abundant evidence that industrialization was a massive response to new opportunities. New goods were made by new methods and sold under new conditions. Perhaps never before or since has the climate for entrepreneurial activity been so favorable in the United States. Population and income growth as well as transport improvements in-creased demand for most goods, and con-sumers responded very favorably to new items, particularly from 1840 to 1860. The new tech-nologies allowed easy entry into most new oc-cupations; economies of scale were not great, and low capital costs and improving financial institutions eased access to capital. Few large firms were already entrenched in most indus-tries. The legal and social climate was extremely favorable to new ventures. And the improved communications reduced some risks and pub-licized success of others who might serve as role models.

Nor should it be assumed that only the owners of new industrial firms prospered in this period. The range of occupations was far wider than it had ever been. Wider job choices always benefit individual workers: they have a better chance to locate an occupation which makes ideal use of their talents. And with more employers—especially from different indus-tries—competing for labor, wage prospects were enhanced. There were as few barriers to entry for workers as for employers; with many jobs in industries that had not existed a few decades before, lack of experience was expected.

American manufacturing made very effective use of on-the-job training. Once on the job in new industries, workers' productivity gains were typically high and firms small enough so that their sources were recognized. Even within existing industries, work now produced higher and far more varied standards of living with less physical exertion. The gains were not great by modern standards, but those who achieved them had a different basis of judgment. Few of us can imagine the prospects of young adults in a world where the choice of jobs and location was as restricted as in eighteenth-century rural life. America had always offered better opportunities than many people found in Europe. Now it offered improved choices to many of its own people as well.

SELECTED REFERENCES

Cain, L., and D. Paterson. "Biased Technical Change, Scale, and Factor Substitution in American Industry, 1850–1919." *Journal of Economic History* (March 1986).

——. "Factor Biases and Technical Change in Manufacturing: The American System, 1850–1919." *Journal of Economic History* (June 1981).

Chandler, A., Jr. *The Visible Hand: The Managerial Revolution in American Business.* Cambridge, Mass.: Harvard University Press, 1977.

Clark, V. *History of Manufactures in the United States.* Washington, D.C.: Peter Smith, 1949.

David, P. "Learning by Doing and Tariff Protection: A Reconsideration of the Case of the Antebellum United States Cotton Textile Industry." *Journal of Economic History* (September 1970).

——. *Technical Choice, Innovation, and Economic Growth.* Cambridge, England: Cambridge University Press, 1975.

Davis, L., et al. *American Economic Growth: An Economist's History of the United States.* New York: Harper & Row, 1972.

Field, A. "Land Abundance, Interest/Profit Rates, and Nineteenth-Century American and British Technology." *Journal of Economic History* (June 1983).

Habbakuk, H. *American and British Technology in the 19th Century.* Cambridge, England: Cambridge University Press, 1962.

Hounshell, D. *From the American System to Mass Production, 1800–1932: The Development of Manufacturing Technology in the United States.* Baltimore, Md.: Johns Hopkins University Press, 1984.

James, J., and J. Skinner. "The Resolution of the Labor-Scarcity Paradox." *Journal of Economic History* (September 1985).

Kendrick, J. *Productivity Trends in the United States.* Princeton, N.J.: Princeton University Press, 1961.

North, D. *The Economic Growth of the United States, 1790–1860.* Englewood Cliffs, N.J.: Prentice-Hall, 1961.

Rosenberg, N. *Technology and American Economic Growth.* New York: Harper & Row, 1972.

Schmookler, J. *Invention and Economic Growth.* Cambridge, Mass.: Harvard University Press, 1966.

Temin, P. *Iron and Steel in 19th Century America: An Economic Inquiry.* Cambridge, Mass.: MIT Press, 1964.

U.S. Department of Commerce, Bureau of the Census. *Historical Statistics of the United States: Colonial Times to 1970.* 2 vols. Washington, D.C.: Government Printing Office, 1975.

Zevin, R. "The Growth of Cotton Production after 1815." In R. Fogel and S. Engerman, *The Reinterpretation of American Economic History.* New York: Harper & Row, 1971.

CHAPTER 8

BANKING, FINANCE, AND COMMERCE

*I*n any economy with an output of physical commodities growing as rapidly as in the mid-nineteenth-century United States, an expansion of the institutions, services, and products that aid production of these goods must occur. Expansion of the marketplace through aggregate growth and increasing interdependence placed greater burdens on the monetary and financial sectors of the economy. In such circumstances, if goods are to be exchanged for money, either an increase in the money supply or a decline in money prices must occur. The form of this response, and the nature of the institutions through which it occurs, can significantly influence the patterns of economic activity.

MONEY AND THE ECONOMY

Economists have developed an equation that illustrates the relations between money and other economic activity. The equation of exchange, or quantity-theory equation, $MV = PQ$, summarizes a great deal in a few symbols. M is the supply of money; V is velocity, or the rate at which a unit of money is spent; P is the aggregate price level; and Q is the volume of transactions or real output.

Velocity is determined by individuals' demand for money balances and by the structure of monetary institutions, neither of which changes rapidly. Thus, changes in the money supply must affect the price level, or output, or both. The level of prices times the volume of real output is a shorthand formula for the money value of aggregate economic activity, and thus the equation provides the link between the money supply and gross national product. If current economic conditions are known, the equation allows predictions of the results of a change or variation in the rate of change in the money supply.

For example, if all resources are in use (the economy is at full employment), Q cannot rise much in response to increases in the money supply. Since V is stable, the effect of money supply increases will be concentrated on the price level, which will rise. If unemployed resources are available, an increase in the money supply will raise both P and Q. Decreases in the money supply must decrease PQ, but it is important to distinguish between these two variables. If all prices fell in proportion, leaving real output unchanged, overall welfare would not be affected. But if real output declines, in a world where scarcity exists at least some people must be worse off. Not only will fewer goods and services be available, so that real incomes are lower, but some of those employed in making the previous volume of output will lose their jobs.

Economists have altered their opinions on the relation between price and output declines several times in the past few decades. Today it appears that prices are more flexible than in the immediate past, when they fell, if at all, only under severe unemployment. In the nineteenth century, prices were quite flexible, as Table 8.1 indicates. Prices both rose and fell; they certainly were not stable.

Rapid inflation might be quickly succeeded by sharp deflation, as in the 1835–1843 period. If there was a long-run trend in this period, it was toward lower prices. Short-term deflation might cause considerable distress, but it did reduce the decline in real output and employment otherwise necessary to accommodate decreases in the money supply.[1] Despite severe deflation, the period from 1839 to 1843 was one of substantial real economic growth.

[1] P. Temin, *The Jacksonian Economy* (New York: Norton, 1969), pp. 160–165.

Bimetallic Money

In 1792 Congress had defined the dollar as containing either 371.25 grains of silver or 24.75 grains of gold. A gold dollar, had such a coin been minted then, would have contained one-fifteenth as much metal as its silver counterpart. The government offered to buy and sell unlimited amounts of gold and silver at the 1:15 ratio and to coin either metal free of charge for anyone bringing it to the mint.

Since American coins were pieces of pure metal, they were valuable for that reason as well as for monetary purposes. But this created a problem. As long as an ounce of gold exchanged for 15 ounces of silver in the bullion markets, where gold and silver were sold as commodities, all was well. However, if the relative values of gold and silver as metal differed from the 1:15 ratio, people would exchange the overvalued metal for the one the mint undervalued.

Early in the nineteenth century, gold brought 16 times its weight in silver in the bullion markets. It was possible—and profitable—to bring 15 ounces of silver to the U.S. mint, exchange them for an ounce of gold, use the gold to purchase 16 ounces of silver in the bullion markets, and repeat the transaction until the mint either ran out of gold or changed the ratio. Since American gold coins were more valuable as metal than as money, they disappeared from circulation. After prolonged debate, Congress changed the mint ratio to 16 to 1 in 1834. But events had moved faster than politics: by this time the 16:1 ratio overvalued gold. Silver coins became so scarce that postage stamps and fractional paper currency were used as substitutes. Before the situation could be rectified, the discovery of gold in California in 1848 and in Australia three years later made it even worse.

Aside from the difficulty of keeping both types of metallic money in circulation, the use of commodity money was inefficient. In general, it does not pay to use any commodity with

Table 8.1 Wholesale Prices, 1815–1860
(1910–1914 = 100)

Year	Price Level	Year	Price Level	Year	Price Level
1815	170	1831	94	1847	90
1816	151	1832	95	1848	82
1817	151	1833	95	1849	82
1818	147	1834	90	1850	84
1819	125	1835	100	1851	83
1820	106	1836	114	1852	88
1821	102	1837	115	1853	97
1822	106	1838	110	1854	108
1823	103	1839	112	1855	110
1824	98	1840	95	1856	105
1825	103	1841	92	1857	111
1826	99	1842	82	1858	93
1827	98	1843	75	1859	95
1828	97	1844	77	1860	93
1829	96	1845	83		
1830	91	1846	83		

Source: U.S. Department of Commerce, Bureau of the Census, *Historical Statistics of the United States: Colonial Times to 1970,* 2 vols. (Washington, D.C.: Government Printing Office, 1975), p. 201.

higher-valued alternative uses for purposes that produce less income—the cost is the foregone income. Gold and silver not only had other uses as commodities, but their production for monetary uses required resources that otherwise might have produced either other goods or metal for nonmonetary purposes. To the extent that other forms of money were substituted for metal, the total output of the U.S. economy could be greater.

Until the California gold rush, precious metals were not produced within the United States in significant quantities. Gold and silver were obtained through international trade, as in colonial times. Sales of American goods or services to foreigners or foreign investment in the United States allowed the country to import specie or bullion—at the cost of other foreign products. There was a minor gold rush in the southern Appalachian Mountains in the 1820s and 1830s. It had little effect on the money supply, but it cost most of the Cherokee Indians their ancestral homelands, as gold seekers swarmed onto Indian lands in violation of treaties. Most of the Cherokees were forcibly removed to what is now Oklahoma by the army; many died on the journey.

International Monetary Considerations

When the United States defined the dollar as containing a specific amount of gold or silver, it also determined the exchange rate between the dollar and foreign currencies whose metallic content was fixed. Dollars would exchange for British pounds sterling in proportion to the rate at which each could be exchanged for gold. Gold in turn could be converted into sterling at known ratios. Prior to 1834, a pound sterling exchanged for about $4.58; after the change made at that time, the ratio was one pound for $4.87.[2]

The stable rate of exchange between the dollar and foreign currencies could affect domestic monetary and real activity. Precious metals not only furnished part of the U.S. money supply, they were also the reserves against which commercial banks issued their own money. If American prices rose, foreign goods would cost Americans less, because the exchange rate would not vary despite inflation in the United States. But this inflation would raise the prices of American goods to foreigners. Thus, inflation in the United States would tend to increase imports and reduce exports, and gold would flow out of the country. Deflation would have the opposite effect. And as the monetary base changed in the United States, both price and real output changes might occur.

Foreign investment, mining activity, or changes in international trade flows might affect the American money supply, interest rates, or investment by increasing or decreasing a most important component of the U.S. money supply. The role of gold flows was magnified because changes in bank reserves could cause much larger changes in the amount of bank money in circulation. Since gold could move freely between nations, the United States could control its own monetary affairs and maintain fixed exchange rates only to a limited extent.

■ Commercial banks issued their own currency, like this $100 note of The Bank of The Manhattan Company (c. 1850).
Source: Courtesy of Chase Manhattan Archives.

When an individual takes out a bank loan, he or she exchanges a personal promise to pay, which is not money, for the bank's promise to pay—a check or a credit to a checking account. These are widely accepted as payment: they are money.

Prior to the Civil War, checking accounts had already become widespread, particularly in eastern business transactions. But unlike today, banks could also print bank notes (currency), which they could lend.

From modest beginnings in the 1780s, banking became a growth industry after 1800. During the next 50 years, the number of banks grew at four times the rate of population growth, and bank assets, note circulation, and deposits grew faster still.

BANKS

Gold and silver coins were only part of the U.S. money supply. Most money was manufactured by commercial banks. In a sense, commercial banks, at least in aggregate, can create money.

Banking Fundamentals

Banks do not derive income from accepting deposits; indeed, deposits per se only increase their operating costs. A bank's income is derived from the interest paid on loans made by the bank or received on securities that the bank has purchased (which represent loans made by someone else). Contrary to popular impression, bankers do not like to refuse loan applications. To do so costs them income—the interest that the loan would generate.

[2] L. Officer, "Dollar-Sterling Mint Parity and Exchange Rates, 1791–1834," *Journal of Economic History* (September 1983).

■ The building of the Erie Canal was facilitated by a $385,000 loan from The Bank of The Manhattan Company.
Source: The Bettmann Archive.

Since money's value, especially that of bank money, depends on its scarcity, banks' ability to increase the money supply is limited. Nobody would sacrifice any real resources to obtain bank money if it were not accepted in trade. Bank money will not be accepted if it is not readily convertible into legal tender (forms of money acceptable in the discharge of debts). In the nineteenth century, legal tender meant specie—gold or silver. Banks had to be able to exchange their notes or checking deposits for legal tender on demand. Under normal circumstances, however, only a small fraction of any bank's outstanding note or deposit obligations would be presented for conversion on any given day. Usually some coin would be deposited with the bank simultaneously, so no net outflow of specie would occur. Thus banks needed to keep only one-tenth to one-third of their current note or deposit obligations in the

form of specie; the rest could be loaned to increase their income.

Banks do not like to hold larger reserves than needed to satisfy current transaction demands. Excess reserves cost the bank interest on foregone loans, and large accumulations of specie attract the attention of bank robbers. Under normal circumstances, the larger the portion of the bank's assets held as reserves, the smaller the bank's profits.

Fractional-Reserve Banking

Fractional-reserve banking allows banks to increase the money supply. If all banks hold 10 percent of their assets as reserves, a new deposit of $100 in gold coin will result in a $1,000 increase in the money supply as banks increase their loans. Under these conditions each bank has a dollar in assets for every dollar of liabilities, but it has only ten cents in reserves immediately available to meet demands for conversion of bank money into other forms. Repayment of bank loans, since it takes money out of circulation, reduces the money supply. If all banks attempt to increase their reserves by calling in loans, the money supply will be reduced by the same multiple of the reserve ratio by which it was expanded. Banks' lending attitudes thus influence the money supply.

What if circumstances are not normal? Usually, people who believe that they can convert their bank money into legal tender are content not to do so. Both paper-money currency and checking accounts are safer and more convenient forms of money than large amounts of coin. But if for some reason many of those holding bank money wish to convert it into legal tender, they will not be able to do so simultaneously in any fractional-reserve system. Unless the banks can sell their nonreserve assets for legal tender or borrow funds, there is no way they can meet the unanticipated demand for conversion. Further, just as any single depositor or bank note holder, but not all at once, can convert bank money into other forms, so any one bank, but not all simultaneously, can sell or borrow from other banks. If all banks try to sell their loans or securities at the same time, prices of such assets will fall, perhaps so much that their sale will not produce sufficient funds to meet the demand for legal tender. If all banks try to borrow from each other, the total amount of reserves (nonbank money) is not increased.

Banks loan money chiefly to people who use the funds for investment purposes. The lenders tend to increase the economy's capacity by promoting commercial or other productive activity. In the nineteenth century, banks made virtually no other types of loans. Banks also serve as financial intermediaries, links between savers and investors, allocating funds to uses that generate the highest possible return. Since their information about investment possibilities is likely to be more comprehensive and accurate than that of individual savers, banks may allocate a given amount of savings more productively than could people with less information.

Antebellum Banking Practices

The history of American banking in the antebellum period is colorful. Banking was a new occupation, not yet well understood, in which profits could be very high. Proper rules of operation had not yet been formulated, and their enforcement lagged even more. Banking attracted the ambitious and sometimes the unscrupulous. Since banks were usually corporations, states were able to restrict their operations through the terms embodied in bank charters (at this time, each corporation had to receive its charter through a separate act of the state legislature). But both the aim and enforcement of early regulations were often deficient. Sometimes banks were required to keep reserves against their capital (the amount paid in by the banks' owners) or only against their outstanding note issues, not their checking accounts. Although the intent of such laws was

to make banks safe by insuring that depositors and noteholders could obtain legal tender on demand, laws requiring banks to maintain reserves against capital discouraged the formation of banks with large amounts of capital. Capital provides a "cushion" of safety for depositors and noteholders, since their claims have to be satisfied before those of the banks' owners. Requiring reserves only against notes in circulation encouraged banks to expand their checking liabilities instead, but checking accounts were the same type of current liabilities as notes. In any case, formulating bank regulations is one thing; before 1860, enforcing them was often quite another. Provisions for bank inspections were often designed to discover the extent of fraud rather than prevent it.

Still, as Table 8.1 indicates, prices did not rise uncontrollably from 1815 to 1860. Moreover, this was a period of very substantial real growth and generally low unemployment. To some extent, the large number of independent banks was a check on any individual institution's tendencies toward excess. If a single bank were to expand its loans much faster than the average of all banks, most of the checks and notes that it issued would be deposited in other banks. Banks receiving these deposits would return them to the bank of issue with a demand for payment in legal tender. This would tend to reduce the expanding bank's reserves and hence its ability to meet further demands for conversion from either its own customers or other banks. If a bank's ability to convert its own money into other forms was in doubt, that money would be accepted in trade and at other banks at less than its face value. This discount would vary with the degree of uncertainty about the issuing bank's eventual ability to redeem its obligations in full. Since information about the stability of banks generally became more difficult to obtain the more distant they were, most banks' obligations were discounted at rates rising with the distance from their point of issue. Local and regional clearinghouses, institutions for settling interbank debts by offsetting credits against one bank with debits against another so that only the net debt need be paid or credit received, also placed limits on individual banks' enthusiasm. They settled debts more quickly than could individual banks, and the clearinghouses might threaten to exclude a bank that ran consistent deficits with other members.

Attempts at Regulation

Various attempts to regulate banks' performance—particularly their note issues—were made in the antebellum era by both private and governmental agencies. States often contributed to a bank's capital and thus gained some control as stockholders. Indiana, Missouri, and Iowa established state-owned banking systems, an indication of Americans' experimental and pragmatic attitudes about relations between government and commerce. At the other extreme, Wisconsin "regulated" banks by making them illegal.[3]

In general, banking laws specified the amount of capital that had to be subscribed by the bank's owners, limited its note issue, and made some provision for inspections to ensure compliance. The extent of regulation and its enforcement varied; laws were stricter where merchant communities were well-established—for example, on the Eastern Seaboard and in Louisiana. In the newer states, laws often reflected a very imperfect understanding of banking and tended to be either lax or flat prohibitions. The Northwest was torn between two goals: it was a debtor region, eager for more capital, but also a stronghold of hard-money opinion, which frowned on banks and paper money.[4]

The Suffolk Banking System

Led by the newly established Suffolk Bank, the Boston banking community developed one form of regulation in the early 1820s. Boston banks had to compete with those outside the city limits. Since the rural banks kept smaller reserves and thus could make loans on more favorable terms than Boston banks, their notes became the common form of circulating currency within the city. Time and travel were required to redeem the notes of rural banks, so they were discounted—accepted at less than their face value—by Boston merchants. Boston banks would not accept notes from rural banks at all, increasing the incentive to discount them. In retaliation, rural banks returned the notes of Boston banks for redemption in specie as they were received. Boston banks found it difficult to keep their notes in circulation under these conditions.

In 1820, the Suffolk Bank offered to accept the notes of any rural bank that would keep a permanent $5,000 deposit over and above the funds required to cover its notes received by the Suffolk. It also allowed rural banks to redeem their notes at the same rate of discount at which the Suffolk had accepted them. Rural banks that did not cooperate found that the Suffolk Bank would accumulate large quantities of their notes and present them for redemption at face value in specie with no prior notice. Such a practice was embarrassing to rural banks with their low reserve ratios. The combined stick and carrot were effective, and most Boston banks joined with the Suffolk in enforcing the system. The Suffolk system did more than improve the competitive position of

[3] B. Hammond, "Banking in the Early West: Monopoly, Prohibition, and Laissez Faire," *Journal of Economic History* (May 1948).

[4] T. Cochran and T. Brewer, eds., *Views of American Economic Growth: The Agricultural Era*, vol. 1. (New York: McGraw-Hill, 1961), p. 171. The point is made in a comment on the article by Hammond, "Banking in the Early West."

Boston banks. It caused the notes of all New England banks to circulate within the region at or very close to their face value. This made bank money a better and more easily used medium of exchange within the system, and it facilitated exchange.[5]

The Safety Fund System

One major source of the U.S. banking system's difficulties was that the many small local banks of which it was largely comprised were vulnerable to failure. In good times, they were tempted to issue too many notes in relation to their reserves, making it difficult to redeem notes in specie if large numbers were presented at once. Fractional-reserve banking is not secure against this difficulty unless most depositors think it is and act accordingly. Unfortunately, bank failures were too common (and suspensions even more so) for nineteenth-century Americans not to consider the possibility that their bank's money might lose part or all of its purchasing power. Small banks' loans tended to be heavily concentrated on local industry, adding to their instability.

For depositors or noteholders, the risks were real and large. Even if the assets of a bank closed by a "run" could cover its obligations, the process of liquidation could take months, with no certainty about the portion of the bank's debts that could be repaid. Such difficulties were real enough for local banks, but information on the solvency of distant banks was so hard to obtain that their notes might circulate only at large discounts, if at all.

New York State attempted to alleviate this instability through an institution similar to the modern Federal Deposit Insurance Corporation. In 1828 the state required that all banks in New York contribute 0.5 percent of their capital annually (up to a maximum of 3 percent) to a fund that would make good the notes of failed banks whose assets could not cover their outstanding notes. Banks were required to join the system as a condition for renewal of their corporate charters. The law provided for effective enforcement and contained provisions forcing banks to keep reserves against notes and checking deposits, not capital.

The "safety fund" was an improvement over most contemporary banking laws, although it still based contributions on capital, not current liabilities. It had other deficiencies: it shifted some risk of loss from individual banks to the system, and at least initially it insured all creditors of the banks, rather than just depositors and noteholders.[6] Although the safety fund apparently was capable of protecting investors against the occasional failures of individual banks, it proved insufficient to deal with the widespread bank collapses of the late 1830s. The state government had to contribute nearly $1 million to make up the difference between the fund's obligations and its resources.[7]

State Bank Instability and Its Consequences

Left to themselves, most state banking systems had serious weaknesses. Regulation varied greatly between states. Since most banks were small and made most of their loans in the immediate vicinity, their solvency was closely linked to the health of the local economy. All too often, if local business was bad, the banks that served it would be forced to suspend payment or fail, making a bad situation worse. The entire U.S. banking system was unstable because there was no dependable source of additional reserves for the entire system. If enough people began to fear that their bank notes or

---

[5] Davis et al., *American Economic Growth: An Economist's History of the United States* (New York: Harper and Row, 1972), p. 356.

[6] I am indebted to Professors Thomas Ulem, of the University of Illinois, and Kenneth Ng, of Cal State, Fullerton, for this information.

[7] R. Robertson, *History of the American Economy*, 3d ed. (New York: Harcourt Brace Jovanovich, 1973), pp. 180–181.

checking deposits could not be converted into specie, the ensuing bank run would invariably prove them correct. Banks faced difficult choices in responding to each others' requests for aid. It was risky for any bank to loan to another institution facing a run. To be effective, the loan had to be large. If such a loan allowed the other bank to meet its depositors' demands, well and good. If not, there was a strong likelihood that one bank's failure might spark runs on others, which would have to face them with depleted reserves.

Nevertheless, antebellum banks' inability to maintain the convertibility of their obligations was not always as catastrophic as it later became. If it appeared that the bank would be able to redeem its obligations at face value after it had time to sell some of its assets or call in loans, its notes and checks drawn on it would continue to be accepted, but at a discount. In this case, the bank had "suspended payment"; it was not redeeming its assets in specie. In "panics," all the banks in a region or even in the country might suspend payment, and specie would either disappear from circulation or command a premium over paper money.[8]

Left to themselves, private, profit-seeking banks have a tendency to accentuate macroeconomic instability, to feed booms and starve depressions. When business conditions are good, it is easy to find borrowers willing to pay high interest rates and offer good security. Consequently, additional bank loans may increase the money supply when full employment limits the economy's ability to increase real output, causing inflation. In bad times, each bank may wish to call in existing loans and make few new ones, because interest rates are low and risks high. Again, what makes sense for one bank may worsen the downturn when followed by all banks. The record of growth and price changes over 1815–1860, however, does not

indicate that these tendencies caused major difficulties for the American economy.

The Central Bank Concept

Central banks attempt to restrict private banks' destabilizing tendencies. The proper function of a central bank is not to make profits, but to regulate the money supply to ensure that it does not contribute to macroeconomic instability. Ideally, central banks attempt to prevent rapid changes in the money supply, which tend to contribute to inflation or recession. The main device for this purpose is their control over private banks' reserves and their ability to change them.

Central banks often provide other services that aid the smooth functioning of the financial sector. They serve as government depositories and disbursing agencies and perform clearinghouse functions for the settlement of interbank debts. These institutions also transfer funds from one region to another and oversee international finance, whether under a gold standard or not. In the early nineteenth century, no nation had fully developed the central bank concept or devised mechanisms for carrying it out, but the United States had two banks with some central bank characteristics.

THE BANKS OF THE UNITED STATES

In 1791, Congress had granted a federal charter to the first Bank of the United States. This institution was unique among American banks of its era because it had a number of branches and did business throughout the country. Because of both this and its position as a government depository, the first Bank of the United States could return notes of other banks deposited with it for prompt collection. While this

---

[8] Temin, *Jacksonian Economy*, pp. 114–118.

may have made currency values more uniform, it also restricted the lending of other, smaller banks, which did not endear it to them. It was a bone of contention between Hamilton and Jefferson, and its stock was largely owned by foreigners. Its charter expired in 1811, and the bill to extend it failed by a single vote.[9]

Origins of the Second Bank of the United States

The government's efforts to finance the War of 1812 were hampered by the lack of a large institution to use as an intermediary or borrow from, so an attempt was made to establish one. In 1816, just too late for the war, Congress granted a charter to the second Bank of the United States, with much the same privileges and structure its namesake had enjoyed. The bank was intended to aid the sale of government bonds for war finance. Bank stock could be purchased with bonds, and because the bank was expected to be profitable, it did increase bond sales.[10] The federal government contributed one-fifth of the bank's total capital of $35 million and appointed one-fifth of the bank's directors. The capital was an enormous sum for 1816, and only one-fourth of the privately subscribed capital was paid in specie. The bank was headquartered in Philadelphia, then the country's financial center, and had branches in all regions of the United States. It served as the federal government's depository, receiving all payments to the government and handling many disbursals as well. It also accepted deposits and made loans (issuing both checking accounts and its own notes) like any commercial bank.[11]

The second Bank of the United States was much larger than any other bank in America. It also followed more conservative lending practices. Consequently, its reserves were both relatively and absolutely large in relation to those of other banks. Because the Bank of the United States was a government depository, tax and tariff payments and the proceeds of land sales, usually in the form of notes issued by state banks, tended to flow into its vaults. Its own policies and its position as the government's depository ensured that the Bank of the United States consistently accumulated more obligations of other banks than they did of its liabilities. Nevertheless, the Bank of the United States remained a profit-seeking if not entirely privately owned bank, primarily concerned with generating income for its owners.

The bank's start was inauspicious. Its first president was incompetent, and the second agreed to an accommodation with state banks from which the Bank of the United States was able to extricate itself only by a drastic and highly unpopular credit contraction. Fortunately, at least for the short run, in 1823 the bank came under the direction of Nicholas Biddle.[12] Under Biddle's presidency, the Bank of the United States assumed a role in which some scholars see central bank characteristics.

Overseer of State Banks

The Bank of the United States began to use its position as a net creditor of the state banks (private banks that had received their corporate charters from state rather than federal government) to control their note issues. As it accumulated the notes of other banks, it returned them for payment in specie or its own notes. It could easily do this because its branches allowed it to transfer funds from one part of

[9] S. Lee and P. Passell, *A New Economic View of American History* (New York: Norton, 1979), pp. 112–113.
[10] C. Nettels, *The Emergence of a National Economy, 1775–1815* (New York: Harper and Row, 1962), pp. 335, 340.
[11] Temin, *Jacksonian Economy,* Chap. 1.

[12] Ibid., pp. 46–49.

the country to another with far greater speed than was possible through alternative institutions. The state banks could do little about this policy. They could not prevent the use of their own notes for tax payments if they were to be acceptable at all.

Because of this policy, the state banks were forced to limit their note issues in relation to their reserves. They now had to anticipate that their notes might be returned to them in much less time than previously, even if they had been issued far from the bank. If they could obtain Bank of the United States notes, they could return these instead of specie. However, the conservative lending policies of the large bank made its notes scarce, and because its reserves were so large, the notes were as expensive as specie. State banks had little choice but to hold larger reserves and reduce their loans.

An Unpopular Policy Bears Fruit

The Bank of the United States had many enemies. Bankers who had lost income and advocates of "cheap money" disliked it for purely economic reasons. But once the bank's policy became effective, the notes of most banks circulated at close to their face value throughout the country. Prior to this, New England banks' currency had been accepted at par (face value), and currency from Mid-Atlantic states' banks for only slightly less. But the currency of Kentucky, Tennessee, and Alabama banks was accepted at 75 percent of its face value or even less. During the 1820s, this discount fell to no more than 5 percent.[13] Notes issued by state banks were finally really usable in distant as well as local markets, and people conducting business far from their own banks did not have to undergo the difficulty and danger of carrying specie or wonder what discount rate their money might fetch. Money was now more nearly

"a good traded in all markets," the classic definition of a medium of exchange.

Was the Second Bank of the United States a Central Bank?

With its large reserves, the Bank of the United States could also function as a source of emergency reserves for state banks—the "lender of last resort" that the American banking system had lacked. However, its performance in that role fell well short of the central bank ideal. Although it did make specie loans to state banks experiencing temporary difficulties, the Bank of the United States loaned with an eye on its own reserve position and prospective profits, rather than state bank needs and the effects its actions had on the economy. Moreover, it sometimes acquired reserves to meet a crisis by selling bonds to the public for specie—which in itself reduced the money supply. This was the exact opposite of modern central bank practice. Nor would the bank expand its loans sufficiently to become a net debtor to the state banks. [14] No really major crises occurred during the 1820s, but had one taken place, it is very doubtful that the Bank of the United States would have loaned sufficient amounts to state banks to prevent a banking collapse.

As a result of these policies, the second Bank of the United States was able to regulate the quality of money (its convertibility into coin) and to exert some downward pressure on state banks' expansion ratios. By relaxing its practice of returning state banks' notes to them, it could in effect loan to these institutions, but apparently did not do so. On the other hand, its policies were ill-suited to lender-of-last-resort functions in a widespread banking crisis. Since the bank could not control the amount of re-

---

[13] Ibid., pp. 48–50.

[14] Ibid., p. 55.

serves held by state banks, it could not expand the money supply. Nor could it contract the amount of bank money in circulation if state banks had ample hard-money reserves. In sum, the second Bank of the United States could not fulfill the primary role of a modern central bank: it could not, in most circumstances, control the money supply.[15] Its influence was nevertheless beneficial. The stability and efficiency of the American banking system were improved by its policies, and as a result banking became an aid rather than a hindrance to regional trade and specialization.

THE BANK WAR

In 1832 President Andrew Jackson vetoed an attempt to renew the federal charter of the Bank of the United States. Jackson's action could have sprung from any or all of a long list of motives: his own dislike of banks, centers of private power, and Nicholas Biddle himself; considerations based on partisan politics; and some very confused economic analysis. When Jackson was overwhelmingly reelected after his veto, the bank's special relationship with the federal government was clearly at an end.

The "Pet Banks"
Although the Bank of the United States obtained a Pennsylvania charter and continued to operate until 1841, federal deposits were withdrawn and placed in banks owned by Jackson's political allies—the "pet banks."[16] After the Panic of 1837, in which the government lost much of the money deposited in such banks, government funds were kept in an independent treasury. The federal government, it was de-

cided, would avoid such losses in the future by collecting, holding, and disbursing all its own funds. Moreover, in 1836 the government refused to deal in bank money. The Specie Circular of that year announced that henceforth only gold and silver would be accepted in payment of obligations (chiefly land, tariff, and tax payments) to the government.

The Distribution of The Federal Surplus
Another program not directly related to the demise of the Bank of the United States has been alleged to have affected the banking system. For most years after 1815, the federal government had a budget surplus. The excess of receipts over expenditures had been used to pay off the national debt, that is, to retire government bonds as or even before they matured. However, in 1835 the debt had been completely retired, and the accumulating surplus had grown embarrassingly large. Twenty-eight million dollars in federal surplus funds were distributed to the states in 1837. The panic of that year ended the program: trade and tariff revenues were so diminished by the slump that the government had no further surplus to distribute.[17]

Economic Instability
Shortly after the veto of the Recharter Bill and during the other policies' implementation, economic affairs in the United States took a much less favorable course than in the early 1830s. After the government began to reduce its deposits with the Bank of the United States, a sharp credit contraction occurred, possibly due to the bank's response (or overresponse) to the loss of government funds. Then in 1835 prices began to increase rapidly. A massive boom, fueled by high crop prices and the resultant market in western lands, occurred. By 1837 prices were nearly one-third higher than only two years before. A severe panic with wide-

---

[15] Ibid., pp. 50–54.
[16] The identity of the owners of the "pet banks" is in some dispute. See H. Scheiber, "The Pet Banks in Jacksonian Politics and Finance, 1831–1841," *Journal of Economic History* (June 1963).

[17] Ibid., p. 129.

spread bank failures then developed, and after an unsteady recovery in 1838 and early 1839, an intensified slump began. Full recovery did not occur until 1843.

The Role of the Bank of the United States

To what extent were these events linked to the demise of the Bank of the United States' control over state banks? Some researchers see a clear relationship. The termination of the bank's special relationship with the federal government, they believe, removed the only restraint on state banks. Lacking the control shown by the Bank of the United States, the state banks expanded the money supply far beyond the safe limits of their reserves. The boom-time atmosphere encouraged speculation, particularly in land. This plus the reckless monetary expansion caused inflation. But the reserves of the state banks were not large enough to support the claims on them, and the situation was ripe for collapse. The final straw was the distribution of the federal surplus, which moved specie from the conservatively managed banks of the East to the reckless western banks, which responded to the windfall by increasing their loans and hence expanding the money supply still further. When the Specie Circular drew much of what little coin remained out of circulation, a banking collapse became inevitable.

This is what might be expected if a central bank's controls were removed suddenly because the proponents of monetary expansion found them too limiting. However, the monetary history of the late 1830s is now thought to be related far more to events beyond U.S. borders than to President Jackson's attack on the Bank of the United States, misguided though it may have been. In particular, Jackson's ancient enemies, the British, played a larger role in the American inflation and depression of 1839–1843 than did internal economic forces. The British actions were based on Far Eastern trade and the British harvest, as we shall see.

An Increased Money Supply

Inflation, as always, was a consequence of rapid monetary expansion. The money supply rose sharply between 1834 and 1836. As indicated in Table 8.1, prices rose by over 25 percent in that period. But the expansion in the money supply was not caused by an increase in banks' willingness to loan against given amounts of reserves (a rise in the expansion ratio). The ratios of reserves to bank money and of specie to all money did not fall. Moreover, reserve ratios were higher, not lower, in western banks than in the East (see Tables 8.2 and 8.3). Banks did increase their loans and raise the money supply, but they did so on the basis of larger specie reserves.

The silver came from Mexico, where it was a commodity export. Furthermore, Mexican silver was being driven out of domestic circulation by the monetary policies of the Santa Ana regime. More silver came from Europe as a consequence of British investment in the United States and the payment of an indemnity by France. Interest rates were higher in the United States than in Britain, and investment funds flowed to America as a result, especially into "safe" state government bonds issued to finance transportation projects. Previously, much of the specie entering the United States had been used to finance trade with China, but now conditions in that trade changed.

The Chinese Connection
Americans had long desired Chinese tea, silk, and porcelain, but the Chinese preferred silver to most American goods. The few items the Chinese found acceptable from the Americans, such as Pacific sea otter skins and Hawaiian sandalwood, required extended voyages and could only be procured in limited quantities.

Table 8.2 Reserve Ratios of State Banks by Region, 1834–1837*

End-of-Year Treasury Data	New England	Middle Atlantic	Southeast	Southwest	Northwest
1834	.06	.22	.24	.13	.46
1835	.07	.16	.21	.15	.28
1836	.07	.14	.18	.14	.30
1837	.09	.19	.24	.13	.32
Van Fenstermaker's Data					
1834	.10	.21	.26	.21	.39
1835	.11	.16	.25	.17	.27
1836	.10	.16	.20	.13	.31
1837	.12	.26	.24	.13	.36

*Reserve ratios are the ratios of bank reserves to notes outstanding and demand deposits.
Source: P. Temin, *The Jacksonian Economy* (New York: Norton, 1969), p. 75.

But in the 1830s, the Chinese began to buy large amounts of opium from British India (and smaller quantities that Americans brought from Turkey). To pay for the opium, the Chinese wanted credit in London, rather than silver. American traders could now finance their purchases in China with drafts on London bankers. The Chinese used this credit to pay their drug bills.[18] While the British were buying large quantities of American cotton and investing heavily in this country, Americans had no difficulty in obtaining advances from London.

The silver that had formerly flowed to China now tended to remain in the United States, and the developments noted previously increased the flow to this country. Part of the silver naturally found its way into bank reserves, and banks thereupon expanded their loans. The British played a large, if incidental, role in the decline after mid-1837 as well. The British increased their grain imports after a series of poor harvests, and their balance of trade deteriorated. Specie flowed out of Britain, and to prevent further loss of reserves, the Bank of England sharply restricted credit. Interest rates rose in Britain, offering better alternatives to foreign investment, and the British demand for American cotton also fell.

The Panic of 1837

The 1835–1837 expansion in the United States had been largely based on the cotton boom, and a major proportion of bank loans was linked to cotton in one way or another. When cotton brokers and the banks with which they dealt began to fail, runs on banks occurred throughout the country. Twenty-three percent of all American banks failed, and many others suspended payment. The money supply fell by 34 percent from 1839 to 1843.[19] The surplus distribution and the Specie Circular apparently influenced the situation only minimally. Transfer of specie from eastern banks apparently did not cause them to fear for the adequacy of their

[18] Ibid., pp. 79–82.

[19] Ibid., p. 157.

Table 8.3   The Supply of Money and its Determinants, 1820–1839

End of Year	Money (Millions)	Annual Rate of Change	Specie (Millions)	Reserve Ratio	Percentage of Money Held as Specie
1820	$85		$41	32%	24%
1821	96	12.4%	39	30	16
1822	81	−15.6	32	21	23
1823	88	8.6	31	25	15
1824	88	0.0	32	27	13
1825	106	20.5	29	19	10
1826	108	1.9	32	20	12
1827	101	−6.5	32	20	14
1828	114	12.9	31	18	11
1829	105	−7.9	33	22	12
1830	114	7.9	32	23	6
1831	155	36.0	30	15	5
1832	150	−3.2	31	16	5
1833	168	12.0	41	18	8
1834	172	2.4	51	27	4
1835	246	43.0	65	18	10
1836	276	12.2	73	16	13
1837	232	−19.0	88	20	23
1838	240	3.4	87	23	18
1839	215	−10.4	83	20	23

Source: P. Temin, *The Jacksonian Economy* (New York: Norton, 1969), p. 71.

reserves. Indeed, some eastern banks proposed shipping specie to England after the surplus distribution.[20] Given the pattern of reserve ratios indicated by Table 8.2, specie movements were toward regions where banks had high rather than low reserve ratios.

If the Specie Circular had any effect at all, it caused a flow of specie (potential bank reserves) into land purchases. But land purchases would reduce inflationary pressures rather than increase them. Given the huge acreage available, land prices were unlikely to rise, and the money devoted to buying land would be withheld from further circulation by the Treasury.

[20] Ibid., p. 135.

Had the second Bank of the United States retained in 1837 all the powers it possessed in 1832, events would not have turned out very differently—at least if the bank's policies resembled those it employed before the withdrawal of government funds. The bank clearly could not have prevented an increase in the money supply based on a more than proportionate expansion of reserves, so it could not have prevented the inflation. It certainly did not control British foreign lending or foreign policy, to say nothing of the British harvest. The Bank of England's reaction to a gold outflow was a long-established policy. But the demise of the second Bank of the United States did leave Americans with greatly reduced regulatory programs for banks. In some cases, regulations were to be still further eased before new and more effective rules were developed.

THE FREE BANKING ERA

In 1838 Michigan and New York passed laws greatly easing the restrictions imposed on would-be bankers. No longer were new banks in these states required to obtain individual charters from the legislature, which permitted at least some chance to scrutinize their proposals. Instead, depositing approved securities of a stated face value with the state's banking officials and observing a few basic regulations entitled any individual or group to enter the banking business. Other states instituted their own "free banking" laws, and the number of state banks rose from 691 in 1843 to 1,520 in 1860.[21]

A Colorful History

State regulations often were not well designed, and enforcement might be lax. These conditions gave rise to some spectacular evasions of the basic financial responsibilities associated with banks. However, it now appears that some of the most colorful tales about antebellum banking have survived precisely because the events described were unusual even then. Nevertheless, the stories are worth repeating.

The bonds of some states, particularly in the early 1840s, were all but worthless because the states were paying neither interest nor principal on them (see Chapter 5). But some "free banking" laws did not exclude such securities from eligibility for deposit with the state as surety for banks' performance. Unscrupulous in-

dividuals might put up only enough cash to allow the bank to acquire these "assets." The state might then allow the bank to begin operations, whereupon the bank's owners would print notes and begin to make loans. The first loans might be to the bank's own stockholders, who sometimes used the proceeds to complete payments on their bank stock. Such a bank would have no real reserves—or even assets. Its success depended on receiving deposits or loan repayments in something other than its own currency.

"Wildcat Banks"

Some such banks were called "wildcat banks" because they were located where there were "more wildcats than people." Another favorite location was among Indians whose pacification was uncertain. Like other banks, wildcat banks employed guards, but in this case their duty was to discourage customers—not robbers—from making withdrawals. These measures were taken for good if not admirable business reasons. Failure rates among such banks were very high. Nor were these failures only the concern of bank owners. People who were left holding the notes of failed banks found that the currency was now worthless, but the loans they had contracted still required payment, often to some distant financier to whom the bankers had sold them. One group of bank promoters had the audacity to note (as a selling point!) that 13 of the 27 banks they had already organized were still in business. In fairness, their rivals had experienced 41 failures in 43 tries.[22]

Despite such tales, wildcat banking was not the norm, even on the frontier, as Table 8.2 indicates. Also, such practices became less prevalent as time passed. By 1860 both bankers and regulators knew that banks should keep reserves against liabilities, not capital or just note liabilities. The enforcement of regulation

[21] U.S. Department of Commerce, Bureau of the Census, *Historical Statistics of the United States: Colonial Times to 1970*, 2 vols. (Washington, D.C.: Government Printing Office, 1975), p. 1020.

[22] Hammond, "Banking in the Early West: Monopoly, Prohibition, and Laissez Faire," in Cochran and Brewer, *Views of American Economic Growth*.

improved, and some states conducted periodic examinations. Macroeconomic evidence strongly reinforces the conclusions of several modern studies that wildcat banking—or even all "free banking"—wreaked no serious damage on the aggregate economy. Economic growth was rapid over the 1843–1860 heyday of free banking, even in activities heavily dependent on bank financing. Prices changed considerably in this era, with an upward trend after 1848, but inflation appears to have sprung largely from the California gold rush and the consequent increase in gold and hence bank reserves rather than actions of the banks themselves. The high reserve ratios of western banks do not entirely reflect unusual prudence; small banks have greater risks from any individual loan, and risks on the frontier were in general higher. Nevertheless, the evidence does not support the usual impression of high-risk or totally heedless frontier bankers.[23]

Currency Chaos

The demise of the second Bank of the United States left the country without a uniform national currency. In addition, there was now no agency as effective at maintaining the convertibility of state bank notes. After 1836, virtually the only money accepted at its face value in all regions of the United States, or at least far from its point of issue, was gold and silver coin. The problem was not a lack of other types of money, but an overabundance. By 1860 the 1,500 banks in the United States had issued at least 9,000 different types and denominations of notes that retained at least some value. Many

notes of failed banks and many counterfeits were in circulation as well.[24]

Persons offered unfamiliar currency in exchanges had several choices: they could refuse the note or determine its value either by bargaining with its owner or by referring to one of the numerous bank note reference guides or "counterfeit detectors." These guides attempted to provide up-to-date information on the values of all notes in circulation and the latest discoveries of counterfeits. Although some of these lists were remarkably comprehensive, their information could never be either complete or current; they could reduce the risks of currency transactions, but not eliminate them. Completed transactions involving currency unfamiliar to one of the parties required agreement on two sets of prices: first, that of the goods in "standard" money, and second, the value of the money involved relative to that standard.

The Burden of State Bank Currency

Traditionally, money has been considered to serve three functions. It is a medium of exchange, a store of value, and a standard of deferred payment. State banks' currency performed less than perfectly in all these areas. Further, resources devoted to offsetting the disadvantages of such currency had alternative uses. But the damage to aggregate economic activity was not great. One study has estimated that social savings from the use of inferior paper money rather than specie declined by from one-tenth to one-one hundredth of 1 percent of gross national product.[25] The cost resulting from impaired medium-of-exchange functions (including the time lost determining currency values) was almost certainly greater. But im-

[23] H. Rockoff, "Money, Prices and Banks in the Jacksonian Era," in R. Fogel and S. Engerman, *The Reinterpretation of American Economic History* (New York: Harper and Row, 1971), and in "Varieties of Banking and Regional Economic Development in the United States, 1830–1860," *Journal of Economic History* (March 1975).

[24] Robertson, *History of the American Economy*, pp. 192–193.
[25] M. Shuska, "The Antebellum Money Market and the Impact of the Bank War," *Journal of Economic History* (December 1976); and S. Engerman, "A Note on the Consequences of the Second Bank of the United States," *Journal of Political Economy* (July/August 1970).

perfect as they were, the responses Americans devised were effective, and the macroeconomic impact of the ragbag antebellum currency—while adverse—was not large.

Small Banks' Defensive Measures

The banking system as a whole was unstable, as the substantial changes in the money supply, price levels, and bank failures indicate. One effort to improve the stability of small banks was only partially successful. As noted earlier, banks sacrifice interest income by keeping large reserve balances in their vaults, but they sacrifice stability by reducing their reserves. Small-town banks began to maintain some reserves in the form of checking deposits with banks in larger cities. The city banks in turn kept a portion of their reserves in deposits with banks in New York City. In normal times, such a system addressed both problems. If any individual bank foresaw an outflow of specie, it could obtain more coin quickly and easily by requesting funds from the bank holding its reserve deposit. Such deposits also facilitated clearance of interbank debts, and they paid interest.

Continuing Instability

Unfortunately, the pyramiding of reserves in New York banks was an effective response from the viewpoint of individual banks, not the entire banking system. If many country banks demanded the funds they had on deposit in larger cities, the system might break down. The problem was that all the banks involved were private, profit-maximizing businesses, and no bank was willing to hold large amounts of reserves that did not generate income. New York banks recognized that correspondent banks might suddenly request large withdrawals, so their investments of such funds had to be highly liquid. Consequently, New York banks lent the money "on call," which meant that the loans were re-payable within 24 hours on the lender's request. Only borrowers who could convert assets into cash on such short notice would borrow under these terms. One such group was securities brokers. Further safety was derived from restricting the loans to some fraction, usually no more than one-half, of the value of the securities they helped to purchase. Such loans appeared both safe and liquid.

But although any individual broker could count on selling securities for more than the amount owed the banks, all brokers combined could not. If many brokers attempted to sell at the same time, securities prices might fall so far that the proceeds would not cover obligations to the banks. Even if this did not occur, the sudden decline in securities values might increase pressure on the banking system as a whole. Since it was known that banks invested in securities as well as loans, depositors and noteholders became uneasy when the news from New York or other money markets was bad. Further, small-town banks' need for funds might be difficult to coordinate with securities markets.

MONEY SUPPLY CHANGES AND THE ECONOMY

Today, most economists agree that the initial effect of a decline in the money supply or even of a sizable reduction in its growth rate would be a drop in real economic activity—in production and employment. Recent history confirms this view: witness the record from 1981 to 1983. While they might disagree over the time between cause and effect, most would agree that one to two years would have to pass under modern conditions before prices fell sufficiently to allow real output to recover.

But through the nineteenth century, these conditions did not hold. First, the structure of the economy was different; most Americans were self-employed farmers who would feel the decline chiefly as a drop in prices received for the produce they sold. (Most farms consumed a large proportion of their own output.) The total amount of farm unemployment caused by a monetary contraction would be small. Although the impact would be greater among merchants, the manufacturing sector, and of course banks, they comprised a much smaller portion of the labor force than they do today.

Even where unemployment occurred, a variety of factors limited its duration. Joblessness might be severe among manufacturing workers and bankruptcies widespread among their employers, but price reductions were likely to result both more quickly and more generally than they would today. A worker with no savings and a family to support might have to accept a cut in his money wages, but the general reduction in prices would mean that his standard of living might not decline in proportion to the wage cut. If real wages declined, because wages are a price to employers, employment would increase. Flexible prices thus made the effects of monetary contractions less severe and shorter than might be the case today.

FINANCE

Any economic activity in which time elapses between the start of production and final consumption involves financial considerations. Someone must forego the use of resources while they are being processed, transported, or held in inventories. If people are to continue to do so, and even more, to invest in capital goods with deferred returns, some form of compensation must be available. In addition, many people wish to consume more than their current incomes will permit. If they are to borrow, those lending to them will have to be paid for allowing others to use their funds. Finally, since the resources involved are scarce—they have alternative uses—some mechanism must be developed to direct resources to uses that produce more than their opportunity costs if incomes are to be maximized.

Banks as Sources of Capital

Even today, commercial banks are imperfect devices for meeting some of the financial needs of new industries. Banks are better suited to providing loans for short-term working capital than to financing long-term projects. This holds with particular force where banks are small and local, as they were in the antebellum United States. Financing a railroad or factory involved committing large sums for long periods. The payoff from such an investment would likely be spread over many years. Just a few loans of this type would be enough to tie up a large portion of a small bank's assets. Thus, the failure of any single such project might ruin the bank as well. Worse, commercial banks' liabilities tend to be short-term: depositors are entitled to their funds on demand or within a short time. Particularly where there is no source of emergency funds for banks, investments in fixed capital are not liquid—they cannot be readily sold on short notice. Hence long-term loans involve high risks for commercial banks.

Early Capital Markets

In the early nineteenth century, there were few sources of long-term capital loans other than personal relationships between borrower and lender. When the capital requirements of essential projects exceeded the resources of local merchant communities, the only alternative source of capital was government. The credit and taxing powers of state and local governments were frequently enlisted to raise funds for such capital-intensive projects as canal construction. Not infrequently, as previously discussed (see Chapter 5), such methods of fund raising suffered from the lack of a market test.

Particularly in eastern cities, the tightly knit social structure of wealthy merchants who were invariably well acquainted and often related eased the problems of raising large sums. Nevertheless, the lack of an effective allocative mechanism for the entire economy limited the choice of investments. Reallocation of investments tended to be local. New England witnessed a notable redirection of activity from maritime ventures to manufacturing over the antebellum period, and by the 1850s New England funds were used to build railroads in that region and elsewhere. But the reliance on local sources of investment capital in most parts of the country and the need to combine the savings of many individuals often resulted in high capital costs and an overemphasis on local projects, which might not offer the rates of return available on alternative investments.

Many early industrialists appear to have spent as much time scrambling for financial support as producing and selling their goods. They obtained funds from friends and relatives, used the trust funds of widows, orphans, and churches, and demanded payment with orders rather than on delivery of products, so that their customers assumed some of their financial burdens. Short-term bank loans might be taken out with an understanding that they would be continually renewed. Nor were some would-be industrialists above marrying for money. Somehow, however, the necessary capital was generated.[26]

Lack of capital does not appear to have been an insuperable obstacle to industrialization, although the records of successful firms have been more extensively analyzed than of those that failed or never operated. The portion of income invested in the antebellum economy rose amid signs that the allocation of savings was becoming more efficient. These developments began on a local or regional basis

and appeared in Massachusetts earlier than in the rest of the country. New legal concepts were required to make debts transferable, and new institutions had to be developed to help reallocate savings from agriculture to industry and transportation, but the process was well under way even before the turn of the century—at least in one area of America.[27]

The Local Bias

The Massachusetts developments had by no means become universal by 1860. As late as that year, there was nothing resembling a national capital market. Interest rates even in well-developed local markets, such as Boston and New York, diverged as often as they converged, and higher interest rates in the capital-starved West did not attract significant eastern investment until late in the period. Few people were willing to invest in projects outside their own communities or directed by persons they did not know personally. One Baltimore bank refused the loan application of a firm nine miles distant because "We know nothing of business conditions in the West."

The Rise of New Financial Institutions

Institutions that remedied some of these deficiencies became more common. By 1860, about half the states provided for general incorporation through laws granting charters on petition rather than by legislative approval of each application. Incorporation made pooling the funds of many investors easier, but many of its modern advantages were not yet fully realized. Corporate stock was sold almost ex-

[26] L. Davis, "The New England Textile Mills and the Capital Market: A Study in Industrial Borrowing," *Journal of Economic History* (March 1960).

[27] W. Rothernberg, "The Emergence of a Capital Market in Rural Massachusetts, 1730–1838," *Journal of Economic History* (December 1985).

clusively to the same lenders who had provided funds earlier and was rarely traded. Stock exchanges appeared in most large cities, but they dealt largely in government bonds and, after 1850, railroad bonds. Financial markets were very thin, with only a few securities changing hands each day, and price fluctuations were extreme. Prior to the Civil War, corporate stock other than railroad stock was not sold on the stock exchanges.

The lack of large-scale financial institutions was not the barrier to industrial capital formation that it might appear from a modern view. In most manufacturing industries, the scale of efficient production was small, and adequate capital could generally be raised by individuals or partnerships. As industry developed, firms' retained earnings became the chief source of additional capital. In many new firms, the rate of reinvestment was very high.

Savings Banks and Insurance Companies

Institutions suited to long-term lending had appeared by 1860, but most were still in their infancy. Savings banks and insurance companies, particularly life insurance firms, were able to make long-term loans because they could count on retaining funds deposited with them for considerable periods. In addition, they pooled the funds of many savers and developed a comprehensive knowledge of investment opportunities, which may have reduced capital costs to investors and improved allocation. Both were capable of making large loans. Savings banks and life insurance companies, like most other financial institutions, operated mainly in the East and had little impact on interest rates in the West. As the importance of foreign trade waned and the institutions conducting it changed their fields of operation, trade credit from English merchants became less important than in colonial days. Other forms of foreign investment achieved a new importance that will be discussed later in this chapter.

Southern Financial Institutions

In the South, capital mobility may have developed much further than formal market institutions would indicate. Capital in the form of slaves migrated with its planter owners to the rich lands of the New South. Although its extent, as noted in Chapter 6, is still a matter of controversy, some development of the interregional slave trade also occurred.

Working capital was provided to planters by cotton factors, specialized merchants who bought the crop from the planters and sold it to manufacturers in Britain and New England. As had Scotch and English tobacco factors in eighteenth-century Virginia, the cotton factors also provided loans and other services, sometimes on the security of next year's crop. They obtained their funds from England. Factors either bought cotton outright or sold it for planters on commission, purchasing supplies for planters with the proceeds. Unlike the tobacco factors, the nineteenth-century factors did not serve a single English cotton merchant. Planters and a network of retail and wholesale merchants collected the cotton produced by small farmers and distributed the manufactured goods and other items that they purchased.

INTERNAL COMMERCE

The Rise of the Middleman

As specialization developed first in agriculture and then in manufacturing and throughout the economy, the role of middlemen assumed greater importance. With so large a portion of the work force now turning out only limited ranges of goods and services, those who distributed these products found a steady increase in demand for their services. They too became more specialized as markets grew. By 1860 some people handled only one or two distribution functions or dealt in a narrow range of items, in contrast to the colonial period. Then, true distribution specialists had existed only for the major export crops, and most distribution functions were handled by the original producers. New opportunities appeared for warehousemen, draymen, salesmen, bookkeepers, clerks, and others, especially after 1820.

In colonial times, only the largest cities had markets of sufficient scope to support stores selling less than the total range of imported goods. Now, both demand and supply were vastly greater. Population and incomes had grown, and urban populations were a larger portion of the total. Discretionary spending was possible, since consumers had something left after providing for basic food, shelter, and clothing. The variety of items available was much greater than in the colonial period, and output came from larger numbers of producers. Since the technology of information gathering and transmission had changed very little from the colonial era, the initial response came through increased specialization and large numbers of middlemen that more or less paralleled the rise in the volume of business.[28]

The General Store

The general store was still much in evidence in rural areas and the smaller towns, but even that hallowed institution was beginning to recognize that consumers now had wider alternatives as to what and where they bought. Commodity dealers, who bought wheat directly from the farmers and used grain elevators, organized exchanges, grading procedures, and other new institutions, began to supplement sales to the general store in the 1850s.[29] Even frontier merchants now began to see the wisdom in viewing samples of goods before they bought. Farmers who received cash for their crops were less tied to one store and the credit of its owner.

Once again, the appearance of new occupations, products, and possible life-styles rewarded those with the flexibility and imagination to recognize them and respond quickly. The attitudes of American consumers toward new products raised the returns garnered by those dealing in new commodities.

The Rise of Mass Markets

Rising incomes allowed people to buy larger quantities of the goods they had always purchased. But more importantly, it appeared that American consumers were interested in variety, in new items that made life different from what they had always known. In addition, as Chapter 7 pointed out, production of many items now moved from the home—or from home finishing—to the factory. Style and quality of finish became more important than in the days when few people bought more than staple foods, cloth, and tools. Competition became a real factor in many local markets as market size grew faster than the scale of production and distribution, and transportation broadened the choices of both consumers and individual producers.

New technology had increased the ability to produce, and it was soon apparent that distributing the results was at least equally important. Especially in the case of finished goods, it became increasingly difficult to dispose of factories' entire output by direct sale in local markets. As producers specialized, for example in gingham rather than cotton cloth, or looms rather than textile machinery, this point gained additional importance. Marketing became vital

---

[28] A. Chandler, Jr., *The Visible Hand: The Managerial Revolution in American Business* (Cambridge, Mass.: Harvard University Press, 1977), pp. 48–49.

[29] Ibid., pp. 209–215.

to the success of producers, whereas only a few decades earlier, markets were taken for granted.

New Methods of Distribution

One marketing method was to sell through a commission merchant. These middlemen found retail outlets for a firm's production and received a percentage of the revenue they generated. Commission merchants did not take title to the goods they sold, leaving inventory financing to producers. Some producers also sold their goods at auction.

Such methods did not answer all distribution needs. Commission merchants could not pay producers until they had sold the goods, and retailers often ordered far less than the commission merchants had available. Later, jobbers intervened between commission merchants and retailers. Unlike the former, jobbers actually owned the goods they sold. With assistance from bank loans, jobbers were able to extend credit to retailers. Jobbers' operations gave rise to credit-rating agencies. They also provided market information to producers, advising them about what goods sell. Few consumer goods were sold under brand names in the antebellum economy, and many wholesalers handled the output of several factories. Since few producers had experience responding to consumers' wishes, such services were an important aid. Where markets were still small, functions were less specialized; often large-scale retailers also served as wholesalers in selling to small-town merchants.[30]

FOREIGN TRADE

Foreign trade had been one of the most important sources of higher incomes and economic growth throughout previous American history. After 1815, however, the relative im-

[30] Ibid., Chap. 1.

portance of foreign trade waned. Domestic substitutes appeared for many of the items previously obtainable only overseas. As Table 8.4 reveals, the volume of foreign commerce increased, but the rest of the economy grew faster.

Changing Trade Patterns

The United States had traditionally exported raw materials to Europe in exchange for manufactured goods, a pattern that continued after 1815. But trade patterns were not static: cotton replaced tobacco and breadstuffs as the most important single American export, and the balance of payments changed from that prevailing in the colonial era. In 1820 about 60 percent of U.S. exports were cotton, tobacco, and other crude materials. By 1860 crude materials comprised 68 percent of all exports, with cotton by far the largest single item. Manufactured items were only 6 percent of exports in 1820, but over 11 percent in 1860. In 1821, 56 percent of American imports were manufactured goods, and these still comprised 48 percent of the total in 1860.

Britain was America's principal trading partner over the entire period, providing a market for one-third to one-half of all exports and supplying about two-fifths of all imports. Trade with other nations of North and South America accounted for about 30 percent of imports through the period, but Western Hemisphere trade partners changed, with Canada, Mexico, and Brazil gaining at the expense of the traditional Caribbean trade.

Some new items achieved importance in American trade statistics and others began to fade. In most years the United States imported more than it exported, just as it had from the late colonial period. Shipping earnings now offset a declining portion of the trade deficit. More and more American trade was carried by foreign ships, and freight rates fell.

Table 8.4 Foreign Trade, 1815–1860
(In Thousands of Dollars)

Year	Total Exports	Total Imports	U.S. Shipping Earnings (Net)	Net Capital Flows*	Net Debt	Specie Flows**	Dividends and Interest
1815	$52,558	$85,357	$20,600	$15,000	$94,000	$2,000	$5,000
1820	69,692	74,450	13,900	−1,000	86,700	0	4,807
1825	90,738	90,189	11,600	−7,000	80,300	−2,500	4,792
1830	71,671	62,721	10,500	−8,000	74,900	6,000	4,557
1835	115,216	139,499	8,800	30,000	158,100	7,000	7,042
1840	123,669	100,224	26,200	−31,000	266,400	0	11,888
1845	106,040	115,448	18,800	−4,000	213,000	−4,000	8,674
1850	144,376	180,450	8,600	29,000	222,100	3,000	13,326
1855	218,910	268,121	21,200	15,000	356,300	−53,000	22,320
1860	333,576	367,760	32,500	−7,000	379,200	−58,000	25,122

*Denotes an increased foreign purchase of U.S. securities if positive, American repurchase of U.S. securities held abroad if negative.
**Denotes imports of specie if positive, exports if negative.
Source: D. North, *The Economic Growth of the United States, 1790–1860* (Englewood Cliffs, N.J.: Prentice-Hall, 1961), pp. 233–238; and the U.S. Bureau of the Census, Department of Commerce, *Historical Statistics of the United States: Colonial Times to 1970*, 2 vols. (Washington, D.C.: Government Printing Office, 1975), 2:865–866.

The Importance of Foreign Investment

Foreign investment in the United States became an important component in the trade balance, with the exception of the early 1840s. In effect, some American imports were purchased by exports of securities. Never more than one-third of domestic investment, and usually far less, foreign capital was available in large amounts from Europe's more developed money markets at lower interest rates than in the United States, especially if the costs of borrowing are included. In the case of repudiated securities, such as those of Mississippi, Pennsylvania, and Michigan, the costs actually incurred by Americans were very low indeed, because foreign investors were never repaid.

Foreigners were at least as willing to invest in the American West as were investors from the Atlantic Seaboard. Foreign funds, mainly from Britain, the Netherlands, and Germany, were invested in state bonds and railroad securities. They allowed America to build its transportation system before domestically generated funds were available. As a consequence of foreign investment in America, the flow of dividends, interest, and principal to foreign owners of American capital increased with time. After 1850, two other factors made significant contributions to the flow of money to Europe. Increased immigration, which had begun in the previous decade, generated a flow of remittances to the "Old Country." Often such remittances became passage money for those still in Europe. And once the United States began to produce gold from its California mines, the yellow metal became a commodity export—another means of financing imports and paying for the services of foreign capital.

Tariffs

Even as the physical obstacles to foreign trade were reduced, political barriers replaced them. By the late 1850s, ocean freight rates were about one-fifth their 1815 levels, which greatly reduced the delivered price of foreign goods. But by that time Europe was no longer the only possible source of manufactured goods, and attitudes toward trade barriers had begun to change. In 1816, Daniel Webster was a proponent of free trade, reflecting the views of his New England constituents, shipowners for whom the largest volume of trade produced the greatest income. By the mid-1820s, Webster had become an advocate of tariff protection for his region's growing industry. John C. Calhoun, the great southern spokesman, opposed Webster on both occasions.

East versus South?

Attitudes toward tariffs have usually been presented as a contest between regions with uniform internal views. The South, with its concentration on export crops and dependence on manufactured goods from other regions, was seen as favoring free trade, which would raise the demand for its exports and reduce the price of imported manufactures either directly or by providing effective competition for Yankee industry. The East, and especially New England, was thought to be solidly pro-tariff, at least after investment began to shift out of maritime activities. But an analysis of congressional support for and opposition to tariffs reveals no such clear-cut regional divisions. Even the "Tariff of Abominations" over which South Carolina threatened secession in 1828 attracted majority or unanimous support from the congressmen of no less than seven southern states. The Massachusetts delegation never gave majority support to any tariff proposal between 1812 and 1832, but Ohio congressmen supported each of these bills unanimously.[31]

Under generally poorly reasoned policies, tariffs were raised on all items in 1816. In the 1820s, duties on manufactured goods reached

nearly prohibitive levels—in some cases, half the value of the imported goods. Initially, even goods that could not be produced in quantities sufficient to meet domestic demand, or even at all, were taxed together with items that competed with domestic production. After 1828 tariffs were gradually reduced to no more than 20 percent of the value of imports, and more items were admitted duty-free. But no sooner had these levels been achieved in 1842 than they were increased in the next year. The 1846 Walker Tariff imposed import classification schedules, which levied different duties on goods classified as luxuries, necessities, and raw materials. The Walker Tariff also reduced overall tariff rates to modestly protective levels again (see Table 8.5).

Tariff Fundamentals

The usual rationale for tariffs is that they encourage domestic production and thus provide jobs. Tariffs may accomplish this, but only at the expense of employment in the country's exporting industries, since foreigners cannot buy unless they can also sell their own products. Generally, too, tariffs transfer resources from high- to low-productivity uses and reduce rather than raise the overall level of incomes. There may be one important exception. Protection for an industry in its early stages of existence may be economically justified if the tariff allows the domestic firms to gain the skills and operating experience needed to compete successfully with foreign producers *in the absence* of tariff protection in the future. Rarely, though, do such "infant industries" ever consider themselves sufficiently mature to do without protection from overseas competition.

The Impact of Tariffs

On balance, tariffs did little to encourage the growth of American industry. They probably did allow the survival of less efficient methods of production within the United States—for example, in the iron industry—after free trade would have forced them out. Few industries

[31] Lebergott, *The Americans: An Economic Record* (New York: Norton, 1984), pp. 144–145.

Table 8.5 Tariff Rates and Proportion of Imports Subject to Duty (Dollar Values Expressed in Millions)

| Year | Total | Value of Imports for Consumption* | | Rate of Duties Calculated to Total Imports | | |
		Free	Dutiable	Duties Calculated	Free and Dutiable	Dutiable Only
1821	$44	$2	$22	$19	43.21%	45.0%
1825	66	4	63	32	47.72	50.54
1828	67	4	63	30	44.74	47.59
1830	50	4	46	28	57.32	61.69
1833	83	20	63	24	28.99	38.25
1835	122	58	64	26	21.25	40.38
1840	86	42	44	15	17.60	34.39
1845	106	16	90	31	29.34	34.45
1846	110	19	91	30	27.70	30.35
1850	164	16	148	40	24.50	27.14
1855	232	30	202	54	23.36	26.83
1860	336	68	268	53	15.67	19.67

*Dollar values expressed are in millions.

Source: U.S. Department of Commerce, Bureau of the Census, *Historical Statistics of the United States: Colonial Times to 1970*, 2 vols. (Washington, D.C.: Government Printing Office, 1975), 2:888.

owed their existence or formation to tariffs. Zevin, for example, found no significant tariff effects on domestic demand for cotton textiles from 1815 to 1833.[32] It is claimed, however, that the demand for iron smelted with anthracite was sensitive to the price of competing imported British iron.[33] Since many American imports were mass-consumption goods, consumers paid for the tariff on such items.

However, the tariff generated over 90 percent of all federal government revenue in some years, and alternative sources of tax income would have had to be developed if tariffs were abandoned. A more cogent reason for the persistence of tariffs, then and now, is that the benefits of protection accrued to small, well-organized groups who received monopoly power and profits, while the costs (probably much larger in the aggregate) were borne by a much larger group who mostly suffered only slight individual losses. This situation has always formed a political equation of formidable strength, no less so in 1850 than today.

Even though most economists would grant some validity to the infant industry argument for tariffs, that defense does not appear very pertinent to the nineteenth-century United States. The argument presupposes that protection is only granted to those industries expected to outgrow the need for it, and that the government possesses both the foresight to recognize such potential and the forebearance to restrict protection to the groups that have it. Tariff protection was in fact granted for many

[32] R. Zevin, "The Growth of Cotton Textile Production after 1815," in Fogel and Engerman, *Reinterpretation*, pp. 125–127. Lebergott, *The Americans*, pp. 147–149, reaches similar conclusions.
[33] R. Fogel and S. Engerman, "A Model for the Explanation of Industrial Expansion During the 19th Century with an Application to the Antebellum Iron Industry," in *Reinterpretation*, p. 159.

other reasons, and it was seldom removed for purely economic considerations.

BUILDING A GROWTH INFRASTRUCTURE

Often we forget that economic growth entails much more than manufacturing, agriculture, and perhaps transportation. None of the sectors that produce or move physical commodities could function efficiently, if at all, without support from banking, finance, wholesaling, and retailing. As economic growth proceeds and the variety of goods produced increases, the volume of transactions grows more than proportionally, and the demand for specialized exchange services rises.

Initially, institutions that Europe had developed centuries earlier proved adequate for American needs. But with the increased volume and variety of production, the distances goods were transported, and the opportunities presented by improved transportation and communication, opportunities for new and better methods appeared. Americans were quick to grasp these, in part because there were few entrenched proponents of older methods— particularly west of the Appalachians, where the innovations were particularly influential. Futures contracts, grading standards, credit agencies, and organized exchanges are not generally accorded prominent positions in economic history. Nevertheless, they may help to explain why Americans seemed to be able to reap larger benefits from the same pool of technology available to and largely developed by Europeans who were less willing to transform the balance of their economies. The greater human mobility and willingness to try out new ideas incorporated in the American population may have contributed as much in this area as it did in factories and on farms.

SELECTED REFERENCES

Chandler, A., Jr. *The Visible Hand: The Managerial Revolution in American Business.* Cambridge, Mass.: Harvard University Press, 1977.

Davis, L., et al. *American Economic Growth: An Economist's History of the United States.* New York: Harper and Row, 1972.

Fogel, R., and S. Engerman, eds. *The Reinterpretation of American Economic History.* New York: Harper and Row, 1971.

Hammond, B. *Banks and Politics in America from the Revolution to the Civil War.* Princeton, N.J.: Princeton University Press, 1957.

Kroos, H., and M. Blyn. *A History of Financial Intermediaries.* New York: Random House, 1971.

Nettels, C. *The Emergence of a National Economy, 1775–1815.* New York: Harper and Row, 1962.

North, D. *The Economic Growth of the United States, 1790–1860.* Englewood Cliffs, N.J.: Prentice-Hall, 1961.

Rockoff, H. *The Free Banking Era: A Reexamination.* New York: Arno Press, 1975.

Studenski, P., and H. Kroos. *Financial History of the United States.* New York: McGraw-Hill, 1963.

Taussig, F. *Tariff History of the United States.* 7th ed. New York: G. Putnam's Sons, 1923.

U.S. Department of Commerce, Bureau of the Census. *Historical Statistics of the United States: Colonial Times to 1970.* 2 vols. Washington, D.C.: Government Printing Office, 1975.

CHAPTER

9

INSTITUTIONS AND THE QUALITY OF LIFE

*I*ncome is by no means the only measure of the standard of living enjoyed by any group. But since income is a measure of the goods and services available and hence the range of choices open to its recipients, few would deny that it is an important indicator of the types of life-styles available to its recipients.

Per-capita incomes rose substantially in the United States from 1815 to 1860. In itself, a trend in per-capita income illustrates the range of possible economic effects on individuals, rather than denoting which actually took place. All we can definitely conclude from the increase in per-capita income is that real output grew faster than population, so that the income of each American could rise without a decline in someone else's. Per-capita income figures in themselves give no indication of the nature of income distribution: they do not tell us whether income gains were widely distributed or went largely to the rich or poor. Nor do such increases indicate anything about regional or occupational distribution.

We do know that incomes rose, and almost undoubtedly at a faster pace than ever before. One study concluded that real per-capita product increased 60 percent over the first 40 years of the nineteenth century and a further 37 percent by 1860. Growth rates varied, with the highest occurring in the 1830s and the lowest in the 1850's.[1] The record of the 1850s is biased downward because of business cycles: 1850 was a boom year, but the economy was enduring a recession in 1860. The data—especially for the first decades of the century—are not as trustworthy as those from later periods, so conclusions drawn from them should be regarded as best available estimates rather than facts.

[1] P. David, "The Growth of Real Product in the United States before 1840: New Evidence, Controlled Conjectures," *Journal of Economic History,* June, 1967.

THE DISTRIBUTION OF INCOME AND WEALTH

From 1815 to 1860, two opposing influences affected the distribution of income and, to some extent, of wealth in the United States. The first was that the range of production and consumption alternatives open to Americans and the factors they controlled grew steadily larger over this time, and considerable redistribution of people from low- to high-income occupations occurred. This redistribution occurred both within and between occupations and regions. People and resources moved to regions where their efforts were more productive in the same work, and they also switched jobs in pursuit of higher incomes. This trend produced greater equality of incomes. It reduced the supply of resources in areas where they earned less than average rates of return, thus raising the incomes of the remainder. And it increased the supply of resources in high-income uses and regions, which reduced their prices there. The overall effect of the reallocations was to increase the average incomes of Americans. At the same time, the largest income gains were in sectors of the economy that even in 1860 were fairly small in relation to the whole, which would tend to produce greater inequality. It must be kept in mind that the foregoing analysis refers to how the increased aggregate output was allocated. There is little doubt that the large majority of all Americans experienced at least some gains in real income. But some gained more than others.

Income Distribution

Some data on the functional distribution of income (the flow of output attributable to land, labor, capital, and other factors) are now available. A good deal is also known about the relationships between age, skills, country of origin, and urban versus rural residence. From these we can derive a fuller, though still incomplete, picture of the levels and trends of income and wealth distribution in antebellum America. The usual conclusion drawn from these sources is that incomes and especially wealth were unevenly distributed among the American population in 1815 and became even more so by 1860.[2] In this view, even when wealth in slaves is excluded and the data adjusted for differences in the age, location, and national origin of the population, the concentration of wealth increased after 1820. In the view of one proponent, the distribution of wealth in the United States may never have been more unequal than in 1860.[3] Another view is that the data from colonial days and from 1860 were not derived by the same methods and thus tend to overstate income and wealth inequality in the later period.[4]

Landownership

Land was the largest component of aggregate wealth. Although land was plentiful and cheap and access to landownership extraordinarily easy by European standards, possession of land was by no means universal, even in rural areas. In 1860 only 42 percent of free male adults in the United States owned land, even though this was a country of small farms. Only 60 percent of free Americans owned property (including land) valued at $100 or more.[5] Thirty percent

[2] P. Lindert and J. Williamson, "Three Centuries of American Inequality," in *Research in Economic History,* ed. P. Uselding (Greenwich, Conn.: JAI Press, 1976), p. 60.
[3] Ibid., p. 89.
[4] S. Lebergott, in *The Americans: An Economic Record* (New York: Norton, 1984), pp. 70–73, notes that while colonial income estimates were derived from probate records, those for the later period were obtained from government surveys, without verification. The nineteenth-century income data contain wide and seemingly inexplicable variations in claimed income and wealth among persons whose situations were apparently quite similar.
[5] L. Soltow, *Men and Wealth in the United States, 1850–1970* (New Haven, Conn.: Yale University Press, 1975), pp. 22, 174. Because of the method by which the data for these statements were assembled, Lebergott suggests that they be viewed skeptically. See Lebergott, *The Americans,* p. 73.

of all U.S. real estate was in the hands of the wealthiest 1 percent of all property owners. Absolute figures, regardless of the confidence they inspire, do not tell the whole story. Comparisons with other nations are also useful. In England, the distribution of land was far less equal than in America. There, more than half the total acreage was owned by less than 1 percent of the population. However, we do not have comprehensive figures for any nation at this time.

Other Sorts of Wealth and Those Who Had It

Nonland wealth appears to have been less evenly distributed, especially in the cities, if the data can be trusted.[6] Wealth is defined by economists as stocks of productive goods. Usually wealth and income are directly related, but the link can be very loose. A lawyer who lives in a rented apartment and drives a leased car while spending every cent of a $100,000 annual income may have no wealth as it is conventionally measured, but we could not term him poor. Still, there is no doubt that wealth was distributed unequally in America, and the distribution may have grown less equal than in the colonial era.

Demographic Influences

Even if disparities in wealth ownership increased, they may to some extent indicate the presence of economic opportunity in the United States rather than its absence. Individual wealth tends to be strongly linked with age. If all wealth were the result of individual saving, we would expect the young to have less than the old. The data bear this out: the proportion of property ownership increased threefold between the ages

of 20 and 60 in antebellum America.[7] At least part of the disparity in wealth can be derived from the rapid growth of the American population, which would make for a high proportion of young people, although average age did rise slightly compared with the colonial period. There was also some mobility among wealthholders—the identity of the top wealthholders in various cities changed even while the individuals remained alive. But the demographic factors only reduce the disparities in wealth, they do not eliminate them. Trends in aggregate consumption, which grew at only slightly lower rates than gross national product, indicate that gains in income—if not necessarily wealth—were widely distributed.

Growth and Income Distribution

Some trends in income distribution are related to changes occurring across the American economy. We would expect people who derived their incomes from rapidly growing sectors to fare better than those employed where productivity grew more slowly. Even though the market system "pulled" resources into areas of above-average productivity and "pushed" them out of areas where performance was subpar, making for greater equality, the process was far from completed by 1860. It would continue as long as new opportunities were exploited. Nevertheless, the patterns we would predict from theory appear in the historical data. Incomes in manufacturing were nearly twice the national average, and incomes of skilled machinists or experienced construction workers were higher still. Employment in both occupations rose in relation to the total over this period. Moreover, the wages of skilled labor rose much faster than the national average from 1815 to 1856.[8]

---

[6] Soltow, *Men and Wealth*, pp. 92–108. It must be remembered, however, that colonial wealth distribution studies employed probate records subject to legal verification, while most of the nineteenth-century data are drawn from census questions not subject to any follow-up (Lebergott, *The Americans*).

[7] Ibid., p. 28.

[8] Lindert and Williamson, "Three Centuries of American Inequality," in P. Uselding, ed., *Research in Economic History*, pp. 102–104.

Rural versus Urban Incomes

Urban incomes on average were higher than rural, though they were less evenly distributed. Since the urban population was growing at nearly three times the rate of the total population, this made for increased inequality of incomes. Americans in the forefront of economic change—those who introduced new products and methods, found new markets, or worked for someone who did—might be expected to earn above-average incomes, and they did. Income gains in such areas were also rapid, reflecting the high rate of productivity increase typical of new industries. Those with the skills required to design, produce, and operate new machinery and institutions gained most, but even ordinary workers in such industries gained.

Women and children also increased their share of money incomes. Their wages might be well below the national average, but they had previously had little or no opportunity to earn any wage. Before the appearance of factories and other sources of urban employment, the only occupations open to them were as low-powered but easily trained "work animals" on farms. The disparity of rural and urban incomes is one reason for the flow of labor to nonfarm occupations that occurred during this period.

Income Distribution in the Rural South

There were some exceptions to the general rule that urban incomes and wealth exceeded those of rural areas. The ten counties ranked highest in average inhabitants' wealth in 1860 were all southern and rural. Most were in the sugar regions along the lower Mississippi River. The reason for this great wealth was the economies of scale inherent in sugar planting. Not only did the free inhabitants of such counties own large numbers of slaves, they also possessed large amounts of valuable land and extensive nonhuman capital. Much southern wealth was in the form of slaves, and the sugar plantations had unusually large work forces even by plantation standards.[9]

In 1860, an individual owning just two slaves and no other wealth possessed property valued at nearly twice the average held by all Americans. There were 10,659 planters who owned 50 or more slaves each in 1860. At an average price of $900 per slave, each such planter held a minimum of $45,000 in slave property alone, and of course each possessed large amounts of land and other property as well. Since the dollar in 1860 had eight to ten times its modern purchasing power, these planters were wealthy even by today's standards. With only about one-third the nation's population, the South was the home of 59 percent of America's wealthiest families on the eve of the Civil War.[10] In other forms of wealth, however, the South was below the average for the northern industrial states.

The Frontier

Generally, wealth was concentrated in more densely settled areas. There, a high proportion of the land would be cleared and under cultivation if the area were agricultural, or it would be a site of capital-intensive activity. In either case, the inhabitants would have had some time to save. Frontier areas, thinly settled and not yet fully in use, had below-average wealth. Areas with heavy manufacturing employment and high proportions of native-born inhabitants fared better than did those whose populations were disproportionately young, foreign-born, or both. Low current wealth did not necessarily imply that such circumstances would continue. Investment rates were high on the frontier, and there was great opportunity for capital gains as land values appreciated.

[9] Soltow, *Men and Wealth*, p. 167.
[10] Ibid., p. 101.

■ Sugar plantations, like this one in Louisiana, displayed rural wealth in the form of land, slaves, and refineries.
Source: From the collection of the Louisiana State Museum.

Immigrants

Foreign-born urban residents generally had less wealth than their American native neighbors, but in rural areas, national origin had little relation to wealthholding. In part, these conditions reflected the circumstances of the immigrants who chose each type of area. Those settling in the countryside were better equipped to take advantage of opportunities. Many of the immigrants in urban areas had been poor when they arrived, while those settling in rural areas were more likely to be educated and to have brought some capital with them. As noted in Chapter 6, the investment required for commercially viable farms rose substantially after 1840. Poverty was more common in American cities than in rural areas. With only about one-fifth of the nation's population, the cities sheltered 38 percent of the nation's poor in 1860. Since urban populations contained more than proportionate shares of the young, recent immigrants, and the illiterate, all factors that reduced incomes and wealth, this is not surprising.

Urban Real Wages, 1820s to 1860

From what is known about wages, it seems that urban real wages probably rose in the 1820s to mid-1830s, declined through the early 1840s, then rose to a sharp peak in the boom of the early 1850s. Subsequently they declined, and they had not fully regained the lost ground by 1860.[11] At first glance, this is surprising, since per-capita incomes rose strongly from 1843 to

[11] S. Lebergott, *Trends in the U.S. Economy in the Nineteenth Century* (Princeton, N.J.: Princeton University Press, 1960), p. 490.

■ One form of wealth was the amount invested in slaves. At this slave auction, a field hand might be purchased for $1,500.
Source: The Bettmann Archive.

1860. Capital per worker and productivity both rose, factors that might be expected to increase wages. Even so, it appears that labor's bargaining power diminished. The causes are not completely understood, but three factors appear especially significant:

1. The late 1840s and early 1850s were a boom period in which labor demand was particularly great due to the California gold rush and the economic activity it engendered. As in 1800–1807, conditions were atypical, and wages and incomes reached levels that could not be sustained.

2. The price level rose by nearly one-third from 1851 to 1855. Wages often fail to keep pace with rapid inflation.

3. Immigration, and even more so the labor supply, increased much faster than in previous years.

A high proportion of the new arrivals were unskilled and destitute, with only minimal bargaining power, which would tend to drive down average wage levels. But real wages for specific jobs and individuals may not have declined, a point supported by the data in Table 9.1. If the proportion of low-wage jobs rose, average wage levels might fall even though those for skilled jobs remained constant or even rose. Certainly the premium for skilled over unskilled labor rose substantially over this period.

Another indication of the probable course of income distribution and income levels is the increased production of certain types of goods.

Table 9.1 Daily Wage Rates on the Erie Canal, 1828–1860 (Current Dollars)

Date	Common Labor	Carpenters	Masons	Teamwork (Wagoners, etc.)
1828	$.71	$1.00	$1.50	$1.50
1830	.75	1.25	1.31	1.75
1835	.75	1.25	1.75	2.00
1840	.88	1.50	1.75	2.40
1845	.75	1.00	1.25	1.75
1850	.88	1.50	1.50	1.50
1855	1.00	1.75	2.00	2.50
1860	1.00	1.75	2.00	3.00

Source: U.S. Department of Commerce, Bureau of the Census, *Historical Statistics of the United States: Colonial Times to 1970,* 2 vols. (Washington, D.C.: Government Printing Office, 1975), p. 164.

Furniture, textiles, rugs, stoves, tools, clocks, and amusement services in the cities were all produced in great quantities, indicating that economic gains extended to middle- and low-income groups.[12] The American rich already enjoyed these items and could hardly have increased their purchases enough to account for the increased output.

The Nature of American Prosperity

Foreign visitors all but unanimously recorded impressions of widespread, boundless optimism and a crude plenty. They observed fewer obvious differences in living standards between various income groups than were apparent in Europe. While such evidence is not the stuff of firm conclusions, it is consistent with the limited quantitative evidence on income distribution. It seems safe to conclude that in-

come shares may have changed, yet the variations were not large, and all groups gained in absolute terms. Real income gains were emphatically not restricted to a small, wealthy minority.

Nonetheless, whatever the ideals of the United States may have been, the antebellum economy was not egalitarian. The gains of the poor were not at the expense of the rich, who at least maintained the share of income they had received in the colonial era. Despite the probable increase in income disparities, it is likely that individuals found it easier to move up or down the income scale in the United States than anywhere else. This is important, because it means that individual incomes could rise or fall in relation to the average, and hence there was constant pressure for efficient job performance. The rewards for effort could be substantial in America, and they were much greater than in Europe.

The movements of people to new areas and new jobs indicate that the incentives were effective. Whether they moved from eastern farms to more fertile soil in the West, from rural areas to higher-income cities, or from low- to high-wage jobs in the same industry, the results ob-

[12] R. Andreano, "Trends in Economic Welfare, 1790–1860," in Andreano, ed., *New Views on American Economic Development* (Cambridge, Mass.: Schenkman, 1965), pp. 131–167.

tained by mobile Americans were the same. Resources produced more in new uses, and through their efforts to improve their own living standards, those who moved increased the economy's aggregate production. Americans were as willing to change the nature of existing jobs as they were to move to new ones. Workers were highly receptive to training and new tools that improved productivity. Because of this, innovations were easier to introduce than where the work force feared them as a threat to jobs. In addition, the full potential of new inventions was more nearly realized, and ideas spread rapidly from the areas they were first applied.

URBANIZATION

In 1815, one American in fourteen lived in a city or town of more than 2,500 people. By 1860, that proportion had nearly tripled, to one in five. Some individual cities had grown even faster. New York's 805,000 people in 1860 were more than the entire urban population of 1815, and Philadelphia's 565,000 were not much less.

Cities have certain advantages for economic growth. Markets and labor supplies are likely to be readily available. Information costs are lower—a point of special relevance before modern communication techniques appeared. Highly specialized resources of all kinds tend to locate where markets are large enough to allow them to exploit all existing economies of scale. For example, a shop selling nothing but blue jeans would not locate in a small, isolated village, but even more specialized shops and workers are found in large cities. Supporting services such as housing and shopping for workers, a transportation system to bring in raw materials and distribute products, and schools, churches, and cultural activities can be taken for granted in large urban environments. So can at least the most basic governmental services—police and courts. As a city's population grows, the range of activities it can support generally grows even faster, particularly if transportation is improving as it was in America at this time. Because the range of specialized occupations is greater, urban incomes are likely to average higher than those of the countryside, where the talents of specialists may not be fully exploited.

Conditions of Nineteenth-Century Urban Life

City life has disadvantages as well. With specialization comes a loss of self-sufficiency, although this to some degree is within the individual's control. But crowding, noise, pollution, and other results of life in close contact with large numbers of people are unavoidable. In the middle of the nineteenth century, these problems had not been mitigated even to the extent they are today. Some had not even been recognized.

There were major disadvantages to urban life in all countries, and the United States was no exception. Only the rich could afford to maintain carriages within large cities. Since there was little or no public transportation, the bulk of the population had to live within walking distance of workplaces. The labor-intensive nature of most industry in this era contributed further to the crowding. The poor lived in multistory tenements that were the only means of providing living space for large numbers of people within confined areas. Space was at a premium. Often, in the poorer areas, several families shared a room. This was a potentially lethal situation when the causes and transfer mechanisms of most diseases were unknown. Nor were people the only things in close proximity. Only in the 1850s did large American cities begin to build public water and sewage systems, and these were not extended to the entire urban population until long after 1860. Before the advent of water mains and sewers, wells and privies were only too obviously close together. New York City had one slum that was so crowded it had no room for any sanitary facilities whatsoever. The city eventually purchased the slum and tore it down.[13]

Pollution

Most buildings were made of wood, and fires were common. Streets generally were unpaved and became seas of mud in wet weather. Worse, they were used as dumping grounds for every sort of refuse, which was picked over by children and the hogs that ranged freely through most cities. In 1900, horses deposited 24 tons of manure on New York City streets every day: this source of pollution might well have been worse in the smaller but even more crowded city before 1860.[14] Eventually, the mess would be trampled into the mud or, rarely, cleaned up. Traffic was heavy and accidents apparently at least as common as they are today.

Poor Sanitation

Methods of preserving food had improved little from colonial times. Salting, smoking, drying, and pickling were used, and some ice was available, but little fresh food was within the means of the poor for entire seasons. Food was often contaminated at its source or in processing. Since milk was difficult to transport long distances, many dairy cattle were kept within cities. Feed was expensive in the cities, so cows were fed whatever was available, and even the milk from diseased cows was sold.[15]

Disease

Ignorance and filth combined to produce incredible rates of disease, particularly among children. In the 1850s, 56 percent of all deaths

■ The disparity in wealth was apparent in urban areas such as New York City. The exclusive Century Club existed alongside squatter encampments in Central Park.
Source: (top) *Harper's Weekly*, Nov. 2, 1889, (bottom) *Harper's Weekly*, June 26, 1869. Both from John Grafton, *New York in the Nineteenth Century*, 2d, ed. (New York: Dover Publication, Inc., 1980) p. 147.

in New York City were of children under the age of five. In an especially bad year in Chicago, 70 percent of all children less than one year old died.[16] Chicago faced particularly intractable sewage-disposal problems, and this was not typical infant mortality even there, but the con-

[13] L. Davis et al., *American Economic Growth: An Economist's History of the United States* (New York: Harper and Row, 1972), p. 628.
[14] I am indebted to Professor Thomas Ulem of the University of Illinois for this information.
[15] Davis et al., *American Economic Growth*, p. 629.

[16] Ibid.

trast with modern conditions was enormous. Figures from Massachusetts in the 1850s indicate infant mortality rates comparable to those of some of the poorer Third World countries today.[17]

As if endemic diseases were not bad enough, most cities suffered periodic epidemics as well. Most large American cities were seaports, constantly exposed to the epidemic diseases of the entire world. Immigrants frequently arrived weakened or sick from shipboard conditions that imposed mortality rates as high as or higher than those suffered by African slaves in the "Middle Passage."[18] Medicine provided no relief. Doctors could treat wounds or set broken bones with some success, but for most diseases they could at best relieve pain with drugs. Often their treatments made the affliction worse. Hospitals were mere warehouses for the dying. Maternal and infant mortality were high, in part because the most elementary principles of cleanliness were violated during childbirth.

The Economics of Urban Externalities

In part, urban problems stemmed from the lack of an organized response and the inability of the market system to provide one. As long as all responses were left to free individuals, it would not benefit any person to try to reduce pollution in an urban environment. If one citizen cut his or her personal contribution to the problem and others did not, no noticeable reduction in pollution would result, and the "good citizen" would have incurred costs for no purpose. Even worse, the greater the voluntary cleanup of others, the less the economic incentive for anyone to follow suit if doing so involved costs in time, money, or changed habits—the classic "free rider" problem. Lack of knowledge and means for effective responses made the problems even more intractable.

City governments were nearly as unable to cope with the problems of crime, fire, lighting, and education as with those of urban health. The rural background of most Americans was reflected in political institutions not designed to deal with costs inflicted on the general public by private actions that might be innocuous in more spacious environments. Changes in political institutions as well as science and technology were needed before effective responses to urban problems could be generated.

The Attractions of City Life

Given these conditions (the author has by no means presented the worst examples), why would any sane person choose city life? How could urban populations increase at three times the aggregate rate? Some attractions must have balanced the grim picture just described, or possibly rural life had drawbacks as well. Both appear to be true. By no means did all city dwellers reside in slums, and urban life offered, in addition to higher incomes, much greater variety in consumption and life-styles than the country. Urban occupations often had much better possibilities for advancement; farm laborers might save for years to buy a farm, but there the process stopped. In the rapidly changing cities, however, a dead end in one job might be avoided by changing occupations. Nor should we romanticize rural life at this time. Farm work was physically demanding, and over the years offered little variety. And it was only relatively safer and healthier: life expectancy for the entire country was 35 to 40 years at best, or about half its present level.[19]

[17] U.S. Department of Commerce, Bureau of the Census, *Historical Statistics of the United States: Colonial Times to 1970,* 2 vols. (Washington, D.C.: Government Printing Office, 1975), vol. 1, p. 57.
[18] Lebergott, *The Americans,* pp. 182–183.

[19] U.S. Department of Commerce, *Historical Statistics,* vol. 1, p. 56.

THE STRUCTURE OF THE LABOR MARKET

The employment of large numbers of people in manufacturing, transportation, and commercial firms was a new development. As in other areas of economic life, institutions had to be developed to deal with new situations, most of which had not existed before 1800. Since even the demands of the new jobs were different, emphasizing dexterity or endurance rather than physical strength, or demanding skills that few if any people previously possessed—such as those of a locomotive engineer—it was not even clear what type of workers were needed. In some cases jobs appeared before any recognition of the skills they required, and answers had to be worked out by trial and error. In many instances employers had to recruit labor. When industrialization began, few people were looking for jobs, and cities were small. Especially when manufacturing locations were dictated by power sources or raw materials, employers might have to build housing and sometimes entire towns for their workers.

Labor and employers also had to reach consensus on which aspects of work were areas of mutual concern and which were the primary interest of one party or the other. Absenteeism and tardiness could affect the performance of entire factories, so employers made rules and tried to instill desired behavior in workers accustomed to the less demanding schedules of agriculture. The pace and duration of work was another matter that today would be acknowledged as a legitimate, though not exclusive, concern of employers. The basis and rates of pay were obviously matters in which both sides had an interest.

Initially, many employers appeared to believe that few if any aspects of workers' overall conduct could be trusted to individual discretion. Some employers made it their business to regulate conduct off as well as on the job, requiring church attendance and contributions and regulating drinking, smoking, appearance, and other aspects of behavior. In small towns, where it was difficult to escape attention, such rules might be enforced. In many of these areas, employers were assuming roles previously filled by ministers, local governments, or public opinion, so their rules were not seen as the outrageous infringements on individual freedom that they appear to be today. Paternalism could have its positive side: most firms were small enough to put relations with the employer on a personal basis. Some employers might help workers in times of personal trouble and take pains to mitigate the effects of unemployment, but there was no obligation to do so.

The "Mill Girls"

The first industrial firms appeared before large-scale immigration and while cities were still very small. Wholly new industries might have to create a work force under such circumstances. In northern New England, textile mills obtained a labor force by hiring the young, unmarried women of the surrounding countryside. The "mill girls" were housed in strictly supervised boarding houses that solved two problems: they eased parental concerns about their daughters' moral and physical welfare, and they provided housing where none had previously existed. At this time (1815–1845) it was not hard to recruit young women to work 11 or 12 hours per day in the mills and live where their every action was subject to strict and unforgiving scrutiny, all for two or three dollars a week after room and board. Young women in this era had few alternatives for employment outside their own homes. About all that was available was domestic service or possibly schoolteaching, and both involved living in another family's home. Domestic service meant the same type of work the girls performed at home, and neither job provided much of a cash income.

The mills offered higher wages, the chance to meet a wider range of people than on the farm, and some control over one's own life. Women might save for a dowry, contribute to the support of their families, and obtain a few luxuries for themselves. Although life was tightly restricted by both social and economic limits, it offered more freedom than the farm. In their few leisure hours, the mill girls pursued literary and artistic endeavors, held debates, and followed many of the same activities that their more fortunate sisters might enjoy full time at a boarding school. Ironically, they are better remembered today for their leisure-time activities than for the work that drew them off the farms. Most women spent only a few years in such jobs, which were widely viewed as an interval between childhood and marriage.

The mill girls also organized one of the first employee strikes in American history. In 1828, the female employees of the Cocheco Manufacturing Company of Dover, New Hampshire, "turned out" to protest a wage cut.[20] But the era of the mill girls was brief. By the 1840s, they encountered increasing job competition from immigrants willing to work for lower wages—in part because their personal conduct was not a matter of concern.

Unions

Some formal labor organizations were formed before 1860, but few aspired to permanence. Most were set up to achieve some short-term objective and lasted only until the issue was resolved. Few resembled modern labor unions, and most appeared among skilled craftsmen, who often owned their own shops or were self-employed. The aims of these groups were often reminiscent of those of the medieval guilds.

Not infrequently, they sought to restrict entry into their occupations or fix prices for their products. Their journeymen attempted to organize both for higher wages and to restrict entry of additional employees. Such groups had little influence on the labor force as a whole. About 26,000 people—less than 1 percent of the labor force—were members of any type of labor organization in 1830. Later, membership declined, and the 1830 figure was not regained until 1860.[21]

Obstacles to Organization

Workers who sought effective bargaining power through organization faced formidable difficulties. In many of the new industries, workers were unskilled and readily replaceable. The structure of most industries was another barrier. Typically, many small firms produced similar goods. For each, labor was a large portion of total production costs. Consequently, wage increases would force increases in product prices under competitive conditions, so that all firms in the same market would have to be organized simultaneously. Before any single employer would raise prices to cover a wage increase, he had to know that his competitors were facing the same situation. Even then, firms outside the organized area might be able to invade its markets as transportation improved. If the employer's markets were distant from the plant, the entire industry might have to be organized.

Limits to Workers' Bargaining Power. Wages were low, and labor organizations could not sustain a strike. Lacking personal savings or strike benefits, most workers could strike only until they or their families got hungry. Worker organizations were extremely vulnerable to the swings of the business cycle. If business conditions prompted an employer to cut wages, even the most militant employees might have

[20] G. Taylor, *The Transportation Revolution, 1815–1860* (New York: M.E. Sharpe, 1962), p. 276. The strike was lost because the mill owners were able to find other workers, and they quickly threatened to do so.

[21] Davis et al., *American Economic Growth*, p. 220.

little choice but to accept. Skilled craftsmen, who could not easily be replaced, enjoyed some bargaining success, but for most workers the economic barriers to successful collective action were very strong.

The Legal Climate. The legal and political obstacles faced by would-be unions were even stronger. Government was invariably on the side of the employers and was often willing to send police or militia to protect strikebreakers. Welfare payments were rare and not generally available to strikers; unemployment payments were unknown. Legal doctrine was, if anything, less favorable to unions. Until 1842 judges regarded labor unions as illegal conspiracies under the common law, attempts to benefit members at others' expense. In that year Judge Shaw ruled in *Commonwealth v. Hunt* that unions were not inherently illegal organizations and their purpose had to be considered before a case could be decided. Since the courts took an extremely narrow view of the permissible range of union activities, the ruling did little more than allow unions to exist.[22] It did not grant them the freedom to organize and bargain as they wished.

Ineffectual Labor Leaders. In some cases unions were not oriented to the interests of labor. Often the leaders of labor organizations were intellectuals whose goals emphasized the reform of society more than material betterment of workers within the current system. Many of these leaders advocated replacing the wage system with some form of utopian socialism in which workers would control the entire economic system. Even had they offered workable proposals, the reformers had little hope of success. They never succeeded in attracting more than tiny minorities of workers to their views, and with good reason. They completely misunderstood workers' objectives, which were higher pay, shorter hours of work, improved working conditions, and the modification of laws unfavorable to workers. Even had their views appealed to the workers, utopian proposals for labor's benefit might have been lost in the collective roar of propositions for reform of virtually every existing institution.

Utopian Ideals

The antebellum era witnessed a burgeoning of panaceas: the world, or at least America, was to be improved or the millenium achieved through means ranging from the practical through the idealistic and on to the truly bizarre. Great things were to come if people would eat graham flour, wear woolen underwear, practice vegetarianism, create a utopian socialist state, or perform any of a thousand other religious, quasi-religious, or secular activities. All were stridently advocated as the answer to all questions their proponents considered important. Labor unions and the women's rights movement were not destined to do well in this climate. Would-be supporters within labor's ranks were deterred by early unions' association with such ideas. This experience with social reform left American labor with a lasting distrust of intellectuals or of any leadership not recruited from within its own ranks.

Not surprisingly, most of the attempts at new forms of social and economic organizations failed. Some advocated a return to agriculture and attracted people who tended to substitute romanticism for farming experience. Some goups could not agree on the most basic goals. Others sought unattainable goals. But a few efforts proved durable, usually in cases where the membership was united around strictly defined purposes. Religion was often the bond that held these groups together. Some isolated themselves either geographically, as did the Mormons, or socially, as did the Amish.

---

[22] C. Gregory and H. Katz, *Labor and the Law,* 3d ed. (New York: Norton, 1979), pp. 27–30.

Others, such as the Oneida and Amana communities, actively participated in the wider economy while maintaining group cohesion.

Some idealistically motivated projects for social betterment had positive, if limited, impacts. Savings banks were established to provide low-income individuals a place to keep their savings at interest (and to promote thrift among the "spendthrift" lower classes). Savings banks would accept very small deposits, while other financial institutions would not. The real difficulty faced by persons with low incomes, of course, was accumulating savings in the first place.

Changes in Social Institutions

A few of the goals of American labor organizations and workers in general were achieved in this period. Imprisonment for debt was abolished, and the use of convict labor in competition with free workers was curtailed. Mechanics' lien laws allowed workers to place liens against the property of someone who failed to pay for services rendered. Education became more widespread and available to working-class children. Work hours were reduced: the average workday fell from 12 hours or more to 11 by 1860. Some states imposed laws restricting the workday of children to 10 hours, and federal employees gained a 10-hour day in 1840. These hours of work were partially mitigated by a slower pace than demanded by modern jobs, but the implications for leisure time are obvious.

These developments resulted from the efforts of many groups, only a portion of which represented organized labor or workers. Reductions in work hours and restrictions on the employment of children indicate growing affluence: society now felt it possible to sacrifice small amounts of production for leisure, or sought long-term gains through education rather than current output.

Occupational and Geographical Mobility

The U.S. work force had certain characteristics that distinguished it from those of European nations. The average age of workers was lower, reflecting both rapid population growth through natural increase and the influence of immigration (most immigrants were young adults). Above all, American labor was both occupationally and geographically mobile in comparison with European. The implications were profound: workers sought only their own betterment in moving, but reallocation of labor increased the efficiency of the American economy and pressured employers to use existing work forces more productively and to pay them in proportion. Mobility was aided by high levels of education: most American workers were literate. Fewer people were stuck in jobs that did not suit them than in less flexible societies, and a larger portion of labor had an opportunity to develop whatever special talents it possessed. The continuing relative shortage of labor in the United States also increased worker acceptance of technological change, which aided economic growth. Labor-saving machinery was welcomed as reducing the load on human muscle. There was less reason to fear displacement from a job when others were easy to obtain.

These work force attributes also increased the productivity of innovations. Foreign observers noted repeatedly that American workers' response to a new machine was not merely to use it, but to try to understand its basic operating principles and often to improve it. This attitude, when combined with labor's mobility and literacy, aided the rapid spread of new technology from its initial geographic and sectoral areas of application. Wide use and modification of inventions helped achieve their full potential. Workers changing jobs often carried useful ideas with them. Men trained in such nineteenth-century citadels of "high technology" as Colt, Brown & Sharpe, Waltham Watch, and the government arsenals were welcomed throughout American industry. In addition, many small but cumulatively important improvements were made within existing plants through labor's efforts.

By no means was the American labor market perfectly competitive. Wide differentials in wages for basically similar jobs occurred—sometimes even within the same city—and geographic variations were still larger and more commonplace. Nevertheless, the mobility of the work force was a powerful mechanism for reducing income variations not based on productivity, and it was developed in this country far more than in Europe even a century later. In a few cases, labor with especially limited mobility and bargaining power might face exploitation in the sense of being paid less than the value of its product, just as slaves were. The textile industry, which employed a high proportion of female and child workers who had few good job alternatives, is one such example.[23]

IMMIGRATION

Before 1830, immigration had been only a minor influence on U.S. population growth and the work force. It accounted for less than 5 percent of American population growth. Not until 1828 did more than 25,000 people move to the United States in a single year. In the 1830s, the flow increased to almost 60,000 people annually, and in the 1840s it expanded even more. The peak for this era was between 1850 and 1855, when over 2,000,000 immigrants arrived in America. They accounted for nearly half the total population growth of this period.

[23] R. Vedder, "The Slave Expropriation (Exploitation) Rate," *Explorations in Economic History* (October 1979).

Most of the immigration originated in northern Europe, as in the colonial era, but as time passed, immigrant nationalities began to change. The portion of the inflow coming from England, Scotland, and Wales diminished and that from Ireland and Germany rose. There was also an influx from eastern Canada, although its numbers did not compare with those of the European migrants.

It seems clear that the immigrants' primary motives were economic. They had other motives: the Irish had endured centuries of social and religious persecution before the potato famines of the late 1840s. Wars, revolution, and repression spurred the German migration, especially after 1848. Nevertheless, economic considerations were paramount for the bulk of the immigrants. Even though most countries accepted immigrants without restriction at this time, the United States, with its higher levels and growth rates of income, attracted most of them. In addition, American immigration correlates with favorable economic conditions in this country after 1830. Immigration increased in good times and fell off about a year after slumps began.

The Immigrants' Reception

Were the immigrants' hopes of a better material life fulfilled? How well did they fare in the new land? The new arrivals met hostility, discrimination, and sometimes violence. The Irish in particular were desperately poor, unskilled, illiterate, and willing to take almost any job even at low wages. To some Americans, they were an economic threat undermining the established wage structure. To others, the Irish were Catholic, had no great love for established authority, and were easily identified. Any of these characteristics might be "reason" enough to hate them. As were many later immigrants, the Irish were derided for their life-styles and scorned for their poverty. German customs and language also appeared strange to many Americans. The Germans, however, often brought capital and skills. In light of their reception, it is hardly surprising that many immigrants tended to cluster in communities of their own. Often the core of such a group settlement would be earlier migrants from Ireland or Germany, sometimes even from the same village. Here the new arrivals found advice about jobs, housing, and other aspects of life.

Those who disliked immigrants soon added another chorus to their complaints—immigrants were "clannish" and reluctant to associate with those who sought to deny them jobs and on occasion burned their churches. Political groups, especially the American Nativist or "Know Nothing" party, were organized to oppose immigration. But the numbers tell the story. America's economic pull was stronger than the social opposition of some inhabitants.

In the U.S. economy, the demand for all types of labor was generally strong. Manufacturing, construction, and distribution could use workers with any degree of skill, and immigrants found jobs plentiful. Pay was often low by American standards, and foreign-born urban residents had not achieved economic parity with American natives by 1860.

If immigrants were illiterate or unable to speak English, they found it difficult to take full advantage of America's economic opportunities. Immigrant groups had more than their share of factors associated with poverty among all Americans: youth, illiteracy, and limited work experience. They were also likely to be poor people from countries far less affluent than the United States. Even without the discrimination that some encountered, it is not surprising that immigrants were more likely than native Americans to be poor.

In rural areas, especially on or near the frontier, immigrants apparently gained economic parity with those born in this country rather quickly. Even so, these were areas where average incomes for all inhabitants were below the national norm. Immigrants' average age probably remained below that of native Amer-

icans throughout the period, since so many were young adults who had arrived within a decade of 1860. As it did for all Americans, youth reduced both incomes and particularly wealth: there had not been time to gain job experience or accumulate assets.

The Irish and the Germans

The Irish tended to settle in urban areas. Most of them were too poor to start a farm immediately, and their experience with agriculture in Ireland could hardly have encouraged another try in America. Lacking funds for travel, the Irish tended to settle in the port cities of the Eastern Seaboard. German settlement reflected their better economic circumstances: it was more evenly divided between sizable communities in growing western cities such as Cincinnati, St. Louis, Milwaukee, and Chicago and considerable farm settlement in the Midwest.

The "America Letters"

The incomes and living conditions of immigrants may not have equalled those of native Americans, but they were undoubtedly superior to what the new arrivals had experienced at home. Average per-capita incomes were higher in America, often considerably so. Even more important from the immigrants' viewpoint were two other considerations: American income distribution was more equal than in Europe, so their incomes here were likely closer to the national average, and there was far more opportunity to rise in the income scale (which itself was rising) than in the "Old Country." Not only are immigrants' "America letters" to those left behind full of references to the better life they now enjoyed, but they also urge those in Europe to come to the New World. More convincing still, the letters often contained money to supplement the incomes of European relatives or finance their voyage to America. Sometimes the letters contained prepaid steamship tickets—evidence that the immigrants could have returned to their native lands.

Instead, they persuaded and helped their friends and relatives to join them in America.

Apparently it took two to three years for a male Irish immigrant to save enough money to finance passage for his family. In Ireland, accumulating the same amount required much more time and greater sacrifice. The trans-Atlantic flow was heavily in one direction—west. Although many people gave evidence that they had earned enough to return to Europe, few chose to do so. Whatever their situation in the eyes of those determined to dislike immigrants, the new arrivals' actions reveal that they were far better off in America.

The Value of Human Capital

Immigrants contributed far more than just unskilled labor to the American economy. According to one study, the human capital (in work skills and education) that America acquired through immigration in the 1850s almost equalled the value of physical investment in the same period.[24] The aggregate value of imported human capital thus far exceeded the sums Americans borrowed in European financial markets during the same period. As before and later, the immigrants were not typical of their native lands. They were largely young, with most of their working lives before them (which increased the potential benefits of emigration), and they possessed above-average skills and education (by the standards of their native countries if not the United States). It is obvious that they were ambitious. In an economy that allowed personal mobility and rewarded responses to opportunity, such traits gave a welcome boost to American economic growth.[25]

[24] P. Uselding, "Conjectural Estimates of Gross Human Capital Inflows to the American Economy," *Explorations in Economic History* (Fall 1971).
[25] R. Gallman, "Human Capital in the First 80 Years of the Republic: How Much Did America Owe the Rest of the World?" *American Economic Review* (February 1977).

EDUCATION

Widespread literacy aids economic de[velop]ment by encouraging the exchange of acc[urate] information. This reduces the risks of op[er]a-tions in new or distant markets and allows new methods and products to be more widely and quickly used. As noted earlier, it also hastens the adaptation of innovations to the needs of other industries.

Well before 1860 the United States was a world leader in basic education. The Northwest Ordinance of 1784 had provided land to finance public education in each township, and some existing states already had school systems by that date. Literacy and general school attendance in the United States equalled or surpassed those of any country in Europe. Not all of this was due to public education: only by 1860 did government provide the majority of educational expenditures.[26] By that time, 57 percent of all white children between the ages of 5 and 19 were enrolled, and over 90 percent of the adult white population was literate. Literacy rates were highest in New England and lowest on the frontier and in the South, but variations were not great (see Chapter 6). In the 1850s, southern and midwestern states followed the East's example in establishing public schools. Education accounted for about one-fifth of all state and local government expenditures by that time.[27]

American educational achievements should not be overrated. Few students received the equivalent of a junior high school education. Very few attended high school, and only a tiny minority went on to college. The school year was much shorter than it is today. In agricultural regions, planting and harvest seasons required children's full-time labor in the fields,

[26] A. Fishlow, "Levels of 19th-Century American Investment in Education," *Journal of Economic History* (December 1966).
[27] Ibid.

■ Educational facilities were limited, as is evident in this country schoolroom
painted in the 1860s. Public schools were often primitive and had minimal
supplies.
Source: Painting by E. L. Henry. Yale University Art Gallery.

and the school year was adjusted accordingly.
Parents could sometimes be an obstacle to education. Poor urban families often tried to keep
their children out of school; the additional income that a child might earn was valued more
than education and its possible future benefits.
It appears that the opportunity cost of foregone income in this era of widespread child
labor at least equalled the direct costs of public
education in 1860. Low-income families bore
much of the burden of educational costs, particularly in the cities.[28]

Educational Quality

The quality of education was uneven. In some
rural schools, children "graduated" when they
grew large enough to beat up the teacher. Few
teachers had much more schooling than the

oldest of their students. In technical and scientific education, the United States lagged far
behind Germany and France. Only one scientific journal was published in the entire nation
before the Civil War. (This may not have been
the handicap it seems, given the state of nineteenth-century science.)

Blacks and Women

Nor was schooling universally available. Education was legally prohibited for slaves in most
if not all southern states. Even in the North,
only the bravest and most idealistic teachers
would ignore public opinion and open the
classroom to blacks. Women found it all but
impossible to obtain advanced education. In
1850, school enrollment rates were about 10
percent higher for white males than for females, and those of whites were 20 times or
more than those of blacks.[29]

[28] Ibid.

[29] U.S. Department of Commerce, *Historical Statistics*, vol.
1, pp. 369–370.

Yet the results were impressive. By stressing communications skills and arithmetic competence, the schools made it easy for Americans to exchange information and approach practical problems with open minds. American formal education was more easily combined with training on the job than in many other nations. In a world of rapid yet basic technological change, perhaps such schooling was better suited to economic growth than any other. Although the quantity and quality of antebellum education compare unfavorably with today's, we must remember that this is hardly the appropriate frame of reference.

GOVERNMENT'S INFLUENCE ON THE ECONOMY

Every form of government influences the economic activity under its jurisdiction. Indeed, without government to make individuals secure in their property and persons, it is difficult to see how any but the most elementary activity would occur. In addition, it is generally through government that people develop institutions that shape the process of economic development, even in market-oriented economies.[30] Government sets the limits of legitimate and illegitimate activity, and through tax policies, safety and environmental regulations, command over the money supply, and redistributional programs it provides incentives or barriers to individual activity.

By curbing two widespread, understandable, but basically harmful tendencies, government can aid economic growth. People are likely to perform acts whose costs are borne by others if given the opportunity, and they are also likely to try to benefit from activities paid for by others, avoiding even contributions much less than the value of their personal benefits. Both lead to economic inefficiency. Persons are likely to push actions whose costs are borne elsewhere beyond the point where the benefits to society equal the costs. Further, if most or all individuals can avoid contributing to the cost of providing services, they will not be performed even though their cost may be far less than the value of the benefits they produce. Government can increase economic efficiency in the short run and raise growth rates over time by instituting policies that equate private and social rates of return.[31]

At the same time, government can be used to further private concerns with little or no consideration of the costs to society or groups within it. Grants of monopolistic privilege are an example: these raise the monopolists' incomes, but at the cost of a larger aggregate reduction in the income of the rest of the economy. Economists term such activities "rent seeking." Whether, on balance, government actions will further or hinder economic efficiency cannot be determined by theory. The answer depends on the popular sense of proper activity and on government's response to the various groups seeking to use it for their own purposes.[32]

The Record of Antebellum Government

In the antebellum period, as in every other, the record of government was mixed. By providing strong support for property rights through the Constitution and a series of laws and court decisions, economic activity in general was encouraged. Contracts were enforced, and the producers of new ideas were given property

[30] See, for example, D. North, *Structure and Change in Economic History* (New York: Norton, 1981) and M. Olson, *The Rise and Decline of Nations: Economic Growth, Stagflation, and Social Rigidities* (New Haven, Conn.: Yale University Press, 1982).

[31] D. North et al., *Growth and Welfare in the American Past: A New Economic History*, 3d ed. (Englewood Cliffs, N.J.: Prentice-Hall, 1983), Chap. 2.
[32] Ibid.

rights to them—but not the right to extend their monopolies beyond the original patent, copyright, or use grants. Crime, even violent crime, was not abolished, but most individuals apparently believed that their goods were secure enough to make long-term plans for investment and invention. Moreover, there was very little attempt to restrict individuals' generation or use of whatever incomes they might produce, a situation fostered by the multiplicity of legal jurisdictions within the United States. Taxes were very low, and virtually no laws redistributed income from those who produced it. In addition, resources under government control (public lands) were rapidly transferred to private ownership.

At the same time, government action or inaction reduced overall welfare at times. The tariff might be one example. Government support for slavery cost the slaves more than it profited slave owners, textile producers, and consumers. The problems of urban life were another clear example of government failure to promote the general welfare. It might be argued that at that time there were no known effective responses to city problems, but measures to prevent fires and epidemic disease had become increasingly effective in Europe in the eighteenth century.[33]

Evaluation Criteria for Government Activity

In another area, government influenced the course of development by direct action: it invested in projects designed to raise aggregate income levels. Professor North has proposed three criteria by which this aspect of government's impact on the economy might be evaluated.

1. Was the social rate of return (the increase in aggregate income rather than that accru-

ing directly to the causal factor) greater than the private returns? That is, were incentives to private activity less than the true value they produced for the aggregate economy?
2. Were government investment policies concentrated in such areas of high social returns?
3. Was the overall level of government investment large enough to exert a significant effect on the economy?

Professor North concluded that the overall contribution of government investment projects in the antebellum economy was not large. In general, government efforts were simply too small to have major effects, even had they consistently met the first two criteria.[34] Federal government spending accounted for less than 3 percent of gross national product in this period. Moreover, much federal spending could hardly be termed investment: over a third was for national defense, which had few direct effects on economic development.

The State and Local Record

State and local government spending were considerably greater than federal spending in aggregate, but much of it failed to meet the first and second criteria. The bulk of state government spending on canals—particularly after 1840—apparently reduced rather than increased aggregate income, although we lack a comprehensive evaluation of canals' social returns. Public subsidies to railroads were more productive, but these were a minor portion of government expenditure before 1860. Education did yield high returns, but the patterns of educational financing prior to 1860 suggest that much public spending would have been replaced by private efforts had it been reduced. In sum, government investment was neither large enough nor directed toward areas of high

---

[33] E. Jones, *The European Miracle* (Cambridge, England: Cambridge University Press, 1981), Chap. 7.

[34] North et al., *Growth and Welfare*, Chap. 8. See also earlier editions of *Growth and Welfare in the American Economy*.

social benefits consistently enough to produce substantial positive effects on income.

Indirect Influences on Income Distribution

Government investment projects were not the only mechanism to influence economic development. As noted in the introduction to this section, government sets the framework of rules within which economic activity occurs. Also, while there were no important attempts to redistribute income between groups, government policies did redistribute income geographically as a consequence of collection and expenditure patterns. Since federal revenues were overwhelmingly derived from tariffs, they were collected largely in New England and the major ports, and they were spent in the South. Frontier states typically paid more to the federal government in taxes than they received, at least after their Indians had been pacified.[35] Patterns of federal taxation and spending indicate at best a minor role for the federal government in the redistribution of income. Funds were transferred from two capital-rich areas and one capital-deficient region to locales that fell in between.

The Economic Climate of Antebellum America

The major economic impact of government on the antebellum economy was its provision of a climate where vigorous expansion by the private economy could and did occur. Government's role in capital formation diminished as private institutions developed and expanded— and as government influence over areas such as incorporation and contracts became more favorable to private enterprise. In cases such as bank regulation and the provision of social overhead capital in the cities, an argument can be made that government's role was too small.

Tariffs on balance probably reduced economic growth rather than aiding it as they were intended to do. For the Indians, of course, government policies for at least the first century of U.S. history were disastrous. Immigration policy, or the lack of one, may have had larger beneficial effects over time than any other single program.[36]

In this period, American attention was strongly centered on economic growth. In pursuing that goal, institutions were developed and expanded that proved admirably suited to their purpose. Both through the temperament of its people and the institutions that supported innovation, the United States offered an extremely favorable climate for expanded and innovative economic activity. Decisions as to the appropriate agency for any purpose were based on pragmatism. Governments owned and operated arsenals, banks, railroads, and canals—which of course was socialistic—not out of ideological conviction, but through a perception that private institutions were less effective than public agencies. The gradual abandonment of many semimercantilistic regulations, especially in the older cities, reflects not a commitment to laissez faire, but a recognition that they were ineffective. If we compare the results actually achieved in this period with those that might be expected from a market economy with the absolute minimum of government intervention, we may conclude that the overt effects of government activity on the U.S. economy were not great.[37]

SELECTED REFERENCES

Anderson, T., and P. Hill. *The Growth of a Transfer Society.* Stanford, Calif.: Hoover Institution Press, 1980.

[35] L. Davis and J. Legler, "The Government in the American Economy, 1815–1902: A Quantitative Study," *Journal of Economic History* (December 1966).

[36] Ibid. See also comments immediately following this article by D. McDougal.

[37] J. Hughes, *The Governmental Habit* (Charlottesville, Va.: University of Virginia Press, 1976) proposes greater governmental impact than seen here.

Commons, J. *History of Labor in the United States.* 4 vols. New York: A. Kelley, 1918.

Davis, L., and D. North. *Institutional Change and American Economic Growth.* Cambridge, England: Cambridge University Press, 1971.

Furnas, J. *The Americans: A Social History of the United States.* New York, Putnam, 1969.

Hughes, J. *The Governmental Habit.* Charlottesville, Va.: University of Virginia Press, 1976.

Lebergott, S. *The American Economy: Income, Wealth, and Want.* Princeton, N.J.: Princeton University Press, 1977.

Lindert, P., and J. Williamson. "Three Centuries of American Inequality." In *Research in Economic History*, edited by P. Uselding. Greenwich, Conn.: JAI Press, 1976.

North, D. *Structure and Change in Economic History.* New York: Norton, 1981.

Olson, M. *The Rise and Decline of Nations: Economic Growth, Stagflation, and Social Rigidities.* New Haven, Conn.: Yale University Press, 1982.

Soltow, L. *Men and Wealth in the United States, 1850–1970.* New Haven, Conn.: Yale University Press, 1975.

———, ed. *Six Papers on the Distribution of Wealth and Income.* New York: National Bureau of Economic Research (distributed by Columbia University Press), 1969.

U.S. Department of Commerce, Bureau of the Census. *Historical Statistics of the United States: Colonial times to 1970.* 2 vols. Washington, D.C.: Government Printing Office, 1975.

CHAPTER 10

THE CIVIL WAR

*T*he American Civil War is often presented as a watershed event in political history. In many ways it was, but its influence on the economic history of the United States is widely misunderstood. Even the war's effects on the economy are still the subject of controversy, especially since we can only compare the actual events of the war's aftermath with hypotheses of "what would have happened if . . . ?"

Some conclusions about the war are now well established. At one time, it was thought that the Civil War initiated American industrialization, but economic historians now agree that the United States had developed a large manufacturing sector before 1860. Both the quantity and variety of manufactured goods produced in this country had been growing at impressive rates for three or four decades before the war. Nevertheless, in 1860 the United States was still primarily an agricultural economy. By 1890 it had become largely industrial. What role did the Civil War play in this transformation? What was its effect on the pace and pattern of economic growth? By what mechanisms was the war's influence exerted? How significant were these effects?

THE COST OF FRATRICIDE

No other war of the United States has been more costly in terms of human lives than the holocaust that consumed the nation between 1861 and 1865. Over 600,000 men died—perhaps 6 percent of the work force. These deaths were disproportionately concentrated among young men, who tended to be more than normally productive members of the work force and whose contributions might have been expected to increase. Additionally, there were hundreds of thousands of wounded as well as many civilian casualties. In relation to the total population, the military death rate was over 65 times that which the United States endured in the Vietnam War. Had the casualty rates there equalled those of the Civil War, the Vietnam conflict would have cost this country 3.95 million American deaths. Even World War II, in which 405,000 Americans died in military service, pales in comparison—especially since the 1940 population of the United States was four times that of 1860.

The direct money costs of the war, including measures of the loss to future output through premature deaths, have been estimated at as much as $6.6 billion in 1860 dollars.[1] Even though this figure is probably a maximum estimate, it is difficult to regard the war itself as anything other than a catastrophe for the United States. It has been pointed out, however, that some of the declines in income in the South after 1865 sprang from causes largely independent of the war.[2] In addition, some nonmoney income gains produced by the war are difficult to quantify: we can assign a lower limit to the value of freedom to the ex-slaves, but its actual valuation cannot really be assessed economically.

Long-Term Effects

Despite the limitations of the Goldin and Lewis study, a summary of its conclusions gives some idea of the possible effects of the war on the United States in subsequent years. The full effects of the war include the retarded economic growth during the war and the reduced consumption required to catch up with the output levels that continued prewar trends would have produced. The resumption of prewar economic growth rates after the war required higher levels of saving from lower incomes (greater consumption sacrifices) than would have been necessary in its absence. When these factors are included, the total cost of the Civil War may be as great as $9 to $15 billion in 1860 dollars. Full recovery (in terms of consumption levels), the study concluded, was not achieved until 1879 in the North, and the South reached the levels of consumption it might have enjoyed in the war's absence only in 1909.[3] Even though other estimates are more modest, by any one of them the war produced a reduction in the physical welfare of most Americans that was both sizable and long-lived. We cannot know what might have happened to economic growth and per-capita consumption had the war not taken place, but even if we assume only a continuation of prewar trends, the conflict reduced incomes to less than their potential for at least a decade and a half.[4]

The real market value of 3.9 million slaves at $1,000 each (probably a sizable overestimate) was almost certainly less than the direct cost of the war. Thus, the war was an expensive method of freeing the slaves; purchasing them out of public funds would have been cheaper. It is difficult to imagine that compensated emancipation could have produced the social and political divisions generated by the war, which may still not be completely dissipated for any region or race. In addition, emancipation as it actually occurred imposed very substantial costs on the ex-slaves themselves.

[1] C. Goldin and F. Lewis, "The Economic Cost of the American Civil War: Estimates and Implications," *Journal of Economic History* (June 1975). This estimate is controversial, both because of data limitations and methodological problems. See S. Lee and P. Passell, *A New Economic View of American History* (New York: Norton, 1979), Chap. 11.
[2] P. Temin, "The Post-Bellum Recovery of the South and the Cost of the Civil War," *Journal of Economic History* (December 1976).

[3] Goldin and Lewis, "The Economic Cost."
[4] Temin, "Post-Bellum Recovery."

CAUSES OF THE WAR

Since the Civil War was so incredibly costly in lives, wasted resources, property destruction, and retarded economic growth, why did it occur? Was it a tragic mistake as well as a tragedy, or did some groups benefit even though aggregate well-being was reduced? Those who had been slaves before the war clearly gained from its outcome, but it strains credulity to suppose that they initiated the conflict. Could the war have been the result of calculation—even on faulty data or by flawed methods—that war was cheaper than available alternatives? Or were the causes wider than the slavery issue? Were tariffs, access to western land, the subsidization of a transcontinental railroad, the question of states' rights per se, or some other differences major contributors to the outbreak of war?

Slavery

Undoubtedly, the slavery question was the primary cause of the southern states' secession from the Union, which in turn was the immediate impetus for the war. The South had an enormous economic stake in slavery. Slaves comprised a major portion of southern wealth, and slavery raised the incomes of free southerners above the U.S. average. Slavery may not have benefited all or even most southern whites, and it certainly reduced the welfare of blacks. But slave owners had influence in southern politics far beyond their numbers, and they reaped large gains from continuation of the "Peculiar Institution." So rapidly were slave prices rising in the 1850s that the capital gains on an investment in slaves at the beginning of the decade were alone enough to pay the costs of their maintenance, even if the slaves were not employed in any form of production.[5] A threat to these levels of income and wealth could hardly fail to rouse the people who enjoyed them. It might also be supposed that slave ownership would not predispose planters to accept orders from others.

On no other topic was southern opinion so nearly unanimous as on the proposition that slavery must be preserved and shielded from any threat. As detailed in Chapter 6, economic forces posed no danger to slavery in 1860. Market forces, if anything, were increasing its profitability. Even southerners who did not own slaves might see slave-based agriculture as their most promising avenue to riches. The danger came from political, moral, and social forces.

The Extension of Slavery

Congressional records show that no other issue engendered the same fierce unanimity of opposition from southern representatives as any proposal for limitations, however slight, on slavery. Even the extension of slavery into new territories was a political rather than an economic question. Before 1860, there was no meaningful political challenge to slavery where it was already established. But the South was keenly interested in securing the rights of slave owners (almost invariably, other slave owners) to settle new areas. Only on the issue of slavery did southern views on states' rights differ significantly from those of other areas.

Since the South still had within its 1860 borders far more land than the existing slave population could work, extending slavery to new territories might appear unimportant. The prices of slaves were rising in relation to those of land, which indicated relative trends in the supply of both.[6] But if slavery were excluded from new territories, the admission of free states into the Union might in time threaten the South's veto power in the Senate. Rapid population growth in the Northwest had already

---

[5] Y. Yasuba, "The Profitability and Viability of Plantation Slavery," *Economic Studies Quarterly* (September 1961).

[6] G. Wright, *The Political Economy of the Cotton South* (New York: Norton, 1979), pp. 131–134.

eroded the South's power in the House of Representatives, and it appeared that even if free states had thus far evinced no real antipathy toward slavery, they had no strong interest in maintaining it. Even though there had been little nationwide support for John Brown and his efforts to raise a slave rebellion in 1859, northern opinions might change.

Even after Lincoln's election, only a scant one-third of Congress voted against a proposed constitutional amendment guaranteeing slavery's perpetuation where it already existed.[7] Thus, not only were slave owners rich and getting richer, but the political threat to their property, if any, did not appear to be growing. Yet the South attempted to secede over the issue of slavery. Why?

Maintaining Investment Values

One explanation has been offered by Professor Wright.[8] After noting the enormous wealth in slaves possessed by the South, he stated that each slaveholder's wealth was to some extent dependent on the conduct of others. The market value of slaves to any single master was determined largely by the expectations of *all other* slave owners. Regardless of any individual slave owner's views on the probability of emancipation, or even of the future markets for slaves or the crops they produced, the market value of slaves depended on the actions of other slaveholders. If enough slave owners offered their chattels for sale, prices would fall and the wealth of all would be reduced, whether they tried to sell slaves or not. To reduce the chance that any substantial group might become worried enough to sell slaves, Wright argued, the South continually sought new assurances from Congress that slavery would be maintained, even when the challenges were trivial. Secession, in this view, would end any possibility of a political

threat to slavery arising from those who had no stake in its continuation.

The Compromise of 1850, the Fugitive Slave Act (1852), and the Kansas-Nebraska Act (1854) were significant to the South not because they affected sizable numbers of slaves or planters, but because they represented other regions' recognition of slavery as an institution, revealed the absence of current opposition, and thus raised the value of slaves. The ownership of human property or the income derived from it was not seriously affected when slave owners were prevented from pursuing runaway slaves through northern states or when they incurred the risk of changing their slaves' status if they brought their bondsmen to free states. These circumstances seldom occurred, and it was easy to avoid bringing slaves to free territory.

Opposition to Slave Imports. The actions of the Confederacy lend strong support to Wright's thesis. No southern state, or even the Confederacy itself, supported measures to reopen the Atlantic slave trade. Indeed, there was widespread southern opposition to such a move. The articles of secession passed by several states specifically prohibited such actions, and the Confederacy even refused to allow the importation of slaves from within the boundaries of the United States.[9] Either measure, by increasing the supply, might have reduced the prices of slaves already owned by southerners.

Slavery's Prospects in 1860. Whether because of the political situation or favorable cotton markets, the evidence indicates that slave owners were becoming increasingly optimistic about the future of slavery and plantation agriculture. Not only were slave prices rising sharply in the late 1850s; they were also rising in relation to the rental rates for the same slaves.[10]

---

[7] Ibid., p. 156.
[8] Ibid., Chap. 5.

[9] Ibid., pp. 150–154.
[10] R. Fogel and S. Engerman, *The Reinterpretation of American Economic History* (New York: Harper and Row, 1971), pp. 382–383.

This indicates increasing confidence that slaves would be a profitable long-term investment: people will not pay higher prices for capital assets if they expect to lose them in the near future. The North had no clear economic basis for opposing slavery, although it may have had somewhat different feelings about its expansion. The abolitionist movement was not strong even in the North.

Northern Views on Slavery

Even the political events of 1860 hardly indicate strong opposition to slavery outside the South. If Lincoln supported the abolition of slavery (and this was by no means certain at the time), he was a minority president. Although he received 59 percent of the electoral votes in 1860, Lincoln was the choice of less than 40 percent of the voters. He owed his election to a split in the Democratic Party.[11] The South underestimated the determination of the North and especially of Lincoln to preserve the Union. The North probably underestimated the South's sense of insecurity. Once the fighting began, neither side felt able to back down on its demands.

THE ECONOMICS OF WAR: THE SOUTH

Southern Weaknesses

It is ironic that many of the conditions the South fought to preserve or further proved severe handicaps to the Confederacy's war effort. The prewar concentration on agriculture left the South largely dependent on foreign sources for arms and other manufactured goods. This should not be interpreted as evidence of economic weakness in the antebellum South, but only of the irrationality of war. Within the Confederacy's borders, only the Tredegar Iron Works in Richmond, Virginia, was capable of producing rails, artillery, and other heavy iron products when the war commenced. The Confederates built another foundry at Selma, in Alabama, but throughout the war, the South had to depend on prewar stocks and on what could be brought through an increasingly effective Union blockade, captured from Union forces, or obtained in trade with the enemy. Partially because of the nature of warfare, and also because of the frequency of Union Army defeats early in the war, arms supplies were largely adequate: blockade runners' cargoes were largely civilian consumer goods until late in 1863.[12] Heavy metal goods may have been an exception. By 1864 the South was forced to tear up branch railroads to obtain rails to keep its main lines in operation.

Population

The South was outnumbered two to one in population, but slavery deprived the South of more than one-third of its potential military manpower. The region's attitude toward the possibility of slave revolts, however, is revealed by the fact that some regions were unhesitatingly stripped of virtually their entire white male populations. In its last desperate days, the Confederacy even began to employ slave troops—long after the Emancipation Proclamation had been widely publicized.

A Weak Central Government

Adherence to states' rights doctrines undermined the adequacy of given quantities of material in the South. The central government of the Confederacy was unable to compel state

---

[11] U.S. Department of Commerce, Bureau of the Census, *Historical Statistics of the United States: Colonial Times to 1970*, 2 vols. (Washington, D.C.: Government Printing Office, 1975), 2:1074.

[12] S. Lebergott, "Through the Blockade: The Profitability and Extent of Cotton Smuggling, 1861–1865," *Journal of Economic History* (December 1981).

contributions toward the cost of the war. The Confederate government could only request men, funds, and supplies from the states. In 1865, Lee's forces were half-starved and facing hopeless odds not only because of the damage and casualties that the South had already endured, but also because some Confederate states would not release troops or supplies for use beyond their borders.

Finances

Finances were another of the Confederacy's crucial weaknesses. Since the central government effectively had no powers of taxation, it borrowed. But bond sales within the South did not raise the enormous sums required for the war. Borrowing abroad was only slightly more successful. Especially after the middle of 1863, European financiers wanted more assurance of success than the Confederacy could offer. Unable to obtain funds in any other way, the Confederate government resorted to the printing press. But as war needs grew and the area under Confederate control shrank, an increasing supply of money was applied to the purchase of declining amounts of real goods and services. Prices accelerated as people learned to anticipate inflation and to spend money as soon as they received it. In terms of the equation of exchange, velocity rose. The result was the only runaway inflation since the American Revolution. Prices rose in terms of Confederate currency until people refused to accept such paper money, and the desperate army began to confiscate goods it could not buy. Obviously, these developments caused further economic disruption.

Crucial Miscalculations

Several miscalculations worsened southern disadvantages. Britain's and France's dependence on southern cotton was overestimated. Many southerners had thought that a cutoff of cotton exports would force Britain and perhaps France to pressure the Union government to allow secession. However, the 1859 and 1860 cotton crops had been enormous, and most of the cotton had already been exported when hostilities began. Although cotton prices rose outside the South, Europe had sufficient inventories to last until new sources could be developed in India, Brazil, Egypt, the Caribbean, and areas of the South now controlled by the Union. Initially, the South had tried to restrict its own exports of cotton, but by the time the failure of this policy was evident and exports resumed, the Union blockade made the effort dangerous and expensive.

There had been some hope in the South that the Midwest would remain neutral in any conflict over slavery, but that region's Union sentiment proved strong. As war proponents do in almost all cases, the South underestimated its military tasks, perhaps because it could not imagine that its foes could maintain their resolve. Once the North learned to use its population and industrial advantages effectively, the southern cause was lost. In a long war, brilliant southern generals could not compensate for the fact that their troops were outnumbered and increasingly dependent on defeating a stronger enemy to obtain supplies. After the North finally found military leaders who could exploit their advantages, southern prospects grew bleaker still.

THE NORTHERN ECONOMY IN THE CIVIL WAR

Northern Strengths

The North began the war no less optimistically, if perhaps with less enthusiasm, than the South. President Lincoln's first call for military volunteers was for 75,000 men for three months. Before the war ended the total strength of the Union army exceeded one million. The North

■ During the Civil War, economic growth rates slowed as labor was diverted to military service. From the state of New York alone, 110,000 volunteers joined the Union army.
Source: *Leslie's*, March 19, 1864. From John Grafton, *New York in the Nineteenth Century*, 2d ed. (New York: Dover Publications, Inc., 1980), p. 21.

had population, industry, organization, and superior access to foreign goods on its side. Union control of the seas was never challenged. These gave it a margin with which to offset the many errors of the first years.

The North's transportation system was improved while the South's deteriorated, and the South had no hope of breaking the blockade with its own resources. In addition, the North also enjoyed superior financial institutions and a strong central government that eventually proved capable of marshalling resources for military purposes.

Before the full weight of the North's strength was used, piecemeal employment of these advantages was not enough to offset timid or incompetent northern military leadership. Eventually the Union found generals who could exploit the disparity in resources effectively enough to overcome the great southern commanders. In the meantime, Union armies might lose battle after battle, but the Confederates always found yet another army facing them. Every battle was crucial to the Confederacy, but the Union army had only to avoid outright destruction to continue the pressure on the South. Confederate attempts to achieve conclusive victory earned only a costly draw at Antietam (1862) and a strategic defeat at Gettysburg (1863) in the East. In the West, the war became a series of disasters for the Confederacy. What victories the South won there

■ The Georgia Railroad roundhouse at Atlanta was devastated by federal troops. Destruction of the South's transportation system hampered its war effort.
Source: Records of the Office of the Chief Signal Officer: National Archives.

were far too costly to offset the defeats that led to Union control of the Mississippi River (depriving the South of virtually all resources from its western regions) and ultimately the loss of Atlanta (1864).

WAR FINANCE

To finance the war, the Union government increased taxes. Tariffs were raised well above levels that had provoked southern protests ear-lier. Excise taxes were levied on a wide variety of domestically produced goods, and an income tax was imposed. Although these measures increased federal revenues from $56 million (including the South) in 1860 to $334 million without the South in 1865, expenditures rose much faster, from $63 million to $1.293 billion.[13] Less than one-fifth of wartime expenditures was tax-financed.

[13] U.S. Department of Commerce, *Historical Statistics*, vol. 2, pp. 1106, 1115.

To finance the unprecedented deficits of the war year, the Union government borrowed, selling large amounts of bonds. The national debt rose from $64 million to $2.678 billion. By the war's end, interest payments on the debt were almost three times total government expenditures in 1860.[14] Bond sales proved difficult, and the government turned to Jay Cooke. This financier organized teams of salesmen supported by newspaper advertising, testimonials, and appeals to patriotism to market the bonds both in the United States and abroad. The experience gained by buyers and bond salesmen alike proved useful in raising funds for private investment after the war. Cooke also used political pressure on the existing banking system to further bond sales.

■ During the Civil War, Congress authorized circulation of government-issued paper money for the first time since the Revolutionary War.
Source: Courtesy of Chase Manhattan Archives.

Paper Money

The government also printed money, both directly and indirectly. For the first time since the Revolutionary War, Congress authorized the issue of paper money. In 1862, $150 million in non-interest-bearing notes called "greenbacks" was placed in circulation. These notes were declared legal tender for all private debts and most obligations of the government as well. Greenbacks were not redeemable in specie and soon drove gold and silver out of circulation at their face value as money. "Hard money" continued to be available at a premium in currency. The total amount of greenbacks authorized ultimately reached $450 million.

The National Bank Act

In a time-honored measure designed to increase the sale of federal bonds, Congress passed the National Bank Act in 1862. This time, however, it did not set up a single large

bank. Instead, it offered federal charters to existing banks or to people forming new ones. The act allowed currently operating banks or groups of five or more would-be bankers to receive corporate charters from the federal government if they met its requirements for paid-in capital. These varied with the size of the city in which the bank was located. Each bank chartered had to deposit a portion of its capital with the U.S. Treasury in the form of government bonds. In return, the bank would receive National Bank notes to 90 percent of the bonds' face value. This currency could either be used as bank reserves, as specie had been, or circulated as the banks made loans. National Bank notes were of standard design, although the identity of the issuing bank was noted on one side. They were accepted at face value anywhere in the United States.

The National Bank Act contained provisions requiring the banks it chartered to maintain reserves as minimum proportions of their outstanding notes and deposits. Since the act imposed greater restrictions on bank lending than state banking laws, few banks were chartered under the National Bank Act until 1865.

[14] Ibid., p. 1104.

In that year Congress imposed a 10 percent tax on all outstanding state bank notes. The tax burden exceeded the interest income state banks had received from loans made through currency issues and effectively ended state bank notes' use as currency, apart from a few that were kept in circulation for advertising purposes and prestige.

After the passage of the 1865 legislation, the number of banks chartered under the National Bank Act rose from 467 to 1,294—over 75 percent of all banks in the United States. The act solved one of the country's prewar financial problems: the United States now had a uniform currency, the National Bank notes. It also provided better-designed and enforced regulation of banks. But the most serious failings of the banking system remained: there was neither a lender of last resort—a bankers' bank that could provide emergency reserves—nor a banking institution that could directly control the money supply.

The Effects of Inflation

Since the supply of money increased much faster than goods and services during the Civil War, prices rose. By 1865, prices were 70 to 100 percent above prewar levels. Periods of rapid inflation usually produce redistributive effects—those selling items whose price increases exceed the general rise gain; those selling goods whose price changes lag suffer losses in purchasing power. Much the same is true for purchases: if an individual buys items whose prices rise disproportionately, he or she is a victim of inflation; gains can be obtained if purchases concentrate on goods whose prices increase less than the overall average. Redistributive effects are especially likely if inflation is rapid and unforeseen.

Although wages rose, they may not have kept pace with price increases, especially for imported goods. The extent of the decline is still under dispute, but real wages probably fell during the war. At one time it was believed that profit recipients gained what workers lost, but it now appears that the portion of income paid in wages rose slightly during the war.[15] Both workers and employers paid higher taxes during the war; the one certain gainer from inflation was the federal government, which greatly increased its command over the economy's output.

The law required that greenbacks be accepted in payment of debt. These notes were fiat money—defined as legal tender by the government. Greenbacks and, until 1865, state bank notes became the circulating media. Gold and silver were worth as much as ever in terms of foreign currencies and hence of foreign goods, so they were either exported or hoarded. Since specie could only be obtained by paying a premium in American paper currency, foreign goods' prices in paper money rose.

The Abandonment of the Gold Standard

Specie flowed out of the United States, and the war made it impossible to reduce the domestic price level. Consequently, the United States was unable to remain on the gold standard: a paper dollar could no longer be exchanged for its face value in specie. The U.S. mint could no longer sell gold for paper currency at the price fixed before the war. At that price there would have been an abundance of gold buyers, but no one willing to sell gold to the mint, and the mint's supply would soon have been exhausted.

Under these conditions, the value of the U.S. dollar in international transactions was set by supply and demand, and it fell as Americans bought more foreign goods than their real exports would finance. The exchange rate rose as foreigners made their currencies available to the United States through purchases of Amer-

---

[15] See R. Kessel and A. Alchian, "Real Wages in the North During the Civil War," *Journal of Law and Economics* (October 1959) and S. DeCanio and J. Mokyr, "Inflation and Wage Lag During the Civil War," *Journal of Economic History* (June 1975).

ican exports or securities. At one time the greenback exchanged for only 35 percent of its face value in gold. One traditional source of foreign exchange declined sharply. Merchant shipping tonnage fell as ships were lost to Confederate raiders or natural disasters or sold to avoid capture. The industry had been declining before the war, but now it suffered a blow from which it never recovered.

DID THE WAR AID INDUSTRIALIZATION?

To some historians, the Civil War was a major economic as well as political divide.[16] To them, the antebellum United States was an agricultural nation, with institutions and values reflecting its people's occupations, and political control in the hands of southerners hostile to northern industry and western settlement. These historians believed that the war directly encouraged industrialization, as several later wars clearly did. They thought it also helped create a political climate much more favorable to the changes that occurred after the war. In the absence of southern representatives, Congress could pass measures favoring transcontinental railroads, the Homestead Act (which provided that government land be distributed virtually free of money charges to bona fide settlers), and steep increases in tariffs (which limited competition from foreign manufacturers). The National Bank Act, the financial markets developed through massive wartime sales of government securities and investors' greater familiarity with financial instruments, and the redistribution of income from labor to capital through "profit inflation" aided postwar industrial financing, in the eyes of this group.

Scholars of this group argued that repayment of the national debt after the Civil War further transferred income from those with a high propensity to consume to people who tended to save and invest large portions of their incomes. Even in the South, despite serious war damage, effects favored this process. The abolition of slavery allowed more flexible and rational uses of labor, since blacks were now freer to respond to economic incentives. Northern agriculture, it was thought, mechanized rapidly during the war to compensate for the loss of manpower to the military.

The Modern View

Implicit in each of these contentions is the idea that the result was both positive and significant for American economic growth. However, today every one of these points is under severe challenge, if not totally refuted. Using nineteenth-century statistics not available when the previous ideas were formulated, historians now increasingly view the aggregate economic impact of the Civil War as negative, and possibly disastrously so.[17]

The Revision of the Optimists' Views

The earlier, positive view of the Civil War's economic influence was based on impressions, not accurate data. Some writers tended to generalize from the U.S. experience in World Wars I and II, in which massive government spending eliminated prewar unemployment, and at least in World War II, significant technological spinoffs aided postwar civilian goods production. Some of the conclusions may result from two of the most common errors in economic reasoning: failure to assess alternatives (foregone options) properly and the belief that his-

---

[16] See C. Beard and M. Beard, *The Rise of American Civilization* (New York: Macmillan, 1930) and L. Hacker, *The Triumph of American Capitalism* (New York: Columbia University Press, 1940).

[17] T. Cochran, "Did the Civil War Retard Industrialization?" *Mississippi Valley Historical Review* (September 1961) was the seminal article in this reformulation.

torical sequence implies causation. Although the U.S. economy underwent massive economic transformation and growth after the Civil War, that is not proof that the war was responsible.

In general, the case against the view just stated is that the war used scarce resources and thus denied them to alternative uses. Large numbers of men and horses previously employed in agriculture, manufacturing, and distribution were transferred to military purposes. To employ these resources in war meant that their output in civilian uses was forfeited. The true gain (or loss) from their diversion is the difference in the value of their output in the two uses.

Economic Costs of the War's Destruction

Since the primary "product" of resources' military employment was death and destruction, the war reduced overall welfare while it occurred. The cost was not only the direct results of military activity, but also the less noticeable forfeiture of civilian goods that were not produced. If men were replaced by less experienced or otherwise less productive workers—women and children—the loss would not be total. But there must have been some overall reduction in output since these alternative (and lower-paid) labor sources were not used while men were available.

General Sherman's "Bummers," Sheridan's devastating forces in the Shenandoah Valley, and General N. B. Forrest's raiders destroyed productive resources and left vast areas unproductive until the damage could be repaired. Both the winners and the losers in the Civil War were Americans, and their war efforts damaged the same economy. The direct result of military action, therefore, was that output from people, physical resources, and institutions was lost, and other resources had to be devoted to their repair or replacement before the country regained its prewar productive potential.

The Demand for Industrial Goods

Modern war, which is waged at least as much with materials as with men, is capital intensive. But the Civil War was not a modern war. Masses of men armed with rifles were the chief military instrument of both antagonists. There was little artillery and virtually no sophisticated machinery. This meant that the war imposed very light demands on industrial production and virtually none on heavy industry. Naval construction might be an exception, especially after the appearance of ironclad warships, but naval activity was only a minor part of the war effort. More iron was devoted to small arms production than to any other item used by the Union army. The second greatest use of iron was in horseshoes, and the two combined required only about 2 percent of total iron production during the war.[18] With the partial exception of weapons, both armies demanded much the same items for their troops as the men had consumed in civilian life. Only the inherent wastefulness of a military establishment in wartime increased demand for food, clothing, and similar items above peacetime levels.

The Effects of Fiscal Policy

It might appear that a large expansion in government spending financed by the highly inflationary methods employed in the war by both sides would stimulate economic activity. If people obtained more money, they could be expected to spend at least most of it. However, although the volume of spending can rise almost indefinitely, the amount of real output that can be produced at any instant is always limited. Once all productive resources are in use, little or no further increase in real production is possible without changes in technology, resource supplies, or the institutions governing their use. Such changes almost al-

[18] L. Davis et al., *American Economic Growth: An Economist's History of the United States* (New York: Harper and Row, 1972), p. 56.

ways require considerable periods of time. The Civil War neither created more resources nor improved the efficiency with which existing stocks were used; indeed, the primary effects of the war were just the opposite. Approximately 25 to 35 percent of the labor force was diverted to less productive uses,[19] if not to outright destruction. Thus, in the 1860 context, a large-scale increase in spending merely diverted resources from one use to another, and a less productive one at that. The increase in spending generated price increases rather than gains in real output. When the war began, the economy was at or close to full employment; there were few resources whose reallocation to military uses did not involve direct opportunity costs.

Wartime Growth

The U.S. economy did not cease to grow entirely during the Civil War, but the rate of growth was much slower than it had been in the two prior decades or would be again in the 1870s. The total output of goods and services had been growing at a 4.6 percent annual average rate from 1840 to 1860, and it grew at 4.4 percent from 1870 to 1900. The rate in the 1860s, however, was only 2 percent. Manufacturing's share of total production increased faster before the war than it did afterward.[20] Heavy industry became a larger portion of total manufacturing production during the war, but it did so largely by default; consumer goods output grew very slowly or in some cases even declined. There was no great spurt of growth in heavy industry.[21] Some important industries were badly hurt by the loss of southern markets, particularly boots and shoes and cotton textiles. The latter was also adversely affected by the restricted supply of raw cotton.

Despite the completion of the Union Pacific, the first transcontinental railway, railroad construction declined. In the 1850s, 20,000 miles of railroad track had been laid in America; the next decade saw only 16,000 miles of new right-of-way, and most was built after the war.[22] In many other industries, the same pattern appears; growth, but at lower rates than in the previous decade, or even absolute declines in production. Nor was slower growth in output offset by qualitative improvements. The 1860s were the only decade in the entire century in which labor productivity in manufacturing declined, indicating that the diversion of first-line workers to the military was not offset by the use of more or better capital.[23]

The war itself produced no innovations that profoundly impacted the productive potential of the postwar economy. Standardized clothing sizes and widespread use of canned goods were the most important new developments. In other sectors of the economy, the picture is similar to that in manufacturing. Northern agriculture did grow faster than industry during the war, but the pace of mechanization slowed rather than accelerated. In any case, much of the increased production of wheat and corn was exported, and the growth in foreign demand can hardly be attributed to the war.

Southern agriculture was of course badly disrupted by the war and its aftermath. It did not fully recover for decades, although not all of the South's difficulties can be attributed to the war.[24] Per-capita income in the South fell 38 percent from prewar levels; much though not all of this decline was due to the reduction in the labor force caused by the abolition of

[19] Ibid.
[20] Fogel and Engerman, *Reinterpretation*, p. 371.
[21] Ibid., p. 372.

[22] U.S. Department of Commerce, *Historical Statistics*, vol. 1, p. 372.
[23] Fogel and Engerman, *Reinterpretation*, p. 372.
[24] Temin, "Post-Bellum Recovery."

slavery.[25] Although the reduction in hours worked and labor force participation indicates a gain in leisure time or household activity, and thus the loss in income is overstated by these figures, the drop in southern incomes was real and large.

Delayed Effects?

It has been argued that the war's beneficial economic effects were delayed rather than immediate. This opinion views the rapid economic growth of the economy in general and manufacturing in particular in the 1870s as deferred effects of the war. Whatever the immediate effects of the war, proponents of this position believe that its long-run results were favorable. But growth rates in the 1870–1900 period were higher than in the 1860s in part because of a catch-up effect: the economy grew faster in this period than in the war decade because it had missed so many opportunities then. The postwar increase in growth rates would not have been necessary or could have proceeded from a larger base had growth in the 1860s been normal. In addition, it is not clear just how the war could have added to growth capabilities if it neither increased resource supplies (in the case of labor, it clearly reduced them) nor introduced important new technology.

Another view of the war's effects finds beneficial but long-delayed results. The Civil War destroyed nearly all the South's economic institutions, and with them the familiarity which allowed rent-seeking activity by various organized groups. Until a new set of institutions could be devised, there would be few barriers to new types of competitive economic activity. Only after the new environment became familiar would rent-seeking activities, with their tend-

ency to reduce economic growth, again become possible. This theory has been tested, and appears to have some relevance to regional growth rates. However, it would be more convincing had the southern economy developed new forms of activity berfore 1900.[26]

THE BENEFITS OF WAR?

The strongest case for beneficial effects of the war on economic growth appears to be in the area of financial and monetary developments. The claim that inflation transferred income from labor to capital during the war is weak, but postwar debt repayment may have had this result. During the war, the chief beneficiary of income transfers was the federal government; redistribution within the private sector during the war now seems unlikely to have had significant effects. Postwar retirement of public debt, financed largely by regressive taxes mainly paid by low- and middle-income groups rather than the rich, did transfer income from consumers to investors. However, it accounted for no more than a fraction of the increase in investment that took place from 1866 to 1900. One study claimed these transfers caused no more than 3 percent of the increase in investment. Others are more generous, but all indicate that investment would have risen to 90 percent or more of actual levels without the aid given by the form of debt repayment employed by the U.S. government.[27]

---

[25] R. Ransom and R. Sutch, *One Kind of Freedom: The Economic Consequences of Emancipation* (Cambridge, England: Cambridge University Press, 1977), Chap. I. See also Temin, "Post-Bellum Recovery."

[26] See M. Olson, *The Rise and Decline of Nations: Economic Growth, Stagflation, and Social Rigidities* (New Haven, Conn.: Yale University Press, 1983), Chaps. 2, 4, 5.

[27] Fogel and Engerman, *Reinterpretation*, p. 378. This estimate (by Engerman) is the lowest. See also J. Williamson, "Watersheds and Turning Points: Conjectures on the Long-Term Impact of Civil War Financing," *Journal of Economic History* (September 1974) and Lee and Passell, *A New Economic View*, Chap. 11.

Banking and Investments

The National Bank Act did improve the banking system's operation to some extent. However, the evidence indicates that the ragbag currency of the antebellum period imposed only slight burdens on the economy or its rate of growth (see Chapter 8). Furthermore, the National Bank Act affected attempts to return to the gold standard in the postwar period in a manner that could not have aided economic growth. The money supply was restricted to the point of severe deflationary pressure, which clearly resulted in real economic distress. Nor did the act eliminate the instability of the banking system. Institutions similar to those provided by the National Bank Act could have been developed without the war, even though the legislation itself was spurred by the needs of war finance. If the war caused them to be introduced sooner than they would otherwise have been, it was a horribly expensive catalyst.

The improved methods of securities marketing that appeared during the war were useful in the postwar period, but again, it is difficult to argue that the war's absence would have done more than delay their implementation. Nor can these methods have been the source of the postwar increase in investment. In fact, the proportion of gross national product devoted to investment had been rising before the Civil War, and its rate of increase declined after the conflict.[28] On balance, the war-induced changes in monetary and financial institutions favored investment and economic growth, but they reinforced already evident trends, and their influence was not great. That the war was the immediate cause of these changes hardly makes their benefits greater than the costs of the conflict.

[28] Fogel and Engerman, *Reinterpretation*, p. 373.

Politics

Few of the political arguments for the war's favorable effects on long-term economic growth now appear strong. The proposition that the war shifted political control to groups more disposed toward industrialization and economic growth is weak. The war's immediate cause now appears to have been the realization that Dixie was *already* losing control of Congress or was very likely to do so. Some of the consequences attributed to the shift in sectional control of Congress were not in fact points of contention between the North and South; indeed, almost no issues aside from slavery united either area. The South was not opposed to government aid to construct a transcontinental railroad, although it wanted the eastern terminal in New Orleans rather than St. Louis. Neither the North nor the South was united on the tariff issue. As Chapter 8 indicated, the trend in prewar legislation was toward lower rates, generally thought to be what the South desired. Easy access to western land was opposed by the South for political reasons, and the Homestead Act was passed during the enforced absence of southern representatives from Congress. But the point is not merely whether the South or the North favored or opposed legislation, but whether the laws actually spurred or curtailed American economic growth.

In the case of the Homestead Act, for example, the results were minor and probably adverse. Despite the reduction in money costs of government land, the act imposed nonmoney costs that apparently were at least as onerous. In any case, most western land was transferred to private ownership under other laws after 1862. Even if the Homestead Act increased the temporary allocation of resources to agriculture, this was a transfer to low-productivity uses in relation to the other opportunities available to labor. As such, it would have reduced incomes rather than increased them.

Tariffs

High tariffs increased the monopoly power of American producers, very much at the expense of consumers and probably of employment as well. It is difficult to view the postwar continuation of the tariffs (which were instituted to raise revenue for the war) as stemming solely from their wartime origin. Attempts to measure the results of all the legislation so far discussed have concluded that none of these measures, including the transcontinental railroad, accounted for more than a fraction of 1 percent of U.S. economic growth. By 1865 the American economy was large and diversified. Even measures that doubled or halved the production of most sectors of the economy (and none of this legislation approached such an impact) would have a far less significant impact on the aggregate economy or its growth.

The Source of Industrialization?

Another point made in defense of the war's economic impact is that it favored a shift from agricultural to business attitudes and thus allowed more rapid growth. The point is impossible to quantify, as are most psychological propositions in history. But it surely involves a misunderstanding of the primary motives of antebellum agriculturalists in North and South alike. The attitudes of American farmers in general and southern planters in particular appear to have been typified by a high degree of economic rationality from as far back in history as the data permit conclusions. Economic theory provides an accurate basis to explain and predict farmers' responses to prices, new technology, and markets. The contention that attitudinal shifts fostered economic growth would be strengthened had the South been ruled by

values that consciously sacrificed economic advantage to other values, or if the southern economy had been poor or stagnant compared with nonagricultural areas. But the South was none of these. It is seldom noticed that the noneconomic values which supposedly pervaded the South could equally be charged against the Midwest, which had achieved less economic success than the South.

The American Civil War, then, was a costly diversion of resources to uses that reduced the rate of economic growth and possibly even the level of incomes. During the war population growth slowed. Immigration faltered. Birthrates fell because of soldiers' enforced separations from their families, and the heavy losses incurred by both sides meant that some of this population loss might be permanent. The labor force reductions, it must be noted, occurred in an economy where labor was less plentiful and more productive than in Europe, and where increases in the labor force were the largest single source of economic growth.

THE WAR-DAMAGED ECONOMY

The Civil War, in aggregate, was no aid to American economic growth. The rate of increase in total production, although not production itself, fell during the war. When we realize that the war occurred after three or four decades of rapid economic growth and diversification, it is difficult to view it as anything other than a tragic interruption of increasingly successful peacetime pursuits. The war marked no transition to industrialization, because that process began 30 or 40 years before the conflict.

The war's impact on various regions differed. It was, as we have seen, not beneficial to the northern economy. In the South it was ruinous. Physical destruction, particularly of

■ Freedmen continued as agricultural laborers but also took advantage of education offered at night after their fieldwork was completed.
Source: Courtesy of The Newberry Library, Chicago.

bellum financial institutions and the extensive capital losses suffered by the planters all but destroyed any chance to substitute capital for labor, or to invest in other sectors of the economy. Cotton prices were extremely high immediately after the war, which increased the incentives for a return to agriculture. But the long-term growth in demand for cotton was slowing, adding to the difficulties generated by disruptions in supply. The South did not regain prewar levels of per-capita income until the 1880s. (Incomes from the two eras are not really comparable due to the sweeping changes in the status of blacks.) This period, not the prewar years, was the source of the South's relative poverty.[30]

buildings, railroads, and other fixed capital, was widespread, but repaired in a surprisingly short time. Southern railroads and manufacturing apparently regained or exceeded prewar levels of production by 1870.[29] These sectors, however, were not the core of the southern economy. Agriculture was, and the South's agricultural recovery was much slower. The abolition of slavery did not immediately generate new methods of organizing agricultural production or employment. People unfamiliar with anything but the slave-operated plantation could only gradually work out new arrangements. Blacks found that the choices opened by freedom were sharply constrained by their lack of property and skills. Since freedmen did not obtain landownership with emancipation, they had little choice but to continue as agricultural labor.

One consequence of emancipation was that black women and children spent much less time in field labor, greatly reducing the South's effective labor force. Destruction of the ante-

SELECTED READINGS

Andreano, R. ed. *The Economic Impact of the Civil War*. Cambridge, Mass.: Schenkman, 1962.

Beard, C., and M. Beard. *The Rise of American Civilization*. New York: Macmillan, 1930.

Davis, L., et al. *American Economic Growth: An Economist's History of the United States*. New York: Harper and Row, 1972.

Fogel, R., and S. Engerman. *The Reinterpretation of American Economic History*. New York: Harper and Row, 1971.

Hacker, L. *The Triumph of American Capitalism*. New York: Columbia University Press, 1940.

Lee, S., and P. Passell. *A New Economic View of American History*. New York: Norton, 1979.

Ransom, R., and R. Sutch. *One Kind of Freedom: The Economic Consequences of Emancipation*. Cambridge, England: Cambridge University Press, 1977.

Studenski, P., and H. Kroos. *Financial History of the United States*. New York: McGraw-Hill, 1952.

U.S. Department of Commerce, Bureau of the Census. *Historical Statistics of the United States: Colonial Times to 1970*. 2 vols. Washington, D.C.: Government Printing Office, 1975.

Wright, G. *The Political Economy of the Cotton South: Households, Markets, and Wealth in the Nineteenth Century*. New York: Norton, 1976.

[29] Ransom and Sutch, *One Kind of Freedom*, pp. 40–42.

[30] Ibid., Chap. 3.

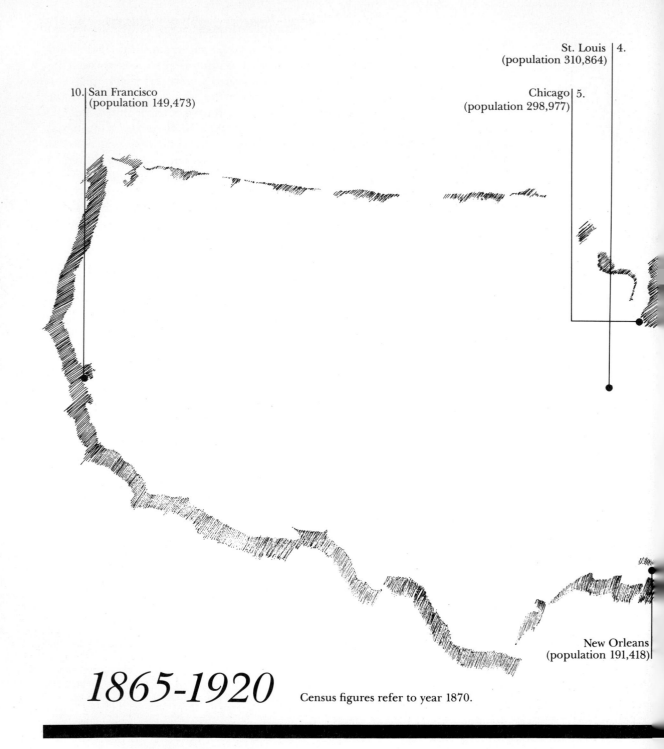

St. Louis | 4.
(population 310,864)

Chicago | 5.
(population 298,977)

10. | San Francisco
(population 149,473)

New Orleans
(population 191,418)

1865-1920 Census figures refer to year 1870.

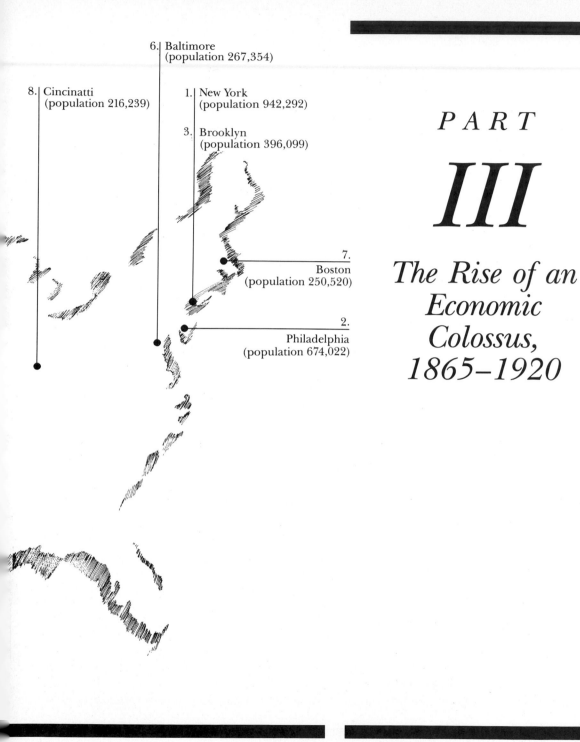

6. Baltimore
(population 267,354)

8. Cincinatti
(population 216,239)

1. New York
(population 942,292)

3. Brooklyn
(population 396,099)

7.
Boston
(population 250,520)

2.
Philadelphia
(population 674,022)

PART

III

*The Rise of an
Economic
Colossus,
1865–1920*

P hotographs depicting Americans at work between the Civil War and the end of World War I often seem intended to convey an impression of capability and achievement. Typically, they show a construction crew, a factory work force, a shift of miners, or a group of lumberjacks posed in front of some product of their efforts. Another favorite pose is the business leader at his desk acting as the "captain of industry." Both employees and employers appear to radiate capability, confidence, and satisfaction in these photos. The poses reflect more than the conventions of portraiture in this era. Americans had achieved a great deal, and they knew that no other nation had done more in the economic sphere by 1910. In the field of economic endeavor, Americans had reason to feel pride and satisfaction in the results they had produced.

In 1860, the American economy had been among the most productive in the world in terms of both aggregate output and the per-capita incomes provided. By 1910, however, Americans had developed their economy into the unchallenged world leader. Per-capita incomes were higher in the United States than in any other nation and growing faster than in most. At the beginning of the period, America was very much in Europe's technological debt, although it had shown a talent for innovation. A half-century later, American technology was the world's best in a growing range of applications, and the country's ability to generate new ideas was increasing rapidly. This position had already been achieved by 1910: with the terrible losses and disruption that Europe endured as a consequence of the First World War, the United States no longer even had close rivals as the world's most productive economy.

The Dimensions of Growth

American economic growth in this period was in part extensive; it resulted from increases in the amount of resources available. U.S. population growth continued to be rapid by world standards. The 37.5 million Americans at the close of the Civil War had grown to 99 million by 1914 and to 106 million by 1920. Expansion of economic activity into previously undeveloped regions continued for much of the period. The area of the contiguous United States had been stable since 1853, but many regions at that time unsettled and unused were now integrated into the national economy. The addition of Alaska in 1867 and the acquisition of Hawaii and an overseas empire were less economically significant than the degree to which the entire continental area was brought into use. Even though settlement extended over the entire 48 states by 1910 and the frontier as a physical limit no longer existed,

Table III.1 Aggregate and Per-Capita Gross National Product

| Date | Current Dollars | | 1972 Dollars | |
	Total (Billion)	Per Capita (Dollars)	Total (Billion)	Per Capita (Dollars)
1870*	$7.4	$170	$100.2	$2,300
1880**	11.2	205	183.9	3,359
1890	13.1	208	228.7	3,626
1895	13.9	200	271.6	3,904
1900	18.7	246	333.7	4,385
1905	25.1	299	418.2	4,990
1909	33.4	369	488.2	5,395
1915	40.0	398	521.9	5,189
1920	91.5	859	578.3	5,432

*1869–1878 average
**1879–1888 average
Source: U.S. Department of Commerce, Bureau of the Census, *Bicentennial Statistics* (Washington, D.C.: Government Printing Office, 1976), p. 393.

enormous potential remained for further development of America's natural bounty.

Although population had nearly tripled, in part because of the greatest wave of immigration any nation had ever received, the total output of the economy had grown much faster. Real gross national product for the 1869–1878 decade had averaged $27.1 billion in 1958 dollars. In 1914 the figure was $125.6 billion, and the 1920 gross national product reached $140 billion.[1] Table III.1 gives rough estimates of aggregate and per-capita GNP growth in 1986 dollars. Consequently, real per-capita income was from two and one-half to three times the Civil War–era level by 1920.

Americans enjoyed per-capita incomes about half again as large as those of the most successful European economies in the years just prior to World War I. Not only were American incomes higher, they were growing faster than those of most other nations. Only Canada and Germany—both much smaller economies—came close to matching American per-capita income growth.[2] Sweden and Japan may have generated equal aggregate growth rates,

[1] U.S. Department of Commerce, Bureau of the Census, *Historical Statistics of the United States: Colonial Times to 1970,* 2 vols. (Washington, D.C.: Government Printing Office, 1975), 1:224.
[2] Ibid., p. 225.

but from much lower income bases. In both national product and its rate of growth, the United States had outstripped Britain, France, and Germany. No other nation had achieved the combination of rapid growth in both income and population to the extent recorded here.

Urbanization

Growth of these dimensions indicated changes, and changes were obvious in the American economy. Population patterns changed, both between geographic areas and between urban and rural dwellers. Cities grew much faster than the aggregate population. In 1860, 19.7 percent of the population lived in cities and towns of 5,000 or more. Two decades later, 28.1 percent of the population was urban, and by 1900, 39.7 percent. After World War I the United States was an urban nation: just over half the population lived in cities.

The United States contained no cities of one million or more inhabitants in 1860, and only two with more than half that number. More than ten million people lived in such cities 50 years later, and the number of cities of all types had increased more than sixfold. As might be expected, this shift in living patterns indicated new employment patterns: the variety of jobs tends to expand at least as fast as urban populations. The proportion of workers engaged in manufacturing, transportation, and services was much higher than it had been in 1860, and the percentage in agriculture lower. The agricultural population had peaked in 1910: the number of people earning their livings from farming has been declining ever since.[3] Construction and domestic service also showed declines in employment. Even so, agricultural production did not fall. Instead, it more than tripled from 1860 to 1900.[4]

New Regional Patterns of Production

The location of production changed within almost all sectors. By the close of this period, the Midwest, particularly the North Central states, had become an industrial region as well as the nation's agricultural heartland. Ohio, Indiana, Illinois, Michigan, and Wisconsin all exhibited faster industrial growth

[3] For all regions but the South, the agricultural population had begun to decline a decade or more before 1910. Only the very high proportion of the southern population engaged in agriculture kept the national figures from indicating this trend by 1900. See G. Wright, *Old South, New South: Revolutions in the Southern Economy Since the Civil War* (New York: Basic Books, 1986), Chap. 3.
[4] Ibid., p. 482.

than the old centers in New England and the Middle Atlantic states. Lumbering and mining shifted westward to a greater extent than did agriculture, but beef and wheat production were now centered west of the Mississippi River. The West became a region of cities and diversified, highly productive agriculture. After 1900, the natural resources and low-wage labor of the South began to attract industry, even as southerners began to migrate to northern cities in search of higher incomes.[5]

These reallocations, which indicated a degree of human mobility greater than even the United States had ever seen before, began to reduce regional differences in wages. Capital, too, became more mobile as financial markets improved, and after 1900 regional interest rate differentials fell, with rates over large areas indicating nearly complete integration into national markets.[6] This relocation of people and industries toward the areas of highest returns led to increasing regional specialization. With specialization, as Adam Smith had pointed out a century before, came interdependence. In nearly all walks of life, Americans used tools, raw materials, and services produced by others as essential elements in their jobs. In addition, their consumption was now largely of goods made by other specialists either wholly, or as in the case of food and clothing, through a larger share of the initial processing and preparation.

International Economic Relations

Domestic changes were paralleled by alterations in the economic relations between the United States and the rest of the world. Traditionally this country had been an exporter of raw materials and semiprocessed goods and an importer of manufactured goods. Its trade deficits were balanced by borrowing abroad. After 1874 the chronic U.S. trade deficit became a surplus, as manufactured exports increased. After 1900 the United States had become an exporter of capital, with growing investments in other countries, and its international indebtedness had begun to shrink. By 1914 America was an industrial power without peer: the country's manufacturing output was equal to that of Britain, Germany, and France combined.[7] In the next half-dozen years American industrial preeminence would grow even greater.

[5] Ibid. Wright stresses that this migration encountered formidable barriers.
[6] L. Davis, "The Investment Market, 1870–1914: The Evolution of a National Market," *Journal of Economic History* (September 1965).
[7] J. Hughes, *Industrialization and Economic History: Theses and Conjectures* (New York: McGraw-Hill, 1970), p. 126.

The Sources of Growth

Natural Resources

Before 1860, most U.S. natural resources had yet to be utilized. Many had not even been discovered, or uses for them found. After the Civil War, exploitation of the nation's mineral and agricultural potential proceeded rapidly. Ample deposits of almost every mineral important to contemporary industry were discovered and exploited. Moreover, in many cases these resources were easy to use where they were, or transportation links could readily send them where they were needed. For example, in the southern Appalachians, coal and iron ore were discovered in the same geological formation, which gave rise to the great steelmaking center in Birmingham after 1871. Elsewhere, natural resources were conveniently located for water transportation. Where minerals, water resources, or soils were not so conveniently situated, Americans developed tools and methods to make them productive. Improvements in transportation, both extensive (the railroads were extended to nearly every corner of the country) and intensive (in the form of innovations such as refrigerated railway cars), made the cost of products from distant regions much lower after 1900 and encouraged regional specialization. Other aspects of distribution also improved, and the proportion of final goods' prices that reflected wholesaling and retailing charges fell.

Labor and Capital

America's generous raw materials endowment contributed less to economic growth than did increases in the nation's labor force and capital stock. The labor force grew even faster than the population, because the declining birthrate increased the proportion of adults in the native population, as did longer life spans. Immigrants, as previously noted, tend to be young adults, and immigration—particularly in the 1900–1914 period—was enormous. Social changes also contributed to the growth of the work force: the portion of women employed outside the home rose from 18.9 to 25.4 percent of the female population over 1890–1910.[8] In the early decades of this period, children worked in factories and other urban jobs, but the portion of children so employed declined after 1900.

[8] U.S. Department of Commerce, *Historical Statistics,* vol. 1, p. 133.

Table III.2 Percentage Contribution of Inputs and Productivity to Growth of Net National Product, 1840–1960

	1840–1960	1840–1900	1900–1960
Annual growth rate	3.56%	3.98%	3.12%
Labor	42.7	47.2	34.8
Land	5.9	9.6	2.5
Capital	22.8	25.9	18.6
Productivity	28.6	17.3	44.1

Source: L. Davis et al., *American Economic Growth: An Economist's History of the United States* (New York: Harper and Row, 1972), p. 39.

Qualitative changes, which had begun to contribute significantly to economic growth in the previous era, assumed a greater importance. The work force gained increased industrial experience and skills, education was extended to more children and the length of schooling expanded, and more sophisticated management techniques appeared. Not only did each worker have twice the amount of capital assisting his efforts in 1909 as in 1869, but the capital was improved.[9] Such changes in factor proportions contributed a substantial share of the increase in output per worker. Gross investment as a portion of American GNP has never been higher than at the turn of the century—some 30 percent.

According to one investigator, growth of the labor force accounted for about half of all American economic growth between 1840 and 1900. Capital accumulation produced another quarter of the total, and the increased development of natural resources one-tenth. The remaining source of growth, about one-sixth of the total, was obtained through productivity increases—through raising the amount of product each unit of inputs turned out.[10] (See Table III.2.) Much of the new capital was designed to produce very large amounts of output; that is, it offered economies of scale. Often such capital had to be combined with extensive support facilities and large amounts of

[9] R. Higgs, *The Transformation of the American Economy, 1865–1914: Essays in Interpretation* (New York: John Wiley and Sons, 1971), p. 33.
[10] L. Davis et al., *American Economic Growth: An Economist's History of the United States* (New York: Harper and Row, 1972), p. 39.

labor. Consequently, large firms became increasingly common in manufacturing, transportation, and at the very end of the period, distribution.

Economic Mobility

Growing interdependence, new technology, urbanization, and easier, cheaper transportation increased the range of jobs open to the typical worker. Especially since many of the jobs were new, either to the area or often to the entire economy, there were few barriers to occupational mobility. As might be expected in a period of rapid economic growth, economic mobility was a noteworthy feature of the American economy. Those clinging to old production methods or old products often found their incomes falling in relative if not absolute terms, while workers opting to reinforce change by making new goods in new ways moved up the income ladder. In a few cases gains were spectacular, but the aggregate effect of millions of modest changes was far more significant for American use of its human talent.

New Technology

As time passed, new growth sectors replaced those whose rapid initial growth had "pulled" the economy forward. Steam power, steel, and the railroads had figured largely in early growth. Before 1914 they had given way to a new technology based on industrial chemistry, electricity, and the internal combustion engine—techniques and tools geared to the needs of the wealthy, urban society that consumed their products. The formal application of scientific methods to economic activity had previously been limited to a few areas within engineering, marine navigation, and little else. Now it was found that such approaches paid dividends in large-scale manufacturing, public health, and even agriculture. Moreover, the employment of scientific procedures made it easier to identify cause and effect. This allowed for a rapid dispersion of productive ideas through the economy and their successful adaptation in new circumstances.

Another feature of the economic growth of this period that may appear surprising to modern students is that much of it occurred during a period of sustained deflation. From 1865 to 1896, the average level of prices fell by about one-half. After 1896, inflation appeared, but at modest rates—1 to 3 percent annually. In World War I, inflation was severe: prices doubled in less than four years, and prices were still rising in early 1920.

The Uses of Wealth

Higher real incomes increase individuals' well-being in two ways. First, they allow their recipients more of the things they have already been consuming. Were this their total effect, the attractions of greater purchasing power might quickly pall for most persons. But increased incomes also allow people to obtain variety, and this desire is insatiable. It appears to be no less true of nations than of individuals. The United States used most of its new productive capacity to increase private consumption and investment, so that the amount and variety of consumer and capital goods rose. But there was something left over to devote to new purposes. Child labor could be reduced, either because people now felt wealthy enough to forego output produced in such a manner, or because they recognized that investing in more education would increase children's productivity and incomes in the long run. As wealth and technological capabilities increased, the cost of imperialistic ventures as a portion of income fell, tempting Americans and their leaders into a new role in world politics.

Government's Role Expands

The role of government also expanded at home. Growing urbanization made responses to problems of public health, police and fire services, lighting, and utilities more essential. The growth of interdependence made accurate information more necessary, and government agencies appeared or were expanded to provide it.

Laws regulating working conditions, restricting monopoly, and protecting natural resources were also passed in this period. So, too, were new types of laws designed expressly to redistribute income. Cities and to a lesser extent states had always provided some support for the needy, even in the colonial era. Now, however, the first laws intended to change the overall distribution of income toward greater equality appeared. In the view of some scholars, a fundamental change in the legal climate took place. Instead of protecting individuals' property rights, the law now began to encourage rent-seeking—the use of government to transfer income from its producers to special-interest groups (which might or might not be poorer than those from whom the income was transferred).[11] If the process began in this period, it had not begun to reach the dimensions it has attained today.

[11] T. Anderson and P. Hill, *The Growth of a Transfer Society* (Stanford, Calif.: Hoover Institute Press, 1980). See also D. North, *Structure and Change in Economic History* (New York: Norton, 1981) and M. Olson, *The Rise and Decline of Nations: Economic Growth, Stagflation, and Social Rigidities* (New Haven, Conn.: Yale University Press, 1982).

American economic success and the ability to extend it to a large proportion of the entire population perhaps caused many people to consider their economic and political system superior to any other. In some cases, this led to attempts to impose it on people who might have different values, such as American Indians and Filipinos. The efforts expended in such causes might well have been better spent on problems within the American economy and society.

The Mixed Blessings of Progress

Nor was the achievement without its costs—people faced pressures to adjust to new circumstances at a pace never imagined before, and some found the demands difficult or impossible to meet. If economic expansion offered opportunities for most people, it also threatened ruin for those who found it difficult to change; like any economic process, change involved both costs and benefits. Nevertheless, there is no doubt that the gains achieved by most Americans during this period were real and substantial. Considerable evidence indicates that by 1920 even some traditional "have-not" groups such as southerners, blacks, farmers, and immigrants were beginning to share in the increased output. Gains in life expectancy and literacy, the conquest of many epidemic diseases, and drastic declines in infant and child mortality were unarguable improvements in living standards in which the entire population shared.

Suggested References

Anderson, T., and P. Hill. *The Growth of a Transfer Society*, Stanford, Calif.: Hoover Institute Press, 1980.

Chandler, A., Jr. *The Visible Hand: The Managerial Revolution in American Business*. Cambridge, Mass.: Harvard University Press, 1977.

Davis, L., et al. *American Economic Growth: An Economist's History of the United States*. New York: Harper and Row, 1972.

Fogel, R., and S. Engerman. *The Reinterpretation of American Economic History*. New York: Harper and Row, 1971.

Higgs, R. *The Transformation of the American Economy, 1865–1914: An Essay in Interpretation*. New York: John Wiley and Sons, 1971.

Kirkland, E. *Industry Comes of Age: Business, Labor, and Public Policy, 1860–1897*. New York: Holt, Rinehart, and Winston, 1961.

North, D. *Structure and Change in Economic History*. New York: Norton, 1981.

North, D., et al. *Growth and Welfare in the American Past: A New Economic History*. 3d ed. Englewood Cliffs, N.J.: Prentice-Hall, 1983.

Olson, M. *The Rise and Decline of Nations: Economic Growth, Stagflation, and Social Rigidities*. New Haven, Conn.: Yale University Press, 1982.

Rosenberg, N. *Technology and American Economic Growth*. New York: M.E. Sharpe, 1972.

Rosenberg, N., and L. Birdzell. *How the West Grew Rich.* New York: Basic Books, 1986.

U.S. Department of Commerce, Bureau of the Census. *Historical Statistics of the United States: Colonial Times to 1970.* 2 vols. Washington, D.C.: Government Printing Office, 1975.

Vatter, H. *The Drive to Industrial Maturity: The U.S. Economy, 1860–1914.* Westport, Conn.: Greenwood Press, 1975.

Wright, G. *Old South, New South: Revolutions in the Southern Economy Since the Civil War.* New York: Basic Books, 1986.

CHAPTER

11

AGRICULTURAL ADJUSTMENT AND CHANGE

American agriculture produced a declining share of gross national product in the 1865–1920 period. Nevertheless, its output grew, both in aggregate and in terms of output per person. Farmers had gained access to virtually all the high-quality agricultural land in the United States before the First World War. By 1920, they had adjusted local patterns of production to fit the characteristics of each area. The implements developed before the Civil War had been refined and modified and were now in widespread use. Tools and particularly knowledge developed after 1865 had also extended farmers' capabilities by 1920. There was no longer any question of whether agriculture was integrated into the rest of the economy or independent of it: the value of implements and tools used on American farms had risen thirteenfold, while the number of farms had little more than doubled. In contrast to the colonial period, few of these tools and even a declining portion of the techniques employed had been developed or produced on the farms.

GROWING ECONOMIC INTERDEPENDENCE

With the exception of cotton, the centers of production for most crops had reached their modern locations by 1920. The techniques of production, however, have continued to change at ever-accelerating rates, a process begun in the period we are now examining. The influence of markets was now pervasive throughout agriculture. Not only did farmers employ tools and techniques from the rest of the economy, their output was largely for sale rather than for personal consumption. As regional specialization increased, farmers grew dependent on a growing chain of specialists who transported, processed, and marketed their produce.

One example of the growing interdependence of agriculture with other sectors will illustrate the point. After the Civil War, the northern Great Plains were found to be particularly suited to the production of spring wheat, if more disease-resistant varieties could be found and a method of transporting the crop to market developed. A search by the new Department of Agriculture turned up a type of Eastern European wheat that flourished in the soil and climate of the Great Plains and was less susceptible to plant diseases than previously grown varieties. The Great Northern Railroad solved the transportation problem, but it was then discovered that the new wheat, when ground by existing methods, produced gray flour that was unacceptable to consumers. Another search resulted in the adoption of roller milling, a Hungarian innovation.

Productivity Improvements

Particularly before 1900, most of the growth in output originated in extensive agricultural growth—it was the product of increases in the amounts of land, labor, and especially capital.[1] But after 1900 little good land remained unused, and after 1910 the farm labor force ceased to grow. Thereafter, productivity improvements became an increasingly important source of production increases. The productivity of farm labor, aided by increases in the amounts of land and capital per farmer, had already improved considerably, as indicated in Table 11.1. In 1870, the average U.S. farmer produced food and fiber sufficient for 5.1 people. By 1920, the figure had risen to 8.3. Output had risen faster than population; the proportion of farm production exported had approximately tripled (see Table 11.2).[2]

The International Connection

As the increase in exports indicates, a growing portion of American farm production was consumed abroad. The demand for food is price inelastic, so the prices of farm products would have had to fall more than in proportion to the increases in output to allow the domestic sale of all that American farmers turned out. The demand for most farm products is also income inelastic: the quantity demanded changes less than in proportion to income variations. Thus, even growing per-capita incomes within the United States did not ensure a market for all that farmers were now producing at previous price levels.

U.S. farmers soon discovered that export markets exhibited the same problems. World production of grain and meat was growing faster than population at this time, just as it was in America. More, conditions in the export markets exerted a strong, even dominant influence on domestic prices. Bumper crops elsewhere in the world might severely reduce grain prices within the United States, even though the domestic crop was small that year. Or crop failures in other major food-exporting areas might mean high prices for American grain and meat despite a large harvest in this country. Political considerations also affected export markets. Some food importers gave protection to domestic producers or favored imports from colonies or political allies, a problem that would become more serious after 1920.

Output per acre rose only modestly for most crops (see Table 11.1). In part, this reflected the relocation of agriculture to the Great Plains, where soil fertility was lower than in the

---

[1] L. Davis et al., *American Economic Growth: An Economist's History of the United States* (New York: Harper and Row, 1972), pp. 374, 377.

[2] U.S. Department of Commerce, Bureau of the Census, *Historical Statistics of the United States: Colonial Times to 1970*, 2 vols. (Washington, D.C.: Government Printing Office, 1975), 1:374,377.

Table 11.1   Farm Productivity

Year or Annual Average	Wheat			Corn for Grain			Cotton		
	Man-Hours per Acre	Yield per Acre (Bushels)	Man-Hours per 100 Bushels	Man-Hours per Acre	Yield per Acre (Bushels)	Man-Hours per 100 Bushels	Man-Hours per Acre	Yield per Acre (Pounds)	Man-Hours per Bale
1800	56.0	15.0	373	86.0	25.0	344	185	147	601
1840	35.0	15.0	233	69.0	25.0	276	135	147	438
1880	20.0	13.2	152	46.0	25.6	180	119	188	303
1900	15.0	13.9	108	38.0	25.9	147	112	189	284
1910–14	15.2	14.4	106	35.2	26.0	135	116	201	276
1920–24	12.4	13.8	90	32.7	26.8	122	96	155	296

Source: U.S. Department of Commerce, Bureau of the Census, *Bicentennial Statistics* (Washington, D.C.: Government Printing Office, 1976), p. 407.

Midwest. Farmers compensated by cultivating larger acreage to maintain or increase their incomes.

As urbanization, higher incomes, and better methods of preservation and transportation affected markets, some crops acquired new importance and others began to lose markets. The demand for meat, fruit, vegetables, poultry, and dairy products increased relative to population, while that for grain and other starchy foods leveled off. Pork lost ground to beef. Prepared foods, such as canned goods and bakery products, increasingly supplanted items made in the home from basic ingredients. As a consequence, the farmer was separated from those who ultimately consumed his output by another layer of specialists.

THE END OF THE FRONTIER

At the onset of the Civil War, settlement extended approximately to the western border of Iowa and into eastern Kansas in the North. Southern settlement reached into eastern Texas. Beyond that line were a few pockets of farmers, miners, and ranchers in Oregon, California, and Utah. Gold rushes had just begun to swell the populations of Colorado and Nevada. Elsewhere, the West was still the domain of the Indian and the buffalo, little traveled and not much better known than a half-century earlier.

This situation changed with amazing rapidity. By 1890, the Department of the Interior issued its famous, though premature, announcement that the frontier no longer existed. Between 1900 and 1910, pronouncement became reality. Although settlement was very thin in large areas, and considerable pockets were still essentially wilderness, the frontier as a continuous line beyond which population density was no greater than two people per square mile no longer existed. By eastern standards the West was not densely populated, nor is most of it even today. But by the eve of World War I, very little land remained unsettled because its potential had not been examined.

Natural Resources

The end of the frontier emphatically did not mean that America had exhausted or even discovered all its usable natural resources. Grad-

Table 11.2 Agricultural Growth, 1860–1920

Year	Number of Farms (× 1,000)	Farm Acreage (× 1,000)	Total Value of Agricultural Produce*	Wheat**	Corn**	Cotton (× 1,000 bales)
1870	2,660	407,735	$2,694	254	1,125	4,352
1880	4,000	536,082	4,129	502	1,707	6,606
1890	4,565	623,219	4,990	449	1,650	8,653
1900	5,740	841,202	6,409	599	2,662	10,124
1910	6,366	881,431	7,495***	625	2,853	11,609
1920	6,454	958,667	15,944***	843	3,071	13,429

Year	Cattle (× 1,000)	Hogs (× 1,000)	Horses (× 1,000)	Mules (× 1,000)
1870	23,821	25,135	7,145	1,125
1880	39,676	49,773	10,357	1,813
1890	57,649	57,427	15,266	2,253
1900	67,719	62,868	16,965	3,039
1910	61,804	58,186	19,823	4,101
1920	66,640	59,346	19,767	5,432

*Millions of 1910–1914 dollars
**Millions of bushels
***Realized gross farm income, millions of current dollars
Source: U.S. Department of Commerce, Bureau of the Census, *Historical Statistics of the United States: Colonial Times to 1970*, 2 vols. (Washington, D.C.: Government Printing Office, 1975), 1:456–520.

ually, developments in this period made clear that the supply of economically usable natural resources depends far less on the earth's total endowment than on resource prices and the technology for exploiting them. For example, even though the number of cultivated acres has declined in recent years, the volume of crops produced has increased. Farmers have substituted knowledge and other forms of capital for raw labor and land, and they have increased the output per acre more than enough to compensate for the reduction in tillage.

In general, as the value of any privately owned resource increases, its owners find it more profitable to safeguard it and use it more carefully. America's richest and most accessible mineral deposits were the first to be mined, and initially little attempt was made to extract every bit of metal from ore. It was cheaper to increase overall output by exploiting new mines.

But as demand for such resources increased faster than supply, their prices began to rise, provoking new responses. Raw materials users found it in their interests to use such inputs more productively and to consider using substitute materials. Simultaneously, increased raw materials prices made it possible to use more distant, lower-quality, or less accessible deposits. Higher prices, by increasing the rewards for discovery of new deposits, not only encouraged discovery, but also created incentives to develop new tools to aid in exploration and production. As we have discovered in the case of oil and natural gas in the past decade, the amounts of any raw material currently available reflect the intensity of the effort to find and exploit it. To the present day these market responses have more than offset diminishing returns for the majority of raw materials. New discoveries continue to be made, and the efficiency with which existing materials are produced and used increases as well.

MINING

Many of the earliest western settlers were not farmers. Transportation in the region was initially so poor that there was little economic point in anything but subsistence farming—costs of moving farm products to market were often greater than their value to final consumers. Gold and silver mining attracted numbers of people to areas where "strikes" had been made, but the precious metals had a limited impact on settlement patterns. Mining, especially under nineteenth-century conditions, was a self-destroying industry. As the scores of western ghost towns indicate, once the rich ore bodies were worked out, moving on was cheaper than working lower-grade ore. Precious metals are relatively easy to transport. They combine high value with limited bulk and weight. This had two implications: first, there was little incentive to develop transport links to mines, and second, any single producer was competing with others throughout the world. Since mines in the American West had to compete with the new discoveries in Australia, South Africa, Canada, and the Alaska-Canada border, if production costs rose, it might be more profitable to seek new deposits than to improve efficiency in the current location.

The characteristics of gold and silver mining influenced other forms of economic activity in addition to transportation, which of course was no aid to diversified activity in the vicinity of the mines. Mining created a local demand for food and lumber, but little else. Gold and silver furnished the initial impetus for settlement in Colorado, Idaho, Montana, and Nevada, but long-term population growth depended on activities with stronger links to the rest of the economy. In later years, copper, lead, and coal were also mined in the Rockies.

These minerals required larger quantities of inputs and better-developed transportation, and so furnished a basis for diversified activity.

LUMBERING

In this period, the center of lumber production was relocated several times. Its original strongholds were in Maine and the Maritime Provinces of Canada. Timber production was also incidental to land clearance for farming in much of the East. But as the eastern woodlands were cut, timber production shifted first to the upper Great Lakes region, and as that area in turn was depleted after 1910, to the Pacific Northwest, the South, and the higher slopes of the Appalachian Mountains.

Lumbering required transportation for its bulky, low-valued product, but it too was a short-lived industry—at least locally—during most of this period. Since it was cheaper to move on to new areas than to manage existing forests for sustained yields, the prevailing philosophy among lumbermen was "cut and get out." This was enhanced by institutions that reflected the historical fact that timberland had higher values in other uses, since lumber was cheap. Only as primeval timber stands were depleted and wood prices rose did it become profitable to manage forests for sustained yields. It also became apparent that some forestland had little or no alternative use: it could not compete in crop production with more fertile or advantageously located acres. As timber prices rose after 1900, both private and public conservation efforts began to appear.

RANCHING

Cattle ranching had long been a frontier activity in America, even before settlement reached the Appalachians. The abundance of

■ Mining "strikes" briefly created towns but had little permanent effect on settlement.
Source: Courtesy of Nevada Historical Society.

unclaimed land meant plenty of cheap, wild pasture on which free-ranging cattle flourished. Nowhere was this more evident than in Texas. There the Spanish and Mexicans had developed their own ranching methods later imitated all over the West. In addition, great numbers of wild longhorn cattle, descendants of strays from the original Spanish herds, were roaming central Texas. These animals were legally the property of whoever captured them and drove them to market. Doing so, however, required considerable effort. Natural selection over the centuries had produced an animal well adapted to survival in a harsh environment without human assistance. The longhorns' primary attributes were mobility and toughness;

they prospered even on the scant vegetation of this drought-plagued region. An adult bull was no mean adversary for a grizzly bear, and sometimes more than a match for inexperienced cattlemen. If these wild cattle could be rounded up and marketed, those who did so might garner high profits, since they would not have to pay anyone for the cattle.

Although wild longhorns had no human owners, the costs of getting them to market were not negligible. Well before the Civil War, herds of longhorns had been driven to New Orleans and even as far as Chicago. But losses of both men and cattle were high on the long drives, and better forms of transportation were sought. As railroads were extended west, the herds were driven to the railhead towns, shortening the drives and reducing costs. Towns such as Dodge City and Abilene quickly developed atmospheres no television serial would dare to portray realistically even today. The men who made the long drives had to be tougher than the cattle they herded and the hazards of the trail. In these towns the surviving cowhands received their pay and sought their own vivid forms of relaxation.

After 1865 lush grazing lands were discovered—and their Indian inhabitants evicted or killed—at the foot of the northern Rockies. Shortly thereafter, herds of longhorns were driven north from Texas to stock the Montana and Wyoming ranges. The range-cattle industry soon began to experience technological change. The qualities that enhanced the longhorns' survival on the range did not make them tender on the steak platter. Worse, the breed not only grew slowly but put much of its growth into bone and sinew. After 1880, new breeds were introduced, sometimes in crosses with the longhorn. These cattle required more care and could not be driven great distances without heavy loss of weight and life, but they grew faster and their beef was more palatable. By this time the railroads had been extended into the northern Plains, reducing the need for long drives.

of the country and the ways of cattle, a small herd might be expanded into the basis of a fortune. But this also made free rangeland a thing of the past: as cattle numbers grew, one herd's grazing and water requirements might infringe on another's. Private ownership of land supplanted the earlier institutions.

Some of the "cattle kings" acquired ranches whose dimensions appeared princely even to the European noblemen who visited them and occasionally tried their own hands at ranching. But the era of the cattle kings was brief. Overstocking the range drove prices down and increased competition for grazing land and water. In the late 1880s, a series of disastrous winters killed thousands of cattle already weakened by inadequate pasturage. New competitors for the land appeared: sheep ranchers and farmers. By 1890 the open-range cattle industry had largely been replaced by fenced, privately owned ranches where natural grazing was supplanted by hay and other feed, often grown under irrigation on the ranches. After considerable and often violent conflict, sheepherding became concentrated in the mountains and the Great Basin, the region between the Rockies and the Sierra Nevada. Farming in this region was restricted to small areas with favorable soil and water conditions.

The End of the Open Range

In the first years after ranching began in the high Plains, cattle were allowed to graze on the open range. Technically this land still belonged to the government. As long as the government did not enforce its exclusive property rights, and while settlement was scattered enough to allow ample grazing for each herd, such methods were practical. But the development of highly specialized meat-packing plants and refrigeration rapidly increased the demand for western beef, and it was easy to enter the ranching business. With luck and some knowledge

Western Institutions and Innovations

As mining and ranching spread through the West, they required new institutions, both physical and legal. Laws had to be developed or adapted from those of other regions to determine which mine had the right to follow a vein of ore beneath the earth's surface. Ranchers had to find new ways to care for cattle and methods of sharing grazing land. In this region, access to water was crucial to success in ranching as well as farming. Some ranching operations were much more effective in cooperation with neighbors, and it was clearly better to have commonly accepted property rights than to work out individual agreements with every neighbor. The registry of cattle brands, rules for division of new calves between various owners at roundup time, and laws on water rights allowed ranchers to operate in close proximity even before the land was fenced.[3]

Several physical innovations also figured prominently in western settlement. Barbed wire was an effective answer to the problem of obtaining fencing material in areas with limited timber, and it also permitted farming in close proximity to livestock—a consideration of growing importance to ranchers dependent on raising feed as well as to farmers. Windmills gave farmers and ranchers greater access to subsurface water, allowing more intensive agricultural activity on the Great Plains. However, the new laws, institutions, and innovations did not always appear in time to prevent bitter and sometimes violent conflict over access to water, land, and minerals.

■ Wheat was the most significant agricultural crop of the Great Plains.
Source: The Bettmann Archive.

THE GREAT PLAINS

The primary crop of the Great Plains was wheat. As far west as eastern Montana, the northern Great Plains were well suited to spring wheat, and the Kansas-Nebraska region to winter wheat. Corn, as the new settlers discovered, required too much water to grow well on the Plains, and the centers of corn production remained further east, particularly in Illinois and Iowa. The vast, level lands of the Great Plains were not as fertile as the Midwest, nor was rainfall as heavy. But low land costs made it possible to substitute extensive acreage for high output per unit of land, and the area was ideal for

agricultural machinery that allowed a farmer to spread his labor over large amounts of land. Consequently, the typical farm was large compared to those farther east. Even so, the economies of scale had their limits. Early attempts at truly large-scale agriculture, the so-called "bonanza farms," comprised thousands of acres of land farmed by hired labor. But they soon disappeared: they had no cost advantages over smaller farms operated by the owner and his family, usually with extra help at harvest time.

By 1909 the chief wheat-producing states were the Dakotas, Nebraska, Kansas, and Minnesota. Far from markets, they depended heavily on railroads as a link to suppliers and customers. A second major center of wheat production developed in the 1890s. The "Inland Empire" of eastern Washington and Oregon was even more distant from markets than were the Great Plains. Its wheat was shipped halfway around the world to Europe or the eastern United States. The ability of such regions to compete in world markets is testimony to the efficiency of ocean transportation by this time.

[3] T. Anderson and P. Hill, "The Evolution of Property Rights: A Study of the American West," *Explorations in Economic History* (April 1975).

■ Farmers sometimes felt at the mercy of grain elevator operators, who often were scarce enough to possess monopoly powers.
Source: *Harper's Weekly*, Dec. 22, 1877. Drawn by W. P. Snyder from a sketch by Theodore R. Davis. From John Grafton, *New York in the Nineteenth Century*, 2d ed., (New York: Dover Publications, Inc., 1980), p. 229.

Innovations Shape Great Plains Farming

A number of innovations aided Great Plains farming. Some may even have made it possible. The variety and efficiency of agricultural implements grew steadily. By the late 1880s, a single machine both reaped and threshed wheat. These "combines" were vast, unwieldy implements, often powered by steam engines and pulled by a score or more of horses. Since efficient harnessing and control of such large teams was difficult and the feed they consumed costly, farmers were very receptive to new and more compact sources of power when these appeared after 1910.[4] By 1920, about 20,000 tractors were in use on American farms. Note the increase in farm output after 1910 in proportion to that of draft animals revealed in Table 11.2.

Plows, rakes, cultivators, and other agricultural machines became more efficient and common. But the two great barriers to agricultural development on the Plains were the difficulty of keeping livestock out of field crops

[4] Davis et al., *American Economic Growth*, pp. 386–386.

and the need for dependable water supplies. As Table 11.2 and pictures of farm life at this time indicate, even farms that raised no cattle, sheep, or hogs required motive power: draft animals were indispensable. Barbed wire solved the fencing problem simply and economically. It did not require the amounts of wood needed for the traditional split-rail fence nor the labor required to construct ditches, hedges, or board fences. The barbs effectively restrained livestock. Springs and streams were few and far between on the Great Plains, and windmills provided a power source to pump subsurface water for irrigation and often for other farm needs.

Other innovations appeared off the farm but had no less an impact in raising the efficiency of Great Plains agriculture. In addition to the railroads, an efficient system of grain elevators and market innovations such as grading systems, futures contracts, and other developments allowed many farmers' output to be concentrated and transported to distant markets at steadily decreasing costs. Ocean transport rates fell sharply through this era, extending the market for American agricultural products to most of western Europe. Railroad rates in the West, however, did not decline decisively until after 1896.[5] Nevertheless, farmers received a rising portion of the price paid by the final consumers of their products, despite a more elaborate chain of distribution.[6]

THE CORN BELT

The movement of wheat production from its antebellum centers in the Ohio and upper Mississippi river valleys caused these areas to con-

centrate on producing corn and the livestock that ate most of that crop. The area from Ohio to eastern Kansas and Nebraska became one of the world's most productive agricultural regions. It had many natural advantages: deep, highly fertile soil, abundant and dependable rainfall, and a lengthy growing season with warm summer nights. These allowed production of a wide variety of crops, but conditions were particularly well suited to the cultivation of corn, which had no rival as the region's chief crop. Corn is an ideal food for livestock, but it is less portable than other grains, so much of the crop was used to fatten cattle and hogs on the farms where it was grown.

The inhabitants of the Corn Belt developed institutions and attitudes that made the most of the region's natural advantages. On the typical Corn Belt farm, the owner faced a continual stream of business decisions. First was the choice of product: he could grow corn or possibly another field crop or fatten cattle or hogs. In addition, he operated in a highly competitive market, in which the chief hope of higher incomes lay in the rapid adoption of cost-reducing innovations. Such an environment encouraged a high degree of economic rationality among farmers. Given the alternatives they faced, most became highly responsive to innovations of all types.[7] The region's arable land was fully utilized by 1900, so there was little hope of increasing income through "more of the same" expansion. Farmers sought lower production costs both through mechanization and rapid adoption of new techniques. As farmers had always done, they used the fruits of their own experience. But they also began to find useful the new ideas based on research by the region's agricultural schools, the Department of Agriculture, and the farm implement companies. Innovation had its rewards; by 1920, the value of output per farm in Iowa and Illinois was equalled or exceeded only by

[5] R. Higgs, *The Transformation of the American Economy, 1865–1914: An Essay in Interpretation* (New York: John Wiley and Sons, 1971), pp. 99–101.
[6] D. North et al., *Growth and Welfare in the American Past: A New Economic History*, 3d ed. (Englewood Cliffs, N.J.: Prentice-Hall, 1983), pp. 107, 129.

[7] Davis et al., *American Economic Growth*, pp. 393–395.

states where the average farm was much larger or by regions producing high-priced specialty crops, such as California and Hawaii.[8]

THE NORTH AND EAST

Other regions felt the competition from midwestern and Great Plains agriculture to a much greater extent than in the antebellum period. Their great efficiency, coupled with declining transport costs, forced a continuation of the readjustments begun in the previous era. If agriculture was to survive in regions less favored in soil and climate, new crops or new methods had to be discovered. The East had locational advantages. Some farmers took advantage of their proximity to large urban populations by specializing in dairy products, poultry, fruit, and vegetables—all items with relatively high income elasticities of demand. As incomes grew in eastern cities, these adjustments proved lucrative. In other areas, even the activities chosen in response to western competition were displaced. Sheep flocks in New England and New York dwindled. As it became possible to ship meat from the great packing plants of Kansas City and Chicago, livestock raising became less profitable on the Atlantic Coast. Feed prices fell as cheap western corn flowed into eastern markets, aiding the region's dairy and poultry farmers.

Changing Agricultural Markets

Just as they had productive capabilities, developments elsewhere in the economy affected eastern farmers' welfare. As cities and per-capita incomes grew, so did the demand for fruit

[8] U.S. Department of Commerce, *Historical Statistics,* vol. 1, pp. 458–464.

and vegetables. Canning was now practical for a wider range of items than before the Civil War, and specialization in such crops was now practical: what was not sold as fresh produce could be vended to canning factories. Dairy farming benefited from cheap feed, as well as from agricultural research, which developed breeds of cattle with higher milk and butterfat yields, and improvements in butter and cheesemaking. Some regions found that the development and enforcement of grading standards for their products more than repaid the cost. Transporting fresh milk was now possible, at least within the region, and the cities gained as the number of cows stabled within them diminished.

Some foods that only decades before had been special treats for holidays or beyond the purses of all but the very rich now became regular items in the general diet. Areas with favorable climates, such as California and (later) Florida, began to supply citrus fruit and "out of season" vegetables to the cities. Demand for these items stemmed both from rising per-capita incomes and from changes in life-styles, particularly among urban residents. Fewer city folk now performed constant heavy labor, and demand for grain and other starchy foods declined. And as always, one of the things people bought with higher incomes was variety, in diets as in other goods.

The Dairy States

The upper Midwest has shorter growing seasons and more rolling terrain than regions farther south and west. Thus, it was not as well suited to corn (at least as a grain crop) as the Corn Belt, nor were its fields as receptive to machinery as the Great Plains. But the region was well suited to hay and other forage crops, including silage corn, and parts of Minnesota, Wisconsin, and Michigan became specialized dairy regions. Many of their farmers had been dairymen either in the East or in Europe. Once again, growing urban markets and improved transportation allowed income-raising specialization. Institutional changes also aided the region: its great land-grant universities produced a variety of useful agricultural innovations after 1900, and quality control standards administered by state government ensured ready markets for the region's products.

POSTWAR SOUTHERN AGRICULTURE

The South exhibited developments similar to those in other agricultural regions. Agriculture became more specialized, with greater dependence on other areas and sectors for inputs and markets. But the South showed far fewer signs of agricultural prosperity. Its performance slipped badly compared to that of other agricultural regions in most indices. In 1860 the average value of output per farm in the South had been $3,455, slightly above the national average. In 1870, southern farms averaged only $1,456 of output, a figure that did not rise significantly until after 1910, by which time farms in the South averaged only 43 percent of per-farm national output. Even if we acknowledge that the definition of a farm in the South changed as a result of the abolition of slavery, the increase in the number of southern farms is not great enough to account for such a difference. What is more, the figures quoted fail to indicate the full decline in some subregions within the South; they are inflated by the inclusion of border states such as Kentucky and Maryland and by areas settled after the war, such as central Texas, Florida, and Oklahoma. These regions performed better than the centers of antebellum cotton culture.[9]

The antebellum South had been self-sufficient in foodstuffs, but now the cotton-producing states became heavy net importers of food. The stagnation of southern agriculture might have had no more serious implications for the region than did that of New England. But unlike that area, the South had few employment alternatives outside agriculture. Developments within agriculture largely determined southern incomes because manufacturing was a minor employer until after 1900, and wages there were heavily influenced by agricultural incomes. In other regions, sizable nonagricultural sectors typically generated larger incomes than did farming. The roots of the South's poverty lie in two facts: not only was the region heavily concentrated on agriculture, but that agriculture fell far short of the performance elsewhere in the United States.

The dimensions of the southern income debacle are not completely clear. Income figures for free southerners in 1860 and 1870 are not really comparable, because of the abolition of slavery. If we use Easterlin's 1860 figures, which include all persons free and slave alike, southern incomes were about 80 percent of the national average (see Table 6.3). By 1870 southern incomes were only 51 percent of the national average, and they grew no faster than the national rate until after 1900. For at least 35 years, then, the gap between southern and nonsouthern incomes either increased or remained constant in relative terms, and the size of the gap increased in absolute numbers.[10] When slaves are included in the prewar population and their maintenance added to income, the postwar income decline diminishes but by no means disappears, and the rate of recovery is no different.

[9] Ibid., p. 463.

[10] R. Fogel and S. Engerman, *The Reinterpretation of American Economic History* (New York: Harper and Row, 1971), pp. 40–41.

The Economic Consequences of Abolition

There is little doubt that the Civil War and the consequences of emancipation explain much of the South's decline. Incomes fell most in those states where plantation agriculture had been most prevalent before the war. Physical war damage explains little: the South sustained no destruction impossible to repair, nor did it suffer a permanent reduction in its potential male labor force. In fact, manufacturing output in the South exceeded prewar production by 1870. But manufacturing was only a tiny portion of the southern economy.[11] Livestock losses took longer to make up, but the evidence that they caused any real handicap to agriculture is at best very weak. As in more recent instances, it appears that developed economies have surprisingly little difficulty putting the pieces back together again after wartime destruction. The job is done much more rapidly than the initial growth process: witness Germany and Japan after World War II. The most serious casualties for the South were antebellum institutions; their replacements may have been significantly less productive, at least in measurable terms.

The abolition of slavery freed blacks, but emancipation gave them no land, capital, or skills other than those they already possessed. Only half-hearted attempts were made to provide blacks with education, although their response was noteworthy: by 1900, most were literate. Blacks' skill acquisition and job mobility were hampered, though certainly not prohibited, by racism.

At the same time, the loss of slaves imposed a huge capital loss on their ex-owners, most of whom had also lost other forms of capital in the war. The war had destroyed the South's credit institutions. Nearly every bank in the region was ruined, and the antebellum system of cotton factors had disappeared. Prewar landowners by and large retained title to their soil, but they lacked both the labor and credit needed to resume production.

The New Environment of Labor

Not surprisingly, the ex-slaves desired above all else the control over their own lives that servitude had denied them. Freedom allowed them to claim a larger portion of the value of what they produced (it reduced exploitation), but equally important, it gave them a voice in determining their new conditions of labor. One immediate response was that the characteristics of the black labor force became much more similar to those of the white labor force than under slavery. Black women and children were no longer available for field work at the landowner's discretion. Some reduction in the hours and number of days worked by adult black men may have occurred as well, although the work year under slavery is not a settled matter. The reduced labor force participation occurred regardless of the wages offered, and is therefore a comment on slavery. The added hours of work required of them as bondsmen were worth more to blacks as leisure or opportunity for household duties than the money income they now generated. Thus, a voluntary fall in money incomes would not indicate a reduction in the welfare of the ex-slaves, had such a decline occurred.[12]

From this evidence, it could be argued that a good part of the apparent economic efficiency of plantation slavery was its ability to coerce slaves into labor conditions for which they could not receive adequate compensation as free people. Blacks were also unwilling to work under the gang system employed under slavery. The changes substantially reduced the

[11] R. Ransom and R. Sutch, *One Kind of Freedom: The Economic Consequences of Emancipation* (Cambridge, England: Cambridge University Press, 1977), Chap. 3.

[12] Ibid., pp. 2–9.

labor force of the cotton-growing South. One study estimates the reduction at between 28 and 37 percent.[13] Blacks also wanted to free themselves from another vestige of slavery: they preferred to live in homes scattered among the fields rather than in closely grouped cabins in what had been the plantation slave quarters. These changes, however, largely indicate what blacks would no longer do. The institutions and conditions of labor that would replace them were yet to be determined in 1865.

Participation in a (Relatively) Free Labor Market

Immediately after the war, cotton prices were very high, creating great incentives to resume production. The new circumstances imposed difficulties. Blacks had no option but to work for their former owners: their only asset was their labor. Landowners just as clearly needed blacks' labor services: the ex-slaves were the only work force available, and without them the land would not produce. But new conditions of employment and payment had to be worked out.

In the first few years, landowners attempted to hire blacks under much the same conditions as before the war—they simply offered cash wages in addition to the food and lodging traditionally provided. The arrangement proved unsuccessful. Blacks disliked it because there was so little change in working conditions. They preferred to work on a more individual basis, with less supervision. In addition, their new mobility caused landowners in regions with acute labor shortages to offer higher wages. If there was anything plantation owners had never had to face, it was a mobile work force. Their first response was an attempt to compel blacks to remain on the plantations through the season and to keep wage levels very low. But the "black codes" proved unworkable: even where state laws could be passed, no state

with a labor shortage respected the regulations of another, and even individual planters within such jurisdictions might prefer labor at illegal rates to none at all. In addition, the federal government soon rescinded these laws.

Adjusting to Labor Mobility

Planters were little more satisfied with the new system than their new employees. Given the severe labor shortage, they were vulnerable to an exodus of their work forces before the harvest was completed. Some workers left for better offers, others demanded higher wages for the arduous work involved in picking the crop. Landowners might be hard put to provide cash wages, food, and other supplies before the crop was sold, because of the destruction of normal channels of credit. They had lost one major item of loan collateral, and the decline in land values throughout the South indicates that land was not the security for a loan that it once had been.

Sharecropping

With the reduced labor force, output was lower—at least for the first decade[14]—and the losses were especially pronounced on large- to medium-sized plantations, where the coercive force of slavery had been greatest.[15] However the advantages of large-scale production had been achieved in the antebellum period, they no longer existed. By 1868 a new arrangement between landlord and farmer had appeared. A sizable portion of plantation land was divided into plots each farmed by a single family. A contract was made between the landlord and the farming family: the landlord agreed to furnish a house, tools, work animals, and (usually)

---

[13] Ibid., p. 45.

[14] U.S. Department of Commerce, *Historical Statistics,* vol. 1, pp. 517–518.
[15] Ransom and Sutch, *One Kind of Freedom,* Chap. 4.

seed. The tenant provided labor and his own subsistence until the crop was harvested. After deducting the expenses of both parties, the proceeds of the crop were shared—usually half went to the landlord and half to the sharecropper. If either party made unusual contributions to the joint effort, the division could vary. Farm workers could still work for wages, rent land for fixed payments, or buy their own land, but sharecropping became the most common single form of farm organization for black farmers in the postbellum South. Nevertheless, it was by no means universal.

New Methods of Agricultural Finance

Since few sharecroppers had the money to buy food and other subsistence needs before they received income from cash crops and harvested their own food, they made a second contract, borrowing against their share of the crop at the nearest country store. Such loans were be secured by a lien against the crops. Sharecropping allowed a division of risks between the landlord, who would bear them all if he hired labor for wages, and the sharecropper, who would shoulder the entire burden if he rented the land. The storekeeper who held the sharecropper's lien also shared the risks. All parties benefited if the crop was good or prices high. Although the sharecropper was hardly an independent farmer under such an arrangement, the system gave him more control over his own work than he had previously enjoyed. A landlord or storekeeper might keep a close eye on croppers whose abilities were unknown, but those with established reputations were largely left to their own devices.

These basic features of sharecropping mask considerable diversity in individual cases, as well as some fundamental differences in the interests of the concerned parties. Since landlords had only a finite quantity of land available to farm, they tried to make each sharecropper's farm as small as possible so that the cropper could only get a large income by producing a great deal per acre. The sharecropper, on the

other hand, wanted the largest amount of land he could get because he received a fraction of the total crop. They might also disagree over the division of the crop, provisions for emergencies, the quality of land, tools, and animals, and the division of the tenant's efforts between raising cotton for sale and corn or other crops for food.

The Controversy over Sharecropping

Sharecropping is a controversial topic; it has been blamed for most of the South's agricultural problems by some historians and absolved or viewed positively by others. Several myths should be dispelled early in any discussion of this institution. First, sharecropping was only one of several commonly used types of agricultural organization. In 1880, only 15 years after emancipation, 20 percent of all southern black farmers owned their own farms. Another 26 percent rented. By 1900 these figures had increased to 27 and 36 percent.[16] Thus, sharecropping did not become more prevalent with time, at least for blacks. Second, sharecropping was not restricted to blacks or even to the South alone. Whites performed an increasing share of the field labor necessary to harvest cotton, a share that nearly quadrupled (to 60 percent of the total) by 1900.[17] Finally, the incomes of southern blacks did not fall after emancipation: they rose by 14 to 29 percent in material terms and more if the value of leisure and work conditions (for which they sacrificed money income) is considered.[18]

Other conclusions about the institution hold only under special circumstances. Sharecropping, it was claimed, provided no incentives to croppers to increase productivity, particularly if the lease were renegotiated each year. If an especially good crop were produced,

---

[16] Lebergott, *The Americans: An Economic Record,* (New York: Norton, 1984), pp. 253–255.
[17] Ibid., p. 260.
[18] Ransom and Sutch, *One Kind of Freedom,* p. 210.

the landlord would increase his share of the following year's crop, which committed the tenant to additional effort for no increase in income. But this is unlikely. If tenants were free to move to other landlords, good farmers would be able to play one landowner off another. Further, *both* parties gained from a good crop. Rational landlords were not likely to remove all incentives from the actual producers, since they had long-term interest in raising their land's productivity.

Sharecropping was also thought to reduce long-term investment by either landlord or tenant. Tenants would be unwilling to finance improvements whose yields would be received in future years because they feared the landlord would evict them and negotiate terms reflecting the improvement with the next tenant. Landlords would be reluctant to make improvements if tenants were mobile, it was claimed, because the tenant might abuse the improvement or neglect maintenance to increase his short-term gains. Once again, these arguments ignore the point that gains from greater productivity were shared between landlord and tenant. As long as the opportunity to gain from investment exists, either party has an incentive to make the investment and "bribe" the other with anything short of the improver's full share of the increased income. In any case, landlords have a strong incentive to at least maintain land fertility over time.

The Influence of Southern Labor Force Characteristics

The question of sharecropping's effect on incentives is thus tied to the nature of labor markets. If labor is mobile and informed, landlords will find it difficult to pay tenants less than the value of their output. If the supply of labor rises relative to that of land, sharecroppers' bargaining position will deteriorate because it will now be in the landlord's interest to increase the number of workers per unit of land. Even so, workers will still receive the value of their output, but under constant technology, this will be less per worker.

When the theoretical view of sharecropping is compared to postwar southern reality, when the supply of labor was rising in relation to that of land, sharecropper incomes might be expected to fall as a portion of the value of total agricultural output. Also, southern labor markets fell short of the conditions required for perfect competition between sharecroppers and landlords, particularly for blacks. Information about employment conditions elsewhere was obviously imperfect, especially before widespread literacy. There were also attempts to coerce both blacks and landlords to keep black incomes low and black labor immobile.[19] However, evidence on black land purchases and mobility, at least within the South, indicates that coercion fell far short of its goals. A recent study found that labor mobility—at least between agricultural employers—was quite high. For blacks, the study concluded, the difficulty was that there were few jobs outside of agriculture.[20] The growing portion of white sharecroppers also indicates that black labor was not so abundant that landlords could dictate terms of minimal subsistence to blacks.

The Structure of Southern Credit Markets

The role of the country store has also figured in the critique of sharecropping. Professors Ransom and Sutch, among others, have alleged that sharecroppers, both black and white, were seldom able to pay off their obligations once they had fallen into debt to the country stores. Worse, they could not leave the sharecropped farm or even control their own production activities until they did so. Nor did external de-

---

[19] Ibid., pp. 86–87, Chap 9.
[20] G. Wright, *Old South, New South: Revolutions in the Southern Economy since the Civil War* (New York: Basic Books, 1986), pp. 65, 177–186.

■ Some researchers believe that the country store exacerbated sharecroppers' problems. Once the sharecropper became indebted to the store, the storekeeper insisted that he raise the cash crop of cotton despite falling prices.
Source: Records of the War Department General and Special Staffs: National Archives.

velopments favor sharecroppers. Farm technology was nearly static, cotton prices low until 1900, and population pressure on the land increasing. Debt tended to increase because storekeepers insisted that sharecroppers produce the cash crop (cotton) once they had fallen into debt. As a result, total cotton production rose and the price fell even more. This increased sharecroppers' dependence on the stores for food. The credit market, in this view, was highly imperfect: it might cost the farmer a full day's travel to visit only two or three stores. Thus, each store had considerable monopoly power and used it to charge very high rates of interest on loans—50 percent and even more per year.[21]

The process, in the opinion of Ransom and Sutch, created a vicious downward spiral of incomes. Storekeepers' insistence on cotton production in the face of inelastic demand resulted in lower net income from its production, because total revenues were reduced and total

costs increased. Southern banks, which might have offered an alternative source of credit and more farsighted regulations on tenant production, were slow to recover after the Civil War and confined their loans to urban borrowers. They had little interest in agriculture. Nor would the stores' extremely high interest returns attract competition: they were not large enough in aggregate to induce entry into the rural credit market.[22] Credit was so expensive and returns in cotton markets so unpredictable that neither landlords nor tenants had incentives to invest in long-term agricultural improvements. Only fertilizer, which yielded an immediate return, seemed a worthwhile investment, and the South used far more of it than any other area. But fertilizer merely kept soil fertility from declining.

In this view, the South was locked into cotton cultivation more securely than it had been in the antebellum period. Now, however, the only beneficiaries were the owners of the country stores. Sharecroppers' futures grew bleak as their numbers rose. Only after two developments external to this system did southern incomes improve. The boll weevil forced agriculture to shift its concentration from cotton, particularly after 1910, and industry moved to the South and created jobs outside farming. Neither had much impact before 1900.

Every major point of Ransom and Sutch's views on sharecropping and the causes of postbellum southern poverty has been attacked.[23] It has been shown that southern banks recovered from the war quite rapidly and even grew faster than the national average after 1880. The banks at least had the capacity to provide agricultural loans.[24] However, no one has as yet shown that the banks actually extended agricultural credit. Credit markets in

---

[21] Ibid., Chap. 8.

[22] Ibid., Chap. 7; and R. Ransom and R. Sutch, "Debt Peonage in the Cotton South after the Civil War," *Journal of Economic History* (September 1972).
[23] W. Brown and M. Reynolds, "Debt Peonage Reexamined," *Journal of Economic History* (December 1973) and Lebergott, *The Americans*, Chap. 21.
[24] Ibid.

the South appear to have offered few barriers to entry, and if so, returns as far above competitive levels as Ransom and Sutch claim the country stores obtained should have attracted competition. Ransom and Sutch found no reduction of credit charges over time, but others are reluctant to accept the combination of rates and trend that they portray.[25] In addition, the agricultural labor mobility noted by Wright and others does not conform to the "debt peonage" structure postulated by Ransom and Sutch.

Some scholars have seen the shifts toward lower food production and the consequent loss of self-sufficiency as rooted in causes other than merchants' insistence on cotton production. Certainly under sharecropping neither landlord, merchant, nor sharecropper gained from policies that increased output of a less profitable crop (cotton) at the expense of one yielding greater income (corn or other food). Merchants, especially, would gain from greater food production. Not only could they market a more valuable commodity than cotton, but their customers' incomes would rise, and they would sell more goods at their monopoly markups. Nor were landlords, with far greater wealth and influence than merchants, likely to accept policies so disastrous to them without protest, but no such outcry is discernible for three or four decades.[26]

Specialization was increasing in all regions, and the South was not exempt. In addition, a larger share of total cotton production now came from highly specialized areas such as east Texas. The smaller size of production units under sharecropping might also reduce food production, but it has been claimed that the average sharecropping unit had ample land and labor capacity for full or partial self-sufficiency in food.[27]

U.S. monetary policies, which caused the dollar to appreciate against the British pound until 1879, have also been viewed as slowing southern recovery because the price of cotton to British purchasers rose.[28] This argument would be more cogent were the British demand for cotton price elastic: as reported by other investigators, the elasticity of demand for cotton was quite low, implying that increasing output in the face of such a slowly rising and relatively unresponsive demand made cotton production less profitable.[29] One effort to test the responsiveness of cotton production to price changes failed to support the thesis that the South was "locked into" cotton production regardless of price changes. Rather, it appears that the supply of cotton was as price elastic as that of wheat.[30]

The Causes of Southern Poverty

Where does all this discussion leave the debate? It appears difficult to place the entire weight of southern poverty in the postbellum South on sharecropping. The mechanisms by which it has been alleged to have reduced incomes appear to depend on an unlikely combination of economic irrationality—especially of the merchants—and failure by others to respond to opportunity. Such phenomena do occur, but among millions of people for 35 years?

Clearly, even though the incomes of southern blacks rose after emancipation, poverty among them and their white neighbors was real. Blacks received below-average incomes in a society that was poor by the standards of the rest of the United States. That they were able to record the gains they made in landownership,

[25] Lebergott, *The Americans*, pp. 263–267.
[26] Ibid.
[27] Ibid.

[28] M. Aldrich, "Flexible Exchange Rates, Northern Expansion, and the Market for Southern Cotton," *Journal of Economic History* (June 1973).
[29] G. Wright, *The Political Economy of the Cotton South* (New York: Norton, 1978), Chap. 6, and Fogel and Engerman, *Reinterpretation*, p. 330.
[30] S. Decanio, "Cotton 'Overproduction' in Late 19th-Century Agriculture," *Journal of Economic History* (September 1973).

literacy, and income under such circumstances is testimony to their ability and determination.

The causes of the South's poor economic performance between 1865 and 1900 appear to lie in its lack of diversification and its demographics. The South did not begin to develop significant employment alternatives to agriculture until the turn of the century. At the same time, its population growth nearly equalled that of regions offering wider alternatives. The South put too many people into its major industry, and its low labor costs may have created little incentive to mechanize agriculture, regardless of the credit situation.

Southern Labor Mobility—or Its Absence

Another mystery is the very slow rate of migration from the South before 1900. This was a well-tested mechanism for income gains, yet it was not employed by the poorest region of the country to anywhere near the same extent as elsewhere in America. It is true that southern agricultural labor would have had to forfeit most of its skills, even if it shifted to farming in other regions, but many Americans and immigrants made much greater transitions. Unlike many immigrants, southerners spoke English, most were literate, and they came from a much more advanced economy than many Eastern European immigrants at this time. Lower levels of education in the South hardly seem a full explanation, even if they had adverse effects. Low incomes made saving to finance a move difficult, but again, many immigrants from overseas overcame far greater barriers. Recently, it has been claimed that the American South constituted a separate labor market from the rest of the United States, with weaker ties to the national economy than even foreign labor.[31] For whatever reasons, the South failed to make the same use of its people's talents as other regions, and the cost was high.

[31] Wright, *Old South, New South.*

GOVERNMENT LAND POLICIES

The land policies of the federal government as well as the market for agricultural commodities played a significant role in the postwar development of American agriculture. The major changes in government land policy from antebellum procedures were the Homestead Act and subsequent legislation expanding and modifying that law, plus land grants to railroads.

Under the Homestead Act, anyone who would live on a plot of land, cultivate it for five years, and erect a house would receive title to 160 acres (320 for a married couple) after paying only nominal filing fees. Later amendments modified the act to encourage settlement in areas where 160 acres were not sufficient for a viable farm, provided access to timber or stone for settlers' personal use, encouraged irrigation or tree planting, or allowed even larger acreage grants in regions suited only to livestock grazing.

In the period between 1850 and 1871, the railroads were granted almost 200 million acres of government land; they actually took title to about 131 million acres, an area roughly twice the size of Colorado. This land was given as a construction subsidy; it had not yet been settled.

Both policies have been the subject of intense controversy, not lessened because they appeared to operate at cross-purposes. On one hand, the government made "free" land available to final users; on the other, it gave land to the railroads to sell to these same final users at the highest possible price.

The Economics of the Homestead Act

The Homestead Act and other related legislation resulted in the transfer of almost 250 million acres into private ownership between 1862 and 1920. All of the land distribution acts were poorly drawn, loosely enforced, and widely abused. It should be obvious that land was not "free" under such policies: the costs of obtaining land legally were compliance with the conditions in the acts. If these terms could be evaded, the actual cost of the land was lower. Many settlers apparently considered the costs of land under homesteading terms higher than under previous land purchase laws, because more than three times as much land was purchased under older laws than was homesteaded in the first four decades after 1862. The costs of evading the act or complying with its requirements may have dissipated much of the potential income from the land.[32]

Mining, timber, and ranching firms filed homesteading claims through their employees or obtained land through a variety of fronts. Although one requirement of the Desert Land Act of 1877 was that the settler provide irrigation, the law failed to specify what constituted irrigation. The Homestead Act required the construction of a permanent dwelling "twelve by fourteen," with no units of measure. Constructing a cabin of those dimensions in inches and moving a house mounted on wheels from one plot to another to be witnessed in each were two of the more common frauds. Laws allowing settlers to cut timber for local use on government land were often flagrantly violated. After 1890, the most convenient vehicles for fraud were repealed or altered. Still, especially in the face of lax enforcement, these violations of the law's letter and intent were not surprising. Given the chance to reduce the cost of obtaining a valuable commodity, many people furthered their own interests.

The real controversy over the Homestead Act concerns its efficiency as a vehicle for the transfer of government land to private ownership. Here the question is confused by various scholars' ideas of the ultimate goal: was the act to promote efficient economic use of the land, or was it directed toward another goal, perhaps not closely related to economic ends? Still other critics regard the Homestead Act as entirely too successful in promoting noneconomic ends; to them, the prospect of free land attracted too many resources into agriculture rather than too few. In this view, the act wasted human labor and capital that would have been more productively employed in other sectors of the economy. By attracting ill-qualified farmers, it may have caused irreparable soil damage.

One point seems clear today: homesteading was not an escape outlet for poverty-stricken people from the urban East. Farming by this time required investments in both knowledge and physical capital that were beyond their means. In addition, movement to the West occurred in good times, not in periods of economic distress. If settlers were the best judges of their own welfare, the fact that they bought more land from federal, state, and local governments, the railroads, soldiers' warrants, and private sellers than they homesteaded indicates that, at a minimum, the Homestead Act was not the only efficient land-transfer mechanism—or even the cheapest. These points gain weight in areas where the minimum size of a viable farm exceeded Homestead Act limits, or where land was not suited to the uses required by the law.

Neither abuses of the Homestead Act nor the restrictions it required made much long-run difference. Land acquired under the act was freely transferable after title was obtained. The large quantities of land available from a variety of sellers ensured that its price would remain close to the $1.25 per acre minimum required for government land sold at auction. Any settler wishing to buy land of given characteristics and willing to search for it (or finance others' searches) generally had a choice

[32] T. Dennen, "Some Efficiency Effects of Nineteenth-Century Federal Land Policy: A Dynamic Analysis," *Agricultural History* (October 1977) and G. Libecap and R. Johnson, "Property Rights, Nineteenth-Century Timber Policy, and the Conservation Movement," *Journal of Economic History* (March 1979).

of land and methods of acquisition. In such a market, land speculation had no adverse effects, whether by the railroads, by land companies organized for the purpose, or by the many individual speculators, large-scale and small, dealing in raw land or land developed and worked for decades. Land markets were very competitive, and no informed buyer needed to pay more for land than its value in his intended use. Often final users paid less.

Unquestionably, land speculation was widespread (and people acquiring land through homesteading participated in it), but some scholars have substantially misunderstood its nature and effects. Speculators do not gain by buying assets or withholding them from the market; they gain from selling. Holding land, even land acquired without a cash outlay, involves costs. Only if land values are appreciating faster than the rate of interest on money obtained from the current sale of land is it profitable for a speculator to hold land instead of other assets. Few speculators acquired land at no cost, so to the costs already mentioned we must add the interest foregone on any money tied up in the land. Speculators had few opportunities to obtain income from their land while they waited for land values to increase, because very few settlers wanted to rent. Speculators would gain most by selling soon after they had acquired land, especially if large amounts of land were available from other sellers, and thus long-run gains were likely to be small.

A few speculators—particularly those who had accurate information about the lands they purchased—obtained above-average rates of return on their investments, but this is normal in any activity: superior information is likely to produce better results.[33] Speculation, whether large- or small-scale, would not change the land's physical properties; if land were best

[33] A. Bogue and M. Bogue, " 'Profits' and the Frontier Land Speculator," *Journal of Economic History* (March 1957).

suited to small-scale farming, it would not be to the speculator's interest to sell only large plots, and if it were only suited for uses requiring a great deal of land, selling small parcels would reduce the return to sellers. Much of the originally homesteaded land was eventually sold and consolidated into large parcels, an indication of its highest-value use.

The Homestead Act and U.S. Income Distribution

Whether the land distribution favored the rich or the poor is unclear. Obviously, the policy favored land recipients over those who paid higher taxes because the government sacrificed land sale revenues.

Had all land been given away to "bona fide users," government and the railroads would have had to find alternative sources of funds. The structure of federal taxes at this time was regressive (federal revenues were derived from excise taxes and tariffs, which raised the cost of commodities looming larger in the budgets of low-income consumers), so more extensive land distribution under the Homestead Act would probably have increased tax burdens on the American poor. In addition, agricultural incomes were lower than incomes in most other sectors of the economy, and increasing the number of small farmers still further was hardly the way to raise them.

As long as the land's value to its owners depended on the uses to which they put it, either giving land away or selling it in competitive markets would be likely to produce an efficient allocation over time if the land could be resold among its new owners. The only difference in results would be the identity of the recipients of land's rental value. The government would obtain the rental values if the land were sold at auction, because prices would be bid up to the land's capitalized value. If land were given away with no charges in money or otherwise (as it was not), the new owners would receive the rents. Even the charge that the act misallocated resources has only short-run validity. High rates of failure on homesteaded land transferred its ownership to more efficient users. Damage to the land's productivity from inappropriate use may be another question.

Railroad Land Grants

Much critical attention has been directed at government grants of land to the railroads. Typically, the federal government land grants followed a checkerboard pattern along the right of way. Railroads thus obtained only half the land fronting their tracks; the rest remained in government hands for disposal either by sale or (less often) homesteading. The idea behind the land grants was that the railroads could sell most of the land they received to obtain funds to actually build the railway. Grants were made to encourage new construction. Lands adjacent to a railroad sold for higher per-acre prices than those at some distance away, especially in the Great Plains. In that region, the distances to market were enormous, and no alternative means of transportation was available.

The Distribution of Benefits from Land Grants

The charge frequently made is that too much land was given to the railroads, who sold it at such high prices that the farmers who purchased it received little or no benefit from their access to transportation. Allegedly, the railroads not only charged very high prices for land, but their freight duties were so steep that farmers using the railroads to ship their produce paid out all the gains that accrued from proximity to the rails.

The evidence belies this contention. First, land adjacent to the railroads was eagerly sought by farmers, even though land of similar physical qualities was available at lower prices elsewhere. This continued long after farmers had gained experience with railroads' freight rates. Second, government land close to the railroads was also available, and buyers bid up prices to levels comparable to those charged by the railroads—evidence that such land was expected to produce higher incomes than more remote acreage. The value of privately owned lands along the railroads rose relative to that elsewhere, indicating that such land returned higher incomes. Finally, transportation costs for wagon freightage were so high that even land purchased at more than three times the government minimum of $1.25 per acre yielded a higher return than did "free" homesteaded land requiring a long wagon trip. This holds even when interest on the price of railroad land is included in its cost.[34]

The Grants' Effect on Economic Growth

Several careful studies have concluded that railroad land grants had positive effects on economic growth. The grants' importance is increased when we realize that western settlement might have been considerably delayed without them. Since the social rate of return on the western railroads was nearly double the private rate of return, the economy benefited from the grants by much more than the returns generated for the railroads.[35] Without the access to markets that the railroads provided, western farmers' lands would have been worthless. However, the railroads were not able to capture the full value of the increased land values for themselves: most of it accrued to the farmers. The government also benefited from increased land sales revenues and from the railroads' carriage of troops, mail, and government freight at below-market rates. By 1940 the value of these services is claimed to have more than equalled that of the land grants at currently adjusted prices.

If the goal of land grants and the Homestead Act was the rapid settlement of the West, they must be judged a huge success. In 40 or

---

[34] Lebergott, *The Americans*, p. 271.
[35] L. Mercer, "Rates of Return for Land-Grant Railroads: The Central Pacific," *Journal of Economic History* (September 1970).

50 years, an enormous area was settled, about as much as in the entire previous history of the country. The speed of settlement makes it difficult to envision an alternative method that could have done the job faster. It constitutes a strong argument against the view that there were substantial barriers to land acquisition and settlement.

THE AGRARIAN PROTEST

At many times in the three decades after 1865, the most rapidly increasing crop appeared to be farm discontent. Especially from the 1870s to the mid-1890s, farmers' unhappiness with their circumstances supported a series of political, social, and economic protests and proposals for change in American institutions. Led both by established politicians and such colorful types as Mary Lease, "the Kansas Pythoness," "Sockless Jerry" Simpson, and "Pitchfork Ben" Tillman, farm protest was a feature of American politics. The movement culminated in the populism of the 1890s, almost as much a crusade as a political movement. Although they differed in emphasis, groups such as the National Patrons of Husbandry (the Grangers), the Greenback party, the various Alliances, and the Populists agreed on the source of farmers' difficulties and what should be done about them.

Sources of Agrarian Discontent

To the farmers, the highly commercialized agriculture of the postwar period, with forward and backward linkages tying farming to the rest of the economy, had exacerbated some old problems and created some new ones. They believed that the prices they received for their crops were falling in relation to prices of the goods and services they bought. To the farmers, the reason was clear enough: they sold their produce in competitive markets, but nearly everything they bought came from sellers who seemed to possess greater or lesser degrees of monopoly power. Railroads, grain elevators, farm implement producers, banks and mortgage companies, and even the sellers of consumer goods all were far less numerous than their customers. They seemed able to raise their prices while simultaneously reducing those paid to farmers. Speculation was also viewed as a major source of farmers' ills. It seemed wrong that someone might be able to gain from buying or selling goods that he had not grown, transported, or processed, particularly when he might gain from a reduction in farmers' incomes.

Prices of the major grain crops such as wheat and corn, as well as of beef and pork, were now heavily influenced if not determined by supply and demand in international rather than domestic markets. Nor was the macroeconomic situation to growers' advantage. Farmers, especially those in newly settled regions, tend to be debtors. In any case, it appeared to many farmers that the interest rates lenders charged them were higher than those paid by other borrowers—yet another indication of the monopoly power that they believed was exploiting them. The general deflation of 1865–1896 added to their burdens. As prices fell, farmers had to repay debt in dollars of greater purchasing power than those they had borrowed. If farm prices fell faster than others, it would take more units of farm goods to buy a given quantity of nonfarm commodities.

Proposals for Reform
The solutions advocated by farm groups generally involved some mechanism to curb or eliminate monopoly among the groups from whom farmers bought. Regulation of railroads and grain elevator charges by state commissions was proposed by the Grange. Other groups proposed that the government should

■ Cartoons like this demonstrated a righteous anger about the farmers' plight.
Source: The Granger Collection, New York.

operate some railroads and use its experience to set "fair" rates, or that all railroads should be nationalized and operated in the public interest. Curbs on monopoly power throughout the economy were sought through regulation, public ownership, or cooperative action by farmers to provide their own supplies and services. Banks and mortgage lenders of all sorts were special targets of reform and control proposals. Farmers were often joined by other advocates of institutional reform. At this time, some urban groups were agitating for municipal ownership or regulation of the new firms that had appeared to provide cities with water, gas, and other essential commodities and services.

Monetary Expansion. Many farmers thought that if the money supply could be expanded, they would benefit as prices rose (obviously they

thought farm prices would rise at least as fast as all others). Several programs seemed to promise this end. The Greenback Movement, which attained the status of a political party in the late 1880s, advocated an expanded supply of the greenback currency issued during the Civil War. Since that time, the number of greenbacks in circulation had either been reduced or held constant. The political appeal of a rapid expansion of inconvertible paper currency was not great while memories of Civil War inflation remained fresh. At its high point, the Greenback party won 22 electoral votes in the presidential election of 1892 and gained a handful of congressional seats.

Silver offered another route to the goal of monetary expansion. After 1860, most of the great mining discoveries in the American West had been of silver rather than gold. Consequently, the value of silver had declined relative to that of gold. The Populists, or at least the party's western wing, advocated the coinage of silver in unlimited amounts. Understandably, this idea was enthusiastically supported by western miners, but it too found only limited success.

Several other agrarian ideas have a distinctly modern ring. The Alliances proposed that the government set up a system of warehouses where farmers could deposit their crops and receive loans of up to 80 percent of the crops' value in the form of greenbacks. They also proposed that the federal government enter the farm-financing business by offering greenback loans of half the value of any farmer's property.

Until the early 1890s few of these proposals were put into operation. The courts endorsed the idea of state regulation (in *Munn v. Illinois*) in 1877, allowing state governments to impose regulations on businesses "imbued with a public purpose" within their own borders. But in 1886 the Supreme Court forbade state regulation of interstate commerce, which effectively removed the railroads from their control. Cooperative efforts at both supplying inputs to farmers and marketing their products met with little success. Farmers learned that replacing a middleman who served no useful function or charged monopoly prices for his services was one thing, but doing without or replacing those whose charges reflected the cost of service was quite another—particularly where economies of scale or highly specialized inputs were involved.

The Populists

Political efforts were the most visible aspect of the Populist effort. This group was an amalgam of farm protest with the reform movements then active in large cities. As such, it gained considerably more strength than its rural predecessors, which had never even succeeded in uniting the agrarian population.

The Populists advocated control over monopolies by the whole range of devices suggested by their predecessors. But it is the advocacy of the free coinage of silver, given voice by the passionate oratory of William Jennings Bryan, for which the Populists are best remembered. Despite the Populist fusion with the Democratic party, they were defeated. William McKinley, the Republican advocate of "sound money" and a gold-based currency, won the election of 1896. Bryan proved unable to carry areas such as the Midwest, where agriculture was well established. Ironically, the long decline in prices was reversed in 1896 for reasons having little to do with politics, and for the next two decades farm prices rose faster than the general rate of inflation. The years from 1900 to 1914 were an era of prosperity for American farmers, and the evidence of unrest rapidly disappeared.

Were Farmers' Complaints Justified?

No doubt farmers thought they had legitimate grievances. The numbers of farmers involved in the protest movements and their fervor were evidence of that. But moral outrage is a poor substitute for accurate information or coherent analysis. Much of the data related to farmers' complaints does little to support them.

Changes in Relative Prices

Prices for farm products continued to fall for three decades after the Civil War—but so did all other prices. Farmers still had a grievance if the prices of their products were declining faster than the average. But it now appears that the prices of goods farmers bought declined slightly relative to those of goods they sold (see Table 11.3). Since farm produce remained essentially unchanged over this period while the quality of both capital and consumer goods that farmers bought substantially improved, the actual trends in real prices favored the farmers.[36]

---

[36] R. Robertson, *History of the American Economy*, 3d ed. (New York: Harcourt Brace Jovanovich, 1973), p. 315.

Table 11.3 Farm Prices Received
and Paid (1870 = 100)

Year	Prices Received for Livestock and Crops	Prices Paid for Farm Machinery	Midwest Interest Rates	Freight and Distribution of Cost of West North Central Wheat
1870	100	100	100	100
1880	76	68	83	60
1890	64	48	68	45
1900	63	45	55	35
1910	95	45	52	24

Source: S. Lebergott, *The Americans: An Economic Record* (New York: Norton, 1984), p. 302.

These price trends also refute the farmers' contention that manufacturers were exploiting them through the exercise of monopoly power. On the other hand, despite the long-term trends noted above, in some periods, especially the 1870s, farm prices fell sharply. In general, farm goods' prices were far less stable than prices of other goods.[37] Thus, while the data do not indicate that farmers were consistently injured by relative price movements, it would hardly be surprising if they, like most people, were moved to public outcry when prices moved against them.

The Role of the World Market

In addition, the 1870–1900 period was the heyday of U.S. exports of grain and meat. The farmer was now participating in a world market, where prices might change for no reason visible to him. Moreover, such changes were impossible to predict. Bountiful crops in the United States might bring high prices and prosperity to American farmers if those in Argentina, Australia, Canada, and Eastern Europe were poor. If foreign producers enjoyed large harvests, prices might be very low. Poor American harvests might be compensated by high prices, but abundant crops overseas could compound American farmers' difficulties. Uncertainty over prices might have been as great a burden as the price changes themselves.

Railroads

The "exploitation" of farmers by railroads and middlemen, particularly grain brokers, was another source of complaints. Rail freight charges fell at about the same rate as all prices and continued to decline thereafter (see Table 11.3). However, especially in the Great Plains, they showed no tendency to decline in relation to grain and cotton prices prior to 1897.[38] Freight rates varied widely from year to year, and often between regions as well. In the early 1890s, high rail freight charges coincided with farm protests. Such protests centered in the West, where freight charges were largest in proportion to the value of goods shipped, and rate changes could make the difference between a good year and a bad one for many farmers.[39] Also, whatever the overall levels of rail charges, few railroads hesitated to employ whatever monopoly power they possessed in local markets—

[37] J. Bowman and R. Keehn, "Agricultural Terms of Trade in Four Midwestern States, 1870–1900," *Journal of Economic History,* (September 1974).

[38] Higgs, *Transformation*, p. 89.
[39] Ibid., pp. 99–101.

or to price their services at or below cost to customers with good alternative means of shipment. The rising value of farmland near railroads suggests that despite their best efforts, the railways were unable to squeeze the full value of their services from customers. But it was not for lack of effort.

The Impact of Middlemen on Farm Income

The farmers' case against commodity speculators and other middlemen appears to have little factual basis. The essence of speculation is the purchase of an asset at low prices in the hope of future sale at higher prices. In pursuing this goal, speculators add to current demand, which increases current prices, and also to future supply, which reduces later prices. For farm commodities, speculators' actions tended to raise prices immediately after the harvest, when most farmers were eager to sell, and to reduce those paid by consumers later. While speculators no doubt wished that prices received by farmers might be very low, their actions produced just the opposite effect. Also, grain speculators suffered losses before 1897.[40]

In light of this evidence, it is difficult to see just how speculation injured farmers. During the period when agrarian complaints were at their loudest, the difference between the final prices paid for grain and meat and the prices received by farmers fell substantially, indicating that the efficiency of transporting, processing, and distributing those commodities increased and the savings were passed on to farmers and consumers. Farmers may have compared their own incomes with those of middlemen serving hundreds or even thousands of farmers. From this perspective, the middlemen might have appeared to be receiving huge (and unjustified) incomes.

Farm Debt

The actual burden of farm debt fares little better in the light of historical evidence. Falling prices generally do make it harder for debtors to repay what they have borrowed, especially if the price of whatever they produce falls. However, the severity of the injury depends on the rate of decline in prices and the length of time over which the loan extends. Nineteenth-century farm mortgages were for only three to five years, a period over which deflation was unlikely to add much to a farmer's debt burden. On the other hand, in such a short time the impact of one bad year of reduced output might be critical. A poor crop, whether it resulted from illness or injury, bad weather, or any of the myriad other possibilities, or just unusually low crop prices might reduce the income available for debt repayment by one-fifth to one-third. A further point tending to downgrade the impact of debt burdens is that the value of farm property rose in every decade from the 1870s through the 1890s. Farmers were receiving capital gains, even after allowing for the burden of their mortgages.[41] For many of them, these were not just "paper profits": the turnover in ownership of individual farms was substantial.

Mortgage rates were higher for farms in the West than in the East, and highest of all on the frontier. Two very real causes were responsible: high demand for loans in relation to supply in areas where few people had had time to accumulate wealth, and greater risks due to distance, lack of information, and the vagaries of western agriculture and ranching. Drought, blizzards, fires, insects, or even wolves and bears with tastes for sheep and cattle could turn an apparently sound investment into a total capital loss in an incredibly short time. All of these

---

[40] Ibid., pp. 87–90.

[41] R. Fogel and J. Rutner, "The Efficiency Effects of Federal Land Policy, 1850–1900: A Report of Some Provisional Findings," in W. Aydelotte et al., *Dimensions of Quantitative Research in History* (Princeton, N.J.: Princeton University Press, 1972).

dangers were either new or far more acute than in the East.

Western interest rates may have exceeded those in the East, but the evidence indicates that if anything the differential did not compensate for the greater risks of lending in the West. By the 1880s there was considerable competition among western mortgage lenders.[42] A classic study of western agricultural finance indicates that most farm borrowing was for expansion, not caused by distress. In the 1890s, bankruptcies among farm mortgage companies were common, indicating that they had charged too little, rather than too much.[43] Nor were all or even most western farms mortgaged, although it is significant that the proportion of farms mortgaged was greatest and the interest differential highest in Kansas and Nebraska, both hotbeds of political activism. In most areas, less than half of all farms were mortgaged, and not a few midwestern farmers were lending money rather than borrowing. This may explain Bryan's poor showing in the older agricultural regions.[44]

Farm Incomes

The evidence on both capital gains and trends in farm incomes per se indicates that farmers' incomes rose in every decade if not in every year. Gains were less (and short-run losses worse) in the 1870s than in other decades, but the general trend of farm incomes was upward. Even so, agricultural incomes were not rising as rapidly as those in other sectors, despite the absolute gains. Moreover, there were regional differences.

Incomes rose substantially in the Midwest and the West, but farms in the South and East recorded lesser gains or none at all during the protest era. After 1896 the general improvement in farm incomes was again unequally shared, and it failed to keep pace with income trends elsewhere in the economy. As long as additional land of good quality remained unused, agricultural incomes were unlikely to show substantial long-term gains. Farming was a highly competitive industry with few barriers to entry, so that any short-term improvement in farmers' prospects would spur a flow of resources into the activities in which the proposed incomes were generated. Only after the supply of usable land became less elastic would an increase in demand for food result in a permanent rise in real food prices. This apparently occurred after 1900, as population continued to increase rapidly and the number of farms rose at a much more modest pace.

The Burdens of Interdependence

Commercialization of agriculture, particularly in the West, may have been a factor in farmers' complaints if not necessarily in their real difficulties. As agriculture became more market oriented, farmers may have felt their control over their own activities slip away. They were more dependent on specialists to market crops, to supply tools, credit, and supplies, and to provide the transportation needed for these linkages. In earlier times, farmers had been able to perform many of these functions for themselves and had in any case been far less dependent on production for the market. The new conditions provided "outsiders" on which to focus discontent.[45] They also increased uncertainty: farmers could no longer trade off money income for self-sufficiency, as they might (but seldom did) in earlier times.

Farmers were losing their social and political position as well. From being regarded as

---

[42] D. North, *Growth and Welfare in the American Past*, 2d ed. (Englewood Cliffs, N.J.: Prentice-Hall, 1974), p. 133.

[43] A. Bogue, *Money at Interest: The Farm Mortgage on the Middle Border* (Ithaca, N.Y.: Cornell University Press, 1955), 1968 reprint.

[44] Higgs, *Transformation*, pp. 96–97.

[45] A. Mayhew, "A Reappraisal of the Causes of Farm Protest in the United States," *Journal of Economic History* (June 1972).

the backbone of the nation and the embodiment of all its virtues, they became the butt of city jokes about hicks and hayseeds. Others lived better than the farmer—any photograph of small towns on market days reveals only too clearly who lived in town and who did not. The conditions of urban life improved rapidly during this era, but those on the farm improved less, and in some regions—especially the Great Plains—may have deteriorated. Farming in that region meant an insecure life of unending hard work, incredible isolation, and little variety. Women on Great Plains farms might literally not see friends or other nonfamily for six months at a stretch. That such a life was the reward for farmers' efforts might well occasion protest when others apparently did less and gained more.

It may have been that while entry into farming was easy, exit was difficult. If farmers felt themselves "locked into" an occupation where market forces offered little hope for rises in income, their protests may be viewed as attempts to seek income transfers (rents) outside the market. The early attempts largely failed, except in the case of railroad regulation,[46] but they may have encouraged farmers in more successful rent-seeking efforts several decades later.

THE BEGINNINGS OF CONSERVATION

For two and a half centuries, Americans had regarded natural resources as inexhaustible, if not locally, at least nationally. For most of that period, natural forces had been enemies to be conquered by any means at hand. As representatives of the natural order, the Indians bore the burden of this attitude. They were regarded as obstacles to progress, to be destroyed or barely tolerated if they converted to the "superior" ways of their conquerors. The Plains Indians were subjugated as much through the destruction of the buffalo on which their economy depended as through direct military action. In both cases the job was thoroughly done: the Indians were decimated, and from herds estimated at 25 to 60 million in 1800, only 541 wild buffalo remained in the entire country in 1889.

Vast areas were stripped of timber, and in the process forest fires sometimes destroyed as much timber as harvesting. A single forest fire in Wisconsin burned several thousand square miles and took 1,500 lives in 1871. It went almost unnoticed, because at the same time the great Chicago fire destroyed most of that city.

Increasing Resource Costs

By 1900, it appeared that some resources might not last forever under current practices and rates of use. It was also realized that some were being used in a manner that reduced incomes in other sectors, creating social costs. All too often erosion and massive flooding resulted from mountainside lumbering. Lumbermen who owned only the lands they cut (if those) were not liable for the reduced productivity of downslope farmland. Previously, the aggregate costs of such damage were slight, because plenty of new agricultural land could be settled if older regions became less fertile. But after 1900 this was less true. Urban pollution was a similar problem.

In the first tentative steps, a few areas were reserved from settlement as national parks, which were to remain forever in their natural state. Yellowstone National Park was established in 1872; by 1914 seven others, all in the West, had been set up.[47] More important than

---

[46] A. Martin, *Enterprise Denied: Origins of the Decline of American Railroads, 1897–1917* (New York: Columbia University Press, 1971).

[47] One of the first tourist parties to visit Yellowstone Park found it considerably more "natural" than they had bar-

the parks was the idea that some resources, particularly timber, could be produced indefinitely if methods were changed. This thought began to influence both private and public attitudes. As timber resources dwindled and wood prices increased, lumber companies began to acquire forestland and manage it for sustained yields—sometimes over government opposition.[48] In 1891, some of the more flagrantly abused land acquisition acts were repealed and enforcement was tightened. During the second Cleveland administration, the federal government began to set aside mineral and timber reserves and to lease waterpower sites rather than selling them outright. Forest reserves (national forests) outside the national parks were to be managed for continuous production.

The federal government began a series of irrigation projects in the West and a program of navigation and flood control improvements in the rest of the country. While some of the latter projects may generate social benefits, in large part they have now become the center of congressional "pork barrel" legislation, designed more to protect incumbent congressmen from floods of votes for the opposition than for economic benefit to the country. In 1911 Congress approved a program of land acquisition under which the government purchased mountain land in the East to preserve its forests and prevent floods.

The early conservation measures were heavily oriented toward timber and the preservation of resources rather than their intelligent use. They paid little attention to soil erosion and pollution control except where needs were overwhelming. In many cases they may have been too chary of infringing on the "rights" of private property even where social costs were involved. Nevertheless, they marked the inception of a new attitude.

State governments also began to develop some concern for conservation. Wildlife was protected through the regulation of hunting, and later by the establishment of game refuges. Previously, wild animals belonged to whoever could kill or capture them, especially from public land. Hence, there was no reason for anyone to refrain from securing all that he could. If private property rights were not to be established for game animals, government intervention was required. Ecological relationships were still unknown, however, so most of these measures were directed only at game species.

It may be that such concern for the future could only be generated by the forces that brought it into existence in the United States (the evidence that wildlife, if not all natural resources, could be destroyed permanently). Americans also had a sense that they were now wealthy enough to view some natural resources not merely as potential sources of immediate money income, but as something to enhance the leisure time that increasing numbers of them now possessed. At no time were the overall costs and benefits of conservation or preservation assessed: this was not an economic movement. But it bought time to allow later, more scientific analysis.

SELECTED REFERENCES

Atherton, L. *The Cattle Kings.* Bloomington, Ind.: Indiana University Press, 1962.

Bogue, A. *From Prairie to Corn Belt: Farming on the Illinois and Iowa Prairies in the Nineteenth Century.* Chicago: University of Chicago Press, 1963.

———. *Money at Interest: The Farm Mortgage on the Middle Border.* Ithaca, N.Y.: Russell (reprint), 1968.

Davis, L., et al. *American Economic Growth: An Economist's History of the United States.* New York: Harper and Row, 1972.

---

gained for. They were attacked by Indians: one person was killed and several others scalped. My thanks to Professor Robert Gallman and Grand Teton National Park Museum for this anecdote.

[48] Lebergott, *The Americans,* p. 273.

DeCanio, S. *Agriculture in the Postbellum South: the Economics of Production and Supply.* (Cambridge, MA: MIT Press, 1974).

Hicks, J. *The Populist Revolt.* Lincoln, Nebr.: University of Nebraska Press, 1961.

Higgs, R. *Competition and Coercion: Blacks in the American Economy, 1865–1914.* Cambridge, England: Cambridge University Press, 1977.

———. *The Transformation of the American Economy, 1865–1914: An Essay in Interpretation.* New York: John Wiley and Sons, 1971.

North, D. et al. *Growth and Welfare in the American Past: A New Economic History.* 3d ed., Englewood Cliffs, N.J.: Prentice-Hall, 1983.

Ransom, R., and R. Sutch. *One Kind of Freedom: The Economic Consequences of Emancipation.* Cambridge, England: Cambridge University Press, 1977.

Shannon, F. *The Farmer's Last Frontier; Agriculture, 1860–1879.* New York: M.E. Sharpe, 1977.

Swierenga, R. *Pioneers and Profits: Land Speculation on the Iowa Frontier.* Ames, Iowa: Iowa State University Press, 1968.

U.S. Department of Commerce, Bureau of the Census. *Historical Statistics of the United States: Colonial Times to 1970.* 2 vols. Washington, D.C.: Government Printing Office, 1975.

Wright, G. *Old South, New South: Revolutions in the Southern Economy Since the Civil War.* New York: Basic Books, 1986.

———. *The Political Economy of the Cotton South.* New York: Norton, 1978.

CHAPTER

12

INDUSTRY, TRANSPORTATION, AND THE RISE OF BIG BUSINESS

Manufacturing had been well established in the United States before the Civil War, but in the half-century after 1865 it became the dominant sector of the economy and a chief source of its growth. In 1859, agriculture had contributed about 62 percent of the total value added in commodity production in the United States. Industry (broadly defined) produced 38 percent. By 1880 the contributions of the two sectors were about equal. In 1909, however, industry's share was almost three times that of agriculture: 74 percent versus 26 percent.[1] Since agriculture expanded substantially over this period, the figures indicate that industrial growth must have been more rapid than that of the overall economy. And so it had. American industrialization had made this country a giant among the world's manufacturing nations.

In 1914, not only was the United States primarily an industrial economy, but its manufacturing output dwarfed that of any other single nation. With about 36 percent of the world's industrial capacity, the United States equalled the combined production of Germany, Britain, and France, its three closest rivals. American industrial primacy was not merely quantitative. In many types of manufacturing, the United States was now the world's technological leader. In 1860, the country had been an importer of capital goods and the ideas they embodied. Now it exported both capital goods and expertise in production methods. American technical leadership was not universal: German performance in industrial chemistry, for example, was still unrivalled. But the previous picture of the United States as weak in basic and applied science was no longer valid.

[1] R. Fogel and S. Engerman, eds., *The Reinterpretation of American Economic History* (New York: Harper and Row, 1971), p. 27.

Developments in transportation were scarcely less impressive. Before the end of the nineteenth century, railroads had been extended throughout the United States and their operating efficiency greatly improved. Mileage of main railway track had increased more than sevenfold from 1865 to 1914, and their carrying capacity had risen even more because of steady technological progress. Railroads had important forward and backward linkages to the rest of the economy: they were major consumers of steel, other heavy industrial goods, and coal, and their services transformed the nature of competition and distribution in America.

THE EFFECTS OF POSTWAR GROWTH

As always, sustained growth within any economic sector meant change. The location and type of industrial activity altered, as did the goods produced. An increasing portion of manufacturing was located in the Great Lakes region, an area endowed with basic raw materials such as coal and iron ore plus a system of natural waterways that allowed cheap transportation of inputs and finished goods. Industry in this region grew faster than in the older manufacturing centers in the Middle Atlantic states and New England (particularly the latter). Once the East North Central states became centers of iron and steel production, they began to produce a growing variety of other items. Nor was this the only new industrial center. After 1900 the South increased its industrial growth, mainly in labor-intensive commodities such as textiles and tobacco products, but also in iron and steel.[2]

Both capital and labor showed greater mobility than in previous eras, responding to the opportunities revealed by factor price differences. The South, for example, had abundant labor and some types of raw materials, but relatively scarce capital. Consequently, wages there were low and the return on capital high. Capital was transferred to the South, although most southern industry was locally financed,[3] and Southern workers began to migrate to the North, where greater capital endowments per worker raised productivity and wages. In the tight labor markets of World War I, this trend accelerated, particularly for blacks.

Leading Industries

The identity of leading industries and the nature of their production processes also changed. In 1860, most American manufacturing involved raw materials processing or was characterized by modest capital requirements, as in the textile and boots and shoes industries. Although some of the leading industries of 1860 retained their importance in 1910, a number of new ones had gained prominence (see Table 12.1). The figures do not indicate another important development: the decline of home manufacturing. Not only did consumers buy more manufactured goods, they now bought more in finished or more nearly finished forms—for example, ready-to-wear clothing rather than cloth and bakery products rather than flour.

The development of some of the new industrial sectors reflected changes in both demand and supply. New technology, increased capital, and improved mechanisms for its allocation affected supply. Demand was influenced by increased population and incomes and also by changes in products, which increased the demand for industrial commodities as in-

[2] G. Wright, *Old South, New South* (New York: Basic Books, 1986), Chap. 5, 6.

[3] Ibid., p. 131.

Table 12.1   The Largest Industries in 1910

Industry	Value Added (Million $)	Employees (Thousands)	Value Added per Worker (Thousand $)
Machinery	$690	530	$1.29
Lumber	650	700	.93
Printing and publishing	540	260	2.06
Iron and steel	330	240	1.37
Malt liquors	280	55	5.01
Men's clothing	270	240	1.18
Cotton goods	260	380	.68
Tobacco manufactures	240	170	1.44
Railroad cars	210	280	.73
Boots and shoes	180	200	.91
All manufactures	8,529	6,615	1.29

Source: L. Davis et al., *American Economic Growth: An Economist's History of the United States* (New York: Harper and Row, 1972), p. 447.

termediate goods. Machinery and railroad car manufacturers needed steel, and printers and publishers required paper, dyes, and specialized machines. Changes in the nature of the population also influenced industrial rank. Heavy Northern and Eastern European immigration no doubt spurred the growth of the brewing industry.

The lists of leading industries from 1860 and 1920 mask as many changes as they reveal. Growth rates between industries continually varied. The late 1860s and early 1870s witnessed a continuation of antebellum product and technique trends. But in the 1870s, the era of iron, firewood, and waterpower began to give way to one of steel, coal, and steam engines. In turn, the period of coal and steel primacy was superceded by one where the major sources of industrial growth and change were electrically powered factories that produced chemicals and capital goods. The new motive force was well on its way to supplanting steam as the chief source of industrial power by 1910; by 1929 it had done so. A decade into the new century, automobiles plus petroleum and its

ever-widening range of products were leading industrial growth. Older industries showed continued growth and technological progress even after their primacy, and many others showed rapid growth even though the value of their output never placed them in the "top ten."

New Products and Methods

Typically, newly introduced products show very rapid growth as customers become more familiar with them and find additional uses for them. Then, as supply increases because of increased competition, better knowledge of production processes ("learning by doing"), and economies of scale, prices fall and larger quantities are demanded by both previous customers and those only now able to buy. After this period of rapid initial expansion, the industry's growth rate is likely to slow to that allowed by increases in population and incomes, or perhaps even less. Increases in supply are more likely to stem from refinements of existing technology, not the breakthroughs

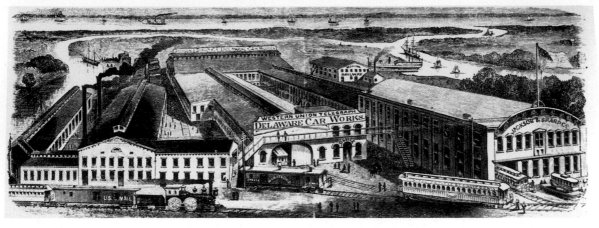

■ In 1910, automobile manufacturers were among the leaders of industrial growth.
Source: *Great Industries*. From *The Picture Reference File*, Volume 1. (New York: Hart Publishing Company, Inc., 1976), p. 134.

of the industry's early years. For these reasons, the continuous rapid growth of an economy is contingent on the appearance of new sectors to supplement or replace those whose growth rate flags, ceases, or even declines.

Obviously, an economy in which both producers and consumers are receptive to new ideas has an important edge in long-term growth. Such an environment fosters efforts to produce new commodities, introduce new methods, and find new markets for existing goods. It also favors resource reallocations and changes in consumer demand that are critical to new product acceptance. As has been stressed throughout this book, economic development is critically dependent on change in the long run. In all these areas, the United States enjoyed advantages over more rigid societies.

The new products, methods, and fuels were economically significant to a much greater extent than their immediate effect on total production and incomes might indicate. Many of them had important linkages to other sectors and fostered growth there. Most of the new growth sectors were highly capital intensive, allowing low unit costs only if large volumes of product were turned out. Often they demanded the coordinated efforts of large quantities of capital and labor. Still, it would be inaccurate to describe American industry as typified by huge factories in 1914. As late as 1900, the average American factory had about two dozen employees. This was more than twice the figure for 1859 (although the earlier data include handicraft shops not counted later), and growth in firm size apparently was accelerating. By 1921, the average factory would employ almost 40 workers, a two-thirds increase.[4] But even the 1921 figure implies the existence of many small- and medium-sized plants as well as the highly visible giant firms.

[4] U.S. Department of Commerce, Bureau of the Census, *Historical Statistics of the United States: Colonial Times to 1970*, 2 vols. (Washington, D.C.: Government Printing Office, 1975), 0:666. The earlier edition of *American Economic History* included an erroneous interpretation of the data on the number of employees per firm. My thanks to Professor A. O'Brien of the University of Georgia for calling this to my attention. See A. O'Brien, "A Note on the Increase in Factory Size in Manufacturing, 1849–1919," (working paper), Department of Economics, University of Georgia.

New Business Practices

With larger firm size and more complex operations, new methods of organization, information collection, and decision making were required. In earlier times, the firm might be small enough, the range of products sufficiently limited, and operations straightforward enough to allow the owner to supervise production from the shop floor. Now, however, firms produced a variety of products and often sold them in markets with very different characteristics, and the pace of technological as well as market change was much faster.

The nature of the products and their markets primarily determined the changes in the structure and organization of firms.[5] Improved accounting methods were nearly as important as new engineering techniques for the successful operation of firms producing a variety of items or performing many operations, both increasingly common in this period. Marketing assumed a new and greater importance as customers' choices between sellers and products increased. Advertising and other forms of product differentiation—brand names and packaging—were used to establish and maintain sellers' reputations for quality. Again, the marketing approach varied with the type of product. In marketing capital goods, more emphasis was placed on designing goods to meet the customer's specific needs and on terms of sale than on attempts to persuade along other lines. Finally, as the number of firms, the amount of output per firm, and the transportation network grew, firms were forced to respond to new competitive circumstances many had never encountered before.

The enormous increases in the production of manufactured goods caused the prices of industrial products to decline relative to those of other commodities throughout this period. In some cases, price declines were truly spectacular. Metal goods in 1910 cost consumers little more than half their 1865 prices in real terms—and the modern goods' quality was far superior. The absolute price declines for manufactured goods exceeded those for farm products, reflecting a much more rapid rate of productivity growth in industry than in agriculture.[6]

OLD AND NEW INDUSTRIES

Rapid manufacturing growth in the latter half of the nineteenth century produced many varieties of change. Some established industries grew at relatively stable rates. Others employed or were affected by innovations that drastically altered their growth. In other cases, entirely new industries appeared, some producing goods never seen before, and others turning out familiar items in unheard-of quantities.

Textiles

Factory production of woolen and cotton cloth had been one of the earliest manufacturing industries to appear in the United States. The growth rate of cotton textile production had peaked and was already declining in the 1830s. The industry's postwar growth was only slightly greater than could be accounted for by in-

---

[5] The following discussion owes much to the work of Alfred D. Chandler, Jr. See "The Beginnings of 'Big Business' in American Industry," *Business History Review* (Spring 1959); *Strategy and Structure: Chapters in the History of American Industrial Enterprise* (Cambridge, Mass.: Harvard University Press, 1962); and *The Visible Hand: The Managerial Revolution in American Business* (Cambridge, Mass.: Harvard University Press, 1977), among others.

[6] U.S. Department of Commerce, *Historical Statistics*, vol. 1, pp. 200, 201.

creased demand caused by the rise in population and per-capita income. Cotton textile prices in real terms did not fall, indicating an absence of technological breakthroughs in this older industry. But the industry was not stagnant. New machinery was introduced and widely adopted. Ring spindles—more nearly automatic looms that replaced empty yarn bobbins without human intervention and stopped if the yarn broke—and other innovations allowed employment of less-skilled labor than previously. The new features allowed one worker to tend several looms. Nevertheless, the gains in productivity that resulted from such innovation were now commonplace, as relative price trends indicate.

Since technological change was limited, other means of lowering production expenses were sought. The industry began to relocate, seeking lower input expenses. In New England, the traditional center of cloth manufacture, output continued and grew. But the pace was faster elsewhere. By 1910 the South, chiefly along the Atlantic Seaboard, had two-thirds as many spindles as New England.

The causes of this relocation are not clear. The postwar South had large quantities of labor not really required in agriculture (where its marginal product was low). By 1890, population pressure on the available farmland made these workers available at very low wages. The South also had a relative shortage of capital, so that returns on investment were higher there than in other regions. These two inducements help to explain the movement of northern capital into southern manufacturing, but they do not explain why investment concentrated so heavily on textiles. Wright's view that most southern textile investment was locally financed would help to explain this through the industry's low capital requirements; the South had difficulty generating investment funds, and capital requirements in textiles were modest.[7]

The shift in textile expansion away from New England is not difficult to understand. Power sources were a growing problem in the old textile centers. New England had no coal and had used nearly all its high-quality waterpower sites by 1900. Further growth required either higher costs or some technical breakthrough.

Relocation of textile production to Georgia and the Carolinas, rather than throughout the South, provides one answer. Agriculture was less profitable in those states than farther west, encouraging a diversion of local investment from agriculture to industry. Prior to emancipation, landowners in the Old South could either move to more fertile areas or compensate for the quality of their soil by selling another crop—surplus slaves—to more productive farming areas. Now, of course, they no longer had this option, and landlords may have sought new directions for investment.[8] The new developments in textile machinery made possible the employment of unskilled labor, especially women and children. Given the labor requirements of the new machinery, the South's educational deficiencies were a lesser handicap than for other types of work.

Steel

More than any other product, steel typifies the late nineteenth-century development of American industry. Perhaps no other single product aided the development of so many other industries, or increased capabilities beyond those possible with substitute materials. And in no other product did America rise to such total dominance before 1900.

Steel is iron containing a small portion of carbon. It is intermediate between the two types of iron. Cast iron contains more carbon than steel; wrought iron, none. Steel was not a new

---

[7] Wright, *Old South, New South,* Chap. 5.

[8] L. Davis et al., *American Economic Growth: An Economist's History of the United States* (New York: Harper and Row, 1972), pp. 438–441.

commodity. As the sword blades of Damascus and Toledo and those crafted for the Japanese Samurai attest, it had been made for many centuries. But steel had always been so expensive and difficult to produce, particularly in large quantities, that it was used only in applications where quality of performance had a high priority over price. Even more than ironmaking, the production of steel was an art whose intricacies could only be mastered through long experience. The crucible process by which it was made involved adding small amounts of carbon to molten wrought iron. It was all but impossible to make large quantities of uniform-quality steel, since each crucible had only a very limited capacity, and each was prepared individually. Since the scientific nature of the process was only vaguely understood, it proceeded by rules of thumb and experience. All in all, steelmaking bore a closer resemblance to the work of a skilled cook than to modern industrial processes. And just as in cooking, great variations between individual batches of steel might occur.

In 1850, all available substitutes for steel had serious shortcomings. No single alternative metal combined all the properties of even crucible steel. Wrought iron is tough, but soft and malleable, and it cannot be given tensile strength. Thus, it was not suitable for applications involving high speeds or heavy stresses. Cast iron was hard, but it was also brittle, and it could not be worked once cast. Nor could it resist shock. Iron tools and machinery could be strengthened only by adding material, a self-defeating process for moving mechanisms: so much energy would be required to move heavily reinforced machinery parts that little would be left for the machine's task. No available metal was cheaper than or physically superior to iron.

The Bessemer Steelmaking Process
In 1856 it was discovered that steel could be produced by blowing air through molten pig iron, a process that removed most of the impurities from the metal. The discovery was made

independently by William Kelly, an American, and Henry Bessemer of England. Kelly failed to make his discovery commercially successful, but Bessemer found a ready market for the steelmaking process that was given his name. The new process was rapid, requiring only about a quarter of an hour, and it greatly increased the quantities that could be made in a single batch.

Soon thereafter, those who tried to use Bessemer's steelmaking process found themselves unable to repeat his success (see Chapter 7). Only after the source of the difficulty was identified as phosphorus in the iron ore was it possible to counteract its effects. This early triumph of industrial chemistry was the key to making the Bessemer process usable and its results more predictable. The United States had large, though highly localized, deposits of suitable ore, and further chemical research developed new linings for furnaces that permitted the use of a wider range of ores. Still more research resulted in changes in the Bessemer process that allowed more exact control of the metal's carbon content and the production of true steel. Once the initial difficulties had been overcome, production of Bessemer-process steel increased rapidly in both Europe and the United States.

Initial Steelmaking Problems. Although Bessemer steel was ideal for some applications, such as railroad rails, both it and its manufacturing process had some drawbacks. Bessemer steel was subject to mysterious fractures, now known to be caused by nitrogen dissolved in the iron by the air blown through it during the refining process.[9] At the time, however, discovering the cause of this problem was beyond the scope of industrial chemistry. In addition, the Bessemer process could employ only a limited range of ores, and American deposits of suitable ore were

[9] Ibid., p. 443.

Table 12.2   Steel Production in the United States
(Thousands of Tons)

Date	Total	Bessemer	Open-Hearth	Crucible	Electric
1860	13			13	
1865	15			15	
1870	77	42	2	34	
1875	437	376	9	52	
1880	1,397	1,203	113	81	
1885	1,917	1,702	149	66	
1890	4,779	4,131	566	82	
1895	6,785	5,494	1,219	72	
1900	11,227	7,481	3,638	109	
1905	21,880	12,231	9,537	112	
1910	28,330	10,478	17,672	122	58
1915	35,180	9,178	25,838	108	55
1920	46,183	9,841	35,846	79	417

Source: U.S. Department of Commerce, Bureau of the Census, *Historical Statistics of the United States: Colonial Times to 1970*, 2 vols. (Washington, D.C.: Government Printing Office, 1975), 2:695–696.

highly concentrated geographically and thus subject to monopoly control.

The Open-Hearth Steelmaking Method

Shortly after the Bessemer process came into widespread use, a second method was developed. The Siemens-Martin (named for its German-English and French inventors) or open-hearth process used a huge, open pan in which the heat from exhaust gases, which previously had been wasted, was employed to raise furnace temperatures. The open-hearth method could use both scrap iron and a wider range of ores than the Bessemer process, and the chemical composition of the steel could be more precisely controlled. Initially, however, the process was less efficient than Bessemer's method. As Table 12.2 indicates, the open-hearth process was not widely used until the latter 1890s, but after that open-hearth steel production expanded rapidly.[10]

[10] Ibid., pp. 442–443.

The Steel Revolution

Steel gave its users increased capabilities compared to iron. Steel railroad rails, for example, lasted up to 17 times as long as iron rails. In addition, their greater strength allowed the passage of heavier, faster trains with greater safety. Not only were the railroads thus enabled to increase train speed and carrying capacity (steel cars had greater payloads per unit of car weight), but they lost far less time to track replacement. Steel ships were stronger and safer than their iron counterparts and had greater carrying capacity per ton of displacement, and their steel engines produced greater speed and higher fuel economy.

In construction, steel produced a veritable revolution. For the first time, structural strength could be achieved without resorting to huge masses of wood or stone. Buildings made from these traditional materials had practical height limits of no more than six or eight stories, because the supports for the upper floors had to be so large that the lower stories had little usable space. Steel frames greatly reduced this limitation and made it possible for cities to expand upward as well as outward.

Steel was also well suited to high operating speeds and could be worked to much closer tolerances than iron. These properties made possible both improved machine tools and better-functioning products. As time passed, steel prices fell until they were well below even the previous price of iron, encouraging still wider use of the world's first really cheap metal. Industrial chemistry produced a growing range of new alloys, and steel could be given properties that no metal had ever possessed before.

Productivity Gains in a New Industry

As with most new industries, productivity grew rapidly in steelmaking, and costs fell dramatically. After 1880, the real price of steel fell, making it not only physically superior to most other materials, but steadily cheaper as well. Producers learned to build plants that reduced the heat loss between operations and to use previously unwanted by-products such as furnace linings and coke-oven gases. American engineers quickly developed the skills to design integrated plants that took maximum advantage of the new technology and were unmatched anywhere else. They were aided by the extremely rapid growth of the industry; many new plants were being constructed, and most were completely new ventures.

Steelmaking also produced experience with the problems involved in moving great masses of material, shaping and finishing metal, and performing other tasks with applications outside the industry. Energy conservation yielded double dividends: not only was a fraction of the coal required to smelt a ton of iron in 1860 needed to produce a ton of steel by 1900, but materials handling, waste disposal, and other expenses were also reduced. Such developments taught plant designers to view the steelmaking process as an integrated whole rather than a series of separate operations.

The market for steel rails flagged with the completion of most of America's rail network in the 1880s, but in place of railway demands, those for sheets, plates, and structural shapes more than filled the gap.

Industry Relocation

The pattern of natural resources in the United States was highly favorable to the steel industry. Steelmaking requires iron ore, coal, and limestone. Limestone is widely available, but many regions of the earth lack one or both of the other two. Great deposits of iron ore were available in the upper Midwest, and the huge ranges of northern Minnesota could be worked with steam shovels rather than expensive deep-mining techniques. After construction of the Sault Sainte Marie Canal connecting Lake Superior with the other Great Lakes in 1855, the ore could be shipped by cheap water transportation to ports on the Lakes' southern shores, from which it could be easily transported by rail to the coal of the Ohio Valley. (Initially, a greater weight of fuel than ore was required to produce a ton of steel.)

Toward 1900, coal was sent to lake ports such as Cleveland, Erie, and Toledo on the return trip of the ore cars. Another great steel center developed at the southern tip of Lake Michigan, where the coal of Indiana and central Illinois was put to use in Gary, Michigan City, and other steel towns. Near Birmingham, Alabama, coal and iron ore were found in alternating layers in the same geological formation, allowing the development of yet another steel-producing area.

Automobiles

The automobile is the twentieth-century economic counterpart of nineteenth-century steel. Like steelmaking, automobile manufacturing was a rapidly growing industry with major links to other sectors of the economy. No other nation has developed its production or altered the other features of its economy in conse-

■ In 1890, America was the leading steel manufacturer in the world.
Source: Thomas Anshutz, American 1851–1912, The Ironworkers' Noontime, ca. 1881. Oil on canvas, 17⅛″ × 24″. Gift of Mr. and Mrs. John D. Rockefeller 3rd, 1979. 7. 4. Reproduced by permission of The Fine Arts Museums of San Francisco.

quence of the mass-produced automobile so fully as the United States.

By the end of the nineteenth century several reasonably practical automobile designs had been developed in a quest almost as old as the first steam engine. Europe was an early leader in invention, but the United States was very strong in innovation. Even so, developing cars suitable for everyday use was a formidable task.

Early Automobiles: The "Toys of the Rich"

The early cars were expensive. Especially when contemporary income levels are taken into account, they cost far more than most modern counterparts, and were even more expensive to maintain. Only the rich could afford to operate automobiles in 1900, in no small part because the early cars were so unreliable that prudent owners who were not experienced mechanics required the full-time services of a combined chauffeur-mechanic. Service was all but unobtainable except in large cities, and repairs might require that the owner make as well as install replacement parts. Gasoline was initially sold by drugstores, in quart bottles, as cleaning fluid. Tire life was measured in hundreds rather than thousands of miles, and drivers carried several spares plus a patch kit and pump as a matter of course. Roads were unbelievably bad, almost totally bereft of either hard surfaces or road signs.

These barriers to ownership were gradually reduced. Auto manufacturers found that sales increased if they provided service, and the sources and normal sales units of gasoline became better suited to motorists' needs. Organizations of car owners allied with bicyclists to press for improved roads; by 1910, they had achieved some success.

Henry Ford's "Better Idea"

The real breakthrough for the automobile industry came from Henry Ford. But Ford's major contribution was not the moving assembly line, which he neither originated nor introduced into the auto industry. Rather, it was Ford's recognition that a truly low-priced car could be sold in vastly greater quantities than were possible while cars remained high-priced toys for the rich and adventurous. The moving assembly line, with its enormous volume of fixed investment, made sense only if its costs could be spread over unheard-of numbers of cars. Ford's vision of a mass market for automobiles was not widely shared. One banker told W. C. Durant, one of the founders of General Motors, that no responsible person would ever lend him money until he ceased his wild talk about the United States eventually producing 50,000 cars in a single year—and refused him a loan.[11] After similar encounters, Ford eventually got his financing from nonbank sources. In the process, he developed a lasting distaste for banks.

The Model T: An American "People's Car". In 1908 the Ford Motor Company began to produce a light, simple motor car called the Model T. Hedging its bets, the company also made a larger, more expensive car similar to those made by other firms. In that year, despite the banker's views, the American auto industry produced and sold 63,500 cars, 5,986 of which were Fords. The differing versions of the Model T were priced at from $825 to $1,000.

In the following year, Ford announced that henceforth he would simplify his model line: he would produce only Model Ts in two versions and "any color the customer wants, as long as it's black." In 1909 Ford production reached 12,292 cars. Two years later Ford began to build a new plant, and by 1914 the moving assembly line was in operation, turning out 260,720 Model Ts. Prices were $440 for the runabout and $490 for the touring car. Just as with modern cars, there was an optional accessories list. If the customer did not wish to start his car with a crank, he could buy an electric starter for $15. That began and ended Ford's list of accessories. By 1916, Ford sold over half a million cars at $345 and $360. This was nearly 40 percent of all U.S. auto production. By 1924, despite the inflation caused by World War I, Ford was able to reduce the price of a Model T roadster to $260.[12]

The Model T was a simple car; many people could perform all their own maintenance work on it. For those unable or unwilling to do so, Ford established a chain of dealerships that were obligated to maintain service facilities. The car was also rugged and reliable, safe and easy to drive, and ideally suited to American conditions. Above all, however, the Model T was cheap—a car for the middle class and even for many who could lay no claim to such status.

The Economic Consequences of Mr. Ford. Ford, who had bought out his initial partners, earned a huge fortune from production of the Model T. But the Ford Motor Company gave the people of the United States far more than just affordable cars in return. The mass-produced

---

[11] T. Cochran and W. Miller, *The Age of Enterprise: A Social History of Industrial America* (New York: Harper and Row, 1968), p. 186.

[12] A. Chandler, Jr., *Giant Enterprise: Ford, General Motors, and the Automobile Industry* (New York: Harcourt, Brace, and World, 1964), pp. 32–33.

■ Henry Ford mass-produced fifteen million identical Model Ts from 1908 to 1927.
Source: Courtesy of Ford Motor Company.

automobile gave Americans greater freedom than any other people had ever experienced. Owning a car conferred a much wider range of choices of places to live, shop, and work— and these choices meant greater freedom. Workers were no longer forced to deal only with those employers within walking distance of their homes (or to live in areas with only proximity to jobs to recommend them). Farmers no longer had to face the "take-it-or-leave-it" offers of a single grain elevator or general store.[13] The automobile made a huge contribution to the American specialty of efficient human resource allocation. It literally made it easier to put the right people in the jobs for which they were best suited. Compared to this, its contribution to American life-styles and leisure hours was unimportant.

[13] J. Hughes, *The Vital Few: American Economic Progress and Its Protagonists* (New York: Oxford University Press, 1973), pp. 291–294.

Further Consequences

The automobile industry had enormous forward and backward linkages. Manufacture required large amounts of steel, rubber, glass, paint, and other materials, and automobiles' special characteristics (together with those of bicycles a few decades earlier) spurred the development of alloy steels, bearings of several types, and other innovations that had wide application in other types of manufacturing. Engineers from many other industries studied the moving assembly line and adapted it to make other goods, just as Ford's engineers had. The automobile increased the demand for fuel, tires, service, and roads as consumer goods. Less directly, it made the suburbs possible, although not really until after 1920.

Automobile production by all America's car manufacturers grew rapidly after 1908. Unit sales exceeded 500,000 in 1914. By 1916 they were over 1,500,000. (In 1900 only 4,000 cars had been sold in the United States.) The moving assembly line's introduction was eased by the use of some other American production specialties, such as interchangeable parts. In 1906, the Cadillac factory created a sensation in Europe by shipping three cars to England, disassembling them and scrambling the parts, and then reassembling them with only hand tools and no fitting, an impossible feat for European carmakers at that time.[14] Note that this feat occurred before Ford built either his new car or the assembly line.

Other Industries

The foregoing industries are only well-known examples of the widespread industrial development sweeping the United States after 1865. Table 12.1 indicates that no single American

[14] D. Landes, *The Unbound Prometheus: Technological Change and Industrial Development in Europe from 1750 to the Present* (Cambridge, England: Cambridge University Press, 1969), p. 315.

industry produced as much as one-tenth of total value added by manufacturing, nor employed more than one-ninth of all industrial workers. Not only did the range of products spilling from American factories expand, but developments in one sector often permitted or encouraged growth in another.

Customer acceptance of more fully processed foods allowed the rise of canning and baking firms. The great meat-packing companies such as Swift, Armour, Hormel, and Cudahy owed their formation to the development of western railroads and refrigerated cars. Local slaughterhouses strongly opposed competition from meat killed a thousand miles from its markets. To ensure access to consumers, the western packers were obliged to build up their own marketing organizations. Boot and shoe production benefited from improved sewing and cutting machines and began to relocate to the Midwest to be near the supply of hides from the large meat-packing plants there. The use of standardized sizes and versions of the new machines also employed by the shoemakers allowed factory production of many articles of men's clothing to replace custom tailoring or home production for all but the very rich, a development that allowed ordinary people greater variety and often better quality clothing than before. Some items of women's clothing were also produced in factories now, but manual labor was still widely employed in making most women's garments and men's shirts.

Communications and Publishing

Increases in income, leisure time, and education stimulated the market for books, magazines, and especially newspapers. On the supply side, the publishing industry was the beneficiary of cheaper paper made from wood pulp rather than rags and of new production devices such as the linotype machine. Communications improved as the telegraph network was extended and incorporated new advances. In the 1890s, telephones became increasingly common. Over a million telephones were in use by the turn of the century, and that figure would rise thirteenfold by 1920. It was possible, although very expensive, to make a coast-to-coast long distance call by 1915.

Electricity

Electric lighting became practical with the development of the first central generating stations in the 1880s. Once the superiority of alternating current over direct current was established (an argument in which Thomas Edison uncharacteristically found himself on the wrong side), the lighting of American cities, both indoors and out, could be greatly improved. Steam-powered street railways could be replaced by quieter, less pollution-prone electric trolleys.

Growth in industries associated with electrical manufactures as well as in power generation and distribution spurred copper production. With an assist from new refining methods that allowed copper production from much lower-grade ore, copper output rose from 9,520 tons in 1865 to 744,036 tons 50 years later.

Electric motors revolutionized the design and layout of many American factories after 1900, allowing much greater productive efficiency in many industries. The use of electric motors made the orderly flow of material possible through the factory and eliminated the dangerous and power-consuming maze of belts, shafts, and gears which characterized plants using steam or waterpower. The electrical industry was the first science-based manufacturing establishment in the United States, and its research operations developed a variety of alloys, insulating materials, and plastics useful in other industries as well as at their point of origin.

Machine Tools

As they had earlier, machine tools and their makers played a central role in disseminating new technology through the economy. Machines themselves were improved as steel allowed higher operating speeds, closer tolerances, and greater strength. New developments in metal cutting, grinding, finishing, and polishing were widely applied. More importantly, the machine tool manufacturers served as specialized problem solvers for their customers, producing machines that addressed buyers' new requirements. Often the solution to one industry's needs proved to be just what another required in a different application or could be adapted for use in another context.[15] Yet one more indication of the diversified growth of industry was that the American machine tool industry became highly specialized, with many producers making only a narrow range of tools. As many others did, the machine tool industry relocated to be near its customers. Firms moved to the Midwest, seeking proximity to the steelmakers, to whose product their own was applied.

NEW FUELS AND POWER SOURCES

In 1865, the most common form of nonhuman energy used in American industry was waterpower. Wood was the most widely used fuel, furnishing 81 percent of all fuel-generated energy for the economy at that date. Fuel and energy sources changed rapidly: by 1880 coal had largely replaced wood as the fuel for steam engines, and steam power had supplanted waterpower in manufacturing. By 1900 steam generated about 80 percent of all the power used in factories. Waterpower accounted for 15 percent, but it was important only in textile, paper, and lumber production. Coal now furnished about three-quarters of the fuel energy required by the entire economy and a still higher portion of that used in manufacturing. Thenceforth, coal's share remained approximately

---

[15] N. Rosenberg, *Technology and American Economic Growth* (New York: Harper and Row, 1972), pp. 100–102.

constant, while that of wood declined in favor of petroleum, in the form of both oil and natural gas.[16] Although we are accustomed to a world powered by mineral fuels, these sources of energy have been in widespread use for little more than a century.

The application of power also changed. Replacing waterpower with steam allowed more flexibility in plant location and reduced interference from weather. Steam power sources could be divided into smaller units, a very difficult proposition with waterpower. Even so, there was a minimum practical size for steam engines, and conversion of their to-and-fro motion into rotary movement wasted energy. It was difficult to vary the speed of operation efficiently. Power transmission devices in steam-driven factories were both inefficient and a major source of industrial accidents. Because of the limits of power transmission, all machines performing a certain function had to be grouped together, working off a shaft turning at the proper speed. Material had to be transferred from these machines to those grouped around another power source for the next operation, losing time in the process. It was difficult if not impossible to design a plant where materials could be moved from one machine to another in a continuous line.[17]

Electric power changed this. Even though the ultimate source of electricity might be mineral fuel or (much less likely) waterpower, it could be used in vastly more flexible forms. Electric motors could be designed to meet the specific requirements of any operation. They eliminated most of the energy loss through transmission, and most of all, they allowed the rearrangement of materials flows through factories along the lines most conducive to continuous operations. This was especially important in producing items requiring many successive stages of manufacture. The moving

assembly line is hardly conceivable without electric motors. Electric power was even more flexible than steam: for the first time, it was possible to transmit power economically over long distances from its point of generation.

PLANT SIZE AND NEW MANAGEMENT TECHNIQUES

The growing size and complexity of many industrial plants and the increasing need to integrate all operations caused men to begin to study the plant as a whole instead of a series of individual operations whose relationships to each other were unimportant. Many firms found that the rise in competition resulting from lower transportation and distribution costs made it increasingly difficult to pass on production inefficiencies in the form of higher product prices, as had once been possible. In part, this trend was a natural outgrowth of specialization.

The New Managers

After 1900 a new generation of plant managers appeared, more oriented toward improving the efficiency of production than the previous owner-managers had been. The early managers had tended to pay little attention to production once the plant was in operation; they specialized in obtaining finance and in sales. The new men combined engineering with management skills, and they developed more efficient plants and improved productivity in those already in operation. Smaller amounts of fuel, labor, and raw materials were used per unit of output as a result of better plant organization, reduced heat losses, increased use of by-products either as inputs in the basic production process or as separate products, recovery and reuse of scrap,

[16] Ibid., pp. 158–160.
[17] Ibid., p. 161.

and a host of other measures. Often these measures had not been taken previously because they were worthwhile only at high volumes of output.

Mass Production

One result of these systematic changes in production was the development of mass production: the production of large amounts of a uniform commodity through the coordinated efforts of a large work force employing large amounts of highly specialized capital. The key element in mass production is coordination. When every worker performs as part of a larger team, there are no small mistakes. Any error affects the flow of product farther down the line, and possibly ahead of the mistake as well. To minimize costs in such an organization, it is essential that each task fully occupy the labor and machine time available to perform it. Any slower pace wastes production potential and raises costs; any attempt to exceed capacity causes breakdowns, errors, and spoiled work.

Scientific Management

With these principles in mind, engineers began to study how each worker's job fit into the whole. Led by F. W. Taylor, who developed what he called "scientific management" (the term was first used in an 1895 paper he presented), they tried to apply production theory to the workplace. The task involved studying the mechanics of each worker's job, attempting to improve performance by the use of either specialized tools or work methods, and using incentives to motivate workers to accept the new methods.

Since scientific management, where successful, increased production rates, workers might—and often did—regard it as a speedup. But scientific management was far more than just a faster work pace. Taylor opposed work rates that unduly taxed workers' stamina, because a pace that the laborer could not maintain efficiently resulted in mistakes and accidents. Nor did scientific management nec-

■ Frederick Winslow Taylor introduced "scientific management" in 1895.
Source: Dictionary of American Portraits. (New York: Dover Publications, Inc., 1967), p. 610.

essarily reduce the worker to a high-speed automaton. Really simple repetition was better delegated to machines than to men, Taylor thought, and his system was designed to avoid worker fatigue and boredom.

The new system's results did not accrue only to management. Taylor and his disciples were aware that few employees would be willing to change their work patterns just to set production records, so a fundamental tenet of scientific management was that improved performance must be recognized and rewarded. Thus, the new methods resulted in higher pay and shorter hours for workers. Other benefits were reduced physical effort and lower accident rates.

As often occurs with innovation, many employers were not willing to accept the full spectrum of changes recommended by Taylor and his students. Nor was it always possible to persuade workers to accept them. But scientific management helped firms reduce costs while making jobs safer, physically less demanding, and better paid, if not always more interesting.[18] The changes did, however, reduce workers' control over the pace of their efforts and often over the manner in which they were performed.

The American Industrial Environment. This attention to plant design and detailed management was uniquely American. It was developed earlier and to a far greater extent in this country than abroad. Various aspects of Taylor's ideas, but never his complete system, were used by railroads, the Remington Typewriter Company, Yale and Towne, and the steel and machine-tool industries.

Possibly scientific management's American reception was greater than in foreign countries because it was easier to introduce changes in methods, tools, and compensation where the tasks were new, and the United States had many new plants where they could be incorporated from the start. Even experienced American workers were more accustomed to the introduction of new machines than were those in Europe. Such alterations appeared less threatening in the labor-scarce environment of the United States. There was also less owner and managerial inertia to overcome. In circumstances of heavy financial or psychological investment in older methods, it was often difficult to institute change or realize its full potential within particular firms or industries. Even so, there was seldom any effective opposition to change in the United States. The promoters of managerial changes in America sowed their seed in fertile soil.

NEW BUSINESS STRUCTURES

The structure of American firms began to change along with the nature and volume of their output. In 1865, with the exception of the railroads and a few companies producing large metal goods, American manufacturing firms tended to be engaged in processing agricultural products or other raw materials. They were dependent on local markets for both inputs and sales. Typically, they produced consumer goods that required additional finishing before they were ready for final use. Most firms were small in absolute size as measured by sales volume, number of employees, or the amount invested in them. After the Civil War, the completion of the railroad system and rapid urbanization made markets larger and frequently regional or national in scope. By the turn of the century, electricity and the internal combustion engine created a new set of pressures for change.[19] All of these developments were both causes and results of changes elsewhere in the economy. They created new linkages as well as changes in the firms most directly affected.

The Birth of "Big Business"

The transition to "big business" in the modern sense of large corporations selling goods in national or even larger markets began in the consumer goods industries.[20] By the early 1890s it was well established. As transportation improved and new production methods appeared that offered lower unit costs only at much larger volumes of output than previously, firms often attempted to expand their sales areas. Many times these efforts resulted in a head-on col-

---

[18] Chandler, *The Visible Hand*, pp. 275–277.

[19] Chandler, "Big Business."
[20] Ibid.

lision with other similarly inclined producers. Where the products of various firms were standardized or at least similar, as many consumer goods were, the usual initial response to rivals—an attempt to destroy them—often gave way to efforts designed to eliminate competition.

Firms made agreements either on price and output or else on the division of markets between them. These collusive developments appeared first among the railroads and spread to producers of standardized consumer products such as flour and cigarettes. In a few cases, the erstwhile competitors formed pools in which they agreed to share profits on the basis of sales or some other acceptable formula. But such "gentlemen's agreements" were illegal under the common law, and there was no way to enforce them. Worse, it paid any individual firm to make such an agreement with its rivals in the hope that the other parties would keep it. If they did, cheating on the compact was highly profitable. Thus, such pools and cartels proved highly unstable. The prices fixed by such arrangements were of course higher than those prevailing in markets before the agreements were reached. At least some of the parties to such price fixing would have unused productive capacity that could be employed to produce goods for sale for less than the agreed-upon price. As might be expected, the businessmen who would make such illegal agreements did not become any more scrupulous when they spotted a profitable opportunity to break them. So long as individuals retained their freedom of action, they were likely to use it for their own benefit.

Mergers

A more successful response to the problem of competition was mergers, which eliminated independent action by bringing firms under common management. But mergers did not eliminate competition in consumer goods industries. Instead of many small firms, a few large ones might share the market—a market structure called oligopoly. It is not even clear that actual competition was reduced, a point that will be discussed later.

In addition to their attempts to combine horizontally, firms in consumer goods industries soon began to integrate into other stages of production and distribution. Producers buying their inputs in competitive markets where supplies were readily available at prices very close to production costs chose to integrate forward rather than back: they purchased retail outlets to ensure access to customers.[21] Producers of new consumer goods often found it necessary to set up their own marketing organizations to ensure adequate presentation of their goods to consumers, as in the cases of cigarettes and bananas. Manufacturers of items for which service after the sale was important—sewing machines, bicycles, and later, automobiles—developed closely controlled dealer networks and sometimes furnished their own credit arrangements as well. In some cases retail outlets established to sell one item were profitably diversified. Meat packers, for example, discovered that the stores they had founded to sell pork, beef, and mutton could also market poultry, eggs, and dairy products.[22]

Firm Structures

The nature of the product affected the firm's internal structure. If a company sold only one item or a narrow range of similar goods, its operations tended to be tightly controlled by a central office and its divisions along functional lines such as sales, production, accounting, and so forth.[23] Firms selling a variety of different goods tended to be organized by product divisions; their structure and operating methods will be discussed later.

[21] Ibid.
[22] Ibid.
[23] Ibid. See also Chandler, *The Visible Hand*, Chaps. 12–14.

Changing Competitive Patterns

In addition to the difficulty of forming cohesive combinations, another factor contributing to the survival of competition was the entry of new firms into established industries, which remained possible throughout the period. If existing firms' profits became tempting enough, others were likely to set up similar businesses to try to garner some of the gains for themselves.

One attempt at monopolization that failed to adequately respond to entry possibilities ended in disaster. In the 1890s an attempt to form a monopoly in the distilled liquor industry occurred. The would-be monopolists purchased nearly all the existing distilleries. Although the liquor trust was able to gain control of over 90 percent of distilling capacity at one point, it defended its position by buying out any new firm that appeared. Unfortunately for the monopolists, an efficient distillery could be constructed for only a modest investment, and when it became clear that all such plants were certain to be purchased by the liquor trust, a new industry was born—the production not of liquor, but of distilleries. Eventually, the trust failed.[24]

Vertical Integration

Firms in the capital goods industries faced a different situation. They were not affected by market changes as early as the consumer goods industries, and no attempts at consolidation among firms occurred until the 1890s. Vertical integration among capital goods producers was generally backward, into sources of inputs, crucial transport links, and preliminary fabrication and processing.

The buyers of most capital goods were or soon became well equipped to judge quality for themselves; indeed, many capital goods were designed to customers' specifications. Since sales in these circumstances were made on the basis of price, delivery terms, and product performance, there was little point in elaborate marketing efforts. As it had elsewhere, vertical integration generally followed a combination movement. In these industries Chandler considered vertical integration to have been a largely defensive measure, designed to ensure the firms' access to resources needed for continued operations, not to increase monopoly power.[25] A more recent study concluded that for at least some firms, particularly U.S. Steel, vertical integration provided useful barriers to the entry of new firms into the industry.[26]

In most of the industries where it occurred, vertical integration was also designed to increase operational efficiency by improving coordination between successive stages of production and reducing scheduling difficulties.[27] Capital goods often passed through many stages of production before reaching finished form, and vertical integration might give users of inputs such as steel and copper bargaining power with their producers or with the ultimate users of electrical goods, bridges, pipe, and other items.

Diversification

These integrated firms, particularly after 1900, began to sell a greater variety of goods. It might be that the optimum (cost-minimizing) scale of operations in successive stages of production was different. One level of the firm might need to produce a larger volume of output than the next division could use if it were to cut unit costs to their lowest possible level. The finished capital good might require some inputs that had simply never been produced elsewhere. These developments were especially prevalent in new industries such as electrical goods, automobiles, oil refining, and chemicals. Such in-

[24] Chandler, *The Visible Hand*, p. 328. See also N. Lamoreaux, *The Great Merger Movement in American Business, 1895–1904* (Cambridge, England: Cambridge University Press, 1985), p. 181.

[25] Chandler, "Big Business."
[26] Lamoreaux, *The Great Merger Movement*, Chap. 5.
[27] Chandler, "Big Business."

dustries began to sell not only the goods for which they were named, but also alloys, insulation, plastics, farm machinery, diesel engines, locomotives, tractors, dyes, and many other goods.

Other firms discovered that the engineering talent needed to design and build their production facilities was more than sufficient to operate them and diverted part of it into research and development. In one case, the electrical industry began to produce not only the heavy generating and power-distribution equipment in which it originally specialized, but also appliances. These were not only profitable in themselves, but they increased demand for the firm's primary output as well.

Yet other firms diversified out of desperation. As the scale of operations increased, problems of waste disposal often rose more than in proportion. When the quantity of waste products was small and governments more obliging, they were simply thrown away. But as the greater volume and rising public concern over some types of pollution made this more difficult and expensive, some firms tried to reduce the amounts of waste. Meat-packing plants turned offal, bones, horns, and hooves into products ranging from pharmaceuticals to fertilizer. Steel firms sold used furnace linings as high-phosphorous fertilizer.

Firm Structure and the Nature of Production.

In diversified firms, the head office exercised little control over division operations, and divisions were generally organized along product lines rather than by function. The head office would handle finance and make basic decisions such as whether to construct a new plant, but production and often marketing were handled by the individual divisions almost as though each were a separate firm.[28]

The path-breaking studies of Alfred D. Chandler, Jr., concluded that the primary influence shaping the development of American industry before 1900 was the establishment of the large corporation. It in turn resulted from the appearance of a national market as transportation and communications improved. After 1900, Chandler found that the primary influences were innovations in products and in research.[29]

THE RAILROADS

From 1865 to 1915, the total length of railroads in the United States grew from 35,000 to 250,000 miles. These figures include only main track outside railroad yards; the railroads had another 140,000 miles of tracks in double lines and yards.[30] Transcontinental lines, beginning with the Union Pacific in 1869, linked the West Coast with the rest of the country; trunk lines served new areas or paralleled existing routes; feeder lines connected local markets with the national economy; and special-purpose roads served isolated logging and mining camps.

Railroad efficiency improved as a result of standardized track gauges, steel boilers, track, and couplings, better brakes, telegraphic traffic controls, and centralized or "union" stations. Pullman cars made long-distance travel more comfortable. The speed and weight of trains rose, indications of the increased carrying capacity resulting from a combination of more miles per unit of rolling stock and larger loads per trip.

Railroads' Economic Impact

Railroads played an important role in the economic development of the United States after the Civil War. The advent of really efficient

---

[28] Ibid.

[29] Chandler, *Strategy and Structure* and *The Visible Hand.*

[30] U.S. Department of Commerce, *Historical Statistics,* vol. 2, p. 728.

overland transportation aided the economic unification of America, furthering regional specialization and interdependence. Railroads also fostered the growth of regional hubs such as Atlanta, Chicago, and Kansas City. Until 1900, the railroads absorbed a larger share of aggregate investment funds than any other single entity. Foreign investment in American railroads had been significant in the antebellum period, and much of the railways' equipment (particularly rails) had been imported in that era. But now the railroads' linkages were to the domestic economy. Rails and other equipment were now manufactured within the United States and sometimes exported. The role of foreign investment also declined.

The Indispensability Controversy

Measuring the railroads' contribution to the American economy has attracted the attention of many scholars. All have concluded that the railroads were indeed important in the economic growth of the United States. One study by Robert Fogel, however, has attracted a great deal of critical attention.[31] To test what he termed the "axiom of indispensability"—the idea that American economic growth would have been impossible, or at least seriously impaired, without the nineteenth-century railroad system—Fogel constructed a model of the U.S. economy identical to historical reality with one important exception: it did not contain railroads. Fogel assumed that the transportation system of his hypothetical economy consisted of the best alternative methods of transportation then available: a greatly expanded network of canals and improved rivers combined with a system of feeder roads. By comparing the national product of his hypothetical economy with that actually achieved in

[31] R. Fogel, *Railroads and American Economic Growth: Essays in Economic History* (Baltimore: Johns Hopkins University Press, 1964). Fogel's latest response to his critics is "Notes on the Social Savings Controversy," *Journal of Economic History* (March 1979).

1890, Fogel hoped to measure the railroads' contribution to economic growth.

Surprisingly—and to many historians, not conclusively—Fogel discovered that his postulated road-canal-river transportation network was technically feasible well out into the Great Plains. This would have placed about 98 percent of all the agricultural land actually in use in 1890 within 40 miles of water transportation, a distance over which wagon transportation was economically possible. To maximize his estimate of the railroads' impact, Fogel assumed that the locations of economic activity were the same as those that actually developed with their aid. Presumably some activity would have relocated away from areas where alternatives to the railroads were especially poor.

The next step was to compute the costs of transporting 1890s agricultural output from production to consumption points and compare the costs of doing so with those actually incurred. Ton-mile charges would have been lower, not higher, on the water and wagon system, but direct freight charges alone understate the railroads' contribution. When allowances are made for the costs involved in using a slower form of transportation (inventories, insurance, and losses), together with the seasonal shutdowns on many water routes, the savings generated by the railroads are positive, as they logically had to be. But the study found they were quite modest. Fogel concluded that national income in 1890 was only about 5 percent higher with the railroads than it would have been without them, even when the cost of transporting all goods, not merely agricultural products, was considered. (Fogel never actually computed costs for nonagricultural products and he excluded passenger transportation, basing the aggregate estimate on the proportion of agricultural to total income.) Five percent of national income was less than two years' economic growth at late nineteenth-century rates. If no railroads had been available to carry freight, Fogel concluded, the United States would have achieved the income actually produced sometime in 1888 by the end of 1890. Railroads were important, Fogel stated (no other industry's absence would have caused as large an effect), but they could not be termed indispensable.

The Critical Response. Some criticisms of Fogel's work are methodological. Specifically , some critics objected to his use of a counterfactual proposition (the railroadless economy). Since this never occurred, they said, it could not be used in historical analysis. However, such counterfactual propositions are in fact implicit in every statement of cause and effect, historical or otherwise.

The more interesting debate is over the dimensions of the railroads' contribution. Virtually every aspect of Fogel's procedures has been attacked. Critics are not convinced that water transportation could have been expanded to the network Fogel assumed, nor do they believe that such canals could have handled the volume of traffic that Fogel assigned to them. The rates charged by various forms of transportation have been challenged, as has the extrapolation from agricultural products to all freight. Others have pointed out that another study concluded that the railroads were already contributing 5 percent of national income as early as 1860,[32] and it is highly unlikely that their impact was not greater when they served large regions with much poorer access to water transport than the settled area of 1860.

The consensus of one group of critics is that the railroads' contribution was considerably greater than Fogel's estimate—perhaps 9 to 14 percent of national income in 1890, rather than 5 percent.[33] Another group, impressed by the very high social rates of return generated by the transcontinental railroads, have argued

■ Railroads' role in American economic growth was significant.
Source: Union Pacific Railroad from the Association of American Railroads.

that the true benefits were greater than 14 percent, perhaps even more than 20 percent of national income.[34] Whether even the latter conclusion would have made the railroads literally indispensable is still a matter of debate. There is no doubt, however, that the railroads' role in American economic growth during this period was greater than that of any other single industry.

Railroad Finances

Much postwar railroad construction took place under very different circumstances from that done before 1860. The earlier lines were built

[32] A. Fishlow, *American Railroads and the Transformation of the Antebellum Economy* (Cambridge, Mass.: Harvard University Press, 1965).
[33] S. Lebergott, "United States Transportation Advance and Externalities," *Journal of Economic History* (December 1966) and M. Nerlove, "Railroads and American Economic Growth," *Journal of Economic History* (March 1966).

[34] H. Boyd and G. Walton, "The Social Savings from 19th Century Rail Passenger Service," *Explorations in Economic History* (Spring 1972) and J. Williamson, "The Railroads and Midwestern Development: A General Equilibrium History," in *The Old Northwest*, eds. Klingamen and Vedder (Athens, Ohio: Ohio University Press, 1975).

to serve settled regions where markets for transportation services already existed.[35] Many postwar railroads, especially in the West, were built in undeveloped, sometimes almost unpopulated, regions. These areas would remain undeveloped until transportation was available to send their bulky, low-unit-value products to market. No accurate measure of the volume of traffic railroads would generate in such regions could be made, because their potential would not be explored until they were linked to settled locations. The extent of the settlement that the railroads would eventually attract was unknown, and so was its rate of growth. Competing rail lines might be built into the same area. For these reasons, investments in railroads built into unsettled areas were viewed as risky, especially since it might be years after funds were committed and construction commenced before an accurate assessment of returns could be made.

Either optimistic or pessimistic conclusions could be reached under these conditions, and those who built the railroads tended to be optimists. They apparently overestimated the amount of development that would take place along the lines they built and underestimated the construction costs, the extent of competition that new railways would face, and the time required for both construction and settlement. Investors, on the other hand, tended to be pessimistic. Very high rates of return were demanded on funds invested in western railroads, indicating that such projects were deemed risky.

The Financial Track Record

Some of the methods railroad promoters used to obtain funds for construction raised the costs of capital still higher. As a result, although the railroads generally earned at least a competitive rate of return on the funds actually used for construction, the costs of obtaining these funds were so high that their overall financial record is poor. One source of later difficulties was that the people who built the railroads did not intend to operate them, and they received high payment for their efforts immediately, not from the proceeds of railroad operations. As a result, the railroad network was overbuilt.

The construction companies that actually built the railways were paid largely in bonds, not cash. These bonds were accepted by the construction companies at far less than their face value, even though the railroad was obligated to pay interest and principal in the amounts specified by the bonds. Other bonds were issued to "sweeten" sales of corporate stock, sometimes for no cash payment whatever. The deflation of 1865–1896 added to railroads' interest and debt burdens, and the depressions of the 1870s and 1890s reduced their earnings. As noted above, the railways' earnings on the sums actually expended to build them were adequate, but still far less than sufficient to discharge their obligations. Construction companies might skimp on their work; one railroad was described as "two streaks of rust across the prairie" only a few years after its completion. Poor construction work added to operating costs. The result was that the railroads were burdened with enormous fixed debts on which interest had to be paid before any dividends could be paid to stockholders. Often operating income did not even cover interest and principal payments on bonded debt. The social benefits of western railways were quite high—they raised customer incomes by considerably more than customer fees for their services—but returns to investors, particularly stockholders, were often low or nonexistent.[36]

Rate Wars. In addition, the burden of fixed debt left the railroads vulnerable to any development that might reduce traffic volume, whether competition from other roads or cyclical slumps in economic activity. Railroads had

---

[35] Fishlow, *American Railroads.*

[36] L. Mercer, "Building Ahead of Demand: Some Evidence for the Land Grant Railroads," *Journal of Economic History* (June 1974).

little choice but to try to retain traffic by any means available in adverse conditions. Since railroad transportation is essentially a homogeneous good, they had to compete in price. The result was a series of rate wars, in which railroads tried to undercut each other. Attempts to collude and fix profitable prices were seldom successful. A rate cut would attract a large volume of traffic to the road offering it, provided all others maintained their rates at agreed-upon levels. Any traffic that more than paid the costs of loading and unloading it at least produced something to apply against the railroads' fixed costs, which had to be met to avoid bankruptcy.

Price Discrimination. The same pressures led to forthright exercises of monopoly power against any customers unfortunate enough to have no alternatives to service from a single road. The burdens of railroads' financial problems pressured them to engage in tactics their customers found incomprehensible—or infuriating. The railroads' actions may have been mere attempts to survive in an uncertain environment while carrying heavy fixed costs, but they provoked punitive legislation from outraged state legislatures. One authority claims that the rates allowed railroads under regulation by the Interstate Commerce Commission did not even allow them to maintain their equipment in proper working order after 1900.[37] At one time or another before 1914, nearly every major American railroad declared bankruptcy, and the industry was in constant turmoil.

OTHER FORMS OF TRANSPORTATION

The railroads expanded in part at the expense of older forms of transportation. Especially on smaller rivers, steamboat traffic declined, since steamboats' disadvantages relative to railroads were greatest on such waterways. Many of the canals so laboriously constructed before the Civil War were now abandoned. Some of their towpaths became railroad beds.

Faded Glory: Barge and Steamboat Traffic

There were exceptions to the general decline in water transportation. Water still offered advantages where cargo volumes were large or values per unit low. Traffic in grain, ore, coal, and building materials on the Mississippi and Ohio rivers continued to increase for several decades after 1860. But only two canals remained important commercial arteries after 1870. Traffic on the New York State Barge Canal System, which included the Erie Canal, continued to increase until 1880. After that, despite the widening and deepening of the major routes to permit passage of larger barges with lower unit costs, and even the abolition of tolls, traffic declined to only half its 1880 peak by 1900 and failed to rise thereafter.[38] The Sault Sainte Marie Canal, which linked Lake Superior with the other Great Lakes, experienced a rapid increase in traffic when the iron mines of northern Minnesota and wheat from the prairies of the United States and Canada furnished "exports" after 1885. Settlement of these regions furnished a market for the coal the ore boats carried on their return trips. Traffic on the other Great Lakes also increased. For the most part, however, the lower prices charged by water carriers did not compensate for their lack of speed and convenience compared to the railways.

The Decline of the U.S. Merchant Marine

Coastal commerce continued to grow, even as the U.S. Merchant Marine carried less overseas trade. The carrying trade between U.S. ports

---

[37] A. Martin, *Enterprise Denied: Origins of the Decline of American Railroads* (New York: Columbia University Press, 1971).

[38] U.S. Department of Commerce, *Historical Statistics*, vol. 2, p. 765.

was reserved to vessels built and operated by Americans by a law reminiscent of seventeenth-century mercantilism. Even so, the gains in coastal traffic did not offset the losses in overseas commerce, and the volume of merchant shipping built in American shipyards after 1865 never approached the levels of the 1850s and was often only one-third to one-half that built in the glory days of American clipper ships.[39]

One reason for the decline of American shipbuilding was technological backwardness. American wooden sailing ships were the best in the world in the antebellum period, and their sailing records and ready markets abroad proved it. But when construction shifted to iron and then steel ships and to steam propulsion, American yards were slow to adopt the new techniques. In part, this may have been due to their location: downeast Maine had plenty of wood and men skilled in working it, but it was far from supplies of metal and had few trained metalworkers. Foreign countries subsidized their vessels, sometimes with lucrative mail contracts, and American shipping costs, particularly for labor, were high.

Urban Railroads

Railways had their urban counterparts. Even before the Civil War, some cities had horse-drawn car systems that ran on rails set in the streets. Steam power was a logical replacement for horses, and after 1890 electric traction was used. As cities grew more congested, some moved their street railways overhead, creating the elevated rails, or "els." Urban railways became an important component of aggregate investment after the construction of interregional railways began to slacken in the 1880s. The appearance of a cheap and reasonably efficient system of mass transportation allowed better housing for city dwellers, who could now reside farther from their jobs. It also encouraged the

[39] Ibid., pp. 749–750.

development of specialized financial, shopping, and industrial districts within cities.

Few, if any, of the interurban and urban railroads survive today, but the system was extensive in the early twentieth century. Not only were there lines in all large and most middle-sized cities, but they also connected many different urban areas. It was even possible, although certainly not comfortable, to travel the entire Eastern Seaboad from Portland, Maine, to Richmond, Virginia, via interurban railway.

The Road System

Before 1900 little had been done to improve the quality of roads since the early national period. The road network had been extended with settlement, but that was about all. Farmers used the roads primarily in seasons when there were few other demands on their time, such as after the harvest, and would have borne a large share of the property taxes needed to improve roads. Consequently, rural areas exerted little pressure for better roads before the twentieth century. American roads tended to be dirt- or at best gravel-surfaced, poorly drained and graded, and without signs. Tales of potholes so large that horses drowned in them may be apocryphal, but no doubt most roads became all but impassible in wet weather. In 1910 the United States had almost five million miles of rural roads, only 200,000 of which were surfaced.

Under pressure from bicycle and automobile owners, states began to construct roads and mark and maintain them. By 1914, most states had organized construction programs and highway departments. In 1916 the federal government began making grants to the states for highway construction. Even so, it was only after World War I that the combination of improved motor trucks and adequate highways offered a practical alternative to railway transportation, and even then only for short distances.

NEW COMPETITIVE PATTERNS

The opportunities revealed by new manufacturing techniques and access to more distant markets made firms increasingly aware of competition from other producers. Many of the new methods of production involved high fixed costs. This meant not only that large production volumes were needed to gain the reduced unit costs such methods made possible, but it was costly to produce at lower volumes or shut down. Interest costs on investment had to be paid whether the capacity it had financed was met or not. Thus, when competition appeared, some response had to be made: it was suicidal to simply reduce production. Even if a firm were content with its traditional markets and made no effort to expand, it had no assurance that others would show similar forebearance. In sum, for many industrial firms there was no place to hide, and often compelling reasons to expand.

Growth in firm size offered several advantages. Often there was no other way to profitably employ the new, highly capitalized production methods. The lower unit costs they produced offered higher profits if prices remained stable and constituted the ultimate defense against competitors.

If firms' size increased relative to their markets, they might also gain some degree of monopoly power. Labor-saving, capital-intensive changes accounted for some but by no means all of the changes in market structure that occurred in this period.[40]

If a firm's size increases to allow use of economies of scale under competitive market conditions, it will be forced to pass its lower costs on to consumers. Under such circumstances, not only is productive efficiency increased, but the product's price reflects these gains. Such changes are beneficial to the entire economy. On the other hand, if firms become large in relation to their markets, they may be able to increase profits by selling smaller quantities at higher prices than under more competitive conditions. Since the same resources produce less in the monopolist's hands than they would under competition, overall welfare is reduced. Monopoly of any type is thus likely to be far more popular with its owner than with those forced to pay its price or do without its products.

The Effects of Monopoly

Compared to competition, monopoly creates an artificial shortage: under the same cost and demand conditions, monopolies produce less and charge more than competitive industries, even though their productive ability is the same. Such policies add to the monopolist's profits, but the monopolist gains less than the aggregate economy loses, and overall well-being is reduced. To retain the profits achieved by these means, a monopolist must be able to prevent others from entering the market and competing them away: it must prevent the market system from reallocating resources to uses where the value of their output is greatest. Thus, monopoly reduces both short- and long-run efficiency by distorting resource allocation.

In one instance, that of "natural monopoly," the results produced by monopoly—while still short of ideal economic efficiency—may be superior to those resulting from competition within the industry. If the most efficient scale of operations—that which minimizes unit costs—is very large in relation to the market for the product, then a single seller may be able to reduce production costs so much that its price (which might nonetheless include a substantial monopoly profit) is lower than those prices smaller firms must charge to cover their costs. In such a case, a larger quantity will be sold at

[40] J. James, "Structural Change in American Manufacturing, 1850–1890," *Journal of Economic History* (June 1983).

these lower prices. It is important to note, however, that economies of scale are generally available only within a single plant. The acquisition of additional plants, especially through mergers rather than new construction, will not reduce unit production costs significantly. When we note that the number of employees per plant rose only modestly in U.S. industry before 1900, the conclusion that the primary goal of increased firm size was increased market power rather than economies of scale is strengthened.[41]

The Competitive Jungle

Attempts to gain monopoly power were as varied as their results. Rarely was a firm able to achieve economies of scale more rapidly than its rivals and drive them from the market by sheer superior efficiency. More commonly, a firm's initial response was to try to destroy its competitors—sometimes literally rather than in a business sense—and when that effort failed, to adopt other tactics. Some firms attempted "cutthroat competition" (sales at less than rivals' costs of production in an attempt to bankrupt them). However, cutthroat competition works only if the price-cutting firm itself has either lower costs or the financial reserves to survive short-run losses. Further, if rivals are driven out, the victor must acquire their assets. Otherwise, their sale at bankruptcy-proceedings prices to new owners simply creates a new rival which is even more dangerous because its costs are lower than its predecessor's.

Even where such tactics succeeded, there was no assurance that the victor could recoup the costs of eliminating competition nor against further attempts to enter the industry. Tactics such as suborning rivals' employees, arson, buying labor unrest for rivals from corrupt union officials, impugning the quality of rivals' products (Royal Baking Powder encouraged rumors that alternatives to its product contained poisonous ingredients),[42] or selling spoiled goods under rivals' trademarks had drawbacks as well. Not only were they illegal, but their outcome was uncertain—and they invited retaliation in kind.

Price Fixing

The usual result of attempts to destroy competitors was a conclusion that those who could not be beaten might more profitably be joined. If all firms in an industry can agree on a common price and restrict output to no more than the market will absorb at that price, they may be able to obtain nearly the same total profit as a single-firm monopolist. The first attempts at collusion involved agreements on price, output, or both. These seldom succeeded for long: if only price *or* output were controlled, even colluding firms would alter the other dimension, and it would be impossible to sell total output or maintain all firms' market shares. Even if agreements covered both price and output, they were unenforceable under the common law and contained irresistible incentives to cheat. Pressures to undercut collusive agreements on prices were increased by the general deflation prior to 1896 and by the boom-and-bust business cycle. When demand for an industry's product fell during a depression, individual firms were strongly tempted to try to regain lost sales through price cuts, particularly if they had high fixed costs and the industry had not existed long enough for the firms to gain competitive experience, as was often the case in manufacturing.[43] Even so, the short-run profits from a price-fixing agreement could be high, and attempts to collude were common.

Trusts

Because agreements between independently managed firms were so unstable, even when they were elaborated into "pools" in which the

---

[41] Ibid.

[42] Lamoreaux, *The Great Merger Movement*, p. 157.
[43] Ibid., pp. 61–62, 87.

parties agreed to share total profits under some agreed-upon formula, other institutions were developed. Trusts were one response to the cheating problem. In a trust, the stockholders of competing firms would transfer voting control of their shares to a central group of trustees, in return for certificates on which they would receive dividends. Since the trustees now controlled the stock of all participant firms, they could manage the industry as a multiplant monopoly. Trusts were organized in a number of consumer goods industries from 1880 to 1900. Holding companies (firms whose assets were the stock of other corporations) were a logical extension of the trusts. But the purpose of such devices was transparently anticompetitive, and they began to encounter difficulty in state and federal courts almost as soon as they appeared.

Mergers

Mergers might be another route to increase market power. A merger is the acquisition of one firm by another, a combination of two or more firms into one. The merger of previously competing firms must always reduce competition if it has any effect. If there had been only two firms in the market, such a merger would eliminate competition. Such mergers are unlikely to produce offsetting benefits through increased efficiency; the merger changes only the ownership of physical assets, not their productivity. Unless the acquired firm was badly managed, horizontal mergers will not reduce production costs. Indeed, many of the firms most eager to merge are likely to have production costs above the industry average.

Vertical mergers occur between firms that previously bought from or sold to each other. A paper mill, for example, might integrate backward by obtaining a pulpwood company or forward by buying a factory that uses its paper to make shopping bags. Both types of mergers increase firms' absolute size, but only horizontal mergers increase firms' size relative to their markets. Vertical mergers increase the *number* of markets in which the firm operates. A merger movement in American industry began in the 1880s and ended by 1905. Its changing features indicate the motives behind mergers and their effects on competition.

The first great wave of mergers occurred among firms producing long-established consumer goods. Typically, there had been many such firms in each industry, most serving local markets. Expanded output caused supply to rise faster than demand, and prices fell. Often, after the failure of less formal attempts at restricting competition, firms began to merge.

Standard Oil

Once the mergers were complete, the larger organizations sought improved operating efficiency through rationalization and the centralization of functions where economies of scale were available. Oil refining was consolidated by John D. Rockefeller and his associates into the Standard Oil Company, which by 1870 controlled 96 percent of all refining capacity in the United States. Contrary to popular belief, however, Standard Oil achieved this dominance through a series of purchases in which the owners of independent firms were often at least as eager to sell out as Standard Oil was to buy, rather than by cutthroat competition.

The assets of competing firms were worth more to Rockefeller as components of a monopoly than they were to their original owners as competing firms. Thus, Standard Oil's first move in an attempt to acquire an independent oil company was an offer to buy it at a price highly favorable from the owner's viewpoint. This was generally sufficient.[44] Rumors of cutthroat competitive tactics (or worse) were undoubtedly useful to Standard Oil, but there is little evidence that they were ever widely employed.

---

[44] J. McGee, "Predatory Price-Cutting: The Standard Oil (N.J.) Case," *Journal of Law and Economics* 137 (1958).

Once its control was established, Standard Oil improved its plants' operating efficiency. This was the primary basis of the firm's market power. Standard Oil was able to force railroads to grant it rebates on shipments of both its own oil and (very briefly) those of its competitors. Largely as a result of Rockefeller's cost-cutting efforts, the prices of refined oil products fell to one-seventh of their 1865 levels by 1884.[45] Once new sources of oil began to appear and refining techniques changed in response to new uses of petroleum, Standard Oil's monopoly eroded. Standard Oil was unusual in achieving virtually complete, if temporary, control over its industry through mergers. In most cases, the first merger wave resulted in oligopolistic market structures, in which three to six firms controlled a large part of the industry's total production.

Changes in the Merger Movement

According to Chandler, the characteristics of merger activity changed in the decade after 1895. The second wave of mergers took place among the producers of capital goods and newer types of consumer goods, particularly those for the urban market. While some horizontal mergers occurred as they had earlier, the emphasis was now on vertical mergers to protect sources of supply or access to final markets. Capital goods producers tended to integrate backward to protect their sources of inputs and crucial transportation links, while the producers of new consumer goods integrated forward, buying outlets to maintain their access to markets.[46]

Recently, this view has been challenged. According to Naomi Lamoreaux, horizontal mergers intended to produce monopoly or at least greater market power predominated in the post–1895 merger wave. Of 93 consolidations, 72 percent controlled at least 40 per-

cent of the product market, and nearly one-third obtained a market share of at least 70 percent.[47] Her study concluded that merger was especially prevalent in oligopolistic industries that had been growing rapidly before the depression of 1893, had high fixed costs, and had experienced traumatic price wars in that slump. Most also had a record of unsuccessful collusion prior to the merger activity.[48]

The Role of Financiers

Especially after 1897, a new motive for mergers appeared. Before then the desire for mergers had originated within the participating firms, but now financiers took an active role. Previously, financiers had dealt mainly in railroad and government securities, with little interest in industrial stocks and bonds. But railroad issues had compiled a dismal record in the depression of the early 1890s, and industrial stocks had fared better. Equally important from financiers' viewpoints, mergers often involved the issue of large volumes of additional securities and invariably required services on which fat commissions and fees could be obtained. Thus, financiers may have been more interested in the mergers themselves than in the firms that resulted from them. The high rate of failures among the firms so formed does little to dispel this view. Some mergers resulted in the issue of "watered stock," securities backed neither by tangible assets nor by justifiable hopes for increased monopoly profits. In most cases, however, it now appears that financiers aided but did not initiate such mergers: the motive forces were within the industries concerned.[49]

The Great Steel Consolidation. The financiers' ultimate triumph was the formation of the United States Steel Corporation in 1902. Com-

[45] S. Lebergott, *The Americans: An Economic Record* (New York: Norton, 1984), pp. 325–334.
[46] Chandler, "Big Business."

[47] Lamoreaux, *The Great Merger Movement*, p. 2.
[48] Ibid., p. 100.
[49] Ibid., pp. 112–115.

panies whose assets were valued at $700 million before the consolidation were combined into a single firm controlling well over half the steel-making capacity of the United States. The same assets now had a book value of $1.4 billion, reflecting their increased value because of reduced competition within the industry. The steel corporation fulfilled the financiers' hopes: it earned handsome profits even on the new asset valuations.

Central to the great steel consolidation had been the acquisition of Carnegie Steel Corporation. A ruthless competitor, Andrew Carnegie had used his firm's superior operating efficiency to undercut his rivals' prices. Carnegie scorned attempts at price fixing; if his representatives attended collusive meetings, they did so largely to learn the level of prices that Carnegie Steel would undercut.[50] The new United States Steel Corporation was formed with very different goals in mind: it was designed to reduce if not eliminate price competition in steel. Its prospects for success in this endeavor enhanced the value of its stock.

The Merger Era Ends

After 1905, merger activity greatly declined. Some mergers had failed outright or produced only disappointing profits, and the really promising merger opportunities had largely been acted on. Changes in technology and resource supply favored new firms, reducing the attractions of mergers still further. In view of the fact that potential entrants often had lower costs than the consolidated firms, there might be no effective barriers to entry. Lamoreaux found that in many cases high short-run profits from consolidation had by 1904 provoked successful entry into the industries where they occurred.[51] Economic growth was rapid after 1900; under

such conditions, there was little need to reduce output to generate higher profits.

The federal government did break up two large firms built by merger (Standard Oil and American Tobacco), and it used the Sherman Act to prevent a merger between two railroads (the *Northern Securities* case, 1904). However, legal pressures appear to have played a smaller role in the decline of mergers than did economics. Probably the most significant legal development affecting competition was the *Addystone Pipe* case (1899), in which the Supreme Court ruled that price fixing was illegal under any and all circumstances. The ruling made collusion between firms more difficult, and although it did not change the structure of existing industries, it provoked a greater degree of competition from the industrial economy. In at least one view, however, antitrust rulings favored vertically integrated firms by allowing barriers to entry stemming from intrafirm practices that were prohibited between independent firms.[52]

DID COMPETITION DECREASE?

There is no question but that in the 1870–1914 era many U.S. manufacturing and financial companies became larger than any business organizations the country had ever seen before. It is equally clear that the managers of many of these new large firms sought control over their markets. The results of these changes in size and (perhaps) in business leaders' intentions, however, are less certain.

Any introductory economics text states that monopoly produces less and charges higher prices than would competitive firms in similar circumstances. Except in the case of natural monopoly, the monopolist's gains come at the

---

[50] Hughes, *The Vital Few*, pp. 231, 238–239.
[51] Lamoreaux, *The Great Merger Movement*, Chap. 5.

[52] Ibid., p. 191.

expense of the economy in which it operates. However, even while the drive for monopolization was at its peak from 1865 to 1914, prices of manufactured goods and transport and financial services—the products of the sectors in which efforts to gain monopoly power were centered—fell in real terms, and their output rose much faster than aggregate economic growth.

Dynamic versus Static Monopoly

The results appear exactly opposed to the textbook prediction, but they may not refute it as decisively as a first reading would indicate. First, there is some question as to whether most firms actually gained market power or merely operated in new and larger markets. The size of individual firms undoubtedly increased, but it did so in an economy that was rapidly enlarging its aggregate dimensions. Firms grew, but so did the markets they served. It is the firm's size relative to the market that constitutes the basis of monopoly power, not absolute size.

Second, it is a serious mistake to think of the antebellum economy as perfectly competitive, or close to it, just because the average size of firms was small. Before 1865, most industrial firms served only local markets, and typically few if any close substitutes existed for the products of any one manufacturing company, except in the largest cities. In such circumstances individual sellers had very considerable market power. With the advent of regional or even national markets after the Civil War, the number of sellers actually competing in each local market may have risen even when the number of producers in the United States remained static or even declined, as it rarely did. Competition may well have increased despite the growth in firm size.[53]

Third, examination reveals that although many firms sought monopoly power, few attained it and even fewer managed to retain profitable monopoly positions for long.[54] Most industries retained a number of sellers; even the most concentrated markets were oligopolistic rather than monopolistic. In such markets, there may not have been any fewer sellers than in the more fragmented local markets of the antebellum era.

Finally, modern studies have shown the actual impact of monopoly power on the economy to be surprisingly small. The chief cause appears to be the diversity of the American economy: few people spend a large portion of their incomes on the products of any single industry or even any small number of industries. Table 12.1 indicates that this point had considerable validity even in 1910. No modern study has concluded that the cost exacted by the exercise of monopoly exceeds 6 percent of national income, and most conclude that the toll is considerably lower.[55]

A Dynamic Economy

Also, the textbook case against monopoly is static. It assumes that technology, demand for the product, and consumer alternatives do not change. The 1870–1914 economy in which the competitive or anticompetitive developments actually occurred was one of far greater change in all these factors than ever before. Nor was the macroeconomic climate favorable to the exercise of monopoly power. It is difficult to imagine less favorable circumstances for static monopoly than a falling general price level, rapid growth in both technology and the ag-

---

[53] Some authorities have little doubt that this was the case. See, for example, Lebergott, *The Americans*, pp. 310–316.

[54] Lamoreaux, *The Great Merger Movement*, p. 189.
[55] The maximum (6 percent) estimate is from D. Worcester, Jr., "New Estimates of the Welfare Loss to Monopoly, United States, 1956–1969," *Southern Economic Journal* (October 1973). See also D. Kamerschen, "An Estimate of the Welfare Loss for Monopoly in the American Economy," *Western Economic Journal* (December 1966). Since these estimates were made, competition has clearly increased within the American economy.

gregate economy, and a legal and social climate that favored the growth of new firms. The number of new corporations formed during the merger wave was more than ten times the number that disappeared through merger or acquisition.[56]

Consumers were not helpless in their struggles against large firms at this time. Their rising incomes gave them better alternatives, especially in regard to manufactured goods, than they had ever enjoyed before. Many of the new goods produced by large firms were objects of discretionary spending, not necessities. In these cases, attempts to exert monopoly power in sales of one good, even though no exact substitutes were available, would shift consumer demand to other goods meeting the same broad desires. Sellers of sporting goods (a broad category in itself) might find that their customers considered live entertainment, books, magazines, the local beer parlor, card games, and even gossip as substitutes. In sum, the historical data as well as economic reasoning provide little support for any claim that monopoly power seriously reduced the welfare of the typical citizen in this period. The balance of the evidence appears to indicate that competition grew rather than declined.

THE ROBBER BARONS

When business activity in the late nineteenth century is discussed, the names of those who founded and directed the great industrial firms, banks, and railroads invariably crop up. Many of these business leaders achieved wealth beyond the dreams of most Americans, and some were equally successful in spending the fortunes they had amassed. To at least one author, these men were robber barons—a title that has

endured despite the questionable evidence supporting it. In this view, the gains made by the robber barons came at the expense of the rest of the population. In addition, they owed far more to their lack of scruples than to conventional business ability.[57]

The Morals of the Gilded Age

Some of the tactics used in business at this time would not be credible in the most lurid television serial today. Fraud, bribery, forgery of securities, deliberate destruction of one's own firm for private gain, mob violence, arson, and even an occasional murder (in labor relations murder was not occasional) were all employed often enough so that even businessmen who did not use such methods had to learn to deal with those who did. The last battle involving artillery fought in New York was between two gangs of hired thugs contesting the ownership of the Susquehanna Railway.

The law was not an effective shield. The New York State legislature once publicly censured one of its members in a bribery case. In the opinion of his fellows, the legislator had sold his vote for too little, which might endanger the bribery fees charged by others. In many other states, standards of political morality were no better. Judges might decide cases in favor of whoever offered the largest bribe.

In general, the moral standards of the Gilded Age do not compare favorably with any other period, including our own.[58] The values of this era put considerably more stress on the accumulation of wealth than on the details of its generation. Neither law nor social usage imposed many restrictions on business activity, and some men did not bother to develop their own. The business world was a complete jungle,

---

[56] N. Rosenberg and R. Birdzell, *How the West Grew Rich: The Economic Transformation of the Industrial World* (New York: Basic Books, 1986), p. 286.

[57] M. Josephson, *The Robber Barons* (New York: Harcourt Brace Jovanovich, 1962 reprint).
[58] For a survey of political corruption in this period, see Cochran and Miller, *The Age of Enterprise*.

and those who succeeded often reflected the environment in which they operated.

The Robber Barons: An Assessment

It would be a serious error, however, to regard all successful business leaders of the period as a pack of thieves whose influence was entirely negative. They were hardly saints, and for some the preceding paragraphs constitute unduly generous praise, but their impact for the most part was beneficial. The economy in which their activities figured so prominently was the scene of rapid economic growth, most notably in manufacturing, finance, and transportation, which all grew faster than sectors not afflicted with such leaders. Output increased, quality of products improved, and real prices fell in these sectors in relation to the rest of the economy. Further, workers' real wages rose and their hours of labor decreased, indicating that by no means were all the gains restricted to the rich.

None of the foregoing should be interpreted as an argument that these developments were solely due to the efforts of business leaders or even reflected their primary intentions. But in the face of concentrated gains in the sectors where these men's activities were prominent, it is difficult to conclude that the great entrepreneurs' impact was wholly negative.

Ford, Morgan, and Carnegie

Many of the business leaders exhibited a curious combination of traits. Aside from his one truly better idea, Henry Ford contributed very little. He was a narrow, inflexible man whose passion for independence from outside sources of supply and inability to tolerate opposition nearly contributed as much to the ruin of his great firm as his vision of the automobile market had done to build it. In company with many other businessmen of his generation, Ford saw only one appropriate response to organized la-

bor—total opposition. J. P. Morgan's mathematical training may have reinforced his love of order, and competition is not an orderly process. Morgan's penchant for mergers and high returns on investment reduced competition in the industries in which he was active. But "Morganization" improved the operating efficiency of industry, financial markets, and railroads, reducing the instability that had plagued the latter two. Carnegie's record with organized labor—or that of his lieutenants—is brutal, but his operating methods, like Rockefeller's, made the product of his industry cheaper than ever before, and consumers gained a large share of the gains.

Even the enormous fortunes that some of these great entrepreneurs amassed must be viewed in light of their achievements. In many cases, they succeeded where it was plain the rewards for success would be great and entry was easy, but accomplishment extraordinarily difficult. In short, they did what no one else could.

Henry Villard, for example, raised $60 million to build the Northern Pacific Railway. For two years' work, Villard received a commission of $3 million. This sum would be equivalent to at least $20 million today, and was not subject to income taxes. But the railroad raised the incomes of those living in its operating area by many times the amount Villard received; and continued to do so every year. Furthermore, Villard was by no means the first to attempt to raise funds for the railroad—only the first to succeed. The point is not whether such men were worth every penny they received—that is really a moral, not an economic judgment—but that their contributions were both substantial and unique.[59] Some engaged in extensive philanthropy, but that pales in comparison to the contributions they made in giving America cheap steel, oil, and automobiles.

---

[59] Hughes, *The Vital Few,* is an excellent assessment of the careers and contributions of some of the business leaders of this period.

The Rogues' Gallery

Of course, some business leaders of this era can be charged with considerably more than perhaps being overpriced. The only legacy of men like Drew, Fisk, and Hyde was less perfect financial markets because investors (rightly) hesitated to venture their savings in markets where such men were free to hatch their schemes. Nevertheless, the business community was not composed solely or even largely of such types.

Since the income, wealth, health, and education of the average American all increased substantially while the business leaders were piling up their fortunes, perhaps the most sweeping charge that can be levied against them with any validity is that welfare might have improved even more without them. Even if some of them were thieves, however, they tended to rob each other; the rich attract such attention more than the poor because the costs per dollar stolen are lower. Few Americans of average means had funds invested in corporate securities at this time. We must also judge such men, if we can, against the background of their era, not ours, and in light of its ideals and standards. Finally, the introduction of new goods, processes, and applications did much to raise the incomes of all Americans, and it was here that the great entrepreneurs made their contributions. They may have gained much, but they also took enormous risks that daunted many others. Their vision made the new ideas work.

SELECTED REFERENCES

Chandler, A., Jr., *Strategy and Structure: Chapters in the History of American Industrial Enterprise*. Cambridge, Mass.: Harvard University Press, 1962.

————. *The Visible Hand: The Managerial Revolution in American Business*. Cambridge, Mass.: Harvard University Press, 1977.

Cochran, T. *200 Years of American Business*. New York: Basic Books, 1977.

Cochran, T., and W. Miller. *The Age of Enterprise: A Social History of Industrial America*. New York: Harper and Row, 1968.

Davis, L., et al. *American Economic Growth: An Economist's History of the United States*. New York: Harper and Row, 1972

Fishlow, A. *American Railroads and the Transformation of the American Economy*. Cambridge, Mass.: Harvard University Press, 1965.

Fogel, R. *Railroads and Economic Growth: Essays in Economic History*. Baltimore: Johns Hopkins University Press, 1964.

————. *The Union Pacific Railroad: A Case in Premature Enterprise*. Baltimore: AMS Press, 1960.

Hounshell, J. *From the American System to Mass Production, 1800–1936: The Development of Manufacturing Technology in the United States*. Baltimore: Johns Hopkins University Press, 1984.

Hughes, J. *The Vital Few: American Economic Progress and Its Protagonists*. Cambridge, England: Cambridge University Press, 1973.

Josephson, M. *The Robber Barons*. New York: Harcourt Brace Jovanovich, 1962 (reprint).

Lamoreaux, N. *The Great Merger Movement in American Business, 1895–1904*. Cambridge, England: Cambridge University Press, 1985.

Nelson, R. *Merger Movements in American Industry*. Princeton, N.J.: Princeton University Press, 1959.

Rosenberg, N. *Technology and American Economic Growth*. New York: Harper and Row, 1972.

Rosenberg, N., and R. Birdzell. *How the West Grew Rich: The Economic Transformation of the Industrial World*. New York, Basic Books, 1986.

Scherer, F. *Industrial Market Structure and Economic Performance*. Chicago: Rand McNally, 1970.

Temin, P. *Iron and Steel in Nineteenth-Century America: An Economic Inquiry*. Cambridge, Mass.: M.I.T. Press, 1964.

U.S. Department of Commerce, Bureau of the Census. *Historical Statistics of the United States: Colonial Times to 1970*. 2 vols. Washington, D.C.: Government Printing Office, 1975.

Vatter, H. *The Drive to Industrial Maturity: The U.S. Economy, 1860–1914*. Westport, Conn.: Greenwood, 1975.

CHAPTER

13

MONEY, BANKS, AND FINANCIAL INSTITUTIONS, 1865–1920

The close of the Civil War found the United States with a monetary situation and financial institutions very different from those with which it had entered the conflict. The cost of the war had forced the Union government to borrow and to print money. In turn, the expanded money supply had caused inflation, abandonment of the gold standard, and changes in financial institutions. For at least half this period, financial and monetary developments were influenced by the legacy of the Civil War. The long-term result was a series of remarkable changes: by 1920 the country would have a new central bank, a new currency, and a vastly expanded role for financial intermediaries.

WAR-INDUCED CHANGES

Two new types of paper currency were in circulation in 1865, and state bank notes, the previous (if heterogeneous) medium, were rapidly being withdrawn. Both developments stemmed from war-induced changes in monetary institutions. Internationally, the United States was no longer on the gold standard. Since paper currency no longer exchanged for gold at fixed rates, it no longer held a fixed value in relation to foreign currencies either. The value of the dollar in terms of foreign currency was determined by supply and demand; that is, by the quantity of dollars furnished to sellers of U.S. imports versus the amount of foreign currencies generated by U.S. exports. Thus, the exchange rate of the dollar for foreign currencies was determined by international trade and investment flows and relative price level changes within nations, rather than by fixed gold prices.

A new type of commercial bank had also appeared. Banks could now receive charters either from state governments, as formerly, or from the federal government—a privilege hitherto accorded only to the two Banks of the United States. With the appearance of the national banks came changes in banks' ability to issue paper currency, which eventually produced important changes in the composition of the nation's money supply.

The Greenback Controversy

The Civil War had not been funded on a pay-as-you-go basis. The Union government had sold bonds, but revenues from this source had become increasingly uncertain in the early years of the war, and some opposed the government's dependence on supersalesman Jay Cooke for bond sales. After 1862, the federal government had begun to print and issue a new form of paper currency officially called United States notes. The public termed these notes "greenbacks" (one side of the notes was green). About $414 million in greenbacks was in circulation in 1865. This amount was slightly greater than the entire currency circulation (including gold) in 1860, and about two-thirds of the entire money supply for the last prewar year.[1] Greenbacks were "fiat money"; an act of Congress had declared them legal payment for debts, but they were not legally redeemable for their face value in specie. In effect, they were money because the law said they were. Greenbacks did exchange at face value for bank money (state bank notes and deposits).

As explained in Chapter 10, real output could not increase at a pace even remotely similar to the rate at which the money supply rose during the Civil War, and consequently inflation approximately doubled the overall price level. Since the supply of greenbacks had increased so rapidly, their purchasing power and

that of other forms of inconvertible paper money (banks suspended payment during the war) declined.

Suspension of the Gold Standard

The supply of gold coins had not increased, and gold retained its value in terms of foreign currency and thus of foreign goods. The owners of gold could still use it to buy foreign goods at stable prices, even though the same goods would cost far more in U.S. paper currency. Consequently, gold could be obtained for greenbacks only by paying a premium. No longer could an ounce of gold or its equivalent in coins be purchased for $20.67 in standard paper currency, as it could before the war. The price of gold varied with the fortunes of the Union army and the trade balance. At one time the greenback price of gold reached nearly $60 an ounce—another way of saying that $1 in greenbacks exchanged for approximately 35¢ in gold at prewar prices. In California, gold was the normal medium of exchange, and greenbacks circulated there at discounted face value. Elsewhere, gold disappeared from normal circulation within the United States.

Since the major trading partners of the United States had not experienced similar domestic inflation, the high prices here did not allow immediate postwar resumption of free convertibility of paper currency into gold at $20.67 per ounce, the antebellum price. Had it been attempted, there would have been swarms of buyers for gold and no sellers, because gold would be nearly the only thing whose price had not risen since 1860. Far more imported goods could be obtained for an ounce of gold than for $20.67 in inflated paper currency. Had resumption been attempted, the U.S. Mint soon would have run out of gold to sell at such a bargain price. Such a policy would have reduced the prices of foreign goods to Americans by over 40 percent, an opportunity too good to pass up. Before resumption at prewar rates could succeed, the U.S. internal price level had to be reduced.

---

[1] U.S. Department of Commerce, Bureau of the Census, *Historical Statistics of the United States: Colonial Times to 1970*, 2 vols. (Washington, D.C.: Government Printing Office, 1975), 2:993, 1020.

Greenbacks had clearly been a major cause of the wartime inflation that in turn prevented the convertibility of paper money and resumption of the gold standard at prewar rates. Stable convertibility could have been regained in several ways. The simplest, from a modern perspective, would have been to ratify the existing situation by increasing the official dollar price of gold to market levels. However, this was politically impossible in the nineteenth century: it would have been considered a violation of previous government commitments.

If devaluation was impossible, the practical alternatives were limited to measures that either reduced the supply of money in relation to goods or raised the supply of goods in relation to money. Either approach would reduce prices within the United States. As long as American citizens were free to use gold in international transactions, there was no way to raise the supply of gold in the United States alone. Whether it was mined in California or obtained through international trade, gold would flow out of the country as long as its purchasing power was greater overseas. If gold had exchanged at $20.67 per ounce for greenbacks whose purchasing power was no greater than in the immediate postwar period, this would have been the case.

Attempts at Deflation

Congress first attempted to reduce the number of greenbacks in circulation. The reasoning was straightforward: as the supply of paper money dwindled, it would become scarcer in relation to other goods and services and its purchasing power would rise. As this process continued, the premium on gold would eventually disappear.

Deflation was already under way in 1865; a slightly reduced supply of greenbacks had to cover transactions in the South as it came back under Union control. Thus, a smaller amount of money had to cover a larger volume of transactions, and the price of money in terms of goods rose. But the cost of deflation was high.

The government ran surpluses in the immediate postwar years; it received more in taxes than it paid out for current expenditures. It was able to reduce the quantity of greenbacks in circulation to $356 million by mid–1868. At the same time it also retired several other types of government currency totaling about $208 million.[2] The result was deflation, but also a drop in the level of economic activity, accompanied by unemployment and general economic distress. As the results of the greenback retirement program became clear, Congress limited the rate of greenback withdrawal in 1866 and stopped it entirely in 1868. The lesson was not forgotten: in a severe depression in 1873–1874, Congress even raised the legal limit on the number of greenbacks in circulation.

Resumption of the Gold Standard

Congressional reluctance to reduce the volume of greenbacks in circulation left only one policy available. The expansion rate of the money supply was limited to less than that of real economic growth, so that the supply of goods and services rose faster than that of money, and prices fell. This approach took time, but it was ultimately successful. It may, however, have been overdone.

In 1875 a lame-duck Republican Congress, fearing what the incoming Democrats might do, passed a law committing the Treasury to redeem greenbacks at par in specie (meaning gold) on demand not later than the first day of 1879. Over the interval between passage of the Resumption Act and its scheduled implementation, the supply of high-powered money (currency and commercial bank reserves, the basis on which the supply of bank money could be increased) did not rise. The money supply in all its forms (bank money, government money,

[2] J. Kindahl, "Economic Factors in Specie Resumption: The United States, 1865–1879," *Journal of Economic History* (February 1961).

and gold) rose only slightly.[3] Prices fell, but at a real cost. In 1879 the goal was achieved: gold and greenbacks exchanged at par. There was a sharp recession as the policy was instituted, but real growth in the later 1870s was rapid despite the deflation. By selling bonds for gold, the government was able to accumulate a gold reserve to satisfy those who might wish to test greenbacks' convertibility, but after redemption became possible the reserve was not needed under normal circumstances.[4] The United States was effectively back on the gold standard.

■ This cartoon illustrates some of the fierce objections to the use of greenbacks.
Source: The Granger Collection, New York.

National Banks and Notes

In 1863 and 1864, Congress had passed the National Banking Acts. While the real purpose of this legislation was to aid the wartime sale of government bonds, the acts contained provisions influential long after 1865. Banks had been offered the privilege of federal charters and the right to issue a new type of bank note, the national bank notes, but both were contingent on compliance with much more stringent federal regulations than most states imposed. Capital and reserve requirements stricter than those of most states reduced banks' prospective profits, so the 1863 act found few banks willing to accept the new charters.

The total amount of national bank notes in circulation was to be restricted to $300 million, apportioned among the states on the basis of population. Within the states, banks were required to deposit government bonds equal to one-third of their capital with the comptroller of the currency, a new federal officer. In return, the banks received national bank notes. No bank's note issue was to exceed 90 percent of the par value of the government bonds it had deposited with the Treasury. Since the 1863 legislation resulted in few charter applications and little increase in bond sales, Congress reduced banks' alternatives. In 1865 the tax imposed on circulating state bank notes was quintupled, to 10 percent. At this rate, it was no longer profitable for banks to make loans in currency.

In the short run, this policy had the desired effect: the number of banks converting to national charters rose sharply (see Table 13.1). In less than a year, the majority of all banks were operating under federal charters. In the long run, however, banks emphasized an alternative to currency loans: they extended their own credit, in the form of checking accounts, instead. Once banks saw this opportunity, the stricter lending regulations, reserve requirements, and inspection standards of national banks encouraged the renewed growth of state banks. Even so, national banks remained somewhat larger on average than state banks.

[3] U.S. Department of Commerce, *Historical Statistics*, vol. 2, p. 993.
[4] Kindahl, "Economic Factors."

Table 13.1 U.S. Commercial Banks and Assets, 1860–1920

Date	State Banks	Total Assets (Millions)	National Banks	Total Assets (Millions)
1860	1,562	$1,000	—	—
1865	349	231	1,294	$1,127
1870	325	215	1,612	1,566
1875	586	395	2,076	1,913
1880	650	482	2.076	2,036
1885	1,015	802	2,689	2,422
1890	3,594	1,539	3,484	3,062
1895	5,086	2,085	3,715	3,471
1900	8,696	4,115	3,731	4,944
1905	12,488	7,217	5,664	7,325
1910	17,376	9,432	7,138	9,892
1915	19,793	12,316	7,597	11,790
1920	22,267	24,242	8,024	23,267

Source: U.S. Department of Commerce, Bureau of the Census, *Historical Statistics of the United States: Colonial Times to 1970,* 2 vols. (Washington, D.C.: Government Printing Office, 1975), 2:1025–1031. The series on state banks is not complete.

A New Currency

National bank notes and greenbacks replaced state bank notes as the country's circulating currency. They were an improvement over their predecessors. Such notes were uniform currency that did not depreciate with distance from the bank of issue, making long-distance transactions and regional specialization easier. The bargaining over the value of currency in "standard" money involved with the old heterogeneous state bank note issues ended. However, as Chapter 8 indicated, this problem had been much less significant than persons accustomed to modern institutions might imagine.

The supply of the new paper currencies was fixed. As previously noted, the volume of greenbacks in circulation was held constant or reduced, with one minor exception in 1874, and the supply of national bank notes was originally fixed at not over $300 million. Although this ceiling was removed in 1875, the actual supply of national bank notes might not even reach the original legal maximum. The amount in circulation depended on Treasury policy and the loan prospects of national banks. To obtain national bank notes, the banks had to buy government bonds and deposit them with the Treasury. As profit-seeking institutions, they would not do so unless the rate of return on federal bonds and on loans made with the currency so obtained at least equalled the rate obtainable on other types of investments, especially loans.

The Role of Treasury Policy. Treasury policy was important because it influenced the prices of outstanding bonds and hence the rate of interest that could be obtained by purchasing them. If bond prices rose, their interest yield fell; the fixed amount of interest payable would be a smaller percentage of their price. If bond prices fell, the rate of return rose.

Through much of this period, the government ran surpluses and used the proceeds to

■ By 1865 state bank notes were replaced by national bank notes and greenbacks.

Source: Records of the Public Buildings Service: National Archives.

retire Civil War debt. This reduced the supply of bonds, and consequently their prices rose. As Table 13.2 indicates, the volume of national bank notes in circulation rose through the early 1870s, and again in the early 1880s, attaining a nineteenth-century peak of $352 million in 1882, after which it fell to less than half that amount by the early 1890s. Thereafter the volume of national bank notes began an increase that ended only after they were replaced by federal reserve notes after 1915. The national bank notes had an importance far beyond their value as currency: they were a major component of state banks' reserves, and so were an important factor in the growth of the money supply, since banks in aggregate could increase the amount of checking accounts they held by a multiple of their reserves.

As the Civil War experience had shown, a rate of monetary growth that exceeds the rate of real output, at least for any extended period, will cause inflation unless the demand for money (to hold rather than to spend) also rises. Extreme inflation, as the Confederacy discov-

ered, can result in a collapse of the exchange system, which is built on money as a medium of exchange. Too slow a rate of monetary increase will reduce the pace of real economic growth unless prices are flexible downwards (as they were at this time). Even with flexible prices, however, sudden large changes in the money supply or its rate of change can outpace the ability of prices to respond and produce unwelcome short-run effects. A steep decline in the money supply, or even in its rate of growth, is likely to cause a decline in real output and consequently in employment as a first effect. An important study of this era concluded that all major declines in economic activity in the period were associated with prior declines in either the money stock or its rate of growth.[5]

The composition of the money supply, as well as its amount, changed over this period. The data reveal that the proportion of "bank money," or deposits, rose from about 52 percent of the total money supply in 1867 to 67 percent in 1900, 78 percent in 1915, and 79 percent in 1920. The aggregate supply of money rose at a considerably faster long-term rate than real output over the entire period. The pace was uneven, however, with aggregate monetary growth considerably more rapid after 1897 than before. A particularly rapid increase occurred during World War I, once again because of the demands of wartime finance. Growth was very slow in the mid-1870s and early 1890s, and prices fell sharply in both periods.[6]

The equation of exchange ($MV = PQ$) indicates that increases in the money supply that exceed those of real output must produce inflation. There are physical limits to the available stocks of goods and the ability to increase them at any given time, and velocity tends to be quite stable, varying only in response to private attitudes toward holding money and changes in

[5] M. Friedman and A. Schwartz, *A Monetary History of the United States, 1867–1960* (Princeton, N.J.: Princeton University Press, 1963).

[6] Ibid., pp. 91–92.

Table 13.2   U.S. Money Stock, 1867–1920 (in Billions)

Date	M2 (Currency plus Deposits)	Monetary Gold	Silver*	Greenbacks	National Bank Notes	Federal Reserve Notes
1867	$1.28	—	$.01	$.319	$.287	
1870	1.35	$.23	.01	.325	.289	
1875	1.72	.09	.02	.350	.341	
1880	2.03	.33	.07	.328	.327	
1885	2.87	.54	.184	.331	.309	
1890	3.92	.64	.408	.335	.182	
1895	4.43	.53	.549	.319	.207	
1900	6.60	.93	.626	.318	.300	
1905	10.24	1.24	.639	.332	.480	
1910	13.34	1.66	.690	.335	.684	
1915	17.59	2.00	.689	.310	.782	$ .07
1920	34.80	2.88	.425	.278	.690	3.064

*Includes silver certificates, treasury notes of 1890, and all silver coinage.

Source: U.S. Department of Commerce, Bureau of the Census, *Historical Statistics of the United States: Colonial Times to 1970*, 2 vols. (Washington, D.C.: Government Printing Office, 1975), 2:992–995.

monetary institutions. However, both the latter variables did change.

Despite increases in the money supply, prices fell from 1865 to 1896, with only one short exception in the 1880s. Velocity must have fallen to produce these results, and it did, to only about 42 percent of its 1869 value by 1915.[7] This decrease in the velocity with which money circulated more than offset increases in the money supply from 1879 through the early 1890s. The decline in velocity appears to have resulted from the growing proportion of bank money in the aggregate money supply. Bank deposits earned interest and thus were likely to be spent more slowly than currency or coin. The public was also increasingly confident that prices would continue to decline in the period before 1896. These factors reduced the costs of holding money and contributed to the decline in velocity. After 1896, faster money supply growth overcame the decline in velocity,

[7] Ibid., p. 774.

and mild inflation replaced the long post–Civil War deflation.

Gold and the Gold Standard

The achievement of convertibility between paper currency and gold at prewar rates in 1879 did not end the controversy over gold's role in the American monetary system. Even so, after that date the United States was on a de facto gold standard. But the process of attaining and maintaining it was neither smooth nor free of conflict.

Defining the U.S. dollar as legally equivalent to a stated quantity of gold and enforcing this standard through gold purchases or sales at the mint had both international and domestic consequences. Internationally, it defined the value of the dollar in relation to foreign currencies whose gold content was also fixed by law. At this time an American dollar was equivalent to about five French francs, four German marks, or slightly more than one-fifth of a British pound.

In all the countries that subscribed to the gold standard, gold constituted a major component of commercial banks' reserves. If prices rose in one country, foreign goods would become relatively cheaper in terms of gold because it was one commodity whose price would not have risen: currency convertibility was guaranteed. At the same time, foreigners would find goods from the country experiencing inflation more expensive since their currencies would buy only the same amount of foreign money, and in its native land, that money bought fewer goods. Consequently, gold would flow out of the high-price country to finance the difference between increased imports and decreased exports. As banks' reserves dwindled, they would react by reducing their loans and tightening up the money supply. The reduction in the money supply would lower prices in countries suffering gold outflows, while inflows of gold in other nations would add to their banks' reserves, money supplies, and price levels.

Results of the International Gold Standard

As long as each nation "played the game" by changing its money supply in response to gold movements, the gold standard more or less automatically kept all participant nations' prices in line with each other. Notice that this does not ensure an absence of inflation or deflation, merely that all nations will be similarly affected by changes in the supply of gold. After 1895, the world's supply of gold began to increase rapidly because of new mining discoveries in the Yukon, Alaska, and South Africa and because of more efficient mining and smelting methods. These additions to the gold stock were a major cause of the inflation that occurred after 1896.

The process outlined above was complicated to some extent by international investment flows. During most of the nineteenth century, Europeans loaned funds to the United States because interest rates were higher in this country. This allowed a somewhat higher American price level than would otherwise have been possible. Essentially, however, the system operated as described. The United States was able to accumulate a gold stock to cover temporary outflows because after 1874 it consistently sold more to foreigners than it purchased abroad, and because of foreign (largely British) investment in the United States.

Internally, the fact that bank money was convertible into gold limited banks' ability to expand the money supply. Banks had to keep a certain fraction of their assets in gold to meet demands for conversion. Consequently, the degree to which the banking system could expand its loans was limited by the amount of gold it held. If people's confidence in banks diminished, they were free to demand conversion of bank money into specie. In addition, there was likely to be a demand for gold to finance foreign transactions. Banks defended themselves against the possibility of large-scale demands for conversion by trying to ensure that they could meet routine demands with some margin of safety. In keeping their loans proportional to their reserves, banks restricted increases in the money supply.

The 1890s Gold Standard Crisis

In the early 1890s the gold standard was threatened in the United States. Government policy since 1879 had been to redeem all paper money, including that issued as a result of silver purchases, in gold if the presenter requested it. Such demands increased as a result of the concern generated by the free silver movement (the political demand for unlimited coinage of all silver brought to the mint), and the Treasury's gold stock dwindled. Worse, silver was overpriced at the mint, and it was more profitable to sell silver to the government than in the metals market. A combination of lower tariff revenues and increased government expenditures forced the reissue of silver certificates as fast as they were redeemed. This meant that the certificates would shortly be presented for payment in gold again.

As though this were not enough, widespread loss of confidence in banks and bank money occurred, especially in the West, adding further to the demand for gold. The more likely the suspension of free convertibility, a political victory for the free silver forces, or both appeared, the worse the situation became. The depression of the early 1890s made matters even worse. Finally, with the help of J.P. Morgan, the government was able to sell bonds for gold and build up its reserves.[8] Some of the legislation that had generated the increased supplies of government-issued paper currency (the Sherman Silver Purchase Act of 1890) was repealed, and with the end of the depression, the threat to the gold standard was over.

In 1900, Congress passed the Gold Standard Act, placing the United States on a full monometallic gold standard in law as well as in fact. The dollar was defined solely in terms of gold, and silver's monetary role was ended. But in the two previous decades the issue of silver's monetary role had been one of America's greatest political controversies.

Silver and the Money Supply

Even before the Civil War the legal definition of the dollar in terms of both silver and gold had caused difficulties. Whenever the official mint ratio at which the government offered to exchange the two metals differed from the bullion market rates, the mint was deluged with sellers of the metal it overvalued while the metal it undervalued disappeared from circulation (see Chapter 8). In the 1850s, the market ratio of silver to gold had been less than the official 16 to 1 rate, and consequently silver coins had almost completely disappeared from circula-

■ The Republicans passed the Gold Standard Act in 1900 despite the objections of silver supporters.
Source: Library of Congress.

tion. As expensive money, silver was hoarded or used for nonmonetary purposes where its value was greater than as coin.

Civil War inflation drove the price of silver in even subsidiary (less than $1 denomination) coins above their face values, and the few silver coins still in circulation disappeared. They were replaced by fractional paper currency or special ungummed postage stamps. In 1873, when Congress voted to resume coinage of silver, the mint was instructed to buy only the amounts required to coin dimes, quarters, and half-dollars. Silver dollars had not been in circulation since 1836, and they were not included in the new coinage. At the time the new law went almost unnoticed, because silver was still slightly undervalued at the mint. Yet in a few years the coinage act was being denounced as "the crime of '73."

The Silver Glut
This sudden reversal of attitudes resulted from events in both Europe and the American West. Many European countries abandoned bimetallic or silver standards after 1870 and released

---

[8] R. Robertson, *History of the American Economy,* 3d ed. (New York: Harcourt Brace Jovanovich, 1973), p. 422.

large stocks of silver from their bullion reserves. At the same time, silver production in the United States had begun to soar. The famous Comstock Lode in Nevada contained huge amounts of silver but relatively little gold, and it was only one of a number of such "strikes." Additional silver discoveries were made in Idaho, Montana, and Colorado. Prior to 1870 the United States had mined at most ten million ounces of silver in any single year. But by 1878 that figure had tripled, and it doubled again by 1892. Gold production declined over the same period.[9] Silver prices began to fall after 1875, and they plummeted in the early 1890s. In 1875, silver's market value relative to gold was equal to the mint ratio of 16 to 1. It continued to decline, reaching 33 to 1 in 1894.[10]

Silver producers responded to their product's declining price by attempting to sell to the one buyer whose price had not fallen, the United States Mint. But the mint's response to the flood of silver infuriated would-be sellers. The mint bought only the amounts of silver actually needed for coinage, an amount far short of those silver producers wished to sell. The official price remained at 16 to 1 relative to gold—but at that price the Treasury was not buying.

The Free Silver Movement

As silver prices in the metals markets declined still further, agitation for government help for the silver interests increased. From 1876 on, a growing number of bills providing for increased silver purchases were introduced in Congress. These were clear examples of "rent seeking": the silver producers were requesting that the government, and through it the taxpayers, increase their incomes above those obtainable through the sale of their output in the marketplace. The western miners' greatest strength was in the Senate, where their states'

sparse populations did not determine representation. When farmers, greenbackers, and labor began to believe additional silver coinage would meet their demands for an expanded money supply and higher prices, the silver forces gained strength in the House as well. Their ranks included articulate spokesmen such as Congressman Richard "Silver Dick" Bland of Missouri.

All these groups recognized that if the government purchased unlimited quantities of silver at 16 to 1 versus gold, large amounts of silver would be brought to the mint. The result would be an end to deflation as the money supply increased, as well as an increase in silver prices. Yet the results desired by free silver's advocates might not have occurred even had their policies been followed. Inflation lowers debt burdens only if it is unanticipated, so that the interest rates on borrowed money do not include an allowance for its decline in purchasing power. If an individual borrows $100 for one year at 5 percent interest and prices are stable, the $105 that must be repaid at the end of the year gives creditors $5 in compensation for the borrower's use of their money over that period, plus a return of the same purchasing power loaned. If prices rise by 10

■ As a result of gold and silver discoveries, eager miners quickly established towns but often just as quickly abandoned them.
Source: Helena, Montana, 1865. Montana Historical Society.

[9] U.S. Department of Commerce, *Historical Statistics,* vol. 1, p. 606.
[10] Ibid.

percent over this year, and lenders do not anticipate this inflation, the $105 that borrowers return in 12 months will buy about 5 percent less than the $100 original loan principal. Under such circumstances, debtors gain, because they return less purchasing power than they borrowed. If the inflation is correctly anticipated, however, interest rates will rise to compensate lenders for the deterioration in money's value as well as their loss of the use of their funds while they are loaned out.

Since the history of nineteenth-century America provides abundant evidence that if anything lenders overestimated the inflationary potential of free silver, it appears doubtful that borrowers would have gained from loans made after the passage of a free silver bill. Only those obligated to repay loans taken out before the passage (or anticipation) of such a bill would have gained. In sum, any gains to debtors from free silver were likely to be temporary.

Inflation raises the prices of all goods and services, not merely farm products and labor. For farmers and laborers to gain from inflation, the price of their products would have had to rise more than the general rate of increase. Whether this would have occurred depends on relative supply elasticities, which were generally high for farm products before 1900. Moreover, an increase in U.S. farm product prices would reduce their markets abroad. The large-scale immigration of the period indicates substantial response to price changes in the labor market also. Nevertheless, it is true that industrial output was rising faster than either labor inputs or prices; inflation might have had the desired effects.

The Silver Purchase Acts

The silver advocates never achieved the "free and unlimited coinage of silver at 16 to 1" that they sought, but they had some partial successes. In 1878, the Bland-Allison Act required the Treasury to purchase between $2 million and $4 million worth of silver per month. Though the Treasury accumulated $380 mil-

■ Silver dollars diminished in popularity due to the difficulty in circulating them outside the mining states.
Source: From *The Picture Reference File,* Volume 1. (New York: Hart Publishing Company, Inc., 1976). p. 99.

lion of silver under this legislation, silver prices continued to fall. Most secretaries of the Treasury limited their purchases to the minimum required by law. Also, it proved difficult to circulate silver dollars since most people disliked their bulk and weight. After 1886, the Treasury was allowed to issue silver certificates—paper currency backed 100 percent by silver—instead of the coins popular only in the West.

As the 1880s ended, deflation had not ceased (see Table 13.3). When western senators found themselves holding the balance of power in a key vote on the new McKinley Tariff, legislation very important to Senate Republicans, they seized their opportunity. In return for their support on the tariff, the silver forces were able to exact approval of the Sherman Silver Purchase Act of 1890, which provided for the monthly purchase of 4.5 million ounces of silver by the Treasury at the going price. These purchases were to be made with yet another form of currency, treasury notes of 1890, which were to be redeemable in either gold or silver.[11]

The new legislation disappointed both its boosters and its opponents. No sooner had it been passed than silver prices began another sharp decline, which reduced the value of Treas-

---

[11] Robertson, *History of the American Economy*, p. 422.

Table 13.3 Price Indices, 1860–1920 (All Items)

Date	Wholesale Price Index* (1910–14 = 100)	Consumer Price Index (1967 = 100)
1860	93	27
1865	185	46
1870	135	38
1875	118	33
1880	100	29
1885	85	27
1890	82	27
1890	56.2 (1926 = 100)	25
1895	48.8	—
1896	46.5	25
1900	56.1	25
1905	60.1	27
1910	70.4	28
1915	69.5	30.4
1920	154.4	60.0

*Warren-Peason Index to 1890, Bureau of Labor Statistics, 1890–1920
Source: U.S. Department of Commerce, Bureau of the Census, *Historical Statistics of the United States: Colonial Times to 1970*, 2 vols. (Washington, D.C.: Government Printing Office, 1975), 1:200, 201, 211.

ury purchases to only about one-third more than under the Bland-Allison Act. The overall decline in prices continued. Proponents of "sound money" noted the increasing doubts about U.S. ability to maintain the gold standard, and the sudden gold outflows that seemed directly related to political developments. They argued that these declines in monetary reserves produced severe economic distress. The mid-1890s were indeed a period of severe depression.

The two silver-purchase acts combined resulted in the addition of over $500 million to the U.S. money supply. But the goal of free silver was never achieved. In 1892 the Senate passed a bill mandating unlimited silver coinage at 16 to 1, but the House refused to approve it.

The Triumph of the Gold Standard

The election of 1896 marked the high tide of free silver sentiment. The Democrats formed an alliance with the People's party, or Populists, and the party platform advocated the free coinage of silver at 16 to 1.[12] The campaign can be viewed as a contest between the whole spectrum of values held by the small towns and rural areas and those of the large cities and industry, but these issues tended to be swamped by that of free silver. William Jennings Bryan, the Democratic nominee, made his famous "Cross of Gold" speech denouncing the deflation caused by the gold standard in accepting the party's nomination. Even the Republicans felt compelled to propose a world conference on the adoption of bimetallic money in their platform. In an election that produced all the political fervor—and excesses—of a crusade (some eastern workers were informed that if Bryan won, they need not appear for work after the election because their jobs would no longer exist), William McKinley, the champion of sound money and the gold standard, defeated

[12] Friedman and Schwartz, *A Monetary History*, p. 110.

Bryan. The "Boy Orator of the Platte" lost the midwestern agricultural states as well as the East; he carried no state outside the traditionally Democratic South, the Great Plains, and the mining states.

Ironically, the cause for which Bryan campaigned was already becoming a reality, but through the mechanism of cheap gold rather than silver. Rich new gold discoveries and the new cyanide process, which greatly increased the amount of metal recovered from a given quantity of ore, poured a stream of gold into the world's coffers. The long deflation ended in 1896. As gold stocks and financial institutions for expanding the money supply based on such reserves grew, the rate of growth of the money supply increased. Moderate inflation, a little over 2 percent annually, replaced deflation.

PRICES AND ECONOMIC STABILITY

From 1860 to 1910 the American economy experienced deflation, inflation, and a boom-and-bust business cycle (see Table 13.4, page 361). The growth of real output, unemployment rates, and price changes all varied considerably. Prices, for example, fell sharply just after the Civil War, in the later 1870s, and again from 1890 to 1896 (see Table 13.3). They rose in 1879–1882 and again after 1896, but the latter inflation, though prolonged, was modest by modern standards. Similar price trends occurred throughout the developed world at this time.

In periods of recession or depression, unemployment among manufacturing workers and other urban employees could be high—from 8 to 13 percent in the mid-1880s and up to 18 percent in 1894.[13] The 1890s in particular were

an era of great distress and substantial labor unrest. It must be remembered that the impact of unemployment on those out of work was far worse in the nineteenth century than it is today. Not only was there virtually no public assistance for the unemployed, but the labor force was also comprised of adult heads of families to a far greater extent than today, when many families contain more than one wage earner and the proportion of single individuals in the labor force is much higher. Even though the long-term trends in output, employment, incomes, and well-being were strongly upward, the path was hardly smooth, and increases in welfare were interrupted by periods of great hardship for some workers.

The Real Effects of Money Supply Changes

In their monumental study, Milton Friedman and Anna J. Schwartz found a close relationship between aggregate economic activity and changes in the money supply.[14] More particularly, they tracked changes in the supply of "high-powered" money in relation to changes in economic activity.

When gold exports or Treasury retirements of currency or the bonds that backed national bank notes occurred, the money supply either fell or grew more slowly. Expansion of these items raised the money supply. To some extent, changes in velocity tended to offset the effects of monetary expansion, because the long-run trend in velocity was down: each dollar did less work (was spent less often) as time passed. At least over time, flexible prices offset declines in the money supply, allowing increases in real output even in periods of substantial deflation such as the late 1870s. Nevertheless, sharp declines in high-powered

[13] R. Fogel and S. Engerman, eds., *The Reinterpretation of American Economic History* (New York: Harper and Row, 1971), pp. 79–80.

[14] Friedman and Schwartz, *A Monetary History*.

money were associated with decreases in real output or its rate of growth.

Only after 1896 were trends in the growth of high-powered money, the ratio of bank reserves to bank money, and velocity sufficient to produce a sustained increase in price levels. Prior to that time, declines in velocity were more than enough to offset monetary growth, which was slightly higher than that of real output.[15] After 1896, a larger portion of the money supply was bank money, which turns over more slowly than hand-to-hand currency. The decline in velocity was also influenced by rising income levels. At that time people increased their money holdings more than in proportion to increases in income.

INSTITUTIONS AND THEIR EFFECTS ON STABILITY

Although the United States lacked a central bank until the very end of this period, the country was not entirely bereft of institutions with some stabilizing effects on monetary affairs. If existing laws had been interpreted literally, the actions of the United States Treasury would have made matters worse. The laws required payment of customs duties, the government's chief source of revenue, in gold. At least initially, the government was forbidden to deposit these proceeds in commercial banks. Under such rules, a substantial portion of the country's potential bank reserves might be beyond the banks' reach, available only as the government made expenditures. Even before the Civil War, secretaries of the Treasury had circumvented this requirement by depositing government funds received from other sources with the banks and by prepaying interest and principal on government bonds in times of financial

stringency. These techniques were developed and expanded later in the period. In 1911 Congress finally allowed the payment of customs duties by certified checks rather than gold.

Commercial banks themselves also developed some devices to reduce the risk of bank failures inherent in any fractional-reserve banking system. When depositor demands for currency were high, many banks—particularly in the South—employed clearinghouse certificates, normally used as evidence of interbank debts, as emergency currency as well as to settle their accounts with each other. Banks also made growing use of certified checks drawn on themselves under such circumstances, and a growing variety of other money substitutes—scrip, factory paychecks, and so forth—were devised by nonbank institutions.[16] Such measures, however, were stopgaps. They could ease banks' difficulties when the demand for currency exceeded their ability to meet it and might prevent bank failures, but they also indicated that the basic situation had not changed. Further, while such expedients were in use, the United States would have two or more types of "currency" in circulation, with varying exchange rates between them, at least until the bank emergency was ended. This, of course, resembled the days of state bank notes.

J.P. Morgan: The Banker as a Central Bank

Bank failures were still common. In 1907, a particularly disastrous collapse of the New York banks and the stock market was averted not by institutions, but by an individual. J.P. Morgan, by sheer force of will and the respect engendered by his vast knowledge of financial matters, was able to pool the resources of the New York banks and the major trust companies to

---

[15] Ibid., p. 774.

[16] Ibid.

Table 13.4 Prices, Velocity, and Real Gross National Product, 1860–1920

Date	Consumer Price Level (1967 = 100)	Velocity	Real GNP (1929 Prices, in Millions)
1860	27	—	$7,300
1865	46	—	8,822
1870	38	4.12	11,028
1875	33	3.99	13,568
1880	29	4.97	16,832
1885	27	3.43	20,366
1890	27	2.93	26,196
1895	25	2.71	31,082
1900	25	2.53	38,197
1905	27	2.18	47,870
1910	28	2.20	56,499
1915	30	1.90	60,424
1920	60	2.20	73,313

Sources: Price data from U.S. Department of Commerce, Bureau of the Census, *Bicentennial Statistics* (Washington, D.C.: Government Printing Office, 1976), p. 390; velocity data from M. Friedman and A. Schwartz, *A Monetary History of the United States, 1867–1960* (Princeton, N.J.: Princeton University Press, 1963); and GNP data from Berry, *Revised Annual Estimates of American Gross National Product* (Richmond, VA: Bostwick Press, 1976), p. 46.

meet runs on the banks and prevent a collapse of stock prices. Morgan assembled the bankers and informed them on successive days how much money was required (on one occasion he demanded $23 million in cash within 20 minutes) and how much each was to contribute. The bankers took their orders, and Morgan distributed the funds to banks in desperate need of cash to satisfy long lines of depositors eager to withdraw their funds or allowed institutions he judged beyond saving to fail.[17] Morgan had done the same thing on a lesser scale several times before, but he was 70 years old in 1907. No other individual could hope to function as Morgan had in 1907—as a one-man central bank.

[17] J. Hughes, *The Vital Few: American Economic Progress and Its Protagonists* (New York: Oxford University Press, 1973), pp. 439–453.

The Instability of the Private Banking System

Morgan was a titan, but he was also mortal. Without him the basic weaknesses of American commercial banks remained. Although the banks themselves, and particularly their local and regional clearinghouse associations, might devise means of using existing reserves more effectively, bankers had no means of increasing the aggregate volume of reserves in an emergency. The clearinghouse associations developed rules for their members designed to reduce the likelihood of trouble, such as capital and reserve requirements; the admission, disciplining, and expulsion of members; and regular reports and audits. They also instituted issuance of loan certificates based on the assets of all banks in any clearinghouse, rather than a single institution, in times of crisis. But such measures merely reduced the risks and were

■ In 1907, J. Pierpont Morgan prevented the collapse of the New York banks and the stock market by spearheading a massive collective effort of New York's bankers.
Source: Library of Congress.

and many prohibited all branches or sharply restricted them. Often such laws had the enthusiastic support of bankers eager for local monopolies. But such small banks were vulnerable to the business slumps of their specialized clienteles, and there were no local institutions with more diversified activities from whom to request emergency aid. Both bankers and depositors knew that the system was vulnerable to a sudden change in depositors' demand for cash. Pyramiding reserves (see Chapter 8) sometimes added to the system's difficulties. News of either a major stock market crash or an increase in the bad debts of New York banks was likely to make banks that had deposited their reserves with those institutions attempt to withdraw them while it was still possible.

Even outflows of funds due to no more than normal seasonal demands of farmers might cause major fluctuations in the securities markets. When withdrawals exceeded normal or expected levels, so-called panics resulted, with stock and bond prices plummeting and call-loan rates reaching extremely high levels. Even though some state governments were beginning to insure bank deposits within their borders, for most people the only sensible reaction to news of a bank run was to attempt to withdraw their own deposits before the bank failed or suspended payments.

only as sound as the clearinghouses, most of whose members were likely to be affected by any regional downturn in economic activity.[18]

The structure of the American banking system contributed to its weakness in emergencies. Far too many American banks were small and tied to a limited range of economic activities in a small region. In part, this resulted from their own efforts to avoid competition. State laws forbade the banks to open branches outside the states where they were chartered,

[18] G. Gorton, "Clearinghouse and the Origins of Central Banking in the United States," *Journal of Economic History* (June 1985).

The Federal Reserve System

The Panic of 1907 had two major effects. First, it was the last straw for many Americans who had endured a series of bank collapses, suspensions, and the accompanying economic distress. Second, J. P. Morgan's rescue operation indicated that successful responses to such situations were possible. Although there was widespread agreement that a new institution was needed to prevent further financial collapses, disagreement over the form it should take and the source of its management was equally widespread.

As a stopgap measure, the Aldrich-Vreeland Act of 1909 formally permitted banks to use emergency currencies backed by commercial paper (loans made to businesses), rather than gold, in times of crisis. This legislation also provided minimum size requirements for the bank associations permitted to form clearinghouse arrangements in panics. And it set standards for the redemption of clearinghouse certificates after the return of normal conditions.[19] More importantly, the act established a National Monetary Commission of 18 congressmen and senators to recommend a more permanent solution. After prolonged study and debate, the commission's report formed the basis of the Federal Reserve Act passed in 1913.

Debate over the form that the new institution would take was long and bitter. Both sides wanted a central bank, but agreement ended there. The Democrats and farm interests thought that such an institution should be free of Wall Street control. They wanted a system of regional central banks, with control centered in the federal government rather than the banking community, and a favorable attitude toward expansion of the money supply, if necessary through the isuue of fiat money. The bankers and their eastern Republican allies wanted a single central bank largely independent of government control and a gold-based currency.[20] As might be expected, the result was a series of compromises.

The New Institution

The Federal Reserve Act gave the United States a central bank, or rather a group of 12 regional central banks. The act provided a new currency—federal reserve notes—which was to be issued by the new banks and backed by gold and commercial paper. This currency was thus less subject to limits on its total amount than greenbacks or national bank notes, and it could be increased at the request of commercial banks. Federal reserve notes could be used as reserves by commercial banks, which could obtain them by "discounting" their loans—selling them to the Federal Reserve—or by borrowing with the loans as security. At long last, the commercial banks had a lender of last resort.

Member banks were required to keep their reserves in the Federal Reserve banks. All national banks were required to join the Federal Reserve System, and state banks were eligible to do so if they could meet the system's requirements, which were stricter than those of the states. In practice, nearly all large banks did join. Ownership of the system lay with the member banks, which bought Federal Reserve stock in proportion to their own capital. The system imposed new standards of conduct, regulation, and inspection upon its members. In addition to its primary duties, the Federal Reserve became the federal government's bank of deposit, and it served as a far more efficient national clearinghouse for checks than anything the country had ever possessed before.

Defining the Fed's Role

The country now had a central bank, but the Federal Reserve's role, the lines of authority within the system, and even its personnel were yet to be determined. If the Federal Reserve Act were taken literally, the new central bank's mission was to expand the money supply in response to the "needs of trade." If it did so, the new bank would do little to ensure greater economic stability, because it would fuel the commercial banks' ability to make additional loans even in periods of inflation, and it would do little or nothing to offset depression. In addition it was not clear which Federal Reserve officials were to make which decisions and where the ultimate source of authority within

---

[19] L. Davis et al., *American Economic Growth: An Economist's History of the United States* (New York: Harper and Row, 1972), p. 361.

[20] R. Johnson, *Historical Beginnings: The Federal Reserve* (Boston: Federal Reserve Bank of Boston, 1977) gives a detailed view of the politics and personalities that figured in the initial establishment of the Federal Reserve Banks.

the system lay. The authorizing legislation went to considerable lengths to minimize the representation of bankers on the boards of the district banks, but it was much less clear about their relations with any central authority. Nominally, the system's control was vested in the Federal Reserve Board, a seven-member body composed of the Secretary of the Treasury, the Comptroller of the Currency, and five presidential appointees. In practice, the 12 district Federal Reserve banks had a good deal of autonomy, far more than they do today.

On-the-Job Training for Central Bankers.
Equally serious was the question of personnel. The Federal Reserve Act and practical politics were both oriented toward reducing the influence of the commercial banking community over the new institution, but the absence of one type of qualification or experience is hardly proof of another. The real problem, however, was that the Federal Reserve System was a new type of institution for the United States, and no one had practical experience in the role it was to perform. The tasks and objectives of central banking are quite different from those of commercial banking, but the only Americans with banking experience had gained it in commercial and investment banking. Thus, the personnel of an institution whose operations were crucial to the entire economy would have to learn on the job.

Defining a Mission.
A further difficulty lay in the implementation of monetary control. The purpose of a central bank is to control the money supply rather than make profits as commercial banks strive to do. Today, the Federal Reserve has three instruments for carrying out monetary policy: changes in the reserve requirement (the ratio of reserves to deposits that member banks must maintain); open-market operations (the purchase or sale of government bonds to change member banks' reserves); and finally, rediscount policy (variations in the interest rates charged on loans to member banks).

In 1914, only the last was thoroughly understood. Open-market operations were legally possible but difficult and one-sided until the Fed built up its own portfolio of bonds. Whether the aggregate effects of open-market operations were understood even in the 1920s is still a matter of debate among economists.[21] The Federal Reserve had no authority to vary reserve requirements until 1935. Of the three control instruments, rediscount policy is the least effective.

In summary, the new central bank of the United States had all the powers of such an institution but was staffed by people who did not understand central banking. They had no clear policy directives to follow, and the methods for accomplishing bank goals were as unclear as the lines of authority among them.

CHANGES IN FINANCIAL INSTITUTIONS

In 1865 the financial markets of the United States were mainly local. Few lenders would extend credit where they could not literally "keep an eye on it." Capital transferred between regions generally moved with its owners, and much the same was true of transfers between uses. Local businesses, no matter how bright their prospects, had to depend on local lenders and their own retained earnings to finance expansion. Rates of interest for similar investments showed large regional variations. Farm mortgage rates might be three times as high on the frontier as in the East, where capital markets were better organized. Institutions to marshal savings and make them available to

[21] E. Wicker, *Federal Reserve Monetary Policy, 1917–1933* (New York: Random House, 1969) argues that the Federal Reserve's officials did not understand monetary policy in the Twenties. Friedman and Schwartz, *A Monetary History,* do not agree.

investors were almost entirely geared to short-term loans.

Such a situation made investment less productive than it might have been. Yet the weakness of American financial markets hardly prevented investment: Americans had accumulated well over a billion dollars' worth of capital prior to 1860, and investment rose as a portion of gross national product. The problem was that allocation of investment funds was inefficient. Despite high rates of return, projects in new areas where savings were scanty and loan rates high might be starved for funds. Meanwhile, those in the East, even though they might yield far less per dollar invested, had no difficulty obtaining financing because the supply of loanable funds was larger and markets for their allocation within the region better organized.

Gradually, however, these problems diminished. Interest rates in all sections of the country began to fall, becoming similar to those in New York City, the financial center of the nation.[22] Institutions were devised to ease the transfer of financial capital from one region to another. In addition, new areas became sources of interregional capital transfers. The Midwest was supplementing the traditional capital-surplus areas of the Middle Atlantic states and New England as a lender to the West by 1900. Even before that time, it had furnished a substantial market for eastern securities.[23]

Building a Financial System

These developments were aided by better and more current information that sprang from a variety of sources. Accounting and communication standardized the data and aided its transfer, and institutions such as commercial paper houses specialized in buying short-term

loans from bankers in capital-short regions and selling them to banks unable to find local uses for all their funds. The first credit-rating agencies appeared in the 1840s and by the 1870s had set up extensive networks that allowed lenders to assess risks in distant markets without traveling to them.[24] These developments made information about investment opportunities cheaper and more accurate than ever before. Their effects were concentrated on short-term credit markets at first; long-term interest rate differentials fell, too, but not as far as short-term lending rates.

The interest rate convergence was least apparent in the South, indicating that the region's credit markets were less well developed and integrated into the national market than those in other sections of the country. Since the South was also a capital-deficient area, this is another indication of the sources of its poverty. Not only did the South have more difficulty generating capital internally because of its low incomes, but its poorly developed capital markets did a relatively inferior job of attracting capital from other regions.[25] It may have been deficient in allocating the available investment funds as well.

Companies specializing in western farm mortgages reduced the risks of such lending for the individual eastern creditor (too much, given the unhappy history of most such firms). By competing with each other and a growing list of other lenders, these firms brought down the rates paid by frontier agriculture. As general incorporation laws were enacted in more states, easier incorporation made it less difficult to raise the initial investment required for large-scale firms.

Savings banks and life insurance companies furnished a new and important source of

[22] L. Davis, "The Investment Market, 1870–1914," *Journal of Economic History* (September 1965).
[23] Ibid.

[24] A. Chandler, Jr., *The Visible Hand: The Managerial Revolution in American Business* (Cambridge, Mass.: Harvard University Press, 1977), pp. 221–222.
[25] Ibid. See also Davis et al., *American Economic Growth*, pp. 328–330.

investment funds. The assets of such firms grew from only $64 million in 1865 to over $5 billion by 1915. Because they sought long-term investments, an area where American capital markets' deficiencies had previously been greatest, life insurance investments filled a most important gap. They were far better suited to finance investments in transportation or heavy industry, where the sums required might be large and the payoff period very long, than were commercial banks. The latter were better suited to short-term and highly liquid investments. Savings banks and other similar institutions were also beginning to appear. With the life insurance companies, they reflect the income gains experienced by a great many Americans. Members of the middle class were now able to set aside funds for long-term savings. With the exception of rural landholding, where saving was largely due to capital gains, savings had previously been primarily restricted to the rich.

The Stock Market

The quantity and variety of securities handled by the stock market were greatly extended, even as it became more concentrated in New York City. Even before the Civil War, most large cities had possessed "stock exchanges"—something of a misnomer because typically these markets dealt almost exclusively in bonds. Stocks of industrial companies were rarely sold, and only the Boston exchange quoted their prices on a regular basis. Even the steel industry's initial capital came largely from individuals who dealt directly with the promoters of firms, such as Andrew Carnegie. Really new industries, such as automobiles, had great difficulty obtaining financing from established institutional lenders even after 1900. If the auto industry is viewed as it appeared to investors then—as a new product of highly uncertain prospects requiring both huge amounts of capital for development and production and a long delay before any returns—lenders' timidity is easier to understand. The auto industry is said to have centered around Detroit because only

there would the banks lend at least some automakers money.

With the extensive marketing of bonds during the Civil War, many Americans had become familiar with investments in which the lender had no direct management interest. This made it easier to sell railroad stocks and bonds, in the postwar period, and after 1897 those of industrial corporations as well. Gradually, banks ceased discriminating against industrial securities in making brokers' loans and assessing collateral. By 1914, industrial stocks were fully accepted as high-grade investments.

The Investment Banks

Another late-nineteenth-century innovation in American finance was the investment bank. These institutions do not accept deposits and make loans as commercial banks do. Their business is the marketing of securities. They buy securities or accept them on consignment from the firms issuing them and sell them to final customers. The investment bank extends the advantages of its knowledge to both the issuing firm and the securities buyers. It sells stock at higher prices or obtains lower interest rates on bond issues than the issuing firm could achieve on its own. And it gives customers the benefits of its knowledge of the investment and its prospects, thus reducing their risks.

In this period, the firm of J.P. Morgan & Co. had no peer among investment banks. Often Morgan provided firms that sought to sell stocks or bonds more than just access to the money market. In return for its services in selling securities, Morgan's firm might assume an active role in the client firm's management. The company's debt structure might be changed, with stock replacing bonds. Ineffective officers might be fired and high-cost operations discontinued. Especially when the firm was experiencing difficulties, the money might come with one of Mr. Morgan's bright young men, who often received a seat on the firm's board of directors to make sure that the money was profitably employed. The new man would report directly to J.P. Morgan, and no firm defied the wishes of the "Napoleon of Wall Street" lightly.

Such practices did more than safeguard investors' funds: they made securities much easier to sell. Once it was known that an ailing firm was being "Morganized," its securities assumed a new value. Not at all incidentally, this also raised the fees J.P. Morgan & Co. could charge for its services. Especially in the railroad industry, with its heavy debt burdens and seemingly intractable competitive problems, smaller firms might be consolidated into large systems by investment bankers.

The Morgan influence may have led to cooperation among firms that accepted his direction. Individual firms were far less likely to cheat on collusive agreements in cases where Morgan and his men were privy to the decisions of all firms. By 1910 Morgan or his associates held seats on over 100 corporate boards.

The "Money Trust." Although the Pujo Committee, a congressional body set up to investigate the "Money Trust" in 1912, did find that there were "common interests" among the members of the financial community, it was not able to establish that competition among either financial intermediaries or the firms they served had been eliminated. This finding probably reflected the facts. First, by no means did all industrial firms or railroads require the services of investment bankers. Nor were all who did controlled by them. Second, in many cases the bankers' remedies worked: firms regained profitability and with it lost the need for outside financing or direction. Third, J.P. Morgan & Co. was not the only investment banking concern. There were many others, not all in New York. Fourth, in some cases successful industrial firms used their profits to diversify into investment banking. The most prominent example is the Standard Oil Company. On balance, it appears that investment banks did more to mobilize capital and improve operating efficiency for the firms they served than to re-duce competition among them. As Chapter 12 has shown, if competition declined during this period, the decline was slight, and the probability that competition actually increased is at least as great.

The Increase in Savings and Investment

The levels of aggregate saving and investment in the American economy increased substantially after the Civil War. The proportion of investment to GNP was the highest ever recorded, between 25 and 30 percent. The reasons are not completely clear. Undoubtedly, the improvement and extension of financial intermediaries that channeled savings into productive uses was one factor. Individuals found that lending their funds was safer and more lucrative on an aggregate basis than before, because capital was now allocated more efficiently. At one time, the distribution of income in this period was thought to be so heavily weighted in favor of the rich that savings had to rise. The rich, it was claimed, made so much money that they simply were unable to spend it all. But today there is little evidence of a massive shift in income distribution toward greater inequality during this era. If there was an increase in the share of income received by the upper income groups, it was far too small to account for the increase in aggregate savings.

The unprecedented rate of technological change may have been a significant cause of the upsurge in investment. Producers found that they had to continue investing in new equipment or lose their market positions. In any case, gross investment reached 28 percent of GNP in some years. Since such large-scale capital accumulation was a recent phenomenon for the United States, a very large portion of this investment represented net additions to the country's capital stock, not the mere replacement of depreciation. Furthermore, the investment was increasingly from domestic sources and represented firms' use of retained earnings and depreciation reserves, not new securities isssues or other external sources.

Unquestionably, the increase in investment was an important factor in aggregate economic growth: the nation's capital stock rose twice as fast as the labor force, and the new capital was a vehicle for the introduction of technological change. These developments cast further doubt on claims that the business leaders of the period played no positive role: they reduced the proportion of their own incomes devoted to consumption while raising their employees' incomes to levels at which saving was a practical possibility.

SELECTED REFERENCES

Allen, F. *The Great Pierpont Morgan*. New York: Harper, 1949.

Davis, L., et al. *American Economic Growth: An Economist's History of the United States*. New York: Harper and Row, 1972.

Friedman, M., and A. Schwartz. *A Monetary History of the United States, 1867–1960*. Princeton, N.J.: Princeton University Press, 1963.

Hughes, J. *The Vital Few: American Economic Progress and Its Protagonists*. New York: Oxford University Press, 1973.

James, J. *Money and Capital Markets in Postbellum America*. Princeton, N.J.: Princeton University Press, 1978.

Johnson, R. *Historical Beginnings: The Federal Reserve*. Boston: Federal Reserve Bank of Boston, 1977.

Kroos, H., and M. Blyn. *A History of Financial Intermediaries*. New York: Philadelphia Bank Company, 1971.

Kuznets, S. *Capital in the American Economy: Its Formation and Financing*. Princeton, N.J.: Princeton University Press, 1961.

Myers, M. *The New York Money Market*. New York: Columbia University Press, 1931.

Sylla, R. *The American Capital Market, 1846–1914: A Study of the Effects of Public Policy on Economic Development*. New York: Arno Press, 1975.

U.S. Department of Commerce, Bureau of the Census. *Historical Statistics of the United States: Colonial Times to 1970*. 2 vols. Washington, D.C.: Government Printing Office, 1975.

West, R. *Banking Reform and the Federal Reserve, 1863–1923*. Ithaca, N.Y.: Cornell University Press, 1977.

CHAPTER

14

LABOR, UNIONS, AND THE STANDARD OF LIVING, 1865–1920

Nearly all dimensions of the American economy increased in this era of growth, and the labor force was no exception. The total work force more than tripled, rising from 12,506,000 people in 1870 to 41,614,000 in 1920. This rate of growth is slightly overstated. It includes only those workers over 15 years old, and the proportion of child labor was higher in 1870 than it was in 1920.[1]

CHANGING WORK FORCE DEMOGRAPHICS

Despite the decline in child labor, the proportion of the population available for work outside the home rose. Falling birthrates, longer lives, and heavy immigration raised the ratio of adults to the total population. Also, the labor force participation rate of adult women rose by about 25 percent, from 18.9 to 25.4 percent over the 1890–1910 period.[2] This increase was the result of rising urbanization, smaller families, changes in social attitudes towards working women, and an increased number of jobs for which mere strength was not a primary requirement. By 1920, about one adult woman in five was employed outside the home, although the proportion was much higher for single than for married women[3].

Other characteristics of the work force also changed. Over the period, a substantial accumulation of labor skills occurred. Although difficult to quantify, it is certain that workers

---

[1] U.S. Department of Commerce, Bureau of the Census, *Historical Statistics of the United States: Colonial Times to 1970,* 2 vols. (Washington, D.C.: Government Printing Office, 1975), 1:129.
[2] Ibid., p. 133.
[3] Ibid.

Table 14.1 Occupational Distribution of U.S. Labor, 1860–1920

Date	Agriculture, Forestry, and Fishing	Mining	Manufacturing and Construction	Trade, Transport, and Finance	Service	Total*
1860**	59.0%	1.6%	18.3%	7.4%	13.2%	99.5%
1870	50.4	1.5	23.2	11.4	13.6	100.1
1880	50.1	1.8	23.0	12.0	13.2	100.1
1890	42.8	2.0	26.1	14.8	14.2	99.9
1900	37.6	2.6	27.5	16.7	15.6	100.0
1910	31.6	2.9	28.7	19.3	17.6	100.1
1920	27.4	3.0	31.4	21.7	16.5	100.0

*Totals may not add to 100.0% because of rounding.
**Data are not strictly comparable with later years.
Source: Calculated from U.S. Department of Commerce, Bureau of the Census, *United States: Colonial Times to 1970*, 2 vols. (Washington, D.C.: Government Printing Office, 1975), 1:138.

gained useful expertise in the increasing variety of new jobs that appeared in this era, even after allowing for the obsolescence of skills made redundant by new methods and products. The amount of formal education possessed by the average American worker increased, but on-the-job training contributed at least as much to the growth in skills, and that has yet to be measured.

Evidence on the massive redistribution of the labor force is much clearer. The period began with most American workers engaged in agriculture. It ended with an even greater preponderance of employment in manufacturing, trade, and other urban occupations (see Table 14.1). By 1920 agricultural employment had begun to fall in absolute as well as relative terms. Labor growth trends reflected industry trends: manufacturing and construction employment grew rapidly in the early decades after the Civil War, but as their growth rates slowed, fields such as public utilities, transportation, trade, education, and government employment furnished a growing portion of new jobs.[4]

Geographic shifts in the labor force occurred as well. While New England and the Middle Atlantic states retained more than their proportionate share of manufacturing jobs, their traditional predominance in that sector was declining. The states bordering the Great Lakes and the Ohio River combined rapid urbanization and a large share of the newer, more rapidly expanding types of industry to achieve a growing share of industrial employment. The Great Plains states were largely unsettled in 1865, and their new populations concentrated heavily on agriculture; they grew rapidly until the land was settled, then saw their growth rates slow. The South, with its high birthrates and limited opportunities outside a not-very-productive agricultural sector, experienced persistent outmigration after 1900.

Overall, these changes in labor allocation were along the lines predicted by economic theory. Labor moved from areas and occupations where wages and incomes were low to those where they were high. This was also, of course, a movement from areas where labor was relatively abundant to those where it was particularly scarce. Labor movements were

[4] Ibid.

slow, however, and affected by many factors besides wage disparities.[5]

The Black Labor Force

After 1900, southern blacks began to migrate from the farms where they had been employed since the war to northern cities. This movement became especially pronounced after World War I raised the demand for labor while shutting off immigration. In this instance, the greater freedom, relatively greater civil rights, and greater personal dignity available through migration carried greater weight than noneconomic motives had for most other migrants. Yet the black migration was primarily a search for economic betterment, because it was greatest from those southern regions where incomes were especially low.[6] In addition, it was directed toward the highest-wage jobs open to blacks.

Female and Child Labor

A growing proportion of women began to work outside the home. Both demand and supply changes were behind this trend. The rapid expansion of job opportunities in trade, the mechanization of manufacturing, and changing social attitudes created more jobs in which women's performance was equal or superior to men's. Urbanization reinforced a shift toward smaller families and later marriages. Even so, as late as 1920, marriage spelled the end of outside employment for most women. In that year, about half of all single women were gainfully employed, compared to only one-tenth of their married sisters.[7]

Labor force participation by women produced greater freedom and wider experience as well as income. Child labor was less beneficial. This institution, of course, did not begin with industrialization; it is at least as old as agriculture. Farmers have long regarded their offspring as supplements to their own labor. However, industrial work for children could have some different characteristics. On the farm, children worked under their parents' supervision, but in factories they might be under the direction of people who had little or no personal interest in their welfare, and their working conditions were seldom open to inspection by their parents. Nevertheless, it appears that child labor was by no means the norm, and even in this period, most children in the labor force worked with their parents, on farms or in small businesses. Even in these cases, the proportion of working children in the United States was far less than in Europe.[8]

The work forces of some industries with low skill requirements included children no older than 6. In the early years of industrial and urban expansion, the number of children in the work force increased to a peak of about two million employed youngsters between the ages of 10 and 15 in 1910—18 percent of all children in this age group and about 5 percent of the total work force.[9] After this date the incidence of child labor declined rapidly under the combined pressures of growing incomes, which rendered children's contributions less necessary, compulsory school attendance laws,

[5] L. Galloway and R. Vedder, "The Mobility of Native Americans," *Journal of Economic History* (September 1971). One study claims that labor was especially immobile in the South. See G. Wright, *Old South, New South: Revolutions in the Southern Economy Since the Civil War* (New York: Basic Books, 1986).

[6] L. Davis et al., *American Economic Growth: An Economist's History of the United States* (New York: Harper and Row, 1972), p. 215.

[7] U.S. Department of Commerce, *Historical Statistics,* vol. 1, p. 133.

[8] S. Lebergott, *The Americans: An Economic Record* (New York: Norton, 1984), pp. 369–370).

[9] G. Walton and R. Robertson, *Growth of the American Economy,* 4th ed. (New York: Harcourt Brace Jovanovich, 1979), p. 324.

■ By 1900, women (particularly those in urban areas) were joining the work force.
Source: Records of the Public Buildings Service: National Archives.

the growth in incomes in this period. People began to believe that the economy could now afford to sacrifice the output achieved through such an offensive practice, especially if children's lifetime earnings were likely to be higher if their formative years were spent in school. It might be noted that much of the opposition to legal restrictions on child labor came from the parents of working children, who bore the direct burden of such changes. By 1920, many states had laws setting maximum hours and minimum wages for women. Wages and hours for adult men, however, were still largely de-

termined in a marketplace where employers' bargaining positions were strong.

PRODUCTIVITY, WAGES, AND HOURS

Although productivity increases contributed more to economic growth in this period than at any time in the past, most of the increase in total production stemmed from increased in-

■ Although young boys were still employed in mines, by 1920 there was a general decline in child labor.
Source: Records of the Children's Bureau: National Archives.

which it works. In the late nineteenth and early twentieth centuries, the supply of capital grew much faster than that of labor. This is another way of saying that the number of tools available to the average worker rose: their quality improved as well. Thus, workers' output increased in part because they had more and better tools at their disposal. If a resource's productivity increases, its price can be expected to reflect its greater value to employers, and resource prices, of course, are incomes to resource owners.

Real Wages

The evidence on real wage trends over the 1860–1920 period bears out this reasoning. For the period as a whole, real wages of nonfarm employees increased, even after allowing for the effects of unemployment. From 1865 to 1920, real wages slightly more than doubled.[11] The pace of real wage gains almost exactly matched that of productivity, which is no surprise: barring some major shift in the compensation of nonhuman resources, workers' real incomes cannot increase faster than their output. In aggregate, resources' combined output is income: it is the goods and services available to be purchased by the sum of payments made to them.

If the base date of Table 14.2 is taken as from 1860 rather than 1865, the growth in real wages is considerably less, about 47 percent. However, two factors cause this increase to be understated. The 1920 figures allow for the effects of unemployment, and those before 1900 do not, even though some years of the nineteenth century saw substantial joblessness. Second, the higher 1920 wages were earned in

puts, just as it always had. Still, for the period 1889–1913, real output per unit of input grew at 1.3 percent annually, about one-third of total growth over that time. Labor productivity increased three times as fast as capital productivity.[10]

Caution should be used in drawing conclusions from these data, however, because the productivity of any input is partially determined by the amounts of other resources with

[10] J. Kendrick, *Productivity Trends in the United States* (Princeton, N.J.: Princeton University Press, 1961), p. 60.

[11] C. Long, *Wages and Earnings in the United States, 1860–1890* (Princeton, N.J.: Princeton University Press, 1960), pp. 109–118. See also A. Rees, *Real Wages in Manufacturing, 1890–1914* (Princeton, N.J.: Princeton University Press, 1961), pp. 3–5.

Table 14.2   Real and Money Wage Trends, 1860–1920

Date	Money* Earnings per Year	Real Earnings**	Loss from Unemployment	Real Earnings after Loss from Unemployment**
1860	$363	$457	—	—
1865	512	328	—	—
1870	489	375	—	—
1875	423	403	—	—
1880	388	395	—	—
1885	446	492	—	—
1890	475	519	—	—
1895	438	520	—	—
1900	483	573	$42	$523
1905	550	621	35	582
1910	634	669	58	608
1915	692	684	93	591
1920	1,426	714	104	672

*Current dollars
**1914 dollars
Source: S. Lebergott, *Manpower in Economic Growth: The American Record Since 1800* (New York: McGraw-Hill, 1964), pp. 524–528. Reprinted in L. Davis et al., *American Economic Growth: An Economist's History of the United States* (New York: Harper and Row, 1972), pp. 212–213.

a shorter workweek, but the later income figures include no allowance for the increased leisure time, even though it represents an addition to workers' well-being. Finally, Table 14.2 includes only nonfarm incomes. These were considerably higher than farm incomes, and over 1860–1920 the proportion of farm to nonfarm workers greatly diminished, so more of the work force enjoyed nonfarm wages.

Another noteworthy feature of Table 14.2 is the great short-run variation in incomes, which reflects the violent gyrations of the American business cycle. Simple money income figures are an especially misleading gauge of welfare during this period. Although money incomes declined over 1865–1879, the price level fell even faster, and deflation continued until 1896. Thus, in some years real wages rose even though nominal wages fell. On the other side of the coin, although money wages more than doubled from 1915 through 1920, real wages

increased by a scant 14 percent because World War I generated rapid inflation. Finally, the figures are averages for all workers and do not reflect changes in the relative earnings of skilled and unskilled workers. The data indicate that the gap between skilled and unskilled workers' incomes grew for most of the period, then declined rapidly during World War I.[12]

The overall picture, then, is one of substantial increases in the purchasing power of the average worker's wages from 1860 to 1920. But the dimensions of the increase are quite sensitive to the choice of base and terminal years. Prices in 1914 dollars were about one-tenth their 1986 level, so the average nonfarm wage around the start of World War I was

[12] P. Lindert and J. Williamson, "Three Centuries of American Inequality," in *Research in Economic History*, ed. P. Uselding (Greenwich, Conn.: JAI Press, 1976), p. 64.

equivalent to slightly less than $7,000 in modern real income. These trends are averages, and wages varied widely between occupations and regions of the country, and sometimes even between similar jobs in the same town. Although these disparities had diminished by the end of the period, they were still much greater than today.

Shorter Work Hours

Workers also gained from a reduction in the number of hours worked per day or per week over the 1865–1920 period. These gains may appear greater than they really were because of the shift from farm to nonfarm labor. Although farm labor worked extremely long hours at planting and harvest seasons, it enjoyed substantially decreased work hours at other times, particularly winter. Factory and other urban jobs offered a more regular pace of work and more hours of employment per year. In 1860, the average manufacturing workweek was about 65 hours over six days. By 1880, the workday averaged 10 hours, and by 1920 it was 9, with a half-day on Saturday. At this time the weekend began to mean something more than Saturday night and Sunday.

Some skilled or privileged workers had even shorter hours. Construction craftsmen generally worked about an hour less per day than was customary in manufacturing, and miners were more successful in obtaining shorter hours than were most other workers. Federal government employees had a 48-hour workweek throughout the period. There were also less fortunate workers. Because continuous operations were more fuel-efficient, steelworkers put in 12 hours a day, seven days a week, which meant a 24-hour shift at the end of each week or whenever the shifts changed. In some "sweated" industries, the hours of labor were limited mainly by workers' physical endurance. In general, the greatest gains in workweek reductions came after 1890.

Unemployment

American workers had made considerable progress in terms of wages and hours, but the transition from farm to urban occupations imposed new types of costs. For the farmer, bad times meant poor crops, low prices, or both, which caused income reductions, but—unless there were additional circumstances, such as a mortgage falling due at the same time—no loss of livelihood. For the industrial worker, bad times could mean lower pay or shorter hours, but they could also mean the loss of a job. In this period, unemployment meant a total loss of income as well. As employment patterns changed (see Table 14.1), a growing portion of American workers became vulnerable to this possibility. Unemployment was more than a remote threat: depressions were tragically common over the years from 1865 to 1900. A substantial amount of unemployment occurred from 1873 to 1879, and from 1893 to 1898 the nation endured continuous unemployment rates of 11 percent or more, with a peak of 18.4 percent in 1894.[13]

These figures understate the impact of unemployment on industrial workers, because they represent the portion of the total work force without jobs. A large percentage of the work force was still employed in agriculture, where unemployment had little effect. Thus, the rates of joblessness among urban workers were much higher than these figures indicate. In periods of high unemployment, many who retained their jobs had only part-time work and suffered reduced wages. Labor turnover in manufacturing was very high by modern standards, however, so the figures do not necessarily represent long-term suffering for those affected.

After 1900, unemployment became less severe, but even in the "good years" from 1900 to 1914, rates varied from 1.7 to 8 percent,

[13] S. Lebergott, *Manpower in Economic Growth: The American Record Since 1800* (New York: McGraw-Hill, 1964), pp. 164–190.

averaging over 4 percent for the period. The lower figure indicates about the absolute minimum rate of unemployment achievable in a market economy, at least under early twentieth-century conditions.

About 2 to 4 percent of all workers are generally in the process of changing jobs, entering the work force for the first time, or suffering short-term layoffs, even when the number of unfilled jobs equals or exceeds the number of those seeking work. These rates vary with social institutions (in our period, unemployment compensation and welfare assistance), demographics (work forces with high proportions of new jobseekers and second earners have higher rates), rates of technological change, and social attitudes, all of which seem to have raised the "normal" or "frictional" unemployment rate in the 1970s and '80s. However, very high rates of unemployment indicate that, at least temporarily, there are more unemployed workers than job vacancies, and those out of work may have great difficulty finding any sort of labor, particularly in the hardest-hit regions. Other factors affect the impact of unemployment as well. For example, few workers had substantial savings on which to draw when out of work in this period.

Industrial Accidents

Other problems facing labor were industrial accidents and diseases. In many industries, particularly commercial fishing, mining, railroading, and steelworking, accident rates were very high. Men new to industrial work labored long hours near machinery designed with little or no concern for safety, and some worked under conditions that no modern worker, let alone private or governmental safety inspector, would tolerate today. Noise, heat, and lighting deficiencies were the most obvious difficulties, but at least they were partially recognized as problems. Other sources of illness and premature death were not even known. Medical research

was in its infancy and had not yet focused on the long-range effects of exposure to dust, soot, noise, and fumes from a variety of chemicals. We have little information about the incidence of job-related disease, but it must have been very high. And of course, if the causes of disease were unknown, there was little hope of instituting successful preventive measures.

The Legal Climate and Job Safety

Those suffering injury on the job could expect little or no compensation. A few employers might give small payments to accident victims or their families, but they were under no legal obligation to do so. Individual insurance was far beyond the means of most workers, and without accurate information on the incidence and causes of occupationally related diseases, insurance protection could not even be offered. The law offered job-related-accident victims little relief. Even if an injured worker hired a lawyer and sued his employer, there were several lines of defense. If the employer could show that the worker had been aware of the hazards of the job when hired, or that his injuries were due to the actions of other workers, the plaintiff could not collect damages. In cases of industrial illnesses, there seldom were methods of tracing the disease back to the job. Even if these existed, the employer could use the same defenses as in accident cases. Even pensions were rare: old age was feared as a time when people who could no longer work would be dependent on others for support.

The Supreme Court repeatedly struck down statutes and reversed lower court decisions that attempted to ameliorate these problems. In particular, it voided state laws establishing employers' responsibilities for industrial accidents and took an extremely one-sided view of virtually all contracts of employment. Shortly before World War I there were a few signs of change. After 1908, railroad workers were covered by a workmen's compensation act that allowed them to collect payments for injuries suffered on the job. From 1914 on, a growing number of states passed such laws in forms the courts would accept. In addition, safety procedures began to be devised and enforced by both legal authorities and employers themselves. Employers discovered that it might be cheaper to prevent accidents than to pay compensation to victims or, at least in the case of skilled workers, endure the loss in output from their absence.

Increases in safety that have costs are not unquestionable improvements in well-being. Only if the marginal benefits of improved safety exceed the costs of providing them does aggregate well-being increase. It is possible that the benefits from improved safety might be worth less than the costs that they impose on employers, consumers, and the workers themselves. For example, a change in work rules that reduced paper cuts received by bank tellers in handling checks at the cost of a doubling in depositor service charges would appear to be a substantial cost for a trivial gain in safety. However, while such considerations may have validity today, they were much less valid in the high-accident work environment of the nineteenth and early twentieth centuries, particularly when the absence of accurate information about the risks of different occupations is taken into account. When moves for increased workplace safety began, they almost certainly resulted in benefits that exceeded their costs.

IMMIGRATION

America has been a nation of immigrants—or their children—from the first European settlements. But the latter half of the nineteenth century and the first decade and a half of the twentieth saw an unprecedented volume of immigration to the United States. From 1865 to 1920, over 28 million people entered the United States—nearly equal to the nation's entire population just prior to the Civil War. Immigration had slowed during that conflict, but it soon increased again, reaching the peak levels of the 1850s by 1873. Then it declined again as America endured the depression of the 1870s. From 1880 on, the volume of immigration rose to unprecedented levels, peaking in the decade from 1905 to 1914, when over a million persons per year entered the United States.

The "New Immigrants"

As the volume of immigration rose, the origins of the immigrants began to change. The influx of northern Europeans—Scandinavians, British, Irish, and Germans—that made up the bulk of new arrivals before 1890 began to decline. In its place came even greater numbers from southern and eastern Europe—Italians, Poles, Russians, and other Slavic peoples. In addition, immigrants came from Canada, the West Indies, and even from Asia—from China before 1882, and Japan.[14] The new arrivals sprang from cultures whose religions, languages, and customs differed more dramatically from those of the United States than had earlier immigrants'. A much smaller proportion spoke English, and the percentage literate in any language was also lower than among the "old immigrants," with the possible exception of the Irish. The portion of skilled and professional workers may also have been lower, though it is possible that the official statistics understate the human capital possessed by the immigrants. In religion, the "new immigrants" were heavily Roman Catholic, with substantial numbers of Jews and Orthodox Christians.

Motives for Migration
The data make it clear that the primary motive for immigration had not changed. The chief attraction of the United States was the hope for a better material standard of life than the

---

[14] U.S. Department of Commerce, *Historical Statistics,* vol. 1, pp. 107–108.

immigrants had known in their native lands. Eastern and southern Europe furnished their inhabitants with abundant reasons to seek betterment or even survival elsewhere: poverty, tyrannical governments, social structures that restricted opportunity for the talented and ambitious, population pressures on the land, and ancient conflicts and hatreds were all common. For the Russian Jews, such pressures were particularly acute. Religious persecution and a government that made them the scapegoat for all the real and imagined evils that flourished in Czarist Russia gave them little reason to stay in their ancestral lands.

Despite these "push" factors, the "pull" of the United States was more influential in the Atlantic migration. In this era of low steamship fares and minimal restrictions on travel between nations, emigrants from Europe could literally have gone anywhere on earth, yet in overwhelming numbers they chose the United States. Even more significantly, immigration to America was strongly correlated with periods of high demand for labor in the U.S. economy, much more so than with events in the countries from which the immigrants came.[15] Immigrants came to America in periods of full employment and rising wages, rather than in response to wars, famines, or political repression in Europe. And they came in huge numbers. From 1890 to 1914, almost 15 percent of the American population had been born abroad, the highest such rate since the colonial era, though only a 10 percent increase over the percentage of foreign-born in 1860.

Immigrants' Regional and Occupational Distribution in the U.S.

The new Americans may have come largely from rural backgrounds, but they settled mainly in the cities of the East and Midwest. Most immigrants found jobs in mining and manufac-

turing. They comprised more than half the work force in copper and iron mining, clothing factories, and steelmaking and held about one-fifth of all jobs in American industry by 1910. Immigrants comprised 34.5 percent of all mining employees and 25.1 percent of those in manufacturing. In agriculture, the professions, and clerical work, they were less well represented. Even so, the picture of all immigrants as unskilled peasants or laborers is incorrect. A sizable portion obtained skilled jobs in industry or were craftsmen of every variety imaginable. Others became or were foremen. In the professions, such as chemistry, engineering, designing, and medicine, the immigrants' representation was roughly proportional to their share of the population.[16] One study has concluded that the value of the human capital that the immigrants brought may have exceeded European direct investment in the United States.[17] Since immigrants tended to be disproportionately male and in the prime of working life, their labor force participation rates were very high. As might be expected of an urban population with low incomes, so too were those for immigrants' children.

Immigrants had come to America seeking a better life and prepared to work to achieve it. However, most accounts of immigrant life at this time paint a grim picture of desperate poverty in fetid, disease-ridden slums, with entire families working long hours for wages that barely permitted survival. Writers such as Jacob Riis found situations in the New York slums comparable to those in Calcutta.

Prejudice and Discrimination

The efforts and ambitions of immigrants were not admired by native Americans, and in some cases were even more fervently derided by those

---

[15] R. Easterlin, "Influences in European Overseas Migration Before World War One," *Economic Development and Cultural Change* (April 1961).

[16] A. Niemi, *U.S. Economic History: A Survey of the Major Issues* (Skokie, Ill.: Rand McNally, 1975), pp. 217–219.

[17] L. Neal and P. Uselding, "Immigration: A Neglected Source of U.S. Economic Growth, 1790–1913," *Oxford Economic Papers* (March 1972).

■ Immigrants came to America to improve their lives.
Source: Jacob A. Riis Collection, Museum of the City of New York.

who themselves had once been immigrants. Their speech, dress, religions, customs, and poverty were objects of scorn and ridicule. Such views were not merely the unpleasant if understandable reactions of those forced to compete with immigrants for jobs and housing, they extended to American intellectuals and business leaders, too.

There were blatant attempts to take advantage of immigrants' handicaps in obtaining information about jobs, wage levels, working conditions, and the means of redressing wrongs available to those who understood American political and legal systems. Immigrants might be met on the docks by agents of some manufacturer or mine owner, offering jobs that the new arrivals had no means of evaluating against American alternatives. Once hired, the immigrants might find themselves in some isolated company town where the employer controlled housing, stores, and the police in addition to jobs. Moreover, full advantage would be taken of all aspects of these monopolies. Even if they lived in large cities, language barriers and long work hours might make it very difficult for immigrants to obtain information about job markets or consumer alternatives. If any of them truly expected to find America's streets paved

with gold, discovering that those in their slum were not paved at all must have been the least of the immigrants' disappointments.

All these things and more happened to some immigrants. In the case of illegal aliens, many still do. Even so, there is massive evidence that immigrants' conditions of life in America were very different from *their* point of view than they appeared to middle- and upper-class American observers. The conditions under which immigrants lived, bad as some may have been, have to be compared to those from which they came and continued to come in increasing numbers. Significantly, the flow of immigrants increased as letters from friends and relatives in America told those in the "Old Country" that conditions were much better than in Poland, Sicily, or Russia. People who had found American life superior urged those left behind to join them. Often they were able to give more than advice: they financed the voyage, or assisted in obtaining jobs and housing in America. In 1909, 90 percent of the immigrants passing through Ellis Island had prepurchased railroad tickets to their ultimate destinations within this country.[18]

If immigrants used their money to bring their families and friends to America, it is clear that they could have returned to Europe had they chosen. But as in earlier waves of immigration, the flow was heavily toward the United States. About a third of the immigrants did eventually return to their homelands. Some had failed to find opportunity here, and others found the difference in culture or separation from old acquaintances too much. Still others returned as rich men by the standards of Italy or the Balkans. In light of their decisions, then, the behavior of most immigrants indicates clearly that they had found what they sought in America.

Immigrants suffered social and religious discrimination. Upon arrival, each new group

[18] R. Vedder, *The American Economy in Historical Perspective* (Belmont, Calif.: Wadsworth Publishing Co., 1976), p. 131.

■ Unrest on the West coast made Chinese
people the victims of racism. Note the
stereotyping even in this sympathetic cartoon.
Source: Thomas Nast, *Harper's Weekly*, 1869.

was labeled "dirty," "criminal," "ignorant," or
other even less complimentary terms. The
Chinese, especially on the West Coast, were
frequent victims of blatant racism. Not only
were they victims of mob violence, but barriers
to the ownership of property were imposed on
them. In 1882 further Chinese immigration was
forbidden, the first instance of such conduct
in U.S. history. The Japanese were treated differently only in degree.

Economic Discrimination. Economic discrimination, however, was considerably less evident.
Wages of most immigrant groups were lower
than those of native Americans, but so were
the immigrants' skill levels and ability to speak
and read English. When these factors are taken
into account, virtually the entire differential
between immigrants' and native Americans'
wages disappears. Ethnic groups containing
high proportions of unskilled or illiterate workers or workers unable to speak English received
incomes well below those of groups that did
not have these disabilities.[19] The initial study
which took these influences on immigrants' in-

comes into account provoked a good deal of
controversy, but has since been confirmed for
both sexes by several other researchers.[20] One
study did conclude that the wage differential
for southeastern European immigrants was approximately 10 percent greater than could be
explained by performance-related characteristics. However, even in this case, the authors
hypothesized that the lower wages for this group
were likely to continue only as long as immigration from southeastern Europe continued
to be very high. This is an indication that the
American labor market had not been able to
adjust fully over the 1890–1914 period, but
not that it would not do so. Also, it presents
ample evidence that economic discrimination,
if it existed, was not a barrier to further immigration.[21]

Market conditions in America gave immigrants some protection against discrimination.
In most years of heavy immigration, the demand for labor was high. No employer wants
to pay very much, if anything, for labor, but
what he or she must pay to obtain it depends
on labor's alternatives. If the employer has to
choose between paying workers what they can
obtain from other employers or going without
labor, it pays to hire any worker who can be
obtained for less than the value of what he or
she produces. Within the limits imposed by what
the laborer can obtain elsewhere and the full
value of his or her product, if the choice is
between increasing wages or losing labor, employers will raise wages. They will not knowingly pay any worker more than the value of
his or her product, but they may not be able

[19] R. Higgs, *The Transformation of the American Economy: An Essay in Interpretation* (New York: John Wiley and Sons, 1971), pp. 114–119.

[20] P. Hill, "Relative Skill and Income Levels of Native and Foreign-Born Workers in the United States," *Explorations in Economic History* (January 1975); M. Shergold, "Relative Skill and Income Levels of Native and Foreign-Born Work-ers: A Re-Examination," *Explorations in Economic History* (October 1976); and M. Fraundorf, "Relative Earnings of Native and Foreign-Born Women," *Explorations in Economic History* (April 1978).

[21] P. McGouldrick and M. Tannen, "Did American Man-ufacturers Discriminate Against Immigrants Before 1914?" *Journal of Economic History* (September 1977).

to pay much less and retain the laborer's services if there are other jobs in which labor is equally productive. It will raise another employer's profits to offer a worker some additional fraction of the difference between current pay and the full value of output, and laborers tend to be as alert to their own best interests as employers.

Immigrants' Standard of Living

Immigrants quickly discovered that it was to their advantage to obtain as much information about job markets as possible. There were many sources of such information: acquaintances (one reason why non-English-speaking immigrants tended to cluster together—information costs were lower), employment brokers, and employers themselves. Clearly it paid to increase one's capability to speak English. Since the newcomers tended to settle in large cities with many different employers, labor markets quickly became competitive for most immigrants. Not surprisingly, those who had been in the United States longest tended to have the highest wages, the most job skills, and the best information.

Whatever their native tongues, most immigrants learned English and sent their children to school. The children did well in their parents' adopted country: although the proportion of laborers, service workers, tailors, and other low-wage occupations among immigrants was above the American norm, the occupations of immigrants' children indicated substantial progress. The proportion of physicians, engineers, lawyers and judges, and scientists within this group was at least twice as great as among their parents, and in most cases above that for native stock as well (see Table 14.3). The proportion of salespeople showed a similar rise, indicating that economic discrimination could not have been a major burden for this group. Over the same period, the percentage of people of foreign stock in low-wage, low-skill occupations fell, often by as much as one-half to two-thirds.[22] For the immigrants and their children, the idea of America as the land of individual opportunity and progress was no myth.

The Economic Impact of Immigration

Immigrants were hated and feared by many Americans. They claimed that immigration, by adding to the labor supply, would drive wages down. Since real wages did not fall, the simplest form of that statement is false. Immigration did not actually depress wages, particularly as it was so strongly correlated with periods of full employment. Yet it is probable that immigration did prevent as rapid an increase in wages as might otherwise have occurred. Although there was a good deal of political action to restrict entry into the United States, proponents of such policies had very limited success before World War I. They did succeed in barring the Chinese and sharply restricting Japanese immigration. In addition, entry into the United States was subjected to various restrictions and taxes. During World War I, a bill to restrict immigration through a literacy test was passed.

Throughout this period, the contribution of immigration to the U.S. economy was highly positive. On a macroeconomic basis, immigration added to the work force in an era when most economic growth stemmed from additional quantities of inputs, and labor was by far the most important. As noted earlier, immigrant labor was a bargain for the United States, not so much in terms of wages paid, but because other nations had borne the costs of rearing and educating a large, strongly motivated body of labor that was now aiding the American

---

[22] S. Lebergott, *The Americans: An Economic Record,* pp. 342–343, 370–376. Data from E. Hutchinson, *Immigrants and Their Children, 1850–1950* (New York: Norton, 1956).

Table 14.3 Occupational Concentration in 1910
(Overall Concentration = 100)

	Foreign-Born	Foreign Stock
All occupations	100	100
Accountants	62	131
Engineers	47	104
Lawyers	25	102
Physicians and dentists	45	86
Teachers	39	75
Domestics	173	87
Charwomen, porters	208	104
Janitors	168	102
Construction laborers	169	84
Transport laborers	224	58

Source: E.P. Hutchinson, *Immigrants and Their Children, 1850–1950* (New York: Wiley and Sons [for the Social Science Research Council], 1956), Table 39 (excerpts) pp. 204–206. Reprinted in S. Lebergott, *The Americans: An Economic Record* (New York: Norton, 1984), Table 26.4, p. 344.

economy. The population growth resulting from immigration made the utilization of economies of scale profitable in many industries because it expanded markets. On the microeconomic side, the roll call of immigrants who made significant individual contributions to their new country is long and varied. Not only does it extend over every field of human endeavor, it includes activities in which native Americans had shown little or no aptitude.

One group that did suffer heavily from discrimination was not composed of immigrants. After all possible influences on job performance (skill, location, age, literacy, and experience) are taken into account, American blacks received from 15 to 20 percent less for equivalent work than whites.[23] Black immigrants from the West Indies, however, did considerably better.[24] In the South, many of the new industrial jobs that appeared for the first time after 1900 were foreclosed to blacks.[25]

[23] Higgs, *Transformation*, pp. 120–123.
[24] T. Sowell, *The Economics and Politics of Race* (New York: Morrow, 1983).
[25] Wright, *Old South, New South*, pp. 177–186.

PERMANENT LABOR UNIONS

As Chapter 9 has shown, labor unions had been formed in the United States before the Civil War, but they were beset with enormous difficulties. The prevailing legal and social climate was bitterly hostile. Unions faced two even more formidable economic obstacles in demonstrating to prospective members that it might be worth risking the community's wrath to join. First, employers found most workers easy to replace, whether with other people from the same labor market, workers imported from another city, or products made by nonunion labor. And second, labor unions were unable to survive depressions. Consequently, few were able to achieve permanent wage levels above those resulting from competitive market operations.

It was less difficult to organize a union in periods of full employment when labor markets were tight and employers might be willing to agree to higher wages, since under these conditions they could pass them on through higher product prices. But when business conditions were bad, it was nearly impossible for unions to function. Then employers wanted to cut wages, reduce employment, or both, and the threat to strike against an already unprofitable firm was an empty threat. Before 1870, very few American labor unions had survived a severe depression, and if anything, the severity of the business cycle increased after 1870. Yet additional forces appeared that made American workers more willing to seek the benefits of cooperation. By 1914 unions had at least discovered the formula that permitted permanent organization, and in a few industries they had succeeded in raising their members' wages above the competitive market level.

Changing Labor-Management Relations

As the size of business firms increased, older forms of labor-management relations were lost. Formerly, most shops, craft establishments, and manufacturing firms were small, and their owners often knew their workers personally. Some owners spent most of their time doing the same work as their employees. Supervision was a simple task because there were at most only a few stages in each firm's operations, and many of the workers were familiar with all of them. But as plant size and specialization increased, this relationship was often lost. The owner would now have to delegate close supervision to foremen and might even cede executive duties to a salaried manager. Relations with the labor force became impersonal and sometimes bureaucratic. Job security was threatened by both cyclical unemployment and rapid technological change, and the individual worker had little or no voice under such conditions.

These circumstances, together with the traditional concerns over wages, hours, and working conditions, encouraged the formation of organizations to represent workers. While today we think of labor unions as centered in the manufacturing sector of the economy, this was not the case before World War I. Most successful labor organization occurred in trades more closely allied to traditional methods, such as printing and various craft skills, not the new manufacturing industries.

The combination of wage-eroding inflation and tight labor markets during the Civil War had sparked increased interest in union formation. Many unions were formed, initially on a local basis. They soon realized that they needed to confront all employers in an industry, or at least in the local market, simultaneously. They then attempted to form common fronts between the employees of different local firms and between those performing similar work regardless of location or industry. These efforts bore some fruit: in the early 1870s several hundred thousand workers may have been enrolled in unions. But in 1873 began the slump that historians termed the "Great Depression" until the 1930s brought new dimensions to that term. It crushed all but a handful of unions. Labor had yet to find an effective counter to unions' most fundamental weakness: they were most successful in periods of full employment, when workers' bargaining position improved even without organization. When it deteriorated in slumps, they either had no effect or converted wage cuts into unemployment.

Labor and Political Action

Some labor leaders began to believe that if the social and political institutions of the United States could be made more sympathetic to labor, workers' goals might be achieved by changing the economic climate. It might be possible to obtain a larger voice in the distribution of income and the organization of production through political action than through bargaining with employers.

The first such effort after 1865 grew out of dissatisfaction with the results of more narrowly economic efforts. The National Labor Union (NLU) began as a combination of the local unions of several cities and a few national craft unions. Initially, its goals were largely economic: better wages, hours, and working conditions. But a union cannot expect much success unless it represents a large portion of the labor producing a particular item, and the NLU had organized only a minority of the workers in any single labor market. Since its efforts under such conditions were unsuccessful, the NLU expanded its vision. It began to ally itself with groups seeking an increase in the money supply and an end to private monopoly. In addition, it sought to replace private ownership with worker cooperatives, an idea then much in vogue among British workers. After a crushing defeat at the polls in 1872, however, the NLU disappeared.

The Knights of Labor

The next effort to reform society—along which lines was never completely clear—bore the resounding title of the Noble and Holy Order of the Knights of Labor. The organization grew slowly for the first decade after its founding in 1869. One of its handicaps was an elaborate ritual and secrecy, which to many Catholic workers (or their priests) bore too close a resemblance to the Masons. The Knights advocated an eventual end to the wage system. They emphasized education and cooperation and sought to enlist the entire working class.

Membership in the Knights was open to everyone, including employers and even the unemployed. Only Pinkerton detectives, lawyers, and liquor sellers were excluded. In pursuit of their goal, the Knights tried to organize all the workers in a region into a single "mixed local" without regard to the nature of their work. More importantly, the Knights paid no regard to whether people had joined as individuals or as members of an existing (usually skilled) craft union. An organization such as the Knights is inherently unsuited to bargain with either individual employers or even an entire industry. This did not bother the Knights' leadership, however, because they were opposed to attempts to shorten hours or raise wages by collective bargaining anyhow. They also opposed strikes in pursuit of such objectives.

A Rapid Rise—and Fall

Ironically, it was a strike against one of Jay Gould's railroads—a strike the Knights' leadership opposed on principal—that gained the Knights a huge increase in membership in 1885 and 1886. If there ever was an authentic "robber baron," at least in public opinion, it was Jay Gould. The news that a labor organization had challenged such an ogre and won spread like wildfire among American workers. In fact, the Knights had done little more than survive the conflict: they did not regain the pay cut that had triggered the strike. Nevertheless, the event attracted hordes of new members for the Knights, many of whom expected the organization to compensate for their lack of bargaining power. Within a year the Knights had over 700,000 members. It was by far the largest labor organization yet seen in the United States. But many who joined the Knights in that 1886 surge had thoroughly unrealistic expectations of the organization in which they had enrolled. While unskilled workers saw the Knights as an avenue to achieve labor's traditional goals, the leaders of the Knights were opposing a national movement for an eight-hour working day.

The organizational weaknesses of the Knights and the disparity between the goals of leaders and rank and file caused a collapse as spectacularly swift as the rise had been. By 1900, the Knights of Labor existed mainly on paper. Their demise was due more to self-inflicted wounds and inept leadership than to employers' opposition. At no time did the Knights' leadership appear to understand that few workers were willing to wait until the organization gained sufficient political power to restructure the entire economy before obtaining any material betterment. The leaders were willing to forfeit short-term opportunities to improve wages, hours, and working conditions in pursuit of this goal: to most members, this was incomprehensible.

Defection of the Craft Unions. Craft unions, whose skilled members had some bargaining power versus employers because they were difficult to replace, were very reluctant to merge with much larger numbers of primarily unskilled workers in the mixed locals that the Knights favored. As the craft unionists could see, such a move diluted whatever bargaining power they might have, while it did nothing to improve the lot of the unskilled. Yet the Knights were unable to resist the temptation to form mixed locals, and attempted to "raid" craft unions for members. Craft unions recognized this threat to their hard-earned gains, and after repeated warnings to the Knights had no effect, they withdrew from that organization and formed the American Federation of Labor in 1886.[26]

By their very nature, the Knights of Labor could be no more than a debating society. Its membership was too small to exercise significant political power, and its leaders could neither appreciate workers' needs for immediate economic gains nor hold them to the desired policies. In reality, workers found the Knights offered only a rapidly fading hope.

The defection of the craft unions was not the only blow the Knights suffered in 1886. The organization had promoted a rally in Chicago's Haymarket Square to generate enthusiasm for a general strike in belated support of the eight-hour-day movement—a move in which the Knights' leadership reluctantly followed the rank and file. Someone (it was never determined whom) threw a bomb into the ranks of the police. The police responded with gunfire that killed or wounded many of the demonstrators. Four men were hanged for murder and several others sentenced to long prison terms as much for their anarchist politics as for any clear association with the crime. All those convicted were probably innocent, but so high were the feelings engendered by the affair that Governor John P. Altgeld's pardon for those imprisoned cost him his political career. It now appears almost certain that the violence was not instigated by the Knights. Nonetheless, many people regarded it as typical of the entire union movement. The repercussions of the affair made labor's relations with the legal system even worse than the bitter hostility that had existed prior to the events in Haymarket Square.

The Knights' basic problem was obvious: to achieve their goals, they had to organize a large portion of the American electorate. Probably even the entire American work force would not have been sufficient to give their policies the necessary support. But many workers would not risk joining the Knights because, unless the organization achieved that unlikely goal, membership was dangerous. Worse, there was no short-term material reward. To have any hope at all of success, the Knights required a huge membership (and, in all probability, a much clearer sense of direction). They never came close.

The American Federation of Labor

The American Federation of Labor (AF of L) achieved one long-sought goal of American labor organizations: it was the first large-scale union to achieve permanent organization, surviving both depression and the worst employers could offer. The Federation succeeded by being virtually everything the Knights were not. The AF of L was exclusive, limiting its attempts at organization to skilled workers with some bar-

[26] G. Grob, "The Knights of Labor and the Trade Unions, 1878–1886," *Journal of Economic History* (June 1958).

■ The Chicago Haymarket Riot of 1886 is a vivid example of the conflict between labor and the legal system.
Source: Library of Congress.

gaining power. The new union was not interested in people who hoped to draw on its strength rather than increase it. It was resolutely nonideological. When Samuel Gompers, its long-term leader, was asked what the Federation's goals were, he is said to have replied, "More."

In contrast to the centralized leadership of the Knights, the AF of L was locally organized and controlled: basic decisions were in the hands of men close to local conditions and the wishes of their members because all worked at the same type of jobs. The Federation would not indulge in symbolic gestures; it was reluctant to strike unless it saw some prospect of gaining union objectives by doing so. Protests against wage cuts in periods of poor business were thought to be losing propositions by the Federation's leaders—quite correctly. Almost without exception, such strikes had ended in failure, and unions could not gain from them.

New Goals and Results

To employers, the Federation unions were antagonists, but no threat to their own survival, as some other unions proclaimed themselves to be. The AF of L accepted the basic institutions of capitalism, seeking only a larger share of its products for union members. An attempt by socialists, led by David DeLeon, to gain control of the AF of L in 1893–1895 failed. Henceforth in their bargaining the Federation unions would continue to seek agreements with employers, not class warfare. The railroad brotherhoods, like the AF of L organizations of skilled workers, followed similar procedures.

The American Federation of Labor needed more than astute bargaining strategy and effective organization to succeed. Under Gompers' direction, it was able to provide other benefits for its members. Because its members were skilled and well paid for the time (and able to extract further concessions from some employers), the unions levied sizable membership dues. These were used to accumulate strike funds, which gave the union some staying power in disputes, and also to pay sickness and death benefits to members. Under such policies, membership benefits could be maintained, and the AF of L was far more successful in keeping its members than earlier unions had been.

Even so, success was modest. Ten years after its formation—largely from existing unions—the AF of L had perhaps 270,000 members. But the Federation had already survived the severe depression of the early 1890s, something few other unions had done. In the prosperous years after 1900, it achieved considerably more. There were 1,500,000 Federation members by 1904 and 2,000,000 on the eve of World War I.[27] In each of these years about one-third as many workers belonged to independent unions. The Federation had few if any members in mass-production industries. Most of its strength was in skilled crafts such as printing, molding, and carpentry. At no time before 1914 were all unions combined able to organize as much as 8 percent of all American labor.[28] Given this data, the wage and hours gains achieved by American labor over this period cannot be attributed to organized labor.

Labor's Left Wing

Ideological unionism was not dead, but it produced almost as many leaders as followers. Often left-wing unions showed as much vitality in fighting each other as in bargaining with employers, perhaps because they could hope to achieve results in the internal conflicts. Aside from generalized opposition to the private ownership of productive resources, the left wing of the American labor movement never suc-

ceeded in presenting a unified program, let alone instituting it. The small socialist, communist, and anarchist unions, a few of which were affiliated with the AF of L, achieved no lasting successes.

One group, the Industrial Workers of the World (IWW), gained some strength in western mining, lumbering, and farm labor. The IWW also won a spectacular victory in a textile workers' strike in Patterson, New Jersey. It was an anarchist organization that advocated the overthrow of capitalism. The penchant of the Wobblies, as the IWW were nicknamed, for flaming rhetoric, strikes, and a readiness to at least associate with violence made the organization a target for all the power of both employers and the law. The IWW had equally serious problems in its relations with workers: it was not particularly interested in day-to-day gains or permanent organization, both of which reduced its already limited appeal. Its opposition to American participation in World War I intensified the public vendetta against it, and the organization was all but wiped out in the early 1920s.

Labor in an Unfriendly World

Almost to the very end of this period, American labor unions had to face relentless and united hostility from most of the other institutions in the country. The legal status of unions was hazy. Although unions themselves had not been illegal since 1842, even their most basic objectives and policies, such as organizing to raise wages, might be. Labor unions by their very nature are concerted actions to raise members' welfare; as such, they resemble price-fixing agreements by product sellers. Like these, unions are more effective if they control all labor in the pertinent market—that is, if they have monopoly power. The Sherman Act had declared "conspiracies in restraint of trade" illegal, and the earliest successful prosecutions

[27] U.S. Department of Commerce, *Historical Statistics*, vol. 1, p. 177.
[28] Ibid., pp. 126, 178.

under this legislation were of labor unions whose activities were held to fall under this definition. In the *Danbury Hatters* case (1901), a small union was held liable for the business losses suffered by employers during a strike.

Employers naturally were hostile, but in addition, management could usually count on support from the courts, police, the press, and often some intellectuals and clergy as well. Popular opinion tended to regard unions as strange and somehow un-American. Prevailing economic doctrine stressed the idea that unhindered competition produced ideal economic results in all markets. It followed that attempts to interfere with the competitive process, especially through joint action to raise prices, would make the situation worse.

Anti-Union Activity

Friendly courts gave employers weapons that made effective action by unions all but impossible. They might issue injunctions against union activity that forbade even the payment of union officers or denied them access to their own records. Employers might force workers to sign agreements not to join unions (yellow-dog contracts), under which the employees could be sued for violations of contract if they engaged in union activity. Names of union members might be circulated to all potential employers (blacklisting) and union membership lists obtained through company informants. Government could be counted on to limit or forbid picketing, to provide police or militia protection for strikebreakers, or even to send federal troops to break a strike by railroad workers that interrupted mail deliveries.

Where the courts failed to restrain unions, some employers went beyond the law. Attempting to organize a union was physically dangerous: many union organizers were beaten or even killed. Where the police or militia could not or would not intervene, Pinkertons or gangs of thugs might be hired to threaten striking workers, to protect strikebreakers, or to provoke an incident as an excuse to attack workers. Some

workers were not averse to similar tactics, meeting guns and clubs with bullets, dynamite, and fire. Some labor disputes, particularly in mining, read like small-unit combat reports rather than labor-management disputes. In this area as in most others, however, the advantages generally lay with the employers.

Disparities in Bargaining Strength

Above all else, employers could often afford to wait, and unions, especially if strikes had been called to force employers to recognize the union, could not. In such cases, unions had seldom had an opportunity to prepare for a long period without pay. Before 1900, only a few unions had strike funds, and they might be denied access to them by blanket injunctions. Fewer still could support their members, even at subsistence levels, for more than a few days or weeks, especially if large numbers were involved. The plight of their families might soon force strikers to return to work on the employer's terms.

Many of the new manufacturing firms were owned by self-made men to whom a union was an intolerable interference with management prerogatives. Such men believed that crushing unions was a matter of principle. A series of famous and often bloody disputes whose very names have become symbols of bitter conflict— Homestead, Pullman, and Ludlow—resulted in the destruction of most manufacturing unions and many in mining as well. Recessions continued to plague unions, even if they now knew how to endure them. In such an atmosphere, the ability of some unions to survive and even expand was near-miraculous.

A Change in Attitudes toward Labor

After 1900, the climate in which labor unions operated softened a little. Employers had organized the National Association of Manufacturers in 1902, largely as a propaganda organization to sell the public on the advantages of the open shop (in which no worker could be required to join a union under any circumstances, including the employer's recognition of a union) and other antiunion views. The NAM was quite successful, but at least its approach was persuasive rather than confrontational. It marked a transition from the days when employers felt no need to enlist public opinion as long as force was available.

The aims and effects of the National Civic Federation were less clear. This group's membership included some established leaders in the business, financial, and political fields, as well as union leaders such as Samuel Gompers and John Mitchell. It provided a forum in which labor's point of view could be presented and solutions to labor conflicts developed. The National Civic Federation urged a more conciliatory approach, including collective bargaining and mediation of disputes between labor and management.

In 1912 another goal of American labor was attained. The Clayton Act of that year, stating (incorrectly) that "the labor of a human being is not an article of commerce," exempted labor unions from the antitrust laws. At about this time, some groups' attitudes toward unions had begun to soften. Segments of the clergy and the press now took either favorable or neutral stances instead of their previous opposition. Some other goals, such as the abolition of debtors' prison, expanded free (meaning without tuition charges) public education, and shorter working hours were gained through the concerted efforts of unions and a variety of other groups by 1914.

U.S. Labor Unions: A Breed Apart

The basic characteristics of American labor unions that persist to this day emerged during this period, especially in the AF of L and the railroad brotherhoods. In this country, unions have been chiefly concerned with the pragmatic pursuit of economic goals. So-called "bread and butter unionism" is primarily interested in wages, hours, and working conditions. Such unions have shown little interest in the ideological concerns of many European labor unions, such as class struggle and the abolition of private capital. The roots of these differences are unclear, but it can be argued that they reflect the greater mobility of workers in the United States, both between employers and through promotion on the job. In the American atmosphere, unions were viewed as devices to increase labor's bargaining power immediately, rather than mechanisms oriented toward changing the entire economic system as a necessary prelude to any improvement in the worker's lot. American workers, who believed that their current jobs were not necessarily lifetime commitments, designed their unions with a view toward short-run gains within the existing system.

Class consciousness did not develop in the United States to any great extent. American society was far more open and mobile than European, and both labor and management were new to their status. Those people most likely to be imbued with a sense of class differences were recent immigrants, for whom the American contrast with Europe must have been particularly great.

Such attitudes also encouraged labor to connect wages with performance on the job and made American labor more receptive to technological change than were European workers. These attitudes helped produce higher incomes, new opportunities, and still further flexibility.

Pragmatism also played an important role in the development of American unions. Bread and butter unionism worked: such unions made progress toward many of their goals, even though for only a small portion of the work force. A union organized for other purposes, such as the long-term transformation of the existing economy, is unlikely to be either motivated toward or effective at achieving day-to-day improvements within the existing system.

American unions' failure to follow a more radical path does not appear to be linked to any systematic effort to exclude immigrants with such views from the United States. There is little evidence of such a policy, and in a world without fingerprints, passports, or social security numbers, even less indication that it could have been effectively carried out. Nor has the United States ever lacked the ability to produce its own radicals. The problem for both the home-grown and imported varieties was attracting a following, and neither group achieved much success.

In consequence, American labor unions have been far less politically oriented than many European labor groups. Even the association between the Democratic party and organized labor dates from the 1930s, not this period. Nor can even the modern connection really be compared to that between British unions and the Labor Party. The American Federation of Labor announced a policy of "rewarding labor's friends and punishing its enemies" at the polls. Given the small numbers of union members, this strategy was more effective than close affiliation with any political party might have been.

INCOME DISTRIBUTION AND THE RESULTS OF ECONOMIC GROWTH

There is no question that working people in the United States increased their material welfare from 1865 to 1920. Their wages provided greater purchasing power, and they worked shorter hours. Moreover, a larger portion of workers were now in high-wage occupations than in 1865, which meant that the gains of labor were more widely shared. But this does not tell us whether the gains in aggregate income were more or less equally distributed. How large were workers' income gains in relation to those of capital and its owners?

Did the Rich Grow Richer?

Enormous fortunes were accumulated by some business leaders, and in this period few hesitated to flaunt wealth. In his will, J.P. Morgan bequeathed to New York City about one-quarter of his art collection, which became the Metropolitan Museum of Art. Yet John D. Rockefeller described Morgan as "not even rich." Such accumulations of wealth have been presumed to indicate growing inequality of both income and wealth. The distribution of wealth almost certainly did shift in favor of the rich in the two decades prior to 1914. However, the evidence on income distribution is less supportive of any conclusion that substantial alterations occurred.

Income distribution, as indicated in earlier chapters, had not been equal in America since the earliest colonial period and may well have become less so in the first century after independence. But the changes in income distribution between 1875 and 1914 were not large.[29] Data from income tax returns (the United States levied income taxes during the Civil War and until 1872), while fragmentary, indicate no increase in income inequality.[30]

These trends should be placed in context. The American population was becoming increasingly urban and contained a larger portion of foreign-born persons after 1850. Both these factors tended to increase income inequality. Thus, the development of at most a weak trend toward greater inequality of income over this period is a remarkable phenomenon. The rich certainly became richer in an absolute sense between the Civil War and 1914. But there is little to indicate that their incomes rose at a faster pace than that achieved by the poor and the middle class. It must also be remembered that the Civil War conferred a huge in-

[29] Lindert and Williamson, "Three Centuries of American Inequality," pp. 92–95.
[30] L. Soltow, "Evidence on Income Inequality in the United States, 1865–1965," *Journal of Economic History* (June 1969).

crease in incomes on American blacks and imposed a great capital loss on their former masters. Moreover, blacks made further relative income gains in the postbellum period. Equality of relative income gains, of course, does imply that the absolute income gains of the rich were greater.

The Effects of Labor Mobility

Improved labor mobility would tend to reduce income inequality compared that produced in time when people were more limited in their choices of jobs and locations. It made those owing their incomes to inherited wealth less secure, and it gave people whose talents and ambition were their only inheritance more scope to receive returns on that endowment. It should also be realized that in an economic environment with a good deal of individual mobility, people can move up and down the income scale even if the scale itself does not change. That is, even if the proportion of income received by the poorest or richest 10 percent does not change over time, each group may contain a substantial number of different persons as time passes. American workers tended to be mobile, both geographically and occupationally, and the result was a substantial reduction in differences between per-capita incomes in various regions of the country, as indicated in Table 14.4.

The Effects of Urbanization

The increase in urbanization would tend to overstate any increase in inequality. Although urban incomes were higher in money terms, they purchased a lower quality of life than in rural areas in this period, especially in food quality, the incidence of pollution, and living space per person. Since living costs were higher in the cities, the gap between urban and rural incomes was not as great as comparisons of money income indicate.

At the same time, the growth of cities produced important gains in economic efficiency and hastened their dispersion through the economy. Cities made communications easier, so markets functioned better in urban areas. Urban conditions encouraged specialization and the use of economies of scale and even fostered invention.[31] Capital and labor were more readily available to innovators within cities, and highly specialized versions of both were likely to be found only in large cities. Selling costs were lower in urban markets. As with international migration, it appears that the attractions of city life—higher incomes and a more varied life-style—improved relative to the disadvantages, provoking a relocation of population toward the cities.

Changes in Urban Life

After 1900, city life had begun to lose some of its old terrors. A combination of new technology and new economic institutions had produced dramatic improvements in public health. Improvements in medical knowledge as well as the technical capacity to improve the purity of water supplies and provide adequate sanitation were not sufficient in themselves. To be effective, these innovations required participation by the entire population. Laws had to be devised to force everyone to use sewers and observe public health regulations and to contribute to their cost through taxes. Much the same was true of police and fire protection, lighting, water supply, and even traffic control. Urban conditions involve far more externalities than rural life: one person's activities influence the quality of his neighbors' lives as well as his own. Once this was recognized, laws could be formulated to increase the costs of actions that reduced others' welfare, or prevent them.

The Results of Preventive Medicine

The new pipes, filters, pumps, and chemicals now available made it possible for doctors to apply what they had learned about disease

---

[31] Higgs, *Transformation*, pp. 72–76.

Table 14.4 Regional Personal Income per Capita Relative to the National Average (National Average = 100)

Regions	1880	1900	1920
Northeast	141	137	132
New England	141	134	124
Middle Atlantic	141	139	134
North Central	98	103	100
East North Central	102	106	108
West North Central	90	97	87
South	51	51	62
South Atlantic	45	45	59
East South Central	51	49	52
West South Central	60	61	72
West	190	154	122
Mountain	168	139	100
Pacific	204	163	135

Source: R. Easterlin, "Regional Economic Trends, 1840–1950" in *American Economic History*, ed. S. Harris (New York: McGraw-Hill, 1961), p. 528. Modified (data for the West in 1900 changed) and reprinted in R. Higgs, *The Transformation of the American Economy, 1865–1914* (New York: Wiley, 1971), p. 108.

causes and transmission agents. In 1914, American cities were still noisy, polluted, and more crowded than ever, but the epidemic diseases that had been the scourge of urban life for as long as cities had existed were being conquered. The urban death rate had fallen by almost one-third in about 25 years, and the improvement in child and infant mortality was even greater: infant mortality in Massachusetts, for example, declined 41 percent fron 1870 to 1919.[32] Death rates from typhoid, scarlet fever, cholera, smallpox, and diphtheria had all fallen by 50 percent or more. Life expectancy at birth for all Americans increased from 47.3 to 54.1 years in the first two decades of the twentieth century.[33] One estimate of the benefits from public health measures in this period concluded that they returned twenty-five cents annually for every dollar invested in them.[34] The

payoffs came in longer working lives, fewer days lost to illness, and lower costs of treatment, all of which allowed the same work force to produce more goods and services. In addition, people suffered less, both in terms of their own pain and through the loss of loved ones, especially children.

Education

Another area in which investment yielded high returns to society was education. By the 1890s all states had public school systems, and no other country educated so large a portion of its school-age population as the United States.[35] The quality of education also improved. Even after the Civil War, the school year had been no more than three months in many areas. Now it was extended, and education was required for more

[32] U.S. Department of Commerce, *Historical Statistics*, vol. 1, p. 57.
[33] Ibid., p. 55.
[34] E. Meeker, *The Economics of Improving Health, 1850–1915*,

unpublished dissertation, University of Washington, 1980. Cited in Higgs, *Transformation*, p. 72.
[35] A. Fishlow, "Levels of Nineteenth-Century American Investment in Education," *Journal of Economic History* (December 1966).

years. The number of high schools and colleges also increased. A growing number of American universities now had science programs worthy of the name. Land grant universities and the Department of Agriculture began to apply formal science to areas long approached only through folklore, tradition, and rule of thumb. The result was a growing awareness of why and how processes produced results, making efforts to improve them more predictable.

There was a strong correlation between expenditures on education and per-capita incomes in each state. The extension of education, as noted earlier, was linked to the decline in child labor. The cost of providing additional education thus was not merely the expenditure on schools and teachers, but also the foregone output of children. The cost was well worth paying: education was a high-yield investment.[36] As growth became increasingly centered in productivity increases rather than additions to the supply of resources, the policy made good use of the one resource whose productivity was unlimited: people. Education also promoted labor mobility.

The increase in labor mobility fostered the movement from low- to high-productivity jobs (see Table 14.4) and thus increased overall economic output. The ability to respond to a greater range of employment opportunities also increased personal freedom and expression. It reduced the monopsony power of local employers and gave people a better chance of employment that provided both high wages and personal fulfillment.

■ **Leland Stanford** founded Stanford University as a memorial to his son when the emphasis on education was becoming more prevalent.
Source: Engraving by H. B. Hall's Sons. *Dictionary of American Portraits*. (New York: Dover Publications, Inc., 1967), p. 583.

A BETTER LIFE?

Were Americans better off in 1914 or 1920 than in 1865? In material terms, their incomes were higher, allowing them to spend more on nonessential items—the things that make life interesting. After food, clothing, and shelter had been provided, the new higher incomes allowed scope for people to express their own personal desires and develop a culture. For the average American, the range of attainable choices had widened, and it is this that distinguishes rich from poor economies.

Choices had not widened in consumption alone. The enormous changes in location, occupation, education, and social structure during this period indicated that many people's contributions to economic life as well as rewards from it had changed. By no means does this imply that everyone could rise from poverty to millionaire status by hard work and clean living. A very few, like Andrew Carnegie, had actually done so. But the real test of social and

[36] Ibid.

economic mobility is whether people in any line of work may realistically aspire to something they consider better than their current situation, or know that their personal failings could cause them to lose things they value. By and large, most Americans lived in such circumstances. On average, they gained, but by no means equally or even in proportion to status, talent, or effort.

Inherited riches have never been a disadvantage to those also born talented and ambitious, especially in an age such as this, where economic success was all but worshipped. Others, less selective in their choice of parents, might reap lesser rewards for equal or even superior effort. On the other hand, some were burdened with disadvantages not of their own making. American blacks had barely shed the worst of slavery's heritage and had not yet obtained equal opportunity. American Indians were still denied the right to try to improve their lives, both by law and in practice. Even so, the dividends on human capital were higher in the United States than anywhere else.

The Measurement of Well Being

Incomes, leisure, health, and even ranges of choice are all measurable, and all had increased for the average American. But can we conclude that Americans enjoyed life more at the end of this period than at its beginning? We have no way of knowing. Economists have yet to devise ways to measure the enjoyment different individuals derive from consumption, especially over long periods of time. Also, the persons who reaped the benefits of the period's economic growth were often not those who had produced it. In material terms, life was more abundant. But it was also different—faster-paced—and not all the changes were unmitigated blessings.

Some of the gains from improved economic capabilities—better health and reduced infant mortality, for example—appear to be unarguable. In other cases, perhaps the best conclusion can be drawn from observing people's response to the new opportunities. Little prevented at least a substantial number of Americans from living as they had 50 years before. But as the opportunities to participate in the modern economy appeared, few failed to take advantage of them. In sum, the old ways were still available, but even those who complained most about the changes wrought by modern life did not appear to believe that conditions would be improved by turning back the clock.

SELECTED REFERENCES

Brody, D. *The American Labor Movement.* New York: Harper and Row, 1971.

Commons, J., et al. *History of Labor in the United States.* 4 vols. New York: Kelley, 1921–35.

Davis, L., et al., *American Economic Growth: An Economist's History of the United States.* New York: Harper and Row, 1972.

Easterlin, R. *Population, Labor Force, and Long Swings in Economic Growth: The American Experience.* New York: Columbia University Press, 1968.

Erichson, C. *American Industry and the European Immigrant, 1860–1885.* New York: Russell and Russell, 1967.

Gutman, H. *Work, Culture, and Society in Industrializing America.* New York: Random House, 1977.

Higgs, R. *The Transformation of the American Economy: An Essay in Interpretation.* New York: John Wiley and Sons, 1971.

Kendrick, J. *Productivity Trends in the United States.* Princeton, N.J.: Arno Press, 1961.

Kuznets, S., and E. Rubin. *Immigration and the Foreign Born.* New York: National Bureau of Economic Research, 1954.

Lebergott, S. *The Americans: An Economic Record.* New York: Norton, 1984.

———. *Manpower in Economic Growth: The American Record Since 1800.* New York: McGraw-Hill, 1964.

Lindert, P., and J. Williamson. "Three Centuries of American Inequality." in *Research in Economic History.* Greenwich, Conn.: JAI Press, 1976.

Long, C. *Wages and Earnings in the United States, 1860–1890*. Princeton, N.J.: Arno Press, 1975.

Nelson, D. *Managers and Workers: Origins of the New Factory System in the United States, 1880–1920*. Madison, Wis.: University of Wisconsin Press, 1975.

Rees, A. *Real Wages in Manufacturing, 1890–1914*. Princeton, N.J.: Arno Press, 1961

Thomas, B. *Migration and Economic Growth*. Cambridge, England: Cambridge University Press, 1953.

U.S. Department of Commerce, Bureau of the Census. *Historical Statistics of the United States: Colonial Times to 1970*. 2 vols. Washington, D.C.: Government Printing Office 1975.

Wright, G. *Old South, New South: Revolutions in the Southern Economy Since the Civil War*. New York: Basic Books, 1986.

CHAPTER

15

DOMESTIC AND FOREIGN COMMERCE, 1865–1914

From 1865 to 1914, the volume of goods and services produced in the United States increased enormously. Since this increase in production was considerably larger than the increases in either the labor force or total population, we would expect it to also have produced an increase in specialization and exchange and in the variety of goods produced. And it did. The types of goods produced and portion of total output exchanged rose even faster than the aggregate volume of production. This development was aided by improved productivity and transportation, but changes in the institutions of exchange also played a vital role.

As specialization increased, so did the interaction between regions, firms, and individuals. These transactions would not have been possible without improved communication, urbanization, and information. The goods exchanged were often produced for markets distant in time and space from the point of manufacture; producers had to know the characteristics of demand, the creditworthiness of customers, and the nature of competition within new markets. Someone had to hold the goods between manufacture and sale, so financial services were needed. New methods of marketing and distribution were spawned by higher incomes, better information, and often, new competition.

Improved information resulted from the revolution in communications at this time. First the telegraph and later the telephone provided nearly instantaneous transmission of information. Contracts were devised that shifted risks from producers, wholesalers, and retailers to speculators, thus greatly easing access to credit for many market participants. The new institutions (credit-rating agencies, insurance companies, and grading systems) both reduced the cost of information and increased its accuracy.

■ An early version of the phone: the invention of the telephone spawned new approaches to business.
Source: The Bettmann Archive, Inc.

NEW PATTERNS OF POSTWAR COMMERCE

Increases in per-capita incomes and urban populations substantially raised the proportion of consumer income spent on durable goods. As people's incomes rose, they spent smaller portions on food and other survival requirements, leaving growing portions for discretionary purchases. At one time, it was believed that consumer spending on durable goods was closely tied to the appearance of the mass-marketed automobile and installment loans in the 1920s. Now, however, we know that the proportion of consumer incomes spent on furniture and other factory-produced goods was almost at modern levels shortly after the Civil War. Eventually lamps, furniture, and other household items became commonplace, so that demand for them mainly reflected replacement of worn-out items and the formation of new families rather than first-time acquisitions. As this occurred, new consumer durables such as iceboxes, sewing machines, bicycles, and a growing range of leisure equipment replaced the initial goods as mainstays of growth.[1]

In the case of basic furniture, the increased purchases after the war may overstate the change in production. In earlier times, much furniture had been made by users in their own homes. Although not purchased with money, these furnishings were obtained at a cost in alternative uses of the maker's time. In that sense, they still represented a use of income.

New Products and Sales Methods

However, purchases after 1865 included a number of items new to American households. Some were relatively complicated machines often employed in the purchaser's work, such as bicycles or sewing machines. These expensive items were difficult to sell without some assurance that they could be repaired if they broke down. It is no accident that successful automobile manufacturers learned to employ interchangeable parts and to copy the sales methods of makers of farm machinery, sewing machines, and bicycles, establishing chains of dealers trained and equipped to provide ser-

[1] H. Vatter, "Has There Been a 20th-Century Consumer Durables Revolution?" *Journal of Economic History* (March 1967).

vice. Henry Ford was an early leader in providing credit to dealers and customers—yet another example of his grasp of the conditions under which his cars were sold.[2] Agricultural machinery makers had been selling on credit even before the Civil War, and makers of expensive consumer durables learned to emulate them. At the same time, urban sellers of nondurables (groceries and dry goods) began to operate on a cash-and-carry basis; they no longer offered credit or delivery services. They realized that their customers were paid more frequently than farmers, made more shopping trips, and might be difficult to evaluate as credit risks in a large city environment.

The greater volume and variety of consumer goods also forced changes in merchandising. In earlier times, the occasional visits of a peddler whose entire stock was carried in a backpack or a small wagon, plus three or four visits to the nearest market town per year, had to satisfy most Americans' need for goods they could not make themselves. Most antebellum stores served a rural market and carried a wide variety of goods. They might accept payment in goods, farm produce, or occasionally even in labor performed for the store owner, although of course cash payment was always welcome.

Pricing Changes

Determining the price of each item was a time-consuming process. Most of the store's inventory was at least partially handmade, and few items were identical. Because of the nature of such merchandise, and also because bargaining was at once a social process and a source of possible gain for a shrewd haggler, prices were not labeled. Instead, they were determined by bargaining between the store owner or clerk and the customer. Payment in kind, of course, required more haggling.

Such methods were practical only where the volume of transactions was small, store personnel had wide discretion and experience, and the variety of goods was limited. As incomes, population, and especially urbanization increased and new technology created more uniform products, sales methods began to change. While the early types existed, they gave the seller an opportunity for price discrimination. With luck and skill, he might obtain the highest price each buyer would pay for each item, rather than the highest single price at which the same quantity could be sold. Gradually, stores began to post prices, as Quaker merchants had long been doing. This permitted a larger business volume, and reduced the skills required of store personnel. It also reduced the store owners' problems of inventory valuation.

The Guarantee

Greater uniformity in manufactured goods made possible another new practice—guaranteeing items and offering refunds if they were not satisfactory, even when the seller was not the maker of the good. Prior to this time, retailers' policy, at least for goods they had not made, had been strictly *caveat emptor* ("let the buyer beware"). A growing range of items was now packaged or labeled by the manufacturer. This practice had begun with food manufactures as an attempt to gain competitive advantages. There had been no point in trying to establish a reputation for quality when every maker's goods might be mixed together in the store's bins or barrels. But with labels or packaging, the maker was recognizable, and producers might be able to recoup efforts to provide superior quality. Consumers also gained, because food items were now likely to be fresher or cleaner—a lesser consideration when most sales were from bulk stores.[3] In addition, the new methods gave producers an incentive to protect their reputations for quality

---

[2] A. Chandler, Jr., *Giant Enterprise: Ford, General Motors, and the Automobile Industry* (New York: Harcourt, Brace, and World, 1964), pp. 34–35.

[3] ———. *The Visible Hand: The Managerial Revolution in American Business* (Cambridge, Mass.: Harvard University Press, 1977), Chap. 7.

goods by holding to uniform standards over large volumes of output.

New Developments in Retailing

Two seemingly contradictory retailing trends had appeared prior to the Civil War. As urban markets grew because of rising population density and incomes, some stores began to specialize in narrower ranges of products. Another indication of growing discretionary income was the increasing prevalence of "stores" providing services rather than physical items—theaters, beer gardens, restaurants, and other places of amusement. Except in small towns, the general store was replaced by establishments specializing in ready-to-wear clothing, hardware, groceries, meat, books, and often even more narrow categories. These stores were aided by the improvements in transportation, communication, advertising, finance, printing, and sometimes by such specialized supporting services as refrigeration. As cities and the number of stores grew, it became more necessary to proclaim each store's existence, function, and location.

Running directly counter to this development was the appearance of the department store. These French innovations had begun to appear in the largest American cities in the 1850s. After the Civil War they spread rapidly. Few towns of any size or pretense to sophistication were without a department store (or a general store masquerading as one) by 1914.

Department stores were really a series of specialized stores under one roof, with each department separately managed. Sometimes departments rented space from the store's owner. The parallels with the new multiproduct manufacturing firms are clear (see Chapter 12). Department stores used such innovations as fixed prices, guaranteed merchandise, cash registers, and improved accounting methods—they might not have been able to exist without them. The large size of some department stores allowed them to be their own wholesalers (some began as offshoots of established wholesaling operations) and deal directly with manufacturers, seeking quantity-purchase discounts that were invaluable competitive tools.[4] Department stores offered their customers savings in shopping time as well as money now that the pace of urban life was quickening.

The Chain Store

Chain stores also appeared in this era. The Great Atlantic & Pacific Tea Company began operations as a retailer of tea and coffee in 1859. It soon found that its stores could easily sell other groceries as well. Using the same principle of quantity purchases to reduce unit costs that had been the basis of its success in tea sales, the A & P chain had grown to 200 stores by 1900. By 1921, it had 4,500 outlets. In 1920, there were no less than 120 grocery chains and 808 chains of all types.[5] As the chains grew, they too began to perform their own wholesaling functions. By World War I, chain store competition had provoked independent sellers to pool purchases to obtain the same discounts.

The Mail-Order Firm

These three types of establishments all served an urban clientele, but the appearance of mail-order houses allowed farmers to gain some of the same advantages of wider selection and prices reflecting competition and economies of scale. Montgomery Ward began circulating his single-page "catalogue" among members of the Grange in 1872. The enthusiastic response among consumers whose previous choices had been limited to the meager stocks of one or two general stores allowed the new firm to expand both its offerings and its clientele. Sears Roebuck & Company was founded in 1886, and several other mail-order houses followed.

[4] Ibid., pp. 225–229.

[5] U.S. Department of Commerce, Bureau of the Census, *Historical Statistics of the United States: Colonial Times to 1970*, 2 vols. (Washington, D.C.: Government Printing Office, 1975), 2:847.

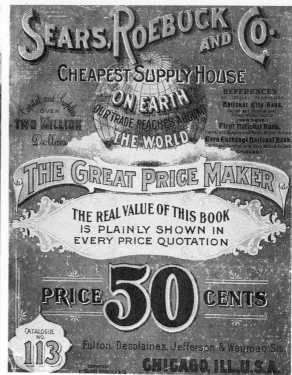

■ Mail-order houses met the need of rural people by expanding their shopping opportunities beyond the supplies of a country store. After its founding in 1886, Sears Roebuck & Co. operated from this elaborate shipping center in Chicago.
Source: Courtesy of Sears, Roebuck and Co.

It is difficult for modern readers to imagine how eagerly isolated farmers and their families awaited the arrival of the Wards or Sears catalogue. Only those whose horizons had been suddenly extended beyond the narrow range of choices offered by small country stores could fully appreciate the worlds opened up by these catalogues. Mail-order houses were initially hampered by the deficiencies of the U.S. Postal System. Rural mail delivery was not begun until 1896, and the parcel post system began operations only in 1913. Farmers' success in obtaining these services from government at considerably less than their full cost was one of their earliest successes in rent seeking. Even

before these innovations, the mail-order houses experienced significant growth after 1900 by using various express delivery companies. By that time, Sears Roebuck & Co. was the largest retailer in America.[6]

It is clear that the new types of retail stores had affected the markets in which they operated by 1900. Owners of more traditional outlets protested the competition they provided. The outcry was due to a reduction in the rents (monopoly profits) that they had previously enjoyed.[7] But the protests were largely in vain:

[6] Chandler, *The Visible Hand*, pp. 230–233.
[7] Ibid., pp. 229, 232–233.

local or even state legislators might be sympathetic, but the Supreme Court struck down attempts to protect local sellers from interstate commerce.

WIDER CHOICES

The economic growth and integration of this period created a greater range of choices for consumers, not only among different items, but also among similar items from a variety of producers. Increased discretionary income meant that a larger percentage of all consumer purchases could be expressions of individual choice rather than acquisitions of basic necessities. This situation undoubtedly aided consumers, but it presented sellers with many problems. More and more of what they sold encountered competition from a widening list of alternatives. Firms selling luxury items might now find their products competing for consumers' dollars against home furnishings, appliances, sporting goods, musical instruments, books, phonographs, and even such services as travel, resorts, and amusements. Under such conditions, adequate sales were no longer assured simply by meeting the prices of similar goods.

An Increase in Advertising

Both producers and retailers responded by trying to make their goods more appealing to consumers. Advertising—in both its informative and persuasive forms—was more widely used. In the cases of bananas, cigarettes, appliances, and other new products, advertising was necessary to inform people of the product's very existence, what it was, and why they might find it desirable. As before, much advertising simply provided consumers with useful information of the "where and how much" variety.

Advertising had earlier been largely restricted to simple announcements in newspa-

■ National advertising helped promote 1910 fashions.
Source: Warshaw Collection of Business Americana, Smithsonian Institution.

pers and handbills, but after 1900 advertisements began to resemble those of the modern era. These developments were aided by improved printing and lithographing techniques and by the great increase in magazines and other periodicals. Advertising could now be directed to specific groups rather than to the general public. Specialized advertising agencies appeared to advise retailers of the appropriate marketing strategies for their goods. As might be expected, some of the most extravagant claims were made for products whose real effects were difficult to ascertain. In that era such approaches were commonly used to market patent medicines; today they are employed to sell sporting goods and cosmetics. Although some ads were deceptive or even fraudulent, most contained at least some information useful to consumers in making informed choices.

Persuading consumers that a product was better, or at least a "better buy," was easier if the product itself could be changed or if its reputation had been firmly established in consumers' minds. The superior performance of some goods, such as Colt revolvers, Winchester rifles, Singer sewing machines, and McCormick reapers, had already earned them favorable reputations. Efforts were made to build such reputations for other goods through advertising (including slogans and testimonials) and through changing the appearance, function, or quality of the product itself. Where the product itself could not be altered, packaging and brand names were used, as with Morton's salt. When such methods succeeded, they allowed sellers to capitalize on the real or fancied differences that made their products better than competitors', encouraging repeat sales and making demand less price elastic.

Brand Names and Consumer Welfare

Prepackaged and branded goods were easier for stores to handle and often more convenient for consumers as well, because of the greater assurance of uniform quality between purchases. Consumers were now able to determine which makers' output to buy or avoid. The registration of trademarks and brand names also allowed sellers to protect their products' reputations against attempts by sellers of lower-quality goods to offer them in similar packages or as the same goods.

Product differentiation could take many forms, including improvements in the goods themselves or modifications to meet specialized needs, as in tools, furniture, or clothing. In some cases, particularly foods and patent medicines, it might entail lacing unpalatable, unwholesome, or useless contents with alcohol, chemicals, or narcotics to increase their appeal while, if anything, impairing their function. Growing consumer sophistication, sensational "muckraking" exposes, and the 1906 Pure Food and Drug Act discouraged the worst of such practices.

On the whole, the result of product differentiation was a wider series of choices for consumers and a greater likelihood of finding products that exactly met needs, wants, or preferences. If the new marketing practices *per se*

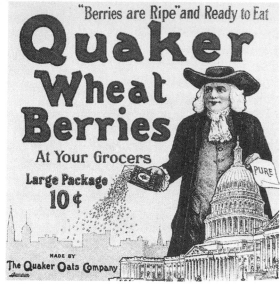

"Berries are Ripe" and Ready to Eat

Quaker Wheat Berries

At Your Grocers

Large Package 10¢

MADE BY The Quaker Oats Company

■ Quaker Oats made a commercial breakthrough by nationally advertising a product that was uniform in size, weight, and price.

added to firms' costs, as they generally did, they might also allow production economies by widening markets and giving access to economies of scale. They also tended to increase competition between sellers and thus lower profit margins. In any case, consumers still had the choice of buying goods produced and distributed under the old methods. The success of new products and practices indicates that most customers considered them worth whatever price increase might be involved.

Wholesaling

Before most goods are presented to the final user, they pass through the hands of people who link the producer with the retailer. The wholesaling function becomes increasingly important in any economy with a high degree of specialization. The concentration of manufacturing in the East and Midwest, and of particular items in even smaller regions, increased the tasks of the distribution system. So did the emergence of expanded and specialized retail outlets, which replaced direct sales by manufacturers to final consumers in local markets. As a consequence, the proportion of the total work force engaged in various aspects of distribution increased by about one-half.

Wholesaling was affected by developments elsewhere in the economy. Improved credit markets allowed wholesalers to begin to supplant commission merchants as early as the 1840s. Commission merchants sold manufacturers' output on consignment; that is, they acted as selling agents for the maker but did not take title to the products themselves. Unlike the commission merchants, who in effect used the manufacturers' credit, wholesalers financed themselves and purchased the goods they distributed. Often, they extended credit to the retailers to whom they sold. Especially in the early years, wholesale and retail activities were intermingled. Some wholesalers maintained retail outlets, and some large-scale western retailers performed wholesaling functions for the smaller stores in their regions. Since wholesale firms employed salesmen who visited retailers, they saved their customers time and travel. Formerly, many retailers had been forced to travel to the East to select each year's inventory. The new methods cut time and money costs and allowed more frequent changes in stocks.

As time passed, most mixed-function businesses tended to specialize in one activity. Wholesalers also increasingly specialized much as retailers had. Firms began to handle only groceries, dry goods. hardware, or other narrow product lines. After 1900, wholesale houses encountered increasing competition from large-scale retailers, such as chain and department stores and associations of independent retailers. The use of brand names encouraged direct sales from manufacturers to retailers. Although wholesalers' sales continued to increase in absolute terms, they suffered an approximately 13 percent drop in the proportion of all items sold at retail in the 60 years after the peak of their power in 1869.[8]

The Role of the Middleman

Those who buy products only to sell them in the same physical form to someone else at a higher price have always had a public relations problem. To many people, it appears that since distributors do not physically change the items they handle, they do nothing but raise their prices. Not infrequently the middleman apparently attempts to persuade customers to pay still higher prices.

There is no doubt that the income of distributors comes from the difference between the purchase prices and sales prices of goods. But this does not make the distributor useless at best and an expensive parasite at worst, one whose only function is to raise prices. Such views are accurate only to the extent that middlemen perform no function of value to ultimate consumers or charge more than the opportunity cost of such services. All too often people forget that corn flakes at the factory in Battle Creek, Michigan, are not as convenient for consumption in Colorado as those in a Denver supermarket. In fact, they are not really even the same commodity. Even if consumers could buy directly from the original producer, they might not find him willing to sell in convenient quantities or to hold inventories to ensure a constant supply. These are the functions of distribution, and clearly they both involve time and other scarce resources and are of value to consumers.

The growing volume and variety of goods that became standard items of consumption in this period and their more extensive geographic markets made the tasks of distribution more complex. Not only did a much greater

---

[8] Ibid., p. 224.

variety of goods and services, many in new forms and quantities, have to be distributed over a wider area, but many—and their means of production and distribution—required continuous servicing. If the proportion of final prices representing distribution costs rose at all during the period, the increase was modest.[9] The task was not accomplished without waste nor to the satisfaction of all consumers. These points, however, did not distinguish distribution from any other economic activity. The quantity, guality, and variety of goods available to consumers all increased dramatically over this half-century, while their prices fell in relation to per-capita incomes.

INTERNATIONAL TRADE

Even though the U.S. share of all world trade nearly doubled from 1870 to 1900 and continued to increase thereafter, trade with other nations became less important to the welfare of the American population. This paradox resulted from the growth of the American economy. Not only did aggregate American economic growth exceed that of nearly all the country's major trading partners, but it also resulted in great diversification. American exports grew at rates equal to or only slightly below that of the overall economy, but imports failed to keep pace. In 1870, imports were 7.9 percent of U.S. gross national product and exports were 6.2 percent. By 1900 the figures were 4.3 and 7.4 percent, respectively, and in 1914 they were 4.9 and 6.1 percent.[10] In the years immediately after World War I, these figures—particularly for exports—rose because the United States was the only undamaged industrial nation, and its food and manufactured

goods helped Europe recover from that catastrophe.

As might be expected, the massive internal changes in the American economy affected international trade. Before the Civil War, the United States had exported agricultural products such as cotton, tobacco, wheat, and raw materials. Its imports were largely semifinished and finished manufactured goods. Since the early days of the nineteenth century, trade had been heavily concentrated on Europe. After the war, as Table 15.1 reveals, these patterns changed. Although agricultural products remained important, cotton and tobacco lost ground to beef, pork, and wheat. Exports of crude foodstuffs (chiefly wheat and beef) peaked in 1880 and then fell as a portion of total exports. Processed foodstuffs (flour, packed meat, and other semiprocessed foods) increased in importance until 1890 and maintained a larger share of total exports than did crude foodstuffs.[11] American industrialization caused the proportion of manufactured imports to decline, while the export of finished goods increased. The proportion of semifinished and finished goods in American exports more than tripled by 1914 and continued to rise thereafter, reflecting U.S. primacy among world industrial powers. However, the growth of American manufacturing had little effect on the composition of exports until the turn of the century.

Concentration on Internal Trade

There is little evidence that export markets were important to any large sector of the American economy except agriculture. For most producers, demand came overwhelmingly from the growing domestic economy. Domestic markets were the primary influence on product devel-

[9] S. Lebergott, *The Americans: An Economic Record* (New York: Norton, 1984), p. 318.
[10] U.S. Department of Commerce, *Historical Statistics*, vol. 2, p. 887.

[11] Ibid., pp. 898–899.

Table 15.1 Composition of U.S. Merchandise Exports and Imports

Exports

Date	Crude Materials	Crude Foodstuffs	Manufactured Food	Semimanufactured Goods	Finished Manufactures	Total*
1860	68.7%	3.8%	12.3%	4.1%	11.4%	100.3%
1870	56.8	11.1	13.5	3.7	14.9	100.0
1880	29.5	31.6	23.4	3.5	11.3	99.3
1890	36.6	15.6	26.6	5.4	15.7	99.9
1900	24.8	16.5	23.3	11.2	24.2	100.0
1910	33.6	6.4	15.1	15.7	29.2	100.0
1914	34.3	5.9	12.6	16.1	31.1	100.0
1920	23.3	11.4	13.8	11.9	39.7	100.1

Imports

Date	Crude Materials	Crude Foodstuffs	Manufactured Food	Semimanufactured Goods	Finished Manufactures	Total*
1860	11.3%	13.0%	16.9%	9.9%	48.6%	97.7%
1870	13.1	12.4	22.0	12.8	39.9	100.2
1880	21.3	15.0	17.7	16.6	29.5	100.1
1890	22.8	16.2	16.9	14.8	29.3	100.0
1900	33.2	11.5	15.6	15.8	23.9	100.0
1910	37.1	9.3	11.7	18.3	23.6	100.0
1914	34.3	13.1	12.0	16.8	23.7	99.9
1920	33.8	11.0	23.5	15.2	16.6	100.1

*Totals may not add to 100.0% because of rounding.
Source: U.S. Department of Commerce, Bureau of the Census, *Historical Statistics of the United States: Colonial Times to 1970,* 2 vols. (Washington, D.C.: Government Printing Office, 1975), 2:889–890.

opment and manufacture as well. With its large, rapidly growing population and high per-capita incomes, the U.S. economy constituted the largest single aggregation of purchasing power on earth. Such a market offered ample scope for economies of scale in any manufacturing process. The design of both consumer and capital goods reflected the conditions of the domestic market, rather than the market for exports.

American agriculture, however, was a major exception to this pattern. As much as one-quarter of U.S. wheat production was exported before 1900, and in periods of rapid agricultural expansion the proportion of the increase

in farm products shipped overseas was higher still. As much as one-half the increase in wheat and pork production was exported.[12] This pattern reflected both increases in American agricultural productivity and changes in European economies. European populations and incomes were also rising at this time, and the attractions of these growing markets, when combined with decreasing barriers to international trade—particularly before 1880—drew a growing stream of food imports from many

[12] L. Davis et. al., *American Economic Growth: An Economist's History of the United States* (New York: Harper and Row, 1972), p. 558.

quarters of the world. Such developments put increasing pressure on the Continent's grain and meat producers, forcing many to produce other crops or even get out of agriculture. The demand for American agricultural products was made more effective by lower ocean freight rates, improved handling and loading methods, and refrigerated ships.

Changing Import Patterns

The changes in imports were less dramatic, but they too reflected the growing wealth and industrialization of the United States and the increasing international specialization that took place at this time. Although imports of manufactured goods fell in relation to total imports, this decline had nearly ceased by 1900. American industrialization produced a growing demand for some inputs such as copper and tin, which were either unobtainable within the United States or not present in sufficient quantities at current price levels. Growing American incomes spurred demand for coffee, sugar, silk, tropical fruits and oils, and other luxuries or their ingredients. With the exception of chemicals and a few resource-specific products that were cheaper to transport as finished or semi-finished goods than as raw materials, imports did not constitute a significant proportion of the needs of any American industry by 1910. The U.S. economy produced a wide variety of goods, most of them more efficiently than any other nation.

New Trading Partners

Changes in the direction of trade also occurred. A larger portion of American exports now went to Canada, Asia, and Latin America, and a lesser portion to Europe (see Table 15.2). The traditional primacy of Europe, and especially Britain, as a destination for American exports declined as new overseas markets were developed—sometimes at European expense.

Still, nearly two-thirds of American exports were sent to Europe after 1900, and only Canada among the new markets rivalled Britain and Germany. Americans might talk of the "limitless markets" of China, but the United States never succeeded in sending as much as 9 percent of its exports to the entire continent of Asia in any single year of this period.[13] As World War I would make tragically clear, the developed nations of the world were each others' best customers.

Europe furnished slightly more than half of all U.S. imports throughout this era, and its share fell only slightly before World War I. Even so, American imports increasingly originated on the Continent rather than in the British Isles. Britain alone had provided a third or more of all American imports before 1860, but she was no longer the only industrial economy in Europe, and British specialties were goods that the United States had little need to import. After 1900 France and Germany combined furnished a larger share of imports than the United Kingdom, and the share of all other European countries approached that of Britain.[14]

Within the Americas, Cuba, with its sugar and tobacco, retained its position as the largest single Western Hemisphere source of American imports. After 1900, however, Cuba's primacy was increasingly pressed by Canada, Brazil, and Mexico. The Americas and Asia furnished the United States with imports, not markets. Exports to these regions were consistently lower than imports.[15]

The Balance of Payments

For virtually its entire history before 1874, the United States had bought more merchandise from other nations than it had sold to them.

---

[13] U.S. Department of Commerce, vol. 2, *Historical Statistics*, pp. 903–904.
[14] Ibid., pp. 906–907.
[15] Ibid.

Table 15.2 The Balance of Trade, 1860–1920
(in Millions of Current Dollars)

Date	Total Exports	Total Imports	Trade Balance*
1860	400	362	38
1870	451	462	−11
1880	853	761	92
1890	910	823	87
1900	1,491	930	570
1910	1,919	1,646	273
1914	2,532	1,991	541
1920	8,664	5,784	2,880

*A positive figure denotes an excess of exports over imports.
Source: U.S. Department of Commerce, Bureau of the Census, *Historical Statistics of the United States: Colonial Times to 1970*, 2 vols. (Washington, D.C.: Government Printing Office, 1975), 2:884–885.

The difference was made up by the earnings of its merchant marine and by borrowing abroad. Foreigners had purchased securities issued in the United States in lieu of goods. In the 1830s and 1840s, the foreign exchange brought in by immigrants could also be applied against the trade deficit. From these sources, plus gold exports after 1849, the United States earned enough to pay interest and dividends on its foreign debts, to finance remittances to the overseas relatives of immigrants, and to cover the travel expenses of Americans in Europe. For about a decade after the Civil War, these trends largely continued, although the war had all but ended the role of the American merchant marine as a source of foreign exchange.

By 1914, however, the picture was very different from that prior to 1874. The United States exported more than it imported—after 1900, far more—and did so in every year but two after 1874. Until 1895, the United States had continued to increase its foreign debts, borrowing more from foreigners than it repaid or invested overseas. The interest and dividend payments made to foreigners had increased with America's foreign debts. After the mid-1890s, American citizens began to make significant foreign investments, and in the twentieth century, the net foreign debt of the United States began to fall.

Another growing source of foreign claims against the United States was immigrant remittances to relatives abroad, a flow that more than offset the foreign exchange they brought into this country. The numbers of those already here and their increasing ability to aid their families in the "Old Country" more than offset the effects of even the heavy immigration in the last quarter-century of this period. As the American merchant marine lost its competitive edge, foreign ships carried a larger proportion of American imports and exports, and shipping charges added to the volume of foreign claims. Still, the balance of payments, unlike the balance of merchandise trade, must always balance: foreign claims against the United States must equal American claims against the rest of the world. America's earnings from the export surplus and the continued flow of European investment were sufficient to meet foreign claims arising from the needs of debt service, shipping payments, and remittances. In fact, a small surplus was left to import gold to add to U.S. monetary reserves or, later, to finance American overseas investment.

The Role of Industrialization

The sources of these developments lay in American economic growth and monetary policies. Industrialization proceeded faster in the United States than in Europe, so that American price levels declined relative to those of other nations. As American goods became cheaper to foreigners, the price of foreign goods rose within the United States. This was the case both before 1879, while the American price level was being pushed down to allow resumption of the prewar gold standard (see Chapter 13), and also after fixed exchange rates had been reestablished.[16] After 1879, the combination of fixed exchange rates and greater productivity increases in the United States than abroad made American goods increasingly attractive buys in foreign markets. Foreigners discovered that while a British pound sterling always bought $4.86—give or take about 3¢—after 1879, that $4.86 purchased a growing amount of American goods. Price levels in the United States were still falling in relation to those of the country's major trading partners on the eve of World War I. The terms of trade continued to move in America's favor in all decades except the 1880s, although the trend was slower than in the first half of the century.[17]

Industrialization increased the variety of items that the United States produced, and as many were goods that had formerly been imported, imports were supplanted by domestic production. Both trends became especially marked after the mid-1890s, and the trade surplus grew with particular rapidity after they took hold.

World War I greatly increased the American trade surplus. It also changed the country from a net debtor on foreign account to the world's largest net creditor. During the war, both private citizens and the U.S. government made huge loans to the Allies. Foreign investments in the United States were sold to finance American exports to the combatants, who could not pay with goods while their economies were devoted to war production. The war hastened America's rise as a creditor nation but did not begin it. American overseas investment and debt repayment had been increasing faster than European investment for over a decade prior to the war. In 1914, American investments in other countries, all privately owned, were about $3.5 billion, while foreign investments in the United States were valued at $7.2 billion.[18]

Tariffs

Trade between nations had become easier after 1870. Both physical and political barriers were reduced: communications improved after transAtlantic telegraph cables were successfully laid, and shipping rates continued to fall. Barriers imposed by government action were also reduced. More and more European nations reduced their tariffs and relaxed other trade restrictions, allowing foreign goods more nearly equal competition with domestic than ever before. This trend was reversed in the 1880s, but while it endured, international trade was as free from political interference as it has ever been, and international specialization increased. There were only two major exceptions to this trend: Czarist Russia and the United States of America.

U.S. tariff rates had gradually been reduced in the 1850s, but they were sharply increased to cover the costs of the Civil War. In 1860, the average tariff rate on items subject to duties had been just under 20 percent and about one-fifth of all imports entered the United States duty free. By 1865, the average tariff was almost 48 percent, and by 1870 virtually all imports were subject to tariffs as the

[16] J. Kindahl, "Economic Factors in Specie Resumption: The United States, 1867–1879," *Journal of Political Economy* (February 1961).

[17] Davis et al., *American Economic Growth,* p. 566.

[18] U.S. Department of Commerce, *Historical Statistics,* vol. 2, p. 869.

duty-free list was drastically reduced. By and large, tariff rates were held at from 40 to 50 percent of the value of the goods until 1914. Then, the introduction of the federal income tax and popular opposition to the tariff provided both an impetus to reduce rates and an alternative source of revenue (customs duties provided nearly half of all federal government revenues between 1865 and 1913).[19] The proportion of duty-free imports was increased after 1872, and by the time rates were finally cut, nearly half of all American imports were not subject to duties.[20]

The Rationale for Tariffs

High tariffs were a cornerstone of Republican party policy, and the Republicans controlled both Congress and the presidency for most of the time between the Civil War and 1912. Even when the Democrats were in power, there was little effective tariff reduction. A few manufacturing interests (and their employees) fervently advocated high tariffs and exerted disproportionate influence on policymaking. Although farmers generally supported tariffs, they received few benefits from this stance: the United States had a huge surplus of agricultural exports at this time, and even if rates on agricultural imports had been made prohibitive, it would have had only a minor effect on the fortunes of American farmers. Although one purpose of tariffs was to furnish revenues for the federal government, there was no real effort to determine whether lower rates might not produce more revenue by increasing imports more than in proportion to the rate reductions.

It may well be, however, that high tariff rates were maintained for so long because they were not very important to most Americans. Tariffs did raise the price of imports and distort resource allocation into less productive patterns, but the aggregate effects on the American economy were small. Imports were not a large portion of domestic consumption for most items, and there was considerable internal competition even in most of the American industries receiving protection that compensated for the lack of that from abroad. Since foreign trade was unimportant to most Americans, the argument that high American tariffs limited foreigners' ability to earn dollars and thus buy American exports would have only a limited impact. With the exception of a few small industries such as tin-plated steel and sugar refining, U.S. producers generally did not need tariff protection to survive or even flourish. Many proved it by successfully exporting their products to the very countries against which they sought tariff protection.

Even so, opposition to high protective tariffs gradually increased. Much of it was based on the general antipathy toward anything that smacked of monopoly, a primary feature of Progressive thought at this time. Charges that the tariff was the "mother of trusts," even if not particularly valid, had widespread political appeal. Such opposition was influential in forcing the rate reductions and expansions of the duty-free list that occurred after 1900. Nevertheless, even the total abolition of all protective tariffs would have only slightly reallocated American resources and had little effect on the overall cost of living. The tariff survived as long as it did because it conferred substantial benefits on a few owners and employees in protected industries at the cost of almost unnoticeable reductions in the welfare of all other Americans. Such a situation produces a political equation of formidable strength today: we should not be surprised to find that it was equally effective a century ago.

IMPERIALISM

From 1870 to 1914, the developed nations of the world extended their political dominion over virtually the entire globe. At the close of this period, few nations were not either exer-

[19] Ibid., p. 1106.
[20] Ibid., p. 888.

■ Grover Cleveland felt it was his duty to reduce the tariffs, but achieved only slight success.
Source: Harper's Weekly, 1888.

fought a war on Chinese soil in 1895 to determine which nation would control the northeastern provinces of the Celestial Kingdom, and the Chinese were unable to even make an effective protest. The islands of the world, no matter how remote, became part of the empires of one developed nation or another. Only Latin America escaped outright loss of sovereignty, and many Central and South American nations were able to preserve no more than nominal independence. The new empires differed from earlier colonies in that most did not attract European settlers in any numbers.

There was one notable exception. Japan escaped the fate of other small, underdeveloped nations by rapidly transforming from potential victim to aggressor in 40 years. Half a century after its "opening" by Commodore Perry's squadron, Japan itself had joined the ranks of the Great Powers. By 1914, the European empires had nothing to teach the Japanese about forcible extension of national power.

The Rise of American Imperialism

The United States began its imperialist career—at least on the new model—rather late. Of course, continuous expansion into territory held by the Indians had occurred since the early seventeenth century, but generally through an extension of settlement. Even the Mexican War had led to acquisition of lands that Mexico had claimed but settled very thinly or not at all. The United States had not expanded into areas held by other "civilized" cultures (California might be a partial exception). Although our attitudes might differ today,[21] from the time of the first

cising control over other regions or subject to another country's control.

Africa was almost entirely divided among half a dozen or so European powers. Only Liberia (where blacks of American ancestry practiced their own brand of local imperialism) and Ethiopia retained their independence. Imperial Russia had expanded into central Asia and was plainly attempting to extend its control into Manchuria, Korea, and China. Britain and France took over all of southern Asia except a few buffer states (Persia, Afghanistan, and Siam) and the crumbling remnants of the Ottoman Empire. China escaped outright partition only because the European powers that nibbled at her borders and extracted a series of humiliating concessions were unable to agree on how to divide so rich a prize. Japan and Russia

[21] It is by no means certain that attitudes would be different. South American governments have made little serious effort to preserve Indian lands against encroachment, and the record of indigenous governments in Southeast Asia is worse. For a discussion of the historical patterns, see Lebergott, *The Americans,* Chaps. 1 and 2.

settlements Americans believed that land left in its natural state by the Indians could be taken at will for more productive uses—and it was, with little regard for prior commitments. The U.S. purchase of Alaska in 1867, largely to keep it from British control, had been in this vein.

The United States was hardly a great military power in the late nineteenth century. In no year from 1870 to 1897 did it have as many as 50,000 men in all its military services combined,[22] and American forces were clearly designed for deployment within North America or, more likely, the United States itself. The country had little capacity for overseas adventures; the United States Navy was hardly worthy of the name. Fortunately, its capacity to defend even the American coast was never tested in this period.

After 1890, the American stance changed with startling speed. The United States began to construct a modern navy and to take a far more active political and military role outside its own borders than it had for decades past. Before this time, there had been no consistent support for interference in the internal affairs of other countries, even when U.S. citizens' lives were in jeopardy. In one instance, the United States refused to intervene to prevent Nicaragua's execution of William Walker, who had attempted to gain political control of that country once too often. But this attitude changed, both in regard to local governments and other nations' efforts to extend their control into areas where the United States had or was attempting to obtain interests.

The Perils of Imperialism

The United States and Imperial Germany came close to violent clashes in Samoa and the Philippine Islands (1898) and exchanged very strong language over German attempts to intervene in South America. After some qualms

[22] U.S. Department of Commerce, *Historical Statistics*, vol. 2, pp. 1141–1142.

by the Cleveland administration, in 1898 the United States annexed a short-lived Hawaiian republic set up by American citizens who had overthrown the native monarchy. The American ambivalence over Latin American adventures ended. At the very least, the United States made no effort to avoid war with Spain, and the Spanish-American War (1898) led to U.S. control over Puerto Rico and Cuba, as well as Guam and the Philippines in the Pacific. When Colombia balked at American efforts to obtain permission to build a canal across the Isthmus of Panama, the United States actively supported a revolt there and prevented its suppression by Colombia (1903). Not surprisingly, the new Republic of Panama granted the United States permission to build its canal.

From about 1900 on, anyone meeting the ultimate authority in a Central American or Caribbean nation was almost as likely to confront a colonel in the United States Marines as a native of the area. Under the Roosevelt Corollary to the Monroe Doctrine, the United States assumed the right to intervene in Latin America any time it appeared necessary—to the United States—to restore order or ensure the payment of debts to foreigners. This policy was to some extent a response to British and German efforts to collect debts with battleships when diplomatic efforts failed.

Even more startling departures from traditional American policy occurred in the Far East. The Philippine Islands and Guam were acquired from Spain when the Spanish-American War ended just before the turn of the century. Especially in the Philippines, American sovereignty was extended over a nation previously told to regard the United States as its liberator from Spanish rule. Moreover, the Filipinos were a civilized people who had been Christian for centuries. It took a brutal war (1899–1901), unpleasantly prescient of a later Southeast Asian expedition, to force the Philippines to accept American rule. The United States may have made no territorial demands on China, but it was most anxious to avoid exclusion from any made by other powers.

The Motives for Imperialism

Imperialism has been defined as "the formal or informal extension of sovereignty beyond the borders within which it was previously exercised."[23] The actions of the United States just described fit the definition, as did those of the Europeans and the Japanese. If there is any difference at all between American imperialism and other nations', it lies in its scale, not its nature. Compared with that of other nations, U.S. imperialism was modest, particularly in view of the country's size and capabilities. But all the imperialists of this time were inspired by similar motives.

What were these motives? Two common, rather contradictory explanations for imperialism are the need for overseas markets to stave off the results of overproduction in advanced capitalistic societies and the need for raw materials not obtainable within home borders. A further motive often proposed is the lure of profitable overseas investments, sometimes thought necessary by a tendency towards falling profits as capitalism develops.

Such motives do not appear to explain American imperialism—or any other nation's—at this time. Even had the market of 100 million Americans possessing the world's highest incomes been unable to absorb all that the U.S. economy was capable of producing, it seems a little strained to envision anyone seeking rescue by adding the demand represented by Guam to this domestic market. Even if all the areas of formal and informal American control are combined, the picture is only slightly less ridiculous. Furthermore, far from adding to American markets, the regions of overseas im-

perialism exported more to this country than they imported from it.[24] Finally, it remains to be explained how markets are expanded by increasing the cost of reaching them. The extension of political control over regions that did not welcome it required the expenditure of money and lives, and whether it made the subjected people more inclined to buy American products is highly questionable.

The need-for-raw-materials argument appears even less justified by the facts. First, the controlled areas were by and large neither known nor suspected sources of raw materials the United States lacked. As Finley Peter Dunne's "Mr. Dooley" remarked, most Americans did not know whether the Philippines were islands or canned goods before their acquisition.[25] Second, there was virtually no thought that the United States' natural resources were inadequate, or ever might be. During this period, the United States produced an export surplus of most important industrial raw materials, and those it imported did not originate within its new empire. Had raw materials been a primary motive for imperialism, the United States would have directed its attentions toward Canada. (Mexico may be a partial exception to this conclusion.) Third, it is not necessary to control an area politically to trade with it. In this era, even the regions controlled by other imperialist powers were open to U.S. trade and investment, often on more favorable terms than those of the controlling state itself.

Imperialism did not provide investment outlets, and investors both in the United States and elsewhere were under no illusions that it did. The areas of imperialistic activity from 1870 to 1914 offered neither better markets nor cheaper resources than already available else-

---

[23] R. Zevin, "An Interpretation of American Imperialism," *Journal of Economic History* (March 1972).

[24] U.S. Department of Commerce, *Historical Statistics*, vol. 2, pp. 903–907.

[25] For a fascinating and humorous commentary on political and social events in the United States at the turn of the century, see Finley P. Dunne, *Mr. Dooley on Ivrything and Ivrybody.*

■ During a period of imperialistic expansion, the U.S. acquired the Phillipines. As this cartoon demonstrates, not everyone was impressed by the results of U.S. imperialism. *Source:* New York *Herald*, 1898.

and Mark Hanna, the voices of financial and industrial capital.

Neither the American empire nor those newly acquired by other nations attracted large proportions of these nations' foreign investment. Much of what little did occur was undertaken for political or military purposes, rather than the prospect of economic gains.[28] No clear-cut evidence of a decline in the rate of profit has ever been demonstrated for this period. Foreign investment by both Europeans and Americans was overwhelmingly in countries well able to maintain their political independence under stable governments. In fact, the United States itself received more foreign investment than any other single country over this period. Other regions of large-scale foreign investment were the self-governing dominions (not the colonies) of Great Britain.[29] Contrary to imperialist slogans, then, trade did not follow the flag in any meaningful sense of that expression.

If the need for markets, raw materials, or profits from overseas investments—indeed any rational economic motive—does not explain American imperialism, then what does? If it somehow developed out of the nature of capitalism, we must then explain why imperialism is at least as old as civilization (the paleontologists would suggest it is older) and has occurred under regimes that under no stretch of the imagination could be termed capitalistic. Cro-Magnons, Assyrians, Imperial Chinese, Aztecs, and Incas were all enthusiastic practitioners of imperialism. The roots of imperialism appear to lie in disparities of political and military power, not the natures of the highly diverse economic systems involved. As befits an activity whose costs have consistently exceeded

where. In the absence of political control, the risks of investment in such regions had proven unacceptably high, which was why only minor fractions of the international investment were directed to them.[26] Although the return on American overseas investment was higher than the domestic rate of return, the difference was slight—no more than would be accounted for by greater risks. Moreover, most American investment abroad was in areas outside U.S. political control, and it amounted to no more than 1 percent of total investment by this country before 1897 and 6 percent from 1900 to 1929.[27] Prominent businessmen in the United States were strongly opposed to imperialistic ventures, and their ranks included J.P. Morgan

[26] See H. Feis, *Europe, the World's Banker, 1870–1914* (New York: Norton reprint, 1965) for a discussion of the prospects and motives for overseas investment at this time.
[27] S. Lebergott, "The Returns to U.S. Imperialism, 1890–1929," *Journal of Economic History* (June 1980).

[28] Zevin, "An Interpretation." See also J. Hughes, *Industrialization and Economic History: Theses and Conjectures* (New York: McGraw-Hill, 1970), Chap 8; W. Woodruff, *The Impact of Western Man* (New York: St. Martin's Press, 1967), Chap. 2; Feis, *Europe, the World's Banker;* and Lebergott, "The Returns to U.S. Imperialism."
[29] Feis, *Europe, the World's Banker.*

its gains, most of the motives for imperialism are noneconomic.

Cultural and racial chauvinism play a large role in imperialism. Americans and Europeans of this period (and perhaps others) were inclined to believe that their political and economic systems were superior to those of any other country. At the time, they had some basis for this opinion. These nations had achieved representative governments, predictable legal systems, and high standards of living, health, and technological progress. Moreover, many had done so within the memories of living men. When they contrasted these achievements with the political chaos then plaguing much of Latin America or the inept brutality that passed for government in many other regions, it is easy to see why outsiders concluded that such conditions could be improved by introducing the institutions that had produced such good results in their homelands. It seldom occurred to them to ask whether the changes were welcome. All too often the less-developed areas furnished "proof" that outside control was needed. The murdered missionary, continuous tribal warfare, slavery, broken contracts with the outside world, or the barbarous mistreatment of their own nationals all appeared adequate rationales to the advocates of intervention.[30]

Today, the notions of "Manifest Destiny," the "White Man's Burden," or the "Civilizing Mission" and other justifications for assuming control over distant nations may appear transparently racist and/or chauvinistic nonsense. At the time, however, they were regarded very differently. Nor were these views held by tiny political or economic elites within the imperialistic nations; they were the opinions of large numbers of ordinary people. President Theodore Roosevelt was cordially detested by much of the American business community, but "Teddy" was the most genuinely popular pres-

■ Domestic economic expansion led to a U.S. policy of interest in foreign markets.
Source: Denver *Rocky Mountain News*, 1900.

ident since Andrew Jackson. His ardent and outspoken imperialistic opinions apparently enhanced the esteem in which he was held by the electorate. The fortunes of those British politicians who opposed the Boer War (over 1899–1902 Britain conquered the previously independent Boer republics of southern Africa) reinforce this view.

The Costs of the Empire

The costs of imperialism may have exceeded its gains but those costs were very low. Industrialization conferred an enormous military advantage on the Europeans, Americans, and Japanese over nonindustrialized nations. Ridiculously small forces with modern equipment, organization, and training could and did overcome large armies using traditional military methods and weapons. Often the imperialistic forces found local allies eager to even old scores, just as they had among American Indians. Nor were imperialist adventures likely to carry great political costs. To oppose the imposition of stable governments and western ideas of justice merely because the prospective beneficiaries did not want them was to seem to favor the continuation of practices that the West found abhorrent. If there were military cas-

[30] Hughes, *Industrialization and Economic History*, Chap. 8.

ualties, the troops involved were long-term professionals, not draftees. Those carrying out the imperialist mission presumably had a clear idea of the risks of military service, which were generally low.

Great Power politics was another factor contributing to imperialism. The United States acquired several areas (Alaska in 1867 and Hawaii in 1898) to forestall their control by other powers, generally Britain. This, of course, could be a self-sustaining process. Nations aspiring to Great Power status required large military forces, and the military tended to seek employment to justify its existence. The United States Navy was powerfully influenced by the seapower theories of Albert T. Mahan. Mahan regarded a strong blue-water navy as absolutely essential for the maintenance of U.S. security. Such a navy required bases, both in the United States and in outposts from which American foreign trade and critical arteries such as the Panama Canal could be defended. If military aspirations were sufficiently grandiose, the acquisition of new outposts might cease only when they reached those of another Great Power.

Finally, even though imperialism was not profitable, the lack of positive returns for the imperialist country as a whole did not mean that some individuals or firms might not extract rents from both their own governments and the subjected areas. They might be able to shift most of the costs of their actions to taxpayers and the military.[31] If the United Fruit Company could count on the support of the Marines without charge, it might be better able to extract concessions from Central American governments that could resist pressure from firms, but not military force. Once again, an opportunity for a small group to reap concentrated gains that were considerably lower than the aggregate cost borne by a much larger, less organized population generated rent-seeking activity. If "glory" could be added to unimpressive empirical returns, so much the better.

Further support for these views lies in the ways most imperialistic ventures were proposed. Theodore Roosevelt urged the American people to "forget their pocketbooks for once" and support the Spanish-American War. Only when the costs of their proposals were questioned did the imperialists begin to talk of markets, fields for investment, or sources of raw materials. There were links between economic development and imperialism, but it was the former that reduced the costs of imperialism. Imperialism may have been cheap, but that did not make it profitable on an aggregate basis.

The imperialism of America and other developed nations during this period was real enough, but its links to economics were weak. The real causes lay in cultural, political, and technological developments, and only secondarily in any rational calculations of potential costs and gains. Whatever the record of U.S. imperialism may have been, the political harvest was almost certainly negative. Latin Americans have shown a lasting distrust of the United States ever since this period. They had legitimate cause to resent both U.S. tactics and the premises on which they were based.

SELECTED REFERENCES

Chandler, A., Jr., *The Visible Hand: The Managerial Revolution in American Business,* Cambridge, Mass.: Harvard University Press, 1977.

Cohen, B. *The Question of Imperialism: The Political Economy of Dominance and Dependence,* New York: Basic Books, 1973.

Davis, L., et al. *American Economic Growth: An Economist's History of the United States.* New York: Harper and Row, 1972.

Feis, H. *Europe, the World's Banker, 1870–1914.* New York: Norton reprint, 1965.

Hilgert, F. *Industrialization and Foreign Trade.* Geneva, Switzerland: League of Nations, 1945.

---

[31] Zevin, "An Interpretation."

Hughes, J. *Industrialization and Economic History: Theses and Conjectures.* New York: McGraw-Hill, 1970.

Maizels, A. *Growth and Trade.* Cambridge, England: Cambridge University Press, 1970.

Ratner, S. *The Tariff in American History.* New York: Van Nostrand, 1972.

Taussig, F. *The Tariff History of the United States.* 7th ed. New York: G.P. Putnam's Sons, 1923.

U.S. Department of Commerce, Bureau of the Census. *Historical Statistics of the United States: Colonial Times to 1970.* 2 vols. Washington, D.C.: Government Printing Office, 1975.

Wilkins, M. *The Emergence of Multinational Enterprise: American Business Abroad from the Colonial Era to 1914.* Cambridge, Mass.: Harvard University Press, 1970.

Williamson, J. *American Growth and the Balance of Payments, 1820–1913.* Chapel Hill, N.C.: University of North Carolina Press, 1964.

Woodruff, W. *The Impact of Western Man.* New York: St. Martin's Press, 1967.

CHAPTER

16

GOVERNMENT IN AN EXPANDING ECONOMY

*T*he 1870–1914 period has long been regarded as the high tide of both the sentiment for and practice of laissez-faire, the philosophy of minimal government intervention in the economy. By modern standards, government's economic role in this period was indeed small, both in terms of aggregate fiscal impact (the proportion of GNP accounted for by government) and the scope and nature of regulation. Still, government's impact on the U.S. economy increased, particularly after 1900.

THE LAISSEZ-FAIRE ERA

Government's aggregate fiscal impact may well never have been smaller than shortly after the Civil War, but our knowledge of local government finances does not permit a firm conclusion. Governments at all levels purchased only a very small share of the economy's total output. Even so, it is clear that all three levels of government—federal, state, and local—were not restricted to the roles prescribed by laissez-faire. It must be kept in mind that laissez-faire does *not* imply no economic role for government. Private property cannot exist without government guarantees of the rights of ownership. Thus, there is a governmental role in a laissez-faire economy, but it is limited to maintaining internal law and order, providing security from foreign attack, settling disputes between citizens through the courts, and little else. Since these activities all require resources, some form of taxation is also implicit.

The Market Economy and Contemporary Thought

The laissez-faire philosophy rests on the belief that a market economy will produce optimum economic results without interference by government. Adherents believe that markets provide more efficient responses to economic stimuli than any other form of economic organization yet devised. In their opinion, the market system expresses the interactions between human wants and scarce means of production. Through the interaction of supply and demand in competitive markets, such a system will provide automatic (though not perfect or instantaneous) responses to changes in tastes, resources, or technology as they occur and generate continual pressure to use resources to produce the most highly valued mix of goods and services available factors of production and techniques will allow.

The market system provides the population with as much as possible of what it wants most through a most unlikely driving force—individual self-interest (a less elegant term is greed). Individuals' efforts to obtain as much as possible for themselves in a system of informed and voluntary exchange lead to concern for others' wants and needs. This occurs because producers' incomes are greatest when they employ their talents and nonhuman resources to provide others with the products they value most highly. The makers of output do so, not necessarily out of love for their fellows, but to increase their incomes so they can obtain more of the items they desire for themselves. Customers will pay more for goods they desire than for items someone else has decided they should have.

Moreover, as tastes or productive capabilities change, the system pressures producers and consumers alike to take the new situation into account. When the supply of petroleum products declined in the early 1970s, producers realized that finding and supplying oil and its derivatives paid more than it had in the past. They were thus encouraged to discover and exploit new reserves or develop techniques allowing greater production from existing resources. Manufacturers of goods that used petroleum products found it in their interest to modify product designs to use less of the scarce resource—to make their goods more energy-efficient. At the same time, higher prices encouraged consumers to drive less, buy smaller cars and more heavily insulated houses, and even relocate to reduce the distance between home and job.

The market automatically incorporates and adjusts to information that other economic systems might be slow to recognize or find difficult to accommodate. It provides a system of feedback that allows rapid and conclusive evaluation of alternatives through prices. It thus provides an efficient and economical response to economic stimuli.

Efficiency

If all participants in a market economy have a wide range of alternatives as both buyers and sellers and accurate information about these choices, the system will eventually produce the mix of goods and services that most nearly satisfies their desires within the limits of the available productive capacity. Productive resources will be allocated to uses where the value of their output is greatest compared with the alternatives perceived by consumers. By producing the greatest value, the resources (and their owners) receive the largest possible real incomes. The system will exert continual pressure to employ more efficient (input-minimizing) methods so that producers either produce a greater value of the same goods or use the resources saved to make other goods: both raise incomes.

Once the economy has completely responded to all available opportunities to increase income (the economist's long-run equilibrium), a competitive market system will turn out the largest possible output of the items most highly valued by consumers permitted by the available means of production. Moreover, it will also generate prices for these goods that reflect their value in terms of foregone alternatives—the real cost of any scarce good. In addition, the system will produce maximum human freedom: each person may produce or consume as he or she wishes, subject only to the costs imposed by foregone alternatives.

As a theoretical construct, no economic system superior to a competitive market has ever been devised—although under certain equally idealized conditions, a fully planned economy can produce identical results given the same human wants and productive capabilities. The market system developed long before any comprehensive analysis of it had been worked out, but by the end of the nineteenth century, economists had formulated a complete theoretical description of its operations.

In part, the theory of the market system developed from a search for better results than those produced by the extensive mercantilist intervention in the economy practiced by most governments in the seventeenth and eighteenth centuries. As with most ideas, the concept of minimal government intervention was selectively applied by many people. Most were willing to reduce government's influence where such action might increase their own incomes, but loath to do so if it might impose costs on them. Allegiance to free markets throughout the economy was and is rare; few persons really welcome competition in their own jobs or for the items they wish to buy or sell.

Social Darwinism

One nineteenth-century doctrine carried the cause of economic nonintervention a great deal further than mere laissez-faire. Social Darwinism was an attempt to apply Charles Darwins's views on the role of biological selection of animal survival characteristics to economic affairs. The theory of markets views income distribution as a reflection of individual productivity. Those resources or their owners that contribute a great deal to others' satisfaction, as indicated by consumers' willingness to pay for the product, will receive high incomes; those making smaller contributions will receive less. The resulting income differences (and a market

system guarantees income differentials unless people have uniform productivity-influencing attributes) provide incentives to self-interested individuals to become more productive—to produce what others want to buy, or to do so more efficiently.

Social Darwinism not only stressed the roles of income differences, it viewed the attributes that generated them as hereditary—much like the characteristics that promoted or hindered survival of an animal species. To Social Darwinists, interfering with income differences determined through the market would not only reduce the incentives for both high-income "donors" and low-income beneficiaries in the short run, but over time would enhance survival of the less productive and discourage further development of high productivity among those receiving the largest incomes. Thus, humanity would become less productive, or at least lose incentives to become more productive. Even more, the proportion of those less able to produce would increase as the incapable passed on their own characteristics to their offspring. The theories of Social Darwinism went a great deal further than either free-market economists or biologists had pushed their ideas; few if any of them believed that productivity was genetically determined.

Even though Social Darwinism was widely publicized by intellectuals, the press, and (surprise!) those with high incomes, it is not clear to what extent nineteenth-century America ever really accepted the idea. There were too many examples of income mobility in both directions and of government actions that curtailed markets yet unquestionably improved general welfare (for example, the restrictions in individual freedom imposed by public health regulations) to make belief in the most extreme versions of this theory tenable. It was obvious that some of the poor were talented and ambitious, and some children of the rich had inherited material possessions but not personal attributes from their parents. But in a world beginning to develop some movements for income redistribution, the theory's conclusions about its pernicious effects were music to the ears of the wealthy. Social Darwinism was a very convenient prop for those opposed to joint efforts by workers or voters to raise incomes through unions or government measures; it viewed these as morally wrong and economically ruinous and stressed the economic virtues of individual rather than joint action. At least in direct form, little redistribution occurred until the very end of the period.

Market Failure

The sweeping changes that occurred with industrialization, the rise of giant corporations, and urbanization changed some institutions of economic activity and created other entirely new ones. When institutions change or are newly developed, individuals will try to shape them to their own advantage or devote resources to protecting themselves from losses that might result from others' attempts to gain. The very increase in incomes and wealth produced by these changes may have convinced some people that some form of redistribution was now worth trying to achieve.

The view of the completely self-regulating market system was honored in the breach as time passed. Both in providing government services, which sometimes had redistributive aspects, and in regulating economic activity, there had always been an element of governmental intervention, however slight. In some cases, measures had favored one group over others or over the general public, as in tariff policy or legal attitudes toward worker or producer organizations. Even when the operation of a competitive economy is fully understood, some of its results may clash with individual ethics as well as self-interest. The idea that, under a market system, people receive the value of what they contribute to others' welfare implies that those with high incomes have a disproportionate voice in deciding what is to be produced,

because they have a great many money "votes" for their own desires. Further, some people's productivity may be very low or even negative for reasons beyond their control (the critically ill, for example). Such persons will have little or no voice in determining what society wants under a pure market system. In consequence, people with a large share of total income can influence what constitutes productivity in others by their purchases.

At the end of the nineteenth century, it was clear that not all markets provided either buyers or sellers with a wide range of choice. The impact of monopoly may well have been overstated at this time, but it was obvious that the economy was not perfectly competitive, and many feared that monopoly was increasing. Nor was the economy completely stable; even though a market system contains automatic adjustment mechanisms that reallocate resources as circumstances change, it cannot prevent such changes and probably makes them more likely than many other economic systems. Reallocative adjustments cannot always be made quickly enough to prevent individual hardship. If jobs are lost in one town or industry because of changing tastes or techniques, the unemployed will be pressured to take their best alternative occupations, but the process may require a prolonged search for those alternatives.

THE ECONOMIC FUNCTIONS OF GOVERNMENT

Even the idealized model of a market economy, in which all markets are perfectly competitive and information is freely available to all parties, contains a very definite role for government. Certain economic activities can only be performed effectively by government: security, the settlement of disputes, and the provision of public goods whose benefits to the economy exceed their cost but for which charges for individual use cannot efficiently be made. In addition, the very process of defining rules—or refusing to do so—influences the climate of economic activity and hence the activity itself. Defining the extent to which individuals are responsible to others for the consequences of their actions changes the scope for economic activity. Also, the refusal of government to influence some element of the economy is not neutral: it carries an implicit acceptance of the consequences of unregulated private action through markets.

The views of most Americans favoring a limited economic role for government were more than mere self-serving justifications of the status quo on the part of those favored by current conditions. As the preceding pages have emphasized, there is ample evidence that most U.S. citizens had prospered under the limited government of this era. Furthermore, American pragmatism had allowed departures from laissez-faire where the gains from such actions were obvious. But increasingly, changing economic conditions demonstrated the inadequacy of institutions designed for a period when most people were small-scale farmers with limited ties to the rest of the economy.

Rent Seeking

Government can also be used by individuals to achieve personal gains regardless of the cost to others. In market transactions, each party pays more or less directly for the items obtained, and sellers will not continue to provide goods whose costs of production exceed their sale prices. But government breaks this direct connection between costs and benefits. Goods provided through government still require scarce resources and thus impose costs on the economy in terms of foregone alternatives. But those costs may be borne by people other than those who receive the government-produced or -funded goods.

There is no such thing as free goods made from scarce resources for the economy. Nevertheless, it is quite possible that individuals may shift the opportunity cost of the items or services they obtain through government action to others. Government can be used to create rents for individuals through income transfers, protection from competition, or other forms of favoritism. Since the recipients of these rents pay less than the full cost of providing them, they are likely to demand more than is economically efficient from the viewpoint of the entire economy. Further waste may occur because those required to pay for such transfers (taxpayers or consumers) are likely to devote resources to preventing such losses. Resources devoted to rent seeking or its prevention can only redistribute or retain existing real income, and the economy sacrifices the alternative output they might otherwise have achieved. In a world of scarcity, this means that total welfare is reduced.

Professors Lance Davis and Douglas North have observed that both the private and governmental institutions of a market system tend to be stable unless some individuals or groups perceive an opportunity for gains from changing them that exceeds the costs of the change.[1] Perceived gains may be in access to economies of scale, externalities, the correction of market failures, attitudinal changes concerning risk, or income redistribution (not necessarily toward greater equality) through the government's coercive powers.

The first four types of change add to total incomes and need not (although they fre-

---

[1] L. Davis and D. North, "Institutional Change and American Economic Growth: A First Step Toward a Theory of Institutional Innovation," *Journal of Economic History* (March 1970). See also L. Davis et al., *American Economic Growth: An Economist's History of the United States* (New York: Harper and Row, 1972), Chap. 17; D. North and L. Davis, *Institutional Change and American Economic Growth* (Cambridge, England: Cambridge University Press, 1971); and D. North, *Structure and Change in Economic History* (New York: Norton, 1981).

quently do) involve income redistribution. Since no one will lose in absolute terms, they may be achieved by purely voluntary means: they are unlikely to generate opposition. For example, legal provision for corporate structures might allow a firm to mobilize sufficient capital to fully use economies of scale in manufacturing. Government aid to railroad construction (at least in the form of grants of otherwise useless land) might be another example—if the railroads were expected to make a much greater contribution to aggregate income than indicated by their receipts alone, and private capital was not available because railroads were regarded as a high-risk investment.

Market failure can result from high information costs. Especially in new markets, information may be difficult and costly to obtain. Once mechanisms to generate it are established, they are often subject to increasing returns: the same mechanisms can provide additional information without a proportional increase in costs. When mortgage companies established their networks of agents in the capital-starved West and sold eastern investors their own securities rather than individual mortgages, they allowed funds to flow from areas of low interest rates and proper assessment of investment prospects to regions where high interest rates had not previously compensated for investors' inability to evaluate risks.[2]

Redistribution and Economic Efficiency

Income redistribution might be direct, through government's tax and spending policies, or through grants or withdrawal of monopoly power to some private group. In these cases, however, there are problems. Since income redistribution can only award to recipients what

is taken from donors, opposition to such programs is inevitable. Further, government actions are less reversible than market transactions. If benefits fall or costs rise, the volume of market transactions will decline, but results less desirable than expected may not be so easy to discontinue if they were achieved through government action. Examples are tax policy, tariffs, the control of monopoly through public utility regulation and antitrust, and the grant of monopoly power to professional groups through laws allowing them to limit their own membership.[3] All these examples and more were areas of government activity from 1870 to 1914.

North and Davis found that government actions had both positive and negative effects on the American economy in this period. Government fiscal powers might be used because private financial markets were poorly developed, for example in canal financing. As capital markets grew and corporations became more common, government aid became less necessary. It was not used to the same extent for railroads as for canals, and was not employed at all for manufacturing. On the other hand, urbanization, with its numerous positive and negative externalities and growing need for public goods, favored the growth and extension of government services. So did the rise of a national market, which placed a premium on the accurate compilation and distribution of information.[4] Government's aggregate size and goals are not determined solely by dispassionate assessments of costs and benefits. Ideology also plays an important role: people develop institutions to further their views on what the economic environment should provide.[5] Through this period, prevailing attitudes very much favored individual responsibility for each person's welfare and action through the market.

---

[2] Davis and North, "Institutional Change and American Economic Growth: A First Step."

[3] Ibid.
[4] Ibid.
[5] North, *Structure and Change,* Chap. 5.

There are thus two possible roles for government in a market economy. On one hand, government is an absolute necessity for the efficient functioning of private markets. But on the other, it is also a mechanism for introducing inefficiency into the system by encouraging rent-seeking behavior in a form that may be very difficult to excise. One authority observed that stable and long-established political systems encourage the formation of rent-seeking groups because any gains are likely to be long lasting and the results of change more predictable. But the same author concluded that the U.S. economy in this period was not stable. Technology and resource supplies were changing rapidly, and effective rent-seeking coalitions were difficult to form while entry into most markets remained open and the federal structure made it difficult to achieve governmental aid that extended over the entire economy.[6] Others view this period as a watershed in which government became increasingly receptive to rent-seeking efforts, rather than devoted to promoting aggregate economic growth.[7]

THE SIZE OF GOVERNMENT

Little is known about the aggregate impact of local government spending before 1902 but that it was larger, probably for the entire period, than either federal or state government spending. Consequently, it is impossible to measure trends in total government spending before the turn of the century. By modern standards, the aggregate fiscal impact of government was very small throughout the period, but

it rose after the Civil War.[8] This increase was concentrated in areas with large urban populations. Spending apparently rose more rapidly than population, although perhaps no more than per-capita income, which rose strongly over this time.[9] As Table 16.1 indicates, the data show no clear trend in federal spending relative to GNP between 1880 and 1913.

Both state and local spending rose after 1902, and state spending may have been increasing even before then, although its 1902 dimensions cast doubt on the idea that it could ever have been much less. Local spending almost certainly rose, perhaps substantially, after the Civil War. Even by 1900, however, total spending by all levels of government was just under $20 per U.S. citizen. Local governments accounted for 45.9 percent of this amount, the states for 16.6 percent, and the federal government for the remaining 37.5 percent. By these measures, government expenditures were 8.3 percent of GNP. Clearly, if the criterion was aggregate fiscal impact, the role of government in the United States was slight. Public spending on goods and services shows no rise in relation to GNP before 1900, remaining at about 5 percent, and it rises only to 6 percent in the first decades of the twentieth century.[10] Transfer payments had become more important, particularly for the federal government, after the Civil War.

The taxes to support this spending were levied on property—almost entirely real estate—at the local level, while the federal government relied largely on tariff income with lesser amounts from excise taxes on liquor and

---

[6] M. Olson, *The Rise and Decline of Nations: Economic Growth, Stagflation, and Social Rigidities* (New Haven, Conn.: Yale University Press, 1982), pp. 94–117.

[7] T. Anderson and P. Hill, *The Birth of A Transfer Society* (Stanford, Calif.: Hoover Institute Press, 1980).

[8] L. Davis and J. Legler, "The Government in the American Economy, 1815–1902: A Quantitative Study," *Journal of Economic History* (December 1966).

[9] Ibid.

[10] Data are from T. Berry, *Revised Annual Estimates of American Gross National Product*, Bostwick Paper #3 (Richmond, VA: Bostwick Press, 1978). These estimates appear to imply lower per-capita income levels than are generally accepted.

Table 16.1 Government Spending, 1860–1920
(Millions of Current Dollars)

Date	Federal Spending	Percent of GNP	State Spending	Percent of GNP	Local Spending	Percent of GNP	Aggregate Percent of GNP
1860	$ 63.1	1.6%	—	—	—	—	—
1870	309.7	3.7	—	—	—	—	—
1880	267.6	2.7	—	—	—	—	—
1890	318.0	2.4	—	—	—	—	—
1902	572.0	2.6	$ 188	0.9%	$ 959	4.4%	7.9%
1913	970.0	2.4	398	1.0	1,960	4.9	8.3
1920	3,763.0	5.1	1,397	1.9	4,567	6.2	13.2

Source: U.S. Department of Commerce, Bureau of the Census, *Historical Statistics of the United States: Colonial Times to 1970*, 2 vols. (Washington, D.C.: Government Printing Office, 1975), 1:224 and 2:1123–1132.

tobacco. The states also relied heavily on property taxes.[11]

The largest single item of federal government spending was defense. Consequences of the Civil War, such as veterans' pensions and interest and principal repayments on the national debt, ranked second. State government spending was distributed over many functions, with only hospitals, education, and general administrative costs receiving sizable portions. Local governments spent most of their funds on education and highways, with public utilities receiving a growing but still small share after 1900.[12]

The Redistributive Aspects of Government Spending

Federal taxes and expenditures had some redistributive effects, at least in a geographic sense. Since revenues were largely derived from

tariffs and excise taxes, their impact was concentrated on eastern seaports and urban areas. Military spending, the largest single federal expenditure, was heavily directed toward the frontier. It was so far out of proportion to the damage from Indians that two students of the period's fiscal policies suggested, only half in jest, that most states would have benefited from importing a few moderately hostile Indians because their presence did so much to raise federal spending. This policy, together with that of establishing post offices in sparsely settled regions where the volume of mail could not finance them, helped transfer income to the new regions of the country. The regions enjoying more than their share of federal spending were the Old South, which contained the District of Columbia and only one major seaport, Baltimore; the Rocky Mountain States, with their army outposts; and New England, which received large sums through repayment of government debt to its bondholders and through veterans' pensions.[13]

There is some evidence that federal expenditures rose in recessions and offered coun-

[11] U.S. Department of Commerce, Bureau of the Census, *Historical Statistics of the United States: Colonial Times to 1970*, 2 vols. (Washington, D.C.: Government Printing Office, 1975), 2:1106–1120.

[12] Ibid., pp. 1119–1120.

[13] Davis and Legler, "The Government in the American Economy."

tercyclical effects, but in view of the overall magnitude of government spending and its variations (and the virulence of the business cycle), the results could not have been very significant. In general, all levels of government were inclined to spend whatever amount was raised by current taxation and to tax any likely source of revenue incapable of effective protest. Little attention was paid to the macroeconomic effects of such programs, and even less was understood about them. The federal government did not even have a formal budget until 1921, and few areas of expenditure were sensitive to the business cycle except as they related to the banking system. Thus, the aggregate tax and expenditure policies of all levels of government were neither oriented toward preventing of major economic fluctuations nor large enough to accomplish this before 1914. Table 16.1 indicates that spending levels for all governments had a tendency to increase permanently after major wars.

GOVERNMENT PROGRAMS AS A SOURCE OF GROWTH

Chapter 9 pointed out that aggregate government spending is only one measure of public expenditures' impact on the economy. Another is the effects they produce in other sectors of the economy. If government expenditures are concentrated on activities that are uncommonly productive (or the reverse), the amount of spending or its relation to GNP may not indicate its effects on economic growth. In this period, there were at least four "uncommonly productive" types of government expenditures.

Railroads. Government aid to western railroads directed capital toward a use where the social rate of return was at least twice that on private capital. Thus, government assistance to

the railroads yielded a rate of return to the aggregate economy twice that obtained by the railroads themselves from such funds. However, it is not at all clear that the railroads' own (private) returns were insufficient to attract construction funds.[14] Much the same is true for government expenditures on education and agricultural research; public health probably required government rather than private spending to be effective.

Public Education. Education appears to have had very high social rates of return, particularly at the primary and secondary levels, where efforts were concentrated at this time.[15] Although high school enrollment began to increase rapidly after 1900, even in 1914 only 1 person in 9 of high-school age or older was a graduate.[16] Colleges in that period enrolled about 1 in every 35 persons in the 18- to 24-year-old age group.

Despite the large numbers of former slaves and immigrants with low literacy rates compared to those of native whites, no nation in the world had higher literacy rates than the United States by 1914.[17] American educators stressed the fact that enrollment in publicly supported high schools and colleges was open to all, but only a small portion of the children of lower income groups attended. In those days of child labor and ready employment for unskilled workers, the cost of education in terms of foregone income rose steeply with age. For

[14] L. Mercer, "Building Ahead of Demand: Some Evidence for the Land Grant Railroads," *Journal of Economic History* (June 1974).

[15] A. Fishlow, "Levels of Nineteenth-Century American Investment in Education," *Journal of Economic History* (December 1966).

[16] Davis and Legler, "The Government in the American Economy."

[17] Fishlow, "Levels of Nineteenth-Century American Investment." See also Fishlow, "The American Common School Revival: Fact or Fancy?" in *Industrialization in Two Systems: Essays in Honor of Alexander Gerschenkron,* ed. H. Rosovsky (Huntingdon, N.Y.: Robert E. Krieger Publishing Company, 1966).

■ Adopted in 1882, the Pledge of Allegiance was one of the Americanizing aspects of education for many immigrant children.
Source: Museum of the City of New York.

all but the most determined of the poor, the cost of advanced schooling was too high.

Nevertheless, the ability to use education was a significant factor in improving economic efficiency. The achievement of American blacks in attaining literacy is especially noteworthy. In 1865, of course, virtually all of the newly liberated blacks were illiterate. By 1900, 55.5 percent of all nonwhites were literate, and by 1920, the figure had climbed to 77 percent.[18] When one remembers that this education came at high costs in foregone earnings for people (especially adults) whose incomes were pathetically small, one can see the determination of blacks to fully participate in the American economy.

Public Health. Public health regulations created a more productive work force and reduced the incidence of premature deaths,

[18] U.S. Department of Commerce, *Historical Statistics,* vol. 1, p. 382.

particularly among children and infants (see Chapter 14).

Agricultural Research. Although the Morrill Act provided federal funds and land grants to support state colleges in 1862, it was not until the turn of the century that the agricultural schools and experimental farms established through this legislation began to produce significant results. Even the principles of basic research procedures were unknown when this effort began, and the contribution that sciences such as chemistry, geology, and statistics could make to agricultural research was not realized. Thus, it took time to develop effective programs. After that time, however, the application of science to agriculture began to greatly increase productivity.

Other Programs. Federal land policy was really a transfer of wealth from public to private hands. It was clear that the land produced far more income for farmers and cattlemen than as part of the public domain. The high tariffs of the period cost more in resource misallocation than they produced in revenue, but their overall impact was slight. Veterans' pensions owed far more to the efforts of pressure groups such as the Grand Army of the Republic than to any degree of economic rationality. They were one of the earliest examples of pure rent seeking. Most defense spending contributed neither enhanced security nor technological spinoffs during this period, but military spending was far below its present dimensions. Expenditures on roads may have had high social returns, but I am unaware of studies on this point. Since the "uncommonly productive" aspects of government expenditures accounted for a large portion of the total, it seems safe to conclude that government expenditures were about as productive as private, although the range of results from various programs was probably wider.

THE INCREASING
SCOPE OF GOVERNMENT

If the fiscal impact of government, even its areas of primary concentration, was modest, another factor to examine was whether and to what extent government modified private economic activity by providing and changing its rules. The details of bank regulation, monetary policy, international monetary considerations, immigration, and the Federal Reserve have already been discussed, as has most of the important labor legislation. In this period government at all levels began to be concerned with many other aspects of economic life. Conditions of life in the cities were of much concern, and government activities aimed at such humanitarian goals as regulating the working conditions of women and children affected labor force productivity and even the size of the work force.

Public Utility Regulation

Some urban developments posed a dilemma. Services such as water, gas, electricity, and sometimes intraurban transportation were subject to great economies of scale. A single source of such utilities, once established, could provide service at lower costs per unit than could a multitude of producers, and it might well be able to serve additional customers at only slightly higher costs. Thus, to minimize the costs of such services—and in some cases, such as telephones, to provide convenient service at all—a single firm had to handle the entire operation. But such a supplier would be a monopolist—and worse, a monopolist controlling a product that had no acceptable substitutes. There was no guarantee that such a monopolist would charge prices reflecting his low costs of production. Indeed, there were sound reasons to believe that such a market position would be turned to the seller's advantage. A more

competitive market structure, however, might involve even higher prices than the monopolist's if economies of scale were large.

Two solutions to this problem were available. Cities might provide the benefits of economies of scale to their citizens by operating such services themselves (a direct expansion of local government), or they might persuade private sellers to accept regulation of their prices, output, and production methods in return for exclusive rights to the entire urban market. The relative advantages of public ownership and regulated monopolies were topics of continuous debate throughout this period, as they are today. In addition, there was the problem of ensuring efficient operation under either system—that is, making sure that prices not only reflected costs of operation, but that those costs were as low as input prices and modern technology allowed. The legal case for regulation received a powerful boost in 1877. In that year, the Supreme Court ruled that firms that operated "in the public interest" were subject to government regulation for the common good. The decision in *Munn v. Illinois* clearly allowed for expanded economic regulation, but did not spell out the forms it might take or the range of activities subject to it. In the opinion of some economists, this decision marked a major change in policy: *Munn v. Illinois* indicated a change in government's role from promoting private economic activity toward redistributing the fruits of current activity.[19]

Regulation of
Interstate Commerce

Concern over the procedures of large, privately owned firms had spurred efforts to control them. The first attempts to do so were at the state level. The operating practices of grain elevators and railroads were of great interest

---

[19] Anderson and Hill, *The Birth of a Transfer Society.*

to farm groups. The so-called Granger Laws were upheld for intrastate commerce by the United States Supreme Court, but it took an extremely restrictive view of what constituted intrastate commerce. In effect, the states' reach extended only to those firms doing business entirely within their borders. As reflected in the *Wabash v. Illinois* case (1886), the High Court in effect removed the railroads from state control and left the regulation of interstate commerce to Congress. As Chapter 12 indicated, railroad procedures, especially pricing policies, were of growing popular concern. Even more, the railroads were beginning to consolidate into regional systems, reducing or eliminating competition between them in large areas.

In 1887, Congress passed the Interstate Commerce Act, bringing under federal control those railroad procedures beyond the states' reach. The act stipulated that railroad rates were to be "reasonable," forbade discriminatory rates, rebates, and other forms of favoritism, and prohibited price-fixing agreements between railroads. To enforce the act, the Interstate Commerce Commission was established and given powers to collect information and issue cease-and-desist orders to the roads. However, by 1891 the Supreme Court had effectively denied the commission power to control rates, allowing it only to rule on the reasonableness of charges and allowing the railroads to appeal such decisions in the courts.

Economic historians are anything but unanimous on the effect of the new legislation. One study concluded that the ICC soon became the captive of the railroads, responsible to nobody but those it supposedly regulated. In this view, the commission became a convenient device for rate fixing, and its "maximum" rates in fact became the minimum rates the roads had never been able to agree upon or maintain among themselves.[20] Another view is

that the commission was captured by railroad customers, particularly farm interests, and their pressure for rate reductions left the railroads insufficient income to maintain their equipment properly or attract new investment. The short-term gains for farmers and other shippers resulted in a near-collapse of the roads during World War I.[21]

The Interstate Commerce Act was revised and strengthened in 1904, 1905, and 1910. The commission received more authority and greater ability to resist challenges to its decisions through the courts. But the first attempt at federal regulation was at best a mixed success. Railroad rates might have been more stable (after 1900 they rose less than other prices), but the railroads' problems persisted. The rate of return on capital invested in them was less than its opportunity cost, yet the railroads' high fixed costs made exit from the industry very difficult. Whether railroads' difficulties stemmed entirely from regulation or had other causes, their ability to maintain existing service became increasingly doubtful.

Antitrust

In another response to public pressure, Congress passed the Sherman Antitrust Act in 1890. Both the Republicans and the Democrats had campaigned for some type of antimonopoly legislation, and the bill sailed through both houses of Congress, gaining approval by a combined vote of 393 to 1. The Sherman Act forbade "contracts, combinations in the form of trusts or otherwise, or conspiracies in restraint of trade" and "monopolization or attempts to monopolize, or combinations or conspiracies to monopolize" in interstate commerce. It was a bill everyone could vote for, and it was left

[20] G. Kolko, *Railroads and Regulation, 1871–1916* (New York: Norton, 1970).

[21] A. Martin, *Enterprise Denied: Origins of the Decline of American Railroads, 1897–1917* (New York: Columbia University Press, 1971).

to the courts to determine what these phrases meant in practice.

Initial Interpretation of the Sherman Act

For the first few years after the act was passed, court decisions indicated that it meant very little. President Cleveland's attorney general had publicly declared that he would not enforce such legislation. The act was used successfully only against labor unions. Nor was it warmly received by the courts. In 1895, the Supreme Court held that although the American Sugar Refining Company controlled 98 percent of the U.S. supply of refined sugar as a result of a series of mergers, the company was engaged in manufacturing, not interstate commerce, and hence was beyond the reach of the act.[22] In all, the government lost six of the first seven cases it brought under the Sherman Act. However, in 1899 the *Addystone Pipe* case established the principle that price-fixing agreements between firms were illegal under the act, regardless of the form they took. This decision effectively reversed that in the American Sugar Refining Company case. The consistent application of this view of collusive agreements has been the most important contribution of antitrust enforcement to this day. Now price-fixing agreements were no longer merely unenforceable under the law, they were criminal offenses.

The Sherman Act was also used to change the structure, rather than just the conduct, of large firms, although with less profound effects. In 1904, the *Northern Securities* case established that the act could be used to preserve at least some elements of a competitive market structure by preventing a merger between two

■ In 1911, the Sherman Act was used to break up Standard Oil Company.
Source: Jersey Journal.

large railroads.[23] The high point in the use of the Sherman Act to promote a more competitive industrial structure was 1911, when the Court ordered the dissolution of the Standard Oil Company and the American Tobacco Company into a number of smaller firms. Both of these large firms had actively sought monopoly power and taken maximum advantage of it once attained. Even so, these decisions marked no attempt to establish a purely competitive structure of many small firms in each market. In both decisions, the Court stressed that the dissolutions were ordered because of the firms' conduct, which made it clear that their market power was the result of long and deliberate attempts to gain monopoly positions. Other firms achieving equally dominant positions through less aggressive methods, the Court

[22] V. Mund, *Government and Business,* 3d ed. (New York: Advocate, 1960), p. 161. N. Lamoreaux takes a very different view. In her opinion, the Court was trying to preserve states' rights to regulate firms by imposing conditions in their corporate charters. See N. Lamoreaux, *The Great Merger Movement in American Business, 1895–1904* (Cambridge, England: Cambridge University Press, 1985), pp. 162–169.

[23] The *Northern Securities* case reflected a change in the Court's attitude toward federal versus state authority. Lamoreaux, *The Great Merger Movement,* pp. 166–169.

hinted, might be exempt from dissolution proceedings.

Consistency was not a dominant feature of the Court's decisions: in 1920, the *United States Steel* case established that mere size—at least at that time—was no offense. The giant corporation was held not to have monopolized the steel industry (as it had been established to do) on the curious grounds that it had only been able to control steel prices through agreements with other steelmakers. Since U.S. Steel had discontinued such practices, the Court said it was not in violation of the Sherman Act.

Once elimininated, competition sometimes proved more difficult to reestablish than anticipated. Although the American Tobacco and Standard Oil companies were split up into a number of smaller firms, the new firms were large enough in relation to their markets to preclude perfect competition. The courts had to divide existing assets so as to produce viable firms in dissolution procedures, and the economies of scale in both cases were considerable. The difficulties were compounded by the fact that the new firms were managed and staffed by the same people who had served their predecessors.

The Clayton and Federal Trade Commission Acts

The Clayton and Federal Trade Commission acts, enacted in 1912, were attempts to clarify the government's antitrust position. Yet they probably produced still greater confusion. The normal organizing and collective bargaining activities of labor unions were specifically exempted from the provisions of the antitrust acts: the nature of unions had previously made them vulnerable to prosecution under these laws. Unfortunately, although the list of prohibited business activities under these laws was clear enough—price discrimination, tying agreements, interlocking directorates, and the acquisition of competing firms' stock were all barred—they were forbidden only if they would substantially reduce competition. The Federal

Trade Commission was established to enforce these acts. The FTC added little to the overall impact of the antitrust laws other than another means of prosecuting firms for activities that were already illegal under other statutes such as fraud or the Sherman Act. The requirement of substantial reductions in competition for offenses under the Clayton Act made it even more subject to court interpretation than the Sherman Act, which it had been intended to clarify.

If antitrust legislation was intended to establish a more nearly competitive structure within most American industries by increasing the number of sellers in each market, it failed. Except for the two major dissolutions, the Sherman Act and subsequent laws left the existing market structure substantially untouched. However, this is an inadequate measure of the total effect of antitrust legislation.

The Sherman Act had clearly established the principle that competition was favored over monopoly. If the courts were not willing to make the existing market structure more competitive, they were equally unwilling to allow less competition than the current structure would produce if firms acted independently. The prohibition of price fixing—which later decisions extended to nearly all attempts to restrict or exclude competition—did not end such practices. But it reduced them and limited their impact. It was now considerably more difficult for firms to collude and all but impossible for them to prevent or punish cheating. As a result, price-fixing combinations became more difficult to form and less effective to operate.

New Government Services

The data on tax burdens indicate that the American taxpayer did not have to part with a large portion of income for government services. Nevertheless, government began to provide a number of new or expanded services during this period. As federal spending grew with the economy, some of the increase was channeled into providing useful information. The Weather Bureau, Bureau of Standards, and Geological Survey were all established in this half-century. Growing concern with public safety led to the foundation of the Bureau of Mines and the Food and Drug Administration. Both agencies were designed to improve standards where the average individual might not be competent to evaluate the problems involved. As noted earlier, a Bureau of Roads was established, and in 1916 the federal government committed itself to constructing a national highway system in partnership with the states. All could in various ways be seen as improving the performance of the market economy by providing better information or an improved environment for private decisions.

Other concerns with economic affairs resulted in the formation of a Department of Commerce and Labor (later divided into separate agencies), the elevation of the Agriculture Department to full cabinet status, the birth of the Forest Service, and a variety of others. Even the conservation movement could be regarded as an attempt to control the use—or misuse— of natural resources through government. The State Department became more concerned with economic affairs. It provided Americans interested in foreign trade with information on foreign markets, products, and regulations to a greater extent than before. Occasionally it even tried to develop overseas interests where none had previously existed.[24] These expansions of the scope of governmental action, while modest, were a substantial increase from that of 1860.

State and local governments had also expanded where they had traditionally been active, such as in schools, public health, and even (very hesitantly) welfare. The small proportion of total output devoted to government may support the conclusion that the United States was still committed to laissez faire in 1914. But the trends were away from this position, as evidenced by the expansion of government activities in general and the passage of child labor and compulsory schooling laws, which were expressly designed to restrict the field of private decision making.

The Income Tax

The United States took another momentous step away from tradition when the Sixteenth Amendment to the Constitution was ratified in 1916. This amendment overcame previous legal barriers to the institution of an income tax. (The Constitution had previously been interpreted as prohibiting the imposition of direct taxes on any basis other than population.) The new tax was enacted the same year. While its initial fiscal impact was slight, the long-term consequences were not. In the first year, only 350,000 returns were filed because tax became effective only at very high income levels.[25] But the precedent that had been set would become much more influential later than even the most pessimistic opponents had claimed.

The tax was progressive—it applied only to incomes above a certain level. As incomes rose beyond the minimum taxable point, the tax rates increased faster. At incomes over $5,000 (equal to perhaps $40,000 to $50,000 in today's purchasing power) the rate increased from 1 percent to a "confiscatory" 6 percent on the portion of income over $1 million per year.[26] Since few Americans had taxable incomes of as much as $3,000 per year in 1913, the income tax was borne by the rich. It was one of the first explicit measures aimed at reducing the inequality of income distribution. Since the income tax replaced tariffs as a major source of government revenue, its effects were doubly progressive: the burden of tariffs had fallen

---

[24] R. Zevin, "An Interpretation of American Imperialism," *Journal of Economic History* (March 1972).

[25] U.S. Department of Commerce, *Historical Statistics,* vol. 2, p. 1110.
[26] Ibid., pp. 1111–1112.

largely on low- and middle-income consumers. As had the Sherman Act and the Federal Reserve Act, the income tax law indicated that American voters were no longer willing to accept all the results of an unhindered market system. In less than a year, events would produce a far larger economic role for government than most Americans had ever thought possible.

WORLD WAR I

When war broke out in Europe in August, 1914, it came as a distinct shock to the nations involved. A conflict between the developed nations of Europe was thought to be impossible—or, at worst, if the unthinkable happened, the war would be very short because the costs would be too great for even such wealthy nations to bear. To strengthen these assumptions, some noted that the workers' movements that had recently gained considerable political strength in many European nations often felt more sympathy for each other than for their own governments, and would never fight in a "capitalists' war." Others pointed to the network of alliances that ensured that each nation, if attacked, could count on help. But French workers' representatives rose to sing the "Marseillaise" after the declaration of war was passed in the French Parliament. In the Reichstag, the song was "Deutschland Uber Alles," but there was no lack of labor support in that body either, and workers of both nations marched off to slaughter each other. In the late summer of 1914 Europeans watched as those alliances, like tumblers clicking into place in a lock, dragged almost the entire continent into war.[27]

It soon became apparent that even the most pessimistic scenarios had drastically underestimated the cost of such a conflict. But the war dragged on for four terrible years. Not only did the conflict consume incredible quantities of men and supplies, but it produced an unforeseen casualty. Trade between the belligerents was, of course, discontinued, and only then did Europeans discover that they had been each others' best customers. The war shattered the network of international trade and monetary agreements that had been so important in Europe's material progress. It would not be reestablished until the 1960s.

The Course of the War in Europe

The Germans had planned to crush the French before aid from France's Russian and British allies could become effective. However, they failed because Russia mobilized much faster than anyone had expected. Consequently, the war in Western Europe became a bloody stalemate. Neither side could advance even a few miles save at a cost that could not be sustained long enough to decide the entire war. The war became a conflict of endurance, a struggle in which the economic potential of the warring nations became increasingly important. The nation that could sustain its military efforts longest would win. Once this was recognized, the belligerents tried to turn their full productive capacities toward furthering their own military efforts while destroying those of their enemies.

The British established a naval blockade of Germany that could not be broken by Germany's smaller and not very adventurous fleet. But the Germans knew that Britain was more dependent on overseas trade than they: Britain imported most of her food, as well as large quantities of industrial raw materials. The Germans attacked British trade with the only weapon they possessed that could reach it—submarines. As soon as the British recognized

[27] B. Tuchman, *The Guns of August* (New York: MacMillan, 1962).

submarines' vulnerability when they surfaced to warn enemy merchant ships before attacking them, losses among the U-boats forced the adoption of other tactics. Submarines had difficulty identifying ships and sank vessels belonging to neutral nations, and there was no means of determining a ship's cargo—or passengers—through a periscope. The British blockade of the Central Powers had little effect before 1916. But as German stockpiles of imported materials dwindled and the substitutes developed by scientific research failed to keep pace with ever-growing lists of shortages, the impact on German living standards grew. In 1917 it became acute.

In Britain and France, the diversion of shipping to military purposes, combined with losses to submarines, also reduced living standards. Even more serious reductions had already been imposed by the diversion of resources, particularly labor, to the war. All the combatants found their productive capacity inadequate in the face of the war's enormous demands. The Germans were almost totally isolated from overseas trade, especially after the British began to control the trade of European neutrals (1916) to shut off that avenue of access to the outside world.

The Early Role of the United States

As the war's costs rose, the Allies began looking to the United States, the only major industrial nation not already involved. They sought additional supplies of both munitions and food as their own productive capacity was overwhelmed. By 1916, the initial trickle of orders from the Allies had become a flood. American producers were eager to deal with buyers in no position to argue about price. After some hesitation, the Wilson administration allowed them to respond to the demand. Table 16.2 reveals that U.S. exports began to increase rapidly, both

to meet European demand and to supply traditional European export markets, such as Latin America, with the goods formerly obtained from Britain and Germany. In the Far East, Japan began to supply markets that had purchased their manufactured goods from Britain and to carry the cargos that had previously traveled in British ships.

The additional source of supply in the United States eased one of the Allies' problems, but paying for the increased imports was difficult. Because they had diverted so much of their productive capacity to war demands, the Allies had little to sell to the United States, which in any case had no increased need for imports. European exports to the United States fell off sharply even as the flow of goods from this country rose. Some form of payment had to be found to meet the widening gap. From 1914 to 1917, U.S. exports doubled, while imports rose only 55 percent. Exports to Europe more than tripled, but imports from that continent fell by almost 40 percent.[28]

Europe had traditionally made up its deficit in direct trade with the United States by running surpluses with other regions from which the United States was a net importer. Now, however, that avenue was no longer available. Europe had few goods to export to any region. Since they could no longer finance imports from America with their own exports, Europeans employed other means. The Allies shipped gold to the United States and sold their portfolios of American securities. As these resources neared exhaustion, they began to borrow from America.

Private Loans to the Allies

British and French bonds were sold not to the U.S. government, but to private citizens in this country. The firm of J.P. Morgan & Co. was active in purchasing war material on behalf of

---

[28] U.S. Department of Commerce, *Historical Statistics,* vol. 2, pp. 903, 906.

Table 16.2   U.S. Foreign Trade, 1914–1920
(in Millions of Current Dollars)

Date	Total Exports	Total Imports	Exports to Europe	Imports from Europe
1914	$2,365	$1,894	$1,486	$ 896
1915	2,769	1,674	1,971	614
1916	5,483	2,392	3,813	633
1917	6,234	2,952	4,062	551
1918	6,149	3,031	3,859	318
1919	7,920	3,904	5,188	751
1920	8,228	5,278	4,466	1,228

Source: U.S. Department of Commerce, Bureau of the Census, *Historical Statistics of the United States: Colonial Times to 1970,* 2 vols. (Washington, D.C.: Government Printing Office, 1975), 2:903, 906.

the French and British governments and in marketing their bonds in the United States. The desperate Allies used this arrangement to its fullest. Any group whose members might be able to buy bonds or influence others to do so could attract a dashing young British or French officer to tell of German "atrocities" and detail how American purchases of his government's bonds would help to preserve civilization and freedom from the "Huns." Inadvertently, the Germans aided these propaganda efforts through their own ill-considered and worse-timed submarine warfare and efforts to obtain help from the Mexican government to keep the United States fully occupied in the Western Hemisphere.[29] The propaganda of both sides appears crude and unbelievable today, but the United States was new to the world of total war. Few of its citizens, not even recent immigrants, knew much about Europe as a whole.

In all, the Allies sold U.S. securities worth $4 billion, shipped over $1 billion in gold to America, and borrowed some $5 billion from private sources in the United States. After American entry into the war, the U.S. government loaned the Allies another $9.5 billion.

[29] B. Tuchman, *The Zimmerman Telegram* (New York: Viking Press, 1958).

From a large-scale debtor, the United States had been transformed into the world's greatest international creditor in only six years.

The Economic Impact of U.S. Entry into the War

The initial effect of the war on the U.S. economy, however, was a financial panic. As Europeans scrambled to sell their portfolios of American securities, stock and bond prices fell so low that the New York Stock Exchange had to be closed. The U.S. unemployment rate began to rise in 1914; it averaged over 8 percent for all of 1915 and reached nearly 11 percent at the depth of the recession (see Table 16.3). At the time European orders for American goods really began to increase, then, the economy had very substantial unused productive capacity. By the fall of 1915, the amount of slack was beginning to fade away, and in 1916 it disappeared in some industries. During the years of active American participation in the war, unemployment continued to fall. At the war's end, it was less than 2 percent. The war had all but ended immigration. After 1916, the American armed forces began to increase rapidly. Under such conditions, the bargaining po-

Table 16.3   The Statistical Impact of World War I

Date	Money GNP (in Billions of Dollars)	Real GNP* (in Billions of Dollars)	Defense Expenditures** (in Billions of Dollars)	Wholesale Prices***	Military Personnel	Unemployment Rate
1914	$38.6	$125.6	$ .348	68.1	165,919	7.9%
1915	40.0	124.5	.344	69.5	174,112	8.5
1916	48.3	134.3	.337	85.5	179,376	5.1
1917	60.4	135.2	.618	117.5	643,833	4.6
1918	76.4	151.8	6.149	131.3	2,897,167	1.4
1919	84.0	146.4	11.011	138.6	1,172,602	1.4
1920	91.5	140.0	2.358	154.4	343,302	5.2

*In 1958 dollars
**War and Navy Departments
***Bureau of Labor Statistics data, 1926 = 100
Source: U.S. Department of Commerce, Bureau of the Census, *Historical Statistics of the United States: Colonial Times to 1970*, 2 vols. (Washington, D.C.: Government Printing Office, 1975), 1:135, 200, 224 and 2:1114, 1141.

sition of workers improved greatly, and wages rose as a portion of GNP.

These circumstances reduced employer resistance to union organization, and government and legal attitudes also favored unions. By 1920, perhaps 12 percent of the labor force was unionized. Blacks began a large-scale migration from southern agricultural employment to urban occupations, chiefly in the North. This was their first significant occupational shift since Emancipation.

American farmers gained as European demands for meat and grain skyrocketed, reflecting the Continent's disrupted trade patterns and wartime resource diversions. High demand was supplemented by government-guaranteed prices after the U.S. declaration of war in April 1917. These circumstances encouraged farmers to expand production by tilling more land, most of it less fertile than the acreage already under the plow. Farmers also increased the amount of machinery employed, which enabled them to spread a diminished labor supply over more land. Much of this agricultural expansion was financed by borrowing, a course that appeared safe enough while prices for farm prod-

ucts were high and rising. In general, despite the moves to increase output, agricultural production had shown only slight increases before 1918 even though the prices of most farm products had at least doubled.[30] The effects of farmers' increased efforts became visible only as the war ended. Farm prices had risen considerably faster than the overall price level. Under such encouraging stimuli, the total debts of American farmers had more than doubled from 1912 to 1920.[31]

The Arsenal of Democracy?

The United States declared war on Germany on April 6, 1917. From the Allies' point of view, the American role was clear. As the world's greatest industrial power, with a population of over 100 million people, the United States would supply the materials and manpower to supplement their own until it was able to mo-

[30] U.S. Department of Commerce, *Historical Statistics*, vol. 1, p. 511.
[31] Ibid., p. 491.

bilize fully. Once that was accomplished, the combined forces would overwhelm Germany. The economic might of the United States would support a military effort much larger than either the Allies or Germany, weakened by years of war, could produce from their own resources.

In fact, despite distinguished records by a few units and individuals, the direct military contribution of the United States to the war was quite modest. At the war's end, only a small part of the American army had seen action. Nevertheless, by fall of 1918 over one million U.S. troops had reached France, and Germany recognized the situation for what it was. After the last-gasp offensive in the spring of 1918 had almost, but not quite, brought a German victory, the Kaiser's forces were nearly spent. With few reserves, and civilian suffering acute, Germany was faced with the prospect of an eventual assault by American forces in overwhelming strength. Accordingly, the German generals told the Kaiser that the war was lost. The speed of the German collapse after the U.S. entry into the war made it easy for Americans to overrate their contribution to the Allied victory.

On the civilian front, harnessing America's economic potential to the needs of war proved far more difficult than anyone had expected. The United States had not fought a major war since 1865, and the Civil War, of course, had been a very different type of conflict. The most recent American combat experience, in 1898, had been a series of blunders in which American failures in supply, medical care, and even elementary sanitation killed five men for every one who died in battle.[32] Troops had been sent to Cuba and Puerto Rico in woolen winter uniforms, inadequately supplied, and with no knowledge of the tropical diseases that proved more deadly than Spanish bullets. Efforts to support the American expeditions in the Caribbean had caused a huge traffic jam on the railroads, backing up traffic from the invasion ports in Florida all the way to the Carolinas.

Only in 1915 had the United States Army exceeded 100,000 men. As a result, there were scarcely enough experienced personnel to train the forces needed for a major military effort in Europe. Supplies of almost all types were even scarcer. In some cases, not even the American military realized what was needed. For all its industrial might, the United States had little capacity to produce some of the tools of modern war, and the American forces fought with French cannon and British combat aircraft.

The U.S. Military Buildup

After 1916, little unused productive capacity remained in the American economy, so increased output of military goods could only be achieved either by expanding overall capacity or diverting resources from the production of civilian goods. The task would be complicated by the diversion of labor into the armed forces. The prewar military strength of the United States had been about 165,000 men in all services combined, but in 1918 the army and navy had expanded to nearly 3,000,000.[33] This military expansion required about 7 percent of the U.S. labor force. Even so, the total number of people employed rose slightly during the war, as unemployment all but vanished.[34] A military draft was no sooner instituted than it became apparent that some skilled workers would contribute far more to the war effort in the factories than they could in the trenches, so a system of deferments was developed. Although 24,234,000 men registered for the draft, the overcrowded training facilities and general chaos of forced-draft mobilization resulted in the actual induction of only 2,820,000.[35]

---

[32] Ibid., p. 1140.

[33] Ibid., p. 1141.
[34] Ibid., p. 126.
[35] Ibid., p. 1140.

Economic Mobilization

Economic mobilization was slightly more successful. By reducing the production of some items for civilian use, diverting others to the military, and discouraging consumption by a variety of devices, including "wheatless" and "meatless" days, more than 20 percent of GNP was devoted to military uses. Even though this was a huge increase in military production over prewar levels, American conversion to a wartime economy was far from complete by November 1918. In that year, for example, the United States produced nearly one million passenger cars.[36] Conversion to war production had, however, built up enormous momentum. Despite widespread cancellation of contracts for military production, spending by the War Department was nearly twice as great in 1919 as in 1918.

Through the war years, despite efforts to increase output from existing resources, output rose only slightly. Real investment rose very little, and what did occur apparently had not been brought into production by the war's end. In sum, the full capacity of the American economy was not yet at the disposal of the U.S. and Allied armed forces when German resistance ended.

The problems of effective conversion did not stem from lack of effort. If anything, the problem was far too many plans for mobilization and far too little coordination among them. This should not be surprising: almost nothing was known about the capacity of individual industries, and less about the inputs various sectors required from each other. In addition, only the most abstract models of sectoral interactions had been devised by economists, and they were useless without empirical data.

Little information on the amounts and types of goods needed for large-scale military action overseas was available, and what there was changed constantly. In addition, the capacities of available resources were unknown under normal circumstances and dependent on a host of contingencies—for example, the amount of steel available for battleships depended on the quantities employed for other purposes. They also depended on the number of experienced steelworkers, miners, and railwaymen drafted to serve in the armed forces.

The Diversion of Production to the Military

Since the demands of the American and Allied military and of the civilian population far exceeded available capacity, a system of priorities was needed. A series of government boards was established to increase the production of vitally needed goods, limit that of nonessentials, simplify designs, and limit varieties of many commodities. Unfortunately, these efforts were poorly coordinated. Some critical problems, such as the relative priority of American and Allied military needs, were never fully resolved. Attempts might be made to prohibit production of some "nonessential" item, for example, only to discover that just a portion of total output met that definition. With consumer incomes soaring as a result of full employment and inadequate taxes, many producers were strongly motivated to continue supplying the civilian market. Producers found themselves facing demand from the military, the Allies, and American consumers, all of whom had seemingly unlimited purchasing power, at a time when it was more and more difficult to obtain labor and other resources.

Government intervention in the economy exceeded the fondest hopes of all but the most optimistic prewar Socialists. In the most extreme case, the federal government took over the management and operation of all U.S. railroads. The railroads had proved unable to handle the strain of a huge increase in traffic, heavily oriented toward the East Coast. The

[36] Ibid., p. 716.

government operated the railroads as a single unit, compensating owners on the basis of the profits generated in the three previous years. This arrangement went far to solve the transportation crisis, but it was a startling departure from peacetime economic policies. Food purchases for the Allies were consolidated under the Food Administration, ably led by Herbert Hoover. The Shipping Board and Emergency Fleet Corporation built merchant ships and coordinated maritime traffic. Efforts to increase shipbuilding capacity were designed to overcome expected losses to Central Powers submarines and increased both production and capacity far beyond peacetime requirements.

The job of tying together the work of several thousand government agencies was given to the War Industries Board, under the direction of Bernard Baruch. The mission and methods of the War Industries Board were not well defined, and it lacked authority over the military's purchases. Some progress was made in standardizing tool design and persuading users to accept these modifications. On the whole, it was impossible to overcome the great barrier to effective planning: the lack of information on both war needs and the capacity available to meet them. Priorities were difficult to establish; even the military was fighting a new type of war and might not know how urgently it needed various goods. Even where priorities were established they were difficult to maintain, because the War Industries Board had no authority over prices and many customers were far more concerned about output than prices—a situation that did not encourage producers to voluntarily comply with the board. In the general euphoria after the war, it appears probable that the effects of all these planning efforts were highly overrated. However, their success in promoting cooperation among the firms in some industries would be a factor in the trade association movement of the 1920s.

War Finances

A large part of government war expenditures were met by borrowing. Such a scheme need not be inflationary if the government borrows funds that would otherwise have been spent for civilian consumption or investment. But government borrowing during World War I far exceeded this limit, and most of it was financed by substantial increases in the money supply. Not only did the Federal Reserve Board urge commercial banks to loan money to individuals for bond purchases, but the banks were assured that if they lacked the necessary reserves to support this extension of credit, the Federal Reserve would lend them, using either bonds or commercial paper as security. Individuals were also told it was their patriotic duty to buy bonds and urged to borrow to do so.

The federal government found that its new central bank was a very convenient mechanism to support its borrowing. Some of the restrictions on the Federal Reserve's ability to expand the money supply were relaxed to aid the process: the gold reserve required for demand deposits was reduced from 100 to 40 percent, and in 1917 member bank reserve requirements were cut.[37]

The Federal Reserve System had only begun operations in 1914, and in its first few years it could only expand the money supply as gold flowed into the United States to finance European purchases. The Federal Reserve lacked a bond portfolio that it could sell, and with the gold inflow, its rediscount policy was ineffective. Even after it acquired bonds that might have been sold to reduce the money supply, the Federal Reserve remained subservient to the wishes of the Treasury, which wanted to keep interest charges on the growing volume

---

[37] P. Studenski and H. Kroos, *Financial History of the United States* (New York: McGraw-Hill, 1952), p. 294.

■ To financially support World War I, Americans were urged to demonstrate their patriotism by buying Liberty bonds.
Source: Records of the Bureau of the Public Debt: National Archives.

of federal debt as low as possible.[38] The U.S. money supply doubled over the war years, and real output increased only modestly, as Table 16.3 shows.

About one-quarter of the war's financial costs were tax-financed, an only slightly greater proportion than in the Civil War. Income tax rates were raised to as much as 70 percent in the top bracket, and the number of persons liable to the tax increased more than twelve-fold. However, the rates were not increased to these levels until 1918, well after federal spending had begun to rise.[39] An excess profits tax was levied on corporate income. Despite the tax increases, the national debt rose by almost $24 billion from 1914 to 1919.

[38] M. Friedman and A. Schwartz, *A Monetary History of the United States, 1867–1960* (Princeton, N.J.: Princeton University Press, 1963), pp. 212–213.

[39] U.S. Department of Commerce, *Historical Statistics,* vol. 2, pp. 1110, 1112.

Much of the increase in production was beyond the reach of civilian consumers. Efficiency of production probably declined, further increasing the extent to which demand outstripped supply for nearly all goods. The result was rapid inflation (see Table 16.3). Prices more than doubled over the 1916–1920 period. Inflation began in earnest in late 1915, and in 1916 wholesale prices rose 23 percent. The next year saw a 37 percent rise. After that the rate of inflation moderated, but massive government deficits continued well into 1919, and prices did not stop rising until the middle of 1920.[40] After the war, as government spending fell, high wages, full employment, and the pent-up earnings of the war years fueled a rapid expansion of consumer demand.

The war's end saw an abrupt cessation of the mobilization effort, and the reconversion to a peacetime economy was as chaotic as the mobilization had been. The armed forces were quickly demobilized and returned to civilian life. Many government contracts for war material were cancelled on the first business day after the Armistice. Yet unemployment increased only slightly. The demand for exports continued, construction increased within the United States, and federal deficits continued for almost a year after the end of the war. Business attempted to rebuild depleted inventories, further bolstering civilian demand.

The Aftermath

The United States, at least in contrast with the European combatants, appeared to have emerged from the war almost unscathed. Some 116,000 U.S. servicemen had lost their lives, over half to disease and accident rather than military action. This loss was about one-fifth that of the Civil War, from a population three times as large. In contrast, Europe's losses were appalling. One estimate is that the Continent suffered 13,500,000 military and civilian deaths.[41] Since these losses were so heavily concentrated among the most productive members of the work force, their long-run portents were even worse than the numbers indicate.

The American economy was fully employed and prosperous, and its productive potential was greater than it had been in 1914. Europe, however, had suffered enormous material losses in addition to the loss of half a generation of young men. The network of international trade that had been a cornerstone of European growth and welfare before 1914 was shattered: it would be further damaged by the peace treaties that formally ended the war. All countries had suffered from wartime inflation, but the extent of price increases greatly varied among nations, which would further complicate the resumption of international trade. Many of Europe's overseas markets had been lost to the United States and Japan. The question of unprecedented levels of international debts incurred not for investment, but for destruction, had not even been recognized for what it was.

The United States was now the financial as well as industrial leader of the world—a role for which it was totally unprepared. It had accumulated some unpleasant wartime legacies of its own: a mass of war-induced private debt plus inflation and considerable overcapacity in agriculture, shipbuilding, and coal—industries that had no prospect of adequate peacetime markets for their current productive potential. But in 1919, neither the internal nor the external problems appeared serious to most Americans. Compared to their own circumstances in 1914, and particularly to those of Europe, Americans were better off than they had ever been. Yet there were signs that the United States was almost as unprepared for the

---

[40] Ibid., vol. 1, p. 199.

[41] J. Hughes, *Industrialization and Economic History: Theses and Conjectures* (New York: McGraw-Hill, 1970), pp. 240–241.

peacetime activity of the Twenties as it had been for war in 1914.

SELECTED REFERENCES

Anderson, T., and P. Hill, *The Birth of a Transfer Society*. Stanford, Calif.: Hoover Institute Press, 1980.

Cochran, T., and W. Miller, *The Age of Enterprise: A Social History of Industrial America*. New York, Harper and Row, 1968.

Davis, L., et al. *American Economic Growth: An Economist's History of the United States*. New York: Harper and Row, 1972.

Faulkner, H. *The Decline of Laissez Faire*. New York: M.E. Sharpe, 1977.

Fogel, R., and S. Engerman. *The Reinterpretation of American Economic History*. New York: Harper and Row, 1971.

Friedman, M., and A. Schwartz. *A Monetary History of the United States, 1867–1960*. Princeton, N.J.: Princeton University Press, 1963.

Goodrich, C., ed. *Government and the Economy*. Indianapolis: Bobbs-Merrill, 1967.

Higgs, R. *The Transformation of the American Economy, 1865–1914: An Essay in Interpretation*. New York: John Wiley and Sons, 1971.

Kolko, G. *Railroads and Regulations, 1877–1916*. New York: Norton, 1965.

Lamoreaux, N. *The Great Merger Movement in American Business, 1895–1904*. Cambridge, England: Cambridge University Press, 1985.

MacAvoy, P. *Economic Effects of Regulation: The Trunk-Line Railroads and the Interstate Commerce Commission Before 1900*. Cambridge, Mass.: M.I.T. Press, 1965.

Martin, A. *Enterprise Denied: Origins of the Decline of American Railroads*. New York: Columbia University Press, 1971.

North, D. *Structure and Change in Economic History*. New York: Norton, 1981.

North, D., and L. Davis. *Institutional Change and American Economic Growth*. Cambridge, England: Cambridge University Press, 1971.

Olson, M. *The Rise and Decline of Nations: Economic Growth, Stagflation, and Social Rigidities*. New Haven, Conn.: Yale University Press, 1982.

Studenski, P., and H. Kroos. *Financial History of the United States*. New York: McGraw-Hill, 1952

U.S. Department of Commerce, Bureau of the Census. *Historical Statistics of the United States: Colonial Times to 1970*. 2 vols. Washington, D.C.: Government Printing Office, 1975.

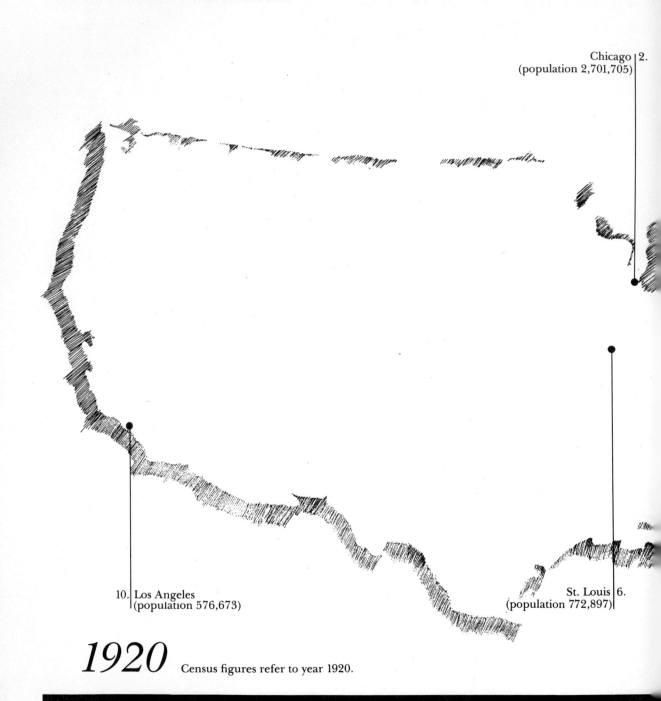

Chicago 2.
(population 2,701,705)

10. Los Angeles
(population 576,673)

St. Louis 6.
(population 772,897)

1920 Census figures refer to year 1920.

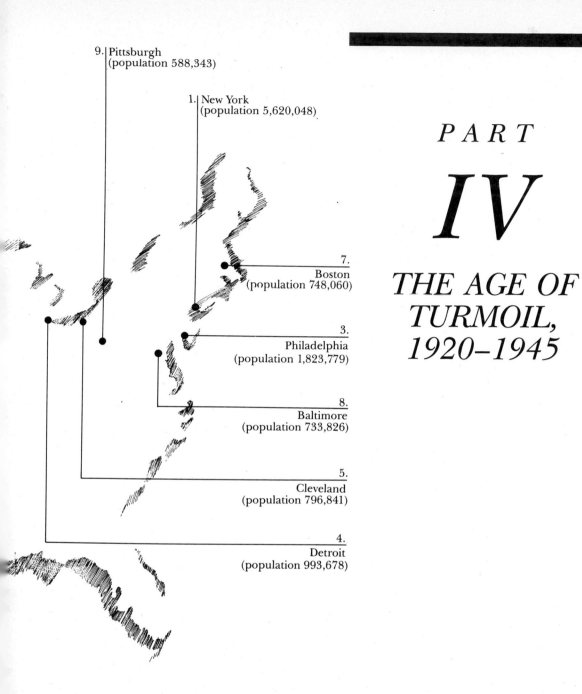

9. Pittsburgh
(population 588,343)

1. New York
(population 5,620,048)

7.
Boston
(population 748,060)

3.
Philadelphia
(population 1,823,779)

8.
Baltimore
(population 733,826)

5.
Cleveland
(population 796,841)

4.
Detroit
(population 993,678)

PART

IV

THE AGE OF TURMOIL, 1920–1945

The two decades between World Wars I and II were marked by dramatic changes in the economy, and even more sweeping changes occurred during World War II. After a decade of "normalcy" following World War I, America endured the greatest depression, the most rapid and far-reaching conversion from peacetime to war production, and the most profound institutional changes in its entire history. The era is even more remarkable because nearly all these changes took place in about 15 years.

The Twenties were a decade of economic stability and growth, stable prices, full employment, and general if not universal prosperity. The beginning of this period, then, gave little indication of what lay ahead. It appeared as though the United States had returned to an improved version of the "good years" of 1900–1914, with the added assurance that government and central bank action could offset any unfavorable (but unlikely) developments in the market economy. It was widely accepted that the U.S. economy would continue to generate improved living standards for nearly all citizens for the indefinite future. But the future proved more indefinite than anyone could imagine.

The Dimensions of Instability

The period from 1920 to 1945 was one of extremes. In nearly every aspect of performance, the dimensions and impact of economic change surpassed any that occurred before or after. Moreover, these changes appeared in nearly every aspect of economic activity. The very nature of work began to change, along with its location, the type of effort involved, and the results it produced. The extremes of macroeconomic performance were even more startling.

The United States was the only major industrial economy to emerge from World War I with all dimensions of its productive capacity not only unscathed, but enhanced. In addition, the country's new position as a center of international finance gave American attitudes an influence in shaping the postwar world that they had never possessed before. Although those attitudes retained the optimism that had characterized previous decades and initially produced conditions resembling those of the prewar era—economic growth and full employment—the very nature of growth was changing.

Productivity advances accounted for a much larger portion of increased aggregate output during the Twenties than in previous decades. Consequently, resources were reallocated between regions, types of production, and types of labor to a greater extent than ever before. Perhaps these reallocations reflected an economy in which a growing portion of income could be devoted to discretionary purchases rather than basic survival needs. They certainly also indicated an accelerating pace of technological change and improvements in communications and transportation that may have provoked increased competition, particularly within local and regional markets.

But it was the changes in output, both positive and negative, that dominated the economic history of the period. These changes, which are outlined in Table IV.1, also produced changes in the other macroeconomic indices that were without precedent over such a short length of time. The expansion of the Twenties gave way to a decline after 1929, which abruptly became the economic cataclysm of the Great Depression. A halting, incomplete recovery in the later Thirties was transformed into an almost frenzied increase in output and activity during World War II. In a complete reversal of Thirties trends, unemployment rates dropped to improbable lows and growth rates soared. Measures of economic performance during these 25 years can only hint at the impact these abrupt and enormous reversals must have had on those who lived through them. As Table IV.1 indicates, this was truly an age of turmoil.

Growth, Price, and Income Shifts

Real growth rates ranged from a decline of 14.8 percent in 1932, as the economy slid toward the trough of the Great Depression, to a peak of 16.1 percent positive growth in 1941. Consumer prices fell 10.7 percent in 1921, and wholesale prices declined more than three times as much at the same time. In 1941, the inflation rate was 12.3 percent, but even the wartime inflation that followed had not brought consumer prices up to their 1920 levels by 1945. Unemployment rates show equally extreme variation, from 24.9 percent in 1933 (which may substantially understate the real dimensions of joblessness) to 1.2 percent in 1944.[1] Few economists familiar with what economic data existed in the Twenties would have believed any of these figures credible. Fewer modern economists would like to see a repetition of the conditions that produced them.

Except in the case of inflation, such rates of change have never been equalled and rarely approached in twentieth-century America. Small wonder that as the period progressed, the American people developed strong desires for economic security and stability! Largely as a result of the upheavals of this period, there was widespread popular support for changing both the

[1] U.S. Department of Commerce, Bureau of the Census, *Historical Statistics of the United States: Colonial Times to 1970*, 2 vols. (Washington, D.C.: Government Printing Office, 1975), 1:135, 200, 210–211, 226–227.

institutions that influenced economic activity and their goals. Most of these changes occurred within government, particularly at the federal level.

Per-capita income exhibited almost equally dramatic shifts. Population growth had slowed in the Twenties. This permitted a 4 percent annual rate of aggregate economic growth (not especially rapid by prewar standards) to produce an increase of about 27 percent in per-capita incomes from 1920 to 1929. The increase would be greater still if 1921 were used as a starting date, because that year saw a severe, though short-lived, recession.

The course of income distribution during the Twenties is unclear, in part because the data for earlier periods are even less conclusive. One study found that income equality lessened considerably even during the Twenties, with most of the population receiving very small gains or even suffering income reductions while the rich garnered the vast majority of the aggregate rise in income. Wealthholdings (which are not income) may also have become more concentrated.[2] However, the statistics on which these conclusions rely had not been adjusted for avoidance of high taxes during the war and early Twenties and greater compliance thereafter. Nor do they reflect the fact that the rich took a substantial portion of their incomes in the form of undistributed corporate profits in the initial portion of the decade and less in the latter half. The data may therefore seriously overstate any increase in inequality.[3] Data on consumption trends in the Twenties indicate that income gains were widely shared.

Per-capita income fell by about one-third in the terrible 1929–1933 period and barely regained its previous level by 1940. The Thirties, then, were an era of zero economic growth. The entire economy forfeited the additional output that normal increases in capacity and technological improvement would have produced. Had the economy grown at a modest 3 percent per year during the Thirties (a 25 percent reduction from the growth rate of the Twenties), 1940 GNP in 1929 dollars would have been $144 billion. In fact it was only $121 billion, 19 percent less. Per-capita incomes rose sharply from 1940 through 1945, but much of the increase represented military production rather than goods contributing directly to improved living standards.

[2] C. Holt, "Who Benefited from the Prosperity of the Twenties?" *Explorations in Economic History* (July 1977) and R. Lampman, *The Share of Top Wealth-Holders in National Wealth, 1922–1956* (Princeton, N.J.: Princeton University Press, 1962). See also U.S. Department of Commerce, *Historical Statistics,* vol. 1, p. 302.

[3] G. Smiley, "Did Incomes for Most of the Population Fall from 1923 through 1929?" *Journal of Economic History* (March 1983).

Even before the Thirties ended, a substantial recourse to government had occurred, both to prevent further recurrence of such extreme instability and to protect citizens from its current consequences. By 1945 there was no doubt that the age of laissez-faire was over both in fact and popular attitudes. Indeed, for a time, the pendulum appeared to have swung very far in the opposite direction: many people seemed to think that all sources of real economic security lay in government. Nongovernmental institutions that promoted individual security through joint action, from labor unions to life insurance, also flourished.

Demographic Change

Population increased, but for much of the period the rate of increase declined, especially in the Thirties. In the Twenties, a prolonged decline in the birthrate was not offset by the spectacular increases in life expectancy that had occurred in the previous two decades (see Chapter 14 and Table IV.2). Despite the economic upheavals of the period, some very considerable and unarguable gains in American well-being occurred: longer life expectancy and a major decline in the infant mortality rate.

There appears to have been a close association between the falling birthrate and urbanization. Growth in the urban population accounted for 85 percent of the total increase in the Twenties, but this implied a slower rate of aggregate increase than when America's population was largely rural. Children were more expensive in the cities, where food and housing costs were greater and they were not productive assets as on the farm.

Immigration, which had gone far to offset a declining domestic birthrate prior to 1914, was sharply curtailed after 1921, falling to less than one-third its 1900–1914 average by the late Twenties. In the Thirties, it declined still more. In that decade, too, marriages and childbearing were deferred because of the depressed economic conditions. With the return of prosperity in the Forties, the birthrate began to rise again, culminating in the postwar "baby boom."

New Patterns of Growth

Population growth was not the only indication that the rate at which the United States was accumulating productive assets was declining. In the Depression, and again during World War II, investment was insufficient to offset deterioration of existing capital stock.

Table IV.1 The Dimensions of Turmoil, 1920–1945

Date	GNP (in Billions of Current Dollars)	GNP per Capita (in Current Dollars)	Real GNP (in Billions of 1958 Dollars)	Real GNP per Capita (in 1958 Dollars)
1920	$ 91.5	$ 860	$140.0	$1,315
1921	69.6	641	127.8	1,177
1922	74.1	673	148.0	1,345
1923	85.1	760	165.9	1,482
1924	84.7	742	165.5	1,450
1925	93.1	804	179.4	1,549
1926	97.0	826	190.0	1,619
1927	94.9	797	189.8	1,594
1928	97.0	805	190.9	1,584
1929	103.1	847	203.6	1,671
1930	90.4	734	183.6	1,490
1931	75.8	611	169.3	1,364
1932	58.0	465	144.2	1,154
1933	55.6	442	141.5	1,126
1934	65.1	514	154.3	1,220
1935	72.2	567	169.5	1,331
1936	82.5	643	193.0	1,506
1937	90.4	701	203.2	1.576
1938	84.7	651	192.9	1,484
1939	90.1	691	209.4	1,598
1940	99.7	754	227.2	1,720
1941	124.5	934	263.7	1,977
1942	157.9	1,171	297.8	2,208
1943	191.6	1,401	337.1	2,465
1944	210.1	1,518	361.3	2,611
1945	211.9	1,515	355.2	2,538

Source: U.S. Department of Commerce, Bureau of the Census, *Historical Statistics of the United States: Colonial Times to 1970,* 2 vols. (Washington, D.C.: Government Printing Office, 1975), 1:135, 199, 224, 226–227, 229.

Even before the Depression, growth in aggregate output was not maintained from its traditional sources. Increases in output became more dependent on increases in productivity, rather than "more of the same" methods.[4]

[4] U.S. Department of Commerce, *Historical Statistics,* vol. 1, p. 225.

Table IV.1   continued

Date	Wholesale Prices (1967 = 100)	Gross Investment (in Billions of Dollars)	Unemployment Rate (Percent of the Work Force)	Growth in GNP (Percent from Previous Year)
1920	79.6		5.2%	−4.3%
1921	50.3		11.7	−8.6
1922	49.9		6.7	15.8
1923	51.9		2.4	12.1
1924	50.5		5.0	−.2
1925	53.3		3.2	8.4
1926	51.6		1.8	5.9
1927	49.3		3.3	.0
1928	50.0		4.2	.6
1929	49.1	$16.2	3.2	6.7
1930	44.6	10.1	8.7	−9.8
1931	37.6	6.8	15.9	−7.6
1932	33.6	3.4	23.6	−14.7
1933	34.0	3.0	24.9	−1.8
1934	38.6	4.1	21.7	9.1
1935	41.3	5.3	20.1	9.9
1936	41.7	7.2	16.9	13.9
1937	44.5	9.2	14.3	5.3
1938	40.5	7.4	19.0	−5.0
1939	39.8	8.9	17.2	8.6
1940	40.5	11.0	14.6	8.5
1941	45.1	13.4	9.9	16.1
1942	50.9	8.1	4.7	12.9
1943	53.3	6.4	1.9	13.2
1944	53.6	8.1	1.2	7.2
1945	54.6	11.6	1.9	−1.7

Not only did the absolute contribution of increases in output per unit of input double in the first three decades of the twentieth century (most of the increase occurred after 1920), but as physical inputs were added at slower rates, the relative contribution of productivity increased still more. Productivity gains had accounted for about one-sixth of all growth in 1900, but in

Table IV.2 Population Statistics, 1920–1945

Date	Total Population (in Thousands)	Life Expectancy at Birth (Years)	Infant Mortality per 1,000 Live Births
1920	106,461	54.1	85.8
1925	115,829	59.0	71.7
1930	123,077	59.7	64.6
1935	127,250	61.7	55.7
1940	132,122	62.9	47.0
1945	139,928	65.9	38.3

Source: U.S. Department of Commerce, Bureau of the Census, *Historical Statistics of the United States: Colonial Times to 1970,* 2 vols. (Washington, D.C.: Government Printing Office, 1975), 1:10, 55, 57.

the Twenties the figure had grown to over two-fifths. In the twentieth century, as much as 80 percent of the gains in real per-capita income were due to gains in factor productivity.[5]

If growth is to be based on productivity increases, the efficient allocation of resources to their most productive uses is vital, and that of the largest single input—human resources—especially so. The period showed rapid and substantial changes in trends of this aspect of economic performance, as in so many others.

The combination of a market economy, geographic, occupational, and social mobility, and an effective system of formal and vocational education had served the United States well in its pursuit of economic efficiency. By no means was all talent instantly recognized, developed, and rewarded. Nevertheless, the barriers to rational uses of human skills along the lines dictated by productivity were lower in America than anywhere else, and in the Twenties several important developments reduced them even further. By the end of the decade, women and blacks had demonstrated that they could perform the jobs previously reserved for white males. The impact of mass-produced automobiles and trucks had greatly increased the range of choices open to both buyers and sellers in local and regional markets. This increase in alternatives forced, through competition, a more rational evaluation of human talent. The gains were tenuous but much greater than the groups affected had experienced previously. In addition, occupational mobility rose across the entire economy. It was easier to move from one type of job to another than it had been.

[5] L. Davis et al., *American Economic Growth: An Economist's History of the United States* (New York: Harper and Row, 1972), p. 39.

The Thirties were a massive setback: an excess of job seekers allowed full rein for the prejudices of employers (and fellow employees). In addition, many government responses to the Depression reduced mobility by attempting to restore the status quo and providing aid only to those who remained in or waited to resume their previous occupations. The lost ground was more than regained in the extremely tight labor markets of the Second World War. By 1945, even though in many instances talented people were denied a chance to improve or practice their skills, discrimination was less common than ever before. Further, the momentum for its continued decline was well established.

Increased labor productivity also stemmed from movements between regions and occupations. These, of course, had occurred from colonial days, but now the pace accelerated. The farm population, which traditionally had lower incomes than other groups, fell in absolute as well as relative terms in the Twenties and Forties. States where average incomes were high and job opportunities plentiful gained in population at the expense of those less favored. Manufacturing employment rose very little during the Twenties, but service employment and "white-collar" jobs showed substantial increases.[6] The Pacific Coast, the area around Washington, D.C., and Florida attracted the largest share of migrants. Appalachia, the Great Plains, and southern rural black populations showed declines. As had the immigrants before them, the internal migrants were responding to economic opportunity.[7] Their moves from low- to high-wage occupations benefited both the migrants and the economy.

As always, new industries appeared, old ones declined, and the growth rates of various sectors of the economy showed wide variation. The Twenties were a period of rapid growth for services, heavy industry, and public utilities and of decline for coal, railroads, and agriculture. Even during the Depression and the war, the changes in occupational patterns continued. In much of the period, however, more growth occurred in government (largely by default) than in the private sector.

Changing Institutions and Attitudes

During the Twenties, it may well have seemed to most Americans that the country had, in President Harding's phrase, "returned to normalcy." While the Twenties were by no means a static era, people accustomed to the econ-

---

[6] U.S. Department of Commerce, *Historical Statistics*, vol. 1, p. 139.
[7] L. Galloway and R. Vedder, "The Mobility of Native Americans," *Journal of Economic History* (September 1971).

omy of previous decades must have found these ten years a time of comfortable growth upon familiar foundations.

But existing institutions appeared utterly incapable of dealing effectively with the Depression. The effects of that catastrophe were not yet over when the military challenge of the Axis threatened the autonomy of the United States, both politically and economically. The last 15 years of this era, then, were a time of profound questioning and readjustment of American political and economic attitudes and institutions.

In the prolonged unemployment of the Depression, the American faith in each individual's responsibility for his or her own welfare was badly shaken. It seemed obvious that large numbers of people could not find any sort of work at any wage. The economy had not adjusted to this excess supply of labor in time to avoid widespread human suffering. Many of the unemployed ultimately had no alternative but to turn to government for immediate relief. They and many others questioned the nature of an economic system that had come so close to total collapse.

One result of this change in attitudes was the institution of government programs such as social security and unemployment compensation, both unprecedented departures from the traditional role of the federal government. Another change was the widespread view that in times of economic emergency the federal government should "do something"—an attitude that may have begun in the mobilization for the First World War. Never again would a president of the United States gain public approval for statements such as this 1921 comment by Warren G. Harding: "There has been vast unemployment before and there will be again. There will be depression and inflation just as surely as the tides ebb and flow. I would have little enthusiasm for any proposed remedy which seeks either palliation or tonic from the public treasury."[8]

For the first years of World War II, the United States paid a terrible price for its recent attitudes on international affairs (such as isolationism, cheating on defense, refusing to acknowledge aggression, and mistaking treaties, like the Kellog-Briand Pact that outlawed war, for reality), and it watched other nations pay still more. The war enormously increased the role of government in the economy, both in the military sphere and by redirecting economic activity toward support of the armed forces. In World War I, American popular opinion had overrated American economic might's contribution to the Allied victory. But the role played by U.S. productive capacity

[8] R. Gordon, *Economic Instability and Growth: The American Record* (New York: Norton, 1974), pp. 21–22.

454

in the second conflict was genuine. In addition, the direct military participation of American armed forces was on an enormously greater scale. The actions taken by government to redirect the economy were generally effective this time. (Their efficiency may have been another matter.) This success probably bolstered the belief that government could accomplish almost any task, given a little time and unlimited spending authority.

The appearance of such attitudes is understandable. So is the fact that actions taken when the political survival of the United States was thought to be at stake were often neither well coordinated nor the best of all possible responses. Extreme pressure and high emotion are no aid to rationality. Both the New Deal and the expansion of production in the early years of the war show no consistent pattern. In each case, the goals were clear enough, but there seemed to be no time to closely analyze the nature of programs, compare them with alternatives, or assess their full costs. Some now-obvious mistakes were made in the pressure-cooker atmosphere in which actions to fight the Depression or the Axis had to be made. But after World War II, few Americans were inclined to question either the efficacy or the efficiency of government intervention in the economy.

Selected References

Chandler, L. *America's Greatest Depression, 1929–1941*. New York: Harper and Row, 1970.

Davis, L., et al. *American Economic Growth: An Economist's History of the United States*. New York: Harper and Row, 1972.

Denison, E. *The Sources of Growth in the United States and the Alternatives Before Us*. (New York: Committee for Economic Development, Washington, D.C., supplementary paper #13, 1962).

Friedman, M., and A. Schwartz. *The Great Contraction, 1929–1933*. Princeton, N.J.: Princeton University Press, 1965.

Gordon, R. *Economic Instability and Growth: The American Record*. New York: Norton, 1974.

Haberler, G. *The World Economy, Money, and the Great Depression, 1919–39*. Washington, D.C.: Brookings Institute, 1976.

Kindleberger, C. *The World in Depression, 1929–1939*. Berkeley, Calif.: University of California Press, 1973.

Temin, P. *Did Monetary Factors Cause the Great Depression?* New York: Norton, 1976.

U.S. Department of Commerce, Bureau of the Census. *Historical Statistics of the United States: Colonial Times to 1970*. 2 vols. Washington, D.C.: Government Printing Office, 1975.

Walton, G. *Regulatory Change in an Atmosphere of Crisis: Current Implications of the Roosevelt Years*. New York: Academic Press, 1979.

CHAPTER

17

THE TWENTIES: GROWTH AND COLLAPSE

*T*here is a tendency to view the decade from 1920 through 1929 as a mere prelude to economic disaster. With hindsight, it seems that surely the portents of the Great Depression must have been obvious to anyone not determined to ignore them. The Twenties have been scrutinized by any number of authors searching for causes of the Depression. After analyzing their proposals, about all that can be said is that some of the phenomena they cited either contributed to the decline or worsened it once it began. But even more than five decades later, there is no single, universally accepted cause of the economic disaster that began in 1929.

Some of the explanations are pretty clearly based on the *post hoc, ergo propter hoc* fallacy in reasoning: they have nothing to recommend them but temporal sequence. The lack of respect for law engendered by Prohibition, greater freedom for women, the values (or lack thereof) of the "Lost Generation," greater concentration on material welfare at the expense of higher ideals—all have been put forward as causes of the Great Depression. None has causal relationships to later events based on much more than its proponents' determination to find a source in previous events.

TWENTIES PROSPERITY

Contemporary observers saw few indications indeed that the Twenties would be the last decade to resemble the "good years" of 1900–1914. During the decade, not only had the United States returned to "normalcy" by dismantling the government control apparatus built up during World War I, but it had achieved some substantial gains over prewar conditions. Real income, productivity, and employment all increased while prices, if anything, fell slightly. The

457

1920s were *not* a period of inflation with all economic activity concentrated on speculation or the New York Stock Exchange. The prosperity of the "New Era" was real and widespread.

The economic data for the period indicate that real output grew at from 3 to 4 percent per year, depending on the base year chosen. This rate was well above that of population growth, so it was possible for the welfare of all Americans to increase simultaneously. (It is claimed, however, that welfare increased at widely differing rates or even that the gains of high-income individuals exceeded other groups' losses.)[1] Productivity rose, particularly in manufacturing, and real wages also increased, although in industry they failed to keep pace with the increase in output. Real production in manufacturing increased 50 percent from 1921 to 1929. Unemployment, after the short but severe recession of 1920–1921, remained very low by modern standards, averaging only 4.6 percent for the entire decade and only 3.3 percent after 1922.[2] Prices fell over the decade: the 1920–1921 recession caused sharp deflation in retail and particularly wholesale prices, but after 1922 the price level was essentially stable until the end of the decade.[3] The 1920s, then, were a decade of full employment, stable prices, and economic growth. The major macroeconomic indicators hardly present clear-cut warnings of the economic cataclysm that ended the decade.

Despite its good overall record, the Twenties began with an intense depression whose causes might have made the discerning uneasy about prospects for future stability. As Chapter 16 revealed, economic activity continued at high levels after the end of World War I, fueled in part by the federal government's continued deficit spending, European demand for American exports, and expansion of the money supply. In addition, there was considerable pent-up domestic demand for both capital and consumer goods, the supply of which had been curtailed by the war.

In 1920, most of these spurs to aggregate demand abruptly declined. European recovery, particularly in agriculture, caused American exports to decline from $8.6 billion in 1919 to only $4.5 billion in 1921.[4] The federal government's budget had a $13.4 billion deficit in 1919, but in 1920 it had a surplus of $291 million, largely due to a sharp reduction in government expenditures.[5] This was a drastic change in the fiscal impact of government on the economy, equivalent to about 15 percent of GNP. A comparable change in 1986 would mean a change of over $500 billion—enough to not only eliminate the current deficit but pay off a sizable fraction of the national debt as well. At the same time, and for related reasons, the Federal Reserve System sharply curtailed credit.[6] The result of these sharp, large-scale policy reversals was a severe recession in the United States. Similar policies created the same results in much of Europe as well. In the United States, the unemployment rate reached 11.7 percent, and wholesale prices fell by about one-third. Although the depression was short-lived (by 1923 the unemployment rate was only 2.4 percent), it had clearly been caused by the government's fiscal policies and the monetary policies that supported them.[7]

That these macroeconomic influences were changed so drastically and with so little regard for their impact on unemployment and output

[1] Holt, "Who Benefited from the Prosperity of the Twenties? *Explorations in Economic History* (July 1977). See also J. Williamson, "American Prices and Urban Inequality Since 1800," *Journal of Economic History* (June 1976).
[2] U.S. Department of Commerce, Bureau of the Census, *Historical S.atistics of the United States: Colonial Times to 1970*, 2 vols. (Washington, D.C.: Government Printing Office, 1975), 1:135.
[3] Ibid., pp. 200, 210–211.

[4] Ibid., vol. 2, p. 884.
[5] Ibid., p. 1104.
[6] M. Friedman and A. Schwartz, *The Great Contraction* (Princeton, NJ: Princeton University Press, 1965), pp. 226–230.
[7] W. Lewis, *Economic Survey, 1919–1939* (New York: Allen & Unwin, 1949), 1969 reprint.

could have been viewed as an augury of things to come, or at least of government reaction to future economic fluctuations. However, it was not, and for the next eight years it appeared there would be little reason for government intervention to improve the macroeconomic situation. The government's actions did indicate that public spending's effects on the economy could no longer be disregarded now that the federal budget accounted for nearly 10 percent of GNP. They also indicated the lack of any real macroeconomic viewpoint. Aside from abstract mathematical models, even economists had not yet developed methods of viewing the economy as a whole. Nevertheless, with only minimal intervention by the Federal Reserve System and a steadily declining role (and taxes) from the federal government, the U.S. economic performance was good. Rates of per-capita income increase were comparable to those of earlier decades; slower aggregate growth was offset by a reduction in population growth. The record compared particularly well with that of nearly all European countries over the same period.

SOURCES OF GROWTH

The introduction to this section indicated that economic growth increasingly stemmed from increases in output per unit of input (productivity advances) rather than mere increases in inputs. Investment rates were high; net investment averaged about 10 percent of GNP during the decade. Not only did the nation's stock of productive equipment grow rapidly, but the capital-output ratio began to fall. This indicated that the new capital was more productive than older equipment: a dollar invested in it produced more output than it had formerly. This reversed the prewar trend, when capital had increased so rapidly relative to labor and raw materials that the effects of increased relative supply swamped those of

technological change. The decrease in population growth, and particularly in the growth of the labor force during and after World War I, was an important influence on investment. Scarcer labor meant rising wage rates, and firms increasingly substituted capital for labor. In addition, the new technology, with electrical and gasoline motors replacing steam and waterpower in factories, tended to produce fewer jobs for unskilled labor.[8]

Manufacturing and Construction

The increase in capital productivity was especially pronounced in manufacturing. A large proportion of all equipment was brought up to the highest feasible levels of performance. Electrical power was quickly substituted for steam power and plant layouts changed to make the most of its advantages. Older, less efficient plants were rebuilt or abandoned, and new factories were located closer to markets, inputs, or both. As a result, manufacturing production rose nearly two-thirds from 1919 to 1929, although virtually no change in manufacturing employment occurred.[9] The increase in manufacturing productivity made nearly the entire increase in the work force available to other sectors, and employment gains were concentrated in trade, services, and construction. Together with public utilities, these sectors grew faster than the aggregate economy.

Significant changes began to occur within some industries. From 1923 to 1925, General Motors began the now-familiar practice of annual model changes in its cars. This practice was an important factor in its rise to the number one position in the auto industry. Many small-scale carmakers found it increasingly dif-

[8] H. Oshima, "The Growth of U.S. Factor Productivity: The Significance of New Technologies in the Early Decades of the Twentieth Century," *Journal of Economic History* (March 1984). See also W. Devine, "From Shafts to Wires: Historical Perspective on Electrification," *Journal of Economic History,* (June 1983).

[9] U.S. Department of Commerce, *Historical Statistics*, vol. 2, pp. 666, 668.

■ The automobile was one of the most visible indications of prosperity in the 1920s.

ficult to compete with the large integrated auto producers who could take advantage of all available economies of scale, often by turning out several lines of cars that shared common components.[10]

Construction was another leading industry. There was a boom in residential building, both of single-family houses and urban apartments, reflecting higher incomes, greater availability of credit and longer mortgage periods, and more widespread automobile ownership. Even so, although many studies of this period have focused on the automobile, construction, and electrical appliance industries, the growth in consumer durables production only slightly exceeded that of the aggregate economy.

The mass-produced, privately owned automobile and the network of roads built in response to it made the growth of the suburbs possible. For the first time in at least six decades, America was becoming a nation of homeowners. During most of the previous urbanization, Americans had lived primarily in rented housing—apartments and residential hotels for the middle class and tenements and boardinghouses for the poor. The housing boom peaked in 1926; thereafter, construction centered on business structures, public-utility equipment, and roads.

Declining Sectors

As always, some sectors grew less rapidly than the entire economy or even declined. Some of these, particularly coal and shipbuilding, suffered from excess capacity installed to meet wartime demands. This was especially true of the shipping industry. Both shipbuilding and

---

[10] A. Chandler, Jr., *Giant Enterprise: Ford, General Motors, and the Automobile Industry* (New York: Harcourt, Brace, and World, 1964), pp. 148–152.

the merchant marine had been greatly expanded during the war, but many of the merchant ships constructed under war emergency programs were not launched until after the hostilities. In the Twenties, these ships had to compete with the results of similar programs in other nations. World trade did not regain its prewar volume until 1924, and even after that was hampered by a web of currency restrictions and trade barriers. The consequence was a worldwide glut of shipping, and the U.S. merchant marine was ill-equipped for the competition that it engendered.

Coal production stagnated in the Twenties, and prices fell as oil and natural gas production more than doubled. The coal industry had internal problems as well. The United Mine Workers pressed for wage increases in excess of productivity gains, raising unit labor costs, and mine owners' investment in cost-reducing technology was limited. In the face of increased competition from cleaner, more convenient fuels, such policies contributed to chronic unemployment in coal-producing regions.

Cotton and woolen textile production, particularly in New England, also failed to keep pace with aggregate economic growth. Rayon, the first widely used synthetic fiber, began to compete with natural materials. A greater difficulty for the textile industry was that consumer spending on clothing grew no faster than the growth of income, or even at a slower pace.

The railroads lost passenger traffic to automobiles moving along the new network of all-weather highways and were hard-pressed to maintain their freight business against growing competition from trucks. Commercial aviation had appeared, but it would not significantly impact other forms of transportation for several decades. Although the railroads had been returned to their owners after World War I, the industry had not yet overcome its prewar difficulties. Some continued to originate in the government. In a misguided effort to aid financially troubled roads, the Transportation Act of 1920 required profitable railroads to

contribute some of their earnings to support lines unable to generate adequate rates of return. There were two major faults in this policy: first, the railway industry as a whole failed to generate profits equal to opportunity costs, so the funds to be reallocated between its components were insufficient, and second, the policy penalized efficient carriers to subsidize those whose performance was below par.

Agriculture

Most studies of lagging sectors in the American economy of the Twenties devote a good deal of space to the problems of the nation's farmers. Even before the war, agricultural employment had begun to decline, and the sector's problems continued in this decade. One source of difficulty had been generated during the war. American farmers had been urged to increase their production of basic commodities by government guarantees of high grain and meat prices. These efforts, often financed with borrowed money, had only become effective after the war ended. The new production efforts were largely based on expanded cultivation of less fertile lands than those already in use and hence tended to be costly. They made economic sense, if at all, only if farm goods' prices remained high. Farm debts to commercial banks alone had more than doubled from 1915 to 1922, and farmers also borrowed heavily from insurance companies and other financial institutions, particularly after 1920.[11] The wholesale prices of farm products fell by more than 43 percent from 1919 to 1922, a considerably greater drop than in nonfarm goods.

At the same time, taxes on farm property increased. Faced with heavy fixed costs, farmers had little choice but to maintain production. If one among the millions of American

[11] U.S. Department of Commerce, *Historical Statisttics*, vol. 1, p. 491.

farmers reduced output, his action would have no noticeable impact on prices but his income would decline because he had less produce to sell. A concerted reduction in output by many farmers might raise the price of their crops, but it was impossible to coordinate. Individual farmers knew that they could benefit doubly from others' output reductions by increasing their own output and selling more at the higher price. No voluntary organization could overcome this problem.

Farm Incomes

Real incomes per farm in the Twenties averaged almost exactly what they had been in the "Golden Years" of 1910–1915. Since farm populations declined through the era, farmers' per-capita incomes rose slightly.[12] Still, the farmers' complaints were based on real grievances. First, farm incomes had been much higher over the 1916–1920 period, and farmers naturally compared the current situation to their most favorable recent experience. Second, the postwar income levels had only been attained by working more acreage and selling a higher proportion of what the land produced. The tractor was rapidly replacing draft animals on American farms, and so less land was required to produce "fuel" in the form of oats and hay, releasing approximately 24 million acres of land for cash-crop production.[13] But even though farmers increased the amount of goods they marketed, their incomes failed to rise relative to prewar levels and their costs of production were higher. While farm incomes were static, or nearly so, others' were not, thus farm incomes declined substantially relative to nonfarm. Farmers had difficulty carrying their debt and tax burdens, and foreclosures on farm property increased. The improved communications of the period made the relative decline painfully clear to the agricultural community.

The disparity between farm and nonfarm incomes was not equally shared. Farmers on marginal land or unable to afford the new, cost-reducing machinery and techniques were more seriously affected than those able to adopt new methods or diversify their crops. The northern Great Lakes states, the Ozarks, and the Appalachians were all areas of considerable farm distress. Farm incomes in California and, to a lesser extent, Florida, which produced citrus fruit and out-of-season vegetables for urban markets, were higher than the average.

The Farmers' Dilemma

The source of most farmers' problems was obvious. The demand for agricultural products was both price and income inelastic. Consumers would not increase their purchases of farm products in proportion to either reductions in their prices or increases in their own incomes. Foreign markets did not offer the outlet from this dilemma that they had before the war: they were declining throughout the Twenties. The changing nature of much nonfarm work, with fewer jobs requiring great physical exertion, even caused a per-capita decline in the consumption of some foods, such as grains.

To raise their incomes under such circumstances, farmers had three choices. First, they could move to higher-income jobs. Some farmers did: despite a rural birthrate substantially above the national average, the farm population fell 1.5 percent in the decade.[14] Second, they could reduce aggregate production, because with an inelastic demand for most farm products, prices would rise more than in proportion to the decrease in quantity. This, however, required concerted action, and there was no agency to coordinate the production plans of all farmers. In its absence, pressures on the individual farmer would continue to reduce the relative prices of agricultural goods. Most of the new techniques reduced costs only at high

---

[12] Ibid., p. 232.
[13] Ibid., p. 510.

[14] Ibid., p. 497.

■ Many farmers chose to move from traditional agricultural occupations to higher-paying urban jobs.

Source: The Depression Years as photographed by Arthur Rothstein (New York: Dover Publications, Inc., 1978), p. 31.

volumes of output, compounding the difficulties of output reduction. Third, they might somehow increase the demand for agricultural products.

Government Aid

Since consumers in domestic markets would not buy more agricultural products, especially at higher prices, farmers requested help from the government. A variety of proposals was made, culminating in the two McNary-Haugen bills passed by Congress in both 1924 and 1928, only to be vetoed by President Coolidge.

Under this legislation, the federal government would have purchased enough of each year's major crops to increase prices to their 1909–1914 relation to all other goods (the parity ratio). These government purchases could not be sold within the United States without reducing prices again, so the government was to sell them on the world market for whatever they might bring. To prevent goods acquired at such bargain prices from being resold in the United States, high tariffs were to be levied on all agricultural imports. This was an admission that the world price would be lower than the American under such programs. The government would lose on its overseas sales, but taxes levied on participating farmers would make up the losses. The greater the difference between the government's purchase price and that in world markets (where its sales would reduce prices) and the larger the quantity sold, the larger the tax required to finance the program. The McNary-Haugen bills contained no limits on aggregate farm production. This was a weak point, because such programs, once enacted, would almost certainly have generated large increases in farm production, and world demand for farm products was also price inelastic.

Farmers did receive some government assistance in the form of loan guarantees and permission to form output-restricting marketing associations. In cases where the affected crops were produced by small numbers of farmers in restricted areas, the associations had some success enforcing output limits. For the major farm crops, however, they were unworkable. In 1929, the Agricultural Marketing Act encouraged the formation of such marketing associations, but it also went a good deal further. For the first time, the government established a fund to buy agricultural products in an effort to stabilize their prices. The purchase fund was swamped by the effects of the Depression. In the face of sharp declines in farm prices, farmers believed they had no alternative but to increase production. With nonfarm incomes declining and pushing agricultural prices even lower, the increased farm production overwhelmed the funds, which were not large enough to buy all the produce offered to them. Farmers' attempts at rent seeking remained on the whole unsuccessful, but they had achieved a more favorable response from government than ever before.

The preceding discussion of declining sectors should not be construed as an indication that the aggregate performance of the American economy was unsatisfactory during the Twenties. The usual macroeconomic indicators (growth, prices, and employment) give an accurate picture of the overall situation. Declining sectors are a normal feature of a market economy: they do not necessarily indicate worsening performance. The aggregate data indicate that the growth sectors more than offset those that declined. Although slow-growing or declining industries were more prone to request government assistance than they had been earlier (perhaps because, in so many cases, their difficulties were linked to government policies), they seldom received it. The prosperity of this decade was almost entirely produced through the private market.

Government Promotion of Trade Associations

One aspect of the government response to requests for assistance was significant. In urging agricultural producers to form trade associations, the federal government was expanding a policy it had already established in manufacturing. Considerable latitude was extended to trade association operations, and government efforts to enforce more traditional antitrust laws were not noted for either vigor or originality of approach in this decade. In particular, after the *U.S. Steel* case (1920), the government made no effort to change the existing structure of industries. Its view of several forthright attempts to restrict competition was also decidedly benevolent.

Trade associations developed from wartime cooperation among firms. At that time they had been encouraged to exchange information on production levels and costs. From this it was a short step to discussing prices, and using this information to restrict competition required even less imagination. Some trade associations compelled their members to furnish other producers with prior notice of all price changes. Others insisted on the use of pricing formulas that made it easy to detect any sales at prices below those "recommended" by the association.

The courts allowed virtually every trade association activity that was not clearly labeled price fixing. At the same time, a wave of mergers occurred. In some cases, they were efforts to achieve economies of scale. Although mergers are a dubious mechanism for reducing production costs within any single production unit, Chrysler and General Motors apparently achieved some success through such methods by adding volume "downstream" from facilities that possessed underutilized economies of scale. Other mergers were vertical or conglomerate, attempts to diversify into new areas. In the public utilities field, some mergers aimed to achieve monopoly. The performance of the stock market in the late Twenties made it easy to obtain funds to finance mergers. In spite of this activity, however, it is unclear whether industrial concentration increased. The shares of total industry output controlled by the largest firms did not change significantly in most industries.

INCOME DISTRIBUTION

World War I had caused a leveling of incomes within the United States. The war increased the demand for unskilled labor much more than for skilled workers, and wage differentials narrowed substantially. Low-income groups also benefit more from full employment than those with higher incomes, because they bear the brunt of joblessness.

After the war, however, there may have been a trend favoring upper-income groups. One study found that by 1929 the distribution of income resembled the patterns observed just before the war.[15] That prewar distribution of income had been substantially less equal than today's. The functional distribution of income was also little changed from earlier decades: the share of income accruing to property in the late Twenties was about the same as two decades earlier, implying that labor's share was also unchanged.[16] In manufacturing, real wages rose less rapidly than productivity, so that the portion of income accruing to property in that sector increased. But this does not appear to have occurred in other sectors of the economy, nor was manufacturing employment an increasing share of all jobs during the Twenties.

The share of income accruing to unincorporated enterprises declined, an indication of the decline of the farm sector rather than of any change in small business. But the proportion of aggregate income going to employees rose almost exactly as much as proprietors' incomes fell. One study claims to have discovered a decided increase in inequality during the 1920s. It claims that the rich, or even just the very rich, received all of or slightly more than the total gains in income generated by the entire economy, while the incomes of middle- and low-income groups remained unchanged or even fell slightly.[17] However, it now appears that this study relied on faulty data and failed to allow for tax avoidance, which may have negated much of the trend toward greater income equality during and immediately after the war. The distribution of income may have become slightly less equal during the Twenties, but the view that the rich obtained all or nearly all the income gains of this decade no longer appears tenable.[18] The evidence that income gains were widely, if not necessarily equally, distributed is very strong.

The 1920s exodus—largely relative—from low-income jobs and regions would tend to pro-

[15] P. Lindert and J. Williamson, "Three Centuries of American Inequality," in P. Uselding, ed., *Research in Economic History* (Greenwich, CT.: JAI Press, 1976).

[16] U.S. Department of Commerce, *Historical Statistics,* vol. 1, p. 236.
[17] Holt, "Who Benefited from the Prosperity of the Twenties?" The rich could get more than the total increase if the non-rich's share decreases, as Holt contends.
[18] G. Smiley, "Did Incomes for Most of the Population Fall from 1923 through 1929?" *Journal of Economic History* (March 1983).

duce greater income equality. The very low unemployment rates previously discussed would be another—these tend to aid the poor far more than those whose incomes already reflect skills or property ownership. Formal studies of income distribution from this era are not really adequate for firm conclusions, but ample evidence suggests that the middle class and many others shared in the prosperity of the Twenties. Increases in single-family housing, in homes with central heating, plumbing, gas, and electricity, and in the ownership of consumer durables such as automobiles, electrical appliances, and more elaborate furniture all represent broad-based income gains, since the rich already possessed these items. Shorter work hours, higher real wages, and longer life expectancy all indicate improvements in the lot of the vast majority of Americans. A larger proportion of all children now attended high school, and child labor continued to decline. New amusements (radio, the movies, professional sports, and the Sunday afternoon automobile ride) made life more interesting. Whether the income gains of the Twenties were equally distributed or not, large numbers of people who could by no means be considered rich obviously gained. The proportion of all families owning houses wired for electricity, indoor flush toilets, and automobiles at least doubled in this decade, and in each case the gains accrued to more than half the total population.[19]

LABOR UNIONS

For labor unions, however, the Twenties were a period of falling membership. Union organization had burgeoned during the war, and by 1920 about 5 million workers were members of labor unions. This was about one-eighth of the work force, by far the largest portion yet organized. After 1923, however, labor union membership did not exceed 3.7 million for the rest of the decade, despite substantial growth in both employment and the labor force. Only 1 American worker in 12 belonged to a labor union in 1930. Nearly half the decrease in union membership was concentrated in the metals, machinery, and mining industries.[20]

On the surface, it seems strange that unions should fail to increase their membership in this period. Tight labor markets should have made it easier to organize and bargain. However, the rapid introduction of labor-saving technology in manufacturing weakened unions' strength in that sector. Much of the growth in employment was concentrated in the service industries, an area of chronic union weakness. Employers' attitudes toward unions had not become more positive in the Twenties, and a vigorous anti-union movement received a good deal of support from the courts. The use of injunctions and yellow-dog contracts was widespread. With the courts inclined to favor employers, such devices could be used to cripple organizing efforts and even allow employers to sue unions that had organized their employees. There was also an extensive development of company unions. These "tame" unions' major purpose was to shield the firms' workers from organizational efforts by unions more likely to bargain vigorously on their behalf.

Despite the legal and institutional opposition that American unions encountered at this time, some labor historians have concluded that the unions' decline owes a good deal to their own lack of effort. Employer opposition to unionization was scarcely a new phenomenon, and American unions had recorded their previous gains under far more difficult conditions than those prevailing in the Twenties. The contemporary union movement, largely restricted

[19] S. Lebergott, *The Americans: An Economic Record* (New York: Norton, 1984), p. 433.

[20] U.S. Department of Commerce, *Historical Statistics*, vol. 1., pp. 177–178.

to skilled craftsmen, may not really have had much interest in expanding within manufacturing or even keeping its toehold there—especially if organizing manufacturing workers meant changes in union structure. Workers in mass-production industries could not easily be organized along craft lines; new institutions would be required to meet their needs. The leaders of American unions at this time were not dynamic or visionary. High wages and steady full employment may ironically have been obstacles to unions' organizing efforts, particularly in manufacturing, the scene of unions' greatest failure in this decade.

FOREIGN ECONOMIC RELATIONS

The First World War had abruptly transformed economic relations between the United States and the rest of the world. Unfortunately, America did not really recognize this fact, and consequently American policies and practices were only slightly modified. The United States continued the practices of earlier decades, when its role in international finance had been of a large-scale debtor with only minor interests in overseas investments. During the war, the U.S. government had loaned nearly $10 billion to the Allies, an unprecedented act for this country. The bulk of the loans had been to Britain and France, but smaller sums had been advanced to Russia, Belgium, Italy, and other countries. The British and French had made larger loans to the other Allies.

Loans to support military expenditures are unlike normal business transactions in that even if they achieve their purpose, they do not produce additional income from which they can be repaid. At best, they are a purchase of political advantage: a consumer expenditure, not an investment. Nonetheless, successive American administrations insisted that the loans be repaid by the Allies. The only concessions made were reductions in the principal due, and only after it became apparent that the loans could not be repaid.

Allied Debt Repayment Problems

For foreign countries to repay American loans, they had to provide this country with more goods and services than they purchased from it, using the dollars so obtained to discharge their obligations. They could also ship gold (the international money), but Allied debts were far too great to be repaid from gold reserves already depleted by the war. Thus Europeans had no alternative but to run a trade surplus with the United States (or at least with other countries). America, however, had traditionally run an export surplus. Prior to the war, this surplus had financed interest and principal payments on American debts to foreigners, with something left over for U.S. investment abroad.

After the war, the structure of international debts was reversed. The United States was now a large-scale international creditor, not a debtor. Nevertheless, the U.S. export surplus continued as productivity gains in this country outstripped those abroad. U.S. tariff rates were increased, making it even more difficult for foreigners to sell their goods in American markets. Duties on imports were sharply raised in 1921 and again in 1922. They remained at about their pre–1914 rates until 1930, when they were raised yet again in a disastrously misguided attempt to export unemployment (the Smoot-Hawley tariff). The Europeans made their own mistakes: the British attempted to return to the gold standard at the prewar pound sterling–dollar exchange rate. At this rate, the pound was seriously overvalued, making British exports expensive to foreign buyers but reducing imported goods' prices within Britain.

Even so, foreigners were able to make some payments on their debts and buy American exports thanks to foreign loans made by private citizens and institutions in the United States. Ironically, many of these loans were extended to Germany, America's chief adversary during the war. American private investment abroad rose by about $10 billion from 1919 to 1930. The Treaty of Versailles required Germany to make reparations payments to the Allies for the damage done to them by German forces during the war. Since the German people were not eager to reduce their own living standards to make these enforced "gifts" to their erstwhile foes, they found loans from the United States very useful. Some of the funds were used within Germany, often for civic purposes with little direct economic payoff, and the remainder financed reparations payments and German investments in Eastern Europe. In effect, any repayment of war debts was funded by the United States itself. Loans to Germany may have prevented some European conflict at this time (the French, in particular, were determined to make Germany pay for the war). At the same time, the loans also delayed recognition that the reparations payments imposed on Germany were utterly unrealistic and probably uncollectible, at least from German domestic resources. Attempts to collect reparations clearly worsened international relations.

The United States had little experience in foreign investment, and almost none at all in lending to governments. A high proportion of its loans to both Germany and Latin America was for extremely dubious projects that might never generate sufficient income to finance repayment. A large portion of American and other international lending at this time was in short-term, highly liquid forms, which did not bode well for international economic stability. Such funds were likely to be quickly withdrawn from the borrowing countries if conditions there became unfavorable. This, of course,

would probably worsen the difficulties of the borrowing nation.[21]

In one instance, the U.S. contribution to international finance was positive, although to some extent after American policies had helped to create the problem. The United States was active in persuading the Allies to scale down the reparations demanded from Germany in 1925 and 1928, and it also reduced the principal on loans to the Allies.

FALSE PROSPERITY?

Given the events of the 1930s, it is tempting to see in the economic conditions of the Twenties the seeds of disaster. In such a view, even the most firmly established evidence of real economic gains is somehow unreal, and those who spoke of the achievement of "permanent prosperity" at the time appear deluded—or worse. But even though the Twenties were followed by a period of economic disaster and a long, halting, incomplete recovery, temporal sequence alone does not establish that something in the course of economic affairs made the Great Depression inevitable.

As the early pages of this chapter have stressed, by the usual macroeconomic criteria the American economy in the Twenties performed at least as well as in recent decades. Who would not exchange the recent record of growth, price stability, and unemployment rates for that achieved 60 years ago? Americans enjoyed a better material standard of life at the end of the decade than at its beginning. People were more educated, their health was better, their work hours shorter and less arduous, and their range of choices wider. Personal freedom,

[21] C. Kindleberger, *The World in Depression, 1929–39* (Berkeley, Calif.: University of California Press, 1973). See also H. Feis, *The Diplomacy of the Dollar, 1919–1932* (New York: Norton, 1950), 1966 reprint.

especially for women, had increased for the average American (except for Prohibition). When the American achievements are contrasted with the lack of similar progress in Europe, they appear even more remarkable.

If the performance of the private economy was good, government's economic policies were another source of satisfaction to most Americans. The federal government consistently ran surpluses, taking in more through taxes than it expended on current public operations. The excess funds were used to reduce the national debt, which fell by about one-third. By modern standards, the tax burden was very light, and over the decade it grew lighter still. About three-quarters of all federal revenues came from income taxes, and these bore more heavily on upper-income groups than had previous federal taxes. The tax structure was made even more progressive over the decade, with rates reduced for all but the very wealthy after 1921.[22] The federal government's share of total income was about 5 percent—very low by modern standards. The minor recessions in 1924 and 1927 had only slightly reduced income and employment and had responded well to open-market operations by the Federal Reserve System. There was considerable confidence in the efficacy of government action: enforcing Prohibition, it was thought, would present few problems to the nation that had recently won the war.

Truly, it must have appeared to most Americans that if they worked hard and saved part of their incomes, they could look forward, if not to riches, at least to growing and substantial prosperity. But in 1929 these rosy prospects disappeared in a 12-year nightmare. Many Americans still bear the psychic scars of a period when there seemed to be no work, no income, and little reason to hope that things would improve.

[22] U.S. Department of Commerce, *Historical Statistics*, vol. 2, pp. 1110–1112, 1120–1124.

■ Bread lines were among the few available sources of relief for the jobless in the 1930s.
Source: Dorthea Lange Collection, The Oakland Museum.

THE GREAT DEPRESSION

The downturn that began in the summer of 1929 initially appeared similar to the recessions of 1924 and 1927. Despite the trend that began in that year, 1929 itself was not a year of high unemployment. The jobless rate for the year was less than 4 percent, and the rate of real economic growth was the highest in four years, 6.7 percent. A slump had been regarded as overdue by most business forecasters; if recent history were any guide, it was expected to be no cause for great concern. But the downturn grew steadily worse for four terrible years, until in 1933 fully one-quarter of the American labor force was unable to find jobs of any kind and at least as many more were working shorter hours or less intensively than they wished. Even

Table 17.1   Unemployment and Unemployment Rates, 1929–1942

Date	Unemployment (in Thousands)	Rate (Percentage of Labor Force)
1929	1,550	3.2%
1930	4,340	8.7
1931	8,020	15.9
1932	12,060	23.6
1933	12,830	24.9
1934	11,340	21.7
1935	10,610	20.1
1936	9,030	16.9
1937	7,700	14.3
1938	10,390	19.0
1939	9,480	17.2
1940	8,120	14.6
1941	5,560	9.9
1942	2,660	4.7

Source: U.S. Department of Commerce, Bureau of the Census, *Historical Statistics of the United States: Colonial Times to 1970,* 2 vols. (Washington, D.C.: Government Printing Office, 1975), 1:135.

after the low point had at last been passed, recovery was agonizingly slow. A severe recession-within-a-depression during 1937 raised unemployment rates to levels surpassed only at the very worst of the Depression. In 1941, after eight years of New Deal policies, and one year of rising defense spending in anticipation of active American participation in World War II, the unemployment rate was still 9.9 percent. It had not been even that low for ten years.

Mere figures such as those in Table 17.1 do not express the human suffering caused by such massive joblessness. There was very little support for the unemployed outside their own resources. Few of the middle class and almost none of the poor possessed savings capable of tiding them over more than a few months without work. Even these meager savings might be reduced or lost entirely in the general collapse of financial institutions. Public programs to aid the indigent were inadequate even under normal circumstances, and in any case were designed to provide only temporary help. They were not intended to provide the sole support of millions of families over years in which there simply were no jobs available. In many cases, the state and local governments providing such assistance proved unable to finance it because their tax revenues dwindled as property values declined and rents fell.[23] Private charities were overwhelmed, and they too suffered from reduced incomes. Some state and local governments were unable to pay the salaries of even their regular employees. They skipped paydays or paid in scrip, which might be accepted for less than half its face value.

Nor can aggregate figures depict the highly uneven incidence of unemployment among industries and regions. In 1932 the American steel industry was producing at one-quarter of its capacity. For cities such as Pittsburgh and Gary, Indiana, this meant unemployment rates

[23] L. Chandler, *America's Greatest Depression, 1929–1941* (New York : Harper and Row, 1970), pp. 47–51, 189.

of 50 percent and more. It should be remembered that unemployment in any single sector has multiplier effects: lost incomes mean fewer customers for other products and hence fewer jobs and lower incomes in other sectors as well.

For those recently hired or subject to prejudice, conditions were still worse. Blacks had only recently gained access to urban and industrial jobs. They bore the burden of limited seniority as well as racism. A 1935 survey of living conditions for American blacks established two yardsticks against which to measure actual incomes. One was a budget sufficient to provide adequate nutrition, but almost nothing else except the most basic clothing and shelter. The other was an "emergency budget" deemed adequate only for the short-term maintenance of life: it jeopardized health if continued over long periods. The income of the average black family met even the emergency budget in only 5 of the 59 cities surveyed.[24] Incomes were considerably higher in the cities than in small towns or rural areas. Under such conditions, mere survival was a noteworthy achievement.

The Psychological Costs

Nor could all the costs of unemployment be measured in terms of lost income or even physical deprivation. To a much greater extent than today, Americans believed that all worthwhile individuals could find and hold jobs adequate to support themselves and their families. Failure to do so meant that there was something wrong with the individual rather than the economy. People had been taught that those unable to find and hold jobs were bums or worse, not really deserving of help. For people holding these values, the effects of years of constant searching for work that produced only short-term jobs with pay and conditions far below

those previously obtained, or even no work at all, can only be imagined. The transition to such conditions was swift—most of the Depression's victims had no warning.

The Depression had consequences not merely for fast-buck artists, who knew they were taking risks, but also for millions of people who had followed the traditional prescriptions of hard work and frugal living. Not only might such people have to endure being told that in effect nobody wanted their efforts, but the savings they had painfully accumulated might be lost in bank failures or declining asset values. The experiences of the Depression left indelible scars on those who lived through them. They go far to explain why the grandparents of today's college students take so much interest in the material possessions, steady employment, and economic security now assumed to be the birthrights of most if not all Americans.

How could the unemployed survive under such conditions? They used up savings if they had any, sold or borrowed against the cherished accumulations of a lifetime, lost mortgaged homes, took whatever help they could from relatives, friends, or charitable agencies, stole—and endured. In 1932, *Fortune* magazine commissioned a sympathetic study of the plight of the unemployed titled "No One Has Starved."[25] The title's premise was almost certainly wrong at the time it was written, and the Depression was to grow worse for two more years. In the first few years, newspapers were full of accounts of those in really desperate circumstances, but as the Depression dragged on, such stories were too commonplace to merit further attention.

Lost Opportunities

In addition to the direct effects of unemployment, the Depression imposed other costs. The economy produced far less than its potential:

---

[24] R. Sterner, *The Negro's Share: A Study of Income, Housing, and Public Assistance* (New York: Negro University Press, 1940), pp. 85–87.

[25] "No One Has Starved," *Fortune,* September 1932.

citizens went without goods that could have been produced. So great was the lost output in the Thirties that if we assume a continuation of the Twenties' rate of economic growth, the additional output would have provided first-class housing and medical care for every American who lacked them. The foregone production was greater than that devoted to World War II in the next decade. A whole decade of growth had been lost: real output in 1939 had barely regained the levels initially reached in 1929. Even after recovery had reached that point, the economy was still capable of producing far more. The unemployment rate attests to that. Real GNP in 1958 dollars was $203.6 billion in 1929. At the trough of the Depression in 1932–1933, it had fallen to only $141.5 billion. By the same measures, gross private domestic investment fell from $40.4 to $4.7 billion.

The rate of investment was far below normal; in some years, it did not even replace depreciation. At least until the New Deal launched its soil conservation and Civilian Conservation Corps programs, even farmland and natural resources suffered from inadequate maintenance. Marriages and birthrates fell.

Few, if any, areas of economic activity were unaffected by the Depression. Labor's aggregate situation worsened with unemployment and underemployment. Surprisingly, however, real wages actually rose in most Depression years—for those who retained full-time jobs.[26] Rent and interest income fell. Landlords and mortgage holders often allowed tenants to stay on even though they could not pay rent or amortization payments. There were no alternative customers with better prospects, and foreclosure might force recognition of the property's true value, possibly revealing the owners to be as bankrupt as their tenants. At the very bottom of the Depression, in 1931 and 1932, corporate profits were negative—incorporated firms

[26] U.S. Department of Commerce, *Historical Statistics*, vol. 1, p. 164.

■ The New Deal initiated many employment programs, including the Civilian Conservation Corps.
Source: AP/Wide World Photos, Inc.

as a whole lost money. It would be a long time before property income recovered. Profits did not regain 1929 levels until 1940 or 1941, and rent and interest income reached its previous peak only in the mid-Forties or even later.

Causes of the Depression

How could such an enormous disaster occur? As with any such calamity, there is no lack of after-the-fact explanations. Some are clearly wrong. A depression, particularly one of this magnitude, is not an inevitable consequence of the prosperity that preceded it. History reveals no other economic collapse of equal severity, and no trend at all for especially severe downturns after periods of high prosperity.

Table 17.2 Changes in Consumption, 1902–1931

Date	GNP (in Billions of Dollars)*	Flow of Goods to Consumers (in Billions of Dollars)*	Column C Divided by Column B
1902–1906	$23.6	$18.2	77.1%
1907–1911	30.1	24.1	80.0
1912–1916	38.9	30.8	79.2
1917–1921	71.6	54.9	76.7
1922–1926	84.8	66.8	78.8
1927–1931	89.9	73.0	81.2

*Figures in current dollars.

Source: U.S. Department of Commerce, Bureau of the Census, *Historical Statistics of the United States: Colonial Times to 1970*, 2 vols. (Washington, D.C.: Government Printing Office, 1975), 1:231. See also S. Lebergott, *The Americans: An Economic Record* (New York: Norton, 1984), Chap. 33.

Moreover, it is difficult to link the Depression's sources with World War I. Although the war did precede the Depression, it was more than a decade past in 1929. The two events were separated by so long and prosperous an era that it is very difficult to see any causation. The Depression was most severe in Germany and the United States, the two industrialized economies probably most and least affected by the war. Although the foreign economic relations of the United States had been drastically altered by the war, they were only a minor part of aggregate economic activity in America.

Both income inequality and monopoly had been at least as pronounced for decades before 1914 as they were in the Twenties, and the previous era had not produced a comparable depression. Indeed, it is regarded as one of high and growing prosperity. Economic growth in the Twenties was concentrated on a few sectors of the economy, but that too is a normal pattern, and if anything the range of growth sectors was unusually broad. Heretofore, new sectors had appeared as old mainstays of expansion waned.

As Table 17.2 indicates, "overcapacity" does not appear to explain many of the events leading up to the 1929 debacle. A few industries (especially automobiles and residential construction) had apparently expanded be-

yond the existing demand for their products at current prices, but the number of people who had not yet obtained modern conveniences in their homes, such as appliances, radios, or other mainstays of 1920s growth, was large. Even more, the variety of products available to consumers was expanding rapidly. The apparent rise in consumption in the 1927–1931 period, however, is more indicative of the collapse of investment late in those years than of any increased tendency to consume.

Also, many business firms still did not have the latest, most productive capital goods. Although farm incomes had failed to grow, the agricultural sector was a smaller portion of the economy than it had been before the war. At best, it appears that such structural explanations can account for only a trifling portion of the Great Depression. While they may have worsened its impact, structural factors were not its cause.

The Stock Market Crash

In many studies of the beginning of the Depression, the spectacular rise and even more spectacular collapse in prices on the New York Stock

■ Among today's collector's items are newspapers recording the stock market crash of 1929.

Exchange play a major causative role.[27] Although the stock exchange was an important instrument of investment and the great crash did occur at the beginning of the Depression, the nature of its effect on the rest of the economy is unclear.

The rise in stock prices had begun in the mid-Twenties. It was solidly based: corporate profits were high, and some years stock prices did no more than reflect the good earnings and excellent prospects of many corporations. Those who had owned stocks at the start of the period or purchased them soon after it began had made good investments. Not only did they receive increasing dividends on their shares, but they also profited from the rising value of the stocks themselves. For some years, yields on stocks remained about the same.

Gradually, however, as the experiences of the early investors became known, there was more interest in purchasing stocks for quick resale as their prices rose—that is, for capital gains rather than dividend income. As long as the speculative demand for stocks continued to increase, so did stock prices. By late 1928, stock prices were increasing considerably faster than dividends, and it had become much less profitable to buy stocks to hold for income at the new prices. This development made little difference to purchasers who expected to sell their

[27] Perhaps the best of these is J. Galbraith, *The Great Crash* (Boston: Houghton Mifflin, 1954).

stocks at enhanced prices in a short time. However, they could do so only as long as even more optimistic speculators were attracted to the market.

Margin Purchases

The profits from stock speculation were increased by the use of margin purchases, among other devices. A margin purchaser might borrow up to 90 percent (in rare cases) of the value of the stocks purchased. In that case, on resale, he received the entire increase in stock prices as a return on an investment of as little as 10 percent of the shares' initial price. Investment trusts, sometimes in several layers, were set up to magnify this process. In these trusts, the majority of the capital gains accrued to the venturesome minority who held the trusts' common stock. Margin loans appeared safe and highly liquid to lenders: the loans were against readily saleable assets whose prices were rising. Stockbrokers were quite willing to lend to their clients. The brokers had no difficulty obtaining financing from banks or large industrial firms, some of which began to consider stock market profits easier and far quicker to obtain than profits from the production and sale of goods.

In the euphoria of the moment, many investors forgot or repressed the idea that such leverage arrangements were equally effective in magnifying losses as well as gains. Further, in a world of scarcity, even the supply of optimists is limited; once stock prices stopped rising, there was no longer any reason to buy them. This was particularly true for stocks purchased on margin. The high interest rates on brokers' loans, which had appeared no burden when large capital gains were expected in a few weeks or months, now imposed higher costs than the stocks' dividend returns. Once it was clear that there was little prospect of any further increase in stock prices, speculators began to sell their shares. As stock prices began to decline, even those not inclined to sell began to receive demands from their brokers to put up a larger share of the securities' prices in their own funds.

If they could not, the brokers would sell the stock to protect themselves and recover the funds they had lent to margin buyers. Thus, once stock prices began to fall, the likelihood was that they would not decline gently but fall at an accelerating pace. And so they did.

As stock prices began their initial decline, pessimistic forecasts and unmet margin calls increased the volume offered for sale, driving prices down still further. Stock prices peaked in September 1929. After that date the price decline quickened, and by late October it had become a collapse. Stock prices declined precipitously, and after one brief rally late in 1929, continued a downward trend for the next several years. Standard and Poor's index of corporate stock values fell from 26.02 in 1929 (1941–1943 = 10) to 21.02 in 1930. By 1932 the index was at 6.93.[28]

Did the Crash Cause the Depression?

The great stock market crash wiped out billions in securities values. It was sudden and (incredibly) almost completely unanticipated, and it affected many of the people who made America's investment decisions. In concert with a falling general price level, the crash sharply raised the price of investment funds.

Nevertheless, it is difficult to assign a major causative role in the Depression to the stock market crash. Stock prices had undergone violent fluctuations before without major repercussions on the rest of the economy. Moreover, it is now clear that declines in real economic variables had begun even before stock prices peaked, let alone began to fall. There may have been some indirect effects because of the reduction in investors' wealth, but for at least a year, investor confidence was not a casualty.[29]

The Federal Reserve System had been disturbed by the massive increase in stock spec-

[28] U.S. Department of Commerce, *Historical Statistics,* vol. 2, p. 1004.
[29] P. Temin, *Did Monetary Forces Cause the Great Depression?* (New York: Norton, 1976), Chap 4.

ulation after 1926 and had attempted to reduce the flow of funds to the stock market by raising discount rates in 1928, using "moral suasion" (attempts to persuade member banks not to lend for stock speculation), and sharply raising the discount rate in the late summer of 1929. As long as optimism prevailed in the stock market, these efforts had little effect. If they had any impact at all, they merely forced those seeking funds for stock purchases to borrow from other sources. The increased interest rates may have discouraged real investment, but with opinions about stock prices at the current pitch of feverish optimism, no conceivable increase in interest rates would have had much of an effect on speculators.

Once stock prices had fallen, the reduced wealth of securities owners may have made them less willing to consume and invest. But only a small portion of the American population actually owned stocks. Stocks represented only a minor portion of the nation's total wealth, and business optimism did not collapse for about a year after the stock market crash.[30]

Most economists grant the crash a minor (and, of course, negative) role in the Depression. In one recent study, however, the crash is seen as a major factor in both initiating the Depression and, because stock prices continued to decline for several years, worsening the economic conditions of the next four years.[31]

Causes of the Depression: The Monetarist View

One explanation of the Depression's causes that has gained credence with a number of economists is that of the monetarists. This group of economists has concluded that changes in the money supply are the chief determinant of short-run changes in real economic parameters. The leading monetary history of this period found that the U.S. money supply declined by over one-third from 1929 to 1933. Further, the money supply had failed to rise in the previous few years. This, the authors concluded, was the real source of the Depression. A series of bank failures caused over one-third of all U.S. banks to fail outright, liquidate, or merge with other banks to survive.[32]

Collapse of the banking system has an effect on market economies similar to that of the failure of the circulatory system on the human body. Money is used in virtually all exchanges, just as blood is essential to the function of all cells in the body. If money is no longer available or its supply suddenly reduced, the impact on all forms of economic activity will be severe, since there are almost no good short-run substitutes for money. The greater the degree of specialization (which in turn indicates the degree of economic development), the more severe the effects of monetary contraction.

The Role of the Federal Reserve System

Professors Friedman and Schwartz found the cause of the monetary collapse (that in turn underlay the collapse of the general economic system) in the actions, or lack thereof, of the Federal Reserve System. The impact of the system's mistakes was worsened by the changes in bank regulations instituted when the Federal Reserve was established in 1913. No longer could banks unable to meet depositors' demands for cash suspend payment, so that their own obligations (bank notes or, more recently, demand deposits) would continue to circulate and be accepted for payments at a discount from face value. Under the Federal Reserve System's regulations, banks unable to redeem their obligations in full had to suspend all operations, which meant that checks drawn on

---

[30] Ibid., pp. 69–74.
[31] F. Mishkin, "The Household Balance Sheet and the Great Depression," *Journal of Economic History* (December 1978).

[32] Friedman and Schwartz, *The Great Contraction*, p. 299.

■ Bank failures like this one in Haverhill, Iowa, were widespread, especially in small farming communities.

Source: *The Depression Years* as photographed by Arthur Rothstein (New York: Dover Publications, Inc., 1978), p. 86.

them would not be accepted no matter how heavily discounted.

It had been assumed that competently managed banks under Federal Reserve System regulation would always have a source of emergency reserves: they could borrow from the Federal Reserve Banks. Moreover, the central banks could always make loans to member banks against good collateral (commercial paper), and thus the member banks could not fail. Even in the Twenties, the evidence was very much to the contrary: 5,882 banks, nearly 1,000 of them

members of the Federal Reserve System, had failed in the decade.[33] If the United States had gained a central bank in the "Fed," its commercial banks had changed little. Many were small and confined most of their loans to their immediate locales, so that if local business were hard-hit, many of the banks' assets would decline in value. Whatever efforts toward bank

[33] U.S. Department of Commerce, *Historical Statistics,* vol. 2, p. 1038.

consolidation or the formation of multibank chains had occurred were largely among similar institutions in the same regions. Not only did these measures do little to promote diversification, but they often tended to be the work of incompetent or unscrupulous promoters. Consequently, they served only to spread trouble within the banking community.

Also, it had been assumed that what the Federal Reserve Banks could do, they would. But no statute clearly defined their obligations to member banks, and few persons in authority within the system had the imagination to see the proper course of action during a bank crisis—or the consequences if it were not followed. Had the Federal Reserve System operated as a central bank was expected to, monetarist analysis would expect only a small reinforcement of the downturn from the monetary system. But the help for member banks that the Federal Reserve System had been established to provide was not forthcoming. During successive banking crises, the system either did nothing to aid commercial banks or actually made the situation worse. The New York Federal Reserve Bank had lowered its discount rate immediately after the stock market crash, reducing the interest rate it charged on member banks' borrowing. But to do more than this, the New York Federal Reserve Bank required support from the rest of the Federal Reserve System. It was not to be had.[34]

Too Little Too Late. No significant action was taken to expand the U.S. money supply until the spring of 1932, when the Federal Reserve System finally began to buy bonds on the open market. By this time, the commercial banks had undergone two waves of runs, each resulting in more bank failures than its predecessor and guaranteeing even greater panic in any recurrences. Under these circumstances, the Fed's purchase of $1 billion in bonds that might have

forestalled the banking collapse in 1929 or 1930 was far too little and much too late. This was the only significant expansionary action in almost four years before the trough of the Depression was reached. In this period, the Federal Reserve Banks essentially refused to operate as a central bank. They acted to protect themselves rather than the commercial banks, evaluating loan requests on criteria appropriate only under normal business circumstances. At no time were the Federal Reserve Banks themselves in any discernible danger of failure, but over one-quarter of all the commercial banks in the United States failed.

There were three waves of bank failures: in late 1930 and early 1931, in late 1931, and again in late 1932. Each was of increasing severity, and the last culminated in the "bank holiday" of the spring of 1933, when all the surviving banks in the United States were closed by order of the federal government (many had already been closed by state governors). The bank holiday gave banks time to sell assets for cash to meet depositors' demands for currency and to be examined and recertified by government examiners. As the banks reopened with government approval, deposits began to flow back into them. The crisis was over for the banking system, but in four years its effects on the rest of the economy had been disastrous. Worse still, the monetarists believe, the banking crisis was almost entirely avoidable.

In the monetarist view, over the crucial 1929–1933 period, the Federal Reserve Banks—the so-called lenders of last resort for the commercial banks—not only imposed stringent terms for loans to banks facing massive "runs," but in some cases actually took actions that increased the pressure on the banks they were set up to aid.

Misguided Policies. In the clearest case, when Britain abandoned the gold standard in 1931 (the Bank of England no longer offered to buy or sell gold at a fixed price in pounds sterling), gold began to flow out of the United States.

[34] Friedman and Schwartz, *The Great Contraction*, p. 363.

Foreigners who held dollars were afraid that the United States might abandon the gold standard or devalue the dollar, and they converted their dollars into gold, which was then exported from the United States. Although at this time the American gold reserves were at almost the highest level yet recorded, and the outflow of gold was obviously not based on changes in the international value of the dollar or the U.S. trade balance, the Federal Reserve authorities reacted by raising rediscount rates within the United States—the traditional remedy for gold movements brought about by inflation relative to price levels in foreign countries. Further, Federal Reserve policy was evenhanded only in its potential for disaster: when gold later began to flow back into the United States, the Federal Reserve Banks "sterilized" it. They paid commercial banks for the gold with bonds, not checks on themselves, which did not allow an expansion of the money supply.[35] (By this time, however, commercial banks may well have preferred bonds to the opportunity to make loans.)

The "Bankers' Bank" and Its Contribution to Collapse.

Throughout the period, the U.S. central bank failed to use all its available resources to aid the commercial banks. If it was restricted by its own regulations, it never asked Congress to relax or change them, particularly not to allow a vigorous program of open-market bond purchases. Not only did the Federal Reserve System treat its own member banks as bad credit risks (which, given its policies, many were), but it allowed its officials to make repeated public statements about the shaky position of the banks, further reducing public confidence in them. Incredibly, even after it was apparent that unemployment was at catastrophic levels and commercial banks were faced with unprecedented demands for cash, some officials of the Open Market Committee not only op-

posed monetary expansion but actually advocated measures to reduce the money supply.[36]

Whether the Federal Reserve System's increasing restrictions on monetary growth in 1928 and 1929 were responsible for the inception of the Depression or not, it seems indisputable that the central bank did little to reduce the slump's impact and that the sum of its actions had a strongly negative effect that extended well beyond 1933. Long after the banking crises ended, the surviving banks did not trust the Federal Reserve System: they maintained reserves far in excess of legal requirements through most of the Thirties. This policy by the commercial banks reduced the effects of expansionary monetary policies caused by the inflow of gold in the period after 1933.

The Monetarist Scenario: A Summary.

The monetarists' scenario for the Great Depression, then, runs as follows. Slow monetary growth before 1930 brought on a recession. Later that year, a wave of bank failures in the Midwest caused the public to try to convert bank deposits into cash. Because the Federal Reserve System refused to increase the money supply in compensation, it fell sharply. As the money supply declined, either prices or the level of economic activity had to fall, and this trend was intensified by an increase in the demand for money to hold (falling velocity). Although prices did fall, the primary result of the decline in the money supply was the catastrophic slowdown in real economic activity that we know as the Great Depression. Under existing circumstances, the Federal Reserve System was the only institution capable of really effective countercyclical action. Not only did the system fail to provide such action, except for its 1932 open-market purchases, but it worsened the situation—particularly in the critical period late in 1931 when a bad recession became a near-total

---

[35] Ibid., pp. 380–384.

[36] Ibid., pp. 384–389.

economic collapse. Had the Federal Reserve taken vigorous action to expand the money supply in the early part of the slump, a recession would still have occurred, but it would have been mild—probably no worse than those of the mid-Twenties. Instead, the Federal Reserve even abandoned policies that would have produced some offsets to declines in member bank borrowing and the gold stock and thus mitigated the aggregate monetary contraction.[37]

Reasons for Federal Reserve Policies. The reasons for the inept policies of the Federal Reserve System seem to have been a failure to recognize both the severity of the Depression and the role of a central bank in internal (rather than international) economic affairs and the absence of clear-cut leadership within the system. Prior to 1929, the New York Federal Reserve Bank, under its governor, Benjamin Strong, had exercised a disproportionate influence on the system's monetary policies. Strong had a better understanding of the proper role of a central bank, both in regard to internal and international policy, than most of his contemporaries. He also possessed the force of character and persuasive powers to bring others to his point of view. But Strong died in October 1928, and his successor lacked the vision, ability, and personality required to turn the entire system toward monetary expansion. The gold outflow in 1931 was a situation that the existing authorities "understood," and their reaction was precisely that prescribed by orthodox central banking procedures under normal circumstances. But circumstances in 1931 were anything but normal.

It may be, as Professor Wicker has claimed, that the Federal Reserve authorities' only criteria were those for international monetary stability, and internal economic considerations had

little or no influence on their decisions.[38] Another study claims that many small, locally-oriented banks were already in shaky financial condition in 1929, often because their assets were heavily concentrated on agricultural loans. For such banks, almost any downturn, whether in agricultural prices, American farm exports, the weather, or general business conditions, would impose severe difficulties. Most of these took place in the early years of the Depression, and tight monetary policy merely hastened the inevitable.[39] Had banks been allowed to have branches, their loans might have been more diversified and their overall position stronger, as was true in Canada, but only a few states allowed even limited branch banking in 1929. Falling bond prices, which reduced the value of another component of bank assets, also impaired bank solvency. But these were consequences, not causes, of the Depression.[40]

Federal Reserve policies may also have been based on incorrect evidence or interpretation thereof. What appeared to be low rates of interest (indicating that monetary policy was "easy") might actually have indicated severe monetary stringency if prices were falling—as they were. For example, a 2 percent nominal interest charge, when combined with 8 percent deflation, becomes a real interest rate of 10 percent, at least if borrowers anticipate deflation correctly.

About all that can be said in defense of Federal Reserve authorities' policies is that they had plenty of company. Fiscal policy at the time was equally misguided. Very few people recognized the Depression for what it was: a massive reduction in aggregate demand. Even fewer realized that once unemployment had reached

[37] P. Trescott, "Federal Reserve Policy in the Great Contraction: A Counterfactual Assessment," *Explorations in Economic History* (July 1982).

[38] E. Wicker, "Federal Reserve Policy, 1922–33: A Reinterpretation," *Journal of Political Economy* (August 1965). See also Wicker, "A Reconsideration of Federal Reserve Monetary Policy during the 1920–21 Depression," *Journal of Economic History* (June 1966).

[39] E. White, "A Reinterpretation of the Banking Crisis of 1930," *Journal of Economic History* (March 1984).

[40] Ibid.

post-1931 levels, recovery through the normal operation of the market system was unlikely to be rapid.

An Alternative Explanation

The monetarists' explanation of the Depression has been challenged by Peter Temin.[41] In the extended discussions that followed the appearance of Temin's book, a somewhat clearer picture of the relation between monetary and nonmonetary causes has begun to emerge. In Temin's view, the stock of money fell through 1930, just as the monetarists claim, but it declined because the demand for money fell, not the supply. The stock of money at any instant is the result of interactions between the supply of money and the demand for money. To Temin, the demand for money declined because of reductions in income, a scenario in which changes in the money stock are a result of income changes rather than their cause. The fall in income in turn stemmed from reduced consumption spending, partially due to the decline in farm incomes and exports of American goods. Changes in wealth caused by the stock market crash and the general fall in securities values also contributed to the decline in consumption. However, the reduction in consumption was too large to be explained by these factors alone, and it was not concentrated on spending for durable consumer goods. This fall in consumption was unique to the 1929–1930 downturn. In similar periods (1920–1921 and 1937–1938), consumption either declined less than the other components of aggregate demand or even increased.

In contrast to the monetarists' explanations, Temin argues that bank failures did not have a significant effect on either the supply of money or aggregate demand. Evidence from short-term interest rates, he concludes, fails to support the monetarists' contention that the

supply of money fell while demand remained stable or increased. Investment spending and the business expectations that influenced it fell no more than in other, less serious downturns. However, the decline in investment spending over 1928–1930 was far more heavily concentrated in construction and equipment than in 1920–1921 or 1937–1938, when the major reductions were in inventory spending. Since plant and equipment expenditures were likely to recover more slowly than other forms of investment, this fact had major implications for the duration of the Depression as well as its severity. Business expectations, according to Temin's findings, remained optimistic until late in 1930.

Moreover, Temin found that the real money stock (the nominal stock of money adjusted for changes in its purchasing power) grew until 1932, long after the Depression was firmly established. While the nominal money stock did fall, it did not do so rapidly enough to offset deflation. Temin further argues that it would have been a year or so after deflation began before price declines became "built into" people's expectations and hence into the expected real interest rate. Given this line of thought, anticipated real interest rates fell until late in 1930, then rose. Temin concluded that banking panics resulted from public reaction to declines in the value of securities held by the banks. The declines in bank asset values, however, in turn stemmed from the previous fall in incomes. Thus the chain of causation, in Temin's view, runs from income to money, rather than in the opposite direction. Monetary forces in this explanation may have contributed to the severity of the Depression, but they did not cause it.

Temin's work remains the center of controversy.[42] Even if fully accepted, it does more

[41] Temin, *Did Monetary Forces Cause the Great Depression?*

[42] For a good summary of the early years of the debate, see P. Passell and S. Lee, *A New Economic View of American History* (New York: Norton, 1979), pp. 372–383. See also White, "Reinterpretation" and Trescott, "Federal Reserve Policy."

to refute the monetarists' contentions than to present a complete alternative explanation. Temin does not explain much of the drop in consumption, which in his view was the ultimate cause of the Depression. Still, his work and that of later analysts has made the monetarist model tenable only under much more restrictive assumptions than initially employed, and it casts grave doubt on the importance of bank failures. It must also be noted, however, that even if Temin's views are fully accepted, the Federal Reserve is not absolved. Temin's analysis does not extend to the Federal Reserve reaction to the gold outflow of late 1931 or to its belated open-market purchases in 1932.

Other Factors Contributing to the Depression

Although the ultimate causes of the Depression remain unclear, some of the reasons it persisted so long are easier to understand. A number of economists have developed theories of investment cycles that place much of the impetus for economic growth on construction and other highly capital-intensive industries. When the long-term trend in construction is up, recessions tend to be brief and mild, especially if other sectors are large-scale users of investment funds. If the construction cycle is in a downswing, however, depressions tend to be severe and prolonged. Those holding such views point out that the construction cycle peaked in 1926 and that public utilities and automobiles, two other major centers of investment during the Twenties, also had excess capacity by the end of the decade.

Whether the "long swing" investment cycle contributed to the onset of the Depression or not, once income and investment declined as they had by 1931, incentives to invest were severely reduced. With only 20 percent of existing durable goods capacity in use, there was little incentive to build more factories or reequip existing plants. Until existing capacity was fully utilized, new investment would depend on the appearance of technical advances or new products.

Unfortunately, the Thirties were not a decade of great technical progress. In consequence, increases in income would have to originate in rises in consumption or government spending rather than investment. International trade was not large enough in relation to the American economy even under normal circumstances to generate a major increase in aggregate demand, and during the Depression foreign commerce had declined even more than internal economic activity. In the view of some supply-side economists, the increase in U.S. tariff rates negotiated in the 1930 Smoot-Hawley tariff was an important causal factor in the decline.[43] However, neither the magnitude nor the timing of the trade restrictions support this contention. U.S. exports declined by only 2 percent of GNP over 1929–1931, and clearly not all of the fall was due to increased trade barriers. Further, the bulk of the decline occurred after domestic economic activity had fallen sharply.[44]

To the extent that growth had centered on durable goods production in the Twenties, there was a further difficulty. The demand for durable consumer goods is in large part a function of how long the owners of such commodities want cars and major appliances to last: they can substitute maintenance and reduced use for new purchases. Spending on capital goods largely depends on the aggregate rate of economic growth and on the use of existing productive capacity. Thus, demand for the products of these sectors would decline, and under Depression conditions it would not be easy to transfer productive resources to new sectors.

[43] J. Wanniski, *The Way the World Works* (New York: Basic Books, 1978).
[44] U.S. Department of Commerce, *Historical Statistics*, vol. 2, pp. 887, 888.

Trade and Fiscal Policies

Government macroeconomic policies were no better than those of the Federal Reserve during the initial years of the Depression. The framework of international trade collapsed as nation after nation sought to export unemployment by raising barriers to the entrance of foreign goods. The idea behind these actions was either to protect existing domestic producers from overseas competition or to generate new import-replacing industries. But when all nations employed similar methods, the result was to reduce business and employment in each country's export industries. Moreover, the jobs lost were in areas of greater relative productivity and hence higher incomes than those gained. The United States, through the Smoot-Hawley tariff of 1930, raised its tariff rates and extended the range of dutiable imports to levels comparable to the high-tariff era before 1900. As nations left the gold standard, they tried to gain advantages for their exports through competitive devaluations of their currencies.

The Hoover Administration's Role. After a brief flirtation with expansionary measures, American fiscal policy was also geared to making the Depression worse instead of better. President Hoover has been vilified as a man unmoved by the suffering of the unemployed, but this is unfair. Personally, Herbert Hoover was a humanitarian, with a distinguished famine relief record in Europe during and immediately after World War I. But his efforts to end the crisis were severely handicapped, not least by his inability to grasp the dimensions of the problem. Government statistics on economic activity in general, and particularly on unemployment, were quite sketchy before the mid-Thirties. Many contemporary economists viewed the possibility of prolonged large-scale unemployment as extremely unlikely.

President Hoover believed that the federal government was obligated to maintain a balanced budget—that to allow revenues to fall short of expenditures for any prolonged period was to invite national bankruptcy. He also believed, apparently quite sincerely, that relief payments to the unemployed without some form of quid pro quo would ruin their moral fiber and bankrupt the country to boot. A few of his advisors, such as Treasury Secretary Mellon, wanted to allow the Depression to "liquidate" the economy as a sort of traumatic process of competition, from which a sounder, more efficient national economy would emerge. There is no evidence, however, that such draconian views ever formed the basis of any Hoover administration policies. In fact, much of what was done required a compromise of the president's publicly stated principles.

In 1929 the federal budget had been in surplus. Revenues exceeded current expenditures by over $700 million. The immediate reaction of the government to the Depression was to cut taxes and increase spending, particularly on public-works projects. This program would meet with the approval of most modern economists as an appropriate response to the downturn. However, the federal budget was so small in relation to the aggregate economy, and the effects of the Depression so great, that these policies had no visible effect.

Government revenues declined. They were heavily dependent on progressive income taxes and thus fell even faster than income as the tax base declined. The budget surplus became a deficit, and the deficit grew. But a deficit large enough to reverse the decline in private economic activity was politically and possibly physically impossible. The Hoover administration's response was to reduce spending.

The deficits continued, and in 1932 a large tax increase was enacted. Since higher taxes could only reduce an already inadequate volume of private spending (and in this case would not finance a compensating increase by the government), this was the wrong policy. Nevertheless, it was supported by both houses of Congress. The Democratic party's presidential candidate, Franklin D. Roosevelt, attacked it—as inadequate rather than wrong.

Higher taxes on shrinking incomes did not balance the federal budget, but they further reduced aggregate demand. At the time, few politicians (or economists) viewed the Depression as a massive shortfall in aggregate demand whose cure lay in additional spending—whether directly, by the government, or, through tax cuts or monetary expansion, by the public. Since no one recognized that these measures might raise the tax base, the tax increase appeared the only means of achieving a balanced budget. That a balanced budget might not be the most appropriate measure under Depression conditions was never considered.

Positive Steps. Some programs that were enacted had positive aspects. The Federal Farm Board purchases of agricultural products in an attempt to maintain or increase farm incomes at least added to aggregate demand, although they also required that recipients remain in farming, where long-term prospects were not good. The Reconstruction Finance Corporation was established by the Hoover administration to extend loans to businesses, including the desperate commercial banks, that were unable to obtain financing from conventional lenders. While this program indicated little recognition of the effects of Federal Reserve policies on money markets, it also shows that the Hoover administration was not a total prisoner of conservative ideology. Most RFC loans went to large firms. Once again, however, the effort was too small. Although President Hoover could not bring himself to support direct federal payments to the unemployed, federal loans to the states to support relief programs were authorized in the last months of his administration.

Herbert Hoover was a political victim of the Depression. He lacked the understanding of macroeconomics and monetary theory needed to effectively respond to the economic decline. But he was hardly alone in that. Perhaps the nation needed to experience a massive failure of the traditional remedies for depression before more imaginative measures became politically acceptable. (Some New Deal measures contained considerably more imagination than coherent reasoning.) The timid moves toward economic expansion made by the Hoover administration were hopelessly inadequate, but their failure probably made government measures on a more adequate scale even more difficult. By late 1932, it was becoming clear that even if the economy did contain forces that would automatically restore full employment, the widespread suffering produced by the Depression required that something be done to speed their operation.

SELECTED REFERENCES

Chandler, L. *America's Greatest Depression, 1929–1941.* New York: Harper and Row, 1970.

Friedman, M. and A. Schwartz. *A Monetary History of the United States, 1867–1960.* Princeton, N.J.: Princeton University Press, 1963. (Chapter 7 of this work has been published separately as *The Great Contraction*, 1965.)

Galbraith, J. *The Great Crash, 1929.* Boston, Mass.: Houghton Mifflin, 1954.

Gordon, R. *Economic Instability and Growth: The American Record,* New York: Norton, 1974.

Kindleberger, C. *The World in Depression, 1929–39.* Berkeley, Calif.: University of California Press, 1973.

Soule, G. *Prosperity Decade: From War to Depression, 1917–1929,* New York: M.E. Sharpe, 1947.

Stein, H. *The Fiscal Revolution in America.* Chicago: University of Chicago Press, 1969.

Temin, P. *Did Monetary Forces Cause the Great Depression?* New York: Norton, 1976.

U.S. Department of Commerce, Bureau of the Census. *Historical Statistics of the United States: Colonial Times to 1970.* 2 vols. Washington, D.C.: Government Printing Office, 1975.

Wicker, E. *Federal Reserve Monetary Policy, 1917–33.* New York: Random House, 1966.

CHAPTER

18

INCOMPLETE RECOVERY AND THE NEW DEAL

DEPRESSION CONDITIONS

In the spring of 1933, the U.S. economy was in desperate straits. The unemployment rate was nearly 25 percent. Even that figure understated the severity of the Depression: many who did have jobs were either working part time or not fully using their productive potential. It has been estimated that nearly half of all American workers were unemployed at some time during the preceding year.

Real GNP was only 70 percent of the 1929 figure; approximately what it had been in 1922. The results of a decade of growth—in addition to the potential growth that might have occurred after 1929—had been lost. Wage and salary income was three-fifths of its 1929 levels, proprietors' income and rents had fallen by two-thirds, and corporate profits had become losses. Farm incomes had fallen more than other proprietors', and delinquencies on farm mortgages had become epidemic. Real wages of the employed had fallen surprisingly little, however: only from $834 to $811 in 1914 dollars. The Depression's real impact on labor incomes, of course, was through unemployment. When adjusted for joblessness, real earnings of the average employee had declined by 30 percent.[1] Prices had fallen, too: by 1933, the consumer price index was at 75 percent of its 1929 level.

Nor was the worst necessarily over. The collapse of commercial banking threatened to become total. By March 1933, more than half the states had ordered all banks within their borders to close temporarily—a tacit admission that under existing circumstances banks were incapable of meeting depositors' demands for

[1] U.S. Department of Commerce, Bureau of the Census, *Historical Statistics of the United States: Colonial Times to 1970*, 2 vols (Washington, D.C.: Government Printing Office, 1975), 1:164.

■ Those whom unemployment had driven to selling apples on the streets were, albeit in a technical sense, employed.
Source: AP/Wide World Photos, Inc.

cash. Banks were caught in a trap. Their efforts to convert assets into cash by selling their securities portfolios drove already depressed bond prices still further down, sometimes impairing the solvency of even those few institutions with no initial need to sell. As for other assets, mortgages were salable for only a fraction of previous values, if at all, and prime commercial paper (high-quality, short-term business loans) did not exist. Declines in asset values put yet more pressure on the battered commercial banks. The Federal Reserve still provided no significant help. Discount rates were increased again in the spring of 1933, and no sizable open-market purchases were made after that of 1932.[2]

Population growth fell as marriages were deferred and couples put off having children. The birthrate fell far below that for the Twenties, which had itself been well below nineteenth-century rates. During the Depression, the American birthrate reached levels not seen again until the 1970s. Demographers predicted that the U.S. population would age and even decline absolutely if such trends continued. Declines in population growth and family formation, of course, affected the economy. An increased supply of labor was the primary source of economic growth (although under prevailing conditions the existing labor supply was only too obviously more than adequate), and the demand for housing was strongly linked to population growth. The social infrastructure (roads, schools, water and sewer systems) was only slightly less directly connected. All had been important factors in the economic growth of the previous decade.[3]

Trends in wages and population growth gave little hope that consumption spending would soon increase. Even if individual incomes somehow rose, the prospects for future unemployment were so great that most of any increase would be set aside for an expected rainy day. Prospects for increased investment spending were even worse. Investment had fallen from $40.4 billion in 1929 to only $5.3 billion in 1933 (figures in 1958 dollars).[4] At this level, capital was not being replaced as fast as it depreciated. Even so, inventories were too large and were being reduced by holding production at less than sales. The huge amount of unused capital would inhibit new investment spending until it was back in use, and that could occur only if aggregate demand somehow increased. New inventions were another avenue of investment spending, but they offered little promise. In contrast to the Twenties' leading sectors (autos, public utilities, appliances, chemicals, and construction), the Thirties developed few new, rapidly growing industries that required heavy investment. Foreign trade had

[2] M. Friedman and A. Schwartz, *A Monetary History of the United States, 1867–1960* (Princeton, N.J.: Princeton University Press, 1962), pp. 324–328.

[3] A. Hansen, "Economic Progress and Declining Population Growth," *American Economic Review* (March 1939).
[4] U.S. Department of Commerce, *Historical Statistics,* vol. 1, p. 229.

declined precipitously: not only was the Depression worldwide, but many countries tried to restrict their imports. American imports and exports were now little more than one-third their 1929 levels.[5]

The final component of aggregate demand was government spending. Increases here were far too small to compensate for the massive declines in other areas of expenditure. The federal government had reluctantly begun to provide loans to railroads, banks, and state governments through the Reconstruction Finance Corporation. A few public works projects, such as Hoover Dam on the Colorado River, had been started. A program to support the mortgage market had just commenced. But these efforts were very small in relation to the shortfall in aggregate demand, and the administration was at least as concerned with their impact on the federal deficit as their potential for increasing employment. State and local governments, lacking the federal government's ability to finance deficits, were grimly attempting to cut spending and increase taxes to finance expenses that could not be avoided.

The Response to Catastrophe

After President Hoover was defeated for reelection in November 1932, there was virtually no cooperation between the outgoing and incoming administrations. The policies of Franklin D. Roosevelt were anything but clear to the electorate, adding uncertainty to the general climate of fear.

Under such conditions, people questioned the viability of capitalism and the market system. An economy that could reach such disastrously low levels of activity was bad enough, but the lack of clear indications of recovery was even more discouraging.

Some contemporary economists added to the gloom: according to their analyses, declining population growth and the end of the geographic frontier had curtailed two of the major traditional uses for investment funds. In an economy where people did not consume their entire incomes, some new uses for these continually rising savings had to be developed to avoid a cumulative decline. Some massive increase in investment spending (on new products or processes) or a large increase in government spending would be needed to bridge the gap between incomes and consumption expenditures. Further, this gap was expected to increase. Without a remedy, the outlook was for continued, even increasing, unemployment with only sporadic growth at best. The "stagnationists" believed that neither of the two potential offsets to this prospect was likely. Although expanded government spending could take up the economic slack, there was little reason to suppose that it would in 1933, especially if the task would grow ever larger.[6]

Four years after the onset of the Depression, it was by no means clear that the economic climate would stop deteriorating. Empirical evidence offered no more hope than the gloomy prognostications of economic theorists. President Hoover's 1932 campaign slogan, "Prosperity is just around the corner," appeared to deserve the cynical mockery with which the electorate received it.

In spite of the desperate circumstances and outlook of the early Thirties, the people who had already endured so much and been given so little reason to expect improvement made no move to rebel. Conservatives feared that the Depression would produce some type of left-wing revolution that would sweep away the basic institutions of capitalism or at least change the form of government, but no such credible movement ever appeared. Farmers prevented

---

[5] Ibid., vol. 2, p. 889.

[6] Hansen, "Economic Progress and Declining Population Growth."

■ Farm auctions were common as farmers became targets of foreclosures.
Source: *The Depression Years* as photographed by Arthur Rothstein (New York: Dover Publications, Inc., 1978), p. 22.

a few foreclosures against their neighbors by force or threats, and some urban protests against evictions and the meager levels of government assistance occurred, along with a march of unemployed war veterans to Washington in 1932. Under the desperate conditions, labor disputes may have had more than the usual quota of violence, and a few new developments, such as sitdown strikes, did occur. But no credible challenge to established authority occurred. The record supports the views of historians such as Crane Brinton, who concluded that revolutions occur when people become dissatisfied with the pace of progress, not in protest against deteriorating conditions.[7]

Despite the rhetoric of right- and left-wing demagogues, some skilled in the use of a new communications medium (radio), the prevailing attitude was one of numbed resignation. Huey Long, Father Coughlin, and Francis Townshend, among others, attracted personal followings. The deficiencies of the traditional system spurred interest in alternatives ranging from technocracy to communism. But it is difficult to see their influence on subsequent events or institutions.

THE NEW DEAL

Franklin Delano Roosevelt assumed the duties of the presidency in March 1933. Obviously, the new administration had a mandate to take

[7] C. Brinton, *The Anatomy of Revolution* (New York: Vintage Books, 1965).

action against the Depression. It was much less clear what form that action would take. During his campaign, Roosevelt had promised the voters a "new deal," but he had not been very specific about proposals designed to end the Depression.

There was no reason to believe that these proposals would include any fundamental changes in fiscal policy. Before his election, the new president had criticized the Hoover administration's budget deficits, and Roosevelt himself apparently believed strongly in a balanced federal budget. Initially, the new administration reduced several types of federal spending, particularly salaries. The only tax changes ever proposed during the New Deal were either increases in existing levies or new forms of taxation. Only after 1938 did the administration explicitly recognize that government might increase aggregate demand when private spending had fallen.

Roosevelt was far more pragmatic than Hoover had been, however, and when it became apparent that the goal of a balanced budget conflicted with other administration programs, he "temporarily" abandoned it. Overall, particularly during its first term, the macroeconomic views and policies of the new administration were merely different from those held previously. By modern standards, they were certainly no more efficacious. The New Deal saw the causes of the Depression in a conjunction of problems within individual sectors (banking, finance, labor, agriculture, and others), rather than a massive shortfall in aggregate demand.[8]

■ F.D.R. effectively used radio to generate support for his many reforms.
Source: Brown Brothers.

recurrence. In the first hundred days after President Roosevelt's inauguration, a wide range of legislation was passed, often after only cursory examination and debate. Some of the new laws enacted relief programs intended to improve the lot of the unemployed or aimed at particularly hard-hit sectors and institutions. Other programs were designed to produce economic recovery. A third set was oriented toward reform. Imbalances in current institutions—for example, in the bargaining power of labor versus employers—were thought to have contributed to the Depression's severity. Consequently, measures were devised to redress them. An expanded scope for government regulation of economic activity was one facet of the reform measures. Another, very sensibly, was the creation of agencies that generated far more information about the economy than had ever been available before.

The "Hundred Days" Legislation

The new administration quickly proposed, and Congress enacted, a series of measures designed to end the Depression and prevent its

[8] R. Gordon, *Economic Instability and Growth: The American Record* (New York: Harper and Row, 1974), pp. 62–64.

Initial New Deal Remedies

New Deal policies were developed to deal with the perceived shortcomings of the economy on a case-by-case basis. Not only were such programs often uncoordinated, but they frequently conflicted. If there was any unifying principle in the New Deal's view of the Depression, it was that prices of various items (labor, farm products, and industrial products) were too low. Conditions would improve if these prices could be raised, generally through policies unique to each sector concerned.[9] This view, however, suffered from two deficiencies. First, it confused symptoms with causes: prices had fallen because of the massive decline in aggregate demand, rather than conditions in specific markets. Second, attempts to raise prices in the face of prevailing low consumer incomes ignored the fact that someone had to buy goods at the higher prices sought by New Deal policy. Unless they somehow increased aggregate demand before or at least simultaneously with prices, policies stemming from this line of thought could not produce useful results.

At best, the piecemeal approach was inefficient. The lack of overall coordination meant that even policies with shared methods and goals were likely to produce duplication and waste, and many New Deal programs were totally independent of any others. Unless instituted on a broad front, these programs were unlikely to succeed, regardless of cost. If the prices of individual goods rose while most consumers' incomes remained depressed, the result would be a decline rather than an increase in the quantities demanded. As production of the now-more-expensive items fell, so too would employment in the sectors that produced them. Thus legislation based on this concept, such as the National Recovery Act, which will be treated in greater detail later, were counterproductive.

[9] Ibid., p. 63. See also L. Chandler, *America's Greatest Depression, 1929–1941* (New York: Harper and Row, 1970), Chap. 13.

Some New Deal policies were experimental and were abruptly dropped, supplemented, or even reversed as alternative programs were developed. These methods had some unfortunate results. In the first place, they allowed the creation of some highly questionable programs, such as the National Recovery Administration. Second, there was no recognition that some programs had relevance, if any, only under Depression conditions. Some were continued long after the only conditions in which they might have been justified had disappeared. As such, they became pure rent-seeking devices that reduced overall economic welfare. Government programs, once instituted, develop lives of their own. These comments are not a criticism of the New Deal's goals. Roosevelt and his appointees were sincerely committed to ending the suffering caused by the Depression and to improving the lot of average and particularly low-income Americans. But intentions should not excuse their efforts from an evaluation based on results, cost, and rationality.

Long-Term Consequences of the New Deal

Some programs had very high long-term costs, not least for the very people they had been established to help. Agricultural policy is a case in point: unquestionably, farmers suffered severe income reductions during the Depression because of declines in the prices of farm products. However, this did not mean that programs to raise the prices of farm products by imposing restrictions on the amounts produced were an efficient answer. These did little for farmers with the lowest incomes and greatest need. Further, increased food prices had adverse effects on hard-pressed consumers. Increased taxes to support such programs had their own burdens. Support for labor unions and higher wages may have benefited the majority of those working when such policies became effective. But they also made finding jobs more difficult for the unemployed.

In a few cases, what appeared at the time to be outright waste might have been the most effective policies under the circumstances. If it was necessary to require "make-work" employment, such as leaf raking, of the unemployed as the political price of rendering them assistance, the compromise was well worth making. It might have been impossible to support the unemployed in any other manner, and such programs were only slightly less efficient than straightforward cash grants.

Still, there was too much emphasis on spreading the existing amount of work among more people under the New Deal, and too little effort—at least *effective* effort—aimed at increasing the overall demand for labor. This reflected a view that only a limited demand for labor existed under any circumstances, and it could not be increased.

Banking and Monetary Policy

One of the first acts of the new president was to order the closing of all commercial banks in the United States. The governors of most states had already ordered banks within their jurisdictions to close by this time (March 1933). The "bank holiday" proclaimed on March 6, 1933, prohibited the usual business operations of commercial banks. In particular, they were forbidden to pay out cash.

To the banks themselves, the next few weeks were anything but a holiday. During the period when they were legally closed, the banks sold securities for cash. The Federal Reserve Banks were ordered to ease their conditions for loans to member banks and to issue more Federal Reserve notes against government bond collateral. The banks were audited by government inspectors instructed to take an optimistic view of the current values of their assets. If the bonds (and even more, the loans and mortgages) in most bank portfolios had been assessed at their actual market value in 1933, nearly all American banks would have been at least technically insolvent.[10]

As banks were found to be in satisfactory condition, they were issued licenses by the Treasury and allowed to reopen. About a month after the bank holiday was proclaimed, Federal Reserve System member banks controlling about 90 percent of the assets of all system members had reopened, and state banking authorities had allowed about 71 percent of the institutions under their control to resume operations, too.[11] Banks found to be in really serious difficulties were not allowed to reopen or had to do business under restrictions imposed by the authorities. About 2,000 banks remained permanently closed after the holiday, but the closings were the result of prior circumstances, not that occasion itself.[12] The bank holiday program was a success. Public confidence in the banks was restored, and the outflow of currency that had placed so many banks in jeopardy was not only halted, but reversed. Cash flowed into the banks, and the waves of bank failures were over.

Shortly afterward, the government began attempts to rehabilitate the debt structure. For those who could not repay their obligations on schedule, loan periods might be extended. In some cases, the government guaranteed repayment of the loan. Many existing business, agricultural, and residential debts were sold by private financial institutions to government agencies such as the Reconstruction Finance Corporation, the Home Owners' Loan Corporation, and the Federal Farm Mortgage Corporation. These agencies also made loans to financial intermediaries and purchased some of their debt and equity issues. Perhaps the most important single measure instituted in the financial sector during this period was the insurance of bank and savings and loan association

---

[10] Chandler, *America's Greatest Depression,* pp. 79–84, 128.
[11] Ibid., p. 146.
[12] Friedman and Schwartz are inclined to be less charitable. See *A Monetary History,* pp. 420–428.

■ A "run" on an Ohio bank, 1933. Thousands of such incidents forced the president to declare a "bank holiday" in 1933.
Source: Brown Brothers.

deposits, which will be discussed under reform measures. Ironically, however, it does not appear to have been part of the New Deal program, although it is widely credited to that source.[13]

Devaluation of the Dollar

The president had been authorized to reduce the gold content of the dollar by raising the price the Treasury would pay for gold. In a series of steps, the price of gold was increased from $20.67 per ounce to $35 by February 1934. This measure reduced the value of the dollar in relation to foreign currencies whose gold content was unchanged and thereby reduced the price of American exports and raised the domestic price of imports. Thus, it increased U.S. exports while it reduced imports.

The primary reason behind the increase in gold prices, however, appears to have been the view that it would somehow increase the general level of prices within the United States and thus stimulate the economy. It was an article of faith within the New Deal that at higher prices business firms would increase output, which would in turn increase employment.[14] To prevent windfall gains and losses, the increase in gold prices necessitated the surrender of all gold coin and bullion to the Treasury at its previous dollar value, and the abrogation of contract clauses requiring payment in gold dollars or their pre–1934 equivalents.

How the increase in gold prices would raise all other prices, let alone how inflation would increase real economic activity and employment, was never explained. But the devaluation of the dollar did have some expansionary effects. Since its price was now higher in this country, gold flowed into the United States

[13] C. Kindleberger, *The World in Depression, 1929–1939* (Berkeley, Calif: University of California Press, 1973), p. 201. See also S. Lebergott, *The Americans: An Economic Record* (New York, Norton, 1984), pp. 447–448, 481; and Chandler, *America's Greatest Depression*, p. 150.

[14] Friedman and Schwartz, *A Monetary History*, p. 465.

from abroad. When the gold was sold to the Treasury as the law now required, that agency paid with checks drawn on its account with the Federal Reserve. These checks, when deposited in commercial banks, increased the banks' reserves and thus their ability to expand the money supply. The stock of monetary gold rose by more than $14 billion between 1935 and 1941, and this increase in "high-powered money" was supplemented by a further $1.7 billion in silver purchases.[15] The latter were intended as a relief measure for western silver producers, as in earlier decades. In the later Thirties, gold also flowed to the United States because of the worsening political situation in Europe.

The United States refused to cooperate with other countries in devaluation policies and thus added to the barriers against international trade springing up all over the world. From this time on, the United States was on a gold-exchange standard. Although there was an official price of gold, the Treasury would only buy gold from American citizens—who were required to sell any gold they acquired through mining or foreign trade—and it would sell to foreigners or for export only under special circumstances.

Monetary Policy and Reforms

The Federal Reserve began a modest program of monetary expansion in 1933, buying some $600 million in bonds and reducing the discount rate. However, for most of the decade the impact of such expansionary measures was blunted by the commercial banks' tendency to hold much larger reserves than required by law. Banks also concentrated their investment policies on purchasing government securities rather than making loans to private borrowers. This did not make monetary policy totally ineffective: the Federal Reserve could deal directly with the public and thus increase the money supply. But it did make monetary expansion less effective. The money supply rose by about 50 percent from 1933 to 1937. The total reserve base ("high-powered money") rose by $6.8 billion from 1933 to 1936. Of this sum, nearly $3 billion was held as excess reserves by Federal Reserve System member banks.[16] Real output grew rapidly from the 1933 trough but was still far from full-employment levels when monetary expansion ceased in 1937.

The Federal Reserve was reorganized in 1935. Responsibility for monetary policy was centered in a new body, the Board of Governors, rather than in the Reserve Banks. The board controlled the Open Market Committee, had responsibilities for setting required reserve ratios for member banks (a new tool of discretionary monetary policy), and approved Reserve Bank discount policy as well. Finally, all the reins of monetary policy were in the same hands. The board's membership was almost entirely new, with only two members from the previous controlling body.[17] Nevertheless, monetary policy was scarcely more inspired than during 1929 to 1933.

Commercial banks had accumulated large excess reserves by 1936. Under existing regulations, they were free to make more loans and thus expand the money supply. The Federal Reserve Board became convinced that if the banks did so, the volume of spending would increase faster than the supply of goods, creating inflation. The board ignored two points. First, the unemployment rate in 1936 was almost 17 percent, and large numbers of unemployed workers mean many idle machines. Thus, a great deal of unused capacity still remained in the economy, and supply would be highly elastic. Second, to the commercial banks those excess reserves spelled safety, not opportunity to expand loans. Bankers viewed those reserves as a first line of defense against a recurrence of the mass depositor demands for

---

[15] Ibid., pp. 483–489.

[16] Chandler, *America's Greatest Depression*, pp. 174–175.
[17] Friedman and Schwartz, *A Monetary History*, pp. 445–449.

cash that many of them had so narrowly survived.

The commercial banks' distrust of the Federal Reserve proved only too well-founded. In three steps over late 1936 and early 1937, the Federal Reserve effectively doubled the required reserves of member banks. The change wiped out about two-thirds of the banks' "insurance policy." The money supply declined only a bit more than 1 percent, but the consequences were much greater.[18] The Federal Reserve's policy had been implemented while an equally ill-advised fiscal program was instituted by the Treasury. Federal spending was cut, and gold inflows were sterilized (they were purchased with bonds, not Federal Reserve deposits) so that they did not add to the money supply.

The "anti-inflation" policy was quite successful, though totally unnecessary. It caused a rapid decrease in economic activity. By 1938, the unemployment rate was 19 percent, as high as in 1935. This was especially disheartening because in 1937 there had been signs that the economy might finally be on the road to complete recovery. Not only had unemployment been dropping, but investment spending had at long last begun to pick up. Once again the Federal Reserve System had acted as though economic conditions were completely normal, despite overwhelming evidence that they were not.

This time, at least the contractionary policy was short-lived. Part of the gold sterilization and reserve requirement changes that had caused the downturn were rescinded in 1938, and federal government spending was increased as well. Banks again began to accumulate excess reserves.

Expansionary monetary policy might have stemmed the slide that began in 1929 if promptly instituted, but now it was much less effective. With a strong assist from the Federal

Reserve, the surviving banks' preferences had been altered in favor of security rather than profits. They now preferred excess reserves and government bonds rather than loans to private borrowers whose profits no longer seemed to outweigh their risks.

From 1933 to 1937, the Federal Reserve authorities did little to promote recovery from the slump they had helped to cause. The increase in the money supply was due more to Treasury policy toward gold than to conscious actions taken by the Federal Reserve. The ineptitude of the Fed and the fiscal authorities in 1937 may have stemmed from the view that the mission of public agencies in countercyclical policy was limited to starting a recovery. Once initiated, it was believed, the recovery would be self-sustaining. Output would rise and unemployment decline without further monetary or fiscal stimulation. How the Fed's leaders could have reached this conclusion in 1937, when recovery still had so very far to go, remains unanswered. Even if they thought that any recovery inevitably proceeded to full employment, it is hard to see how that view sanctioned contractionary policies rather than a mere cessation of stimuli.

Fiscal Policy

In its last two years, the Hoover administration had run budgetary deficits. The Roosevelt administration did the same in every year before 1941, after which the demands of war finance changed the situation almost beyond recognition. The deficit in 1937, however, was very small. Most modern economists agree that if fiscal policy is to counteract the business cycle, the government should attempt to counter the source of the problem. If the economy is suffering from inflation, which is normally caused by too much purchasing power chasing too few goods, the government should reduce the amount of purchasing power available to citizens. It does this by running a surplus, with-

[18] Ibid., pp. 516–534.

drawing more purchasing power through taxes than it injects through its expenditures. The result will be a reduction in excess purchasing power and lower inflation. In a depression, the problem is the opposite: too little spending. In such circumstances, the proper fiscal policy is to increase net injections of purchasing power into the economy through deficit spending. Proper countercyclical policy then requires that the government's expenditures exceed its tax revenues. The shortfall is financed either through the creation of new money by the central bank or by borrowing funds that would otherwise have remained idle. It should not employ funds that would have been spent in some other way.

Given these criteria, the actions of the federal government throughout the Depression appear appropriate, yet recovery was very slow and incomplete. Professor E. Cary Brown investigated this seeming paradox and came to the conclusion that countercyclical fiscal policy had not worked—because it had not been tried. After examining the fiscal record of the 1933–1940 period, Brown found that in only two years (1931 and 1936) were aggregate government budgets (federal, state, and local government combined) significantly expansive.[19] In addition, even with a generous allowance for multiplier effects, federal government deficits that never exceeded $5 billion were insufficient to offset declines in GNP that exceeded $40 billion.

The Aggregate Impact of Government in the Thirties

The federal deficits by themselves give a misleading picture of government's fiscal impact. State and local governments, which in aggregate had been running deficits when the Depression began, generally had balanced their budgets or even achieved surpluses by 1933

and continued this policy through 1940. They did so largely through increased taxation. The subsidiary governmental units were facing heavy welfare and relief demands, but given the minimal government of the time, there were few areas where spending could be reduced to channel more to anti-Depression policies.

State sales taxes became common during the Thirties,[20] and they have a restraining effect on consumption spending. State and even more so local governments cannot be expected to attempt countercyclical fiscal policy in any case, because most of any benefits from their actions would occur outside their borders. The surpluses of state and local governments offset a considerable portion of the federal government's deficits. In 1931 and 1936, the expansionary effects of fiscal policy largely resulted from the payment of large veterans' bonuses. Both bonus bills were passed by Congress over presidential vetoes; President Roosevelt was almost as vehement in his opposition to the 1936 measure as President Hoover had been to that of 1931.[21]

As if this were not enough, the federal tax structure imposed barriers to full employment that became considerably greater as incomes began to rise. The 1932 tax increase, which much more than wiped out the temporary tax reduction of 1929, raised income tax rates at all levels and extended the tax further into the middle class, which had previously been largely exempt. The poor were almost entirely below the income tax threshold, but they did not escape. Both state sales taxes and federal social security taxes bore disproportionately on low incomes. The social security tax, in particular, was strongly regressive at this time. Modifications in 1934 and 1935 did not change the federal tax schedules significantly.

The result of the various tax changes was that for the first years of the New Deal, the

---

[19] E.C. Brown, "Fiscal Policy in the Thirties: A Reappraisal," *American Economic Review* (December 1966).

[20] Ibid.
[21] Gordon, *Economic Instability and Growth*, p. 63.

overall federal tax structure imposed a great deal of "fiscal drag." As recovery proceeded and incomes grew, the government's tax revenues would grow much faster. Given constant levels of federal spending, the budget would be balanced long before full employment was achieved. As incomes rose beyond the level at which the budget was balanced, further growth would be in the face of a growing federal surplus: taxes would remove more income than federal spending plowed back into the economy (even in the unlikely event that welfare expenditures were not decreased). This was the fiscal program of the first four years of the New Deal. Recovery never proceeded far enough to show its full effects.

Subsequent changes in fiscal policy only gradually became more beneficial. In 1937, the unemployment rate was declining, although still over 14 percent. In nominal terms, GNP was 88 percent of 1929's, although since prices were now much lower, it was about equal in real terms. Investment spending was beginning again, and businesses had just commenced adding to their inventories—a most hopeful sign. In view of this evidence of "recovery," the federal deficit was reduced to only $400 million through cuts in relief programs, the end of the "one-shot" veterans' bonus of 1936, and tax increases, in particular the new social security payroll tax.[22] During late 1937 the federal budget was for practical purposes in balance, even though the economy remained far below full-employment production levels. The monetary contraction engineered by the Federal Reserve must share the blame for the ensuing recession-within-a-depression of 1937–1938, but obviously there was little or no thought of the federal budget as a tool that could itself have been used to expand the economy during the crucial years before 1938.

Throughout this period, the New Dealers continued to regard deficits as unfortunate side effects of the costs of specific programs, not as tools to promote general economic expansion. The programs under which expenditures rose were to promote recovery by their direct effects on specific sectors of the economy, rather than by increasing aggregate demand. Moreover, deficits were to be eliminated as soon as falling unemployment allowed spending reductions. There was no consideration whatever of tax reduction as a device for economic expansion.[23] Recent revisions of Brown's work employing more modern theoretical concepts have reached even stronger conclusions. Even the federal budget had a net expansionary effect only in 1931 (under the much-maligned Hoover administration), and then by less than 1 percent of GNP.[24]

After the 1937 debacle, there was more New Deal interest in using budgetary deficits to fill the gap between current and full-employment levels of spending. Marriner Eccles, the new chairman of the Federal Reserve Board, advocated this policy.[25] Even so, the concept was never seriously pursued. The largest federal deficit before World War II was $4.5 billion— far too little, even when its multiplier effects were considered, to offset the shortfall in private demand. For the entire Depression, federal deficits totaled about $30 billion. This was barely enough to offset two or three years' income decline under the most favorable assumptions. From 1934 to 1940, federal spending rose from $6.6 billion to $10.6 billion (the latter figure includes a half-billion dollars for additional defense spending). Total tax revenues rose faster, from $3 billion to $6.8 billion over the same period.[26]

[22] Chandler, *America's Greatest Depression*, p. 140.

[23] Gordon, *Economic Instability and Growth*, pp. 62–64.
[24] L. Peppers, "Full Employment Surplus Analysis and Structural Change: The 1930s," *Expolorations in Economic History* (Winter 1973).
[25] Eccles' ideas have recently been outlined by Professor Jonathan Hughes. See *The Vital Few: American Economic Progress and Its Protagonists*, 2d ed. (Cambridge, England: Cambridge University Press, 1986).
[26] U.S. Department of Commerce, *Historical Statistics*, vol. 2, pp. 1105–1106, 1114.

The policies and record of the New Deal have been termed Keynesian. Supposedly they were derived from the theories of the British economist John Maynard Keynes. Keynes promoted the idea that under certain conditions a market economy might produce substantial unemployment and at best only slowly regain full employment. Should such circumstances occur, Keynes advocated increased government spending and tax cuts to spur the growth of income. Keynes met President Roosevelt, but neither appeared to sufficiently appreciate the other's genius, and nothing came of the meeting. Keynes's ideas, at least in their original form, had little or no effect on American fiscal policy before World War II.

The Failure of Fiscal Policy

Aggregate monetary and fiscal policies did not end the Depression. They were seldom used as such, and when they were, were perversely employed as often as properly directed. In fiscal policy, some excuses can be made. Macroeconomics was still in its infancy. Even had American politicians gained a proper understanding of appropriate macroeconomic programs, they would have had great difficulty persuading the electorate to accept them. The relatively modest deficits of the New Deal were widely attacked as "bankrupting the country" and "destroying the credit of the federal government." The balanced peacetime budget had been a cornerstone of American fiscal policy for so long that it might well have been impossible to gain political acceptance of expansionary policies of sufficient scope to deal with the Depression. It might not even have been physically possible after 1932, given the magnitude of the Depression and the modest size of the budget. American as well as British academics might have concluded that serious depressions required unbalanced budgets, but they had little immediate influence.

In the case of monetary policy, no adequate defenses appear possible. Some monetary authorities, at least, were aware of methods to expand the money supply, and the idea that monetary expansion was an appropriate counter to such conditions was well established. It was impossible to conclude that empirical conditions did not warrant expansion if real-world evidence was taken into account. Monetary policy for most of this period lacks even the fig leaf of ignorance to hide its errors of omission and commission.

Relief of the Unemployed

The Roosevelt administration, unlike its predecessor, accepted responsibility for easing the plight of the unemployed. It quickly launched programs to provide government-funded jobs and relief payments. However, there was still great opposition to direct money payments to the jobless without some sort of quid pro quo. President Roosevelt and Harry Hopkins, the director of the Federal Emergency Relief Administration, both desired measures that would preserve the self-respect and use the talents of the unemployed. It was decided that federal efforts to aid the unemployed would concentrate on the direct provision of jobs.[27] Hopkins' agency began operations in May 1933. It was empowered to make grants to the states to supplement their efforts to provide both direct relief and work relief and to make additional grants without state partnership when necessary. Under the Federal Emergency Relief Administration (FERA), programs such as the Civil Works Administration, Works Progress Administration, and Civilian Conservation Corps—all soon known by their initials—provided several million jobs per year.

The Conflicting Goals of Federal Employment Programs

Projects undertaken by these agencies included construction of social overhead capital such as parks, airports, roads, public buildings, water

---

[27] Chandler, *America's Greatest Depression*, pp. 191–192.

■ WPA projects produced many public works.
Source: The Bettmann Archive.

and sewer projects, erosion control, the reforestation and other environmental work of the Civilian Conservation Corps, and a wide variety of similar undertakings. Some programs sought to use the skills of unemployed artists, writers, teachers, dramatists and other professionals. These programs constructed both physical and intellectual capital: some generated a good deal of useful information, both from direct investigation and on-the-job experience, that aided later governmental decisions. While some of these programs were derided as "make-work," mere excuses to pay the unemployed (in some cases the charge was valid), the basic idea was a humane response to the psychic effects of the Depression. These programs were frankly designed primarily to provide employment and income; the products that resulted were a secondary consideration.

Harold Ickes, the Secretary of the Interior, led a different approach. Under his direction, the Public Works Administration also constructed social overhead capital, generally large-scale projects such as roads and dams. In this case, however, the primary emphasis was on the value of the projects themselves. Every effort was made to complete them as efficiently as possible, using least-cost methods. Whether this meant employing much or little labor was unimportant. Many Public Works Administration projects were highly capital- and material-intensive and increased employment far less per dollar spent than did programs of the FERA. Nor were the jobs or their locations particularly well suited to the capabilities of the unemployed, and they often required a good deal of time to plan before actual construction began. Although the Public Works Administra tion provided a peak of 714,000 jobs in 1936, this was far below the nearly five million employed under FERA programs at their maximum in 1934.[28] The Public Works Administration record provides a good argument against reliance on public works projects as unemployment relief, at least if the projects themselves are to be a primary concern.

Federally funded employment programs provided a cumulative total of more than eight million jobs. Most were designed to minimize competition for labor with private employers. In view of the prevailing unemployment rates, such a precaution was unnecessary. Although the programs were a step in the right direction (at least given the ineptitude of efforts to increase private employment), they were too small and at best provided more or less thinly veiled charity. There was no question that they were a "second-best" response to unemployment, necessitated largely by the New Deal's failure to end the Depression.

However, if New Dealers insisted on treating the symptoms of the Depression rather than its causes, the programs were a response to the economic and human costs it imposed. While these programs did significantly affect the numbers of people totally without work after 1932, it must be remembered that those working under them were not doing the type of work they would have chosen under normal conditions. In many ways, they were similar to a present-day individual collecting unemployment compensation—not without income, but clearly not working at a job of his or her choice, and presumably willing to do so.[29]

Farm Relief

Farming was affected as adversely as any occupation by the Depression. The prices of most agricultural products fell below the none-too-remunerative levels of the Twenties, but farm production costs did not decline proportionately, and fixed costs such as debt service and property taxes scarcely fell at all. In 1929, wheat had sold for $1.04 per bushel and corn for 88¢. Cotton brought farmers 17¢ per pound. By 1932 these prices had declined to 39¢, 32¢, and 5¢, respectively.[30] Price declines for other crops and animal products had been equally dramatic. Even at these prices, unsold stocks of all farm commodities were rising in the face of widespread hunger. The net income that American farmers derived from farming fell to only one-third its 1929 level. Debt and other fixed-cost burdens were becoming unbearable. Slightly less than half of all farm mortgages and over half the total value of all farm mortgage debt was delinquent as 1933 began.[31]

Nor were farmers spared the economic problems of the cities. Bank failures were even more frequent among small-town and rural institutions than in urban areas. When the local bank failed, farmers seldom had easy access to alternative sources of credit. Even agricultural unemployment was not unknown. Mortgage foreclosures, crop failures, and simple economic defeat drove some farmers off the land, and increasing farm mechanization cost some agricultural laborers their jobs as well, particularly in the South. The government would not make direct loans to farmers, and there were no better jobs they could migrate to in the early Thirties.

As in so many other cases, the New Deal response to farmers' plight was unique to that sector. The primary goal of government agri-

[28] Ibid., p. 196.

[29] M. Darby, "Three and a Half Million U.S. Employees Have Been Mislaid: Or, An Explanation of Unemployment, 1934–1941," *Journal of Political Economy* (February 1976). See also J. Kesselman and N. Savin, "Three and a Half Million Workers Were Never Lost," *Economic Inquiry* (April 1978) and Lebergott, *The Americans* pp. 464–465.

[30] U.S. Department of Commerce, *Historical Statistics*, vol. 1, p. 511.

[31] Chandler, *America's Greatest Depression*, p. 64.

Table 18.1 The Economy during the New Deal

Date	Nominal GNP*	Real GNP**	Unemployment (in Millions)	Rate of Unemployment	Rate of Growth
1929	$103.1	$203.6	1.55	3.2%	6.7%
1930	90.4	183.5	4.34	8.7	−9.8
1931	75.8	169.3	8.02	15.9	−7.6
1932	58.0	144.2	12.06	23.6	−14.7
1933	55.6	141.5	12.83	24.9	−1.8
1934	65.1	154.3	11.34	21.7	9.1
1935	72.2	169.5	10.61	20.1	9.9
1936	82.5	193.0	9.03	16.9	13.9
1937	90.4	203.2	7.70	14.3	5.3
1938	84.7	192.9	10.39	19.0	−5.0
1939	90.5	209.4	9.48	17.2	8.6
1940	99.7	227.2	8.12	14.6	8.5
1941	124.5	263.7	5.56	9.9	16.1

Date	Real Annual Wages (1914 Dollars)		Consumer Price Index (1967 = 100)	Index of Manufacturing Production****
	Nominal	Adjusted***		
1929	$ 834	$793	51.3	23
1930	834	725	50.0	19
1931	857	657	45.6	15
1932	838	554	40.9	12
1933	811	526	38.8	14
1934	800	569	40.1	15
1935	816	584	41.1	18
1936	830	633	41.5	22
1937	880	704	43.0	23
1938	868	641	42.2	18
1939	915	699	41.6	22
1940	943	754	42.0	25
1941	1,018	861	44.1	32

*Current dollars
**1958 dollars
***For unemployment
****1967 = 100
Source: U.S. Department of Commerce, Bureau of the Census, *Historical Statistics of the United States: Colonial Times to 1970*, 2 vols. (Washington, D.C.: Government Printing Office, 1975), 1:135, 164, 210, 224, 226–227; 2:667.

cultural-assistance programs was to increase the prices of agricultural commodities. While this, if achieved, would increase farmers' incomes, price-support programs had both short- and long-term drawbacks. Although the Depression had greatly intensified farmers' problems, the primary cause of low agricultural incomes had not changed in decades. There were too many farmers, and their combined output was too large to be absorbed by markets at prices that allowed farmers to earn incomes comparable to those of other occupations. This had been true even in normal periods (it is only relatively less valid for the 1910–1915 period than for the Twenties).

Since the demand for most farm products was price inelastic, increases in output reduced prices disproportionately and lowered aggregate farm revenues. Nor could any individual farmer raise the price of agricultural commodities by reducing output. Because there were so many small-scale producers, no individual production decision changed supply appreciably. Mass action by farmers, at least on a voluntary basis, was impossible. Consequently, the individual farmer had little choice but to produce as much as he could, regardless of the expected price. If prices were low, the farmer's only hope for an adequate income was the largest possible crop from his land. Most farmers had substantial fixed costs that had to be met regardless of the volume of production. Even worse, many farms were too small or badly located, infertile, unsuited to large-scale, cost-reducing methods, or otherwise physically incapable of producing an output that would yield a decent living at any realistic price. In such cases, higher farm products prices might reduce the poverty of those trying to wrest a living from agriculture, but they could not cure it.

The Parity Concept

If farm prices were to rise, some combination of increased demand, reduced output, or both was necessary. In addition, the problem of current farm debts and future agricultural credit supplies required attention. The New Deal's first response was the Agricultural Adjustment Act, a product of the "hundred days" in which the New Deal's basic legislation was enacted. In this law, the federal government accepted the principal of parity as a goal for agricultural prices. Parity meant that farm commodities' prices were to be increased relative to nonfarm goods' until they bore the same relationship they had in some base period, usually 1910–

1914, when farm goods' prices were exceptionally high.

The parity concept ignored relative trends in demand and supply for farm and nonfarm goods. But it allowed farmers to mask rent-seeking as an appeal for "fair" treatment rather than a handout. A parity ratio of 100 would indicate that farm and nonfarm prices had the same relationship as in the 1910–1914 base period. A unit of farm goods, say a bushel of wheat, would exchange for the same number of nonfarm goods, for example sixpenny nails, as it had in the earlier period. In 1933 the actual parity ratio was 64.[32]

Farm Production Quotas

To increase farm goods' prices to or nearer the parity ratio, either supply would have to be reduced enough to cause prices to rise to the desired level, or government could fix a minimum price and then buy any quantity unsold at that price. Since surpluses of many farm products already existed in 1933, it was clear that some method must be found to reduce both existing and future supplies. If not, the government would be forced to buy ever-increasing quantities of agricultural products that could not be disposed of within the United States. The Agricultural Adjustment Act therefore provided a mixture of production controls, benefit payments, and government purchases of surplus agricultural products. Under the act, the government fixed national quotas for the production of virtually all major crops, beef, pork, and dairy products. Qualifications for inclusion in the program were extremely liberal: they extended to sugar cane, flax, and grain sorghums.

The Department of Agriculture was empowered to establish quotas in an attempt to reduce quantities produced and thus push prices toward the parity targets. The national

[32] U.S. Department of Commerce, *Historical Statistics,* vol. 1, p. 489.

quotas were then divided among regions on the basis of past production, and within regions by the vote of the farmers themselves. The process favored the large producers, who had the most at stake. Those participating in the scheme received benefit payments from the government, and all farmers gained to the extent that the agreements resulted in higher prices. To finance the program, a tax was levied on the processors of all agricultural products within the United States.

The whole program, of course, was price fixing on a grand scale, and the act included a provision exempting participants from the antitrust laws. When it went into effect in 1933, some farm production was already in process. Meeting the production quotas for that year required destroying several million young pigs and plowing under a large portion of that year's cotton crop. With an assist from nature in the form of a severe drought in the Great Plains (the beginning of the "Dust Bowl") and other crop failures, the program successfully raised the prices of most farm products.

Net agricultural incomes doubled by 1934 and continued to rise every year thereafter until 1939. Even so, farm incomes did not regain 1929 levels in nominal terms until 1941. Because both price levels and the number of farms (though not the farm population) were substantially lower at the later date, real income per farm was considerably higher in 1941 than in 1929. Real agricultural income per member of the farm population had risen by about 15 percent. By that time the demands of World War II were a greater influence on prices than were crop-limitation schemes. At no time, however, was the goal of 100 percent parity ever achieved.[33] Output restriction became more difficult as farmers adjusted to the new regulations. The production quotas were imposed through acreage limitations, and farmers responded predictably. They withdrew their least fertile land from production and cultivated their most productive acres more intensively. Yields per acre rose for all major crops during this period.[34]

The Agricultural Adjustment Act was declared unconstitutional by the Supreme Court in 1936, but similar programs continued in a new guise under the Soil Conservation and Domestic Allotment Act. This legislation's ostensible purpose was to withdraw land particularly subject to erosion or depletion from cultivation or convert it to less destructive crops. Farmers received government payments for withholding such land from the production of basic crops. This, of course, reduced output and allowed the quotas and benefits of the Agricultural Adjustment Act to continue. A new provision was added: under this law, farmers could borrow against the value of crops they had stored with the government's Commodity Credit Corporation. If the crops' market value rose to more than the value of the loan, farmers could sell their produce, repay the loan and interest, and pocket the difference. If crop prices remained below the loan extended on them, they could discharge the loan obligation by granting the corporation full title to the crops deposited with it.

Help for Farm Debt

Farm finances were improved by several programs aimed at reducing debt burdens and improving farmers' access to credit. Since farms were virtually unsalable, even at a fraction of their pre-Depression values, many private mortgage holders such as the life insurance companies refrained from foreclosing on delinquent loans. They asked merely that the farmers maintain the property and make whatever payments they could until better times. Alternatively, they might allow mortgagees to remain as tenants.

[33] Ibid., pp. 484, 489.

[34] Ibid., pp. 500–501.

Such decisions were not entirely motivated by concern for the farmers' plight. Foreclosure often involved the creditor in a capital loss because resale of the property seldom returned even the principal amount of the original mortgage. Financial institutions holding mortgages as assets against their liabilities were not willing to risk their own solvency with procedures that revealed the extent of the fall in asset values. Nevertheless, a combination of unpayable debts, low commodity prices, and unfavorable weather drove many small-scale or marginal-area farmers from the land, a process portrayed in books such as John Steinbeck's *The Grapes of Wrath*. The western Great Plains, the upper Midwest, and Appalachia were particularly hard hit.

The Farm Credit Corporation was organized in 1933 to restructure existing farm debts and channel federal credit to agriculture. The Federal Land Banks, established during the Wilson administration, were employed to refinance farm mortgages or purchase them from private creditors. Funds were advanced for taxes or other pressing obligations, and in some cases, to purchase additional land. By 1940, nearly 40 percent of all farm mortgages were held by the Farm Credit Administration or its subsidiaries, reflecting both the extent of federal aid to agriculture and the market's evaluation of farming's prospects.

New Deal Agricultural Policies: An Assessment

The agricultural programs of the New Deal were flawed. Above all, they were palliatives rather than solutions, attempts to raise the incomes of farmers by increasing agricultural product prices. Unfortunately, most cases of real poverty among farmers—and they were numerous—stemmed from inability to respond to production incentives. Increasing the prices of commodities that worn-out hill or jackpine farms could never produce in large amounts merely encouraged farmers to continue a struggle that in the long run was hopeless. As

long as no alternative jobs were available for the surplus agricultural population, such measures served as an inefficient form of welfare. After full employment was regained, they tempted people to remain in an occupation offering little or no chance of income parity with other jobs.

The programs were inefficient because they channeled most of the aid to the farmers who produced most efficiently and thus had least need of assistance. Those who were really poor got little under such programs. In the case of cotton production, the new programs encouraged mechanization and actually reduced the labor force required for the harvest.[35]

Another drawback to the agricultural assistance programs is that, by and large, they offered aid only to those who agreed to remain in farming. While few if any alternative jobs were open to those leaving agriculture in the Thirties, the basic provisions of these programs have remained essentially unchanged to this day. Nor, in the face of another farm crisis, does there appear to be much political will to recognize the problem now.

As farm productivity grew, the position of the small farmers became worse, since they were in most cases unable to reduce their production costs to the extent that large-scale farmers could. The programs imposed unnecessarily high costs per dollar of aid actually received by farmers because of the expenses of holding surplus products and administering production quotas. At the same time they gave farmers incentives to increase production, the programs pushed up the price of food and other farm products. Since the New Deal's farm programs clearly involved higher costs to the economy (food price increases, taxes, foregone alternatives) than the aid received by farmers

---

[35] W. Whatley, "Labor for the Picking: The New Deal in the South," *Journal of Economic History* (December 1983). See also G. Wright, *Old South, New South: Revolutions in the Southern Economy since the Civil War* (New York: Basic Books, 1986), Chap. 7.

and thereby reduced overall economic welfare, they are a clear example of rent seeking. Farmers gained less than the rest of the economy lost.

Other Relief Programs

Home mortgages prior to the Depression were typically "balloon mortgages," in which only interest charges were payable until the last few years of the mortgage. Then the entire principal of the mortgage fell due in a few large payments, or even only one. No wonder so many melodramas were built around a single all-or-nothing mortgage payment! Such arrangements were extremely vulnerable to depression conditions. As incomes fell and bank failures increased during the Depression, some mortgagees lost both their current incomes and the savings they had been accumulating for the mortgage payment. Millions of home loans became delinquent from either or both of these causes.

Relief was complicated. Often housing values had fallen so low that foreclosed property could not be resold for even half its value when the mortgage was taken out. Either reducing the loan principal or foreclosing for resale inflicted a capital loss on the mortgageholder. Declining asset values threatened the survival of many institutions holding large numbers of mortgages. Thus, assisting mortgagees on the basis of current market values of their property might further the financial collapse that had already inflicted such great damage on the economy. Even extending the repayment period for delinquent mortgages might produce severe cash-flow problems for creditors.

Government programs in this area were similar to those set up in agriculture. The Home Owners' Loan Corporation extended its own credit, purchased mortgages, and refinanced existing debts. Loans were guaranteed by the Federal Housing Administration, established in 1934. The government began making loans to finance municipally owned public housing in 1937. Finally, institutions also changed: most mortgages issued after this time provided for the now-familiar monthly payments amortizing both principal and interest. This change reduced the risks to buyer and seller alike.

RECOVERY POLICIES

In its efforts to end the Depression, the New Deal achieved less than in its relief or reform efforts. Even its successes were often fortuitous.

The National Industrial Recovery Act

No program more clearly reveals the deficiencies of New Deal recovery policies than the National Industrial Recovery Act, yet another product of the "hundred days" period in 1933.[36] No other New Deal legislation was more firmly rooted in the belief that businesses required the incentive of higher prices (and security against price competition from rivals) to induce them to increase production. Higher production, ran the rationale for the NIRA, would require more workers and thus reduce unemployment.

To achieve these goals, the act authorized the formulation of "codes of fair competition." So-called blanket codes were established as models, but each industry was urged to produce its own. The codes pledged each firm to "fair" methods of competition and employment; they covered such matters as prices, wages, hours, output, trade practices, working conditions, and collective bargaining. They were to be formulated by representatives of business, labor, and consumers. Once a code was

---

[36] Chandler, *America's Greatest Depression,* Chap. 13.

■ Steinbeck's *The Grapes of Wrath* portrayed a dismal fact of life, the migration from marginal agricultural areas.
Source: The Depression Years as photographed by Arthur Rothstein (New York: Dover Publications, Inc., 1978), p. 24.

accepted by the National Recovery Administration, its provisions became binding on all firms in the industry whether they had cooperated in shaping it or not.

In practice, the codes were largely designed by business. Labor generally had only a minor role, and consumers none at all. Not surprisingly, the codes became price-fixing arrangements that the basic NIRA legislation exempted from the antitrust laws. A provision that was to have profound long-term consequences guaranteed employees the right to form their own organizations, choose their own representatives, and bargain collectively with employers. The blanket codes and most industry codes established minimum wages and maximum hours of work. The latter provision was designed primarily to increase the number of workers hired rather than improve their working conditions. By 1935, more than 500 codes covering the vast majority of all industry had been drawn up.

Under the codes, the basic structure of each industry became a cartel for all practical purposes. Firms lost individual control over their own price and output decisions and were required to furnish information to the code authorities that made evading the agreement's provisions difficult. The codes became the instrument by which prices were increased, free from the threat of competition. Wholesale prices rose nearly 23 percent from 1933 to 1935, although consumer prices and the GNP deflator exhibited much smaller increases.[37] Some of this increase probably indicated that wholesale prices had temporarily fallen below levels equating demand and supply at the trough of the Depression.

Flawed Policies

From the viewpoint of economic theory, the National Industrial Recovery Act appears to be exactly the wrong medicine for the Depression. To be sure, as markets shrank, prices had fallen and competition for the remaining business had become intense, but this reflected the overall decline in income. Raising prices in the face of reduced demand could be accomplished only if output were reduced, perhaps substantially.

To the extent that it had any effect, the NIRA could only worsen the Depression's impact. With their incomes low and uncertain, consumers were likely to respond to increased prices by reducing the quantities they purchased. The immediate effect of price increases would be a reduction in the already shrunken purchasing power of consumers, and consequently an additional decline in output and employment. All the unused capacity made it unlikely that such programs could ever be put into effective operation (particularly in the existing circumstances, producers' incentives to cheat, code or no code, would be overwhelming). Even if an increase in aggregate demand could somehow be achieved independent of the NIRA programs, they would reduce its impact. The Supreme Court's decision that the act was an unconstitutional delegation of congressional powers provided the Roosevelt administration with a graceful way out of a thoroughly ill-conceived program.

The next year, policy was completely reversed. Instead of supporting legally sanctioned price fixing, the administration began a vigorous program of antitrust law enforcement under Thurman Arnold, the new head of the Department of Justice's Antitrust Division. While this policy had greater implications for reform than recovery, it certainly would not inhibit the latter. But the abrupt policy reversal did nothing to strengthen the confidence of business leaders, few of whom placed great trust in the New Deal or its leader in any circumstances.

The Fair Labor
Standards Act

After the demise of the NIRA, the provisions affecting labor were quickly incorporated into the National Labor Relations Act, which was destined to play a prominent role in the labor history of the following decades. The Fair La-

---

[37] U.S. Department of Commerce, *Historical Statistics,* vol. 1, pp. 198–199, 210–211.

bor Standards Act (1938) had elements of both recovery (or the New Deal version thereof) and reform.

The Fair Labor Standards Act set minimum wage levels and maximum work hours: initially 25¢ per hour and not more than 44 hours per week. Any additional hours were to be compensated at overtime rates, in the hope that employers would hire additional workers rather than pay more per hour. This legislation, as well as the Social Security Act, attempted to reduce the supply of labor by tightening restrictions on child labor and on the employment of those over age 65.

Imposing a legal minimum wage under Depression conditions was a very dubious policy. Employees might be able to increase both wages and total employment if they were assisted by minimum wage legislation or a labor union in dealing with a monopsonistic employer, but most labor markets were not monopsonistic. Under more competitive conditions, raising the cost of labor to employers, particularly when there was a huge surplus of labor at existing wage rates, was far more likely to reduce than to raise aggregate employment. Such laws may be consistent with other New Deal legislation, but implicit in them is a view that the demand for labor is fixed and cannot be increased, and that buyers' reactions to price changes do not matter.

REFORM MEASURES

The reforms instituted by the New Deal probably represent its most positive contribution to economic improvement. Curiously, the one institutional change of this period applauded by liberals and conservatives alike was not supported by the administration.[38] The Federal

Deposit Insurance Corporation and its twin, the Federal Savings and Loan Insurance Corporation, insured deposits in commercial banks and savings and loan associations. All member banks of the Federal Reserve System were required to join the FDIC, and nonmember banks were allowed to do so. In practice, nearly all banks joined. The result was a major improvement in the stability of the commercial banking system. Bank runs all but disappeared because depositors were now assured of access to their cash from an insured bank in a few days, no matter how many of their fellows had cashed in their own deposits in the meantime.

The Social Security Act

The first steps to publicly assist individual security were initiated—several decades after most western European countries had instituted similar measures. The Social Security Act of 1935 provided a much wider range of benefits than the old-age pensions that normally come to mind when social security is mentioned. Direct aid to those unable to work—the aged, the handicapped, and dependent children—was provided, as was unemployment insurance. The portion of the social security program that provided direct money payments to the needy was the forerunner of our current welfare system. For all its conceptual faults (the program generates revenue as if it were an annuity and disburses funds with little recognition of long-term revenue prospects), the Social Security Act was the first explicit recognition that in a market economy some persons may be unable to provide for themselves.

All facets of the program have been revised and expanded many times since 1935. Despite widespread criticism from many different viewpoints, the act's basic premise that individuals who cannot generate a decent standard of living through their own efforts have a claim on society's resources continues to receive popular support. The reconciliation of views on el-

---

[38] Kindleberger, *The World in Depression*, p. 201. See also Lebergott, *The Americans*, pp. 447–448.

■ Publicity for the Social Security Act of 1935 attempted to reassure individuals who feared such a "radical" new notion.
Source: Social Security Administration.

taining the commitments of the Social Security Act increasingly problematical. Other developed nations have had similar experiences. Originally, the Old Age and Survivors' Insurance portion of the social security program was intended to form a base below which no covered individual's income need fall, but it was not envisioned as an adequate sole income source for the retired.

As did so many other New Deal programs, the Social Security Act contained provisions intended to reduce the labor supply. These included retirement at age 65 and the loss of accrued benefits if insured individuals earned more than a minimal income from labor after becoming eligibile for benefits. The purpose of these features was to spread an apparently insufficient demand for labor over as many individuals as possible.

Social security did remove some of the terrors of old age. No longer did people have to fear literally working until they died, possibly at jobs unsuited to the elderly, to avoid a loss of independence. Prior to the advent of social security, the elderly who lacked adequate savings faced bitter choices. They could depend on their children for support or turn to the public authorities. Public support was both niggardly and subject to demeaning conditions designed to discourage applicants. The legislation probably also encouraged greater interest in private pension plans. Higher income levels have nevertheless contributed more to the potential security of the elderly than social security by increasing their ability to accumulate private savings, either directly or in fringe benefits rather than wages.

Unemployment Insurance

Unemployment insurance was another result of the American experience during the Depression. The program set up at this time was to be self-funding: a tax levied on employer payrolls was used to establish a fund from which payments could be made to those out of work. The length of support was limited to provide

igibility and support levels is another matter and appears no nearer solution today than it was fifty-odd years ago. In addition, the provisions of the act have proved useful instruments for rent-seeking in the hands of various pressure groups.

Social security also provided pensions for the retired. The program was to be financed by taxes on both individual incomes and employer payrolls. Since both taxes increased employers' labor costs, both were borne primarily by employees. Inflation, changing demographics, and rent-seeking politics have made main-

incentives for the unemployed to seek work. The plan was designed to encourage each state to set up its own program and to ensure conformity among the state plans. Once in operation, the program not only provided relief to the jobless but proved valuable in increasing economic stability, since it cushioned the decline in incomes resulting from unemployment and reduced the multiplier effects that spread the impact of unemployment throughout the economy.

The Tennessee Valley Authority

The Tennessee Valley Authority is not easily classified. Originally conceived as a massive public works project designed to raise incomes in one of the poorest areas of the United States, it also represented a significant change in the economic role of government. The federal government built a series of huge dams in the Tennessee and Cumberland River valleys. The dams were primarily designed to generate hydroelectric power, but the project also improved navigation and provided flood control and recreational facilities. To improve the projects' effectiveness in flood control, the TVA began efforts to control erosion through reforestation projects and by teaching farmers soil conservation methods.

The TVA assumed the character of a regional development project. The great dams' cheap electric power enticed industry to an area that previously had few attractions for manufacturing firms. The new jobs that resulted offered much better income prospects than ever before to the valleys' residents. Competition from TVA power drove some privately owned electric companies out of business, and TVA generating costs were used (unfairly, some claimed) as a yardstick in determining the rates allowed regulated utilities.

Other New Deal programs were extensions, sometimes much enlarged, of activities traditionally performed by government, although sometimes not at the federal level. The Tennessee Valley Authority, however, fit the classic definition of socialism: here government owned the means of production. Although similar projects were planned in other regions, little was accomplished before World War II except in the Pacific Northwest.

Private capital had been developing hydroelectric facilities for decades before the TVA appeared. However, it seems most unlikely that private projects would have financed the range of social benefits provided by this vast public enterprise. Some of these were costly (flood control). In other cases it was difficult to assess benefits or assign them to specific individuals or even locations (erosion control). Such circumstances are often used to justify the provision of public goods. The costs and benefits to the national economy from the TVA have never been fully assessed. However, there was little doubt that the benefits in the immediate area were far greater than the costs and that such an undertaking would never have been financed by private enterprise in the Thirties.

The Growth of Organized Labor

The Twenties had not been a good decade for labor unions in the United States. Earlier depressions had always caused substantial declines in union membership, so it could be expected that the Great Depression would be devastating for organized labor, and that union ranks would dwindle.

For the first few years of the Depression, this prediction held true, although the unions lost fewer members than might have been expected. Their membership fell from 3.6 to 3 million—a serious blow, but not a fatal one. Shortly after the trough of the Depression, however, union membership began to increase even though unemployment remained very high. Not only did the unions make up lost ground; they grew larger than ever before. By 1937, there were 5.8 million workers in union ranks, and three years later, almost 9 million. The work force had also grown since the unions' previous peak of strength in 1920, so the gains as a portion of the work force were smaller. Still, the 1940 figure represented about 15 percent of the U.S. labor force, an all-time high. Much of the increase was in industries that had previously defied union efforts: the large mass-production manufacturing firms, most of whose workers were semiskilled or unskilled, not craftsmen.[39]

Labor in a New Climate

These developments were not quite as startling as previous American labor history might indicate. The climate in which labor operated had now changed. The Depression had greatly reduced the public's esteem for business in general and business leaders in particular. By the late Thirties, the social, political, and legal situations had all swung far in the unions' favor. The legal basis for organized labor's new position was the reenactment of Section 7 of the National Industrial Recovery Act as the National Labor Relations Act, sometimes known as the Wagner Act. Together with the Norris-LaGuardia Act (1932), the law now gave labor the legal right to organize. Employers' legal positions were now much weaker. Not only were they obliged to recognize unions that had won representation elections and bargain with them in good faith, but labor relations were now enforced by the National Labor Relations Board and, if necessary, the courts.

The Norris-LaGuardia Act stripped employers of some of their favorite anti-union weapons. Yellow-dog contracts could no longer

be enforced in the federal courts. Employer access to the injunctions that had previously all but paralyzed unions in their attempt to organize employees became only a memory. Instead, not only were labor representatives allowed to organize unions if they could persuade workers to join, but unions could also boycott and picket recalcitrant firms, even if they did not represent the firms' employees (secondary boycotts). Employers were forbidden to interfere with union attempts to organize their workers, to interfere in union organization or internal affairs, to discriminate against their members, or to refuse to bargain with a union that had won the support of a majority of their employees. The laws were broadly drawn, and the courts' interpretation of them tended to be as liberal as it had once been narrow.

New Union Structures

Changes in the nature of union organization were as important to the growth of organized labor as the new laws. Heretofore, nearly all American unions had been organized along craft lines: they were composed of workers who performed the same type of job, such as carpenters or printers. This type of organization was unsuited to large manufacturing plants that employed many different types of skilled worker or even workers with no particular skill. The latter group, for example assembly-line workers, often made up a majority of the work force in such establishments. Even if unions representing all the craft skills utilized by such an employer cooperated—a very difficult proposition in itself—there remained the problem of the laborers whose jobs did not clearly link them with any specific union.

Such firms had been organized in some European countries, but not by craft unions. A new type of organization, the industrial union, had been developed. Workers qualified for membership in such unions on the basis of the

[39] U.S. Department of Commerce, *Historical Statistics*, vol. 1, p. 178.

firm for which they worked and the product it made, not the tasks that they performed. For example, a lathe operator in a small Detroit machine shop might be a member of the machinists' union, together with all the shop's other employees whose jobs were similar. The machinist's cousin performing exactly the same job in Ford's great River Rouge plant might now become a member of the United Auto Workers—together with people working on the assembly line, in the carpentry shop, and even on the janitorial staff. The industrial unions avoided the jurisdictional disputes that pitted union against union, often over issues that had little to do with normal labor-management concerns.

The older craft unions were not inclined to favor the formation of industrial unions, viewing them as a threat to their position within the labor movement. But industrial unions offered many previously unorganized workers an opportunity they had never before possessed. Industrial unions grew rapidly. In 1935, the Committee for Industrial Organization was organized, representing the industrial unions within the American Federation of Labor. After bitter disputes with craft unions over jurisdiction and "raiding" (attempts to persuade each other's members to change unions), the industrial unions formed their own organization, the Congress of Industrial Organizations. The CIO's strength was centered in the industrial unions that had just been organized among the steel, rubber, glass, and automobile industries.

Firms' responses to attempts to organize their employees varied. Some recognized the union as soon as it was obvious that it had the support of most of their workers. Others, such as Republic Steel and Ford, met unionization efforts with company police and hired "goon squads" (sometimes provoking responses in kind). Many injuries and some deaths occurred before the recalcitrants understood that the days of such tactics were over.

New Leaders, New Tactics

New union leadership also played an important role. One reason the mass-production industries' were not organized as this era began was the absence of any serious union efforts to do so in prior years. The new industrial union leadership was intensely interested in expanding aggregate membership. Not only were they starting "from scratch" in most cases, but large gains in membership would improve their own positions within the labor movement. Significantly, John L. Lewis, the head of the only large industrial union within the old AF of L (the United Mine Workers), played a major role in supporting the new efforts.

Industrial union members were more dependent on political support than were the older craft unions. Employers could often replace such workers easily. Consequently, they were far more politically active and partisan than the AF of L had been, generally supporting candidates of the Democratic party. New organizing tactics also were developed. Because employers could readily find other workers to replace them if they struck, the industrial unions made use of the sit-down strike—they stopped working but remained in the plant so that they could not be replaced by strikebreakers.

The Depression's Role in Union Growth

Public opinion toward unions in general had become more favorable, but the change in individual attitudes toward actually joining one was even more beneficial to unions. During the Depression, the old attitudes about the individual bearing sole responsibility for his own welfare had been profoundly challenged.

Even for those who retained their jobs, the idea of inevitable progress—that each job was at least potentially a stepping-stone to another, better position—appeared far less valid than in earlier decades. Such changes in attitude encouraged interest in organizations that promised to improve current conditions. Fear of arbitrary dismissal was one incentive to unionize. Often, nonunion jobs provided no effective appeal against the foreman, who could hire and fire on whatever basis he chose. Unions might be able to offer some benefits in case of layoffs, sickness, or injury, and they were obviously far better situated to negotiate with employers about such considerations. Especially under Depression conditions, unions appeared much better equipped to bargain with employers over traditional concerns such as wages, hours, and working conditions than individual employees. From 1935 on, the annual number of work stoppages resulting from union attempts to organize workers was three to five times the number that occurred during any year of the Twenties.[40]

Union growth in the twentieth century was to be expected. The portion of the U.S. labor force organized was far below that of most industrialized European nations, and even the gains of the late Thirties only partially closed the gap. Even had the laws not been altered so much in unions' favor, the change in attitudes caused by the traumatic insecurity of the Depression (workers are far more interested in improving conditions in their current jobs if there are no other jobs) would have led to increased interest in unions.

But the unions' growth probably hindered economic recovery. To the extent that organized labor gained higher wages for its members, unionization added desperately needed purchasing power to the recovery. But it must be remembered that while wages are income to employees, they are costs to employers, and higher labor costs and greater employer uncertainty were unlikely to aid business expansion. Even the increase in purchasing power accrued to a small minority of workers, so it could not have greatly increased aggregate demand. Indeed, if the demand for labor was elastic, unions' net effect on aggregate wages was to reduce them: they lost more in reductions of people hired than they gained in higher wages for those retaining

their jobs. Since real earnings per employee rose substantially more than output per worker[41] (not, of course, entirely as a result of union activity), the increase in unit labor costs when cost increases were especially difficult to pass on to consumers probably retarded the growth of employment in the Thirties.

Reforms in Financial Institutions

The reforms in the Federal Reserve System that occurred in this period have already been discussed. The stock market crash caused the formation of the Securities and Exchange Commission in 1934. This agency was charged with improving the information available to participants in securities markets. It was also to prohibit some activities that allowed "insiders" with early or unique access to information to increase their profits from securities transactions by capitalizing on their superior knowledge. The scope of holding companies (firms whose assets were the stock of other companies) was greatly reduced. Public utility regulation was tightened.

In almost every area, the presence of government, especially the federal government, increased. These changes took place both through direct regulatory activity and through the requirement of more detailed reports on private economic activity.

THE NEW DEAL: AN ASSESSMENT

Any analysis of the effects of the New Deal must conclude that in one of its major endeavors, if not *the* major endeavor of the Roosevelt administration, it was a failure. It did not end the

---

[40] Ibid., vol. 1, p. 179.

[41] Ibid., vol. 1, p. 164; vol. 2, p. 950.

Depression: the unemployment rate in 1940 was still 14.6 percent. Although this was ten percentage points better than the rate in 1933, it was still intolerably high, and many other nations had done far better even before rearmament spending for World War II became significant. It may be disheartening to realize that the military malevolence of Adolf Hitler and his allies produced a greater decline in civilian unemployment in the United States in three years than all the good intentions and efforts of the New Deal had in seven, but it is so.

Pluses and Minuses

Some positive accomplishments occurred. Certainly by 1940 the American citizen was better shielded from the effects of the Depression than in 1933. There was now some assurance that the loss of a job need not mean a cutoff of all income, thanks to New Deal measures such as unemployment insurance and public employment programs. Nevertheless, it is hard to argue that an early return to full employment might not have done more for economic well-being. Had the primary goal been achieved, the secondary defenses would have been less important—and less used.

Some New Deal policies directly or indirectly retarded recovery. At least one investigation has failed to support the oft-repeated charge that New Deal policies reduced private investment spending and thus slowed recovery,[42] but investment did remain very low throughout the Thirties. Attempts to cure the Depression by reflating prices were ineffective at best. Macroeconomic policy was hardly ever recognized as such and at its best was never more than mildly expansionary. Usually, it exacerbated the situation. The very serious ma-

croeconomic errors of 1937 undoubtedly prolonged the Depression, and they occurred after four years' experience.

If the promotion of monopoly power was eventually abandoned in industry, it continued in agriculture and labor, where, as usual, it restricted resource mobility and reduced aggregate incomes. The long-run effects of such programs were increasingly negative.[43]

The efforts at "planning" were almost without exception disasters. In nearly every instance, the New Deal ignored demand in efforts to promote supply, or vice versa. The attempts to promote recovery within individual sectors of the economy without attention to the impact elsewhere were in the same vein. Even government spending nominally devoted solely to promoting recovery was apparently strongly influenced by political considerations. It was concentrated on "swing states" where it might influence the outcome of elections, leaving states whose Democratic loyalties or irredeemable Republicanism were well established much more to their own devices.[44]

Income distribution apparently became somewhat more equal during the Thirties. However, the change was largely a transfer of income (and perhaps wealth) from the very rich—the top 1 to 5 percent of all income recipients in the country—to the middle class, rather than the poor.[45] The change was largely due to the decline in property income such as corporate profits and rents, which were highly concentrated among the rich. It resulted more from the Depression itself than from the New Deal's social programs or taxes. One study has

---

[42] T. Mayer and M. Chatterji, "Political Shocks and Investment: Some Evidence from the 1930s," *Journal of Economic History* (December 1983).

[43] For discussions of this concept, see M. Olson, *The Rise and Decline of Nations: Economic Growth, Stagflation, and Social Rigidities* (New Haven, Conn.: Yale University Press, 1982) and D. North, *Structure and Change in Economic History* (New York: Norton, 1981).

[44] D. Reading, "New Deal Activity and the States, 1933–1939," *Journal of Economic History* (December 1973).

[45] Lindert and Williamson, "Three Centuries of American Inequality," in P. Uselding, ed., *Research in Economic History* (Greenwich, Conn.: JAI Press, 1976).

Table 18.2 Government Spending and Its Relationship to GNP, 1927–1940*

Date	GNP (in Billions)	Federal Spending (in Billions)	Percentage of GNP	State and Local Government Spending (in Billions)	Percentage of GNP
1927	$ 94.9	$2.8	3.9%	$ 7.9	8.2%
1928	97.0	3.0	3.1	—	—
1929	103.1	3.1	3.0	—	—
1930	90.4	3.3	3.7	—	—
1931	75.8	3.6	4.7	—	—
1932	58.0	4.7	8.1	8.4	14.5
1933	55.6	4.6	8.3	—	—
1934	65.1	6.6	10.1	7.8	12.0
1935	72.2	6.5	9.0	—	—
1936	82.5	8.4	10.2	8.5	10.3
1937	90.4	7.7	8.5	—	—
1938	84.7	6.8	8.0	10.0	11.8
1939	90.5	8.8	9.7	—	—
1940	99.7	9.1	9.1	11.2	11.2

*Figures in current dollars.
Source: U.S. Department of Commerce, Bureau of the Census, *Historical Statistics of the United States: Colonial Times to 1970*, 2 vols. (Washington, D.C.: Government Printing Office, 1975), 2:1114, 1132.

concluded that most income shifts occurred before the advent of the New Deal.[46] Direct transfers either in money, as with welfare payments or unemployment compensation, or through government-subsidized housing, schooling, or jobs undoubtedly contributed to greater income equality; pro-union legislation and minimum-wage laws probably did not.

Aggregate economic security also increased. Even in the areas of the New Deal's greatest failings, countercyclical monetary and fiscal policy, some lessons had (finally) been learned. In the future there would be no gross errors comparable to those of 1929–1933 or 1937. The various provisions of the Social Security Act have thus far lived up to their title.

At the same time they have allowed an ever-expanding cycle of rent-seeking activity.

Survival of the Market Economy

The New Deal left the U.S. economy a largely market-directed system. The TVA and massive government aid to agriculture, particularly through interference in the markets for farm products, are exceptions; for the most part, economic activity continued through the interplay of supply and demand in the marketplace. The role of the federal government expanded considerably, both through direct spending and through programs that funded local and state government activity. A recent study found that the New Deal tended to expand federal and state government activity at the expense of local government.[47]

[46] D. North et al., *Growth and Welfare in the American Past: A New Economic History,* 3d ed. (Englewood Cliffs, N.J.: Prentice-Hall, 1983), pp. 160–161.

[47] J. Wallis, ''The Birth of the Old Federalism: Financing

Table 18.2 indicates that although federal government expenditures did grow in both absolute and relative terms, the increase was modest. Much of the government's relative growth occurred through the collapse of the private economy, not its own absolute increases. Indeed, the greatest proportional increase took place under Herbert Hoover, not Franklin Roosevelt. Had economic growth continued after 1929 at the modest annual rate of 3 percent, the federal government's share of total spending in 1940 would have been 6.4 percent. Even this figure assumes that federal expenditures would not have declined had economic circumstances been better. The rate of increase in total government expenditures was no greater in the Thirties than in the three preceding decades.[48]

The changes made by the New Deal in the basic institutions of the American economy were surprisingly modest. In 1933, it would not have been difficult for the government to nationalize the commercial banks and probably the railroads, but it made no attempt to do so. Its efforts to control operations within various industries may have diverted attempts to direct the aggregate economy. In light of the skills, information, and sense of direction available for such a task in the Thirties, this was probably fortunate. The emphasis was largely on saving the market system, rather than replacing it. The United States has always taken its social reforms the way the frontier took religion and

castor oil—in large, infrequent doses, and only long after the need had become overwhelming.

SELECTED REFERENCES

Chandler, L. *America's Greatest Depression, 1929–1941.* New York: Harper and Row, 1970.

Friedman, M., and A. Schwartz. *A Monetary History of the United States, 1867–1960.* Princeton, N.J.: Princeton University Press, 1962.

Gordon, R. *Economic Instability and Growth: The American Record.* New York: Harper and Row, 1974.

Hansen, A. *Business Cycles and National Income.* New York: Norton, 1951.

Kindleberger, C. *The World in Depression, 1929–1939.* Berkeley, Calif.: University of California Press, 1973.

Klein, L. *Economic Fluctuations in the United States, 1921–1941.* New York: John Wiley & Sons, 1950.

Leuchtenburg, W. *Franklin Roosevelt and the New Deal, 1932–1940.* New York: Harper and Row, 1963.

Mitchell, B. *Depression Decade: From New Era Through New Deal, 1932–1940.* New York: Holt, Rinehart, and Winston, 1947.

North, D. *Structure and Change in Economic History.* New York: Norton, 1981.

North, D., et al. *Growth and Welfare in the American Past: A New Economic History.* 3d ed. Englewood Cliffs, N.J.: Prentice–Hall, 1983.

Olson, M. *The Rise and Decline of Nations: Economic Growth, Stagflation, and Social Rigidities.* New Haven, Conn.: Yale University Press, 1982.

Stein, H. *The Fiscal Revolution in America.* Chicago: University of Chicago Press, 1969.

U.S. Department of Commerce, Bureau of the Census. *Historical Statistics of the United States: Colonial Times to 1970.* 2 vols. Washington, D.C.: Government Printing Office; 1975.

Walton, G. *Regulatory Change in an Atmosphere of Crisis: Current Implications of the Roosevelt Years.* New York: Academic Press, 1979.

the New Deal, 1932–1940," *Journal of Economic History* (March 1984).
[48] Ibid.

CHAPTER

19

THE ECONOMICS OF (ALMOST) TOTAL WAR

World War II's European beginnings in the fall of 1939 had little immediate impact on the U.S. economy. American exports increased by about $1 billion from 1939 to 1940, but only about half that amount represented increased purchases by the combatants, chiefly Great Britain. Nor was there much domestic military spending through this period. Although the United States had 458,000 men and women on active duty in the armed forces (an increase of about one-third over Thirties levels),[1] the American military was far from prepared for war. An arms buildup had just begun. Nevertheless, the United States Army (which at this time included the air force) was smaller than that of Bulgaria. The quality and amount of military equipment were deficient, restricting American military capabilities even more than the raw figures indicate.

After the fall of France in June 1940, it became apparent to many Americans that the war might not be just another European squabble that could safely be ignored, regardless of its outcome. In late 1940, only Great Britain remained actively opposed to Hitler's forces, and the consequences of Nazi supremacy in Europe were not pleasant to contemplate. Japanese-American relations in the Pacific and the Orient were deteriorating, and now the United States could no longer rely on substantial aid from friendly European powers in the event of a Pacific conflict. Rearmament assumed a new urgency.

By early 1941 the economic impact of the war on the United States was increasing. The hard-pressed British began to increase their orders for food and war material from America;

[1] U.S. Department of Commerce, Bureau of the Census, *Historical Statistics of the United States: Colonial Times to 1970*, 2 vols. (Washington, D.C.: Government Printing Office, 1975), 2:1141.

■ After the fall of France, neutrality became difficult. By 1940 Britain sought
U.S. assistance.
Source: Cassel in the Brooklyn *Eagle*; Trustees of the Imperial War Museum, London.

they had already taken over French contracts
made before France's defeat. The United States'
own rearmament program was gaining momentum as well: defense spending more than
tripled between 1940 and 1941.

As Britain's military situation grew more
desperate and its ability to pay for U.S. imports
declined, the ties between the two countries
increased. In March 1941, the Lend-Lease
Program was instituted by the United States.
In return for services rendered by the British
(and a much smaller amount of British war material furnished to American forces), the U.S.
government financed British purchases of war
material in this country. Some of the goods sent
to the British supposedly were loaned for the
duration of the war. British services were only

vaguely specified in the program, but in fact
continued British resistance to Nazi Germany
was invaluable to the United States. It was increasingly obvious that the United States would
not be able to avoid becoming directly involved
in the war. The Lend-Lease Program helped
to keep the situation from deteriorating too far
in the meantime. Had Great Britain surren-
dered and her industrial plant and possibly her
fleet been added to Nazi strength, the war would
have become enormously more costly for the
United States. A trans-Atlantic invasion of Europe without British bases would have raised
the war's costs in American lives as well as material. During the 1940–1945 period, a total
of about $50 billion in Lend-Lease aid was pro-
vided to Britain and the other Allies. In return,

■ When the Japanese attacked Pearl Harbor, all questions about U.S. involvement were silenced.

Source: General records of the Department of the Navy: National Archives.

the United States obtained foreign goods valued at about $8 billion.

U.S. ENTRY INTO THE WAR

With the Japanese attack on Pearl Harbor (December 7, 1941), the United States became an active participant in the war. As in World War I, the conflict absorbed incredible amounts of manpower and materials, and the productive capacity of the American economy was one of the Allies' key assets. Prospects for an Allied victory hinged on the speed and extent of American mobilization. Unlike World War I, however, this time the American contribution was actual rather than potential. The American war effort was based on the ability of the United States to produce enormous quantities of material, and no less important, transport them to the battlefields. The United States produced few really outstanding military leaders (Admiral Raymond Spruance was a conspicuous exception): its victories were largely the result of material superiority.

After the dark days of Allied defeat and retreat through the first half of 1942, the Axis forces were first checked and then forced into a defensive posture from which they never recovered. In the Pacific, an inferior American fleet dealt the Japanese Navy a stunning defeat at the Battle of Midway (June 1942). Japan was never able to replace the skilled pilots it lost there and at Guadalcanal six months later. In the European theater, the offensive power of Nazi Germany was broken in North Africa (1943) and at the battles of Stalingrad and Kursk (1942–1943). The Allies received wholly unintentional help from Adolf Hitler, whose decision to attack the Soviet Union in 1941 was one of the war's great blunders.

The Production War

With the time so dearly purchased by the armed forces, the productive capacity of the American economy was converted to military output. The British, Canadian, and Soviet economies were even more totally mobilized. As a result the Axis forces were drowned in a flood of machines. The United States produced huge volumes of material to equip its own forces and also augmented the supplies of British Commonwealth and Soviet forces.

Once the war became a struggle between the adversaries' productive potentials, the Axis powers were doomed. Only Germany was then an industrial power of the first rank, and ironically, the German war effort was hampered by the Nazis' own propaganda. The German leaders were convinced (in late 1940, apparently with good reason) that the war would be short. Consequently, the German economy was not fully mobilized for war until early 1943.[2] By then it was far too late. Although Germany achieved some remarkable feats of production after that date, the Nazi war effort was fatally handicapped.

In addition to dictatorial and unstable leaders who made the rational weighing of costs

against benefits difficult, the Germans lacked a basic understanding of how the various sectors of their own economy interacted. The Allies, particularly the Americans, had developed national income accounting, a tool that proved invaluable in determining the demands of war production programs upon available resources. Production bottlenecks could be foreseen and cleared up before they hindered production. Fewer unanticipated crises developed in the American, British, and Canadian economies as a result, while the Germans continually had to meet unexpected shortcomings on an emergency basis. By 1944, Allied intelligence experts had a better grasp of the capabilities of the German economy than did Hitler and his followers.

In a long war, neither Italy nor Japan proved capable of equipping their forces sufficiently to offset the Allies' growing numerical superiority. The Japanese admiral who planned the attack on Pearl Harbor had warned his government of precisely that possibility before the war began. This admiral, who had studied at Harvard University and was quite familiar with American industrial capacity, told his superiors that Japan's only hope was to win a position of such dominance that the United States would be unwilling to pay the price to break it. Moreover, he said, this position would have to be attained in less than a year. The Japanese thought the attack on Pearl Harbor would demoralize and divide the United States.[3] This may have been a bigger miscalculation than Japan's underestimation of American economic potential and the speed with which it could be mobilized. Whether the willingness to fight the war through existed in America before Pearl Harbor or not, it certainly did after, and the Japanese military expansion lasted only six months.

---

[2] D. Landes, *The Unbound Prometheus: Technological Change from 1750 to the Present* (Cambridge, England: Cambridge University Press, 1969), pp. 413–415.

[3] G. Prange, *At Dawn We Slept: The Untold Story of Pearl Harbor* (New York: McGraw-Hill, 1981).

CONVERSION TO A WAR ECONOMY

The basic task confronting the United States was that of increasing military production. Initially, there were several avenues by which this might be accomplished. First, the economy's total output could be increased, with the bulk of the added production going to war needs. Alternatively, the composition of existing output could be shifted to favor the war effort. Either method would produce other problems. Increased military output would raise the money incomes of the workers and firms producing it without proportionately increasing civilian goods and services on which the added wages and profits could be spent. Such a situation would produce inflation and reduce incentives, because the additional income would buy few if any more goods. Some means of reducing inflation and maintaining incentives would have to be developed as the economy neared capacity output levels. If additional money would purchase no more—or even fewer—consumer goods, people would not be motivated to produce.

It was soon apparent that this was more than a theoretical problem: the war's demands far exceeded available productive capacity. Therefore, priorities had to be developed to determine which war goods had first call on available means of production and which alternative uses had to be sacrificed first. In addition, the means of military goods production might also have to be determined.

Initially, the wartime buildup caused few difficulties. Unemployment was still widespread in the United States when the war began in Europe, and it continued for almost two years. Under such conditions, additional production was readily obtained by putting unemployed resources back to work. This involved no reduction in current production for the civilian economy. But by the time of Pearl Harbor, the unemployment rate was at 7 percent and falling rapidly. Shortages of some types of labor and services had already appeared and were rapidly becoming more serious. Prices, which had remained almost stable in 1940, were beginning to rise despite informal government inflation-control programs. By mid–1942, increases in war production could no longer be obtained by using previously idle capacity because almost none remained. Henceforth, sacrifices in current or potential civilian output would be needed, or production methods would have to be changed.

Nevertheless, a huge increase in total production occurred. As Table 19.1 illustrates, real output grew by 59 percent from 1940 to 1945, and industrial production approximately doubled. Defense spending, which had been 1.5 percent of GNP in 1939 and 1.8 percent in 1940, reached 37.8 percent in 1944. The overall impact of government demand on the economy's capacity rose even more than these figures indicate. Not only did federal nondefense spending rise slightly more than enough to offset reduced expenditures by state and local governments, but government regulation of all types of economic activity took a quantum leap. By 1944, government spending of all types and levels accounted for 58.2 percent of GNP.

Far-Reaching Changes in the Labor Force

Such a massive increase in government expenditures, combined with expansionary monetary policies, soon accomplished what the New Deal had not: it ended the Great Depression. Unemployment fell to levels many economists had considered impossible. It had been thought that 2 to 4 percent of the work force would always be unemployed as the normal consequence of entry into the labor force, movements between jobs, seasonal and accidental

Table 19.1 The Economic Dimensions of Mobilization, 1939–1945

Date	GNP (in Billions of Current Dollars)	Real GNP (in Billions of 1958 Dollars)	Military Spending (in Billions of Dollars)	Federal Deficit (in Billions of Dollars)	Civilian Labor Force (in Millions)
1939	$ 90.5	$209.4	$ 1.4	$ 2.9	55.6
1940	99.7	227.2	1.8	2.7	56.1
1941	124.5	263.7	6.3	4.8	57.7
1942	157.9	297.8	22.9	19.4	60.3
1943	191.6	337.1	63.4	53.8	64.9
1944	201.1	361.3	76.0	46.1	66.3
1945	211.9	355.2	80.5	45.0	66.2

Date	Military on Active Duty (in Millions)	Unemployment Rate (%)	Price Index* (1958 = 100)	Industrial Production (1967 = 100)
1939	.3	17.2%	43.2	22
1940	.5	14.6	43.9	25
1941	1.8	9.9	47.2	32
1942	3.9	4.7	53.0	38
1943	9.0	1.9	56.8	47
1944	11.5	1.2	58.1	51
1945	12.1	1.9	59.7	43

*GNP deflator

Source: U.S. Department of Commerce, Bureau of the Census, *Historical Statistics of the United States: Colonial Times to 1970,* 2 vols. (Washington, D.C.: Government Printing Office, 1975), 1:132, 135, 198, 224; 2:1105, 1114, 1141.

layoffs, and similar causes. Such levels were the cost of individual freedom and mobility. But over 1943–1945, the jobless rate was less than 2 percent of the work force.

Furthermore, these extremely low rates were *not* merely due to the great increase in military manpower, which removed men from the unemployment rolls. The civilian labor force grew substantially during the war. In part, this reflected normal population growth, but a new and more important factor was the entry of many people who had not worked outside the home in more normal times. Women and those younger, older, or less qualified than the normal range of employees responded to the incentives of high wages, steady work, large amounts of overtime at even higher pay rates, and patriotism. The average workweek in manufacturing, for example, increased from 38 hours in 1940 to 45 in 1944.[4] The low unemployment rates are even more remarkable since the groups contributing most to the labor force increase normally have above-average rates of joblessness.

The male labor force did not shrink during the war, although its composition changed. As did other periods of extremely tight labor markets, the war gave women and minority groups

[4] U.S. Department of Commerce, *Historical Statistics,* vol. 1, p. 169.

■ World War II's economic demands opened up many non-traditional jobs for women.
Source: Library of Congress.

a chance to show that they could handle a much wider range of jobs than previously open to them. About five million women joined the labor force during the war, and the skills they acquired became a vital force in the postwar assault on barriers to female entry under normal conditions. In addition, resource mobility was spurred by the war. Many firms began making products for the military quite different from anything they had manufactured in peacetime, which encouraged postwar entry into new industries and greater competition throughout the economy.

Bigotry, American Style

Minority groups' experience was similar to women's, with one exception. The nisei, Americans of Japanese ancestry living on the U.S. mainland, were interned in thinly disguised concentration camps because they were considered security risks. They were often forced to sell their property for a fraction of its value. The treatment of the nisei was a national disgrace, inexcusable even in the climate of wartime hysteria in which the ornamental cherry trees given to the District of Columbia by the Japanese government were cut down as a "patriotic" act. No nisei ever committed a disloyal act during the war, and the 442nd Regimental Combat Team, all of whose enlisted men were nisei, won more citations for valor and suffered higher casualties than any other U.S. military unit.

restricted war production, the government built factories and leased them to private operators for the duration of the war. The major increase in defense production, however, came from the increase in overall output. The expansion was sufficient to overwhelm the Axis powers.

The Opportunity Costs of War

Diversion of productive capacity proved more difficult than simple expansion of aggregate output. Once the economy was operating at or beyond full-employment levels, military production could only be further increased by diverting resources from their current uses. Production of certain goods that competed strongly with military needs, such as automobiles, major appliances, and housing, was forbidden. Production of a variety of other items was restricted, at least for civilian use. Nevertheless, the United States was the only major combatant able to maintain or even increase aggregate civilian consumption during the war. In real terms, consumption fell slightly in 1942, but by 1944 it was about 10 percent above the 1940 level.[5] These figures, however, are not as reliable indicators of civilian welfare during the war as they would normally be. They contain no allowance for the changes forced by shortages or total absences of some goods or the deterioration in quality of others.

The major diversions of capacity, however, came at the expense of investment, which fell to less than half its prewar levels (even those had been below the long-term norm), and state and local government activities.[6] Under wartime conditions, resources could not be devoted to increasing future productive capacity if the cost was current military production. In a few cases where shortages of capital severely

Extended Controls in the War Economy

The increasingly complex reallocation process was directed by a series of government agencies. Particularly scarce inputs were rationed and in some cases directly allocated to high-priority uses. The extent of government regulation was unprecedented: not even the emergency measures employed during World War I approached it. The War Production Board, established in 1942, was responsible for the overall direction of industry. A system of priorities was established, under which users of materials critically important to the war effort—such as steel, copper, and aluminum—were ranked in order of their estimated contribution to military production. The most vital received first consideration and were guaranteed all the scarce inputs they needed. Lower-priority users received less. In general, civilian production, which had the lowest priorities, had to make do with whatever was left.[7]

Although this method of allocation ensured that high-priority uses received ample supplies of materials and labor, it was not very efficient. It gave users only limited incentives to conserve scarce inputs, particularly since prices for these inputs were controlled by government. Wasted material, or perhaps even some used in war production, might have been used elsewhere at no sacrifice in military goods if production methods had been altered to conserve scarce materials.

---

[5] Ibid., p. 318. See also R. Gordon, *Economic Instability and Growth: The American Record* (New York: Harper and Row, 1974), p. 84.
[6] Gordon, *Economic Instability and Growth*, p. 85.

[7] Ibid., p. 88. See also Robertson, *History of the American Economy,* 3d ed. (New York: Harcourt Brace Jovanovich, Inc., 1973), p. 711.

Other agencies allocated manpower, both between military and civilian occupations and within each. As in earlier wars, conscription was used to fill the military ranks. All men of military-service age who were neither unfit for service nor deemed to be contributing more to the war effort in their civilian occupations were liable to induction. (Definition of the latter category proved a fertile ground for pressure-group politics.)

Transportation was controlled by yet another government agency. Through all these mechanisms, the primary goal of American economic activity was changed from civilian consumption to support of the war effort. The various agencies' activities were coordinated by the Office of War Mobilization, which was set up in 1943.

The control agencies were set up in great haste. For at least the first two years, their operations were conducted with almost frantic urgency. Neither the speed with which they were established nor the need for immediate action allowed reasoned consideration of the available alternatives or the full ramifications of each decision that they made. Inevitably, mistakes—often of duplicated effort—were made. But it is much easier to point to problems in efficiency than to dispute the overall effect. The essential tools of war were produced quickly and in huge amounts. By the end of 1942, the Allies had gained at least quantitative parity with the Axis. Soon thereafter, they achieved numerical superiority, and in many cases a qualitative edge as well.

The Lessons of Government Control

The mobilization process essentially substituted government planning for the normal direction of the economy by market forces. Productive resources remained privately owned, but their owners lost much of their peacetime freedom to decide volume, price, and method of output, subject only to market forces. They were forced to respond to government directives instead. Government controls were pervasive: they extended even to the type, quantity, and price of inputs and the nature and hours of production, as well as the price and amount of output. No doubt government planning achieved most of its major objectives during World War II, including of course the single overriding concern: giving the armed forces the tools required for victory.

However, whether many of the lessons learned at this time can be applied to a peacetime economy is questionable. Virtually all production affected by the planning system was directed to the requirements of a single customer—the government. Moreover, the government exercised a great deal of control over the aggregate amounts of inputs, the conditions under which they were employed, and the ultimate "consumers'" use of the results. (Any history of the war will reveal the military's dissatisfaction with some of the weapons it was issued.) The public authorities had the power to resolve most disputes in their own favor and to make all decisions on the basis of short-term objectives.

Further, even though the demands of modern war were complex, the tasks of meeting them were simple compared to those of a peacetime economy. Under normal conditions, the desires of millions of individuals (most of whom prize variety and the right to change their minds) provide the impetus for production. Under such conditions the priorities for resource allocation are far less obvious or unidirectional, and their direction and speed of change is obviously under less control. Thus, the success of wartime planning over 1941–1945 may not accurately indicate the results if the same planning mechanisms were applied to the needs of a peacetime economy.

It must also be remembered that wartime planning enjoyed the overwhelming support of the American population. Given the circumstances of World War II and the obvious objectives of a powerful enemy, there was a consensus that war needs must be met—at least at the level of sacrifice actually involved. Ideology can be defined as popular opinion about what is acceptable or "fair" regardless of the goals of official policy. As such, it is an important determinant of the actual, as opposed to the theoretically possible, potential of any economic system.[8] It is difficult to imagine such a national consensus under normal peacetime conditions.

MACROECONOMIC PROBLEMS OF THE WAR

Although World War II's demands on the American economy ended the Great Depression, the war created its own macroeconomic problems. The rising level of aggregate demand decreased unemployment, eliminated unused productive capacity, and raised incomes. However, military spending rose when there were no offsetting reductions in other components of demand, resulting in increased pressure on productive capacity and a growing inflationary potential. Some indication of the increase in demand can be garnered from Table 19.1. The labor force grew by over 22 million persons between 1939 and 1945, an increase of about 40 percent. Moreover, virtually the entire wartime labor force was employed, as opposed to prewar conditions, and wages were much higher (military wages were lower than civilian, but the armed forces were paid in kind as well as money and the equipment they were furnished also added to aggregate demand).

At any instant, an economy's ability to produce additional output is limited by the available amounts of labor, capital, raw materials, and technology. Once all resources are in use and all production employs the most efficient techniques available, output cannot be increased without a change in the economy's productive capacity. Unless input supplies can be increased, new technology employed, or the social constraints on the production process relaxed, there is a "lid" on output. Once this point is reached, more of any single product can be obtained only by reducing the amount of something else.

During the 1941–1945 period, few changes in technology occurred, and supplies of some if not all inputs were fixed or even declined. To some extent, however, social regulations on production were relaxed, allowing output to rise. The increasing employment of women outside the home, the opportunities for individuals previously excluded from the jobs they now performed or even from the labor force itself, and the longer workweek are all examples of relaxed social constraints. Even so, in an economy as materialistic as that of the United States, and given the short adjustment period, such changes could not keep pace with the increase in demand.

The Impact of Defense Spending, 1942–1945

By late 1941, it was clear that war demands would outstrip any conceivable increases in output that were readily attainable. Efforts to raise capacity through conventional methods such as investment and human training also used resources, and hence would interfere with production for current use once all resources were employed. The demands of the military restricted expansion of the labor force. In addition, there was the problem arising from the additional incomes earned in production of military goods. There was no corresponding increase in civilian production on which those vastly increased incomes could be spent. The

---

[8] D. North, *Structure and Change in Economic History* (New York: Noreton, 1981), Chap. 5.

multiplier process made the rise in demand greater than just the initial increase in incomes. In total, then, the potential volume of spending was rising beyond the ability of the economy to satisfy demand at current prices. Inflation is an inevitable companion of the extreme levels of demand in times of total war.

Spending could rise without limit, but as the previous paragraphs indicate, there were restrictions on the potential increase in physical output. These constraints grew steadily tighter. Nor was it possible to restrain spending. Government expenditures, particularly in the early years of the war, could not be decreased. Indeed, there was painful evidence that current military spending was inadequate. As resources had to be bid away from other employment, military spending was likely to accelerate. Simultaneously, if consumers found that their higher incomes actually bought fewer goods and services as the output of civilian products fell to allow greater military output, incentives might suffer. They might also suffer if taxes were raised sufficiently to finance the entire volume of military spending. In such a case, even though inflationary pressures might be muted, aftertax incomes would be no greater—or even smaller—than before the war, despite a much greater work effort. Thus, government faced a delicate task. There seemed to be no method of financing the war that avoided the problem of diverting output while maintaining incentives.

Wartime Finance

Increases in government spending could be financed through increased taxes, borrowing, or the creation of new money. In the end, a combination of all three methods was employed. About half the war's costs were tax-financed, a considerably higher portion than in either the Civil War or World War I. As incomes rose, the tax revenues of the federal government increased even faster because of the progressive nature of the income tax. This did not yield sufficient revenues, however, and the tax structure was revised. Rates were increased, and the range of incomes liable to taxation was extended downward in each year from 1940 through 1944. By the latter year, the effective rate on taxable income in excess of $1 million per year was 90 percent, and all incomes of $600 or more were subject to tax. Prior to 1940, all incomes under $5,000 had been exempt. Since prices in 1940 were roughly one-sixth their 1985 level and real incomes were much lower, the changes meant that the income tax now was borne by middle-income groups and to some extent even the poor, as well as the rich. These changes raised the number of persons filing income tax returns from 7.5 million in 1940 to 49.9 million in 1944.[9]

The government also began withholding taxes from wages and salaries as they were paid, rather than allowing individuals to settle their tax obligations with a single annual payment. The corporate income tax was increased and an excess profits tax levied. The changes raised the internal revenues of the federal government from $5.3 to $40.1 billion over the 1940–1944 period. But at the same time, expenditures rose from $9.1 to $95 billion. The result was unprecedented federal deficits—over $45 billion in each of the war's last three years.[10] These were financed largely by borrowing from nonbank institutions and from the public.

Monetary Policy in World War II

Had the government only borrowed funds that would otherwise have been spent by the lenders, its borrowing would not have been inflationary. However, the scope of borrowing was far greater than this source alone could support. On the day after Pearl Harbor, the Federal Reserve assured the Treasury that the central bank would buy at par (face value) all government bonds that could not be sold elsewhere on these terms. This pledge made gov-

---

[9] Tax data are from U.S. Department of Commerce, *Historical Statistics,* vol. 2, p. 1110.
[10] Ibid., pp. 1105, 1107, and 1114.

ernment bonds far more liquid than before. Bond owners could convert them into cash at their face value at any time. The federal government's debt rose by about $215 billion during the war. Of this amount, the Federal Reserve Banks purchased $21 billion. Commercial banks bought another $60 billion.[11] Currency in circulation increased by $17 billion.

The result was a sharp increase in the money supply, which more than doubled over the war years and continued to rise at a slower rate for some years thereafter. As long as the Federal Reserve was committed to supporting government bond prices, the central bank was essentially powerless to control, or at any rate reduce, the money supply. Open-market operations could not be employed, because bond sales might depress prices. The discount rate was no longer a control mechanism, because commercial banks could sell bonds to the Federal Reserve at guaranteed prices in lieu of borrowing. In any case, commercial banks had held large excess reserves when the war began. Reserve requirements had been raised to their legal maximum in 1941, and no further restraint via this avenue was possible without a change in the law.[12]

Inflation

The increase in the money supply, coupled with highly expansionary fiscal policy, made rapid inflation inevitable. The federal deficit was now about ten times its peak in the Thirties, and the economy had unquestionably regained full employment levels. Although there was an increase in the aggregate price level, it was surprisingly small: only about one-third from 1940 through 1945. Most of the increase occurred before the United States was fully mobilized. As Table 19.1 indicates, the general price deflator increased about 21 percent from 1940

through 1942 and then a further 13 percent by the end of the war. Inflation appears less than expected for a number of reasons. First and perhaps most important, consumer spending rose much less than incomes. Income can only be either consumed or saved, and the portion saved during the war was four to five times the normal rate. The savings increase had several sources. It appears that many people expected a return to depression conditions after the war, and they also expected prices to fall. In anticipation, they accumulated money and financial assets.[13]

Furthermore, although high wages, abundant overtime, and increased labor force participation increased incomes during the war, many of the normal avenues for spending increased income were closed or restricted. New cars, housing, and major appliances were unobtainable at any price: they simply were not being manufactured. Many minor luxuries such as meat were strictly rationed. Travel possibilities were limited. All forms of public transportation were very crowded, and military needs had priority. Travel by private automobile was legal: one could drive anywhere within the limits imposed by the basic gasoline ration of three gallons per week and by the fact that tires were all but unobtainable. Many vacation resorts were closed, and overtime work reduced the opportunity for shopping and leisure activities. There were drawbacks to some of the consumer goods that remained obtainable. Price controls and end-of-the-line materials priorities reduced quality and restricted choice. Finally, appeals to support the war effort by restricting consumption and buying war bonds had some effect. The combined influence of all these effects on saving and consumption decreased the velocity of money circulation after 1942, despite high levels of aggregate economic activity.[14]

---

[11] Gordon, *Economic Instability and Growth*, pp. 85–87.
[12] M. Friedman and A. Schwartz, *A Monetary History of the United States, 1867–1960* (Princeton, N.J.: Princeton University Press, 1962), p. 556.

[13] Ibid., pp. 558–561.
[14] Ibid., p. 558.

Rationing and Price Controls

Other more direct efforts were made to reduce the wartime impact of inflation. If money incomes rise and the supply of goods and services fails to keep pace, prices will rise under normal market conditions. But inflation does not affect all people equally: those whose incomes rise faster than the average of all prices will gain an increasing share of all output at the expense of those whose incomes have failed to rise as fast as inflation. In the absence of any other influences on allocation, shortages will be resolved in favor of those with increased ability to pay and at the expense of those whose real incomes have fallen. During World War II, this tendency was reduced through rationing and price controls.

To ensure that all consumers received at least some of such items as sugar, coffee, meat, shoes, gasoline, and certain types of clothing, these goods were rationed. They had to be purchased with ration stamps as well as money. The total supply of ration "points" that could be applied to each item was restricted to approximate equality with the supplies available. Stamps were issued to individuals by local boards. The basic allocation was an equal amount per person, with some adjustments for special needs. In this manner, demand for items whose supply could not readily be increased was held below the demand that would have resulted from the increase in money incomes. Thus, by requiring two types of money to purchase essential items of consumption, the rationing process kept them within the reach of most consumers—albeit in smaller amounts than people were willing to buy at the prevailing prices. The system was not perfect: ration stamps could not be legally exchanged between individuals, which limited the expression of individual preferences. Also, some complained about the decisions of local ration boards.

Another form of inflation control was a nationwide system of wage and price controls. The Office of Price Administration "froze" prices at their March 1942 levels. After this

■ Rationing was a response to war-generated shortages. Ration stamps were required for the purchase of a wide variety of consumer goods.
Source: The Bettmann Archive.

action, sellers were forbidden to charge more than the ceiling prices established.

Some difficulty was encountered almost at once. Food prices and wages could not be controlled for some time, in part because of the political efforts of labor unions and the farm bloc. Price controls, in conjunction with rationing and the lower propensity to consume, reduced the rate of inflation during the war and lessened its impact on those whose incomes lagged the rate of price increase. But prices became an imperfect indicator of consumer satisfaction because many markets did not clear at existing prices: consumers were willing to buy more than was available at prices allowed by these regulations. On the whole, however, the system was reasonably successful for the duration of the war. When production cost increases threatened to make production of some goods unprofitable at controlled prices, thus threatening their withdrawal from the market, government preferred to subsidize producers rather than allow price increases.

Understandably, under such conditions producers concentrated on those items with the greatest profit margins and reduced or discontinued output of others. They also attempted to maintain profits by reducing quality. Some items became virtually unobtainable or disappeared completely, and others bore little resemblance to their prewar counterparts—two factors not reflected in the official price indices.[15]

Since the war raised aggregate demand for farm products and disrupted the normal channels of world trade, American agriculture benefited from swiftly rising prices. America was the only nation with agricultural exports to fill the worldwide gap, and farmers were encouraged to increase output via draft deferments, the elimination of all government restrictions on acreage under cultivation (see Chapter 18), and price guarantees of not less than 110 percent of parity.[16]

Wage Controls

Wage controls proved much more difficult to implement effectively. In 1943, under the "Little Steel" formula, wage increases were to be limited to not more than 15 percent more than their 1941 levels. The rationale was that this would compensate workers for inflation but not add to its pressures. However, the need to remedy both real and imagined inequities, to meet special needs, and to attract labor to crucial programs made it very difficult to hold to this ceiling.[17] Firms resorted to granting "promotions" and to paying a growing portion of total compensation in the form of fringe benefits to attract and hold labor in the face of growing shortages of qualified workers. Overtime also allowed labor incomes to rise even where limits on hourly wages were observed. The wage control program thus had only limited success, and official statistics on wage levels overrate its achievements.

The growth of fringe benefits, such as pensions, medical insurance and programs, and (largely after the war) paid vacations proved very popular with labor. Particularly in unionized industries, where a single organization assembled and presented workers' claims in a unified form, fringe benefits became an increasing portion of employee compensation. Union growth was both legally sanctioned and encouraged by labor-market conditions, and the strength of American unions increased.

The Mixed Success of Economic Controls

The control packages had considerable apparent success in limiting price increases during the war. However, it has been suggested that their impact is overrated. Some observers argue that the controls merely repressed inflation rather than prevented it. This view is supported by the rampant inflation that occurred after controls were abolished in the postwar period.[18] Another consideration not included in the official statistics is the deterioration in quality of many wartime consumer goods.[19]

As always happens when prices are prevented from equating supply and demand, there was evidence of extralegal forms of allocation. Charges that some suppliers were far kinder to favored buyers than to the general public were endemic. Black markets, with prices far above controlled levels, appeared for many products. As economic theory would suggest, black markets were especially common for goods with the

---

[15] Ibid., p. 559.
[16] Robertson, *History of the American Economy*, pp. 525–526.
[17] Gordon, *Economic Instability and Growth*, p. 89.

[18] Friedman and Schwartz, *A Monetary History*, pp. 557–558. See also H. Rockoff, "Price and Wage Controls in Four Wartime Periods," *Journal of Economic History* (June 1981) and "The Response of the Giant Corporation to Wage and Price Controls in World War II," *Journal of Economic History* (March 1981).
[19] H. Rockoff, "Indirect Price Increases and Real Wages during World War II," *Explorations in Economic History* (October 1978).

greatest spread between legal maximum prices and those customers were willing to pay and whose origins could not be traced. There is also some evidence that the controls were more effective earlier in the war. Again, this is hardly surprising: patriotic fervor and support for the war effort was then at its peak, and means of circumventing controls had not yet been devised. This was also the time when controlled prices were closest to market-determined rates.

On the whole, controls were reasonably successful in their primary purpose: achieving a more widespread distribution of articles than under free market allocation. They also probably maintained general incentives (it can hardly be said that they did so for producers of items whose prices were forced down, however). The controls were not in force long enough to cause major distortions in the price structure. Over time, price controls in periods of substantial inflationary pressure prevent the market from allocating resources to their highest-value uses, but the process was not continued long enough in World War II to produce major misallocations.

Obviously, the system was not "fair"; it was impossible to provide solutions regarded as equitable by all parties when supplies were far below normal levels. For that matter, market systems do not produce "fair" distribution of scarce goods either, nor does any other type of system. Mistakes were made, both in allocation and in setting up the mechanics of distribution. The controls worked as well as they did because they received a great deal of popular support. Many Americans were willing to put up with shortages and inconvenience because they were convinced that everyone else shared their situation and that the purpose behind these irritations was worthwhile. It should also be noted that maintaining controls imposed some costs on the war effort. At its peak, the Office of Price Administration employed over 300,000 part-time and full-time workers, and there were 5,400 local price and rationing boards.[20]

THE COST OF WAR

No economist would advocate war as the proper means of ending a depression. In addition to moral considerations, war is a costly human activity. In a world where all economists agree that the available means of production are already insufficient for demand, war destroys some resources and makes many others more scarce. It substitutes the consumption of humans for human consumption as the primary goal of economic activity. Had the United States been able to spend $664 billion (the estimated total cost of World War II as of 1970)[21] on sending people to the movies rather than into combat, the expansive effects on the economy would have been just as great and the effects on human welfare much superior. *Any* massive spending program would have stimulated economic recovery in 1941 or 1933. However, the U.S. role in World War II can hardly be viewed exclusively as a program for economic recovery. Given the nature of the political opponents that the nation faced in this conflict, the war was a necessary price to maintain our political freedoms. It is easy to imagine scenarios in which the war's cost to the United States would have been far greater.

The war may have been a political necessity, but it cannot be regarded as an unmitigated economic boon. A great portion of wartime economic activity was directed toward ends that had no immediate payoff in enhanced human welfare. The statistical record indicates that World War II levels of real per-capita income in the United States were not regained

---

[20] Robertson, *History of the American Economy*, p. 712.
[21] U.S. Department of Commerce, *Historical Statistics*, vol. 2, p. 1140.

until the mid-Fifties. However, these figures treat the military goods that at times accounted for nearly two-fifths of total wartime output as equivalent to the consumer goods of the later period in their contribution to human well-being. While the benefits of life in a world free of the threats that bulked so large in 1941 must not be underestimated, surely the income figures understate the increased welfare that occurred in the decade after 1945. In sum, while we cannot simply subtract the war years' military expenditures from total income to arrive at an accurate measure of welfare, neither can we include them in full.

The Net Result

A few economic gains were spawned by the war. It can at least be argued that only a political emergency of the war's magnitude could have prompted the increased spending needed to end the Great Depression. In this case, the gain was the greater understanding of macroeconomics that resulted from the war. Also, some results of wartime research have proved valuable in peacetime: radar, the jet engine, computers, some medical advances, and—for good or ill—nuclear energy.

Probably a better case can be made for the loosening of restrictions on individual geographic and occupational mobility that wartime changes produced. Women and minorities gained access to a much wider range of jobs as a result of wartime labor shortages. More importantly, these advances—at least in the form of easier entrance—were permanent.[22] Few modern students can imagine how blatantly and smotheringly restrictive racial and sexual discrimination was just five decades ago. Such

practices cost the United States dearly in wasted human talent. Individual geographic mobility was also greatly enhanced in the war's aftermath. A similar process occurred as firms took wartime contracts to produce goods they had never considered making in peacetime and learned new technologies. Shocks to the established order and continuity of social institutions are important in maintaining economic vitality and competition.[23] So was the rapid introduction and dissemination of new technology that occurred in the postwar period, in part as a consequence of the war's effect on the economy.

The costs of the war were borne largely by those who experienced it. Obviously, a very large portion of the war's costs was paid by the 405,000 Americans who died in service and the thousands more who were wounded. Enforced military service cost millions of other Americans the higher incomes they could have earned in alternative occupations. The economy lost the forgone potential of all these misallocated or prematurely ended human resources. Loss of investment—perhaps tempered by war-induced technological progress—was another cost of the war.

After the euphoria of military victory had faded, Americans had a new concern. The high levels of income and economic activity during the war had clearly stemmed from massive government spending. But military spending had been reduced as soon as victory was achieved in Europe, and with Japan's surrender, it had plummeted. As government spending fell and 12 million military personnel returned to civilian life, what would prevent a recurrence of the Great Depression?

---

[22] Gavin Wright has suggested that these effects were especially pronounced in the South. See *Old South, New South: Revolutions in the Southern Economy Since the Civil War* (New York: Basic Books, 1986), Chaps. 7 and 8.

[23] This is a central theme for Macur Olson. See *The Rise and Decline of Nations: Economic Growth, Stagflation, and Social Rigidities* (New Haven, Conn.: Yale University Press, 1982), Chaps. 2 and 3.

SELECTED REFERENCES

Friedman, M., and A. Schwartz. *A Monetary History of the United States, 1867–1960*. Princeton, N.J.: Princeton University Press, 1962.

Gordon, R. *Economic Instability and Growth: The American Record*. New York: Harper and Row, 1974.

Olson, M. *The Rise and Decline of Nations: Economic Growth, Stagflation, and Social Rigidities*. New Haven, Conn.: Yale University Press, 1982.

North, D. *Structure and Change in Economic History*. New York: Norton, 1981.

North, D., et al. *Growth and Welfare in the American Past: A New Economic History*. 3d ed. Englewood Cliffs, N.J.: Prentice-Hall, 1983.

U.S. Department of Commerce, Bureau of the Census. *Historical Statistics of the United States: Colonial Times to 1970*. 2 vols. Washington, D.C.: Government Printing Office, 1975.

Wright, G. *Old South, New South: Revolutions in the Southern Economy Since the Civil War*. New York: Basic Books, 1986.

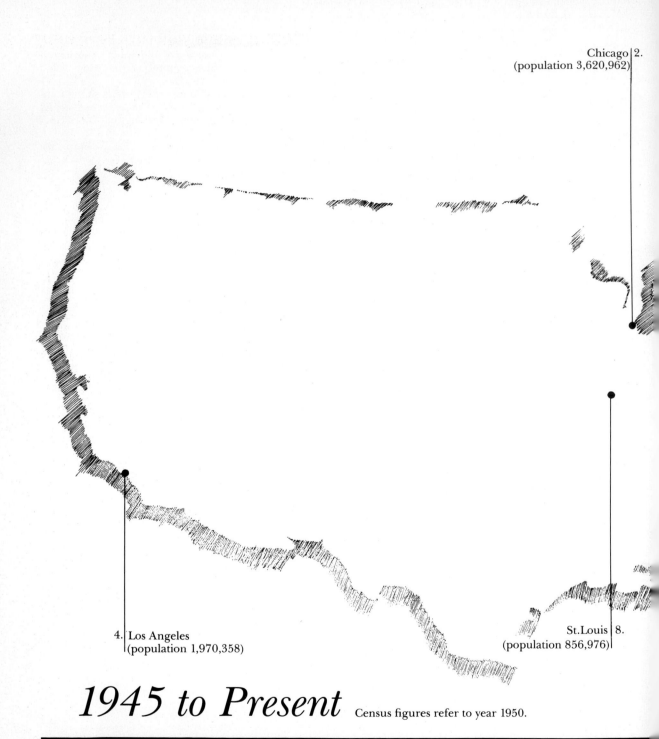

Chicago 2.
(population 3,620,962)

4. Los Angeles
(population 1,970,358)

St.Louis 8.
(population 856,976)

1945 to Present Census figures refer to year 1950.

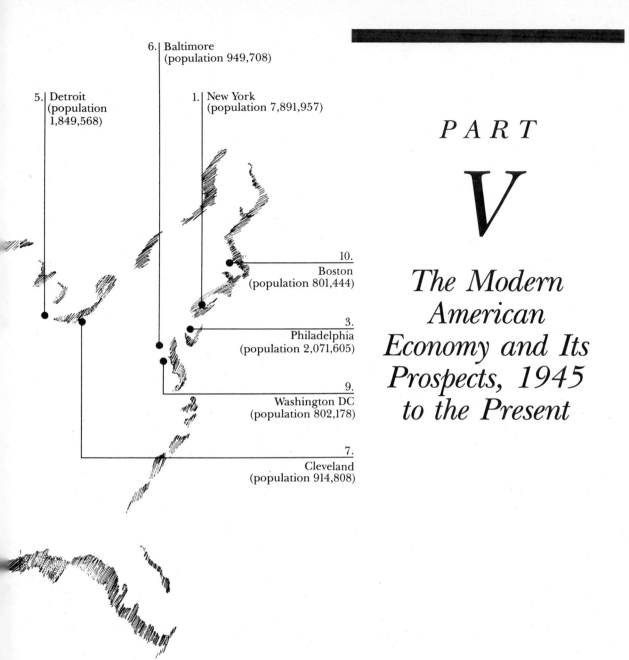

5. | Detroit
(population
1,849,568)

6. | Baltimore
(population 949,708)

1. | New York
(population 7,891,957)

10.
Boston
(population 801,444)

3.
Philadelphia
(population 2,071,605)

9.
Washington DC
(population 802,178)

7.
Cleveland
(population 914,808)

PART

V

*The Modern
American
Economy and Its
Prospects, 1945
to the Present*

*T*he four decades after World War II have in general been characterized by "good times." Most indicators of economic welfare have shown substantial improvement, although at times the pace was irregular or the incidence of improvement uneven. Overall, however, the amounts of goods and services available to each American has risen, and the indicators of well being have improved since the Thirties. Real income has increased. Postwar recessions have been far less severe than the Great Depression or even the lesser slumps of other periods, and their impact on the individual has been muted by a growing range of social welfare programs. Life expectancy and other indicators of health have increased. Levels of education have shown significant improvement. The gains in income have been widely shared: although the distribution and even the definition of income remain controversial among economists, today the arguments center on to what extent income distribution has become more nearly equal.

No previous four decades of U.S. economic history have been free of problems, and the recent economic past is no exception. If there is one source of concern unique to this period, it is inflation. Since 1945 no substantial periods of deflation and few of even approximate price stability have occurred. Moreover, inflation has increasingly become divorced from other economic indicators. At one time inflation was largely associated with high, even unsustainable levels of economic activity, such as the peak of peacetime booms or major wars. More recently, however, even though there is still a loose association between increased inflation and levels of real economic activity, some positive rate of general price increase seems to occur at virtually any tolerable level of employment and output.

The combination of price stability and historically low unemployment rates (say 5 percent or less) has proved impossible to achieve in the past two decades and was rare just before that time. Currently, it appears that the "natural rate" of unemployment has increased to perhaps 6 percent of the work force due to changes in labor force participation rates, demographic factors, and social institutions such as welfare, unemployment compensation, and tax policy. Not only was inflation nearly universal; but the rates of price increases during 1974 and the 1979–1981 period equalled or exceeded those of every year since 1929 except the 1946–1947 reconversion boom.[1] Even though inflation subsided in the Eighties, it did not disappear.

It seemed that even a growing economy could not simultaneously provide environmental protection, increased occupational health and safety, eco-

[1] Council of Economic Advisors, *Economic Report of the President, 1985,* (Washington, D.C.: Government Printing Office, 1985), p. 296.

nomic support for the needy, greater levels of defense spending, and continued improvements in the aftertax real incomes of most Americans—or at least not at the levels desired for each in isolation. In short, the economic situation of postwar America was what it had always been: nothing was free, and efforts to achieve one goal involved opportunity costs elsewhere.

Even more seriously, there was some concern that all new ends might have to be achieved by reallocating existing output from other sectors. In the modern era, economic growth had become increasingly dependent on increases in productivity (increases in output per unit of input). In the Seventies, the rate of productivity improvement apparently declined and in some years even became negative.[2] Although economic growth continued even while productivity apparently fell, the gains were achieved only through sharp increases in labor force participation that more than offset declines in output per worker. These increases in income were welcome, but their source was an obvious long-run dead end. Even in the short run it offered only limited potential for increased per-capita income. In consequence, there was growing interest in the sources and trends of productivity within the U.S. economy.

The Dimensions of Growth

In 1945, the gross national product of the United States in dollars of constant (1982) purchasing power was $1.355 trillion. That figure may have substantially overstated the level of economic welfare, since it was heavily influenced by war production. Perhaps a more realistic base for the era would be 1947's $1.067 trillion. By 1986, real gross national product had risen to $3.677 trillion in the same terms (1982 dollars). Since the 1986 overall price level was nearly five times its 1947 level, the increase in current dollars is much greater, from $235.2 billion to $4,209 trillion. Population increased as well as income, so the rise in per-capita income figures was more modest. Even so, the increase was substantial: real disposable income per person was $10,563 in 1984 compared to only $4,780 in 1947.[3]

The median income of American families in 1985 dollars rose from $14,493 in 1947 to $29,152 in 1985.[4] These figures reflect only one of two

[2] E. Denison, "Explanations of Declining Productivity Growth," Brookings General Series #354 (Washington, D.C.: the Brookings Institution, 1979). An alternative, far more optimistic view is that of M. Darby. See his "The U.S. Productivity Slowdown: A Case of Statistical Myopia," *American Economic Review* (June 1984).
[3] Council of Economic Advisors, *Economic Report of the President, 1987,* (Washington, D.C.: Government Printing Office, 1987) pp. 244–246.
[4] Ibid., pp. 275, 278.

important influences: incomes were growing, but family size was shrinking, so they slightly understate the rise in per-capita income. In addition to this increase in the purchasing power of their incomes, Americans had access to a much wider range of government services than ever before. By at least some measures (discussed in detail in later chapters), income distribution in the United States became substantially more equal as well.

Unemployment rates were lower than in the Thirties. Although recessions occurred in 1949, 1954, 1958, 1961, 1970, 1974–1975, and 1980–1982 (See Table V.1), the jobless rate reached 10 percent of the work force only for portions of 1982 and 1983. For those years and for 1975, the yearly unemployment rate exceeded 8 percent. Despite the lack of extreme levels of joblessness recorded in earlier periods, the average unemployment rate for the 1945–1984 period was somewhat higher than in earlier periods of similar length.[5] The average duration of unemployment rose in the postwar period, perhaps reflecting the "cushioning" effects of unemployment compensation, favorable tax treatment of the unemployed, and changes in the demography of the work force more than any difficulty in finding new jobs. Similar developments took place in the advanced industrial economies of Western Europe, in particular those with generous welfare systems. Certainly there was no failure to produce additional jobs: the number of Americans employed in civilian occupations increased from 60 million in 1950 to 109.6 million in 1986, and the pace of job creation increased after 1970.[6]

The Changing Labor Force

According to a major study, changes in the composition of the labor force assumed a new importance. Richard Easterlin concluded that the proportion of workers of various ages in the labor force—especially the portion of young males—has replaced aggregate growth in the labor force through immigration and other factors as the single most important influence on aggregate unemployment, the distribution of income between age cohorts, female labor force participation, and the birthrate.[7]

In Easterlin's view, before 1960 young males were in relatively short supply because of declining birthrates in the preceding decades and reduced

[5] S. Lebergott, "Changes in Unemployment, 1800–1960," in *The Reinterpretation of American Economic History*, eds. R. Fogel and S. Engerman (New York: Harper and Row, 1971), pp. 82–83.
[6] Council of Economic Advisors, *Economic Report of the President, 1987*, p. 282.
[7] R. Easterlin, "What Will 1984 Be Like? Socioeconomic Implications of Recent Trends in Age Structure," *Demography* (November 1978).

Table V.1   U.S. Economic Performance, 1946–1986

Date	Real GNP (Billions of 1982 Dollars)	Population (Millions)	Per-Capita Disposable Income (1982 Dollars)	Consumer Price Index (1967 = 100)	Civilian Unemployment (Percent)
1946	$1,096.9	141.4	$ 5,115	58.5	3.9
1948	1,108.7	146.6	5,000	72.1	3.8**
1950	1,203.7	152.3	5,220	72.1	5.3
1952	1,380.0	157.6	5,379	79.5	3.0
1954	1,416.2	163.0	5,505	86.5	5.5
1956	1,525.6	168.9	5,881	81.4	4.1
1958	1,539.2	174.9	5,908	86.6	6.8
1960	1,665.3	180.7	6,036	88.7	5.5
1962	1,799.4	186.5	6,271	90.6	5.5
1964	1,973.3	191.9	6,727	92.9	5.2
1966	2,208.3	196.6	7,280	97.2	3.8
1968	2,365.6	200.7	7,728	104.2	3.6
1970	2,416.2	205.1	8,143	116.3	4.9
1972	2,608.5	209.9	8,562	125.3	5.6
1974	2,729.3	213.9	8,867	147.7	5.6
1976	2,826.7	218.0	9,175	170.5	7.7
1978	3,115.2	222.6	9,735	195.4	6.1
1980	3,187.1	227.7	9,722	246.8	7.1
1982	3,166.0	232.5	9,725	289.1	9.7
1984	3,489.9	237.0	10,421	311.1	7.5
1986	3,676.5*	241.5	10,780*	328.4	7.0

*Preliminary data
**The basis of computation has been changed to include only those over 16 years old; formerly those 14–16 were also included.
Source: Council of Economic Advisors, *Economic Report of the President, 1987* (Washington, D.C.: Government Printing Office, 1987), pp. 246, 275, 279, 307.

immigration. Under these circumstances, young men found jobs easy to obtain. Moreover, salaries were generous by their parents' standards and promotions readily obtainable. Because of both the scarcity of young males and long-run social trends, female labor force participation rates increased from 1940 to 1960. (In Easterlin's view, women of all ages have tended to compete for jobs more directly with young males than with older men, whose jobs require greater training and skills than most female first-time job-force entrants possess.) Since young men enjoyed such favorable income and employment prospects before 1960, labor force participation by young women was restricted. Family formation and the birthrate increased sharply because families could afford more children. Women entering the labor force in this period tended to be from the older age cohorts.

After 1960, as the children of the "baby boom" of the 1940s and 1950s entered the labor market, young men faced much less favorable prospects. Their large numbers made competition for jobs much more intense. Labor force participation by older women declined, but that of younger women increased—producing even more severe job competition for young men. The high proportion of young women seeking and holding jobs after 1960 and the less promising long-run job outlook for the generation entering the labor force in the subsequent two decades resulted in lower birthrates. Other consequences of the labor market situation were higher rates of unemployment, divorce, and other indicators of social stress. Easterlin concluded that the relative position of each generation—that is, the effort required to match or better parents' living standards at comparable ages—is fixed for the cohort's entire working life.

If the Easterlin model is correct, the lower 1960–1980 birthrates will result in reduced unemployment in the 1980s and 1990s, an increase in the birthrate, and improved income prospects for younger workers as they enter the labor force. In this model, "long swings" of approximately two generations recur. In the swings, the experience of workers just entering the labor force greatly influences economic growth, unemployment, the birthrate, and other indicators of social well-being. If this analysis is correct, the traditional methods of reducing long-term unemployment by stimulating aggregate demand (the "Keynesian" prescription) will not work, since the unemployment stems from demographic rather than economic factors. For the next few decades, the model's outlook is optimistic: it predicts declining unemployment because the portion of the labor force unusually susceptible to job loss will decline. Moreover, this improvement in new workers' employment prospects will occur whether expansionary macroeconomic policies are followed or not.

Despite its possible effects on the individuals involved, the rapid growth of the U.S. labor force in the Sixties and Seventies contributed greatly to the economic growth of those decades.[8] In spite of widespread impressions to the contrary, U.S. real economic growth in the Seventies almost exactly

[8] Denison, "Explanations of Declining Productivity Growth."

equalled that of earlier, more fondly remembered decades. If anything, it slightly surpassed the gains recorded over 1900–1929 and 1946–1970.[9]

The growth record of the United States since World War II is comparatively modest. Italy, France, West Germany, and especially Japan grew faster than the United States over these four decades.

Sources of Growth

Since prolonged economic growth occurred in this era, we would expect that changes in the American economy spurred the rise in output. Perhaps the most obvious growth-producing change was a major increase in resource mobility. Overwhelmingly, resources were transferred from areas and occupations of low incomes to those where their earnings were greater.

Agriculture, a sector of chronically low incomes, continued to lose workers to other types of employment. The agricultural work force declined from 10 million workers in 1945 to less than 3.5 million by 1984, and the exodus from farm employment was by no means over.[10]

Manufacturing employment increased very slightly from the immediate postwar period to the mid-Sixties, then declined until 1970. After that it recorded an increase of slightly less than one million jobs to 1984.[11] Despite claims that the United States is "deindustrializing," it is the only major market economy (not excepting Japan) to gain industrial jobs over this period. Still, manufacturing jobs declined sharply as a portion of total employment. The bulk of the increased labor force found jobs in services, finance, wholesale and retail trade, and, particularly after 1960, state and local government.[12]

Increased mobility between regions occurred as well. People moved to the Pacific Coast, to Florida, and later to the entire "Sun Belt" along the Gulf Coast and the Mexican border. In more recent years, areas of "high-tech" employment have gained and those centered on high-cost energy production, such as most oil-producing regions, have lost jobs and population. Urbanization increased, even though the populations of many large central cities stabilized or even declined after 1960. By that date, fully 87 percent of the American population lived, worked, or did both in broadly defined

[9] Bureau of Economic Analysis, *Long Term Economic Growth, 1986–1970,* Part V, and *1981 Statistical Abstract* (Government Printing Office), p. 423. Cited in S. Lebergott, *The Americans: An Economic Record* (New York: Norton, 1984), p. 494.
[10] Council of Economic Advisors, *Economic Report of the President, 1985,* p. 340.
[11] Ibid., p. 276.
[12] Ibid., p. 275.

metropolitan areas.[13] A short-lived movement of population back to the countryside and to small towns in the early Seventies was soon overwhelmed by rising energy costs and the continuing decline of agriculture.

Over the period, income disparities between regions declined. Some traditionally low-income regions, such as the South, achieved above-average rates of income gains. Improved communications also bettered the circumstances of even those who stayed put. Capital increasingly migrated to areas where potential returns were greater. Firms located new plants in regions where returns on investment were higher, either because capital was scarce in relation to other inputs (chiefly labor) or because of proximity to new and growing markets.

The Critical Importance of Productivity Growth

To a greater extent than ever before, economic growth now derived from productivity improvements rather than increased inputs. Growth of the labor force was not rapid by nineteenth-century standards, nor was the aggregate rate of investment high. The contribution of raw materials to output decreased substantially over this period. Consequently, maintaining the rate of increase in real GNP at the historical level depended on increasing the amount of output per unit of input. By one estimate, over 80 percent of the increased output per worker in the postwar period can be attributed to productivity increases.[14]

In agriculture, where productivity gains were especially rapid (aggregate output rose despite a two-thirds reduction in the work force and a slight decline in acreage), farmers literally worked themselves out of their traditional jobs as the demand for agricultural products continued to lag behind income growth. In manufacturing, output per worker rose rapidly, but demand for manufactured products rose at about the same rate as aggregate income; consequently, the sector enrolled a declining portion of all workers.

The Marriage of Science and Technology

The sources and nature of technological change were themselves changing. As previously noted, technological progress, impressive though it may have been, had only tenuous links with formal science through most of American

[13] L. Davis et al., *American Economic Growth: An Economist's History of the United States* (New York: Harper and Row, 1972), p. 603.
[14] Denison, "Explanations of Declining Productivity Growth."

economic history. This situation had begun to change well before 1945, but now the changes became dramatic.

Increasingly, technological change now stemmed from controlled scientific investigation rather than seat-of-the-pants tinkering and innovation. As noted earlier, there had been previous indications that science would become more closely linked to industrial progress. Rayon and alloy steels had both resulted from advances in chemistry. But now the application and, even more, the integration of knowledge from various fields of science allowed far more than the production of greater quantities, varieties, or qualities of goods. It became possible to accurately predict the results of new production methods before they were actually in use. In some cases, products with no counterparts in nature, such as fiber optics, were developed. Improvements in the transmission of knowledge and their increasing concentration in a common core of training allowed principles developed for use in one area to be adapted to others, where they often proved even more productive.

Specialization to a previously unheard-of degree has now become not only effective, but less risky than it once was. For example, farmers now use inputs such as herbicides, insecticides, and fertilizers specifically tailored to the requirements of a particular crop and soil. Beyond that, it has become increasingly possible to breed more desirable characteristics into the crop itself.

The new methods have been at least equally successful in developing substitutes for particularly scarce or hard-to-work inputs. As with any other aspect of economic life, however, the gains are not free. Increased productivity achieved through these means requires interaction between researchers and those who use the methods and tools they develop. The ultimate human controllers of an automated assembly line must be familiar with a range of techniques and equipment far beyond the intellectual grasp of even the best engineers of a generation ago. On a more modest level, the use of a word processor may greatly enhance literary productivity, but it also demands an investment in logic from its operator. To broaden the market for such tools, their producers must make them more "user-friendly"—or require an investment in new skills by would-be authors.

These increases in productivity, stemming as they do largely from human ingenuity, allow far more optimistic assessments of humanity's long-run material prospects than ever before. They are based on the one resource that can fairly be termed inexhaustible: human imagination. Moreover, they offer an escape from many of the constraints imposed by other resource trends. Prospects for sizable growth in the American labor force over the next few decades are slim without a revolution in social attitudes. Yet the new methods allow increase in output per person to substitute quite effectively for a larger number of hands. There appears little doubt that productivity increases will be the dominant source of American economic growth over the next 20 years, and probably far beyond.

New Choices and Adjustments in a Complex World

Improved productive capabilities have allowed Americans a greater range of choice in several senses. First, the same amounts of product may be turned out in fewer working hours, allowing for increased leisure time at no sacrifice in conventionally measured living standards. Alternatively, they can be used to raise those material standards or provide newer, more varied, or better goods.

With increased productivity, humanity gains some welcome additions to the attainable range of social and personal choices as well. Growing output reduces the opportunity cost of devoting resources to environmental preservation. It also reduces the cost of aiding the less fortunate, promoting further growth, or in general pursuing whatever ends individuals or society may deem worthwhile.

The new capabilities have also produced new sources of both market and governmental failure. The modern economy is more crowded, both in terms of physical proximity in urban areas and in that more activities can affect the welfare of others without their consent. Use of the air and water as dumps for annoying or even dangerous refuse, traffic congestion, and 4:00 A.M. aerobic dancing to loud disco music in an apartment house are examples of such externalities. Growing international trade and investment necessarily involve political relationships with other countries. Technology may produce new forms of property (air rights over an urban building site) that require new legal forms to secure them.

However, the expansion of government to further worthy social objectives is a two-edged sword. Government action may be used to secure individual property rights, but it can also be used to limit them or transfer some of the proceeds they generate to others. Two facets of recent economic development in the United States have encouraged rent seeking. First, a wider role for government regulatory activity has been accepted, often on rather flimsy grounds. Second, the gains from rent seeking are likely to be much greater in a society where average incomes and wealth are high. The very pace of change threatens some types of jobs, life-styles, and consumption patterns. One result is efforts to prevent such change or to reduce its effects on those who feel adversely affected.

The Continuing Necessity of Choice

Widespread rent seeking is not economically neutral: its effects extend far beyond the redistribution of existing wealth or incomes. Resources must be used to promote such transfers, and those who stand to lose will devote resources to defending their property. Lobbyists, tax consultants, lawyers, environmental and consumer advocates, and a host of others familiar to modern society cannot in most cases simultaneously promote or resist the transfer of income and generate more. As a result of their activities, aggregate output is reduced below potential levels: rent seekers' gains are less than the cost of their activities to society as a whole. However, as long as the direct gains to rent seekers exceed the costs they incur to achieve them, such activities will continue.[15] Rent seeking may not be directed toward clear-cut transfers of income; its goal may be government protection from competition, so that costs are imposed on customers or would-be competitors rather than on taxpayers.

In addition—and this may well be the source of much of our current dissatisfaction—despite all the technological marvels that have enhanced our economic capabilities, we must still choose the ends to which these means may be devoted. Human wants are the ultimate growth industry: they seem to increase slightly faster than the ability to meet them, no matter how rapidly productive capacities rise. At any instant, greater effort in pursuit of a single economic goal means that fewer resources are available to meet some other want. The growth of government may exacerbate economic scarcity: often even successful responses to problems through government—those that permanently resolve the problem—produce an agency in search of a mission. Either it will insist that even vestiges of the original difficulty must be eliminated, regardless of cost (a phrase whose implications for economic efficiency are only too clear), or the agency will look for new dragons to slay. In other cases–for example, the U.S. government's subsidizing both lung cancer research and tobacco production—aims and methods of various agencies conflict.

[15] M. Olson, *The Rise and Declione of Nations: Economic Growth, Stagflation, and Social Rigidities* (New Haven, Conn.: Yale University Press, 1982) provides an excellent statement of this problem.

Selected References

Anderson, T., and P. Hill. *The Birth of a Transfer Society*. Stanford, Calif.: Hoover Institution Press, 1980.

Council of Economic Advisors. *Economic Report of the President, 1985*. Washington, D.C.: Government Printing Office, 1985.

Davis, L., et al. *American Economic Growth: An Economist's History of the United States*. New York: Harper and Row, 1972.

Denison, E. *Accounting for United States Economic Growth, 1929–1969*. Washington, D.C.: Brookings Institution, 1974.

Gordon, R. *Economic Instability and Growth: The American Record*. New York: Harper and Row, 1974.

North, D. *Structure and Change in Economic History*. New York: Norton, 1981.

North, D., et al. *Growth and Welfare in the American Past: A New Economic History*. Englewood Cliffs, N.J.: Prentice-Hall, 1983.

Olson, M. *The Rise and Decline of Nations: Economic Growth, Stagflation, and Social Rigidities*. New Haven, Conn.: Yale University Press, 1982.

Rosenberg, N. *Technology and American Economic Growth*. New York: M.E. Sharpe, 1972.

Rosenberg, N., and R. Birdzell. *How the West Grew Rich: The Economic Transformation of the Western World*. New York: Basic Books, 1986.

Simon, J. *The Ultimate Resource*. Princeton N.J.: Princeton University Press, 1981.

Vatter, H. *The U.S. Economy in the 1950s*. New York: Norton, 1963.

CHAPTER
20

THE PRIVATE SECTOR

At times it appears that the course of economic affairs in the postwar United States has been determined largely by government. Nearly all sectors of the economy are now affected by government to a greater extent than even under the New Deal, and the influence of government is vastly greater and more pervasive than it was prior to the Thirties. The share of income that originates in the expenditures of all levels of government within the U.S. economy has risen from 19.5 percent in 1948 (when normal postwar conditions were established) to 32 percent by 1970 and 36.7 percent by 1986.[1] Despite the fact that government activity grew faster than the overall economy in the postwar period, however, the private sector continued to be the dominant force affecting economic welfare in the postwar United States.

THE CONTINUED DOMINANCE OF MARKET TRANSACTIONS

The market influenced employment patterns, regional growth, and income levels. Although some industries (for example, aerospace and defense-related production) were almost completely dependent on government demand, the gains and losses of most regions, occupations, and industries were largely due to market supply and demand changes. Those industries whose products were in unusually great demand achieved above-average growth. The incomes of low-cost producers were higher than those of less efficient individuals, regions, or

[1] Council of Economic Advisors, *Economic Report of the President, 1987,* (Washington, D.C.: Government Printing Office, 1987), pp. 244, 331, 338.

firms. Transfers of resources into more efficient uses or improvements within the same occupation were even more important for aggregate economic growth than in earlier periods.

As social restrictions on the occupations of women and minority groups loosened, the more efficient allocation of economic resources as well as the correction of long-standing social injustice were made possible. Reduced employment discrimination benefited the aggregate economy as well as the individuals directly affected by allowing the same work force to produce more output. The gains to the American economy from this source were potentially even greater than those already achieved through allocating jobs by merit among the rest of the labor force. These changes reinforced those produced by improved geographic mobility and communications.

Geographic Mobility

Social change combined with geographic mobility to give the United States a work force whose response to new opportunities was nothing short of extraordinary. The legacy of individual mobility that had always characterized American labor was even further developed after 1945. The U.S. population is highly mobile in geographic terms, and the impetus for mobility remains economic. U.S. citizens move to areas of higher wages, better climates, and improved prospects, and they do so as cheaply as possible.[2] This ability to transfer labor readily from low- to high-productivity uses continues to be a major advantage of the United States in a world where markets, resource patterns,

and especially technology change at ever-increasing rates.

The dimensions of geographic mobility are staggering. Although only one U.S. family in six has moved in each year since 1980—as opposed to one in five two decades ago—the decline appears largely due to the increase in home ownership. Crucial mobility indicators such as the portion of families moving outside the original county of residence and of renters who moved have not decreased.[3] Nearly one-half (46.4 percent) of the U.S. population changed residence between 1975 and 1980.[4] The contrast with Europe's current difficulties in reallocating workers between regions and jobs could hardly be more vivid.

Moving in search of better incomes and jobs is one thing: achieving these goals may be quite another. But the data on income mobility for individuals in the United States (see Chapter 21) indicate a high incidence of change. Moreover, conditions that ease relocation, such as education and a reduction in regional differences, appear to be increasing.

Regional Gains and Losses
The latter form of mobility also contributed to increased income levels after World War II. Regions as well as individuals were affected. For nearly the entire postwar period, the Pacific Coast, which combined a favorable climate with rapidly growing electronics, communications, and aerospace industries, attracted massive population flows from the rest of the country. In consequence, although aggregate West Coast incomes grew rapidly, the pace of increase in individual incomes there was modest by national standards. Later in the era, the Sun Belt (Arizona, New Mexico, and the Gulf

---

[2] C. Galloway and R. Vedder, "The Mobility of Native Americans," *Journal of Economic History* (September 1971). See also M. Greenwood, "An Analysis of the Determinants of Labor Mobility in the United States," *Review of Economics and Statistics* (May 1969).

[3] U.S. Department of Commerce, Bureau of the Census, *Current Population Reports: Geographic Mobility Series* (Washington, D.C.: Government Printing Office, 1984), p. 80.
[4] U.S. Department of Commerce, Bureau of the Census, *Statistical Abstract of the United States* (Washington, D.C.: Government Printing Office,1984), pp. 15–17.

States) also grew rapidly. Texas rode its combination of natural resources (petroleum, salt, and sulfur) and petrochemical, electronics, aerospace, and defense industries to spectacular growth. Its decline as oil prices fall may be no less impressive. At one time, prospects for continued high energy costs appeared to point to rapid growth in the Rocky Mountain region, but the rebirth of competition in international oil markets now casts some doubt on that prediction. "High-tech" industries, such as those linked to the seemingly unlimited applications of computers, also contributed to regional growth: the classic example is California's "Silicon Valley."

As economic activity became increasingly centered on service and information rather than manufacturing, resource mobility increased. Many of these new activities have few locational requirements, such as natural resources or access to transportation, to tie them to specific localities. This development was nearly as prominent in the international sphere as within the U.S. economy, and it has greatly increased competition in the markets for these goods.

Areas whose principal industries served slowly growing or declining markets or whose chief products encountered increasing competition experienced chronic high unemployment, slow income growth, and at least relative outmigration. These dismal processes continued until the low-growth regions developed new occupations or lost sufficient population to allow remaining workers' prospects to improve. The coal mining regions of Appalachia and the shoe and textile districts of New England have made their adjustments; regions heavily dependent on agriculture or some types of industry may be forced to do so.

Areas where incomes were far above or below national norms tended to converge toward the average. The South, traditionally a low-wage area, gradually began to gain income parity with other regions.[5] As investment avoided those

states where labor costs were already high, income growth there fell below that of regions with abundant low-wage labor and consequent high returns on investment. Supply and demand operated in textbook fashion in labor markets: where work forces grew rapidly, wages generally failed to keep pace with national rates of increase, and where labor force growth was slow, wage rates grew at better-than-average rates.[6]

AGRICULTURE

If the influence of productivity changes was paramount in any sector of the American economy, it was agriculture. The total output of American farms rose substantially, but changes in the relative weight of various farm products reflected changes in demand. Production of beef (until very recently) and poultry increased rapidly, indicating the high income elasticity of demand for those foods. Cotton output fell substantially, and hog and tobacco production also faced limited futures. A few crops—soybeans were the primary example—assumed new importance in the postwar era. The nature of some farm products was altered in response to changing dietary preferences, such as consumers' growing preference for lean beef.

Only minor changes occurred in the centers of agricultural production from 1945 to the 1980s. Some additional land became available for crop production as a result of irrigation programs or new strains of traditional crops, but in most areas the pattern was one of increased production from lands already in use. Had government agricultural programs not intervened via efforts to raise market prices for

[5] G. Wright, *Old South, New South: Revolutions in the South-*

ern Economy Since the Civil War (New York: Basic Books, 1986), Chap. 8.

[6] Council of Economic Advisors, *1977 Economic Report of the President* (Washington, D.C.: Government Printing Office, 1977), pp. 243–245.

■ From 1945 to the 1980s, the location and types of American agricultural production varied little, while productivity increased enormously.
Source: Pictorial Parade Inc.

farm products through reduced output (as in the 1983 payment in kind measure), output might have risen even more. Gradually, however, it appeared that Congress was more willing to support farmers through high prices than through purchases of surplus output. (This point will be addressed in detail in the following chapter.)

The Productivity Revolution

Trends toward greater output per farm worker had appeared long before 1945, but they greatly accelerated after that date. Production of farm products per labor-hour more than quadrupled between 1946 and 1984.[7] The rate of increase in farm labor productivity was twice that achieved by industrial workers. Farmers were able to increase the per-unit productivity of land as well. Output per acre began to rise after 1950, with the per-acre gains in yields of wheat, potatoes, corn, and tobacco (all of which doubled or more by 1970) exceeding those of hay

and cotton.[8] These output gains enabled each American farm worker to produce sufficient food and fiber for 47 people in 1970, whereas in 1946 the same worker's output provided for the needs of only 14 persons.[9]

Furthermore, this increased farm output came from about 10 percent less acreage than in the earlier period. Although American agriculture was still a very long way from being able to supply the world's wheat requirements from a single flowerpot—or county—the postwar trend was in that direction, both in the United States and in many other regions of the world. One consequence of these productivity advances was a more than 50 percent reduction in the farm labor force after 1950.

Economic analysis would indicate that if the amounts of land and labor required per unit of agricultural output fell, either some other input was increased or technology improved (a shorthand term indicating an improvement in resource quality). Both occurred. The average productivity of land rose, since the small amounts withdrawn from use tended to be the least productive acres. Land productivity increased much more because new knowledge allowed the production of greater yields from the remaining acreage. Such scientific advances were often embodied in more efficient machinery, more systematic choice and application of fertilizer, wider and more specialized employment of agents to control plant and insect pests, and new plant and animal strains.

The improvements in agricultural technology constituted a veritable revolution in farming methods. Modern farmers' market situation is if anything even more competitive than that

---

[7] U.S. Department of Commerce, Bureau of the Census, *Statistical Abstract of the United States* 1986 ed., (Washington, D.C.: Government Printing Office, 1986).

[8] These trends have continued for some but not all crops in the Eighties. Tobacco yields, for example, have shown no gains, while yields of most grain crops continue to rise. U.S. Department of Commerce, *Statistical Abstract, 1986 ed.*

[9] U.S. Department of Commerce, Bureau of the Census, *Historical Statistics of the United States: Colonial Times to 1970*, 2 vols. (Washington, D.C.: Government Printing Office, 1975), vol. 1:498.

of their Populist forebears, so learning about the most modern production methods—and buying the capital that made the most of them—was a matter of survival. The new agriculture required far more than rules of thumb or even application of the best-controlled experiments of a decade or so in the past. In many cases, the new techniques could now be minutely tailored to take even minor variations in soil chemistry or growing conditions into account.

New Requirements in Human and Physical Capital

Many farmers now found that a college education, preferably with training in both agricultural and business techniques, was a valuable tool in the new, rapidly changing environment. Since few of the ideas used by modern farmers originated on commercial farms, and of course the tools, chemicals, and seed employed there had not done so for decades, the last vestige of the American farmer's image as a self-sufficient producer disappeared. In addition to their purchases of fuel, machinery, chemical inputs, and knowledge and a huge expansion in their use of financial credit, an increasing proportion of American farmers now bought nearly all their food from stores.

At least for the basic crops and meat animals, efficient application of the new methods appeared to require larger production units. Economies of scale were fully obtainable only on farms considerably larger than the typical American farm in the Forties. And the increase in optimum size continued with startling speed. In 1950, American farms averaged 213 acres. In 1975, that average had increased to 387 acres, and nine years later it was 445.[10] When we combine the decline in aggregate farm acreage with the increase in average farm size, it is easier to understand why the number of farms decreased from 5.4 to 2.3 million over the same period.[11]

Today the American countryside is dotted with homes that once were farmhouses. The land their owners formerly tilled is now sold or leased to other farmers who have been able to expand. The small farm may still have a place in the production of specialty crops or dairying, but the day of the 100- or even 250-acre farm devoted to grain, cotton, or meat production is now over. Many small units are now farms in name only; their owners subsidize farming losses with income gained in urban occupations. In recent years, farms with annual sales of less than $20,000 of agricultural goods generated net losses from farming. Only at crop sales of $100,000 per year or more did farming generate a majority of the owners' incomes.[12] In most areas, a viable farm is now a small- to medium-sized business in which no less than half a million dollars is invested.

Growing Competition in an Uncertain World

These developments have reduced the cost of food for consumers, but their impact on farmers has sometimes been traumatic. The need for continual new investment and long-term commitments in a market where prices are more unpredictable than ever has inevitably meant that many farmers misjudged their ability to remain competitive. Export markets for major American grain crops are now subject to political events (the 1980 embargo on grain sales to the Soviet Union following its invasion of Afghanistan is only the most spectacular example) and steadily increasing foreign competition as other nations adopt the new agricultural technology and sometimes subsi-

[10] U.S. Department of Commerce, *Statistical Abstract, 1986 ed.*, p. 660.

[11] U.S. Department of Commerce, *Statistical Abstract, 1986,* p. 661, and U.S. Department of Commerce, Bureau of the Census, *Bicentennial Statistics* (Washington, D.C.: Government Printing Office, 1976), p. 405.

[12] U.S. Department of Commerce, *Statistical Abstract, 1986 ed.* p. 646.

dize exports. Reduced domestic inflation also imposed unforeseen burdens on many farmers (and their creditors). Those who borrowed heavily at the interest rates of the mid- and late Seventies in the expectation of long-term world food shortages and continued high farm product prices have been particularly hard hit by the drastic changes in both.

Very large farms, particularly those managed as subsidiaries of large corporations, have shown no productive advantages save in a few specialty crops and have made little headway in the past few decades. Such farms should not be confused with individually or family owned farms that have been reorganized as corporations for tax or other reasons by their owners. These corporate farms constitute nearly 90 percent of all incorporated units,[13] but as such have no implications for competition in agriculture. These incorporations alter neither the size nor the number of farms. If there is any trend toward decreased competition in American agriculture, it is not obvious—least of all to farmers. Reductions in the number of producers have not changed the basic structure of the industry. Developments in transportation and even import competition have increased the intensity of agricultural competition.

Consequences of Technological Change in Agriculture

The introduction of new technology has not been without cost. In addition to the debt burdens some farmers have been unable to carry as they tried to use improved methods, changes that increase output per unit of input while consumer demand for farm produce is both price and income inelastic (and population is increasing more slowly than farm productivity) mean that some producers have to leave the

[13] Ibid., p. 638.

industry. In some cases the transition to alternative occupations has been very difficult for people who had invested most of a working lifetime and a host of emotional commitments to farming.

Mechanical cotton pickers and new strains of vegetables suited to machine harvesting have reduced costs of production and raised consumers' living standards. They have also meant less back-breaking manual labor. The same developments, however, have eliminated the primary occupations of millions of low-income agricultural workers, many of whom lack the education and cultural flexibility to readily find other jobs. This problem appeared even before World War II in the South, and it seems likely to become increasingly serious in California, Texas, and Florida. A small farmer forced from the land may at least be able to sell his land and obtain funds to tide him over the transition. But for an unskilled and barely literate migrant farm worker, displacement from the only job he and his family have ever known can mean the bleakest of prospects. Yet there appears little doubt that the exodus will continue.

In addition, there have been environmental costs. Agricultural chemicals have been applied without proper appreciation of their full impact on wildlife, the crops themselves, or even the workers who handled them. In some cases the danger was realized only after serious harm had been inflicted.

Farm incomes have not risen as rapidly as all others in the United States, and in the Eighties they have undergone substantial absolute reductions. To add to farmers' difficulties, income trends have varied greatly. Net farm income more than doubled in two years (1973–1974), but it declined thereafter and has never regained the levels achieved in the mid-Seventies. Under such conditions, it is hardly surprising that most American farmers earn most of their incomes from nonfarm occupations. Nor does the future appear bright, at least if the farm population declines no faster than at present. Export markets are likely to become increasingly competitive as other nations' farmers adopt new technology. A growing number of nations that had chronic deficiencies in domestic food production are now self-sufficient in major cereal, dairy, and meat products, and some (including India) are at least occasionally able to export as well. U.S. farmers can no longer take export markets for granted.

Government's influence on American agriculture grew to unimagined dimensions in the New Deal. Not only did that era introduce subsidies and production controls but American farmers now began to be affected by many of the same environmental, safety, and land-use policies as the rest of the population, and often to a greater degree. Policies for distribution of government food surpluses had obvious implications. Political considerations became increasingly important, too. Was American food to be used as a weapon, traded as nearly as possible along lines dictated by comparative advantage, or used for humanitarian purposes? Should American farmers be helped still more to maintain their export markets in the face of subsidized competition from other nations? The strength and weakness of the dollar in international trade, the oil crisis, and a host of other phenomena made it clear that American farmers, to a greater extent than most other U.S. producers, were now operating in a world economy.

MANUFACTURING

Manufacturing was another sector of the economy where productive capabilities grew faster than demand. Prices of manufactured goods, particularly consumer durables, fell in real terms after 1967.[14] Unlike in agriculture, however, the decline of manufacturing was relative

rather than absolute. The number of workers employed in manufacturing rose from 15.5 million in 1947 to over 20 million in 1974. Although some claim that the United States is "deindustrializing," about 500,000 more workers were employed in manufacturing in 1984 than in 1970, although this is less than the 1979 peak.[15] Approximately one million new manufacturing jobs were created from 1982 to 1986. Nevertheless, total employment rose from 43.9 to 94.2 million over the 1947–1984 period, so the portion of all nonagricultural workers employed in manufacturing declined from 35.3 to 20.8 percent.[16] By the end of the period, large numbers of those employed in manufacturing performed clerical, distributive, or administrative tasks. Manufacturing's share of the total value of output fell from 28.5 to 20.7 percent over the 1947–1983 period.[17] As these figures indicate, labor productivity in manufacturing rose more than the national average.

Science: A Growing Partner

The sources of growth in manufacturing, as in agriculture, have become increasingly tied to generalized scientific research and its application through technology. There has been more research oriented toward the specific problems of individual firms or industries, based on the common ground of discoveries in pure research. Both the nature of twentieth-century patents (which are increasingly based on the results of formal scientific investigation rather than empirically developed ideas) and the rapid growth in the ranks of technically trained persons support this conclusion.[18] Once the basic principles of atomic and molecular structure were understood, the properties of existing

[14] Council of Economic Advisors, *Economic Report of the President, 1986*, (Washington, D.C.: Government Printing Office, 1986), pp. 294, 297.

[15] Ibid., p. 275.
[16] Ibid.
[17] Ibid., p. 244.
[18] N. Rosenberg, *Technology and American Economic Growth* (New York: M.E. Sharpe, 1972), p. 118.

materials could be made more desirable. In addition, it was possible to produce entirely new synthetic materials that had no counterparts in nature, such as plastics, fibers, adhesives, insulation, and fiber optics.[19]

The tasks of applied science in manufacturing have grown almost immeasurably more complex. Considerations of producer and product-user safety and the environmental impact of products and processes have generated an ever-expanding area of additional scientific inquiry. This concern with the social costs and benefits of new technology is a further indication of America's growing wealth and scientific capabilities, not merely its social values. Yet these investigatory capabilities are still in a very early stage.

The new developments have also reduced dependence on almost all natural resources, particularly the high-quality, high-content mineral resources that were the only usable forms of such resources for most of human history. There are, however, some exceptions to this greater access to alternatives, and they are crucial. There are no substitutes for air and water. Thus, our stocks of these two essentials for human life must be maintained in usable form. "Usable" does not imply absolute freedom from pollution for all or even most uses. It does, however, mean that the costs imposed on mankind by additional deterioration in the quality of air and water resources must not be allowed to exceed the benefits conferred by the activities that produced this deterioration.

The other exception—on which all our newfound and potential ability to generate substitutes for natural inputs depends—is energy. With sufficient energy supplies, the new techniques promise to compensate for limitations in the earth's stock of conventional raw materials through more efficient use of available supplies, greater ability to locate and use lower-grade resources (stocks of which are enormous, relative to current rates of use, in most cases), and the ability to produce substitutes.[20]

By no means will such resources be free or even necessarily cheaper in the future. But natural resource supplies will not impose an insuperable barrier to further economic growth. Copper supplies, for example, may well not be able to support the demands of further growth employing the technology of the recent past. However, copper is being supplanted in its electrical applications by aluminum and fiber optics. The ultimate sources of these copper substitutes—clay and sand, respectively—appear ample for generations. As long as the range of substitutes for various applications of some raw material continues to increase, the lack of a single material that can replace it in all uses becomes less important. Fear that limited natural resources will catastrophically restrict human well-being is at least as old as the Reverend Malthus, who uttered such misgivings with regard to arable land in the early nineteenth century. It appears to be no better linked to reality today than in his day.

The Role of New Industries

The overall growth performance of any economy is a composite of the rate of change in output of all its commodities. As more or fewer sectors exhibit especially rapid or slow growth, their performance influences that of the economy disproportionately. Within sectors, the same is true of individual industries. Typically, industries producing new products just beginning to be accepted by consumers tend to grow particularly rapidly. As customers become more familiar with a new product or service, not only do they use it more, but they find wider uses for it. Often these may be applications scarcely

---

[19] Ibid., pp. 124–126. The following discussion is based on Professor Rosenberg's views.

[20] H. Goeller and A. Weinberg, "The Age of Substitutability." *American Economic Review* (December 1978).

imagined by the original producers. This point is especially germane for items purchased to express individual consumers' tastes, or those, like plastics or computers, which can be adapted to a wide range of applications. In addition, as production of a new good expands, the producers may be able to exploit economies of scale or gain cost reductions through "learning by doing." The success of such new products invites competition from additional producers of identical goods or close substitutes. Any or all of these developments reduce the item's price and further expand its market.

After a while, however, the impact of these factors will be largely complete, and the growth of the no-longer-so-new industry will slow. The same factors that aided the growth of one new item are likely to encourage use of still newer goods as the public gains an appreciation for the benefits of such innovation. As other new commodities appear, they may partially or wholly replace those that preceded them. Potentially, any item that attracts consumer or producer spending competes with every other one, since incomes are limited.

How long a new good enjoys rapid growth depends on its nature. Once demand becomes largely based on replacement needs and aggregate economic growth and the article has become familiar enough to invite competition from new substitutes, growth of the industry will slow to that of the aggregate economy or less. If many good substitutes appear, the initial good's production may decline or even cease. If the new good is a producer input, its growth depends on the demand for the final products in which it is a component and the technology of the industries that employ it. The users may either discover broader applications or develop substitutes for it.

New Products and Economic Growth

As the American economy diversified, the pace of technological change quickened, and the ease and accuracy of communication increased, the potential growth phase for any single product has probably decreased. If substantial economic growth is to be maintained under such conditions, the economy must continually generate new products and the rapidly growing industries that produce them. To accomplish this, there must be as few noneconomic barriers to new competition as possible.

Competition from new products or methods is particularly important to improve overall economic efficiency, both by reallocating resources and exerting pressure on established producers of older products to improve existing methods. Since the established producers are likely to be more influential than new industries, they may attempt to block the growth of new sectors or limit the dispersion of new products or methods to maintain their own incomes. Barriers to occupational mobility, restrictions on the use of new methods, discriminatory taxes, and a long list of other tactics have been employed by those opposed to change. Such tactics impose severe long-run burdens; even if innovations occur, these measures restrict their impact and range of application. In this area, the attitudes and political structure of the United States have conferred important advantages on the economy compared to countries where a central government establishes all rules for economic activity or social attitudes are slower to change.[21]

The Diversity of American Manufacturing

To the casual observer, the postwar American economy appears to have developed few products whose growth was both rapid and large enough in aggregate to significantly impact the national growth rate. However, this impression

---

[21] See M. Olson, *The Rise and Decline of Nations: Economic Growth, Stagflation, and Social Rigidities* (New Haven, Conn.: Yale University Press, 1982) and D. North, *Structure and Change in Economic History* (New York: Norton, 1981) for recent illustrations of this point. Its applicability to non-Western economies is illustrated in E. Jones, *The European Miracle: Environments, Economics, and Geopolitics in the History of Europe and Asia* (Cambridge, England: Cambridge University Press, 1981).

is largely due to the enormous diversity of the economy and to the fact that so many once-new items quickly become taken for granted in the American environment. Few if any single industries have had the postwar economic impact of the railroads, cheap steel, or electricity. Television might be an exception, but there are a host of others which have shown above-average growth, even though each one's aggregate impact has been modest. Production of home freezers, plastics, air conditioning, industrial chemicals, frozen foods, synthetic fibers, and recreational equipment has expanded at rates that bolstered aggregate performance. Computer production and its contributions to other economic activity may prove a greater accelerating factor than any other new postwar industry.

In addition, many individual products or types of products achieved rapid growth even within stable or declining industries. Textile production, for example, has not kept up with the aggregate pace of American economic growth in recent decades, but the output of synthetic fibers has grown far more rapidly.[22] Dacron, Orlon, nylon, and newer synthetic fabrics are supplanting wool, cotton, silk, and even rayon, the first synthetic fiber.

Some idea of the diversity of American manufacturing may be gained from Table 20.1. Even under its very broad definitions, no single industry accounted for as much as 15 percent of all value added by manufacturing. It must also be kept in mind that manufacturing itself now accounts for only about a fifth of all economic activity. A comparison of these data with Table 12.1 indicates the changes that have occurred in the American economy. Few of 1910's leading industries have retained their rank within American manufactures. The greater importance of industries producing highly transformed products, where raw materials ac-

■ The increasing variety of goods available maintained market growth.
Source: The Bettmann Archive.

count for only a minor portion of the final product's value, is a feature of modern industry. In the postwar period, the growth of older industries such as food, lumber, leather, textiles and apparel, and even metals (both fabricated and primary) lagged behind that of all manufacturing, while that of instruments, chemicals, rubber and plastic products, and transportation equipment exceeded it.[23]

The Role of Computers and Automation

Changes in the control of production mechanisms profoundly altered manufacturing. Heretofore, machines had provided either the strength or speed that human muscles could not generate or had performed relatively simple, repetitious operations. In some cases, machines were the simplest method of achieving high uniformity and accuracy over a large volume of production. But such tools generally required close human supervision: they had a

---

[22] L. Davis et al., *American Economic Growth: An Economist's History of the United States* (New York: Harper and Row, 1972), p. 456.

[23] U.S. Department of Commerce, *Historical Statistics*, vol. 2, pp. 669–680, and *Statistical Abstract, 1986*, pp. 745–749.

Table 20.1 Leading U.S. Industries, by Value Added, 1982

Rank and Identity	Value Added (in Millions of Dollars)	Total Employment (in Thousands)	Production Workers (in Thousands)
1. Machinery (nonelectrical)	$102,270	2,189	1,358
2. Food	88,419	1,488	1,047
3. Transportation equipment	84,932	1,595	1,060
4. Electrical equipment	84,605	1,915	1,198
5. Chemicals	77,315	873	508
6. Fabricated metals	58,928	1,460	1,073
7. Printing and publishing	54,423	1,292	711
8. Instruments and related products	33,672	624	363
9. Paper	33,376	606	461
10. Primary metals	33,291	854	638
Total U.S. manufacturing	$824,118	19,094	12,401

Source: Department of Commerce, Bureau of the Census, *Statistical Abstract of the United States, 1986*, (Washington, D.C.: Government Printing Office, 1986), pp. 745–747.

limited ability to make changes or adjustments, for in that area there was no substitute for human judgment. These restrictions began to diminish as computers and sophisticated control mechanisms capable of coordinating a great many processes simultaneously were brought into use.

By programming instructions into a computer, it became possible to devise control mechanisms for whole groups of machines that could deal with variations in the material, move it from one machine in a coordinated group to the next, adjust for missing or defective components, and even switch to the production of different items. Human labor was now required mainly to set up and maintain the system and to make adjustments beyond the computer's information or capabilities, such as major product changes.

Automation and Employment

Two points should be noted in regard to automation. First, it reduces the number of jobs where it is used. Although it makes additional jobs available in other areas, they are unlikely to be suited to the capabilities of the displaced workers. However, it does not create a general reduction in the demand for labor. Purchasing and installing automated equipment is enormously expensive, and such machinery is still best suited to producing large quantities of fairly standardized products. Automation's chief impact on labor, then, is similar to that of previous advances in machinery—in repetitious jobs requiring iron muscles and the intellect of the average acorn squash. We may deplore either the displacement of labor from such occupations or their demeaning impact on the humans who perform them in the absence of automated machinery, but not both simultaneously. The jobs that automation has not affected, as yet, are those requiring flexibility and the continual exercise of judgment.

Second, automation reduces the production costs of the goods it makes, at least compared to other methods. Thus automation gives consumers better or cheaper products, or both, than alternative production methods. Consumers derive the same benefits they obtained from earlier manufacturing innovation. The reduction in product costs made possible by automation allows for an increase in real aggregate demand—consumers' incomes now purchase larger quantities of goods, which may increase employment in many sectors of the economy.

However, the beneficial effects of automation, large though they may be in aggregate, are widely diffused. The adverse effects, though their total impact is less, are likely to be highly concentrated on the displaced. Consequently, there may be a potential for rent-seeking activity among persons trying to protect their current jobs.

Because of the nature of the jobs most likely to be automated, those displaced are liable to have a hard time finding new jobs since their previous occupations did not emphasize flexibility and imagination as the newer jobs do. Often age, lack of education, locational factors, or personal inclinations make the adjustment process traumatic. The adaptability of the human race, or large portions of it, has always exceeded that of individuals who bear the brunt of change. Nevertheless, it now seems clear that even those who plan to spend their entire careers in the same job must expect to relearn it several times during their working lives. Many more persons will have to shift occupations more or less completely.

The New Competition

A cursory statistical examination of the manufacturing sector of the American economy might lead some to conclude that economic power became more concentrated and competition decreased during the postwar period. Ownership of manufacturing assets has gravitated toward fewer hands; the share of all manufacturing capacity and equipment owned by the largest 50, 100, or 200 corporations has increased substantially in the last three or four decades. (This trend, however, was reversed in the late 1970s.) In addition, the absolute size of large corporations, whether measured by dollars of sales revenue or amount of assets (but, particularly in recent years, not employees),[24] has also risen.

None of these developments really gives an indication of competition trends within manufacturing. Absolute size of firms is all but useless when considered in isolation. One example should make the point: by any measure of absolute size, Sears, Roebuck, and Company is one of the largest firms in the United States. Clearly, however, Sears faces strong competitive pressure in every market within which it operates. Monopoly power is conferred not by absolute size, but by size in relation to the market in which the seller operates. In the United States, most markets have greatly expanded as a result of the economy's postwar growth and improved transportation and communication. We hardly think of increased competition in retail markets as one of the consequences of the interstate highway system, but that has been one of its effects. In general, unless the growth of sellers is assessed in relation to that of their markets, no meaningful conclusions can be drawn about the extent of monopoly or its rate of change.

There is little question but that the absolute size of the largest manufacturing firms increased relative to the industrial sector. In 1947, the 200 largest industrial firms produced 30 percent of all value added by manufacture, a figure that had risen to 43 percent by 1970.[25] Large firms grew more rapidly than their smaller rivals. But the growth of such giant concerns was more the result of diversification than of increasing shares of individual markets. Large firms, aided by the revolution in production methods, have generated new divisions that turn

[24] N. Rosenberg and L. Birdzell, *How the West Grew Rich: The Economic Transformation of the Industrial World* (New York: Basic Books, 1986) pp. 295–296.

[25] U.S. Department of Commerce, *Historical Statistics* vol. 2, p. 686.

out products quite different from those the firms originally produced. A much more important factor, however, has been the widespread incidence of conglomerate mergers. The large firms have acquired smaller firms that had no previous economic relationships with them as customers, suppliers, or competitors. Since 1970, however, large firms in many industries have failed to match the aggregate economy's growth.[26]

Conglomerates

Conglomerate mergers do increase the absolute size of firms, but they do not necessarily— or even probably—increase the conglomerate's share of any individual market and thus its monopoly power, as normally measured. Opinions on the economic effects of conglomerates vary. Some economists feel that they constitute a potentially dangerous concentration of economic power through their very size, and offer few or no advantages of increased efficiency in return. A conglomerate merger cannot directly result in enhanced economies of scale, because it has no effect on the size of actual production units, only on their ownership. Furthermore, critics of conglomerates charge, since production is so diversified, most decisions are made within the divisions of such a firm or even at the plant level. The top management of a conglomerate plays little or no role in any but the most generalized decisions. Close central office supervision of widely differing production units is all but impossible, and thus the conglomerate is for all intents and purposes managed as if it were a series of independent firms. Thus there might be little reason to expect conglomerate divisions' performance to differ from that of independent firms. Worse, there may be some reason to expect it to be less efficient.

Some conglomerates were formed in the Sixties for no better reason than ease of financing due to securities market conditions or the profits and tax advantages accruing from their formation rather than their long-term productive operations. When economic conditions changed later in the decade, firms that had grown by this route (Ling-Temco-Vought is an example) recorded very poor performances.

Other economists view conglomerates more favorably. They point out that the most tempting targets for acquisition are firms whose performance under current ownership and management is poor. An acquiring firm might expect a higher rate of return from the assets of a badly managed firm than the owners are currently obtaining. Thus the present value of such a firm is greater for prospective new owners than for current stockholders. In this scenario, the possibility of conglomerate mergers improves overall economic performance among both firms actually acquired and those forced to improve their operations to maintain their independence.

Conglomerate firms, due to their larger size, may have better access to financial markets, advertising, and other inputs. However, for firms large enough to have any effect on national markets, these considerations are unlikely to significantly affect overall efficiency. There is at least one widespread myth concerning conglomerates' operations. It is alleged that such firms, if vertically integrated, can sometimes obtain productive inputs from their own divisions "free" or "at cost" and thus gain competitive advantages against rivals forced to buy the same goods at arm's length. Such a claim is simply untrue: no firm can raise its aggregate profits by reducing those of one division to raise those of another. To be efficient, a firm must earn at least the opportunity cost of capital on *all* its assets, not just a portion of them. About the only point on which there is widespread agreement is that conglomerates are not suited to analysis by the traditional methods developed for single-product firms.

[26] Rosenberg and Birdzell, *How the West Grew Rich,* Chap. 9.

Industry Structures

Economists have traditionally assessed the presence and extent of monopoly power within an industry by the concentration ratio—the share of total industry production controlled by the four or eight largest firms. For example, the concentration ratio in the domestic auto industry in 1986 was very high. The four largest firms (General Motors, Ford, Chrysler, and American Honda) had a combined share of total output that exceeded 97 percent. The concentration ratio in the domestic auto industry was therefore over 97 percent.

Recently another, more comprehensive measure of market structure, the Herfindahl index (the sum of the squared market shares of all firms in a given industry) has been developed. But an examination of the concentration ratios within American manufacturing reveals no pronounced overall trend and few significant changes in recent years. Concentration ratios have increased in some industries (brewing is a notable example), but they have fallen in others (computers), and the overall situation appears little different from that of 1920—or even 1900. If there has been an overall trend, Table 20.2 indicates that it has been toward reduced market power. But even this view understates the degree to which competition has increased in the United States in the past few decades.

Technological change has greatly increased the extent and intensity of competition within most national markets. Today few products' only rivals are goods made by other firms in the same industry. As consumer information and discretionary income have increased, so has competition from dissimilar goods that fulfill roughly the same needs, in some cases enormously. At the turn of the century, there were no economic substitutes for steel; today many other metals, plastics, glass, carbon fiber, reinforced concrete, and even wood compete with steel.

In an era where information is one of the most valuable commodities, a great many different types of firms may offer roughly the same computer services to customers. Virtually any firm with unused mainframe computer capacity, regardless of its primary orientation, may compete for data-processing jobs. Moreover, this interindustry competition is highly resistant to anticompetitive methods. The costs, goals, and procedures of firms outside one industry may be very different from those within it and all but impossible to assess. In addition, information is almost uniquely portable: competition is often nationwide. Thus, price-fixing or market-sharing agreements are extremely difficult to form.

There is no question as to the chief beneficiaries of these developments. The essence of wealth is an extended range of alternatives: these changes have given American consumers at every level a range of choice far beyond that available even a few decades ago.

The Growth of Foreign Competition. In addition, the usual indicators of monopoly power assess only domestic producers and ignore the influence of imported goods. Merchandise imports furnish a smaller portion of total consumption in the United States than in most other nations. However, while they were only 3 percent of U.S. GNP in 1948, they had risen to 8.5% by 1985.[27] In addition, the range of products in which imported goods compete with domestic products has widened. In the 1970s the portion of the world's manufactured goods exported from their country of origin rose from 10 to 25 percent. Today, it seems obvious that the extent and intensity of competition is increasing within most if not all manufactured product markets. In addition, "Big Business" is heavily concentrated within a shrinking sector of the economy. The rapidly growing service sector, at least on a national scale (which may not be an entirely appropriate measure), is highly competitive.

[27] Council of Economic Advisors, *Economic Report of the President, 1987*, p. 360.

Table 20.2   Changes in Industry Structure

Sector	Total Net Sectoral Output (in Billions of Dollars)	Percentage of Each Sector That Was Effectively Competitive		
		1939	1958	1980
Agriculture, forestry, fisheries	$ 54.7	91.6%	85.0%	86.4%
Mining	24.5	87.1	92.2	95.8
Construction	87.6	27.9	55.9	80.2
Manufacturing	459.5	51.5	55.9	69.0
Transportation and public utilities	162.3	8.7	26.1	39.1
Wholesale and retail trade	261.8	57.8	60.5	93.4
Finance, insurance, and real estate	210.7	61.5	63.8	94.1
Services	245.3	53.9	54.3	77.9
Total	$1,512.4	52.4%	56.4%	76.7%

Share of Each Category in Total Output (in Billions of Dollars)		Percentage Shares		
		1939	1958	1980
1. Pure monopoly	$ 38.2	6.2%	3.1%	2.5%
2. Dominant firm	42.2	5.0	5.0	2.8
3. Tight oligopoly	272.1	36.4	35.6	18.0
4. Others: effectively competitive	1,157.9	52.4	56.3	76.7
Total	$1,512.4	100.0%	100.0%	100.0%

Source: W.G. Shepherd, "Causes of Increased Competition in the U.S., 1939–1980," *Review of Economics and Statistics* (November 1982). Reprinted in R. Ruffin and P. Gregory, *Principles of Microeconomics*, 2d ed. (Glenview, Ill.: Scott-Foresman & Co., 1986).

The Status of Industrial Competition in the Eighties. In summary, the recurrent fears of consumer exploitation by "Big Business"—at least in the sense of monopoly power—are now perhaps less justified than ever. Quite simply, when faced with a would-be monopolist's "pay my price or do without," consumers—or other firms—can almost always find alternative sources at little if any additional cost.

ENERGY

The provision of adequate energy supplies has profound implications for long-term economic growth. As noted in the preceding section, the ability to find and exploit a growing range of substitutes for current inputs depends on ad-equate energy supplies. While at present American energy supplies seem adequate for the foreseeable future, developments in the past dozen years allow ample scope for concern. The problem is not physical supplies, the technology to employ them, or the market's ability to produce and allocate them efficiently: it is noneconomic interference with the process.

The actual number of energy sources is far more limited than the forms in which they are employed, as Table 20.3 indicates. Fossil fuels, the sun, falling water, geothermal and nuclear energy, plus a few minor additions comprise the entire list of sources at present. Energy can be applied through a variety of transmission media, such as electricity, but first it must be generated.

Energy use and economic growth are connected, but in recent years it has become ap-

Table 20.3   U.S. Energy Consumption, Total and Per-Capita

Year	All Energy*	
	Total (in Trillions of BTUs)	Per-Capita (in Millions of BTUs)
1920	19,782	186
1930	22,288	181
1940	23,908	180
1945	31,541	236
1950	33,100**	218
1955	38,800	235
1960	43,800	243
1965	52,700	272
1970	66,400	326
1975	70,600	327
1980	76,000	334
1984	73,700	312

*Includes natural gas, coal, crude petroleum, and hydro, nuclear, and geothermal energy
**To nearest one trillion BTUs
Source: U.S. Department of Commerce, Bureau of the Census, *Statistical Abstract of the United States, 1978* (Washington, D.C.: Government Printing Office, 1978 and 1986), p. 606.

parent that the strength of the connection depends on energy price trends. During much of the postwar period, real energy prices fell, and energy consumption increased more rapidly than the rate of economic growth. After the oil price increases of 1973 and 1979, energy prices rose at one and one-half to three times the rate of inflation, and it became apparent that the relationship between energy prices and growth was far looser than had been supposed (or, after 1973, feared). The energy required to generate an additional dollar of GNP declined by about one-quarter from 1970 to 1984, and consumption by the average household fell in about the same proportion between 1979 and 1984.[28] As energy prices rose sharply and appeared likely to go on increasing, the classic market system responses appeared. Consumers learned to use substitutes (from

sweaters and insulation to shorter commutes and new architectural styles), and they reequipped with more energy-efficient cars, machines, buildings, and (over a longer period) habits.

Changing Energy Sources

In recent decades, the sources of energy in America have changed. Over the long run, the importance of coal has declined in most uses as cleaner, less-polluting, more flexible fuels such as oil and natural gas became available. Such fuels are not only more easily transported and applied, but they contain more energy per unit of bulk or weight and pose fewer waste-disposal problems. Coal has retained its importance only in electric power generation and steelmaking. Coal, oil, and natural gas provided 92.2 percent of all American energy in 1975 and still accounted for 89.7 percent of the total

[28] U.S. Department of Commerce, *Statistical Abstract, 1986,* p. 556.

in 1984.[29] The remaining 10 percent or so is provided by hydropower, nuclear, geothermal, and solar energy, and fuel wood. Despite their comparative insignificance in aggregate terms, hydropower and nuclear energy are important in the generation of electrical power.

The change from coal to petroleum and natural gas stemmed in part from their physical properties as well as their relative prices. After the mid-Fifties, however, petroleum prices were determined by government policy rather than market factors alone. The result was that the real prices of oil and natural gas fell, and consumers responded by using more of both and replacing coal-burning facilities with new equipment designed for oil or gas.

■ The U.S. found itself in a unique situation following 1973 OPEC restriction of exports, a position, ironically, largely of its own making.
Source: Lou Grant of the *Oakland Tribune*, © Los Angeles Times Syndicate.

Natural Gas

The price of natural gas in interstate commerce was set by government regulators in the Fifties. Natural gas prices were maintained at this level, which became increasingly unrealistic, through the middle Seventies. Regulation led to growing shortages in states that did not produce gas, while supplies within the producing states, which were not subject to price ceilings, were ample. Gas prices were raised in the late Seventies and price ceilings finally eliminated, but the jump in prices that deregulation initially entailed was politically traumatic. After years of blaming Arabs, OPEC, greedy oil barons, and a host of other villains for high energy prices, Congress was forced to take measures that in the short run clearly increased natural gas prices—and there was no mistaking the immediate agent behind the rise. Restructuring the equipment and habits accumulated over decades of declining real prices required years of unwelcome adjustment for consumers. It also resulted in sharp increases in profits for domestic producers—and a large increase in efforts to find and exploit domestic gas reserves.

[29] 1975 figures from U.S. Department of Commerce, *Bicentennial Statistics*, p. 631; 1984 data from U.S. Department of Commerce, *Statistical Abstract, 1986*, p. 556.

Oil

Nor was oil exempt from the influence of short-sighted policies. In an effort allegedly designed to increase domestic oil production and enhance the nation's defense capabilities, the Eisenhower administration imposed quotas on imported oil. The natural result of this decrease in competition was an increase in domestic oil prices above world levels. It became more profitable to search for and produce domestic oil than to search abroad, leading to a more rapid depletion of American reserves than might otherwise have occurred. One result was that the United States became increasingly dependent on foreign oil in the Sixties and Seventies. As it became more and more difficult to meet environmental restrictions in constructing new refineries, the United States also became increasingly dependent on foreign refining capacity.

The 1973 Energy "Crisis." When the Organization of Petroleum Exporting Countries (OPEC) restricted exports to the United States in 1973 and subsequently began a series of price increases, domestic reserves were lower than they would have been without the import quotas. To make matters worse, to combat inflation, the price of domestic oil had been controlled at far less than world prices. Nevertheless, there were rapid increases in petroleum prices—especially for gasoline, whose price almost tripled—and the Nixon, Ford, and Carter administrations all attempted to restrict the rise in oil prices. American dependence on foreign oil increased as a result of the price ceilings and limited refining capacity, and attempts to restrain imports under these conditions only worsened matters.

Incredibly, the government decreed that the "windfall profits" gained by domestic oil producers should be largely taxed away—and the tax proceeds used to subsidize imported oil. Had the program been expressly designed to increase American dependency on imported oil, it could hardly have been more effective: it reduced the profitability of domestic production while raising that of oil imports. Even worse, by holding down the prices actually paid by consumers, it reduced the incentives to conserve. The policies resulted in long lines at service stations in both the winter of 1973–1974 and spring of 1979. A series of highly unpopular nonprice rationing schemes only exacerbated general dissatisfaction. Significantly, however, when gasoline prices were first allowed to rise and then entirely decontrolled, the lines disappeared. Some price restrictions on gasoline were continued through 1979 despite evidence from natural gas markets that removing price ceilings gave consumers much greater incentives to conserve and expanded supplies because it made finding and marketing gas more profitable. Eventually, the lesson was absorbed, and in 1981 gasoline prices were decontrolled.

Conflicting Views on Energy Production

American policy on energy production, particularly after 1973, has often been confused and contradictory. Environmental regulations, such as limitations on strip-mining of coal and the incredibly complicated (and dubiously effective) licensing regulations for new power plants—particularly nuclear units—both added to energy costs and made future supplies less certain. In some cases, complying with the legal restrictions on power plant construction requires so much time that no meaningful forecasts can be made of demand for the power they will eventually produce. Perhaps the chief source of America's energy problems was a reluctance, particularly by government authorities, to admit that additional energy could not long be obtained for prices that did not cover production costs.[30] After 1981, more attention was paid to market forces, but government interference by no means disappeared.

Other aspects of energy production and use present additional difficulties. Thus far, efforts to control the air pollution caused by coal have proved expensive and not very effective, and alternatives such as in-site burning and coal gasification owe considerably more to engineers' imaginations than to economic practicality. Even oil presents serious problems of pollution in production, transportation, refining, and consumption. Moreover, with the passage of time and the development of alternatives to oil-based fuels, petroleum may one day become too valuable in its nonfuel uses, particularly in petrochemicals, to allow its continued use as fuel. Natural gas is virtually nonpolluting, and the United States apparently has huge reserves of gas in previously unknown deep deposits and dissolved in brine. Both of these sources, however, will be very costly to use and may require further technological breakthroughs to become practical. Other energy sources offer at best limited supplements to current sources. Use of refuse for fuel might ultimately be more valuable for its contribution to waste disposal than as an energy source.

---

[30] R. Hall and R. Pindyck, "The Conflicting Goals of National Energy Policy," *The Public Interest* (Spring 1977).

Wood fuels have a limited potential contribution and have already increased air pollution problems.

Conventional fuels, then, will continue to be available, but it is unlikely that their real prices will ever return to pre-1973 levels. New sources of conventional fuels, such as oil shale, apparently will be even more costly than OPEC oil at the peak of that organization's power.

Hydropower

Hydropower is clean and can be obtained from the same sources virtually forever, but there is little potential for any large-scale addition to the nation's energy resources from waterpower. Virtually all the first-rate hydropower sites in the contiguous United States have already been harnessed. Some abandoned dams could be renovated and returned to operation, but most are small and on streams with irregular seasonal flows—they were abandoned for good reason. New hydropower stations are highly capital-intensive (a lesser barrier than three years ago, as inflation and interest rates decline). But new dams tend to be ruinous to stream ecology. Hydropower, then, is like solar power: by no means a free good, at least in usable form. A few regions of the United States have potential for expanded geothermal power generation, but this is a wasting asset of uncertain duration. Harnessing wind energy appears unlikely to become competitive with less exotic forms of generation, and it suffers from localized and small-scale production potential.

Nuclear Power

Public opinion in the United States still appears strongly opposed to any significant expansion of nuclear power. This is unfortunate, because fewer risks are associated with nuclear power—even after the incident at Three-Mile Island in 1979 (which caused no deaths at the time and no measurably significant long-term increase in morbidity or mortality)—than with some widely used fossil fuels, particularly coal. Thus, our choice of power generation sources apparently implies that certain, but widely diffused, deaths are preferable to a very low probability of fewer total casualties from new causes. Whatever risks are posed by nuclear power appear amenable to reduction by currently available technology. The vitrification of atomic wastes would reduce the dangers involved in their disposal below those of current storage methods. There seems to be no reason why operating standards and equipment of nuclear power plants cannot be improved if necessary.

What does appear certain is that nuclear power will be part of the U.S. energy supply for at least the next few decades. Currently, it provides from 12 to 15 percent of all electric power in the United States: far too much to be replaced immediately by any reasonably priced alternative. Thus, the debate over nuclear power must actually be over the size of its role in energy production for the next generation, rather than whether it should play any role at all.

Alternative Sources of Energy

The use of more exotic sources of energy such as solar, fusion, or artificial fuels remains far in the future, and costs per unit are still pure conjecture. Solar power, as opposed to solar heating, appears far from practical application, and it is not yet clear that its costs will ever be competitive. Even the expanded use of western coal or oil shale would draw heavily against that region's limited water supplies.

Coal

In summary, all currently available energy sources have drawbacks, and in most cases the drawbacks increase more than in proportion to the additional energy they provide. The United States has enormous reserves of coal, perhaps enough for three to five centuries' consumption if some increase in prices is allowed. But aside from the direct effects of coal mining on the environment, the use of coal poses a serious threat to human safety. Contemporary coal use is estimated to cause from 10,000 to 20,000 deaths annually, chiefly through the effects of air pollution. This is at least the equivalent of a major nuclear disaster in an urban area every two or three years. Further, while coal's guilt as a source of acid rain is not completely proven, it would be a major surprise if further knowledge exonerates it completely. Although no source of energy is completely free of threats to health and safety, few others pose the threats involved in expanded use of coal.

The Energy Outlook

Despite these cautions, there is no reason to regard the energy situation as potentially disastrous. Energy will probably be more expensive in the future, but additional supplies will be obtainable and total supplies will grow. Hopefully, an appreciation of the role of higher energy prices on supply and demand has been gained from the debacles of the past dozen years. Increased prices induce both greater supplies and reduced demand, as do increased prices for any commodity in a market economy. Producers are stimulated to develop substitutes for current energy sources; consumers, to practice greater economy of use. Price increases also make it feasible to tap reservoirs that previously would not have been economically exploitable, such as the North Sea, Alaska, and Mexico.

Current energy policy is still affected by the period when it was torn between the need to increase producers' incentives through higher prices and the political benefits of maintaining low consumer prices—at least until the resultant shortages became too inconvenient.[31] American industry's response to higher energy prices has already been noteworthy: firms have reduced their energy consumption with no loss—or even increases—in output. As energy prices decline, industry will not discard the

equipment that produced these savings. Consumer response was slower, but once begun, reduced consumption per dollar of income to a similar extent. Most of these gains are also permanent. The adjustment led to different patterns of economic activity than in a period of cheap energy, but there is no reason why "different" and "worse" need be synonymous.

LABOR FORCE TRENDS

Perhaps the most significant developments in the American labor force in these four decades were its massive growth and changes in its composition. The civilian labor force grew from 59.4 million persons in 1947 to 117.8 million in 1986.[32] This rate of growth exceeded that of the population. Labor force growth stemmed not merely from demographic factors, such as birth and death rates and growth in those age cohorts tending to have high rates of participation, but also from changes in social customs—especially in women's working outside the home. These developments more than offset a decline in participation of adult males, most of which appeared due to increased enrollment in institutions of higher learning and to early retirement. The change in female labor force participation was more significant: by the mid-Eighties, the majority of American women could expect to work outside the home for most of their adult lives. Further, they would do so not merely before they had children or after their families had left home, but even while their children were infants.

Hours of work changed relatively little for most Americans: the average workweek fell only from 40.3 hours in 1947 to 34.8 in 1986. Even that decline appears due to the growing importance of retail trade employment, with its

[31] Ibid.

[32] Council of Economic Advisors, *Economic Report of the President, 1987*, p. 280.

■ Women began to work more outside of the home, especially in the rapidly growing service sector.
Source: Eliot Elisofon, *Life* Magazine © 1956 Time Inc.

large portion of part-time workers. Manufacturing and construction workweeks showed almost no change.[33] Hours actually worked over the year did decline as paid vacations became standard, the number of holidays increased, and sick leave became available. The Seventies saw some experiments with new workweek arrangements, such as flexible hours and three-day weekends, but there seemed to be no great preference for additional leisure. Many workers began to "moonlight" (take second jobs).

Real gross wages for private nonagricultural workers rose from $123.52 per week in 1947 to $171.07 (both in 1977 dollars) in 1986. Even so, the 1986 figure was about 10 percent less than the 1972 peak and about the same as that for 1963. In manufacturing and construction the gains were larger, but the growing weight of retail trade in all employment, especially in the Seventies and Eighties, reduced the average for all workers.[34] Median family income rose slightly from 1970 to 1985: from $27,336 to $27,735 in 1985 dollars. This figure does not indicate the slight decline in family size over that period, but 1970–1985 was not an era of rapid income gains. Male workers fully employed in year-round jobs experienced a decline: full-time year-round female workers received a slight gain over the period.[35] The gross wage figures quoted above do not include fringe benefits, which increased noticeably in the postwar period, or changes in working conditions, so they are not exact measures of well-being. They also do not include the increased government services that taxes on those wages provided, although there was increasing evidence in the late Seventies and Eighties that many people considered those services inadequate compensation for the taxes they paid.

As might be expected, aggregate wage trends masked substantial variations between industries, regions, occupations, and sectors. In manufacturing and construction, wage gains at least through the early Eighties were larger as employment in those sectors remained stable or fell as a portion of the work force, many workers were represented by strong unions, and substantial productivity gains occurred. In retail trade and services, where the supply of labor expanded rapidly in both relative and absolute terms and productivity gains were modest, wage gains failed to keep pace with the average for the entire economy.[36]

Organized Labor

Since, for the most part, employment growth was strong from 1947 to 1986, we might expect that labor unions would have also grown substantially. In addition to the favorable job climate, the political situation was in general far

[33] Ibid., p. 292.
[34] Ibid., p. 293.

[35] Ibid., p. 278.
[36] Ibid., pp. 273–277.

more sympathetic to organized labor than at any prior time save the late Thirties.

For the first portion of the era, these expectations were borne out. Labor unions had grown rapidly during World War II, and in the first postwar decade they improved on those gains. In 1956, about 30 percent of the non-agricultural work force was enrolled in unions, an all-time high for the American labor movement. After that date, however, the union movement faltered; at best, its growth failed to keep pace with that of the labor force, and in some years—particularly the Eighties—union membership declined. In 1945, labor union membership was just under 15 million. This figure increased to almost 18.5 million in 1956. Only in 1970 did union rolls list 20 million workers.[37] In 1984, the 17.3 million union members constituted slightly over 15 percent of the U.S. labor force and just under 19 percent of employed wage and salary workers.[38]

The very limited gains in union membership in part reflected the fact that the economy had changed faster than the unions. American unions are strong in manufacturing and construction, where a large majority of all production personnel, especially in large firms, are organized. But employment in these fields is now a smaller portion of the total: for practical purposes, the number of manufacturing jobs has been stable for the past two decades. Unions have been less successful in organizing most of the rapidly growing sectors of the economy, such as retail trade, government (with some exceptions), finance, and services. They have only recently begun serious efforts to organize in most of these areas, and in general they have found the task difficult.

[37] U.S. Department of Commerce, *Bicentennial Statistics*, p. 389.
[38] U.S. Department of Commerce, *Statistical Abstract*, vol. 1, p. 179.

The Decline of Union Strength

Since it is unlikely that employment in manufacturing will expand significantly (even if the sector does not decline absolutely, productivity gains will have to rise at least in proportion to output if foreign competition is to be met—and since 1982 has actually exceeded that pace), to maintain its current aggregate position, organized labor must expand into new fields. There are few remaining prospects in industry; virtually all large firms' employees had been unionized by the mid-Fifties. After this had been accomplished, the task of organizing the remaining industrial workers involved high costs per member gained, because the firms were small and often highly resistant to organization. In recent years, unions have lost most of the elections through which they sought recognition as workers' bargaining agents, and they have even been repudiated by previously organized workers in a few cases.

Union Failures. Some union efforts at new organization were misdirected. Two highly publicized attempts to unionize previously unorganized labor involved southern textile workers and farm labor in the West. The former are employed in a highly competitive industry vulnerable to foreign competition as well as competition from unorganized American firms. In such circumstances unions can achieve wage increases, if at all, only at a very high cost in reduced employment. The farm workers appear threatened by technological change. Thus, neither industry offers unions a chance to produce long-term wage gains in relation to competitive market levels.

In some cases, the lack of growth is not the result of misdirected effort, but of little or no effort. Many unions appear to have become content with the status quo and are more interested in promoting the interests of their current membership than in expanding. The growing disparity between union and non-union wages in comparable jobs, the resistance of some unions (especially old-line craft unions) to government efforts aimed at reducing race and sex discrimination in admitting new members, and various attempts to insulate themselves from nonunion competition are all classic symptoms of static monopoly power.

Unions in a More Competitive Economy. More recently, even survival has become difficult for some American unions. As noted previously, competition has been increasing in the U.S. economy, due to technological change, improvements in transportation and communication, and the growth in foreign trade. The impact of most of these changes has centered on manufacturing. Industries accustomed to passing union wage increases on to customers in the form of higher prices now encountered much more resistance.

With demand for manufactured products becoming more elastic, unions found that wage increases could now be obtained, if at all, only at the cost of reduced employment. In some cases, they were forced to accept wage reductions, as in the steel, airline, and auto industries. Collective bargaining agreements in the mid-Eighties generally provided for smaller wage increases than those obtained by unorganized workers. Sometimes union wage increases did not even match inflation. In a few cases, such as the airline pilots', unions faced with employer demands for wage or salary reductions had little choice but to accept. Members' current salaries were far above what they could earn in alternative employment. If the choice was between a cut to say one-quarter more than could be earned in the best alternative or no job at all, the choice was easy, if unwelcome.

The results of some union efforts may not even benefit all their own members. If wages are increased faster than the rate of labor productivity gains—that is, if wages rise more than real output per worker—over time the employer must either accept lower profits or pass on the higher labor costs to customers. As markets become more competitive, profit margins are likely to be small in any case, and customers highly sensitive to price increases by individual firms. Under such circumstances, the increased wages will reduce demand for union labor, thus displacing it to nonunion employment, where the increase in supply will force wage levels down. Clearly, some unions have followed exactly these policies. The United Mine Workers, both under John L. Lewis's presidency and in the past decade, are one example. The steel and auto workers are others. In the Seventies, the steelworkers gained large wage increases even in the face of declining productivity and rapidly increasing foreign competition. Only when several large steel firms faced bankruptcy was it recognized that such policies could not be continued.

The Legal Climate. The legal climate in which American labor unions operated became somewhat less favorable after the war. In the late Thirties the Norris-LaGuardia and Wagner acts had given unions wide latitude in their organizational and bargaining activities. The widespread labor unrest of the immediate postwar period resulted in the passage of the Taft-Hartley Act (1947). This amendment to the Wagner Act was an attempt to redress the problem of coercion of individual workers by the unions, both directly and through pressure on employers. Some of the assumptions embodied in the law, especially the idea that agreements negotiated with employers by union leaders might run against the desires of the membership, proved to be wrong.

Nevertheless, unions' freedom of action was restricted by the Taft-Hartley Act. The law provided for 80-day injunctions against strikes in which the president of the United States felt the national interest was involved. It forbade secondary boycotts (in which members of unions not directly involved might refuse to buy or even handle products of firms with whose labor policies they disagreed) and the closed shop (in which employers agreed to hire only union members). The act allowed individual states to pass "right-to-work" laws, which forbade even the union shop (an agreement that all workers in a firm that had recognized a union had to join it to retain their jobs). The latter provision may have had some effect on unions' ability to organize workers in the rapidly growing industries of the southern states, most of which had right-to-work laws, but the chance to earn much higher wages than those previously available was probably a greater barrier.

Evidence of serious corruption and misuse of union funds was unearthed in a few unions (notably the Teamsters). One result was the passage of the Landrum-Griffith Act in 1959. It provided tighter legal controls over union funds, mandated the secret ballot in union elections, and attempted to prevent persons with criminal records from gaining union office. In light of subsequent events, the Landrum-Griffith Act's success has been modest indeed. Despite the changing legislative climate, however, unions' current difficulties appear far more directly linked to economic developments than to changes in the labor laws.

The Future of Organized Labor

It appears that neither popular opinion nor legislation is likely to turn in unions' favor in the near future. Strikes, particularly public employee strikes that seriously inconvenience the general population, have cost the entire union movement goodwill. One example of this shift in attitudes occurred during the air traffic controllers' strike in 1981. Even other unions offered only token support to the strikers, and public opinion strongly favored the president, who fired the strikers. The continuing problems of some unions in financial management, leadership, or both, while certainly not representative of all or even most organized labor, have added to the unfavorable publicity.

Few people now regard unions as oppressed workers' only defense against employer exploitation: Big Labor is now regarded with no more esteem than Big Business. Some of this antagonism may be misdirected; strikes, although highly publicized, are relatively uncommon. In only one year since the end of World War II (1947) have work stoppages due to labor disputes cost the American economy as much as 1 percent of total working hours. But the unions' situation may be revealed by the fact that a growing portion of all strikes now originate in wage and working condition demands, rather than new organizational efforts.[39]

In summary, most American labor unions now appear to be solidly middle-class organizations far more concerned with their current members' welfare than with improving the lot of the working class (however that may be defined in America) or society as a whole. Unions have strongly supported minimum-wage laws (even though their members receive wages far above those mandated) and restrictions on imports. Such actions support the conclusion that union members' gains have come at the expense of consumers and unorganized workers, not employers. Still, unions have been instrumental in the growth of fringe benefits—the pension, insurance, medical care, and vacation provisions—which have become so prominent a portion of most labor compensation.

Postwar Labor History

The structure of the American labor movement changed over the 1945–1984 period. The American Federation of Labor's membership had approximately equalled that of the Congress of Industrial Organizations in 1939. By the early Fifties, the AF of L was about twice as large as the CIO. In part, the growth of the AF of L was due to changes in the affiliation

---

[39] U.S. Department of Commerce, *Historical Statistics,* vol. 1, p. 179.

■ George Meany (left) and Walter Reuther (right) celebrate the 1955 Merger of the AFL–CIO.
Source: AFL-CIO.

AFL-CIO has lost about 300,000 members as gains in government employees, teachers, and service workers have not offset losses in steel and auto workers, machinists, and other old-line union groups.[41]

Two of the claims most frequently made for organized labor in America are not borne out by the facts. First, the union movement does not speak for all American labor: almost six of every seven workers are not organized. Second, despite the spectacular successes gained by some unions in collective bargaining, unions are not the primary source of high wages in the American economy. Wage levels in both unionized and nonunionized industries appear more closely related to productivity than to the degree of organization. As the economy becomes still more competitively structured, this trend is likely to continue.

of some member unions. The United Mine Workers, under their mercurial president John L. Lewis, left the CIO, briefly rejoined the AF of L, and then became an independent union. Other unions were expelled from CIO ranks in the late Forties and early Fifties for communist affiliations.

In 1955 the two major organizations merged, becoming the present AFL-CIO. Even after this time, however, organized labor had difficulty maintaining a solid front. The United Auto Workers disaffiliated from the AFL-CIO in 1968 in a dispute over political policy, and the Teamsters were expelled in the mid-Sixties because of corrupt leadership. Despite the merger, AFL-CIO membership in the Sixties remained between 15 and 16 million. The membership gains of that decade were recorded by independent unions, especially the Teamsters, whose membership swelled from 3 to nearly 5 million.[40] In the last decade, the

BANKING AND FINANCE

Two trends dominated postwar developments in American financial institutions and markets. One was the culmination of developments that began over a century before. As communications became essentially instantaneous, financial markets became far more integrated and lending rates became uniform across the country. Second, the financial sector was strongly influenced by what for a time appeared to be permanent inflation. As the rate of price increase has declined recently, some of the changes made at that time have proved troublesome for financial institutions and their customers alike, as have changing conditions in energy markets.

The responses to accelerating inflation became apparent in the mid-Sixties and grew more obvious as prices, and even more, expectations

---

[40] Ibid., pp. 176–177.

[41] U.S. Department of Commerce, *Statistical Abstract, 1986,* p. 426.

of future prices continued to rise in the Seventies. Savers, borrowers, and the institutions that served them began to respond to what appeared a permanent problem. They became more sophisticated in anticipating price changes and evaluating nominal interest rates. New types of financial assets were developed to meet the changed conditions.

An additional development grew out of the energy crisis. Large amounts of money were deposited in American banks by some of the OPEC nations. In a period when interest rates had been driven to record levels by inflation, the banks had to find ways to employ the funds deposited with them. When inflation declined in the Eighties, it was clear that they had not always done so with prudence.

Commercial banks and other financial institutions adjusted their asset portfolios continuously over the era. Initially, they exchanged the large volumes of government securities that they had accumulated during the Great Depression and World War II for private securities and loans with higher rates of return. Later they adjusted their portfolios in response to changing conditions and prices in financial markets. Unlike during the Great Depression, the risks of lending to private borrowers declined in the postwar prosperity. In the last decade, however, it became apparent that some loans, particularly those to foreign governments, energy producers, and agriculture, were far shakier than they had initially appeared. So too were real estate loans in regions where mainstay industries were in difficulty. In recent years, banks have also been increasing credit card and leasing operations.

Commercial Banks

The assets of commercial banks expanded enormously in the 1945–1980 period, but the number of banks declined. After 1980, the number of commercial banks in the United States stabilized or increased slightly. Banks were affected by new technology: data processing and improved communication, aided by computers, greatly increased individual banks' ability to handle a growing and more varied amount of business. For most of the period, both state and local regulations made it difficult—and if existing banks were opposed, often impossible—to found new banks. Needless to say, such rules had the enthusiastic support of most existing banks. These barriers to entry were relaxed after 1980.

If the number of banks declined, the number of banking offices rose as branch banking expanded. Increasing numbers of states allowed banks to operate more than one office within their own borders or in a wider local area. In 1955, only 12 percent of all commercial banks had branch offices, but by 1970, nearly one-third of all banks had at least one branch.[42] From 1970 to 1984, the number of bank branches doubled.[43] Even so, the establishment of branches in some states remained illegal, and some U.S. banks expanded their operations overseas instead.

Although the absolute size of banks expanded, concentration ratios did not, at least through 1970. The largest American banks controlled a smaller portion of total bank assets in 1970 than in 1940, and their share was not expanding.[44] Since that time foreign banking activity within the United States has substantially expanded as well. The development of truly national or even international markets, at least for large loans, has increased competition within the American banking system. Structurally, the banking system may show only slight changes, but these mask important competitive developments within financial markets.

---

[42] U.S. Department of Commerce, *Historical Statistics*, vol. 2, pp. 1036–1037.
[43] U.S. Department of Commerce, *Statistical Abstract, 1986*, p. 492.
[44] R. Robertson, *History of the American Economy*, 3d ed., (New York: Harcourt Brace Jovanovich, Inc., 1973), p. 496.

Bank Failure Rates

One positive legacy of the New Deal era, if not the New Deal itself, has been a much lower rate of bank failures. As of 1970, fewer than ten commercial banks had failed in any single postwar year—a far cry from the first third of the century, when from fifty to several hundred failures or suspensions occurred even in normal years.[45] More effective regulation and better training for bankers, as well as a generally buoyant economy, deserve most of the credit. But the Federal Deposit Insurance Corporation virtually ended runs on banks rumored to be in financial difficulty, a process that often resulted in precisely the development banks' depositors sought to avoid. In the Eighties, however, this record has been marred. Bank failures have increased to as many as 80 per year. While most of the failing banks were small rural institutions, often heavily involved in local agriculture, several large banks have failed as well—most notably Continental Illinois National Bank in 1983. Changing prospects for energy-related loans and for repayment of loans to foreign governments, especially those in Latin America and Eastern Europe, caused sharp deteriorations in the stability of several large U.S. banks. In most cases involving banks insured through the FDIC, that agency arranged for banks' reorganization or absorption by larger institutions.

Thus far, another aspect of postwar banking has been a very low rate of loss to depositors in bank failures. Well over 90 percent of the funds placed with failed banks had been recovered and returned to depositors as of 1970.[46] Deposit insurance has been gradually expanded; individual deposits are now protected up to $100,000. Most bank failures have occurred in small banks, but the difficulties of large New York and California banks—potentially involving billions of dollars—indicate that the U.S. banking system is not yet collapse-proof. The possible losses in such cases might exceed the FDIC's capacity, although the federal government would no doubt provide support should such a situation occur. Even so, widespread bank failures are no longer an inevitable—and early—feature of any economic downturn.

Other Financial Institutions

Assets of commercial banks totalled more than two trillion dollars by 1984, but as the data in Table 20.4 indicate, those of other financial institutions grew at a faster pace for much of the period. Still, they rivalled commercial bank assets only in aggregate.

This rapid growth of nonbank financial institutions, including pension funds, had several implications. The increased assets controlled by savings-oriented institutions reflected the priorities of an aging and affluent population concerned with retirement. Because of both legal restrictions and their own inclinations, institutions serving such needs place a high premium on the security of the funds deposited with them. The channelling of a growing portion of aggregate savings through risk-averse institutions may have reduced the supply of long-term investment funds available to new (and thus risky) investment prospects. These firms' responses to inflation further reinforced this attitude. The rising interest in venture-capital markets in recent times has gone far to offset such developments, however. Such markets deal almost entirely in investments in projects unable to attract funds from more conventional lending sources.

The response to inflation also changed the roles played by various financial institutions. Some savings institutions devised new forms of deposits that were far more liquid than any previously offered, increasing their role as money substitutes. Certificates of deposit, money-market funds, "NOW accounts," and

---

[45] U.S. Department of Commerce, *Historical Statistics*, vol. 2, pp. 1038–1039.
[46] Ibid., p. 1039.

Table 20.4 Assets of Major U.S. Financial Institutions, 1945–1984 (in Millions of Current Dollars)

Date	Commercial Banks	Savings and Loan Associations	Mutual Savings Banks	Life Insurance Companies	Other Insurance Companies
1945	$ 146,245	$ 8,847	$ 16,962	$ 44,907	$ 7,851
1950	156,914	16,893	22,446	64,020	13,476
1955	199,244	37,656	31,346	90,432	20,305
1960	234,274	71,476	40,571	119,576	30,132
1965	356,110	129,580	58,232	158,884	41,843
1970	534,932	176,183	78,995	207,254	58,594
1975	1,095,400*	388,200	121,100	289,300	94,100
1980	1,855,700	629,800	171,500	479,300	197,700
1984	2,147,700	902,400	206,400	723,000	249,100

*To nearest $100,000,000
Sources: For 1945–1970 data, U.S. Department of Commerce, Bureau of the Census, *Historical Statistics of the United States: Colonial Times to 1970*, 2 vols. (Washington, D.C.: Government Printing Office, 1975), 2:968–1061. For 1975–1984 data, U.S. Department of Commerce, Bureau of the Census, *Statistical Abstract of the United States, 1986* (Washington, D.C.: Government Printing Office, 1986), pp. 494–512.

other forms of deposit, as well as bank credit cards, all tended to increase the volume of transactions that could be supported by a given money supply as conventionally defined. This development complicated aggregative monetary policy; it became difficult to even define the supply of money or its velocity.

As in many other areas, the influence of government regulation was not entirely positive. Interest rate ceilings had been imposed on some but not all savings institutions in an effort to generate rents for firms that could now pay their depositors far less than the rate earned on their funds. As inflation changed the prevailing structure of interest rates but not the legal ceilings, such laws provoked massive shifts of funds. Laws providing for higher interest rates on some types of large deposits produced similar effects. The consequences for institutions that could no longer attract funds at legal rates (savings and loan associations were a primary example) could be serious: rapid withdrawals of small deposits, soaring mortgage rates, and various types of credit rationing even at the unprecedented interest rates that

resulted. Limits in the rates paid on small deposits had another unwanted effect: they discouraged saving by low- and middle-income groups. The resulting increase in consumption at the expense of investment worsened inflationary pressures. Those who saved anyhow were punished by rates of return that fell short of inflation, while the institutions in which they deposited their funds reaped windfall profits.

THE UNITED STATES IN THE WORLD ECONOMY

The economic relations of the United States with the rest of the world in the postwar period may be divided into two distinct episodes. In the first, the rest of the world was unable to generate sufficient claims on the United States, at least through normal methods, to finance the desired level of imports from this country. The United States was a large-scale international creditor, it had a massive surplus of exports over imports, and the international value of the dollar was high. Foreign countries seeking to repair the widespread devastation of World War II needed huge amounts of U.S. goods—everything from food and consumer goods to tide their populations over through recovery to the capital goods needed to accomplish this feat. Yet at the same time, the war's physical damage and disruption of normal trade patterns had impaired their ability to produce and export sufficient goods or services to finance the imports they required.

The worldwide "dollar shortage" was met, in part, by large-scale U.S. foreign aid programs. Initially aid was extended on a country-by-country basis. After 1948, aid to Europe was coordinated under the Marshall Plan. The Marshall Plan was an unprecedented peacetime step for the U.S. government. At least in Western Europe and Japan, it was highly successful. In these countries, even though factories, transportation systems, and other productive resources had been destroyed, the human knowledge and talent behind them remained, as did most of the institutions through which they were applied. Indeed, by sweeping away many of the old monopolistic and social restrictions on output expansion, the war had a favorable effect on institutions (which of course did not totally offset its cataclysmic impact on human and physical capital).[47] When aid was provided to people who knew how to use it and had formulated effective recovery plans, the results were spectacular.

Both in this period and afterwards, restrictions on world trade were reduced, and the world economy began to struggle back toward the relatively free exchange and specialization that had prevailed before World War I. Institutions such as the World Bank were established to aid recovery and further economic development. The financial institutions of the world were revised, and after the Bretton

Woods Conference in 1946, the U.S. dollar increasingly began to supplement gold as an international reserve currency. The dollar was "as good as gold": it could readily be converted into gold at a constant rate of $35 per ounce. In the immediate postwar years, the United States held the bulk of the world's gold reserves, which were further protected by its massive trade surpluses. There was no doubt that it could accommodate any request to exchange dollars for gold.

Changes in the U.S. Trade Balance

In the mid-Fifties, however, this situation began to change. The industrial nations of Europe, plus Japan, recovered from the war. But they achieved much more than this: their economic growth, rather than slowing down, accelerated. As these economies grew, modernized, and diversified, they became less dependent on American exports. Their own exports increased, and they began to compete with the United States in third-party markets and then within America itself. The United States maintained an export surplus until the early Seventies, but it declined as other developments placed more and more dollars in the hands of foreigners.

Foreign aid programs were continued, although their focus shifted from Europe to the underdeveloped areas of the world. In these regions, aid was far less successful in promoting initial economic development than it had been in fostering recovery. In addition, the United States spent large sums on overseas military bases, on supporting its allies' armed forces, and on the wars in Korea (1950–1953) and Vietnam (1963–1974). As Europe recovered and began its economic integration under the Common Market after 1958, many American firms began to invest overseas, lured by the prospect of a large market where incomes were

[47] Olson, *TGhe Growth and Decline of Nations.*

growing more rapidly than in the United States. Further, European demand for some long-time American specialties such as consumer durables was very high. Canada, a traditional recipient of American foreign investment, continued to attract massive flows of American dollars. Prosperity in the United States meant growing demand for both foreign services, such as shipping and tourism support, and imported goods.

As a result, foreign countries began to receive more dollars than needed to finance imports from the United States. At first, the excess over trade requirements was used to bolster foreign-exchange reserves, but this demand was soon satisfied. Foreigners then began to convert dollars into gold or required special incentives, such as high interest rates on dollar-denominated deposits or securities, to continue holding U.S. funds. The "dollar shortage" had become a "dollar glut." Although increased earnings on American foreign investments added to American claims on other nations, they did not offset the effects of additional overseas investment, foreign aid, military spending, and a declining export surplus. The usual process of adjustment would have been a revaluation of the dollar against gold and foreign currencies, but the United States was reluctant to take this step. Many nations held their international reserves in dollars rather than gold, and a U.S. devaluation would impose severe deflationary pressure on them.

In the early Seventies, the American export surplus vanished, and foreigners became unwilling either to hold more dollars individually or to allow their central banks to do so. In 1971, the United States devalued the dollar (the official dollar price of gold was increased). This reduced the amount of foreign currency that could be obtained for a dollar. It made foreign goods more expensive in the United States and reduced the price of American exports in foreign currency. In 1973, a further devaluation occurred, after which the dollar was allowed to "float" (its value in terms of foreign currencies was determined by supply and demand, with some intervention by central banks).

America's Trade Deficit

The predicted effects of these measures, which should have reduced the American trade deficit, were only beginning to be felt in 1973. In the fall of that year, the Organization of Petroleum Exporting Countries (OPEC) began a series of sharp oil price increases. With domestic oil production declining and inept policy responses doing little to reduce demand, the rapidly rising bill for imported oil swamped all other developments through the Seventies. Since that time, the United States has continued to incur massive trade deficits. In 1985, this country became an international debtor; it is now the world's largest.

Developments in international trade were heavily influenced by inflation. The Seventies and early Eighties were a period of worldwide inflation, but the rates of price increase were not uniform among nations. Since inflation rates were lower in the United States than in many other nations, foreigners began to build up deposits in American banks and to buy American securities. The possibility of government instability or restrictions on private economic activity in many countries further increased the flow of funds to the United States. American interest rates adjusted to inflation both more rapidly and more completely than those of many other nations: real returns on funds in America were high, while in many other countries they were negligible or even negative.

Some OPEC nations accumulated massive trade surpluses that they literally could not spend as fast as they accrued. These too tended to flow to American banks. The result was an increase in the international value of the dollar and a further widening of the trade deficit. The financial developments' impact was heightened by deteriorating American productivity gains, particularly in relation to those of major trading partners such as Japan and West Germany. Later the same factors produced growing deficits in direct trade with rapidly growing nations of the Western Pacific. In the mid-Eighties, these factors began to ease; the international value of the dollar declined, and (probably more significantly) productivity growth in U.S. manufacturing substantially improved. Even so, as of early 1987, the trade deficit was only slightly reduced.

The Nature and Direction of Foreign Trade

Early American foreign trade had been largely an exchange of American raw materials and agricultural products for European manufactures and tropical products such as sugar and coffee. American shipping earnings supplemented the incomes gained from exports, and Europeans invested in the United States. Gradually, the American trade position changed. Agricultural exports continued but were supplemented and then surpassed by shipments of manufactured goods to foreign customers as American industrial productivity achieved world primacy. The United States first began to pay off its international debts, and then, in the early twentieth century, to invest overseas.

In the 1945–1984 period, some of these trends were again reversed. Manufactured goods accounted for only two-fifths of American imports in 1947; by 1984, they comprised 68 percent of the total. Manufactured goods were almost 65 percent of all American exports in 1984; they had comprised about three-fourths in the earlier period.[48]

These changes mask still more violent short-term fluctuations, particularly in the Seventies. By 1975, U.S. manufactured imports had slumped to only 53 percent of the total: the current-dollar value of crude material and fuel imports increased fourteenfold between 1970

and 1980, to 38 percent of the total at the latter date. Since 1981, the value of such imports has declined; they comprised 22 percent of all imports in 1984, and their share of the total continues to fall.[49] The composition of exports showed more stability: manufactured goods continued to hold about a two-thirds share through 1984. Agricultural products, however, were 12 percent of all exports in 1970, 15.8 percent in 1975, 14 per cent in 1980, and 12.9 percent in 1984.[50] In 1986, the United States even became a net importer of agricultural goods for a brief period.

New Trading Partners

The identity of major U.S. trading partners remained about the same through 1970, but more recently there have been some shifts. As Table 20.5 indicates, about three-fifths of American foreign trade in both exports and imports is with the developed regions of the world. The proportion of our trade with these areas decreased during the oil shortage: 71 percent of American exports went to the world's developed nations in 1970, and 74 percent of all imports originated there. In 1975, the figures were 60 and 58 percent, respectively. They have since recovered to approximately 62 percent each and may be expected to rise as oil prices fall.

Three quarters of the change in imports and half that in exports during the Seventies was due to changing relations with OPEC nations.[51] Thus, with the exception of oil, whose influence can be expected to decline, it does not appear that the United States is dependent on the underdeveloped nations for either export markets or imports to any great extent. Because of their higher incomes and productivity, the developed nations of the world continue to be each others' best customers, even

[48] Council of Economic Advisors, *1985 Economic Report of the President*, p. 348.

[49] Ibid.
[50] Ibid.
[51] Council of Economic Advisors, *1977 Economic Report of the President*, pp. 298–299.

Table 20.5 Origins and Destinations of U.S. Foreign Trade

Area of Origin or Destination	1950	1960	1970	1975	1984
	Imports				
Canada	23%	20%	28%	23%	20%
Other Western Hemisphere	35	27	15	12	18
Europe	16	29	28	22	23
Japan*	2	8	15	12	18
All Asia	19	19	24	28	37
Africa	6	4	2	8	8
	Exports				
Canada	21%	18%	21%	20%	21%
Other Western Hemisphere	28	19	15	16	14
Europe	30	36	34	28	29
Japan*	4	7	11	9	11
All Asia	16	21	23	27	30
Africa	4	4	4	3	4

*Figures for Japan are included in those for all Asia. Totals will not add to 100 percent because of exclusion of minor items.
Sources: Council of Economic Advisors, *Economic Reports of the President, 1977, 1985* (Washington, D.C.: Government Printing Office, 1977 and 1985) and U.S. Department of Commerce, Bureau of the Census, *Historical Statistics of the United States: Colonial Times to 1970*, 2 vols. (Washington, D.C.: Government Printing Office, 1975), 2:903.

for raw materials.[52] Rapid growth of the nations on the western rim of the Pacific (Singapore, Taiwan, Hong Kong, and South Korea), as well as the continued expansion and diversification of Japan, has increased the importance of that region in U.S. trade, while slower-growing regions have lost ground.

The aggregate importance of foreign trade to the U.S. economy has increased sharply in the past two decades. Imports, which had been about 4 percent of American GNP over most of the postwar period, rose to 6 percent in 1975 and 8.8 percent in 1984. For exports, which had slightly exceeded the relative importance of imports in the early years, the figures rose to 7.1 percent in 1975 but declined to slightly less than 6 percent in 1984, indicating the size of America's trade deficit.[53] The aggregate impact of foreign trade thus increased from about 8 or 9 percent of GNP over most of the postwar period to almost 15 percent in the Eighties. While this is a far smaller percentage of aggregate economic activity than in most developed economies, it leaves little doubt that the U.S. economy is no longer operating in isolation.

Foreign Investment

The private overseas investments of the United States were only $14.7 billion in 1945. By 1970 they had risen to $120.2 billion, and by 1984

[52] E. Fried, "International Trade in Raw Materials: Myths and Realities," *Science*, February 20, 1976.

[53] Council of Economic Advisors, *1986 Economic Report of the President*, p. 348.

to $795.1 billion. At the latter date, foreign assets in the United States were $884.1 billion. Again, with the exception of petroleum, most American foreign investment has been and continues to be in developed countries. Profit-seeking investment will be placed where markets are large and property secure, not where incomes are low and governments both unstable and hostile. About 60 percent of American foreign investments were in Canada and Western Europe in 1970. At that time, about 16 percent was in Latin America and 24 percent in all other areas, some of which, like Australia, were also developed countries.[54] Latin America's share of U.S. investment has increased in recent years, chiefly in Brazil, Mexico, and Argentina.

One result of the massive outflow of dollars in the later postwar period was increased foreign investment in the United States. Although this caused some popular resentment and concern, it was an inevitable outcome of this country's continuing difficulties achieving a balance in its international accounts by other means. As long as the United States continued to make more dollars available to foreigners than they wished to spend for American products or hold in various short-term accounts, foreigners could be expected to use their dollars in their own best interests. By 1985, the total foreign investment in this country exceeded U.S. investment abroad.

While many of the changes in the U.S. international economic relations were due to developments in international monetary affairs, others reflected changes in real factors or political pressures. Western Europe and Japan had increased productivity considerably more than the United States and consequently grew much more rapidly. The Pacific "Gang of Four" (Singapore, Hong Kong, Taiwan, and South Korea) made even greater gains after the mid-Seven-

ties. In these countries, production techniques caught up to or in some cases surpassed those of the United States, resulting in increasing competition for American goods in domestic as well as international markets. Some foreign investment in this country was spurred by fears of increased American trade barriers.

None of this implies that the United States is or should consider itself unable to compete with foreign producers. Rather, it indicates that maintaining American exports requires a constant increase in American productivity and also a constantly changing mix of economic activities. The United States must generate new items for export that make use of its productive and innovative advantages, because competition in virtually all long-established products can only be expected to increase. Indeed, one measure of the success of a modern economy is now the rate at which jobs in long-established industries are eliminated and replaced by work in new sectors: high "job death" rates imply even higher "job birth" rates.[55] Nor should foreign investment be restricted; if foreigners want to provide American workers with new and better tools, they should be encouraged to do so, particularly since domestic savings rates are low.

American industries that have maintained their technological leads, such as computers, chemicals, and aircraft, have had little trouble maintaining or even expanding their export markets. Others have had considerable success in responding to foreign competition through the introduction of new methods. The automobile industry's position seems ambivalent: having made considerable strides in improving both productivity and product quality under the shield of "voluntary" import quotas on Japanese cars,[56] American producers appear unwilling to return to normal terms of competition. Industries that have failed to

[54] U.S. Department of Commerce, *Historical Statistics* vol. 2, pp. 870–871.

[55] Rosenberg and Birdzell, *How the West Grew Rich,* p. 278.
[56] The only agreement which the Japanese made under less "voluntary" circumstances was signed on the deck of the USS *Missouri* in August 1945.

match or exceed the technological gains made abroad, such as shoes and textiles, have lost both foreign and domestic markets to imports.

Prospects for World Trade

World trade appears likely to increase if left to economic factors. The postwar trends in reduced transport costs appear likely to continue, and there is at least a possibility that political barriers to trade will continue to decline. Protectionist sentiment has not yet prevailed in the United States; some of its recent beneficiaries have obviously profited at the expense of American consumers, while doing little or nothing to restore their long-term competitive ability.

If world trade continues to increase, the degree of specialization possible for each member of the world community—and the total incomes of the world's population—will rise. Despite the protests of those industries and workers displaced by foreign competition, there is little doubt that the increase in foreign trade has benefited the United States. It has increased competition and the range of choices open to U.S. consumers in many markets. It has given new opportunities to America's most efficient producers and forced others to change their operating methods. Like all economic changes, this has required adjustments—sometimes sizable ones for certain individuals. But if the adjustments are made along the lines indicated by comparative advantage, they will increase the incomes of American producers—and certainly American consumers. Given the traditional sources of its economic growth, the United States should have little to fear from a process that places a premium on the ability to change.

SELECTED REFERENCES

Council of Economic Advisors. *Economic Report of the President.* Washington, D.C.: Government Printing Office, annual editions.

Davis, L., et al. *American Economic Growth: An Economist's History of the United States.* New York: Harper and Row, 1972.

Feldstein, M., ed. *The American Economy in Transition.* Chicago: University of Chicago Press, 1980.

Gordon, R. *Economic Instability and Growth: The American Record.* New York: Norton, 1975.

Olson, M. *The Rise and Decline of Nations: Economic Growth, Stagflation, and Social Rigidities.* New Haven, Conn.: Yale University Press, 1982.

Rosenberg, N., and L. Birdzell. *How the West Grew Rich: The Economic Transformation of the Industrial World.* New York: Basic Books, 1986.

U.S. Department of Commerce, Bureau of the Census. *Bicentennial Statistics.* Washington, D.C.: Government Printing Office, 1976.

———. *Historical Statistics of the United States: Colonial Times to 1970.* 2 vols. Washington, D.C.: Government Printing Office, 1975.

———. *Statistical Abstract of the United States, 1986.* Washington, D.C.: Government Printing Office, 1986.

CHAPTER

21

GOVERNMENT IN THE POSTWAR ECONOMY

*T*he role of government has expanded greatly in the postwar U.S. economy, through increases in both government's aggregate size and the range of functions it performs. Even more, government influence on private economic actions has increased. This growth of the public sector has been controversial: both its nature and extent have been questioned. Currently, however, there appears to be little consensus on the focus of the critique. Some people question the aggregate dimensions of government; others point to its effects on specific sectors of the economy. Still others note its adverse impact on their own actions.[1] However, growing skepticism is evident whenever the claim is made that government action per se invariably produces gains in overall welfare. In fact, there is evidence that on occasion it fails to do so—even in the areas it directly addresses.

THE DIMENSIONS OF GOVERNMENT

The knowledge that government has expanded is commonplace, but some of the details of its growth are not well recognized. Table 21.1 indicates that since 1929 government employment and spending have expanded faster than GNP and the labor force and thus account for growing portions of both. This trend began well before the postwar period, as detailed in Chapter 18. What may be surprising is the degree to which both expenditures and employment growth have centered in state and local rather

---

[1] A thoughtful discussion of the results of government interaction with economic activity can be found in N. Rosenberg and L. Birdzell, *How the West Grew Rich: The Economic Transformation of the Industrial World* (New York: Basic Books, 1986). See especially Chaps. 9 and 10.

Table 21.1 Government's Economic
Impact, 1929–1986

Date	GNP (in Billions of Dollars)	Federal Expenditures (in Billions of Dollars)	State and Local Government Expenditures (in Billions of Dollars)	Total Government Spending/ GNP*	Federal Civilian Employment (in Thousands)	State and Local Government Employment (in Thousands)
1929	$ 103.4	$ 3.1	$ 7.8	10.5%	533	2,532
1945	211.2	92.7	9.0	48.2	2,808	3,137
1948	261.6	29.8	17.6	17.4	1,863	3,787
1950	288.3	42.6	22.5	21.8	1,928	4,098
1955	405.9	68.4	32.9	24.2	2,187	4,727
1960	515.3	92.2	49.9	26.3	2,270	6,083
1965	705.1	118.2	75.5	25.9	2,378	7,696
1970	1,015.5	195.6	134.0	30.1	2,731	9,823
1975	1,598.4	332.3	235.2	32.1	2,748	11,937
1980	2,732.0	590.9	363.2	31.7	2,866	13,375
1985	3,998.1	946.3	515.8	34.1	2,875	13,540
1986	4,208.5	989.8	557.9	34.3	2,899	13,839

*Net of federal grants to state and local governments
Source: Council of Economic Advisors, *Economic Reports of the President, 1977, 1985, 1987* (Washington, D.C.: Government Printing Office, 1977, 1985, 1987).

than federal government. Federal spending rose in relation to other government spending during the Great Depression. In the wartime period, it skyrocketed. After 1945 federal outlays decreased, but not to prewar levels. Since 1955, however, state and local government spending (aided by federal grants, especially after 1970) has increased about 9 percent faster than federal expenditures.[2] Federal employment has declined as a portion of the civilian labor force and risen only about 27 percent in absolute terms since 1955. Over the same period, however, the ranks of state and local government employees have almost tripled, and they had more than regained their 1980 peak by 1986.

[2] Council of Economic Advisors, *Economic Report of the President, 1986* (Washington, D.C.: Government Printing Office, 1986), pp. 320–321.

In 1984, about one U.S. worker in seven was a government employee.[3]

The figures just quoted should be viewed in context. Two factors modify their aggregate impact. First, in recent years the federal government, and to some extent all others, has increasingly used independent consultants and other experts on a temporary basis. These persons are not included in government employment data. Second, neither government expenditures nor employment figures indicate the growing influence of government on private economic activity. While the figures show that the aggregate dimensions of government are now much larger than in 1929 and have expanded considerably from the low postwar point in the late Forties, they understate the actual expansion.

[3] Ibid., pp. 266, 275.

■ Suburban developments in the 1950s generated demand for additional government services.
Source: Photo Trends.

Causes of Government Expansion

The causes of this expansion are political, social, demographic, and perhaps even historical. After the Second World War, the United States accepted its world power status. This decision entailed large expenditures on American armed forces, aid to those of our allies, and foreign aid. However, the government devoted even larger sums to domestic purposes.

The bulk of the additional state and local government spending financed education, streets and highways, and welfare programs. Growth in state and local government outlays reflected population increases, enhanced interest in education—particularly higher education, the growth of the suburbs, increasing attention to the needs of the less fortunate as average income levels rose, and a general tendency for demand for government services to increase at least in proportion to, and generally faster than, increases in income and wealth. Changing social standards also raised government spending. The larger portion of the population housed in single-family dwellings, often in entirely new communities, raised the demand for social overhead capital of all kinds—roads, utilities, sewers, police and fire protection, and the like. Increased parental aspirations for their children, as well as the greater numbers of children during the "baby boom," raised demands for education. More automobiles and the higher average annual mileage per auto produced demands for additional roads.

The Role of Military Spending

As Table 21.2 indicates, the growth in federal spending, at least since 1955, was not due entirely—or even largely—to increased military spending. Despite the enormous costs of some new weapons systems, the higher military wages needed to attract an all-volunteer force after 1973, and the waste inherent in military procurement, military spending has not risen more rapidly than direct government expenditures on individuals—an area generally linked to efforts to redistribute income and to improve social welfare.

Even when a broad definition of military spending incorporating all the expenses of the State Department, the National Aeronautics and Space Administration, and all support for scientific research is contrasted with a narrow definition of social spending that excludes the areas of most rapid growth, the figures fail to support the contention that military spending has come at the expense of the needy. Individual recipients of government transfer payments now receive almost twice the portion of total output they obtained 30 years ago; the military's portion has increased about 10 percent. Even the peak years of the Vietnam War only slightly interrupted these trends. In 1987, defense spending per se (the narrow definition) is less than 7 percent of GNP, with the massive increases instituted by the Reagan administration essentially complete. The stability or decline of military spending as a portion of GNP, then, does not explain the relative growth of federal spending. Of course, it also has no relation to state and local government expenditures, which have risen even faster.

Table 21.2 Military Spending and Transfers to Individuals, 1950–1986 (in Billions of Current Dollars)

| | | | Transfers to Individuals | | |
| | | | | | Combined as |
Date	Defense Spending*	Percent of GNP	Federal	State	Percent of GNP
1950	$ 17.9	6.2%	$ 10.8	$ 3.6	5.0%
1955	40.4	10.0	12.4	4.0	4.0
1960	49.4	9.6	21.6	5.9	5.3
1965	59.0	8.4	30.3	8.8	5.5
1970	87.3	8.6	55.3**	20.1	7.4
1975	96.5	6.0	131.9	38.9	10.7
1980	152.5	5.6	235.4	65.7	11.0
1985	277.5	6.9	360.8	99.2	11.5
1986	296.6	7.1	380.4	106.7	11.6

*Includes all expenditures for space, science, technology, and international affairs
**Transfer payments to U.S. citizens only
Source: Council of Economic Advisors, *Economic Reports of the President, 1985, 1987* (Washington, D.C.: Government Printing Office, 1985, 1987).

The Role of Public Programs

In recent years, the portion of GNP allocated to government transfers (payments that do not involve performance of services or sale of goods in return for public funds) to individuals has not risen, nor has it fallen significantly. However, spending on transfer programs has been reallocated within that sector, with the social security program gaining at the expense of others.

As American incomes increased in the postwar period, a growing portion was devoted to public programs. In some cases, this reflected changed living patterns. As a larger portion of the population chose an urban life-style, the externalities of city life rose at least as fast. Higher aspirations for children meant more schooling. The ability to analyze and in some cases compensate for unwelcome influences on human existence increased, resulting in greater government activity. Air and water pollution regulations would be examples, as would a growing range of regulations designed to improve safety. Concern with the quality of life gained near-equal status with the acquisition of more goods and services. In all these areas, there was at least some reason to believe government was better suited to respond than the private sector.[4]

New departments were established within the federal government: Health, Education, and Welfare (Education became a separate department in 1977); Housing and Urban Development; Transportation; and Energy. In addition, new agencies were established for environmental and consumer protection, occupational health and safety, and equal employment opportunity. The other levels of government were equally active in these areas, and a noticeable expansion of government activity in traditional areas occurred as well.

Most or all of these areas had been the scene of at least some previous governmental activity, but the new involvement went far beyond its scope and depth, particularly at the federal level. In the late Seventies and early

---

[4] T. Borcherding, ed., *Budgets and Bureaucrats: The Sources of Government Growth* (Durham, N.C.: Duke University Press, 1977).

■ The government provided additional roads to accommodate growing numbers of automobiles.
Source: Bob W. Smith, EPA-Documeria, courtesy of U.S. Environmental Protection Agency.

Eighties, it was recognized that this expansion of governmental activity had economic dimensions, regardless of its primary focus. New programs, regulations, and institutions employed scarce resources and affected the manner in which those they regulated could be used. Once they recognized that programs had costs, policymakers began to evaluate their results in relation to those costs and to scrutinize the costs to determine whether the same results could be obtained at a lower sacrifice in alternatives foregone.

Costs and Benefits of Government Intervention

In some cases, programs had clearly been undertaken with little attention to either current or long-term costs, or secondary and tertiary effects of institutional changes had been ig-

nored. The government's provision of Medicare and Medicaid (1966) is an example. Both programs, however worthy, proved vastly more expensive than their proponents had anticipated. They should have known that when the cost to the individual of additional medical care is suddenly reduced to nearly zero, particularly in cases where those receiving care were deemed unable to afford sufficient amounts from their own resources, the amount demanded will considerably increase. The programs' costs were further increased by payment procedures that offered almost no resistance to price increases by those actually providing medical services.

In other cases, government programs work at cross-purposes. The Department of Agriculture sponsors research intended to increase crop output per acre and publicizes any useful results among farmers. It also imposes acreage restrictions on crops when farmers apply this knowledge too successfully. Government subsidizes both tobacco production and medical research aimed at discovering a cure for lung cancer. The list could be almost indefinitely expanded.

Some of the new goals pursued through public action are extremely difficult to define clearly. The quality of life, in particular, appears to be a highly subjective concept. Programs to enhance it are subject to widely varying interpretations by a variety of pressure groups. In consequence, some programs probably cannot satisfy the very persons or groups that suported them because their goals are so different.

The Political Economy of Activist Government

In some cases, government appeared to be increasingly sensitive to short-run considerations, such as the state of the economy on the eve of the next election, almost regardless of the long-term consequences. For example, government might be more concerned with the state of the economy on the eve of the next election than with the inflation or resource misallocation it causes. Such programs, of course, are generally designed to oppose changes induced by economic pressures. As such, they reduce long-term economic growth. To some economists, the business cyle in the postwar United States appeared to be influenced ever more heavily by political considerations.[5]

Moreover, unlike private economic activity, government programs do not disappear when the need for them ends. The losses incurred by a private firm that produces goods, such as slide rules or buttonhooks, for which demand no longer exists will force it out of business. But no such forces affect government programs, particularly those that are a small portion of total public sector activity. Agencies whose task has been completed seldom die: they may even grow.

Any economic decision involves weighing costs against benefits. If either one or the other is absent, the decision becomes trivial; if not, both must be specified as fully and accurately as possible. Overall welfare is enhanced only if the total benefits of an action exceed its costs, and aggregate welfare is maximized only when benefits of all actions exceed costs and are greater than those attainable through alternative measures. Action through the government often allows proponents of some measure to forget or evade these simple analytical rules. Too often, policies have been determined by assessing only one side of the cost-benefit equation, examining only a portion of the relevant considerations, or ignoring inconvenient objections to preconceived decisions.

It is increasingly clear that government policies that transfer income or other benefits from large numbers of donors (taxpayers) to a much smaller number of recipients are attractive to politicians. So are programs that deny large aggregate benefits to the general public to save a small group a lesser, but concentrated, burden. Donors or recipients faced with small individual gains or losses are unlikely to respond politically, but the small group bearing a more concentrated impact will respond in a manner favorable to the politician who protects its interests. For example, a program that levied a $10 annual tax on 200,000,000 citizens to fund a $1,000 payment to each of 2,000,000 citizens might well be passed in a democracy. The $10 tax might be too small to provoke much opposition, but the prospects of an individual gain of $1,000 would cause prospective beneficiaries (especially if they were already identified) to lobby enthusiastically in favor of the program. Even disinterested legislators who wished only to reflect "the will of all the people" would hear largely from proponents of the measure. Such situations give pressure groups, whose mem-

[5] E. Tufte, *Political Control of the Economy* (Princeton, N.J.: Princeton University Press, 1978), Chaps. 1, 2.

bers would gain or lose disproportionately from legislation, political clout far greater than their numbers. They also give such groups an incentive to organize and increase their effectiveness.

Incumbent legislators are also likely to favor measures that produce immediately favorable effects, regardless of their long-term consequences. This is especially true if elections are scheduled at a time when the favorable effects (tax cuts, spending increases, or jobs "saved" by government assistance) are evident, and the long-term costs (inflation, taxes, or resource misallocation) are not yet manifest. Such circumstances promote rent-seeking behavior, as well as defensive efforts by prospective victims. Since both use scarce resources to determine the distribution of existing output rather than producing more, they reduce potential well-being.

Such considerations are particularly relevant to government aid to "sick industries." The sectors requesting aid are generally sizable. They find it easier to petition the government for help than to reduce costs or increase markets, and they invariably represent older technologies. Aid to such industries can only come at the expense of more efficient, newer sectors. Such measures hinder the long-term resource reallocation that is the key to economic growth. It can well be argued that government in the United States is not indifferent to the wishes of the citizenry: rather, it is far too responsive, particularly to small but passionate groups.[6]

---

[6] See M. Olson, *The Logic of Collective Action* (New Haven, Conn.: Yale University Press, 1983) and *The Rise and Decline of Nations: Economic Growth, Stagflation, and Social Rigidities* (New Haven, Conn.: Yale University Press, 1982); D. North, *Structure and Change in Economic History* (New York: Norton, 1981); N. Rosenberg and L. Birdzell, *How the West Grew Rich: The Economic Transformation of the Industrial World* (New York: Basic Books, 1986); and T. Anderson and P. Hill, *The Birth of a Transfer Society* (Stanford, Calif.: Hoover Institution Press, 1980).

THE ELUSIVE GOAL OF MACROECONOMIC STABILITY

As noted in Chapter 18, the federal government did not succeed in regaining full employment during the Thirties. As the war drew to a close, both concerns about postwar macroeconomic conditions and confidence in the government's ability to influence them increased. As a result, Congress passed the Employment Act of 1946. This legislation committed the nation to the pursuit of "maximum employment, production, and purchasing power." Aside from establishing the Council of Economic Advisors and requiring the president to submit an annual economic report to Congress, the Employment Act did not specify how these goals were to be achieved.

The overall economic performance of the United States in the four postwar decades was far better than in the Thirties. No postwar recession even remotely approached the magnitude of the Great Depression. Economic growth averaged 3.5 percent annually between 1946 and 1970, better than in the Twenties and more than triple the rate of the 1929–1940 period.[7] Even the much-maligned Seventies saw real economic growth of about 3 percent, and in the Eighties U.S. growth rates have been only slightly less than those of other developed countries.[8]

In most years, economic growth was rapid enough to accommodate both the increases in the labor force and the rise in productivity, so that unemployment did not increase. This trend

---

[7] U.S. Department of Commerce, Bureau of the Census, *Historical Statistics of the United States: Colonial Times to 1970*, 2 vols. (Washington, D.C.: Government Printing Office, 1975), 1:226–227.

[8] Council of Economic Advisors, *Economic Report of the President, 1987*, p. 368.

faltered somewhat toward the end of the period, but under circumstances that made the unemployment rate an increasingly dubious indicator of aggregate economic performance. Even in the worst postwar years, the unemployment rate never exceeded 10 percent for a full year, although it did so for some months in 1982 and 1983.[9] On two of the usual macroeconomic criteria, then, the economy's performance was good. On the third, however,—and, as indicated in Chapter 20, in the field of international trade—the record was far less favorable.

The Problem of
Postwar Inflation

Price stability became an increasingly elusive quarry for most of the period. Even the return to low levels of inflation in the Eighties was achieved at such cost that its long-term continuation may be in doubt. It was also clear by that time that at least one of the measures traditionally proposed as a means of controlling inflation (contractionary fiscal policy) was of little practical value. It was not that fiscal policy, properly applied, was ineffective. Rather, there was no political will to take the proper measures to combat inflation, such as reducing government spending and increasing taxes, and even less to do so before the problem had already exerted harmful effects.

Unlike after other wars, prices did not decline after 1945. Instead, severe inflation occurred: the consumer price index rose by about one-third over the 1945–1948 period, and wholesale prices rose over 50 percent.[10] The source of the inflation was clear. Most Americans possessed purchasing power that they had either lacked or been unable to use from 1930 to 1945. During the Depression, incomes had been so low and uncertain as to prohibit buying anything not required for immediate consumption. During World War II, many goods were unobtainable, rationed, or of very low quality, and many workers had little spare time to shop or enjoy new goods. Only after 1945 did consumers enjoy both the ability to buy and the markets to meet their demand. The abrupt lifting of price controls in 1946 and consumers' fading fears of another Great Depression also fed the inflationary pressures of the late Forties.

Monetary policy from 1945 to 1951 was highly expansionary and only slightly offset by federal budget surpluses. High demand for investment goods and American exports further increased the pressures on the economy. This inflation ended with the 1949 recession, but developments at that time set the pattern for the rest of the postwar era. Even in the slump, prices did not decline significantly; they merely ceased to rise or increased at a slower pace.

At the onset of the Korean War, another sharp burst of inflation occurred, no doubt fueled by memories of World War II shortages. After 1952, however, inflation subsided. Consumer prices in 1964 were only 17 percent higher than a dozen years before.[11] Many economists regard rates of inflation this low as no more than a reflection of increases in product quality. At any rate, inflation over this period was very slight. But in the second half of the Sixties, this pleasant interlude ended. Price stability vanished and would not be restored until the mid-Eighties.

From 1967 through 1969, prices rose about 5 percent a year. In the Seventies, inflation became far more severe. Prices rose 11 percent in 1974, and from 1979 through 1982 the consumer price index rose 39.4 percent.[12] Inflation was then reduced to the 2 to 4 percent

---

[9] Ibid., p. 267.

[10] Council of Economic Advisors, *Economic Report of the President, 1977* (Washington, D.C.: Government Printing Office, 1977), pp. 241, 247.

[11] Ibid., p. 241.

[12] Ibid., p. 291.

range and finally to less than 2 percent in 1986, but only at the cost of the most severe recession in the postwar era. Even worse, by the standards of the earlier postwar period, the inflation of the Seventies was accompanied by disturbingly high rates of unemployment and by erratic economic growth. In prior decades, inflation had been linked to very low unemployment rates (4 percent or less) and rapid economic growth. In the latter period, the inflation-unemployment trade-off, if one still existed, became far less favorable.

Government's Contribution to Economic Instability

How much did the government's macroeconomic policies contribute to this record? If the question is directed toward deliberate countercyclical fiscal policies, the answer appears to be "not much," at least before the mid-Sixties. Little use was made of countercyclical fiscal policy during this period, and it was misused as often as not (government spending was expanded to counteract the 1958 recession only in 1959, after recovery was already under way—a case of too much and too late). Most of the changes in tax or spending programs prior to 1964 reflected the need to finance existing programs or those unrelated to stabilization policy or the launching of programs valued for their direct effects rather than their macroeconomic impact. Nor were stabilization efforts effectively coordinated.

The federal government ran sizable surpluses during the immediate postwar period—proper policy in a time of obvious demand-pull inflation. At the same time, however, the Treasury offset its own fiscal policy through its influence on monetary policy.

The Treasury–Federal Reserve Accord

World War II had generated a massive increase in the national debt. To keep interest charges on its outstanding bonds as low as possible, the Treasury held the Federal Reserve System to its wartime promise to purchase at face value all government bonds that could not be placed with other buyers. Although the volume of federal debt did not increase in this period, some bonds were replaced by new issues as they matured, and private bondholders became eager to sell their government securities. The "accord" with the Fed kept the Treasury's interest costs down, but one result was that the central bank could take no effective measures to combat increases in the money supply at a time when the economy obviously suffered from excess purchasing power.[13] American citizens were taxed through inflation rather than by paying taxes to offset higher interest rates on government debt, but the impact on aggregate real incomes was much the same.

Since nominal interest rates on government securities were low (and real rates negative), commercial banks and other financial institutions were inclined to exchange them for higher-yielding private loans and securities. Had they been free to vary, government bond prices would have fallen to reflect their yields, and the prospect of capital losses on bond sales might have inhibited some banks from selling their U.S. securities. As it was, nothing prevented the sale of bond portfolios to the Fed. For commercial banks, such sales increased the excess reserves upon which they could extend additional loans and thus expand the money supply. Commercial banks could not only sell the large amounts of bonds they had purchased during the war but were willing to buy bonds from private individuals and firms, since resale to the Fed was free of risk.

Under these circumstances, the Fed could not use open-market sales to reduce the money supply: there were no buyers for low-interest government bonds at par. Thus, the Fed lost its most important instrument for regulating

---

[13] R. Gordon, *Economic Instability and Growth: The American Record* (New York: Norton, 1975), p. 107.

the money supply. Nor could it employ the others. Reserve rate requirements had been increased to their legal maximum by 1948.[14] Given the banks' easy access to the huge volume of bonds still available in the private economy, rediscount policy could not be used to influence them either. In 1951 the Fed was finally released from the "accord" and used its freedom to allow bond prices to fall and interest rates to rise. By 1953 the Fed had regained effective control of the U.S. money supply.[15]

Fiscal Policy

In the Fifties, monetary growth was slow and fiscal policy became increasingly contractionary. The Revenue Act of 1954 established steeply progressive income tax rates, which reached a maximum of over 85 percent on taxable income of $1 million or more. As the general level of income grew and federal spending failed to keep pace, the unchanged tax rates began to generate a large-scale "fiscal drag." The federal government's tax program generated an increasing surplus at aggregate income levels well below those needed to achieve full employment. Thus, not only did the tax structure hinder the pursuit of full employment, its burden became greater the closer the approach to full employment. If incomes continued to rise, the surplus would grow even greater: the government would withdraw even more from the economy without replacing it through expenditures.

Recessions occurred in 1958 and 1961; recovery from both was sluggish and failed to bring unemployment rates back down to earlier levels. The failure to regain full prosperity gave the Democratic party an issue on which to wage the 1960 election. Aggregate rates of economic growth were low, giving rise to concerns on the

international as well as the domestic scene. The Soviet economy was growing rapidly at this time, and it was widely feared that such growth might either sway the uncommitted nations of the world or promote Soviet expansion.

Nevertheless, the macroeconomic record of this period is not completely dismal. Although countercyclical fiscal policies were little used or misused, the dimensions of government in the economy furnished some stabilizing effects during downturns. The government was now a large source of expenditures that did not decline in recessions, thus reducing the extent to which aggregate economic activity might fall. In addition, spending through these so-called "built-in stabilizers" such as the progressive income tax and some government spending programs (particularly welfare, unemployment compensation, and farm price supports) actually tended to rise in slumps, even though their aggregate impact was not sufficient to eliminate recessions.[16]

The Brief Triumph of the "New Economics"

When the new Kennedy administration assumed office in 1961, it attempted to stimulate the economy. It increased federal spending and tried to increase private investment through such measures as the investment tax credit and accelerated depreciation schedules. Although these programs did induce some expansion, the results were disappointing to an administration pledged to achieve rapid economic growth. Consequently, a massive reduction in personal and corporate tax rates was proposed in 1962. This measure was explicitly designed to increase economic growth and reduce unemployment. It represented the first clear-cut use of countercyclical fiscal policy by any American government. The tax cut program was finally passed by Congress in 1964, after President

---

[14] Ibid.
[15] Ibid., p. 118.

[16] Ibid., pp. 124, 131.

Kennedy's death—a pace that should have caused the more ardent advocates of fiscal policy some serious reflection.

At about the same time, monetary policy became more stimulative as well. Although economists disagree over which of the two causes had the greater effect,[17] there is no doubt of their combined effects. The rate of economic growth increased, and unemployment, which had been 6.7 percent in 1961 and had not fallen below 5 percent since 1958, declined to 3.8 percent of the labor force in 1966.[18] The first real effort at countercyclical fiscal policy was a decided success because these accomplishments were associated with only a slight increase in inflation. Many economists hoped to achieve further gains through "fine tuning" the economy—using specific tax and spending programs to reduce the remaining pockets of high unemployment.

Political Economy Faces Reality—and Flinches

Both Congress and subsequent administrations appear to have absorbed only half the lessons of the 1964 tax cut. Expansionary fiscal measures, such as tax cuts and increased government spending, are politically popular. Monetary expansion, although not the responsibility of Congress, lowers interest rates—at least temporarily—and makes credit more available. Both might be expected to boost the popularity of political incumbents.

If the problem is excess demand rather than unemployment, however, the remedies are less palatable. Tax increases, reduced government spending, and monetary stringency may be effective, but they are no more welcome than any other bitter pill and have several characteristics that make them a politician's nightmare. They are unpopular in themselves, but even more, they require time to become effective. Thus, if instituted to ward off inflation, they reduce incomes before rising prices become obvious; if they are withheld until the problem is evident to the electorate, for a time both income reductions and inflation will exist side by side. Their impact is uneven, and those who bear its brunt, such as the residential construction industry, are unlikely to be forgiving at the next election. Finally, they represent the rectification of past errors, and Congress is no more willing to have its past sins exposed than any other body.

When the need for such policies arose, they proved far more difficult for Congress to pass than expansionary measures—and Congress required two years to decide the distribution of tax-cut benefits after 1962. In 1965, the unemployment rate was low, and there was every indication that the U.S. economy was operating at or very close to its physical capacity. Federal spending was slated to increase through President Johnson's "Great Society" program of social expenditures. American military involvement in Vietnam had just begun, and its eventual costs were as yet unclear. In the end, the bills for both domestic and foreign activity proved far greater than anticipated. In part, the cause was unduly optimistic military and economic forecasts. A greater share of the blame, however, must be laid to a reluctance to admit that the costs were so badly underestimated that the tax cuts of a few years ago now had to be at least partially rescinded.

In any event, no tax increase was enacted until 1968. By that time, inflation had already become well established. The form of the tax increase seemed better designed to reduce political damage than to combat inflation. The new taxes were to be temporary. As such, they were presented as a surcharge rather than integrated into the permanent tax structure. Not surprisingly, they were largely ineffective. Most taxpayers maintained their previous levels of

[17] M. Friedman and W. Heller, *Monetary versus Fiscal Policy: A Dialogue* (New York: Norton, 1969).
[18] U.S. Department of Commerce, *Historical Statistics*, vol. 1, p. 135.

consumption and paid the tax by reducing their savings.[19] Thus, long-run economic growth potential was reduced because the pool of loanable funds diminished. Monetary policy had become restrictive in 1966, but only temporarily. This policy was too limited in impact and duration to stem the pressures for inflation.

Fiscal Policies of the Nixon Administration

The incoming Nixon administration had opposed the surcharge in the election campaign, but found it necessary to retain the increased tax for a year after 1969 and then to reduce this surtax in increments rather than simply abolishing it. The Federal Reserve also began a sharp reduction in the rate of monetary growth. The result was an end to the long era of continuous expansion that had begun in 1962—the longest recession-free period in American history to that date. The contractionary policies that brought on the recession of 1970 would probably have halted inflation had they been continued (by mid-1971 the rate of inflation had declined noticeably), but another consequence was increased unemployment. Worse still, at least from a political point of view, was the timing of these developments: unemployment worsened before the rate of inflation moderated, and joblessness did not decline during the summer of 1971.

A combination of 6 percent unemployment and 5 percent inflation seemed a poor base from which to launch a reelection campaign. Accordingly, in August 1971 President Nixon announced his "New Economic Policy." The dollar was devalued and the Japanese and West Germans were pressed to raise the exchange rates of their currencies. A 10 percent tariff surcharge was imposed on merchandise imported into the United States. The intent was to rectify a growing balance-of-payments problem. Inflation in the United States, massive

overseas spending by the government, and sharp increases in competition from foreign producers had resulted in a large outflow of dollars. Foreigners had become unwilling to use such funds to purchase American goods or to hold them in short-term deposits in U.S. banks, and foreign central banks were unwilling to accumulate further dollar balances. It was hoped that the new measures would raise American exports and reduce imports.

Wage and Price Controls

The most noteworthy aspects of the "New Economic Policy," however, affected the domestic economy. A freeze on all wages and prices was announced, effective immediately. This was the first time wage and price controls had ever been employed during peacetime in the United States. Phase One of the freeze was to be followed by a second phase when price increases would be allowed within the limits imposed by the new Council on Wage and Price Stability. Although the price controls received widespread popular and political support, they proved largely ineffective. In the varied economy of the United States, it proved all but impossible to determine the proper base prices for many items. Wage controls proved difficult to enforce against either mobile individuals or strong labor unions.

In cases where controls could be enforced, they soon began to produce distortions in the structure of relative prices. At best, a price freeze in a market economy allows only price declines as a reallocative mechanism, and price declines are most unlikely to occur under the circumstances that prompt such controls. Nor are price decreases likely to be very effective reallocative devices if underlying inflationary pressures remain strong, as they did in this case.

Employers and workers quickly responded in ways that reduced the impact of the controls. Some goods that normally would have been sold in the United States were exported. Others were simply not produced. Employees who appeared

---

[19] Gordon, *Economic Instability and Growth,* pp. 166–169.

"Your Majesty, according to our study the shoe was lost for want of a nail, the horse was lost for want of a shoe, and the rider was lost for want of a horse, but the *kingdom* was lost because of overregulation."

Source: Drawing by Dana Fradon; © 1980 The New Yorker Magazine, Inc.

likely to quit unless they received wage increases above those sanctioned by the Pay Board (a group of experts assigned the task of determining non-inflationary wage changes) received "promotions" that consisted of higher salaries for the same work under different titles. Businesses changed the names of products or introduced "new" items for which no previous pricing standards existed. These developments made the actual impact of price and wage controls highly uneven and unfair. They also allowed price increases to continue.

Moreover, even though the totally unexpected controls had some impact on inflation when introduced, they were an attempt to cure inflation by treating its symptoms while other government policies exacerbated its causes.[20] Monetary and fiscal policy both became stimulative in 1970, and even more strongly so in 1971. The federal government's 1971 deficit was $20.5 billion, by far the largest ever compiled to that time, and the money supply grew at an annual rate of 10 percent, far in excess of any sustainable rate of real expansion.[21]

Most price controls were dropped in mid-1973, with the portentous exception of those on oil and gas (see Chapter 20). Since the factors that actually produced inflation had, if anything, been strengthened while the price controls were in force, inflation increased after the controls were lifted. By mid-1974, however, the current rate of inflation (nearly 12 percent) was recognized as more than a deferred reaction to the period of controls. Prices had not risen at this rate since the 1946–1948 period. In addition, unemployment rates were climbing toward a postwar high, which they attained in the following year. (The unemployment rate became even higher in 1982–1983.) Unemployment has fallen below 6 percent in only one year since this period—it was 5.8 percent in 1979.[22] Inflation was not brought down to reasonable levels until 1983.

Seventies "Stagflation" and Growing Deficits

During 1970–1979, both monetary and fiscal policy appear to have been overly stimulative. Under any reasonable concept of full employment given the current composition of the labor force, the federal budget showed a large full-employment deficit, and the rate of increase in the money supply, while erratic (in itself a cause for concern to many economists) has averaged out to considerably more than the long-run increase in physical capacity. Even though a variety of changes in the real economy have made stabilization policy more difficult in recent years, it seems fair to conclude that fiscal policy in general contributed to U.S. macroeconomic problems throughout this period, rather than to their solution. For the most part, monetary policy has achieved a better record, although it too has been anything but a consistent force for economic growth and stability.

---

[20] E. Feige and D. Pearce, "The Wage-Price Control Experiment—Did It Work?" *Challenge* (July–August 1973).
[21] Gordon, *Economic Instability and Growth*, pp. 175–178.

[22] Council of Economic Advisors, *Economic Report of the President, 1986*, p. 266.

The macroeconomic situation of the Seventies and early Eighties has been termed "stagflation": a combination of rising prices, slow economic growth, and uncomfortably high levels of unemployment. In the United States, this situation was accompanied by growing federal deficits. The expenditures of the national government grew much faster than its revenues.

The Fed Takes Charge

In 1979, however, President Carter appointed a new Chairman of the Federal Reserve, Paul Volcker. Under his leadership, the central bank began a determined anti-inflation policy. The rate of growth in the money supply was cut or even halted; interest rates increased to unprecedented levels (for a time in 1980, the rate offered banks' most creditworthy customers was over 21 percent);[23] and credit was rationed even at these high rates. Unemployment rose: the recession of 1981–82 was the worst in the postwar period. But inflation declined from 12 to less than 2 percent, and its corrosive influence on economic activity disappeared. High rates of inflation—especially when incorporated into interest rates and borrowers' expectations—make short-term projects more appealing than long-term investments, provide incentives to buy existing assets rather than produce new ones, and encourage consumption at the expense of investment. The Fed received little help from fiscal policy in its endeavors: federal budget deficits remained at (then) record levels throughout the period.

Tax Cuts and Spending Promises

In 1981 a new administration took office. President Reagan and his advisors were convinced that it was necessary to reduce the impact of government on the economy. They planned to cut taxes to raise economic incentives, reduce government spending both for ideological rea-

■ The range and impact of regulation increased far beyond previous levels in the seventies.
Source: Reprinted by permission: Tribune Media Services.

sons and to increase private production, and reduce the regulatory activities of government. At the same time, they planned to increase defense spending even more than the Carter administration had intended after 1980. They expected that the private economy, when freed of excessive government restraints, would respond to these incentives and the rate of economic growth would increase, possibly enough to generate higher tax revenues from lower rates on a greatly expanded tax base.

A large-scale tax cut was enacted in the summer of 1981: the original intent was to reduce personal income taxes by 10 percent for three successive years. The program was reduced to a 25 percent total cut, and in 1982 some additional taxes were imposed, although not on incomes. Far less progress was achieved in cutting domestic expenditures by government. Their rate of increase relative to GNP was reduced or stopped, but as Tables 21.1 and 21.2 indicate, their relative impact did not decline. With a few exceptions, mostly continuations of programs begun under the Carter administration, little was accomplished toward reduction of the burden of regulation.

Economic growth increased sharply in 1982 and reached 6.5 percent in 1983, but since that

[23] Ibid., p. 310.

time growth has been disappointing—less than 3 percent annually. Because the economy has failed to expand as hoped, the Reagan tax cuts have generated huge federal deficits (up to $200 billion after 1983). These have proved sustainable without a catastrophic decline in domestic investment or a resumption of inflationary increases in the money supply largely because of a massive inflow of foreign investment. To date, the goal of simultaneous low unemployment, economic growth at or above historic long-term (3 percent) levels, and stable prices remains unmet.

■ This cartoon demonstrates one view of recent monetary policy.
Source: Reprinted by permission: Tribune Media Services.

Can Stabilization Policy Succeed?

Since the late Forties, economists have developed several views on the most effective methods to pursue macroeconomic policy. No group's boundaries are sharply defined, but at least three schools of thought may be distinguished.

The Intellectual Heirs of John Maynard Keynes

The first group employs ideas developed by John Maynard Keynes and his followers. It regards changes in government tax and spending programs (fiscal policy) as the most effective stabilization tool. Members of this school advocate tax cuts and spending increases (raising the full-employment deficit) as appropriate counters to recessions. Their remedies for inflation are measures that reduce aggregate demand, such as tax increases and reductions in government spending. Many but not all of this group tend to regard market economies as inherently unstable, with a tendency to operate at less than full-employment levels. Monetary policy is a secondary tool in this group's view; it can be used to encourage investment by reducing the cost of capital.

The Monetarists

Another school of thought, the monetarists, regards fiscal policy as having little effect in itself. To them, the primary influence on macroeconomic conditions is the size of the money supply and particularly its rate of change. In this view, if the money supply fails to grow as rapidly as real capacity, the short-run result will be a recession and unemployment. The long-term (perhaps the *very* long-term) outcome will be deflation and a return to full employment. If monetary growth exceeds that of real capacity, the short-term consequence will be inflation and, particularly if the inflation continues, little or no reduction in unemployment as people learn to anticipate price increases. Most monetarists regard the economy as inherently stable, with strong tendencies toward market clearance in all sectors, including labor markets. An intellectual offshoot of monetarism is the rational expectations school, which holds that the economy quickly incorporates all useful information into its expectations of future events and acts logically in pursuit of its goals under the new circumstances. This group, too, views economic stability as the norm, probably to an even greater extent than most monetarists.

The Supply-Siders

At the time of the 1980 presidential election, yet another set of ideas received wide publicity: the supply-side view. Supply-side economists view efforts to achieve full employment and rapid growth by managing monetary aggregates or aggregate demand as inherently flawed. To them, the proper policy is to encourage increases in real output through increased incentives to producers (the term in this context emphatically includes employees). They would achieve this goal by reducing taxes, which would allow producers to keep more of the income they generate, and by relaxing most government regulation of private economic activity. Implicit in their ideas (and sometimes explicit as well) is the acceptance of wide ranges of income inequality. Supply-side economists do not advocate halting all government domestic activity, but they wish to reduce its role to very little more than preserving property rights, settling disputes, and preserving order.

None of these schools of thought is happy with recent stabilization policy. Monetarists believe that the long-term growth rate of the money supply has been excessive, and short-term fluctuations in the rate have been needlessly disruptive. They feel that the Fed's concentration on interest rates (save for a brief hiatus in the early Eighties) rather than on growth of the monetary aggregates has been a primary cause of the poor performance of recent years. They also view federal deficits as competing for loanable funds that might otherwise go to productive investment.

Advocates of fiscal policy would point to problems of timing and magnitude in the implementation of their suggested remedies. Most clearly, there is a lag between perception of the need for fiscal remedies and their implementation. Supply-side economists argue that tax cuts have been insufficient to provide the incentives required for increased economic growth; they are particularly critical of the 1982 tax increases, which they feel blunted much of the potential impact of the 1981 income tax cut. Both they and the monetarists see little progress in reducing the regulatory drag on the economy.

Does an Effective Macroeconomic Policy Exist?

Fiscal Policy. A reasonably dispassionate analysis of all three schools indicates that each has serious shortcomings, at least in practical application. Fiscal policy is at best a one-sided response to macroeconomic problems. Since it is conducted through the political process, it is nearly impossible to employ for anti-inflation programs. Further, changes in spending programs are subject to a "ratchet effect": once a program is instituted, it quickly generates a constituency determined to preserve it, regardless of its purpose or current conditions. In practice, no tax changes are made for their macroeconomic impact alone; indeed, they are one of the most fertile grounds for rent seeking of all government activity. Consequently, tax changes are unlikely to be instituted quickly and all but certain to reflect concerns other than their impact on the aggregate economy. This, of course, applies to both fiscal policy and supply-side programs.

Monetarism Monetarism also has its practical flaws. It is true that monetary policy conducted by the central bank is, at least under normal conditions, relatively free of political influences. However, it is also true that recent institutional developments (wider ranges of money substitutes, such as certificates of deposit, credit cards, money-market funds, and the host of savings programs more or less open to checking), have made merely defining the money supply more difficult than when the monetarists' basic views were developed. Monetarism has other practical difficulties: velocity—the link between the money supply and real economic activity—has recently become less stable, undermining confidence in the real effects of money supply changes. Monetarism provides a program for avoiding the catastrophic errors of the Thirties, but even monetarists admit that the lag between the institution of monetary policy and its impact is long and unpredictable. As yet, there is little empirical support for the rational expectations model in any other than financial assets markets.

Supply-Side Economics. Supply-side economics has as yet offered little more than a series of truisms. It is obvious that a zero tax rate would yield no revenue, regardless of the tax base, and almost equally clear that total confiscation of all proceeds from economic activity (a 100 percent tax on all income) would yield no more, because the tax base would disappear. It follows that some tax rate between the two extremes will yield the maximum total revenue from any given economy. Beyond this, however, the supply-siders have yet to indicate what this optimum rate is, develop any clear indication of whether current tax rates in the United States exceed, equal, or fall short of this level, or indeed explain why a tax rate that yields maximum revenues is necessarily the proper goal. The conditions that some supply-siders have required for a "fair" test of their theories' validity, such as a return to the gold standard, seem designed more to ensure that no such test can occur than to provide a test of their ideas.

Stabilization Policy in a Changing Economy

Failures of the Indicators. A final problem for stabilization policy is that changes within the real sectors of the American economy may require a reassessment of the traditional numerical indicators of success or failure. Figures on industrial capacity and its rate of use—and hence on whether further economic stimulation will produce increased real output or merely inflation—obviously need revision. Currently, they include a good many obsolete facilities that would not be employed under any conceivable peacetime conditions.

The Labor Force. More significantly, the composition of the labor force has changed, and this, as well as macroeconomic conditions, influences unemployment rates.[24] The growing portion of female full-time workers has raised the average level of unemployment rates: such workers have higher unemployment rates than full-time male employees, though not above the overall average. Other changes in the labor force have considerably greater impact. The increased proportion of young workers, minority groups, and those seeking only part-time employment has raised the portion of the labor force subject to above-average jobless rates under any conditions. It has been proposed that the unemployment rate among full-time workers who are also heads of families might be a better indicator of labor market conditions, or that overall unemployment rates be adjusted to incorporate changes in labor force composition. Certainly there are indications that the impact of 7 percent unemployment today equals that of much lower rates—perhaps less than 5 percent—in the Sixties or earlier.

Institutional Change. Institutional changes have also contributed significantly to the changes in observed unemployment rates. For example, in 1972 those receiving public assistance under the Aid to Dependent Children and food stamp programs were required to register with the unemployment agencies. They were thus added to the unemployment rolls, although most were probably unemployable at wages above the legal minimum.[25] More generous rates of un-

[24] R. Easterlin, "What Will 1984 Be Like? Socioeconomic Implications of Recent Trends in Age Structure," *Demography* (November 1978).
[25] K. Clarkson and R. Meiners, "Government Statistics as a Guide to Economic Policy: Food Stamps and the Spurious Increase in Unemployment Rates," *Policy Review* (Summer 1977).

employment compensation and welfare payments, as well as their nontaxability, combine to reduce the income disadvantages of unemployment. They encourage the unemployed to search for work until they locate a job that suits them, rather than to accept the first available offer of paid employment. This phenomenom is particularly obvious in Western Europe: nations with especially generous unemployment programs have high levels of unemployment regardless of the number of job vacancies. Minimum wage laws deter both the employment of unskilled workers and their acquisition of training, prolonging the period in which they are subject to above-average unemployment.[26]

Employment Growth. The recent increase in unemployment rates does not stem from the American economy's inability to generate additional jobs. In the 1965–1985 period, the number of persons employed in the United States increased from 71 million to 109.6 million.[27] Over the same period, however, the labor force grew even more rapidly. Yet if unemployment is concentrated among new labor force entrants and those seeking only part-time work, its implications are different than if the same rates prevailed among full-time workers who were the sole support of their families. If, for example, full-time college students look for part-time work in order to attend more rock concerts than their parents are willing to finance, the increased unemployment rates they generate hardly indicate any great rise in hardship.

A growing number of economists now believe that these demographic and institutional factors, rather than stabilization policies, are the major long-term determinants of unemployment.[28] If there is a trade-off between unemployment and inflation, they think it is a purely short-term phenomenon that depends largely on mistaken impressions about the course of future inflation. If they are correct, the long-term unemployment rate can be reduced only by changes in the characteristics of the labor force, such as their skills, information, mobility, and attitudes, and the institutions that employ it. Only time can alter demographic conditions, but the United States is now at the end of the period of rapid labor force growth.[29]

Prospects for Stabilization Policy: Have We Learned Anything?

Some lessons about inflation and its control have been learned. Increases in the price of any individual good, for example energy in the Seventies, do not constitute inflation, except as they push the index of all prices up. Changes in the prices of individual goods represent the normal operation of the market system rather than inflation. While some goods' price increases were a scapegoat for inflation, an analysis of their relation to price indices indicates that they were not the only source of price increases. This holds even in the case of oil in the Seventies. Further, it is probably much easier to prevent inflation than to cure it. Once inflationary expectations become widely accepted, they tend to become self-fulfilling. The reduced savings rates and the shift from long- to short-term investment that result from this change in attitudes impose real costs on the economy and require more stringent monetary or fiscal contraction to overcome.

In summary, since the late Seventies economists have more and better information about the macroeconomic aspects of the economy than ever before. They also have a great deal

---

[26] M. Feldstein, "The Economics of the New Unemployment," *The Public Interest* (Fall 1973).

[27] Council of Economic Advisors, *Economic Report of the President, 1987*, p. 282.

[28] Easterlin, "What Will 1984 Be Like?" See also Feldstein, "The Economics of the New Unemployment."

[29] Easterlin, "What Will 1984 Be Like?"

less confidence that they can generate the exact conditions their policies are designed to produce—even if their policies emerge from Congress or the monetary authorities in exactly the form in which they were submitted. There is little doubt that enough is now known to prevent either an economic collapse such as the Great Depression or hyperinflation of the sort experienced by some nations in war or its aftermath. Yet more than this cannot be promised.

Economists, if not politicians, now also realize that policy proposals must be scrutinized for their secondary or tertiary as well as their primary effects. Few economists now believe that inflation can be reduced to insignificant levels with no increase in unemployment. Also, they now realize that some stabilization policy efforts have directly or indirectly reduced the economy's long-term growth rate by encouraging consumption at the expense of investment, reducing the level of employment, or slowing the productivity increases that over time offer the only hope of higher real incomes per person.[30] In particular, relief of economic distress must not concentrate on efforts to preserve existing jobs; a rapid rate of "job death," in which old forms of employment disappear and are replaced by new, is essential to growth and the resource reallocation that inevitably accompanies it.[31] The aid provided to large firms such as the Chrysler Corporation in 1979, though temporarily successful, is a most dangerous precedent because it interferes with resource allocation along the lines of highest return. Such measures do not preserve "good jobs": they hinder movement to better ones.

[30] E. Denison, "Explanations of Declining Productivity Growth," Brookings General Series Reprint #354 (Washington, D.C.: Brookings Institution, 1979).
[31] Rosenberg and Birdzell, *How the West Grew Rich,* p. 278. The same study revealed that most jobs, even in the U.S. industrial sector, are not provided by giant firms, and very few additional jobs are created by long-established firms.

THE OLD REGULATION

The American economy has never been regulated by market forces alone.[32] The power of government has always been employed to define and enforce property rights, delineate the boundaries between legal and illegal conduct, settle disputes, define the monetary unit, and in general provide a healthy, competitive climate for economic activity. As the economy became more urban and industrial and the variety and complexity of its products increased, providing useful information, protection against externalities, safety, and a competitive environment assumed new importance. Government activity in all these areas dates from the nineteenth century or even earlier.

In recent years, some government regulatory activities have been extensions of those traditional roles. Most were designed to improve the operation of the market system, not to substitute for it. There were exceptions: a few groups, such as farmers, obtained favored treatment from government. Over time such groups increased. Support of the needy had always been a recognized function of government at some level, and twentieth-century support really represented no more than an expansion of traditional services. Until the second half of the twentieth century, however, facilitation of rent-seeking had yet to occupy the general thrust of government's domestic operations.

Antitrust

The federal government (and some states) continued to enforce antitrust laws. Although the bulk of such activity still revolved around the

[32] J. Hughes, *The Governmental Habit* (New York: Basic Books, 1977) is a good statement of this proposition.

Sherman Act's prohibition of various forms of anticompetitive behavior as it always had, there were some attempts to break new legal ground. In particular, policies were developed to deal with some of the merger activity that appeared after the war. Such policies have had varying degrees of success, and their impact on the overall economy or even individual industries can be questioned. It has been found, for example, that periods of intense merger activity see an increase in the number of firms, rather than a decrease. The number of new firms established by merger far exceeds those that disappear.[33]

In general, the antitrust authorities were successful in persuading the courts that horizontal mergers virtually always had an adverse effect on competition. Horizontal mergers are those between previously competing firms, and the courts refused to permit them in virtually any circumstances where measurable increases in economic concentration could be demonstrated. They followed this policy through the Seventies, in not only national but even local markets. In recent years, this attitude has been relaxed; some large mergers between oil firms have been allowed after evidence was presented that competition would remain vigorous or even increase despite the mergers.

The courts were only slightly less hostile to vertical mergers (those between firms that buy from or sell to each other). Not only were a number of proposed mergers forbidden, but some existing vertical structures were ordered dissolved. Motion picture studios were ordered to sell the chains of theaters they once owned, and the du Pont Company was made to sell its large stock interest in General Motors in 1959. The Clayton Act was amended in 1950 to make it more difficult for one firm to acquire the assets of another, and the courts and the Department of Justice made extensive use of the new law.

[33] Rosenberg and Birdzell, *How the West Grew Rich*, pp. 281–286.

The legal status of conglomerate mergers is not yet clear. The antitrust authorities have not favored such mergers, but existing laws were not designed to deal with them, nor is it easy to demonstrate that they have clear-cut effects on competition. Since 1973, the courts have been unwilling to accept any challenges to conglomerate mergers in which only a potential for reduced competition, rather than an actual reduction, could be demonstrated.

IBM and AT&T

The resolution of two recent antitrust suits indicates that the thrust and enforcement of the law are not completely consistent. After a prolonged trial, the government's case against International Business Machines (IBM) was dropped. The government was unable to prove its contention that IBM achieved its position within the data-processing industry (which changed substantially during the course of the suit) by anything other than superior competitive efficiency. In another case resolved in the same year (1982), the American Telephone and Telegraph Company (AT&T) was required to split off its local-service operations in return for government permission to enter new industries, such as computers. These cases may reflect the last gasp of antitrust efforts based on narrowly defined market shares. Recently, the courts have become more receptive to the idea that many if not most firms now face rivals whose primary operations lie in other industries, and that competition no longer is restricted to that between closely similar or identical goods.

Transportation

The preceding chapters indicate that government has never dealt with transportation at arm's length. Generally, it has either subsidized it or subjected it to discriminatory taxes. Currently, transportation policy appears to be changing from tight regulation of both prices and scope of activity to a greater reliance on competition. But for at least three decades after 1945, the traditional policy of aid to various forms of transportation, often without much coordination, was continued.

Highways. In the waning days of World War II, Congress authorized construction of an interstate highway system. As initially proposed, it was to extend some 40,000 miles and be financed 90 percent by federal funds, with the balance coming from the states where the roads were located. The system, with some expansions and alterations, is now all but complete. The new highway system, in conjunction with regulations that favored trucks at the expense of railroads and technical improvements in the trucks themselves, diverted a large volume of long-distance freight to the highways. For the railroads, the losses were more serious than volume figures alone suggest, because trucks competed most effectively for the high-value shipments that contributed disproportionately to revenues.

Railroads. Rail passenger service had been declining since the Twenties; Americans apparently preferred private automobile travel. After a brief revival during World War II, rail passenger service declined precipitously. In the early Seventies the railroads turned over all passenger service except their commuter lines to a government corporation (Amtrak). Despite large subsidies, Amtrak has failed to cover its operating costs and was forced to discontinue service on some of the routes it took over.

Railroads fared only relatively better in the freight business, largely because of competition from other forms of transportation that received favorable treatment from the government. Water transport, pipelines, and long-distance transmission lines reduced the volume of high-bulk, low-value cargo available to the railroads, just as trucks wrested away a growing portion of the more lucrative small-lot shipments. Although air freight ton-miles rose rapidly after 1960, this form of transportation remains an insignificant competitor in the overall freight market. Its importance is limited to a few instances of particularly valuable or perishable items.

For many years the federal government subsidized most forms of transportation and substituted control by the Interstate Commerce Commission for that of supply and demand. Water transportation and later trucking were particular beneficiaries of federal largesse: the government built and/or maintained their rights of way, charging them far less than the full cost of its services.

Airlines. Air travel was even more heavily subsidized: government-financed airports and navigational and air traffic control facilities and government research on aircraft and equipment are only the most obvious benefits provided. In addition, many air carriers received air mail contracts whose rates tended to be set more in accordance with the airlines' revenue requirements than their costs of carriage.

Beyond the explicit and implicit subsidies, government regulation of various forms of transportation protected many from competition. Rate structures might be set to allow several modes of transportation to "compete" for business even though one had large cost advantages over all others. In most cases, regulators were reluctant to recognize that some forms of transport were not well suited to moving certain types of goods. Almost invariably, they opposed (with the enthusiastic support of their clients) the entry of new firms into regulated markets.[34] The results were what might have been expected: monopoly profits for the protected firms (and their employees) and high prices for consumers.

[34] M. Cohen and G. Stigler, *Can Regulatory Agencies Protect the Consumer?* (Washington, D.C.: American Enterprise Institute for Public Policy Research, 1971).

The Beginnings of Deregulation

Recently, such policies have come under increasingly hostile scrutiny, and many have been modified. In 1978 the first step was taken: domestic airlines were given wide latitude in setting their own fares and were allowed to enter new routes. In addition, the regulation-imposed barriers to entry into the industry were abolished. The outcome followed the predictions of economic theory. Fares were reduced (the prevalence of discount fares is not captured by most statistics), service was increased, and some old-line carriers were unable to meet the new competition. Airline employees found the new competitive climate difficult; many were forced to accept lower wages to retain their jobs. Much the same results were observed after deregulation of the trucking industry (which, with its thousands of small firms, should never have been regulated): increased competition, new entry, and lower profits and wages for established firms and their employees, particularly the members of the Teamsters' union.

Farm Policy

Agriculture began to receive favored treatment from government 40 years after transportation did, but farmers more than made up for lost time. After 1945 it was clear that farm incomes were at least as dependent on federal farm policy as on the current state of markets for agricultural products. Government agricultural policy objectives have been conflicting. One primary goal was to raise the incomes of American farmers through increased product prices. However, this was to be accomplished without accumulating large agricultural surpluses (and without depressing overseas markets for America or her allies). It was also to be done without reducing the number of family-owned and -operated farms.

Given the highly elastic long-run supplies of most farm goods (which stemmed in part from the government's agricultural research and efforts to teach farmers new methods) and the low domestic price and income elasticities of demand for most major farm products, this combination of objectives proved impossible to attain. As noted in Chapter 20, farmers vary widely in their ability to use the cost-reducing technological improvements that give some hope of survival under such conditions. Small farms, at least for the major crops, are increasingly unable to use the new methods effectively. As differences in the amount and cost of output of different types of farms became more pronounced, splits began to appear in the farm bloc. The owners of small farms typically favor very high price supports and, if necessary, strict controls on output, especially from large farms. The operators of larger, more efficient farms are less inclined to favor high price supports if they mean limits on output. The decreasing number of farmers in the total population has worsened the effects of this split. It now appears that small farms are no longer able to compete, even with government assistance, in most major farm crops; the income figures noted in Chapter 20 testify to that.

Payment in Kind and Price Supports

One novel effort to solve several problems of government involvement in agriculture took place in 1983. Surpluses of many agricultural products had been accumulating in government storage, imposing increasing costs. At the same time, the total output of American farms could not be sold on domestic or international markets at the level of government-supported prices. The Reagan administration offered to provide the amount of crops that farmers might have grown out of surplus stocks if they would withdraw their land from production of any similar crops. Recipients of government surplus stocks were free to sell them. Agricultural output declined sharply for that year, and the outlays of the Department of Agriculture rose by about one-half. Market prices for farm products rose slightly. The "payment in kind" experiment reduced government surpluses, but at enormous cost to the taxpayers ($26 billion), and it was not repeated.

The farm program has failed. Government assistance to agriculture has not been able to shelter farmers from the economic pressures that have driven millions of them into other occupations on either a full- or part-time basis. Incomes in nonfarm occupations remain well above those of most American farmers and far above those generated by farming alone. The distribution of agricultural income is less equal than that of the rest of the economy. Laws have been passed that limit total price-support payments to individual farmers to not more than $55,000 annually for each of three crops; it could be argued that attempts to reduce agricultural poverty are overdone in such cases. Price supports have increased the cost of food to American consumers, and surpluses have imposed burdens on taxpayers as well. At the same time, these price supports threaten to drive American farm products from international markets.

Government signals to farmers have been wildly inconsistent. In the mid-Seventies, farmers were urged to maximize output by increasing both acreage and the intensity of cultivation to feed a hungry world. They were also encouraged to make long-term additions to capacity and to borrow to finance them. A few years later, acreage restrictions were once again imposed. Basically, the farm program has been unsuccessful because its objectives simply cannot be realized simultaneously. It is impossible to increase efficiency, maintain high-cost producers, and supply consumers with low-cost food (in terms of both prices and taxes) at the same time. Refusal to recognize this situation can only lead to more wasted expenditure and even more difficult long-run adjustment.

INCOME DISTRIBUTION

Only in the postwar era was government deeply involved in efforts to change the distribution of income generated by market forces. Although public assistance in one form or another dates back to colonial times, historically aid to the needy was intended to provide little more than subsistence incomes for those clearly incapable of generating their own. No effort was made to provide more than bare-bones subsistence, at least by American standards, and applications for aid were not encouraged. There is no evidence to indicate that much more than these goals was ever met, and some that points to failure to achieve even these minimal objectives.

The new trends in aid took both general and personal forms. During the New Deal and particularly after 1960, various stabilization policies were developed and expanded. Aimed at ensuring high levels of current employment and economic growth, they were to provide greater security of private incomes and enhanced opportunity to raise incomes through job mobility. As yet, economic growth has done more to raise the incomes of the poor than any other policy. Rapid growth raises the demand for labor and reduces unemployment. It also promotes gains for those already employed by improving chances for promotions and transfers to better jobs.

Only in the postwar period was it realized that policies that assumed every American was a member of a family with at least one full-time wage earner little helped those whose circumstances were different. For those unable to work or prevented by discrimination from obtaining jobs that fully used their capabilities, macroeconomic policies were not the answer. For the aged, the very young, the handicapped, and increasingly, single mothers with limited work skills, work incentives were a cruel joke. Others might find themselves trapped in depressed areas, unable to move to regions with better job prospects but facing prolonged unemployment if they remained. Such groups are a minority in the United States and do not constitute the entire low-income group, but they were more numerous than many people believed.

The Growth of Public Spending

The general increase in income and wealth provided more job opportunities and better occupational choices for low-income people, but it did more. Concern for providing aid to the less fortunate and broadening the opportunities open to all individuals increased. Education was expanded. Overall, the United States spent about three times the portion of GNP on education in 1983 that it had in 1948. Real spending per public-school pupil more than quadrupled from 1948 to 1970.[35] The average educational level of the population increased, with blacks recording the largest gains, particularly in terms of quality of schooling.[36] The proportions of high school and college graduates among the population and the availability of vocational and special education programs all increased. The government launched a large-scale effort to provide training for low-skilled workers and the hard-core unemployed through the Comprehensive Employment and Training Act (CETA), a program whose costs and results are highly controversial. From 1973 to 1982, 27 million persons were enrolled at a total cost of $58 billion. Only 15 percent of CETA participants found jobs through the program.

Programs that provided aid for those unable to work were also expanded. Welfare programs, such as Aid to Dependent Children,

[35] U.S. Department of Commerce, *Historical Statistics,* vol. 1, p. 373.
[36] R. Margo, "Race, Educational Attainment and the 1940 Census," *Journal of Economic History* (March 1986).

unemployment compensation, and social security, grew in terms of both portion of the population covered and amount of benefits per individual. Programs that provided aid in kind, such as food stamps, Medicare and Medicaid, job training, and subsidized housing, expanded much faster than those providing cash payments. Together, such programs accounted for a major portion of the growth in government expenditures. Transfers to individuals increased faster than total government spending from 1955 through 1975 and maintained their share thereafter (see Table 21.1). This was particularly true of measures providing income in kind and education. By the standards of any previous era, the United States became more generous toward the less fortunate, devoting a growing share of total income to programs designed to assist them.

Trends in Income Distribution

There is no question about the magnitude of the effort. What were its results? At first glance, they appear disappointing. Table 21.3 shows the distribution of pretax money incomes by quintiles of families (the 20 percent of all families with the lowest incomes are the bottom quintile, the 20 percent receiving the highest incomes are the top, and so forth). The table reveals that although there has been some income redistribution toward greater equality since 1929, most of it has occurred through a fall in the share received by the truly rich—the top 5 percent of all families. All other income groups have shared in the redistribution, and the poor, even proportionally, gained only slightly more than the middle class. Moreover, the bulk of the redistribution occurred prior to or during the Second World War. The dominant feature of the American distribution of income since 1945 has been stability. According to these figures, the gains from economic growth have been shared by all income groups, with the possible exception of the very highest.

Table 21.3   Distribution of Pretax Money Incomes by Quintiles and Top 5 Percent of All Families, 1929–1981

Quintile	1929	1948	1955	1972	1981*
Lowest 20 percent	3.5%	5.0%	4.8%	5.4%	4.4%
Second 20 percent	9.0	12.1	12.2	11.9	10.2
Third 20 percent	13.8	17.2	17.7	17.5	16.3
Fourth 20 percent	19.3	23.2	23.4	23.9	23.8
Top 20 percent	54.4	42.5	41.8	41.4	45.3
Top 5 percent**	30.0	17.1	16.8	15.9	18.8

*Data for 1981 are for families and unrelated individuals; income distribution in this group is less equal than for families.
**Also included in top 20 percent
Total may not add to 100 percent because of rounding.
Sources: Data for 1929–1972 from U.S. Department of Commerce, Bureau of the Census, *Current Population Reports*, Series P-60 (Washington, D.C.: Government Printing Office, 1981). Data for 1981 from S. Lebergott, *The Americans: An Economic Record* (New York: Norton, 1984), pp. 498, 501.

In absolute terms, the average incomes of each quintile have risen considerably. The table indicates that if the rich are not growing richer relative to the American average, neither are the poor growing less poor.

However, the figures in Table 21.3 have some serious shortcomings. They reflect only money incomes and neglect income received in kind. Transfers in kind are heavily concentrated among the lower-income groups, but the data in Table 21.3 do not include such income. The value of education, medical care, food stamps, and subsidized housing provided to the poor may be difficult to calculate exactly but is surely positive; were it not, such goods would not be accepted, let alone sought. The data in Table 21.3 also ignore the impact of personal taxes, which make aftertax incomes slightly more equal than pretax incomes. More seriously, the data ignore the impact of demographic factors. Contrary to general opinion, the typical low-income family contains fewer people than a high-income unit. A large proportion of low-income families is composed of young adults and thus contains few children. Another group overrepresented in the low-income ranks is single-parent families. A high proportion of families with above-average incomes have two or more income earners. In any case, the lowest two quintiles of American families as ranked by money incomes contain considerably less than 40 percent of all family members.[37]

When the income figures are modified by these considerations, a very different picture emerges (see Table 21.4). The revised figures indicate a substantially greater degree of income equality at all periods. They also indicate a substantial movement toward greater income equality in recent years.[38] Although the revised figures have not been updated recently, there is little reason to conclude that these trends

[37] President's Council on Income Maintenance Programs, "The Meaning of Poverty," in *Poverty Amid Plenty: The American Paradox, Report of the President's Commission on Income Maintenance Programs* (Washington, D.C.: Government Printing Office, 1969). See also "The Change in Inequality of Family and Individual Income," *Report of the Council of Economic Advisors, 1974* (Washington, D.C.: Government Printing Office, 1974).
[38] E. Browning, "How Much More Equality Can We Afford?" *The Public Interest* (Spring 1976).

Table 21.4   Adjusted Relative Income Distribution
(Shares of Income Received by Quintiles
of Equal Population)

Year	Lowest 20 Percent	Second 20 Percent	Third 20 Percent	Fourth 20 Percent	Top 20 Percent
1952	8.1%	14.2%	17.8%	23.2%	36.7%
1962	8.8	14.4	18.2	23.1	35.4
1972	11.7	15.0	18.2	22.3	32.8

Source: E. Browning, "How Much More Equality Can We Afford?" *The Public Interest* (Spring 1976).

have reversed. Demographic factors, especially the growing proportion of single-parent families, would reinforce them. In-kind transfers have shown, at most, small declines.

The Search for a Definition of Income Distribution

Income is not equally distributed in the United States: the top quintile receives from three to eight times the total income of the lowest quintile, depending on the income distribution measurements employed. Furthermore, the results obtained by analysis are strongly influenced by our definitions of both income and the groups who receive it. Even apparently straightforward changes in the data may not indicate what they appear to. For example, a growing influence on income distribution figures in recent years is the "decoupling effect," which occurs as extended families become less prevalent. The elderly are now less likely to live with their children, and young adults are more prone to establish independent households as or before they complete their educations, rather than waiting until marriage. Both these changes increase the number of families without changing the total income they generate and thus tend to raise the portion of low-income families, but it is doubtful that they indicate reduced well-being. Divorce and other forms of marital breakup by definition divide the fami-

ly's income (perhaps very unevenly) between two units, but do nothing to increase it. Given these trends, it is easy to see why the gains in income equality have been limited, at least by current measures.

One final point concerning income distribution has only recently begun to receive attention. To many persons, poverty (and perhaps wealth) are different conditions if temporary than if lifelong. Different policy conclusions may well arise from the discovery that most people at the income extremes are there only temporarily and not consigned to permanent poverty or assured of permanent wealth. If extreme income conditions for most individuals are temporary, most persons are able to change their relative incomes. This is even more true for the children of wealthy or poor generations.

Income Mobility in the United States

Two recent studies indicate that during their working lives—or even in as little as eight to fifteen years—most Americans experienced sizable increases and/or decreases in their incomes relative to the national average. In short, they moved up or down the ladder of income distribution for some considerable portion of its length.[39] The changes were not trivial: the average movement was over one-fifth the entire income range in the 1957–1971 period, and twice that in 1969–1978.[40] These studies indicate that substantial income changes are not merely possible for individuals in the American economy, they are the norm. This is almost equally true at every income level, high or low. Other studies, most unfortunately concentrating on movements between "high-status" and "low-status" jobs (has a high school shop instructor who quits his $25,000 teaching job to earn $60,000 as a master plumber lost status?) and also between the occupations of parents and their children reveal a very high degree of individual and intergenerational mobility within the United States.[41]

These findings do not support the claim that relative income levels are rigidly stratified for most Americans. They do, however, reveal a lesser income mobility for blacks than for most Americans.[42] Evidence also suggests that different demographic groups and educational levels within the American black community have progressed very unevenly, with young, well-educated blacks at or very near income parity with whites and a widening disparity for less well-equipped groups.

While evidence of income discrimination against women and minority groups (lower pay for the same productivity) is now diminishing, the effects of previous unequal treatment and preparation for employment will linger for years.[43] This has caused some persons to ad-

vocate favored treatment for those groups that were victims of discrimination in earlier periods. But hiring, salary, or job-training preference for current labor force entrants who otherwise would not face discrimination cannot reasonably be regarded as compensation for the disadvantages previously suffered by others. The implications for productivity growth and justice to all stemming from such programs can hardly be favorable.

Clearly the forms and financing of income transfers influence the incentives to individual effort of both recipients and taxpayers. The aggregate effects on income may be quite large. If the evidence of the Browning, Schiller, and Duncan studies is accepted, however, two conclusions emerge. First, income distribution in the United States is more nearly equal than commonly accepted evidence indicates, and it is becoming even more so. Second, individual progress is eminently possible, even probable.

THE NEW REGULATION

In the past few decades, some analysts have claimed that the nature and objectives of much government regulation of the economy have changed significantly. They see a shift in emphasis away from measures designed to improve the operation of a market economy, which left resolution of the basic questions of what, how, and for whom to the interplay of supply and demand. The new regulation introduces governmental judgments (or those of private groups acting through the government) on both goals and the means and methods of their pursuit.

The old regulation did not always fulfill the expectations of those who instituted it. On occasion it became the tool of the very interests it had been designed to control, and it was always more responsive to well-organized groups than to the public at large (the implications for

[39] B. Schiller, "Equality, Opportunity, and the Good Job," *The Public Interest* (Spring 1976). See also G. Duncan, *Years of Poverty, Years of Plenty* (Ann Arbor, Mich.: University of Michigan Press, 1984).
[40] Ibid.
[41] S. Lebergott, *The Americans: An Economic Record* (New York: Norton, 1984), pp. 508–511.
[42] Schiller, "Equality, Opportunity, and the Good Job."
[43] An excellent discussion of this issue is found in T. Sowell, *Race and Economics* (New York: David McKay, 1975).

consumer welfare should be obvious). Even when it fulfilled the role for which it was designed, regulation did not invariably promote the general welfare.

Under the new regulation, however, government does not merely identify a problem (such as automobile-caused air pollution), provide information (perhaps based on government-sponsored research), and provide a mechanism by which injured parties can protect themselves (such as the right to sue for damages). Instead, it might specify both the extent to which the problem is to be addressed and the means: new cars must not emit more than specified amounts of pollution and must achieve these levels through the use of catalytic converters in their exhaust systems. Government may no longer merely inform consumers about hazards contained in goods—it may require specific modifications before they are allowed to be sold. In some cases, government may mandate treatment that clearly would not have resulted from the operation of even perfectly competitive market forces, or perhaps even from the desires of injured parties.

Reasons for Expanded Regulation

Expansion of government's regulatory activity was no doubt inevitable under modern circumstances. Most of the population lives in urban areas; technology both produces more serious pollution problems and offers means for their detection and amelioration, and growing income levels allow more concern for the quality of life. Assessing these conditions, particularly their long-term consequences, often requires expertise beyond the capabilities of the average citizen. This probably also contributed to increased regulatory activities. Social attitudes for most of this period indicated a growing tend-

ency to seek solutions through government rather than through the market.

Regulation's Successes

Some new government programs and agencies have made remarkable achievements. Water pollution, although still a serious problem, is on the decline in the Unites States. The Atlantic salmon returned to New England's rivers after the dams and pollution that destroyed its habitat a century ago were removed. Lake Erie and the Detroit River, once regarded as dead, now support flourishing sport fisheries. A number of endangered species, notably the nation's symbol, the bald eagle, have increased their populations. Death rates in automobile accidents have been reduced because of the safety measures now required as standard equipment on new cars. (Curiously, the use of by far the most effective item of this required equipment—seat belts—is not mandatory in all states.) Some dangerous pesticides have been banned from use, and research on less environmentally disruptive methods of insect and plant pest control continues to produce useful results. Socially, advocates of overt discrimination no longer obtain widespread approval. Opportunities for women and minority groups are vastly wider than they were two decades ago, and there is abundant evidence that these incentives have promoted increased acquisition of job skills.

"Progress" at Any Price?

But there have also been costs, and in many cases they have been much greater than necessary to achieve the results obtained. Any reallocation or modification in the employment of scarce resources involves costs: no more fundamental proposition exists within economics. However, the existence of costs implies that economic well-being will be enhanced only if the benefits received through their incurrence exceed the value of the alternatives foregone. Welfare is increased only when resource productivity is increased, rather than merely changed. It is equally true that the mere existence of costs is no deterrent to economic action: costs and benefits must be compared if rational actions are to be taken. Further, the mere indication that the costs of a given measure are less than its benefits is insufficient; we must also be as certain as available knowledge permits that we could not generate an even greater surplus of benefits over costs by some other use of the same resources. Too often these simple rules have been forgotten.

In some cases, proponents of action in one field ignore the possibility of far greater gains through action elsewhere. Millions of dollars are spent every year to reduce the already statistically infinitesimal risk of death from air crashes or nuclear reactor breakdowns. Even total success in the former area could save at most a few hundred lives annually; best estimates in the latter are for even smaller gains.[44] We also lavish attention on efforts to eliminate food ingredients that pose even smaller risks of cancer. Yet little has been done to rid our highways of drunk drivers, who kill well over 10,000 people each year, generally under circumstances where the casualties had far less choice about exposure to their attentions than the areas of more intense concern.

The aggregate costs of regulation are not trivial, and they are far greater than the budgets of the government agencies that oversee the laws. Actual compliance with the new environmental, safety, and employment regulations alone was estimated to cost over $100 billion annually in the mid-Seventies. The paperwork required to document it cost another $40 billion.[45] All this, of course, is added to costs of production and hence to prices. A large portion of all new investment in the United States is devoted to meeting regulatory requirements, even though the economy desperately needs more modern facilities to meet foreign competition. The services of key personnel may be diverted to responding to the new measures, which reduces growth and increases costs. Perhaps even more serious in the long run, mandated solutions deny the consideration of alternatives that has been a strong point of market responses.

In a few cases, the only result of regulation has been higher costs. By the government's own estimate, the Department of Energy contributed to shortages of petroleum in the Seventies rather than reduced them—at an annual cost of $9 billion. Despite the innumerable regulations it has issued, the fines it has levied, and the inspections it has conducted, the Occupational Health and Safety Administration has produced no change in the long-term trend in industrial accident rates.[46]

None of the foregoing is intended to imply that all regulatory activity—or even all new activity—should be discontinued. Rather, it is a plea for recognition of the fact that if government regulation is to improve the aggregate human condition, its benefits must exceed its costs. Particularly where regulation, however well-intended, interferes with reallocation of economic resources to new uses, the long-run results are unlikely to be positive.

SELECTED REFERENCES

Anderson, T., and P. Hill. *The Growth of a Transfer Society.* Stanford, Calif.: Hoover Institution Press, 1980.

Borcherding, T., ed. *Budgets and Bureaucrats: The Sources of Government Growth.* Durham, N.C.: Duke University Press, 1977.

Council of Economic Advisors. *Economic Report of the President.* Washington, D.C.: Government Printing Office, annual editions.

---

[44] The Union of Concerned Scientists, an antinuclear group, estimates the total U.S. deaths from nuclear power at about 120 per year. B. Cohen, "The Hazards of Nuclear Power," in H. Kahn and J. Simon, *The Resourceful Earth: A Response to Global 2000* (New York: Basil Blackwell, 1984), p. 545.

[45] M. Weidenbaum, "The Economic Cost of Big Government," *Challenge* (November–December 1979).

[46] Lebergott, *The Americans,* p. 520.

Duncan, G. *Years of Poverty, Years of Plenty.* Ann Arbor, Mich.: University of Michigan Press, 1984.

Friedman, M., and A. Schwartz. *A Monetary History of the United States, 1867–1960.* Princeton, N.J.: Princeton University Press, 1963.

Gordon, R. *Economic Instability and Growth: The American Record.* New York: Norton, 1975.

Kahn, H., and J. Simon, eds. *The Resourceful Earth: A Response to Global 2000.* New York: Basil Blackwell, 1984.

Olson, M. *The Rise and Decline of Nations: Economic Growth, Stagflation, and Social Rigidities.* New Haven, Conn.: Yale University Press, 1982.

Rosenberg, N., and L. Birdzell. *How the West Grew Rich: The Economic Transformation of the Industrial World.* New York: Basic Books, 1986.

Sowell, T. *Race and Economics.* New York: David McKay, 1975.

Stein, H. *The Fiscal Revolution in America.* Chicago: University of Chicago Press, 1969.

Tufte, E. *Political Control of the Economy.* Princeton, N.J.: Princeton University Press, 1978.

U.S. Department of Commerce, Bureau of the Census. *Historical Statistics of the United States: Colonial Times to 1970.* 2 vols. Washington, D.C.: Government Printing Office, 1975.

CHAPTER

22

THE AMERICAN ACHIEVEMENT AND PORTENTS FOR THE FUTURE

An assessment of the economic history of the United States of America does not encourage a pessimistic view of the consequences of economic growth. Not only has the American economy's output grown from levels that allowed the early settlers only the most precarious grip on survival, but its rate of increase has far outpaced that of population. Today, with little more than 5 percent of the earth's population, the United States produces between one-fifth and one-fourth of the planet's entire economic output. If meaningful comparisons can be made between very different life-styles, the average contemporary American citizen enjoys a real income somewhere between ten and twelve times that of the typical eighteenth-century colonist. And the colonists were even then among the world's most affluent populations.

Income figures probably give a better indication of twentieth-century Americans' well-being than the colonists'. Income distribution, for example, is far less unequal today than it was when one-fifth of the population was slaves. Also, differences in the life-styles of various income groups are less today than in earlier times. In previous centuries, the rich consumed many items that the poor could obtain not in lesser quantity or quality, as they can today, but not at all. Numerical income comparisons, however, probably mask more than reveal the real differences in economic welfare that have resulted over time. The increased number of material possessions of the average modern American is probably less significant than the increased choices open to that person in the modern world.

THE FRUITS OF ECONOMIC GROWTH

In nearly every possible aspect, Americans in 1986 had far more available choices than citizens of earlier periods. This greater variety of life is a direct consequence of the process of economic growth in the United States. As the preceding chapters have stressed, growth entailed far more than mere increases in total output. Particularly as output increased faster than population or the labor force, its origin was something other than "more of the same." Sustained increases in per-capita output over the length of time observed in this country involved changes in most aspects of economic activity.

Changes in methods, occupations, institutions, and allocation criteria, together with their results, reinforced the belief that change could improve the human condition. As we have seen, that attitude was central to the settlement of America from the earliest days, but American conditions reinforced it powerfully. Receptivity toward new and different methods, products, and people, combined with the automatic evaluation of change provided by the market system, produced America's wealth. Progress in recognizing the benefits of diversity, especially in people, was anything but smooth, but it has been a consistent feature of American economic life. This resulted in a great deal more than more and different material goods: it enabled a degree of individual freedom not possible under any other system.

Even in America, the lesson was not easily learned. It may not be fully absorbed even today. Most Americans of the 1980s would find it difficult to comprehend the laws, and even more, the customs that limited individual expression until the recent past. Even though people migrated to this country because its society imposed fewer restraints on the individual than did other nations, the difference was one of degree, not kind. Only in the very recent

■ The economic roles of women are becoming less limited in the modern economy.
Source: UPI/Bettmann Newsphotos.

past have restrictions limiting the economic roles of women, "outsiders," members of minority races or religions, or other identifiably distinct people been seriously questioned. The iron grip of social custom was often little less confining for majority group members. Both sources of restrictions have proved difficult to eradicate even under American circumstances, where they were less common and less accepted than elsewhere.

American economic institutions were not developed solely through a continuous effort to increase measurable production, nor are they today. The American Civil War is only the most obvious example of evidence to the contrary. The adjustment to institutional changes that stemmed from noneconomic causes, as in Douglass North's concept of ideology, has also played an important role in the process of economic development.[1]

The Role of the Market

Nevertheless, the combination of the American setting, in which basic social institutions encouraged great diversity among agencies and individuals seeking change, and a mechanism

[1] D. North, *Structure and Change in Economic History* (New York: Norton, 1981), Chapter 5.

(the market) that provided an efficient and above all automatic evaluation of efforts to produce change has been extremely effective in promoting economic growth.[2] Societies that promote diversity of effort are likely to be especially successful not only in discovering new ideas, but in selecting the most effective among them and putting them to widespread use.[3] In addition, a market climate that reflects rapid changes in products and methods also encourages rational evaluation and employment of the most valuable resource of any nation—its people. Assessment of each person's productive capabilities encouraged rational labor force allocation to jobs. Asking job candidates "What can you do and how well?" may seem common sense to people accustomed to the American economic environment. In much of the world, however, such a question, if asked at all, still is less important than "Who were your parents?" or " To what tribe, region, or religion do you owe allegiance?" (In such societies, discrimination by race or sex is likely to be so common as to eliminate applications from the "wrong people": these groups have learned there is no point in making the effort.)

On a more dynamic basis, the continuous introduction of new goods and techniques has steadily widened the scope for individual talents as well as increased specialization within jobs. Finally, economic growth creates more range for individual expression within both work and leisure. A rising margin over subsistence needs allows societies to make new choices. Not only are resources now available for cultural expression, but they also permit the forfeiture of some material income to allow more leisure time, more fulfilling work roles,

and greater cultural expression even in utilitarian objects.

The Role of Rational Employment of Human Resources

The attitude that performance was the only relevant criterion for evaluating job applicants did not diffuse throughout the economy at the same pace, nor was it simultaneously accepted by all groups. Technological change might produce sudden breakthroughs in the range of jobs open to individuals, as did factory production or the rise of wholesale and retail trade in the nineteenth century. Changing social attitudes—toward racial differences, women's employment, or even the size of the average family—took longer to produce their effects. However, in the long run, the impact of such innovations may well be greater. Wherever rational assessments of human potential appeared, they became profoundly subversive of older methods based on other values.

Today, as the United States enters a period of declining labor force growth relative to the recent past, it is essential that each individual be allowed to make his or her maximum contribution to aggregate production. Labor scarcity will undoubtedly encourage rational use of human resources, as it consistently has in the past. Compared to other nations, the United States has always been a labor-scarce economy. Even so, it is no accident that especially rapid gains in both incomes and access to particularly desirable jobs have occurred when labor markets were tight, such as during World Wars I and II and the prolonged boom of the Sixties (when demographic trends were also favorable). Since the links between economic activity and government (the most potent mechanism for expressing social attitudes) have traditionally been relatively weak here, the gains for women and minorities have been more pro-

[2] In the view of Rosenberg and Birdzell, this distinguishes the West from virtually all other societies and explains its economic success relative to that of Africa, most of Asia, and elsewhere. See *How the West Grew Rich: The Economic Transformation of the Industrial World* (New York: Basic Books, 1986).

[3] This is a central theme for Rosenberg and Birdzell. See *How the West Grew Rich*, especially Chap. 10.

nounced than in nations possessing both more firmly established social traditions and a greater degree of public control over the economy.

Education

Recent declines in employment barriers have been closely linked with new attitudes toward education. The extent to which individuals could realistically aspire to various careers influenced their development of job skills. For many years, women and blacks were not likely to seek education that prepared them for business or professional employment. Such education was of course expensive, but that was not the major barrier. The incentives to obtain such skills were less than for white males. If only a few employers were willing to hire outside stereotyped roles and fewer still did so on an equal basis, there was little point in incurring high costs to prepare for business or professional work. As an investment, such education yielded a noticeably lower rate of return for blacks and women.[4] In a climate where economic pressures strongly reinforced social barriers, it is hardly surprising that few "outsiders" sought preparation for these occupations. In the past decade, the proportion of female and minority students in business and professional schools has expanded substantially.

The tendency toward rational employment of human resources has done a great deal more for the American economy than merely increase the incomes of the individuals who benefited or satisfy aspirations for social justice. From its earliest days, America has gained from the contributions of persons not permitted to use or develop their talents fully in their native lands. Migration patterns strongly indicate that America provided what such persons sought.[5] The

United States modified its labor market institutions to take advantage of the immigrants' contributions, a process that increased labor force participation rates and the dissemination of skills. Even more, the American economy traditionally borrowed imported techniques, which encouraged both full use of whatever immigrants had to contribute and further innovations from their additions to productive capacity.

DID ECONOMIC GROWTH INCREASE WELL-BEING?

The growth in incomes and, to some extent, in the range of choices that the development process allowed can be measured. Nevertheless, the increases revealed by quantitative assessment may or may not indicate corresponding increases in human well-being. In material terms, no doubt the average American citizen today enjoys a quantity and range of possessions far greater than did his or her forebears. Nevertheless, there is no reliable way to measure the satisfaction that people have derived from such goods at any one period, let alone over centuries. Comparisons of our current situation with the satisfaction our ancestors obtained from their standards of living can only be conjectural.

We have noted that growth in per-capita incomes as conventionally measured has serious drawbacks as an indicator of human welfare. Some items that can reasonably be assumed to produce benefits (for example, increased leisure time) are not assigned values. Others, such as the costs of preventing or treating pollution, crime, and accidents, are treated as additions to welfare although at best they represent the cost of maintaining the status quo, and are really contained within the value of other output. Many government activities treated as final products in the national income accounts are also intermediate goods, which are incorporated in the value of final goods and

[4] A. Niemi, Jr., *U.S. Economic History*, 2d ed. (Chicago: Rand McNally, 1980), pp. 298–303.

[5] J. Hughes, *Industrialization and Economic History: Theses and Conjectures* (New York: McGraw-Hill, 1970), pp. 146–150. See also S. Kuznets, "The Contribution of Immigration to the Growth of the Labor Force," reprinted in R. Fogel and S. Engerman, eds. *The Reinterpretation of American Economic History* (New York: Harper and Row, 1971).

services. In the modern economy, the incidence of such double counting has risen. Finally, per-capita income figures are also only statistical averages: they may mask growing or decreasing deviations from the mean.

Another problem arises from how most people make conclusions about their own well-being. The available evidence indicates that most people compare their circumstances with those of their neighbors and judge their own welfare largely against that standard, rather than in an absolute sense.[6] If so, it is ironic that today's greater income equality may have reduced rather than increased the satisfaction provided by larger per-capita incomes. Not only are more persons' incomes growing at the same rates, but there are fewer exceptions: "keeping up with the Joneses" is just as difficult as ever, and now the fortunes of the Smiths, Browns, Lees, and Hernandezes must also be taken into account. Many people whose real incomes increased at the average rate achieved by the postwar United States consider themselves little better off than they were in 1947, even though their real incomes have doubled. However, this does not mean that growth is not worth the effort. A person whose income remained at the 1947 average would consider it substantially reduced if other persons had shared in the income gains since recorded.

The Dimensions of Improved Welfare

Income. It is not easy to recognize the magnitude of the gains achieved even within a generation or two. By today's standards, nearly 60 percent of all American citizens in the 1947–1950 period had real incomes below the current poverty threshold—about $12,000 in current dollars for a family of four.[7] Yet the late Forties were a period of full employment and rapid economic growth in the United States. Income levels were well above those of any preceding era, and the income gap between the United States and the rest of the world had never been wider. Whether the income gains enjoyed by most Americans in recent decades have added proportionately to their happiness is an open question.

Life Expectancy. However, certain aspects of life in the contemporary United States strongly linked to economic growth can only be regarded as improvements in human well-being. Life expectancy at birth was only 50 years in 1900. Even that figure represented a considerable advance over most of the nineteenth century, to say nothing of the colonial era.[8] Currently, U.S. life expectancy is over 74 years, and it increased by approximately three years over 1970–1984—a noteworthy achievement since much of the gain came through improved longevity at advanced ages rather than reduced infant or child mortality.[9] For black Americans, the increases have been greater, from 33 years in 1900 to over 68 years today.[10]

Health and Disease. Many diseases that had taken a fearful toll of American lives throughout history are now almost or entirely unknown. Others that imposed a heavy cost in suffering, such as polio, have also been practically eliminated. The death rates from still others, such as heart disease, have been curtailed. Partially in consequence, the causes of death have changed. Cancer has become more

---

[6] R. Easterlin, "Does Money Buy Happiness?" *The Public Interest* (Winter 1973).

[7] Council of Economic Advisors, *Economic Report of the President, 1977* (Washington, D.C.: Government Printing Office, 1977), p. 216.
[8] U.S. Department of Commerce, Bureau of the Census, *Bicentennial Statistics* (Washington, D.C.: Government Printing Office, 1976), p. 379.
[9] ———, *Statistical Abstract of the United States, 1986* (Washington, D.C.: Government Printing Office, 1986).
[10] Ibid.

common in the United States, but the two primary sources of this change indicate economic gains and the use (or misuse) made of them. More Americans now live to the advanced ages at which cancer is most prevalent. Further, the association between long-term use of tobacco and lung cancer is now obvious. No age-adjusted increase in cancer deaths (aside from lung cancer) occurred over the 1950–1980 period. Indeed, the death rates from several other common forms of cancer declined substantially over these decades.[11] The United States has reduced infant mortality in recent years, perhaps because the reduced birthrate has allowed higher standards of infant and maternal care. Even so, the 38.5 percent reduction in infant mortality the United States achieved between 1960 and 1975 still leaves the rate well above that of the Scandinavian countries and no better than that of far poorer nations such as Spain, Singapore, and Taiwan.[12]

Preventive medicine has made great strides and has contributed much more to the decline in death rates than curative medicine. Nevertheless, modern physicians now routinely repair damage or cure diseases whose only outcomes not so long ago were lifelong pain or disability for most patients—if they survived at all.

Wider Choices. Improved health standards are obvious evidence of increased well-being. But in other, less conclusive areas, there is also much to reinforce the conclusion that Americans are better off than in previous eras. Compared with their forebears, Americans today enjoy an almost incredible range of choice in jobs, location, diet, life-styles, and amusements. Choice increases welfare because it allows the individual a greater chance of finding the job, location, commodity,

or life-style that exactly satisfies preferences. Convenient forms of travel are within the reach of the large majority today, whereas 150 years ago the only motive power for most overland travel was human or animal muscle.

The Work Environment. Work conditions have also improved. Jobs today require less time, involve far less physical effort and discomfort, and provide much greater scope for self-expression than jobs in earlier periods. Some economists have calculated that including the value of increased leisure time in per-capita incomes would add from 20 to 40 percent to the rate of growth of per-capita product.[13]

Assembly line jobs, supposedly the epitome of mindless drudgery in the modern world, currently employ only a small minority—perhaps 3 percent—of all American workers. The majority of workers have jobs that place varying degrees of emphasis on their judgment and ability to respond to changing conditions. In the nineteenth century, however, the range of jobs open to the average male worker was far more limited. For most women, the choices were restricted to marrying one suitor rather than another, since there were few alternatives to homemaking. In the colonial period, choices were even more restricted.

It is difficult to believe that most Americans were perfectly content with these limited opportunities, given the speedy acceptance of alternatives as these became available. Not all small farmers found their work satisfying in either economic or psychological terms, and many abandoned farming and rural life with alacrity. The idea that all urban workers were "craftsmen" who found their creative jobs both lucrative and emotionally satisfying is of course utter nonsense. Such jobs did exist, but most urban work in the nineteenth and earlier cen-

[11] R. Peto, "Why Cancer?" in H. Kahn and J. Simon, *The Resourceful Earth: A Response to Global 2000* (New York: Basil Blackwell, 1984), p. 533.
[12] World Bank, *World Atlas of the Child* (Washington, D.C.: World Bank, 1979), pp. 32–35. The relative figures had changed little in the mid-Eighties.

[13] L. Davis et al., *American Economic Growth: An Economist's History of the United States* (New York: Harper and Row, 1972), p. 45.

■ Robot welding of automobiles illustrates the decrease of American laborers involved in assembly line work.
Source: Courtesy of Chrysler Motors Corporation.

turies was dull, dirty, arduous, often dangerous, and provided only the starkest subsistence incomes. In addition, the barriers to entry into more desirable jobs were far greater and less "fair" than they are today.

Education. Education is both a source and a product of economic growth. Greater knowledge and the flexibility instilled by the learning process increase overall productivity, especially over time. Only societies that have achieved some

"Merfson, I'm afraid I have some rather unpleasant news for you."

■ Automation caused mixed reaction in the 1950's; its pace and popularity have increased rapidly.
Source: Historical Pictures Service, Inc.

substantial margin above subsistence can afford to withdraw a large portion of their young adults from the work force and invest in increasing their long-term productivity. A properly structured education is both a capital and a consumer good: in addition to raising direct vocational skills or increasing aptitude for further training, it adds to the individual's enjoyment and quality of life. In this area, the United States is without peer among nations. In 1981, 58 percent of the college-age cohort of this country was enrolled in some form of higher education. Even if we concede that quantity is not necessarily quality, the gap between the United States and its closest rivals in this regard is larger than that between them and other nations. Canada and Sweden sent approximately 37 percent of their young adults to higher education in 1981; the United States exceeded this achievement approximately two decades ago.[14] Such educational at-

tainments are an important asset in a world where the ability to respond to change is absolutely necessary for economic success. The largest gains in access to education have been made by minorities and women.

Collective Security. Economic growth has meant a reduction in self-employment, but it has also produced gains in economic security. Individual incomes and wealth have increased, allowing a greater portion of income to be devoted to saving. In addition, they made possible the programs devoted to public welfare that individual efforts alone could not meet. Higher incomes also funded much of the research that resulted in reduced threats to health. It may appear that the largely self-sufficient frontier farmer had little to fear from variations in the business cycle or from unemployment, and this is largely correct. However, he and his family were still vulnerable to bad weather, accidents, disease, and other disasters. Any of these could throw them on the uncertain charity of neighbors, who might be similarly affected and in any case had little to spare beyond their own needs. Old-age security at that time meant that either one or more children would stay with their aging parents or the parents would not outlive their ability to support themselves. We may mourn the disappearance of the extended family in cases where several generations lived together voluntarily, but often the association was a matter of necessity rather than affection.

Quality of Life. The growth of knowledge so closely interwoven with intensive economic growth has allowed the development of concern for other aspects of life. Regard for the human and physical environment is far more likely to generate positive action in rich than in poor societies. If levels of real income are sufficiently low, the only concern is for the next meal. Poor societies cannot afford concern for the unproductive or for the long-term consequences of actions that immediately increase

[14] World Bank, *World Development Report, 1984* (Washington, D.C.: World Bank, 1984), pp. 266–267.

■ The Alaska pipeline is the largest privately financed construction project ever completed.
Source: David Moore/Black Star.

incomes.[15] Often these societies cannot even develop the means to analyze such effects, let alone respond to them. It is now becoming clear that the destructive impact of primitive races upon the flora, fauna, and soil that provided their incomes was restricted more by their limited capacity to inflict damage than by any ethic of conservation or any foresight.

Economic growth provides both a margin over subsistence that reduces the need for environmentally ruinous practices and a wider choice of alternatives to such methods. Further, it increases these abilities over time, generally producing alternatives faster than it generates resource shortages.

Finally, economic growth allows the use of resources in areas other than the satisfaction of basic survival needs. Attention to the areas deemed the highest expressions of human culture—not merely art, literature, and music, but also care of the less fortunate—requires resources beyond those needed to sustain the productive individuals of a society. It is clearly easier to devote some of the fruits of growth to such purposes than to divert some portion

of a fixed productive capacity. Growth also reduces social stress; few persons in any society find their current incomes so large that they are willing to turn over significant portions for others' unrestricted use. Even when transfers are accomplished through the political process, it is easier to divert portions of income gains, which are not already committed to the satisfaction of long-felt wants than it is to tax incomes previously devoted to private purposes.

The Scorecard on Economic Growth

Taking all aspects of economic growth into account, perhaps the easiest way to determine whether it has increased human welfare is to offer recipients of 1986 incomes the chance to live as did middle-class Americans a century or two ago. We might be intrigued by the chance to dine with Thomas Jefferson or talk politics with Benjamin Franklin. Yet it is difficult to imagine that most of us (with the exception of microbiologists) would respond with equal enthusiasm to the food available in the average household at the end of a long winter. The finest medical care available even 50 years ago would evoke only incredulous horror.

Interestingly enough, a close approximation of earlier life-styles is still readily available today, and might be considerably cheaper than the current version of the "good life"; but few practice back-to-the-land life-styles for long. Such efforts, however, are a good way to gain an appreciation of why our ancestors tried so hard to change their lot, saving at high current cost in foregone consumption and routinely undergoing risks that would daunt a Hollywood stuntman today. A realistic assessment of the conditions of life in earlier days reveals a lack of variety and personal opportunity. Life was not only less varied, it was shorter, more arduous, and contained little in the way of amelioration of physical difficulties.

[15] E. Eckholm, *Losing Ground: Environmental Stress and World Food Prospects* (New York: Pergamon Press, 1976).

Economic growth has undoubtedly had some adverse consequences. In addition to the familiar list (pollution, crowding, the possibility of universally catastropic war, and so forth), the modern era is not kind to people who in earlier times might have been able to function in a slower-paced society. If these were the sole results of growth, we might well be better off living as our ancestors did. Fortunately, they are not the whole picture. Growth has provided humanity with a far greater capacity to successfully respond to constraints on income and life that could only be met with endurance not so very long ago. The problems of previous eras appear trivial in light of modern capabilities, but they appeared very different to those who lacked effective remedies for epidemic diseases, famine, or other scourges of the past. No doubt later generations will find our concerns no less puzzling in view of their enhanced capabilities. Although it is often difficult to admit, on close examination all previous "Golden Ages" have large areas of tarnish and even actual corrosion when compared to the life of today's average citizen.

THE SOURCES OF MODERN ECONOMIC GROWTH

From 1920 to 1984, real economic growth in the United States averaged over 3 percent annually.[16] Although this figure is subject to all the reservations pertaining to national income accounting as a measure of welfare discussed previously, it nevertheless indicates that the output of goods and services (adjusted for price changes) increased at a faster pace than population. The amount available for each citizen rose over time.

What have been the chief causes of twentieth-century economic growth, and what do current trends indicate for the future growth of the American economy? This forecast must necessarily be restricted: predictions that extend for more than a decade or so are pure speculation. Meaningful economic forecasts for a generation are probably impossible; those for a century, whether for the United States or the planet earth, cannot be taken seriously. About all that can be said about the distant economic future with any assurance is that it undoubtedly will be quite different from the present. Most long-range forecasts involve so many interrelated assumptions about population growth, the pace and direction of technological change, the influence of social and political factors on the economy, climate, and even the objectives of economic activity that they are at best mere exercises in logic.

For the next decade or so, however, it may be possible to make some statements with confidence. We have fairly good information about current supplies of most productive resources, their probable trends in the near future, and their current contributions to the growth process. With somewhat less confidence, we may predict the course of technological change in the near future. Projecting productivity trends involves more guesswork, but it is probably fair to assume that relations between inputs and outputs will continue to change at rates close to those recently observed. Even so, the reader should be cautioned that the first attempt to predict U.S. economic growth during the Sixties (in 1962) proved to be about 25 percent too low.[17]

[16] For 1920–1970: U.S. Department of Commerce, Bureau of the Census, *Historical Statistics of the United States: Colonial Times to 1970*, 2 vols. (Washington, D.C.: Government Printing Office, 1975), 1:226–227. For 1970–1984: Council of Economic Advisors, *Economic Report of the President, 1986* (Washington, D.C.: Government Printing Office, 1986), p. 356.

[17] E. Denison, *The Sources of Economic Growth in the United States and the Alternatives Before Us,* Supplementary Paper #13 (Washington, D.C.: Committee for Economic Development, 1962).

The common method of measuring the contributions of productive inputs—labor, capital, and raw materials ("land")—to total output assumes that total payments to each factor approximate its current contribution to total output. If so, the share of each factor in national income is an approximate measure of its elasticity of output. If, for example, labor receives 75 percent of all factor payments (in wages, salaries, and fringe benefits) we can assume that a 1 percent increase in total labor inputs, holding the quantities of all other factors constant, would result in a 0.75 percent increase in total output.

Productivity Growth

In modern economies, the growth rate can be expected to exceed the sum of all factor contributions. The difference between the actual growth rate and that attributable to increases in factor supplies is ascribed to productivity increases. Strictly speaking, this method is appropriate only in a fully adjusted, perfectly competitive economy, but most economists agree that it yields useful predictions in the American economy.[18] Over time, increases in productivity have assumed a greater relative importance in the growth of the U.S. economy. Their absolute contribution in the 1900–1960 period was twice as great as in the last six decades of the nineteenth century.[19]

Productivity gains have a special importance: they are the one growth source that by definition means gains in per-capita output, and they compensate for declines in the rate of growth of other inputs. In recent times, they have become the largest single source of American economic growth. Productivity gains accounted for about one-sixth of the total increase in output over the 1840–1900 period, which

was a time of very rapid growth in the labor force, stock of capital, and usable natural resources. In the next six decades, as the growth rates of most productive inputs declined and technical progress accelerated, they were the source of 44 percent of all economic growth.[20]

Labor

Growth in the labor force has always had a greater impact on the aggregate growth rate of the United States than increases in any other input. In the twentieth century, it has accounted for slightly more than one-third of the total. In recent years, as the "baby boom" generation entered the work force and social attitudes toward married women's employment outside the home changed, the labor force growth rate increased. In the Sixties, the American work force increased 45 percent more rapidly than in either of the two preceding decades.

Labor force changes, of course, depend on more than just changes in population size.[21] In recent years, labor force participation rates have increased as a larger portion of the population became available for work outside the home. Primarily, more married women and teenagers began seeking work. Other factors that influence labor's contribution to the growth rate are the number of hours worked per year (determined by social conventions concerning working hours, holidays, and the extent of unemployment) and the ages at which people enter and leave the work force. Changes in the education of the labor force are better regarded as productivity increases than quantitative changes in labor inputs.

In the Sixties, these factors remained constant or rose slightly due to the low rates of unemployment prevailing through that dec-

---

[18] Ibid. See also Davis et al., *American Economic Growth*, p. 35.
[19] Davis et al., *American Economic Growth*, p. 39.

[20] Ibid.
[21] R. Easterlin, "What Will 1984 Be Like? Socioeconomic Implications of Recent Trends in Age Structure," *Demography* (November 1978).

ade.[22] In the Seventies, a rising portion of part-time workers and women (who tend to take less productive jobs than full-time male workers) has reduced or even eliminated the positive contribution of labor force growth.

The Future Role of Labor

It appears that several influences on labor's contribution to growth will affect developments in the mid-Eighties and beyond. First, aggregate growth rates in the work force will decline: the number of potential new entrants is no longer rising rapidly. Second, as the labor force ages, a larger portion of all workers will gain additional skills, and women will probably gain more nearly complete access to the entire job spectrum. These developments will increase labor productivity. Finally, the educational achievements of new workers rose markedly in the 1960–1985 period. It is unlikely that a similar increase can be achieved in the near future. One study claims that when changes in the composition of the work force are considered, the much-discussed decline in productivity of the Seventies never took place: there was no departure from age-adjusted long-term trends in productivity growth. If this is correct, the future should witness above-average increases in productivity, reflecting the increased skills of the large additions to the work force during the last decade or so.[23] Changes in attitudes toward work might occur, but their direction is uncertain and their effect likely to be small.

Institutional and Legal Changes.

Institutional changes may also be influential. Recently, some economists have claimed that changes in labor regulations (as well as failures to change union work rules) and other aspects of the legal climate have affected unemployment rates, labor mobility, and other factors important to productivity. Whatever the intent of these changes, the results, they feel, have not been wholly beneficial. More generous rates of unemployment compensation, favorable tax treatment of such compensation, as well as welfare benefits and private sector innovations such as supplemental unemployment benefits and the increase in multiple-earner families have lengthened the average job search even among persons whose work motivation is high.[24] Minimum wage laws reduce the employment options of the least skilled members of the work force, while at the same time increasing employers' training costs. Government retraining programs may encourage the movement of labor from low- to high-productivity employment, but aid to "sick industries" surely hinders it. At the other end of the scale, steeply progressive tax rates may discourage additional effort by highly productive workers whose skills are extremely difficult to replace on short notice. Taxing interest income at rates that make real returns negligible or even negative discourages saving, especially in periods of high inflation.

One study found that the combined effect of efforts to reduce environmental damage, employee accidents and occupational diseases, and losses due to crime caused a drop of about 0.5 percentage points in the aggregate growth rate. This apparently insignificant reduction is in fact one-sixth or more of the total recent growth rate, and such influences have if anything grown in the decade since the study was completed.[25] It may be that such regulations produce compensating improvements in the quality of life, but these are not measured by

[22] Ibid. See also E. Denison, "Some Explanations of Declining Productivity Growth," *Brookings General Series Reprint #354* (Washington, D.C.: Brookings Institution, 1979).

[23] M. Darby, "The U.S. Productivity Slowdown: A Case of Statistical Myopia" *American Economic Review* (June 1984).

[24] M. Feldstein, "The Economics of the New Unemployment" *The Public Interest* (Fall 1973).

[25] E. Denison, "Effects of Selected Changes in the Institutional and Human Environment upon Output per Unit of Input," *Brookings General Series Reprint #355* (Washington, D.C.: Brookings Institution, 1978).

national income statistics. At best, they are likely to be difficult to assess.

Innovation versus Government Regulation

As this volume has stressed, one strength of the American economy has been its ability to develop a continuous series of new occupations and industries by allowing or encouraging the introduction of new ideas into a market economy, where they were free to compete with those of more established producers. This strength was fostered by receptivity in innovation in consumer goods and investment markets. The institutions of a market economy allowed innovators to reap a large portion of the results of their activities. In the long run, economic growth is critically dependent on innovation and change, and the long run now appears to be a smaller number of calendar time units than it was a few decades ago.

Some recent institutional developments, particularly in government, hamper response to new opportunities because of excessive concern with the inevitable by-products of innovation: reduced incomes for individuals and firms slow to respond and the changing impact of economic activity upon the quality of life. The debate over proper income distribution cannot be resolved to the satisfaction of all interested parties, and the same is true for the trade-off between environmental impact and safety and conventional economic activity. Therefore, any response to these problems must take the form of a compromise.

In seeking a workable solution, the costs of gains in environmental purity, reduced accident and disease rates, and a more "ideal" income distribution must be assessed realistically. These costs are not zero, nor are the benefits infinite; were either true, there could be no rational opposition to maximizing them. Nor are the benefits conferred by increased material welfare a trivial concern for most Americans. These considerations are particularly important in attempts to avoid the effects of change. Attempts to preserve obsolete industries generally result in increased long-term costs, both to those directly involved and in potential lost income in other sectors. "Job death" is not an indication of economic disaster: it is most prominent in periods of rapid "Job birth" in new sectors and industries.[26]

But the political dice are loaded against new industries and new products: although they produced the vast majority of new jobs in the American economy in recent decades while large firms lost more jobs than they generated,[27] new firms tend to be small, diversified, and fully occupied with market activity. Their losing rivals tend to be larger, more concentrated, and convinced that the route to survival lies through government aid rather than increased efficiency—or even a complete reallocation of productive resources. Humankind must have ethical standards, but efforts to keep low-productivity jobs aid no one in the long run.

Investment and New Capital

Increases in the quantity (not quality) of capital have accounted for slightly more than 20 percent of recent American economic growth. This is an area of increasing concern for many students of the growth process. The rate of capital formation in the United States, at least as conventionally measured, is among the lowest of all industrial nations. In the past few years it has continued to decline. This is not only a matter of needing to increase the amount of capital (tools) per American worker: replacement of depreciated capital and rapid growth in the capital stock are the chief mechanisms for introducing technological change into the production process. Thus, low rates of invest-

[26] Rosenberg and Birdzell, *How the West Grew Rich*, pp. 265–269.
[27] Ibid., pp. 297–298, footnote 6.

ment may have a dual impact on long-term growth.[28]

It may be claimed that modern capital formation has assumed a different guise in the United States. The education and on-the-job training of the work force may be increasingly important supplements to growth in the stock of plant and equipment. As previously noted, this is an area in which U.S. performance is very strong. Education is both intensive and extensive and has aspects of both capital and consumer goods. Also, it is linked to productivity growth. Nevertheless, it is difficult to assess this contention.

Inflation

Inflation has played a large role in the observed decline in personal savings (one source of investment funds). It may also have caused corporate management to concentrate on short-term at the expense of long-term goals. Changing investor attitudes toward expected profit levels may have reinforced these alterations in investment policy. Some analysts also point to the impact of government in such varied areas as tax structure, environmental and safety regulations, and direct redistribution of income, all of which have increased consumption or otherwise reallocated resources away from investment.[29]

Even policies that reduce inflation have an adverse short-term effect on investment. Such policies must reduce monetary growth or even the money stock; hence, they impact heavily on sectors sensitive to interest rate changes, such as residential construction. Over longer periods, however, investment should benefit from the greater security afforded by lower rates of price change. In sum, there appear to be no insuperable barriers to increased rates of aggregate investment in the United States.

Natural Resources

The contribution of increased amounts of usable natural resources to the overall rate of increase in output has been quite small (less than 3 percent of the total) in this century, and it has been declining. This is due less to a declining absolute rate of increase in such inputs than to the high capital and labor content of most modern products. For example, few of us would imagine that the price of copper or other raw materials employed in computers is a major influence on their costs. The growing importance of services in the American economy reinforces this trend. Most goods today are far more than processed lumps of raw materials: growing portions of output have little or no raw material content whatever.

Although additional amounts of most raw materials will likely be available only at increased costs per unit, barring some technological breakthrough, raw materials supplies appear unlikely to exert major influences on the U.S. growth rate. As technology increases the range of substitutes for most natural resource inputs, supplies of natural resources exert even smaller constraints on growth.[30]

Aggregate Resource Supply

Prospects for greater amounts of productive resources are not especially promising for the next decade. For all practical purposes, the persons who will join the labor force over the next 18 years are already with us, and their numbers will not increase at the pace of the two previous decades. Indeed, this may be a much longer-term trend: despite changing attitudes toward childbearing on the part of American women, particularly those in their

---

[28] Denison, "Some Explanations of Declining Productivity Growth."

[29] Ibid.

[30] Goeller and Weinberg, "The Age of Substitutability," *American Economic Review* (December 1978). See also N. Rosenberg, *Technology and American Economic Growth* (New York: Harper and Row, 1972), pp. 198–201.

thirties, the birthrate has not risen significantly in recent years. It may have ceased the decline that began about 1960, but that is all.[31]

Labor force participation rate increases offer little more promise; higher-than-current rates would require major social changes, which generally take a long time to become effective. Changes in the rate of investment are within the economy's grasp but would have only about half the direct impact of an equal increase in the rate of labor force growth. Moreover, the investment increases hoped for after the tax reductions of the early Eighties have not materialized. Enormous changes in the growth rates of natural resources would be required to significantly impact the aggregate growth rate of the economy. A 100 percent increase in the rate of growth of all natural resources combined would raise total output by less than 5 percent, or from 3 percent to less than 3.15 percent annually.[32]

The Importance of Increasing Productivity

Given these prospects, the best opportunity for increased rates of economic growth lies in productivity—increasing output by raising the efficiency of production rather than the quantity of inputs. In this area, the outlook is at least potentially encouraging. Not only has the rate of productivity increase accelerated in all but the most recent decades (and possibly even in the Seventies if allowances are made for labor force demographics),[33] but increased productivity has some very desirable effects in addition to increasing aggregate output. Productivity increases can offset declines in quantities of inputs. They encourage more rational use of resources and work against discrimination on any basis other than ability. At the same time, they force consideration of alternative uses of nonhuman inputs as well. Finally, productivity

increases are based on the one productive resource that is truly inexhaustible: the human ability to reason, learn, and apply knowledge. It would take a brave prophet indeed to predict a decline in the pace of technological change in the modern world—the opposite appears more likely.

Raising the rate of productivity increase will mean reducing its opposite—rent seeking. Raising output per unit of input is generally accompanied by large-scale movements of resources from one use to another, rather than by efforts to prevent such changes. Much the same is true of removing social or political barriers to the rational employment of resources. Ultimately, the development of new knowledge and its introduction into economic activity enable possible continuous productivity increases, and they cannot occur without changes in the structure of the economy. Better use of currently available knowledge can yield gains, but without the infusion of really new ideas it is a long-run dead end.

The Importance of New Research

The function of pure research is the generation of new knowledge for its own sake, not its immediate applicability to current problems. As the predominance of Americans among recent Nobel Prize winners in science indicates, pure research has been a strong point for the United States in the twentieth century. Diversity of research efforts has long been a source of economic growth for Western economies, and particularly for the United States.[34] This diversity means that a larger portion of all possible avenues of inquiry is covered and new ideas are evaluated by a large community with few or no vested interests in anything other than the development of knowledge.

The nature of pure research makes it poorly suited to production through the market. The

---

[31] U.S. Department of Commerce, *Statistical Abstract, 1986.*
[32] Rosenberg, *Technology and American Economic Growth,* Chap. 6.
[33] Darby, "The U.S. Productivity Slowdown."

[34] Rosenberg and Birdzell, *How the West Grew Rich,* Chaps. 8 and 9.

knowledge gained may have no immediate applicability, may not suit the productive abilities of the generators, or may be evidence that some line of inquiry is a dead end. Especially when the costs of inquiry may be enormous, these characteristics make pure research ill-suited to the support of private, profit-seeking firms. Furthermore, the end product of research is information, and there is no more mobile commodity. Thus, research efforts in one nation may well find their major economic applications elsewhere.[35]

Even though the private returns on pure research may be low and highly uncertain, the social returns tend to be very high, although often in unexpected forms. For this reason, it is often proposed that pure research be largely supported by government, possibly with a few large firms also contributing within their own areas of interest. Most private activity, in this view, should concentrate on applying ideas developed elsewhere or using existing information to improve current products. These procedures yield quicker and more certain returns and appear to be areas where the market response is swift and effective compared to the responses of other economic systems.

Research Spending Trends. There have been several trends in spending on all aspects of research and development in the past four decades. Expenditures increased from 0.6 percent of GNP (largely private spending on development) in 1940 to over 3 percent in 1970 (still mostly on development, but with a significant increase in funds for pure research).[36] In recent years, the aggregate portion of GNP spent on "R & D" has declined somewhat. Yet this trend may be offset by the growing participation of private firms plus universities and other nonprofit institutions, whose efforts generally yield more immediately productive results than

federal government research concentrating on space technology and national defense.[37] Research in oceanography, climatology, and similar areas might well be more economically beneficial than the current areas of government concentration; certainly its payoffs would be more quickly obtained.

Problems with Government-Funded Research. If private research is narrowly focused and heavily slanted toward development (largely changes in existing products) rather than pure research, government research support also has its weaknesses. As noted above, diversity is essential for efficient generation of new knowledge, and centralization of research funding in one organization does not promote simultaneous funding of a variety of investigations in the same field.[38] In this area, our federal government structure and considerable autonomy for a variety of research organizations have some important advantages over more centralized nations.

Another difficulty is that government often promotes something other than pure research. It may devote funds toward some problem area, but at the same time specify that must be used to develop one specific means of mitigating it, with no consideration of alternatives. Unless bureaucrats who apportion research monies possess more technical expertise than those who actually perform the investigations, results—even if they reduce the impact of the problem—will likely not be optimum. Further, this process may result in slower application of superior methods when they appear; government is far more resistant than the market to change. Government could obtain a higher return on its research dollars, even within specified areas, if it requested only results and left their achievement open to the full range of alter-

---

[35] I am indebted to Professor Gavin Wright for this insight.
[36] Rosenberg and Birdzell, *How the West Grew Rich,* p. 177.

[37] Denison, "Some Explanations of Declining Productivity Growth."
[38] For a cogent presentation of this point, see Rosenberg and Birdzell, *How the West Grew Rich,* Chap. 10.

natives. This point is particularly evident in recent efforts to improve occupational and consumer safety.

The Need for New Knowledge. For all these problems, efforts to generate and apply new knowledge hold great promise as sources of new economic growth. Most of the obstacles here are institutional: if people created them, they can also remove them. The inevitability of diminishing returns to all other growth sources makes continued research absolutely necessary, if only to preserve current living standards rather than raise them. Undesirable consequences of technological change can best be countered by encouraging the broadest possible range of investigation. Nor can we deny the importance of continued economic growth. Barring some revolution in human nature, responding to humankind's problems will require more capabilities than we already possess: our current productive capacity does not satisfy all our wants. The form that economic growth assumes, and the ends to which it is directed, are for us and our children to decide.

SELECTED REFERENCES

Berger, P. *The Capitalist Revolution.* New York: Basic Books, 1986.

Council of Economic Advisors. *Economic Report of the President.* Washington, D.C.: Government Printing Office, annual editions.

Davis, L., et al. *American Economic Growth: An Economist's History of the United States.* New York: Harper and Row, 1972.

Denison, E. "Some Explanations of Declining Productivity Growth." Brookings General Series Reprint #354. Washington, D.C.: Brookings Institution, 1979.

————. *The Sources of Economic Growth in the United States and the Alternatives Before Us.* Supplementary Paper #13. Washington, D.C.: Committee for Economic Development, 1962.

————. *Trends in American Economic Growth, 1962–1982.* Washington, D.C.: Brookings Institution, 1985.

Kahn, H., and J. Simon. *The Resourceful Earth: A Response to Global 2000.* New York: Basil Blackwell, 1984.

Kuznets, S. "Innovations and Adjustments in Economic Growth." In *Poverty, Ecology, and Technological Change: World Problems of Development,* edited by R. Puth. Durham, N.H.: University of New Hampshire Press, 1972.

Olson, M. *The Rise and Decline of Nations: Economic Growth, Stagflation, and Social Rigidities.* New Haven, Conn.: Yale University Press, 1982.

Rosenberg, N. *Technology and American Economic Growth.* New York: Harper and Row, 1972.

Rosenberg, N., and R. Birdzell. *How the West Grew Rich: The Economic Transformation of the Industrial World.* New York: Basic Books, 1986.

U.S. Department of Commerce, Bureau of the Census. *Historical Statistics of the United States: Colonial Times to 1970.* 2 vols. Washington, D.C.: Government Printing Office, 1975.

————. *Statistical Abstract of the United States, 1986.* Washington, D.C.: Government Printing Office, 1986.

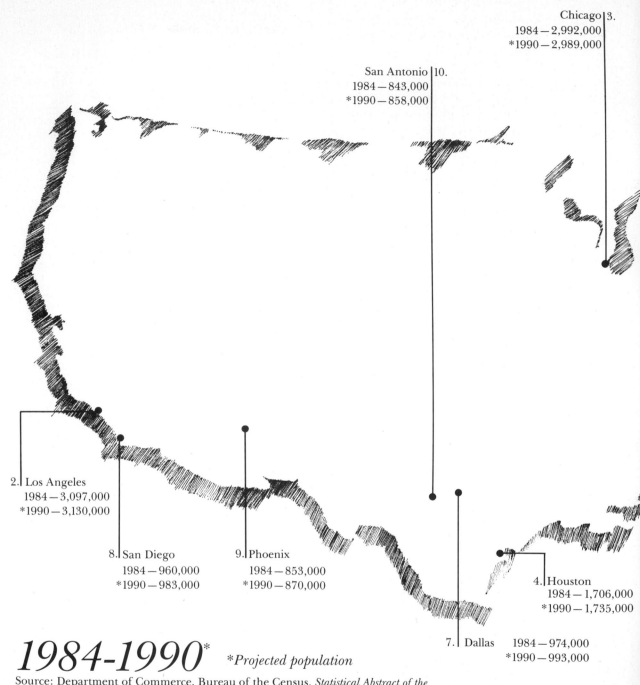

Chicago | 3.
1984 — 2,992,000
*1990 — 2,989,000

San Antonio | 10.
1984 — 843,000
*1990 — 858,000

2. | Los Angeles
1984 — 3,097,000
*1990 — 3,130,000

8. | San Diego
1984 — 960,000
*1990 — 983,000

9. | Phoenix
1984 — 853,000
*1990 — 870,000

4. | Houston
1984 — 1,706,000
*1990 — 1,735,000

7. | Dallas   1984 — 974,000
*1990 — 993,000

1984-1990 *Projected population

Source: Department of Commerce, Bureau of the Census, *Statistical Abstract of the United States, 1986,* Washington, D.C. Government Printing Office, 1986, pp. 16-18.

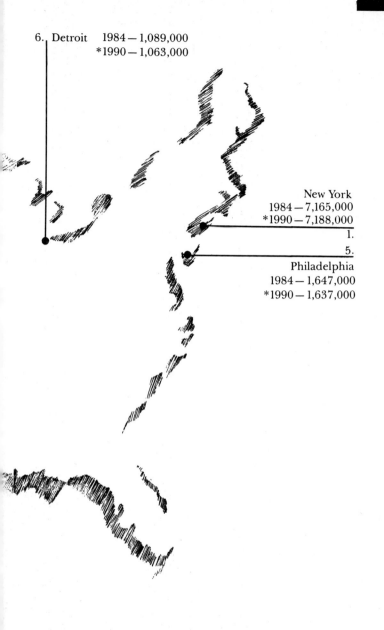

6. Detroit   1984 — 1,089,000
*1990 — 1,063,000

New York
1984 — 7,165,000
*1990 — 7,188,000

1.

5.

Philadelphia
1984 — 1,647,000
*1990 — 1,637,000

INDEX